1999

THE YEAR THE RECORD INDUSTRY LOST CONTROL

(A division of the Wise Music Group
14–15 Berners Street, London, W1T 3LJ)
Cover designed by Amazing15

ISBN 978-1-9131-7277-0

A catalogue record for this book is available from the British Library.

Printed in Poland.

www.omnibuspress.com

1999

THE YEAR THE RECORD INDUSTRY LOST CONTROL

EAMONN FORDE

OMNIBUS PRESS
London / New York / Paris / Sydney / Copenhagen / Berlin / Madrid / Tokyo

To Sonja van Praag – for all time

Contents

INDIES

PIRACY

MP3

STANDARDS

STARTUPS

RETAIL

Prologue

The record business barged into 1999 full of vim, arrogance and certitude.

The record business stumbled out of 1999 full of demoralisation, consternation and shrapnel.

It began as a year promising so much. The CD business, firmly in its imperial period, had been an unprecedented licence to print money throughout the 1990s, with record labels ballooning on profits like never before.

The hubris of the time was such that the major record labels started to look to buy up each other, with Seagram's acquisition of PolyGram in late 1998 creating a new giant among the majors and suggesting even greater consolidation to come. The era of the super-major was here and was symbolic of the period and its three unifying principles: power, scale and profits.

It was not to work out that way, however. 1999 was not going to be just another staging post year on the way to even greater profits. 1999 was to prove to be the start of the end of the old way of doing business and a tearing up of the map, causing cartographical confusion as the majors lurched around looking for not just *the* future, but *any* future.

If the story of 1999 is about anything, it is about control: who had it; who wanted more; who wanted to take it from whom; who wanted to grind the very concept of control into dust.

To the victor belong the spoils. Except in this brutal multiplayer stand-off in 1999, there was so much collateral damage, so much turmoil, that the spoils steadily ebbed away over a decade and a half and became a fraction of what they were in 1999.

There is, of course, great cinematic symbolism in the fact that all of this happened in the final year of the millennium. This was less *fin de siècle* and more a dismantling of the past and a detonation of the future.

This book tells the full story of a phenomenal twelve months in which all the music industry's plans were broken apart by a storm that had been quietly brewing in the background, but which became uncontrollable in June with the launch of a Northeastern University undergraduate's hobby project that aimed to make finding and swapping music MP3 files as simple as clicking a mouse.

This is not the story of Napster alone: rather it is the story of the entire year and how the record business, from January to December, went from towering confidence to utter panic.

Over the past two decades, a narrative around 1999 has slowly ossified into a certain kind of truth: that the record business was fast asleep at the wheel; that it never saw digital coming; that it failed to grasp the long-term implications of the internet; and that, as such, it got what it deserved.

This is very much a misreading of history. This book is not here to make excuses for the record business or absolve it of all its mistakes; but it is here to lay out the complexities of what happened and to show that it was much more than the clichéd notion of the past (the record industry) violently clashing with the future (digital in general and Silicon Valley in particular).

While both record companies and retailers were slowly moving towards certain (and conditional) digital goals, there were also terrible push-pull tensions between them. High-street retailers were demanding that labels should not prioritise the downloading of music or the nascent online retailers over and above them.

There have been several music books that focus on a single year, imbuing it with huge importance. Among them are *1971: Never A Dull Moment* by David Hepworth, *1966, The Year The Decade Exploded* by Jon Savage, *Can't Slow Down: How 1984 Became Pop's Blockbuster Year* by Michaelangelo Matos, *The Beatles 1963: A Year In The Life* by Dafydd Rees, *Beatles '66: The Revolutionary Year* by Steve Turner and *Faster Than A Cannonball: 1995 and All That* by Dylan Jones. These are primarily about music, musicians and wider culture.

Here, I take this calendar year approach and apply it specifically to the record business, considering the forces at play and the height of the stakes at risk. 1999 was the single most important year in the history of the record business and marks not just the last gasp of the old business but also, amid the confusion, the sowing of the seeds of the new business as we know it today.

This book tells the whole story of that single and most singular year

– looking at what the record industry was doing (what it was doing right as much as what it was doing wrong) and how, with the ripe and poetic symbolism that can only happen on the cusp of a new millennium, external forces were going to make the business change forever.

It is only now, a quarter of a century on, that we can look back at 1999 and fully understand just what a seismic, shocking and significant year it was for the record business.

The book stands as a biography of a year: the most important, pivotal, lucrative, exciting, ridiculous, terrifying and chaotic year that the record business has ever experienced.

BEGINNINGS

CHAPTER 1

A Fracture in the Endless Party

(The presumption of control seems unassailable)

The 1990s were a *phenomenal* time for the record business, boosted by snowballing CD sales. They retailed for considerably more than LPs or cassettes and, because they were treated as a 'new' format, despite dating back to 1982, often saw a lower royalty paid through to artists. They were also a way to boost catalogue sales, getting fans to buy favourite albums again on this shiny new format. Every way you looked at the spinning CD, it was a fruit machine where the symbols on all the reels were the same and a jackpot was guaranteed.

The business was awash with money. It felt like every night was a party and that the good times were never going to end.

Each autumn or thereabouts, the IFPI (the trade body for the international record business) would publish its global sales figures for the previous year, and every time they did it felt like they were published to a cacophony of champagne corks popping.

Global record sales by retail value

1989 – $21.6 billion	1995 – $39.7 billion
1990 – $24 billion	1996 – $39.7 billion
1991 – $25.4 billion*	1997 – $38.1 billion**
1992 – $28.7 billion	1998 – $38.7 billion
1993 – $30.5 billion	1999 – $38.5 billion
1994 – $35.5 billion	

* 1991 was the first year that global CD sales passed the 1 billion mark.
** This dip from 1996 to 1997 was blamed on currency rate fluctuations.

Sources: IFPI data as reported in *Music & Copyright* and *Billboard*. These are the numbers reported at the time, year by year. The IFPI reports in US dollars and typically adjusts historic numbers to factor in currency fluctuations (with the trade press flip-flopping between 'current dollar terms' and 'constant dollar terms') when publishing new numbers. For reasons of consistency, I am using the numbers reported by the IFPI when initially published.

In 1999, as the century closed, there was a general air of confidence – or, more likely, arrogance – that the upward sales curve would continue into the new millennium.

There were, inside record companies, small pockets of people who understood that a change was coming and that it was not going to be wholly positive. They had detected a series of early warning tremors, but they were not always listened to by the heads of these corporations, who were luxuriating in their corner offices, paid eye-popping salaries and awarded flabbergasting bonuses for keeping things exactly as they were – selling more CDs and making even more money. The only change they wanted to see was the same except *more so*.

When you live in a bubble, of course, it becomes comfortingly insular and you cannot comprehend a life outside of that bubble. Or that the bubble you inhabited would ever pop.

The story of 1999 is really the story of control. It is the story of an industry predicating on having total control slowly realising that control is conditional and can be snatched away. It is also a story of two different parts of the record business – labels and retailers – fighting each other to get even more control in the relationship, a relationship defined by codependency but but also by distrust and resentment.

The control enjoyed by the major record companies, of which there were six in the late 1990s, was something they lorded over the many independents. When an independent managed to gain some ground, one of the majors would buy it, or try to buy it. Then when all the indies that could be bought had been bought, the majors started to look to buy up each other.

Market share and consolidation were the closest things the majors had to a collective religion. In that regard they were zealots.

But that control was going to be broken apart by developments that had been brewing for decades in northern California and, most spectacularly of all, in the dorm room of a Boston university, over two hundred miles from New York and over 2,500 miles from Los Angeles where the American (and, hence, the global) record business was centred.

As it turns out, 1999 was to prove to be the single most significant year in the record industry's history. It was the year when everything changed; where the certainties and bullishness of the preceding decades started to crack and splinter while the uncertainties of a whole new world and a whole new way of business were set to kick the legs from under everyone.

The defining factors of 1999 were actually percolating in 1998 – both minor and major moves on the chess board that would shape not just the closing year of the 20th century but also the opening decades of the 21st century.

In the art world, as the 1800s came to their end, a whole new creative moment, caught in the split between fear and excitement around the arrival of a new century, was defined as *fin de siècle*. Translated from French as 'end of the century', it was seen almost as a cultural, artistic and moral palimpsest – where the panic around 'social degeneracy' would be wiped away and the seeds of a new beginning planted. This could be a great reset, jumping on the symbolism tied up in a century's closure.

'For decades *fin de siècle* implied a "go to the dogs" feeling that was thought to pervade European "civilised" society in the years around 1900,' argued Mikuláš Teich and Roy Porter. 'Underlying it was a cocktail of lamentation for the past and fears of the future, countenancing the notion that human progress was being brought to a halt, if not an end.'[1]

The closing of a century effectively sparks an existential crisis and a philosophical freefall, with the transition from one century to the next being seen 'as a watershed in many areas'[2] of society and culture.

'By the end of that century, the first *fin de siècle* period, a genuine crisis of reason was underway,' noted Jeffrey Alexander, professor of sociology at UCLA, in his book on the movement. 'Crystallized by new and persistent tendencies in social theory, its repercussions have been felt in disastrous ways, on the right and on the left, throughout the 20th century.'[3]

As Fritz Weber proposes about *fin de siècle*, 'Above all, the term evokes a certain atmosphere, a feeling between doomsday apprehensions and the exhilaration of setting sail for new horizons.'[4]

This sense of schism, of upheaval, of looming disaster in the worlds of art, politics and philosophy in the late 1800s could be equally applied to the record business as it faced the closing of the 20th century.

Alice Teichova drew on these theories and applied them to notions of capitalism at the end of the 1900s. The push towards globalisation defined Western capitalism in the second half of the last century and was reaching a crescendo in the late 1990s.

'[T]he historical reality of contemporary capitalism, far from giving a multitude of independent entrepreneurs a chance of competing in the market to satisfy consumers, confers advantages on the strongest, most forceful companies pursuing oligopolistic and monopolistic aims and competing among themselves for even bigger market shares,' she wrote.[5]

She cited Dutch electronics group Philips (which we will hear much more about soon) regarding its corporate objectives in the 1990s as being about structuring its production to 'a single world concept' while aiming to be a 'global'[6] company rather than a *mere* international one. This was the natural byproduct of a flurry of corporate acquisitions across multiple sectors, leaving Teichova to conclude that '[t]hus the trend is towards mega mergers'[7] in many business areas.

For the record business, the push towards even greater consolidation – and, eventually, a 'mega merger' on a wholly unprecedented scale – in the 1990s was not driven out of panic about a market in decline; it was driven by an arrogant belief that becoming even bigger was a birthright and the natural end game for an endlessly ballooning market.

All this growth and analogous hubris was coming from a shiny new 5-inch disc.

THE CD BOOM: THE GIFT THAT KEPT ON GIVING

The compact disc was developed in late 1976 in a joint initiative between Philips and Sony.[8] It launched commercially in Japan in 1982, with Billy Joel's *52nd Street*[9] being the first album to be commercially released on CD and the Sony CDP 101[10] being the first CD player to be sold in Japan (in October 1982). When it arrived in the UK the following spring, it retailed for £545 (the equivalent of £1,778.75 today).

The high cost of the hardware and the discs, as well as an initially small catalogue of available titles, made it a niche interest, primarily targeting the affluent audiophile market. But costs slowly came down, more hardware manufacturers developed cheaper products and more artists had new and catalogue titles released on the format.

In this dash for cash, quality control was barely a tertiary, never mind a secondary, consideration. Anything and everything that had even the vaguest whiff of commercial potential was put out on CD.

'Suddenly reissues of all kinds, which had previously been the Cinderella wing of the record business, became a priority,' says noted music writer David Hepworth. 'Even run-of-the-mill albums from the past which had been forgotten by everyone but the people who made them could be "rediscovered", thanks to this new, reputedly future-proof format.'[11]

It got its biggest stamp of approval when The Beatles' catalogue was made available on CD in 1987.[12] This was in part down to EMI, The Beatles' label, initially being standoffish with regard to the format, with EMI Records UK publicity executive Brian Southall telling the BBC in February 1983 that macroeconomic factors were behind its hesitancy to move here.

'The British record industry, it's [been] tough over the two or three years – it's dropped between 20 and 30 per cent overall,' he said, noting it was the LP that was most significantly affected. 'The decision with the compact disc is that we will wait and we will observe its introduction and the reaction to it over its early beginnings and see how the public reacts.'[13]

The move by EMI and The Beatles in 1987 was hastened when, the year before, over 100 million CDs were sold globally. This was a clear sign of a boom happening. (A decade later, 2.16 billion CDs were sold globally).'[14]

The slump Southall referred to was a marked decline in record sales between 1979 and 1983, but a rise was reported in 1984. Much of that was put down to not only the introduction of a new format but also its significantly higher retail price compared to LPs and cassettes.[15] In the US, for example, a new LP in the early 1980s would have cost around $8.98, but the CD when it first went to market retailed for around $16.95, almost double the price of an LP.[16]

Philips and Sony were the biggest beneficiaries of this format windfall. They may have shouldered the enormous development costs of the CD but not only were they major manufacturers of CD players, they also received a per-copy royalty from all music companies manufacturing CDs.[17]

US artist lawyer David Braun said label heads were initially hesitant to embrace the CD but once they got behind it, the market exploded. '[T]he CD saved the industry,' he said.[18]

There were some concerned voices in the record business at the time who were suggesting that issuing digital copies of recordings to the public could unleash a potential piracy problem that would come back to bite them.[19]

Al Teller was president of CBS Records at the time of the CD's arrival. He also had a science background, with an undergraduate degree in electronics engineering and a graduate degree in operations research, a subfield of mathematical science. He forecast major problems on the horizon.

'At the time the CD was introduced, I was having a conversation with some old engineering school classmates of mine, several of whom worked in the signal processing area,' he says. 'The conversation basically went as follows: now that the analogue waveform has been digitised, it is now in the language of computers; it's zeros and ones. You can make a computer file out of a song. A couple of my signal processing friends were saying, "You know, we're working on ways to move files from one computer to another in rapid form." We're talking among ourselves [and saying], "One day it's going to be very possible that all music will be digitised and they'll be sent all over the place via computer".'

Albhy Galuten straddles the worlds of music production and technology, with production credits including global hit albums such as *Saturday Night Fever* and Barbra Streisand's *Guilty*. He invented the enhanced CD and held senior technologist jobs at both Sony and Universal Music Group. He says it is understandable that, at the time in the 1980s, no one could have foreseen the digital time bomb the CD was setting off.

'Nobody imagined that there was a copying problem,' he says. 'An audio CD is about 650 megabytes. When that came out, I had a five megabyte and a ten megabyte drive in the computers that I was using for music and it was about $1,000 a megabyte. So no one imagined when they designed the CD that people would be copying 650 megabytes' worth of audio. It was incomprehensible.'

The incoming waves of cash for the industry, however, meant the warnings of the CD Cassandras like Teller were not fully heeded.

The industry's cockiness was exacerbated by the fact that labels used the new format – and the development costs – to rework contracts that would *lower* artist royalty rates by 20 per cent. They also increased the 'packaging reduction' (also known as 'container charge', essentially the manufacturing costs) from 10–15 per cent to 20 per cent.[20] [21]

Author Steve Knopper, in his book *Appetite For Self-Destruction: The Spectacular Crash Of The Record Industry In The Digital Age*, spelt out exactly what the pros were for record labels and what the cons were for recording artists.

'After labels factored in these new fangled deductions, a typical artist received roughly eighty-one cents per disc. Under the LP system, artists made a little more than seventy-five cents per disc. So labels sold CDs for almost $8 more than LPs at stores, but typically artists made just six cents more per record.'[22]

As the CD became a truly mainstream format, production costs fell due to the economies of scale but the wholesale price to retailers and the cost to consumers were not reduced accordingly.

'Profit margins were expanding [. . .] as efficiency gains in compact disc manufacturing brought the per-unit cost of goods below a dollar – a saving that was not passed on to the consumer, who was charged $16.98 retail,' lamented author Stephen Witt.[23]

Never before had the record industry had a music format with such a profit margin.[24] This was the cream that no one ever thought would curdle.

By the 1990s, the CD had ushered in what author Fred Goodman called 'a period of greed and self-interest that was exceptional even for the record business.'[25]

Hepworth defined this period as one of endless and self-perpetuating bacchanalia. 'The mid-nineties turned out to be the high point of the record business,' he proposed. 'Because CDs were still selling, and selling at retail prices which produced an awful lot of fat, much of which could be spent on hype and hoopla, it turned out to be quite a party. In terms of wealth, decadence and even ostentatious drug use in the music business the nineties was the decade the seventies has the reputation for being.'[26]

Hilary Rosen was at the Recording Industry Association of America (RIAA), the trade body for US record labels, between 1987 and 2003, eventually rising to become chairman and CEO. The CD, she says, brought in an era of enormous success for labels.

'The margins on CDs had created a significant financial boom for the record business and a renaissance of the drugs, sex and rock'n'roll era in the 1980s and 1990s,' she said.[27]

It also created a culture of short-termism and myopia as well as greatly rewarding industry executives for merely having the good fortune of being in the right place at the right time. The collective boost to executive egos was chilling.

'The easy windfall from CD profits made some executives who knew nothing about the business look savvy – and it spurred many who did to reach for ever more wealth and executive power,' Goodman noted. 'The result was a generation of label managers who thought almost exclusively about the immediate results that could boost their own bonuses and make them more powerful than their rivals, and not at all about where the business – and particularly the technology supplying its robust growth – was going.'[28]

Jeremy Silver worked at Virgin Records and then at EMI (when it bought Virgin in 1992) between 1992 and 2000, rising to become vice president of new media at EMI Recorded Music Worldwide. He was a digital evangelist through this period but says that the success of the CD made the record business arrogant and greedy, presuming it was bulletproof. It was also, at the senior level, closing its ears to things he was saying about the imminent transformative impact of digital.

'Part of the reason why the industry didn't give a shit was that between 1989 and 1999 it was the most profitable period and highest revenues the industry had ever achieved in its entire history,' he says. 'As far as the old boys were concerned, they were driving towards their bonuses; that was all they thought about. So all of this internet stuff – it was just a bunch of nerds! There was an intellectual gap, I think. There were the techies and us nerdy types who got it.'

Between 1996 and 2000, Ben Drury was working at *Dotmusic* (a consumer-facing music site that was a sister title of UK trade magazine

Music Week). He had come straight from studying for a physics degree at King's College London and was fascinated by the emerging internet, teaching himself HTML.

He was taken aback by the excess he encountered in the record industry in his early dealings with them at *Dotmusic*. He was also frustrated that the success of the CD was making labels indifferent to the coming of digital.

'It was a money-printing machine because often they would just reissue stuff on CDs that people had already bought on cassette – so they were double dipping in a way,' he says. 'It was party time in music! Because everyone had been living off the CD boom, there was a huge amount of complacency around. There were only very few people at the record labels who were interested.'

Silver confirms this with a sigh. 'What became very, very clear was that, fundamentally and strategically, there was not a desire to change,' he says. 'We had maximised the CD opportunity as an industry. Our revenues were sky high at that point, by historic standards. So all we could look at was jam today and jam tomorrow.'

This 1990s boom time in the record business coincided with a boom time in the technology business. There were, as we will see, moments of crossover, but both sectors were caught in the warp speed of their own rapid growth trajectories, too self-involved and too arrogant to really care too much about what was happening outside their own realms.

When the two sectors found themselves really coming together at the close of the 1990s, it was the kind of gentle intertwining one normally associates with a boa constrictor.

UNPLEASANT VALLEY SOME DAY: THE DOT COM BOOM MEANS A LOOMING STORM FOR MUSIC

A particular stretch of Northern California, essentially between San Jose and San Francisco, is known colloquially as Silicon Valley. Its sobriquet has been traced back to a January 1971 article in *Electronic News* by Don Hoefler entitled 'Silicon Valley USA.' He is reported to have first heard the term from Ralph Vaerst, founder of Ion Equipment Corp, as he was researching an article about the computer and hardware industries concentrated in the area.[29] The name took off in the 1980s and is now as much a mindset and an ideology as it is a geographical location.

In his bracing oral history of the place, Adam Fisher wrote, 'History, to Silicon Valley, is the story of the new versus the old: how one technology is vanquished or subsumed by the next.'[30] The impression he gives of Silicon Valley is of a place in constant flux, propelling itself into the future with no regard for the businesses and ideas it tears through and junks. Silicon Valley is always right: it is down to everyone else to keep up.

There is a beautiful symbolism in the fact that San Francisco only became the major city it is now because of the gold rush in the mid 1800s. In 1846, it was a tiny town of two hundred people. Two years later, gold was found in Sutter's Mill in Coloma, just over a hundred miles away, and prospectors descended on the area *en masse*. San Francisco swiftly grew to 36,000 people by 1852 and then rocketed to 150,000 by 1857.[31]

Silicon Valley is now seen as the apotheosis of the American dream, where fortunes can be made in an instant. That same prospecting spirit from the 1850s is traceable to the technological gold rush from the 1960s onwards.

As Ezra Callahan, one of the earliest Facebook employees, put it in Fisher's book, 'It's a place where people with an idea and some talent can make something huge out of something small. It's the success stories of young entrepreneurs with no particular business experience who, within a matter of months, become industry-creating technological celebrities.'[32]

Fisher says Silicon Valley really began with the development of computer game Pong, inspired by the Spacewar! game, by Nolan Bushnell and Ted Dabney, co-founders of Atari, which Allan Alcorn had developed for them as a training exercise.[33]

'Not only did Bushnell single-handedly create an industry around a new American art form – video games – he also wrote what has become the quintessential Silicon Valley script,' wrote Fisher. 'The story goes like this: Young kid with radical idea hacks together something cool, builds a wild free-wheeling company around it, and becomes rich and famous in the process.'[34]

Everything that came in the wake of Atari drew on its story – from Apple and Microsoft to Google, Facebook and Twitter – with the only thing that was different being the speed of change and the scale of the transition from old to new and beyond. Build the future and burn down the past.

'Titans rise, titans fall – that's the nature of the world,' said Jamis MacNiven, founder of the Buck's of Woodside restaurant, where a multitude of tech companies would host their earliest meetings. 'It just happens faster in Silicon Valley.'[35]

In early 1990, there was a frenzy around Silicon Valley, driven in part by a change in financial terms but also in contractual and deal terms. Roger Lowenstein charted the dot com bubble, noting that it was the wider introduction of stock options to CEOs, rather than paying them a huge salary, that changed the rules of engagement.

'Soon, a new model of governance, a new elixir, and not incidentally a new culture was born, and it revolved around the stock option.'[36]

The stock option had fallen out of favour in the 1970s due to the weak nature of the stock market, but things started to change in the 1980s as Silicon Valley 'made stock options seem especially fashionable', making it 'the advance guard of the stock market bubble.'[37]

This made CEOs – and, by default, the companies they were leading – more rapacious in their actions and more ruthless in their ambition to succeed.

Everything was exacerbated in the 1990s when IPOs (initial public offerings[38]) in Silicon Valley were becoming headline news. In 1983, over 90 per cent of stocks in the US were owned by the wealthiest 1 per cent of households, but a major societal shift in attitudes towards stocks and shares had happened by 1998 when over half of American households owned stocks (be that through individual shareholdings or by way of mutual funds).[39]

Stocks had become democratised and Silicon Valley companies were desperate to capitalise on this growing public interest.

Author John Cassidy suggests, 'The discovery of gold on the internet can be dated, with some precision, to August 1995, when Netscape, the maker of the Netscape Navigator Web browser, held its IPO.'[40] At the close of the first day, over 14 million shares in the company had been traded (meaning each of its five million shares had, on average, changed hands close to three times). The company's valuation at the end of that first day's trading was $2.2 billion.[41]

Lowenstein, however, cites eBay's IPO in September 1998 as a major watershed moment, but perhaps not as much of a watershed moment as when theGlobe.com (a company that let people build their own websites) did its IPO that November where shares rocketed from $9 to $97 in five minutes, giving the company a paper valuation of $1 billion.

At least eBay had demonstrable earnings; theGlobe.com had only been going for nine months and had revenues of just $2.7 million.[42]

There was, by this stage, a feeding frenzy where investment was being driven as much by hype and IPO windfalls as it was by solid business ideas.

At the close of the 1990s, the record industry was intoxicated on the profits from CDs; Silicon Valley was intoxicated on merely the *theory* of huge profits from software-centric ideas. Venture capital (VC) firms could not sign cheques quickly enough, with $60 billion being invested in new tech companies in 1999, sharply up from just $3 billion in 1990.[43] In 1996, there were 458 VC firms in the US, with $52 billion under management. By 1999, that had almost doubled to 779 VC firms with $164 billion to invest. The average investment in 1999 was $15 million.[44]

Caution and logic were the first casualties in this VC stampede to get in early with companies that seldom had anything even approaching a solid revenue stream. 'The magic rise of such profitless companies distorted the scales of traditional business, now derisively referred to as the old economy,' cautioned Lowenstein.[45] He added that between 1998 and 2000, investment banks had earned fees of $3.9 billion for brokering deals for companies that rarely showed profitability.[46]

With numbers like these flying around it is far from surprising that this mass distortion of economic reality became not just endemic but the default setting. Lowenstein says, 'the mania of '99 was absolutely breathtaking' and marked a business sector that had spun ridiculously out of control. 'Notwithstanding the Pollyannaish optimism of the late twenties, there was nothing in the Jazz Age (or in any other period in American life) to compare with the dot-com phenomenon, in which scores of companies that were *worthless* from start to finish came to be valued in the billions of dollars and, indeed, at vast premiums to established, profitable enterprises,' he wrote. 'The harm done was massive.'[47]

In his hair-raising account of the dot com boom, Michael Wolff suggests that a 'new American industry was being born' in this time, in large part because the internet business had a cost of entry that was minimal, was subjected to little-to-no regulation and predicated on 'no rules, no religion, no canon, no bullshit.'[48]

The first website was launched on 6 August 1991. It was created by Tim Berners-Lee for the European Organization for Nuclear Research (CERN).[49] By 1993, there were just over a million computers connected to the internet globally.[50]

Wolff, however, argued this remained a highly esoteric world for a few years, with only a handful of websites ('mostly one-page jobs with straightforward hypertext links') in existence by early 1994.[51] In the next few years, there was growing interest in the internet space, but it confounded as many as it excited. 'The world seemed to be dividing cleanly between those who had no interest in the internet, saw no logic or sexiness in it, and those who were just dying to believe in it.'[52]

In 1995, there were an estimated 23,500 websites in existence, up sharply from 2,738 the year before.[53] By 1999, there were 3.17 million websites.[54]

The age was defined by seemingly endless growth and characterised by the arrogance that the wave being surfed would stretch into infinity. Silicon Valley was soon to find out that the good times it thought would never end were rapidly approaching. Yet as Wolff cautioned, 'The zeitgeist [. . .] is an unreliable business partner.'[55]

MUSIC'S EARLY DIGITAL DISCIPLES AND EXPERIMENTERS

The argument that the music business was fast asleep or simply dismissive of the coming digital changes in the 1990s has been repeated so often that it has ossified into fact. Yet there were many label executives and artists pushing the digital boundaries throughout the 1990s. They may have been toiling at the margins, but they were keen to experiment beyond the CD, despite the staggering revenues it was bringing in, and find new pathways to the future.

On 27 June 1994, Aerosmith released 'Head First', an outtake from their *Get A Grip* album sessions, as an exclusive download (as a WAV file), the first major act to release music this way. There were suggestions that it took upwards of ninety minutes to download, but it proved, given sluggish internet speeds and the small number of people online in 1994, reasonably successful, being downloaded by ten thousand CompuServe subscribers in eight days.[56] CompuServe had two million users, so for something so unprecedented, these were impressive numbers.

Jim Griffin was chief technology officer at Geffen Records, Aerosmith's label, at the time. He saw all this as a technological inevitability, but also a more cost-effective means of marketing.

'I'll give you a number – it's firmly in my head,' he says. 'At the time we had calculated that it cost us a quarter of a million dollars to release a track. In other words, we would spend $250,000 to put a single into the marketplace. The people we hired, the way we would put it out there, the stores and the arrangements we made with them. We were effectively buying their shelf space. And with radio we were doing the same; we were buying their airwaves. As a result, we calculated that we would spend about a quarter of a million dollars to test the waters with a new track. That was prohibitive for many things, but it was our sense that, if this evolved, we would have a way to try new music without the gamble. That we could put it out there and read the reaction, without the expenditure of a quarter of a million dollars.'

Geffen Records had been acquired by MCA Music Entertainment in 1990, but its major label owner was not as enthused by digital experiments like the Aerosmith one.

'There was enormous tension about what it was, how it would be used, if it would be used at all,' says Griffin. 'We were the object of memos from the legal department prohibiting things and telling us not to do X or Y and Z. Yet it seemed inevitable to us that we needed to be doing these things.'

He felt that too much marketing money was being wasted with no way of telling what worked – or to what extent. He says that Geffen had undertaken a marketing study that brought back a worrying statistic about record releases in the physical world: they found that 70 per cent of respondents did not know when a favourite act had released a new record.

'I mean, that's disconnected,' says Griffin. 'That is an enormous goal to overcome 70 per cent of these people don't know when their favourite artist has a new record out. And yet we were spending enormous amounts of money on marketing.'

Scott Cohen co-founded music distribution company The Orchard in 1997 with Richard Gottehrer (who had co-founded Sire Records with Seymour Stein in 1966). They originally started working together in 1995 when they set up a label called Sol 3 ('which we very quickly renamed – privately – as Sold 3 because we were so shit that was about the best we could do'). They were both gripped by the potential of the internet to change the rules of engagement for record labels.

'In 1995, we started doing online promotions, which is really early,' he says. 'This was the days of AOL. We had ten computers connected to the internet in our office. We got interns, free interns, from New York University who wanted to be in the music business. We sat them in front of computers. We had twn computers, but only six phone lines, because that's how you got on the internet. And everyone had their own AOL account so they'd have to log on.'

It proved to be a steep learning curve for them. 'You pay every minute you are online to the phone company and every minute to AOL, so you were double charged,' recalls Cohen. 'It was fucking expensive to be online. We went online with those modems and people would take turns. "Hey, I'm going online in five." They'd go on and somebody else would log off. What they were doing was they would go into message boards on AOL where people could talk about music. We'd go into message boards about bands that were similar to ones on our label, but were much bigger, and we would click on their username. It was all very anonymous back then. So it'd be Astroman6004. Click! And you could send him an email. The intern would find it, click, send an email that would be like, "Hey, I see you like so and so. You should check out this band on our label".'

As this was so unusual at the time, he says that they were effectively working on a 100 per cent response rate from the people they were targeting.

'Oftentimes, it was the first email anyone ever received,' says Cohen. 'The first! And it was a targeted, relevant marketing message. It was about music and the genre they liked. People would say, "Where do I find this?" They'd send us $10 cheques in the mail and we'd ship them off the CD.'

It was from this online marketing that the idea of The Orchard was born, spotting not just a different type of delivery system but also a different type of audience engagement to be nurtured that was previously not possible.

While major label employees like Jim Griffin may have felt at the time they were locked in an echo chamber and that the wider industry was not taking them seriously, or simply not listening to them, there were like-minded individuals in other major labels arriving at the same conclusions about the impact that digital was going to have.

In November 1996, Sammy Hagar, who had just left Van Halen that year, became another unlikely digital pioneer by releasing the track 'Salvation On Sand Hill' as a Liquid Audio download.[57] It was claimed the track was downloaded a hundred thousand times.[58]

Three years after the Aerosmith experiment, EMI/Capitol Records made Duran Duran track 'Electric Barbarella' available for free streaming for two weeks from 9 September 1997 as a way of promoting their

Medazzaland album. The original plan was to sell the track, in the Liquid Audio format, for $0.99 and sell a special 'internet-only mix' of the track for $1.99. The commercial release was put back to 23 September, but in the fortnight before that fans were able to stream it or download a 30-second clip for free.[59]

Jeremy Silver was the executive overseeing the Duran Duran project at EMI and had been working on digital initiatives for artists for several years at this stage, having set up The Raft for Virgin Records in 1994. The name was inspired by sci-fi writer Neal Stephenson's *Snow Crash* novel 'which depicted a seminal vision of a virtual world'[60] and became a major focus for Silver.

'It was an artist-led site,' he explains. 'The theory then, as now, is that consumers are interested in bands and they are not interested in labels.'

He admits now that the Duran Duran release in 1997 was mainly a brazen PR stunt.

'At that point, it was just about using it as a gimmick,' he reveals. 'It was a novelty. For the most part, every time we did one of these things, it was a novelty: the fact that Duran Duran claimed to have the first ever track downloaded and sold online. What was the thing that was important about that? It was Duran Duran! Not the fact that there was a download involved.'

Scott Campbell was founder and MD of MediaSpec at the time, dealing in digital post-production technology, with clients including Abbey Road Studios. He was involved in the Duran Duran download and says it was his credit card being used to demonstrate the online purchasing when CNN came to the studios to film a piece about it.

'For Duran Duran, it was big publicity for them, even though it was a relaunch of their career,' he says. Around the same time, he was working with George Michael and Andros Georgiou, Michael's second cousin, on digital initiatives for Aegean Records, the label they had founded together.

'They had Aegean.net at the time, which was like an ISP,' he says. 'We got in AT&T who put together the George Michael fan club experience. You could sign up and get an @agean.net email address and all that kind of stuff. Liquid Audio was part of that production and I helped George with that.'

Silver talks of operating for much of the time in a silo, with other executives often mocking his 'nerdy' interest in digital and the internet. More upsetting than their jibes was the simple fact that few were even listening to him.

'It was a struggle to get anyone's attention to even talk about this stuff,' he says. 'I remember chasing a senior executive down the corridor and into the toilet in order to try to have a conversation with him. The only time I could actually get him to stay still and listen to me was when he was having a piss!'

As the decade progressed, rather than seeing all of this as a new form of marketing, Silver was firm in his belief that it could be an entirely new form of income. 'By 1997 or 1998, it was quite clear that we could be making a lot of money out of this,' he says. 'The bubble of the dot com boom was plain for all to see; that the money tree was shakeable and everybody was looking at where the financial opportunity was.'

Of the few people at the label who did listen, most tended to see the internet as purely promotional and not commercial. Says Silver, 'My bosses would pat me on the head and say, "You've been staying up too late at night on those modems of yours. Go back to your modems. We'll look after the business. You look after the future, Jeremy. We'll look after the business." That was quite frustrating, really.'

Finding like-minded people in digital was not straightforward in the mid-1990s and the media interest around the Aerosmith release promoted Griffin to set up the Pho List, initially as a real-world event in a pho restaurant in Los Angeles and then as an online community.

'At the time [of the Aerosmith release], journalists were calling on the phone,' he says. 'I felt terribly guilty that I did not get back to them quickly so I said to my assistant, "Any time a journalist is trying to get a hold of me, and I fail to get back to them in time, tell them to come to this pho restaurant in downtown LA and I will buy them brunch on a Sunday at noon. Every Sunday at noon, I will be there or I will have someone there to talk to them."'

Journalists and other industry people started showing up to discuss digital and music and word spread so quickly and so widely that even a brace of students from Harvard Business School showed up.

'So we thought that this is catching on,' marvels Griffin. 'People really do want to get together and talk about these things. At the time, hundreds of people from Los Angeles, from Hollywood, were coming, and then the students from the Harvard Business School came. It just became clear that we needed a way to communicate. And so the Pho List was born. It took on a life of its own, like a metaphor for the internet itself.'

Al Teller joined MCA in 1998 and by 1995 had become chairman and CEO of the music entertainment group there. He says he was an advocate for digital, saying that his final keynote at his last MCA conference was '10 per cent congratulating everybody for all the good work they'd been doing' and 'the other 90 per cent was about the coming of the Internet'.

He recalls, 'The line I used in my talk was, "Any record company that does not take the internet seriously and aggressively begin to adopt it and adapt to it is going to find itself left as digital dust on the internet highway".'

He says he also took the same message to the RIAA, where he was on the executive committee. 'At every one of these committee meetings I kept saying, "We need to work as an industry to get on top of the coming of the internet rather than let some folks from the technology world start dictating terms to us".'

He found himself running into a brick wall at the time with the other majors, something which caused him enormous frustration. 'I could not get anyone else's agreement, whether it was Sony, BMG, Warner, PolyGram – nobody,' he says. 'Nobody else was interested in doing this.'

While Duran Duran and Aerosmith were being encouraged and directed by the handful of digital evangelists active within major labels, a number of musicians were independently coming alive to the artistic and community potential of the internet as well as the fact that it could empower them in new ways, allowing them to reach audiences directly without that being mediated and controlled by record labels.

Todd Rundgren had long been fascinated by computers and multimedia. Back in 1978, he organised what *Sound On Sound* called 'the world's first interactive television concert [. . .] during which home audiences could choose what songs would be played.' In 1992, he released his *No World Order* album on CD-I, which sliced all the songs into four-bar segments that enabled listeners to build their own song structures.[61]

He released his *The Individualist* album in 1994 as the first full-length enhanced CD and then launched both www.tr-i.com and www.patronet.com to allow fans to pay in advance for music that would be delivered directly to them online. Through PatroNet in 1998, he began issuing new material and reworking old tracks, suggesting the future lay in creating subscription services for fans. On PatroNet, he had different subscriber tiers with monthly fees ranging from $25 to $60 a year, and new music being sent to subscribers as soon as it was ready. 'The service isn't anti-label but anti-inventory,' he said. It echoed what Kristin Hersh of Throwing Muses had been testing with her Works In Progress subscription service, offering fans twelve unreleased songs a year as MP3 download for a $15 fee.[62]

'The Web will be a great place to find music,' Rundgren told *Wired* in 1998. 'It will make the music of the world more accessible.' He cautioned, however, that artists would have to significantly recalibrate the level of success they would have here. 'If you have blockbuster expectations, you might be disappointed,' he said. 'If you want a million people as fans, this might not be the way to go. I want a loyal following that's interested in what I'm going to do next. It's a lot like bands who throw everything in the van and head out for every podunk town, just to find five people who will come hear them again.'[63]

Prince was similarly prescient here and took the idea behind the NPG retail store[64] in Minneapolis, which opened in 1993, and transplanted it online in 1997. He began selling his *Crystal Ball* CD via the site[65] but soon expanded to add in merchandise.[66]

David Bowie was equally rhapsodic about the possibilities of the internet and had been experimenting with digital for several years. In 1994, he released *Jump*, a PC CD that let fans create their own video for his single 'Jump, They Say' and in 1996 he released 'Telling Lies' online only. The following year, he did a 'cybercast' of a show from Boston.

His biggest move, however, came in September 1998 with the launch of BowieNet, his own branded ISP. Tied to a dedicated website, users could access a large archive of photos and videos as well as a blog and plenty of exclusive tracks and webcasts. Similar to the George Michael ISP, users could get a BowieNet email address. Bowie himself would occasionally host live web chats.[67] It cost fans $19.95 a month for all the different component parts as well as full internet access. At its peak, it had around a hundred thousand customers.[68]

'I wanted to create an environment where not just my fans but all music lovers could be a part of the same community, a single place where the vast archives of music information could be accessed, views stated and ideas exchanged,' said Bowie on the launch of BowieNet.[69]

Bowie's business manager, Bill Zysblat, told *Forbes* that the ISP move was not immediately concerned about the commercial opportunities, but was paving the way for this in the near future. 'Money was not the main reason to go into this,' said Zysblat in September 1998. 'But maybe someday he'll be selling records online.'[70] Within a year, Bowie was to sell music online in a way that upended the old order, set a bomb under traditional retail and sent shockwaves through the industry (see Chapter 15).

Digital music was gathering a head of steam as the 1990s progressed, but it was still an experience anchored to a computer. There was, however, about to be a seismic unshackling of digital music and it was going to become portable and create whole new experiences for consumers, but also whole new traumas for the record industry.

'TAKE THAT FUCKING THING HOME IF YOU KNOW WHAT YOUR JOB'S WORTH': DIGITAL MUSIC PLAYERS ARRIVE

Music listening used to be tied down to a location. You had to go to where musicians were playing or, as technology advanced, listen via a hefty radio set[71], wax cylinder[72] or record player[73] in the home.

The mass untethering of the listening experience, taking it out of the home and making it portable, happened in late 1954 with the launch of Texas Instruments' Regency TR-1 transistor radio. This pocket-sized device was not cheap, however, with the first models selling for $49.50 (the equivalent of $550 today).[74]

The first portable gramophone was developed by Decca back in 1919[75], followed by the Mikiphone (branded as a 'pocket phonograph') in Switzerland in 1924, which was a circular metal container with a diameter of just 11.5cm that had to be unpacked and reassembled, making it an incredibly fiddly experience.[76]

The arrival of the Dansette in the 1950s was significant as it had three speed options (33⅓ rpm, 45 rpm and 78 rpm) and grew in lockstep with the growth of the single from early rock'n'roll into the pop explosion of the 1960s.[77]

The biggest leap forward in music portability, however, came in 1979 with the launch of the TPS-L2, Sony's first Walkman.[78] It initially sold for $200 in the US ($726 today) and was such an immediate hit that there was reportedly a two-month waiting list for it at Bloomingdale's in New York.[79]

Where the Walkman differed significantly from all the other portable music players that preceded it was that it not only played a commercially released audio format (the cassette) but it also played cassettes that users at home could compile themselves from any audio source (cassette, LP, the radio). The Walkman was not only portable, it also allowed users to curate their own listening experience, not one dictated to them by recording artists and record labels on the albums they released.

The cassette Walkman was followed by the CD Discman[80] in 1984 and the MZ-1 MiniDisc[81] player in 1992. By 1999, Sony was reporting global shipments of 196 million cassette Walkman players, 46 million CD Walkman players and 4.6 million MiniDisc Walkman players.[82] Of course, a multitude of other consumer electronics companies had introduced rival players to the market so the number of Walkman-like devices will have been substantially higher than just Sony's official sales numbers.

There was record industry concern around the commercial availability of devices that allowed consumers to make their own recordings at home – as well as significant court cases, anti-piracy campaigns and legislative changes (covered in Chapter 5) – but the audio quality deteriorated when transferred to a compact cassette and, sonically at least, was seen as an inferior offering than commercially released recordings.

The development of digital audio compression, notably the MP3 (covered in Chapter 6), meant that copies could be made endlessly and the audio quality of the digital file would not deteriorate no matter how many times it was copied.

Like the early days of radio and records, digital music listening, even though it was still a relatively niche activity, was restricted to bulky and unportable devices at home. There were prototype MP3 players circulating in the tech industry in the mid 1990s, but none were commercially manufactured. Jeremy Silver recounts Larry Miller from AT&T Labs coming to his London offices in November 1996 with 'the first ever mp3 player' to demonstrate it to him. Silver described it as 'a clunky-looking black box' built into the body of, symbolically, an old Sony CD Walkman and that was '[h]eld together with duct tape,'[83] What made it different was that it had no moving parts. 'Considering the importance of this breakthrough, the effect was unsurprisingly unsexy,' noted Silver, adding that Miller was 'on a mission to evangelise the player and the concept of the MP3 as a new standard', using this 'laboratory prototype' as his calling card.[84]

'It was very interesting that this was a telecoms business that had latched onto this,' he says of AT&T's early move here. 'It would be really interesting if history would have been rewritten, had AT&T taken that initiative, looked at that innovation and thought, "This is going to give us a huge new revenue stream for our networks".'

AT&T never took this nameless MP3 player to market, but the same ideas were percolating elsewhere and the companies behind them had bold commercial ambitions.

Two devices arrived in quick succession in 1998 that were to do for the MP3 what the Walkman did for the cassette. The record industry's panic here stemmed from a firm belief that because no mainstream MP3 paid download services even existed and, even if they did, the major labels had not yet licensed their catalogues for sale this way, MP3 players could only be filled with files that were (largely) pirated online.

The MPMan F10, created by South Korea's Saehan Information Systems, arrived in March 1998.[85] It had a mere 32MB of Flash storage (so could only hold 'a handful of songs') but it seemed to slip under the record industry's radar.

The commercial release of the Rio PMP300, developed by Diamond Multimedia, on 15 September 1998 quickly faced the full wrath of the US record business. It, too, only had 32MB of storage, but it was what it represented that most raised the hackles of the major labels and the RIAA.

Within a matter of weeks of it going on sale, the RIAA claimed it was in direct violation of the 1992 US Audio Home Recordings Act (AHRA).[86] It swiftly filed a lawsuit on 8 October and demanded it be withdrawn from sale. The RIAA managed to secure a ban on 16 October, only to have it withdrawn ten days later.

This court triumph was, as author Steve Knopper noted, down to the fact that Diamond 'had excellent attorneys' who managed to find a loophole in the 1992 act that 'specifically exempted computers'[87] (i.e. the Rio required a connection to a computer hard drive onto which MP3 files had been ripped). The media interest around the case helped Diamond go on to sell 200,000 Rio players.[88]

'This is not an anti-MP3 action,' said Hilary Rosen of the RIAA at the time. 'They (Diamond) are going out to market at a time when the majority of MP3 files on the internet are not legitimate.' She backed this up by claiming that the RIAA, in one afternoon, had found 80 MP3 sites with more than twenty thousand MP3 files online. They said they were almost all illegal recordings by major acts.[89]

Other markets were closely following what was happening with the Rio in the US. Global record company trade association the IFPI called the Rio's arrival in the UK 'damaging' for the industry, arguing MP3 was essentially a pirate format. Mike Edwards, the IFPI's director of operations, told *Music Week*, 'Definitely at this stage it is doing more harm than good. Wherever we find these devices being marketed illegally we will take action.'[90]

Ken Wirt, Diamond's VP of corporate marketing, responded saying, 'We're not promoting the illegal use of music. With the Rio, we've included two hundred songs from unsigned artists who want to distribute their music via MP3.'[91]

The RIAA was far from pleased with its call for an injunction against the Rio being rejected by Judge Audrey Collins, saying it would appeal the decision. Cary Sherman, the RIAA's senior EVP and general counsel, said, 'We think the judge made an error of law [. . .] Everybody has a moral obligation to protect creative works and we want to engage in a dialogue with these companies. We are doing everything we can to move this process along.'[92]

Looking back on the 1998 case, Sherman says it was an important proactive move by the RIAA to try and head off ever bigger problems at the pass. 'The Diamond Rio case was brought because we were attempting to get a music industry and a tech industry technological standards-setting solution to these issues before the problem got out of control,' he explains.

The Rio case dragged into 1999 and Diamond eventually emerged triumphant in June that year, with the 9th Circuit Court of Appeals ruling that the Rio did not qualify as a 'digital audio recording device' and, as such, did not fall under the AHRA. 'The Rio is incapable of independent recording or serial copying and is simply not covered by the act, something we have argued from the beginning of the case,' Andrew Bridges, one of Diamond's lawyers, told *Variety*. The RIAA could only say it was 'disappointed' in the ruling.[93]

'[It] really was only ever used to rip off music,' says Rosen reflecting on the case. 'The industry was determined to send a message to manufacturers that that wasn't going to be tolerated. We sued the Diamond Rio and lost that case because they – 'they' meaning their lawyers, and the court agreed – came up with enough other, in theory, non-infringing uses.'

The early MP3 players, beyond their tiny storage capabilities, were not seen as beautiful pieces of design. Author Steven Levy, when comparing them to the ergonomic elegance of Apple's iPod that followed in 2001, is unsparing in his assessment of their limitations.

'They generally held too little music, had impenetrable interfaces, and looked like the cheap plastic toys given to losers at carnival games.'[94]

Knopper also disdainfully described the Rio as 'ugly and hard to use' as well as 'resembling a walkie-talkie that had shrunk in the dryer.'[95]

Responses within the music industry when they first encountered the Rio were mixed to say the least.

Jollyon Benn was the internet investigations executive at the BPI at the time, working within the body's anti-piracy department. As such he was intrigued by this device that was causing such an uproar in the US.

'Personally – not the BPI's view by any stretch – I bought one so I could play with it and see how it worked,' he says. 'The interface for it was dreadful in terms of getting content from your PC onto it. The Diamond Rio was like the ZX80 of its time. It was just shite!'

For music lawyer and self-confessed 'gadget freak' Cliff Fluet, business affairs manager for the Central Division of Warner Music UK at the time, the Rio was a Damascene moment. 'It was absolutely an avatar for everything that was going on,' he says, but suggests the most senior people at the company were gravely spooked by it. 'Most record industry executives saw it almost like a grenade – in terms of its size and in terms of what it would do to the industry.'

By way of illustration, he recounts having travelled to the US in late 1998 and bringing back a Rio, effusively showing it off to colleagues, loudly extolling its virtues and the industry changes he believed it was a catalyst for. During his show and tell in the Warner offices, a senior executive made their disapproval more than clear. 'I was told, "Take that fucking thing home if you know what your job's worth",' says Fluet.

The attitude within the major labels at the most senior level was often one of protectionism and of either ignoring digital, in all its iterations, or trying to bring it to heel. Bloated on the phenomenal profits of CDs, the majors were keen to bulk up further still. If they could not do it through sales alone then they would do it through accelerated consolidation.

A whole new growth dynamic was about to hit the record business and it was all about ruthless land grabs for market share. The bigger the grab, the better.

THE ERA OF THE SUPER-MAJOR: HOW UNIVERSAL MUSIC BECAME THE BEHEMOTH OF THE RECORD BUSINESS (OR A $10.6 BILLION TRAIN SET)

As a member of the Seagram dynasty, the Canadian distillers that grew to become a multinational conglomerate of staggering power, Edgar Bronfman Jr, on paper at least, seems an unlikely candidate to be the architect of what was to become the biggest record company in the world.

He had a keen interest in the arts, originally hoping to dominate in the film business as well as trying his hand as a song lyricist, notably co-writing 'Whisper In The Dark' (recorded by Dionne Warwick), 'To Love You More' (recorded by Celine Dion) and 'If I Didn't Love You' (recorded by Barbara Streisand). His creative ambitions ran in parallel with his corporate ambitions. His interest in the music business suggests he understood that he could have more impact in the boardroom than in the studio.

Speaking to me in early 2023 for this book, Bronfman looks back on this move and explains the investment appeal to him of entertainment companies.

'At Seagram, we'd always been a company with assets in safe places – North America and Scotland, principally – but sold those products all around the world,' he says. 'It seemed to me that the entertainment business offered the same kind of situation, which was assets that were primarily UK and US, but would be distributed all around the world. I also felt there would be an explosion in distribution capabilities over time, and that there was a limited amount of content – so that global distribution would be enhanced.'

Bronfman initially hoped for Seagram to buy MCA, founded in 1924 by eye surgeon Jules Stein[96] as the Music Corporation of America. He was, however, beaten to the punch by Matsushita Electric Industrial Co who acquired MCA in November 1990 in a deal estimated at $6.6 billion.[97] MCA was also the owner of Universal Studios.

Bronfman did not have to wait so long to take control of MCA, leading a deal whereby he paid $5.7 billion to Matsushita to take over 80 per cent of MCA.

'For Matsushita, selling control of MCA ends a stormy, five-year marriage marked by an openly strained relationship with MCA Chairman Lew R. Wasserman, 82, and President Sidney J. Sheinberg, 60, the longest-running management team in Hollywood,' noted the *Los Angeles Times* on 10 April 1995 when the deal went through. 'That relationship worsened in the past week as Wasserman and Sheinberg deliberately were kept in the dark about the talks.'[98]

By the end of the year, Bronfman changed the corporate name of the company from MCA Inc to Universal Studios Inc – covering all the company's interests in movies, TV music and theme parks.[99]

Doug Morris had been 'the No. 2 executive in Time Warner's record division' but was spectacularly fired after 17 years at the company 'because he had failed to disclose that he knew about the alleged theft of thousands of compact discs from Time Warner's Atlantic Records label', so reported *The Washington Post* in July 1995.[100]

When Al Teller left as the head of the music division at MCA, Bronfman moved to lure in Morris. Morris, then reportedly being courted by both Viacom and PolyGram, was initially cold to Bronfman's overtures.[101]

Bronfman played to Morris's vanity and offered to set him up a well-funded new label within Universal. Morris agreed. The label's name, Rising Tide Records, was a reference to Bronfman's recruitment strategy. He had called Morris and told him to watch *The Shawshank Redemption*, which had been released the year before. Morris replied he'd already seen it and asked Bronfman why he was insisting he watch it. 'Because,' said Bronfman, 'I'm the guy waiting on the beach for you.'[102]

Bronfman had bold ambitions for his new music company and moved in February 1996 to buy 50 per cent of Interscope Records[103] (which had been dropped by Time-Warner amid a furore over rap lyrics). This brought the ebulliently ambitious Jimmy Iovine into Bronfman's company. The Interscope deal saw Universal's market share in music jump from 8 per cent to 14 per cent, whetting Bronfman's appetite for more.[104] Bronfman then offered Morris the chairman role at the rapidly expanding company.[105]

'That really changed the culture of this group of companies forever,' said Morris. 'When you're in front of the parade with cutting-edge music, all of the other artists look to it and admire it. All of a sudden, wow, Universal [was] hot on the East Coast, Interscope on the West Coast. Suddenly we were a force to be reckoned with.'

Bronfman looked to make the music company more professional by cutting down on waste, lowering its expenses and hosting fewer parties – suggesting a slick company culture replacing a hedonistic one.

Laura Martin, at the time an entertainment analyst at Credit Suisse First Boston, said, 'From a Wall Street point of view, as someone who allocates capital, you're more willing to allocate capital to a firm that's becoming more efficient in its use of that capital.'[106]

MCA's sales had largely been in the US. It might have had the biggest market in the world for record sales, but MCA had made little headway outside of the territory, earning it the snide sobriquet of Music Cemetery of America.[107]

Bronfman wanted to stick it to the detractors and had clear global ambitions for his new company with plans to break more of its artists internationally. Biographer Rod McQueen noted that Bronfman was keen to assure the company's employees that 'he was there for the long haul' and that 'he was someone who believed in buying, improving, and keeping companies.'[108]

In wanting to prove the naysayers wrong – about him and about his new music company – Bronfman's acquisition of Interscope was merely the *amuse bouche*. He wanted Universal to become the biggest music company in the world. While deals like the Interscope one could incrementally take him there, he was impatient and was setting his sights on the biggest beasts among the majors. He did not want them to buy Universal. He wanted *Universal to buy them*.

The purchase of Interscope was to prove incredibly straightforward compared to what Bronfman was planning next. It was to greatly test his nerve and his tenacity, but if Universal was to become the dominant music company, Bronfman was assured it would all be worth it. In 1996, he made overtures to Colin Southgate, chairman of EMI Group, about a merger or acquisition of some sort. He also approached Cornelius Boonstra, chairman of Philips Electronics (which controlled 75 per cent of PolyGram) with a similar mission.

The talks with EMI were happening at the highest level, with many senior executives within the company oblivious to what was happening until leaks started appearing in the business press.

Tony Wadsworth was promoted from managing director of the Parlophone label to president of EMI Records UK in 1998. He says rumours of a sale of EMI were circulating from early 1996 when EMI was demerged from Thorn.[109] (Thorn Electrical Industries had originally acquired EMI in 1979).

'It was part of Thorn EMI's gradual divestment of what it regarded as its core businesses,' says Wadsworth. 'The whole thing was to realise as much shareholder value as possible. Eventually Sir Colin [Southgate] gets left with a music company, having divested himself of lightbulbs and electronics and Rumbelows and Radio Rentals or whatever. Then that was his main game and he had to actually make the most of that.'

Despite his senior position at the company, Wadsworth says 'awareness and discussion of these potential mergers was very low', adding that there were 'several layers between me and where all of this stuff was happening.'

This all became purely academic as Southgate rebuffed Seagram, allegedly calling Bronfman a 'bootlegger'[110] (a crass reference to allegations that Bronfman's grandfather transported alcohol over the border to the US during prohibition).

Bronfman invited Boonstra to his Manhattan home for dinner and Boonstra invited along Alain Levy, head of PolyGram, suggesting a deal could be thrashed out. Levy soon disabused him of that suspicion saying, 'Under no circumstances am I working for you.'[111]

Two discussions. Two shocking rejections.

Things changed over the next eighteen months, notably EMI's share price slipping by a third, so Bronfman contacted Southgate again to see if a new deal could be done.

Music & Copyright at the time was reporting that Seagram was 'in many ways a natural partner' for EMI and that it would be 'unlikely that BMG, PolyGram, Sony or Warner would be able to cross the regulatory hurdles involved in buying EMI.'[112]

In January 1998, Bronfman and Southgate agreed on a target price of £6.35 per share for EMI, but due diligence altered Bronfman to the fact that EMI was not in as great a shape as he had hoped. He told Southgate he could not recommend that share price to his board, suggesting it would have to be under £6. Southgate reportedly shrugged and said, 'It doesn't matter because there's no deal if it's less than seven.'[113]

The conversations, disastrous as they were, had taken place behind closed doors, but EMI admitted in April 1998 that it had been approached with an offer but would not say who it was from.[114] It quickly leaked that it was Universal.

Days later, Boonstra got in touch and said he was open to discussions.

David Geffen, founder of Geffen Records and an executive not known for delicate diplomacy, advised Bronfman on the course he should take. 'Do you know what the difference is between PolyGram and EMI?' he reportedly asked Bronfman. 'The first is chicken salad and the other is chicken shit.'[115]

I ask Bronfman if this oft-quoted line from Geffen was true.

'Well, he said it!' he says, laughing. 'That is true. My view was somewhat different. I did not see it that one was good and that one was bad. They both had strengths. But that was David's comment for sure.'

Variety, fanning the speculation further, reported in late April 1998 that the 'acquisition of EMI would be a coup for Bronfman', adding that he 'believes that Universal's biggest growth opportunity is in music.' It fleshed this thesis out by noting that Universal, while holding 12 per cent of the US market, only held 3 per cent of the market outside of the US whereas EMI controlled 17 per cent of the non-US market.[116]

Bronfman says he was conducting talks with both companies concurrently but reveals he always had a clear preference. 'I was negotiating with both of them,' he says. 'Quite honestly, my big preference was PolyGram, but I didn't know if I'd get there with PolyGram. So I was basically talking to both. And all that happened was that Colin Southgate badly overplayed his hand.'

I ask Bronfman if he felt that Southgate was expecting too high a price for EMI.

'Way too much,' he says. 'Way too much. My recollection was that it was £7 – he said he would not even take an offer to the board under £7 per share. That's my memory. I said, "Colin, nobody on earth is going to pay you £7." He said, "Well, we'll see about that." And I said, "OK, well if that's where it is, that's where it is." I don't think he was ever serious about selling the company.'

(Southgate died in July 2021,[117] several months before I started work on this book).

Buying PolyGram – despite more cordial relationships with its heads – was instantly attractive to Bronfman as it would mean, in a single deal, he would own the biggest music company in the world.[118]

PolyGram itself had been aggressively bulking up at the close of the 1980s, buying Island Records in July 1989 for an estimated $300 million[119] and then acquiring A&M in October that same year for a reported $500 million.[120]

The drama of the deals had been playing out across the pages of the music trade press, notably *Music Week* in the UK and *Billboard* in the US, with every twist and turn being catalogued. An anonymous analyst quoted in *Music Week* was cynical about EMI's claims of a serious approach. 'It's not as if we haven't been here before' they sighed. 'I mean it's not like EMI are saying they have had a bid – and approaches are cheap to make.'[121]

A few weeks later, Philips had confirmed that Seagram was in discussions to buy PolyGram although rumours were bubbling that Alain Levy was plotting a management buyout of PolyGram and that EMI was being kept in the wings by Seagram should the PolyGram deal fall apart.[122]

Mere weeks after hyping the EMI/Seagram deal, *Music & Copyright* was now proposing that 'PolyGram is arguably a better fit with Seagram's Universal music and film business' as speculation around the deal ramped up in the music trade press.[123]

Music Week suggested in late May that two other leveraged buyout funds – a consortium of Fortsman Little & Co and Thomas H Lee, and Donaldson, Lufkin & Jenrette – had withdrawn their interest in PolyGram, giving Seagram a clear run.[124]

Bronfman had held his nerve and a complex deal was thrashed out whereby Philips would buy $2 billion of shares in Seagram, 'in effect making Philips participating financiers.' The deal in total was valued at $10.6 billion.[125]

Music Week noted that Bronfman had been viewed as 'a playboy dilettante' by many but that the PolyGram deal 'could be the making of Edgar Bronfman.'[126] It threw a sly dig at EMI saying, 'Sir Colin Southgate must be feeling like Miss Havisham.'[127]

Drawing on market share numbers in 1996 from the *MBI World Report*, *Music Week* estimated that the takeover would give the newly inflated Universal a 23 per cent global market share, putting it far ahead of Sony (15.7 per cent), Warner (14.5 per cent), BMG (14 per cent) and EMI (11.2 per cent).[128] The rest of the market was divided between a multitude of independent labels.

Bronfman says such sheer market dominance was always his goal as soon as he took over MCA. 'The grand vision was to create the number one music company in the world and to do that by combining MCA's strength in the US with PolyGram's strength outside the US,' he says.

Larry Kenswil was head of legal and business affairs at Universal when the EMI and PolyGram bids were in motion. He was general counsel on the PolyGram deal and says it changed the company instantly. 'We went from last to first with that purchase,' he explains.

This was all, he feels, an inevitability. He had been at MCA when Seagram bought it and understood that was just the first step in Seagram's bolder ambitions. 'Obviously they wanted to try and buy a second company. The first thing we looked at was EMI. And then it became PolyGram.'

The *Los Angeles Times* spoke to investors who were effusive about the deal, paraphrasing them that they believed that Seagram was getting PolyGram 'at a good price at a time when the record business is poised for a comeback.'[129]

Bronfman flew to London in late May/early June to meet his new team of around thirty-five executives. Some of the executives who met him were positive when approached for comment by *Music Week*, albeit anonymously. One called him 'very articulate' and 'incredibly brave and he set exactly the right tone', adding that he gave 'a heart-warming speech.'

Another called him 'very charming' and said he is 'so obviously passionate about music.' A third source was less obsequious. 'I felt battered, bruised and betrayed. It was like meeting a kid who's just got himself a $10.6bn train set.'[130]

Bronfman says his changes for the company outside of the US were not greeted with applause from some executives, in a large part because it wounded their egos.

'Effectively we adopted the PolyGram organisation and really got rid of the Universal organisation outside of the US, with one or two exceptions,' he says. 'I remember that some of the senior international Universal management said, "How is that possible? We bought them. We should be taking over." And I'm like, "No, we bought them because they're better than we are. We're not taking them over that. That's why we acquired them".'

There was a waiting process before any restructuring could take place, however, as the deal would have to be referred to the competition regulators at the European Commission (EC) and go through antitrust scrutiny in the US, with suggestions it could take six months or more.

Billboard spoke to the appositely named Stefan Rating of DG4 (the EC's competition department) about the approval process and what would be scrutinised.

'Market share is one concern, but it is only one indication of market power,' he said. 'What we are really concerned about is whether a company has enough power in the market to impose prices on its competitors and whether it has the ability to conduct its business independent of its competitors. We could also investigate [whether] the combination of two companies means all other companies in that sector become minor players.'[131]

Bronfman claims he was never unduly worried about the regulatory process and was convinced the deal would pass smoothly.

'We didn't have a concern about regulators, quite honestly,' he says. 'MCA at the time was only a US label and the smallest of the US labels. We had a few international markets, but we were tiny. We really didn't see that a consolidation with the smallest player in the industry, meaning us, with either EMI or PolyGram was going to run afoul of the regulators. We didn't know that it would pass European regulation so quickly. It ended up being only six months. We thought it maybe would take longer. But we were not concerned. That was not part of our thinking with regard to one or the other.'

He had little to worry about. The European Commission regulators at the time were commonly seen as an easy touch. Of the 1,500 merger/acquisition deals it considered in the 1990s, it blocked just thirteen.[132]

Things moved much faster than was initially anticipated, with the deal being approved in late November by the Securities Exchange Commission, and European regulators giving it the green light in early December.

A report prepared for the European Commission into the proposed Seagram/PolyGram deal, dated 21 September 1998, gives good insight into the thought processes at work here.[133] It noted that the six majors – which it listed as PolyGram, Sony, Warner, BMG, EMI/Virgin and Seagram (interestingly not listing it as MCA) – collectively controlled 78 per cent of global sales in 1996. It referred to Seagram as 'not a major record company' as two-thirds of its revenues are in North America and it has limited market presence outside that territory.' It noted that Seagram's share of the market had 'not grown significantly since 1992 to the detriment of the [other] major five music companies.' (1992 was when it last looked at the music market, concentrating on EMI's acquisition of Virgin Records).

Point 29 of the report reads. 'The oligopolistic structure of the music industry may point to a situation of collective dominance. However, the Commission has concluded that the proposed acquisition would not create or strengthen a dominant position among the five major companies as a result of which effective competition would be significantly impeded in the common market or a substantial part of it.'

It adds that 'Seagram has not pursued an aggressive commercial policy to increase its market share at the expense of the five members of the oligopoly' and, looking outside of the majors' collective dominance, concludes that a 'dynamic competitive force is represented by the independent labels.'

In short, it felt that Seagram buying PolyGram would not really change anything for anyone. This summation was yet more reason for the multitude of independent record labels to start to organise themselves in ways they never had before (covered in more depth in Chapter 4).

The deal approval did immediately affect several people adjacent to it.

On the future of Alain Levy at PolyGram, given his previous refusal to work under Bronfman and the rumoured management buyout that came to nothing, one of his lieutenants put it bluntly to *Billboard:* 'When you've been king of the world, why would you accept being king of half the world?'[134]

Colin Southgate was trying to put a brave face on it, attempting to spin the doomed deal with Seagram as actually allowing EMI to enjoy its independence. He batted down rumours that EMI and Seagram could have merged, saying, 'We never got down to detailed discussions with anyone, and now there's absolutely nobody around. That's the nice thing about [the Seagram/PolyGram deal] – it takes us out of their eyes. We are settled.'[135]

The year ended with artists and their managers worried that the combined company was going to brutally slash its roster. Staff members were also anxious about their futures, as deals on this scale traditionally came with drastic cuts in the workforce and stinging cost-saving measures. Doug Morris tried to quell their concerns when it was suggested that up to three thousand staff, equal to 20 per cent of the workforce, could be laid off in order for the company to achieve the $300 million in annual savings that Bronfman wanted.

Fred Goodman noted that the Morris-led restructuring would be around integrating the PolyGram labels into Universal Music Group to 'structure the new company as a group of allied but competing record labels.'[136]

'We're not prepared to discuss it yet,' Morris told *Billboard*. 'All it does is scare people. It's very unsettling. We felt it was better to get through the holidays before a lot of announcements are made.'[137]

In the same issue of *Billboard*, a garish and self-congratulatory two-page ad was placed by Universal. It read: 'We Proudly Welcome PolyGram To The Universal Music Group.' The word 'universal' in dark blue overlapped with the word 'polygram' in light blue. The phrase 'Music Is Universal' was also stamped across the two pages in English as well as in French, German, Italian, Chinese, Swedish, Portuguese and Spanish.

It sent out two messages to the music business readership of *Billboard*: that the company was truly global; and that the company was powering itself with hitherto unforeseen levels of self-belief and/or arrogance.

Morris was further quoted about the implications of the newly enlarged company in *Music Week*. 'When you look at this company you're going to have much more repertoire and much less expense,' he said. 'Our margins are going to be exceptional – it'll be hard for competitors to deal with the kind of financial results we're going to have.'[138]

Kenswil says the company was working towards serious, and painful, reductions in costs and overheads. 'Layoffs or closing down plants,' he says, were the main focus of the cutbacks. 'The cost savings were built into the deal. There were huge targets for most of the department heads.'

Rod McQueen wrote how the whole process could have teetered on the lip of disaster. 'More than two-thirds of all corporate mergers fail because of corporate cultural problems or because cost-cutting possibilities turn out to be minimal.'[139]

Bronfman himself was bullish about what the combined – and streamlined – company was set to achieve when addressing analysts in New York as the year, the biggest corporate year for him personally, came to a close. 'We sought to acquire a music company with complementary strengths,' he said. 'The new Universal Music Group is now the premier music company in the world. Our music operations will generate strong cash flow with minimal capital requirements.'[140]

The other majors were putting a brave face on things and trying to avoid looking unduly worried that the landscape of the record business had suddenly, and dramatically, tilted away from them and the comfortable positions that they used to not just enjoy but also take for granted.

'We looked at it with a degree of scepticism, to be honest,' says Jeremy Silver. 'There was no question about the strength of PolyGram as an organisation. In some respects, it didn't mean anything, because PolyGram was going to continue to be a power and a force for good. It was going to carry on behaving the way that it behaved, which had a different character from some of the other majors, but it was nonetheless very progressive and aggressive in the market. The thing that was interesting about it was, of course, that change meant that the link between Philips and PolyGram was severed.'

Steve Knopper noted of this new super-major, 'If ever there was a record label built for economic success in 1998, it was the Universal Music Group.'[141]

I ask Bronfman if, at the close of 1998 and with the creation of a new super-major, his deal having cleared the regulators would scupper any attempted merger between the other majors. Was this deal effectively on such a scale that it would offer Universal a buffer zone to not just settle into its new market-leading position but to extend it even more as it was so much bigger than any of the other majors?

'No,' he replies. 'I just felt it was going to make us the biggest company in the world. And that was a platform from which we could continue to grow. What others did wasn't really much on my mind, to be quite honest.'

1998 ended with the ongoing success of the CD and the disruptive arrival of a new corporate behemoth in the world of the majors. If the year was a Venn diagram it would have two circles, one marked 'confidence' and the other marked 'arrogance', that were almost totally overlapping. All the signs projected outwards by the business was that 1998 was a phenomenal year and that 1999 was going to be ever better.

The record business was hardwired for success. The heads of the major labels toasted their own genius, their towering success and their tremendous wealth, wholly confident that nothing could stop them.

A MILLENNIUM BUG, NOT A FEATURE: PREPARING FOR THE END OF EVERY COMPUTER SYSTEM IN THE WORLD (MAYBE)

Like Chicken Licken, slightly concussed by a falling acorn and convinced the sky was falling down, there was mounting anxiety at the start of 1999 that every computer system in the world was going to crash at the stroke of midnight on New Year's Eve. Digital calendars would short-circuit as they flipped into 2000, banking systems would go dark, planes would plummet from the sky.

The Millennium Bug (or the Y2K Bug) was a tremendous concern. We can look back at it, a quarter of a century on, and dismiss it as a grand overreaction; but at the time, paranoia reigned due to what was seen as a 'computer flaw' that was a ticking time bomb getting louder by the day.

'The term Y2K had become shorthand for a problem stemming from the clash of the upcoming Year 2000 and the two-digit year format utilized by early coders to minimize use of computer memory, then an expensive commodity,' explained *Time* magazine. 'If computers interpreted the '00' in 2000 as 1900, this could mean headaches ranging from wildly erroneous mortgage calculations to, some speculated, large-scale blackouts and infrastructure damage.'[142]

Companies assigned large teams and significant budgets to ensure they were Y2K compliant. US president Bill Clinton even urged the US government in 1998 to 'put our own house in order', setting a deadline of March 1999 to have full compliance measures in place.

'The effort will include 'Good Samaritan' legislation to guarantee that businesses sharing information about Y2K cannot be held liable if the information turns out to be inaccurate; a national campaign to promote partnership between industry groups and government agencies; and a job bank to help fill the need for programmers and information technology experts,' noted CNN.[143]

For the music business, it was the biggest existential worry at the start of 1999, with enormous time, money and effort being pumped into safeguarding the industry. It became a rallying of the troops against a worst-case scenario that could rapidly unfold before their eyes.

The biggest concern was among music retailers, with the worry their ordering and stock management system would be wiped out.

EROS (the Electronic Record Ordering System) in the UK was going to be scrapped in June. 'Doubts over the future of EROS arose when it emerged that the 10-year old technology would not beat the millennium bug and a major overhaul of the system, which is believed to cost around £40,000 to run, was needed,' wrote *Music Week* in February 1999.[144]

The following month, *Music Week* reported that the major retailers had IT consultants working on this for the past two years. HMV's own system (Track) had been running software that was Y2K compliant since September 1998 (with around 85 per cent of HMV stock at the time being replenished electronically), while Virgin Megastore had invested heavily to ensure its own Elvis software (EPoS Linked Virgin Information System – EPoS standing for 'electronic point of sale') was compliant.[145]

'The Millennium Bug for a large company like ours was just a straight corporate response,' says Simon Wright, MD of Virgin Retail UK. 'It didn't really impact on our entertainment strategy per se. Every POS [point of sale] system in the world would have been worried about what was going to happen with that.'

Stuart Rowe, general manager of direct and e-commerce for HMV Europe, says that huge amounts of corporate efforts were ploughed into Y2K compatibility that, to an extent, held back some corporate plans and strategies that could have been happening in 1999. 'I think that the Millennium Bug also took everybody's eye off the ball, because they were so worried about all the EPoS systems, shutting down and the whole business coming to a standstill,' he says.

The record labels were also treating this as a deadly serious matter.

'We spent a lot of time on the Millennium Bug,' says John Kennedy, chairman and CEO of Universal Music UK. 'This was going to be bigger than our other problems! We were going to be out of business! Of course, it seems so ridiculous [now]. Edgar [Bronfman Jr, owner of Universal] invested a big sum of money in the Millennium Bug, but it wasn't really coming out of our revenue.'

Darren Hemmings, running IT at Sony Music in the UK, recalls it being an enormous focus for the company because no one dared underestimate the impact it *could* have.

'You look back on it now and you think, 'What on earth was the fuss about?'' he says. 'But at the time, no one was able to confidently say that this wasn't going to bring about the end of days. It was genuinely feared. *Feared.* People were terrified that the infrastructure of the world would collapse. At Sony, they were just terrified that everything would go kaput there, which is entirely legitimate.'

He adds, 'We [the IT team] had to be the ones working on that, which meant a whole bunch of weekend work and extra work. For twenty years, up to 2020, I've never earned more money than I earned in 1999 because we got paid overtime doing Millennium Bug stuff. Weekends were double. I didn't have to work New Year's Eve, but I had to work New Year's Day on triple time. We did celebrations and then we all had to go to the office. All of us had a drink. We'd stagger in and check that the world hadn't ended.'

The world did not end on 1 January 2000, but it was still not a smooth transition into the new millennium.

Martyn Thomas, emeritus professor of IT at Gresham College, led Deloitte Consulting's Y2K efforts internationally in the mid 1990s. Writing in *The Guardian* in 2019, he insisted that this was not something to make trivial jokes about as the threat was real.

'Internationally, correcting Y2K problems cost thousands of person-years of effort and many billions of pounds,' he wrote. 'The UN International Y2K Coordination Centre estimated the cost as between $300bn and $500bn. Then 1 January passed without a catastrophe and the myth started that the threat had been grossly exaggerated. There were many failures in January 2000, from the significant to the trivial [. . .] The millennium bug was real and the internationally coordinated effort was a great success. Tens of thousands of failures were prevented [. . .] Y2K should be seen as a warning of the danger that arises when millions of independent systems might fail because of a single event.'[146]

MAJORS

CHAPTER 2

Getting Away with Merger: Answering the Digital Revolution Through Pepped-up Consolidation

(Guaranteeing control via competitor acquisitions)

1998 ended with the Seagram acquisition of PolyGram clearing all the regulatory hurdles it needed to. Therefore 1999 began with Edgar Bronfman Jr's bold restructuring plans swinging into action.

Meanwhile all the record companies were being affected by digital and were having to think of ways to prepare for the changes coming down the line to ensure they were not washed away by them. At the very top of the companies, digital might have been barely registering (if it was even properly understood), but further down the chain of command, teams of like-minded individuals were formulating plans and trying to get everyone else to not just listen to them but also to take them seriously.

'THE WORLD'S LARGEST SPORTS CAR': BRONFMAN'S NEW VISION FOR THE BIGGEST MUSIC COMPANY IN THE WORLD

Bronfman was keen to be viewed as a different type of company owner in music, one with experience in other business areas and not having, unlike so many label heads who were defined as much by their myopia as their arrogance, spent his entire career in an echo chamber loudly bellowing that the music industry was the centre of the world, drowning out any and all evidence that might have suggested otherwise.

He knew that digital was going to change things. Exactly how it would change things, he was not sure, but he knew his new company needed to be ready for what was coming.

'Even after the merger with PolyGram, Bronfman still fretted that his company wasn't big enough to dictate its own fate, especially on the internet,' wrote Bronfman biographer Fred Goodman. 'He believed that a handful of larger entertainment, communications, and tech giants such as Time Warner, AT&T, Microsoft, AOL, News Corp., and Disney were better poised to define and dominate the online entertainment business and place Seagram at a competitive disadvantage.'[1]

Brian Lane, an artist manager, was quoted in *Billboard* saying that the PolyGram/Seagram deal was akin to a merging of Ferrari and Rolls Royce. 'The result,' he suggested, 'will be the world's largest sports car.'[2]

Calling it 'the world's largest tank' or 'the world's largest steamroller' might have been more apposite.

Given the scale of the deal, Bronfman was keen to ensure that the merger was not just a success but also that the massive market share Universal now found itself with was grown further still through new efficiencies, powers and foresight.

Rod McQueen noted that the company dispatched forty different teams, made up of 250 internal employees and fifty Boston Consulting Group (BCG) consultants, to spend a year working on the integration of Universal and PolyGram.[3]

There were fierce cost-savings of around $300 million to be made, but this came at a human and financial cost. An estimated one thousand artists (solo and groups) were dropped from a combined roster of around three thousand while two thousand members of staff were fired.

At least someone benefited from such axe swinging as BCG was paid around $50 million for its work here (and that $50 million was part of a grander total of $150 million it got for a variety of projects requested by Bronfman). On top of that was $100 million paid to Booz Allen and Price Waterhouse for their 're-engineering' work. This was the age of the consultant and the fees charged reflected the perceived corporate need for their insight teams.[4]

Art Peck was one of BCG's lead consultants but was hired directly by Bronfman as EVP of operations at the start of March 1999. Less than a month later he was out, but no one has said why. Bridges were not totally burned, though, as Peck was able to return to BCG and work as one of its key consultants on the Seagram project.[5]

Acquisitions can be like an affair outside of a failing marriage for some corporate heads: something that obsesses them for an intense period of time but that they quickly tire of before lustily moving on to the next affair.

'Acquisitions have always held a mystique for the would-be builder of an empire,' wrote Roger Lowenstein. 'The new acquirer of a business, instantly expanding his domain by a degree that would require years if left to normal operational growth, is apt to feel a surge of adrenaline, an effusive giddiness [. . .] After the business is acquired, the honeymoon is apt to be short. Whatever the problems were that dogged it before – after all, something drove the previous owner to sell – these ills will most likely reappear. Soon, the acquired business begins to feel old, and the CEO begins to yearn for rejuvenation – perhaps, indeed, for another acquisition.'[6]

Looking back at it from the distance of almost a quarter of a century, Bronfman is pleased with the cost-cutting measures they enacted. 'It was an incredibly successful merger because I think we got the people side of the equation right,' he says.

Key to that, he feels, was the appointment of Doug Morris to run the music operation.

'Doug and I were always in sync about what to do and how to do it,' says Bronfman. 'Doug was very loyal to me and I also to Doug, particularly after what happened with [his sacking from] Warner. He came straight to MCA. We all had really good relationships. And so it really wasn't a struggle. I never needed to make a big deal about a disagreement or take a stand.'

(I attempted to contact Doug Morris several times during the research for this book. Then in December 2022, he was named in a suit filed by Dorothy Carvello against the late founder of Atlantic Records, Ahmet Ertegun. Carvello alleged that she was 'sexually abused and harassed' by Ertegun and Morris when she worked at Atlantic in the 1980s and 1990s.[7] After this point, Morris was utterly uncontactable by anyone).

Bronfman feels that the restructuring of his newly enlarged company was a success around the traditional parts of the business, but with hindsight, that not enough was done initially to make Universal as digitally focused as it could have been.

'I really wanted Universal to become a digital-forward company,' he says. 'But I have to tell you – and this is true, really, of every large company in every industry, it's not anything particularly focused on Universal – innovating from the inside is incredibly difficult. And getting people to create businesses that will ultimately replace the businesses that they're running or that their friends are running is almost impossible. We made real efforts, but they were clumsy and they were not particularly successful.'

Author Stephen Witt claimed that, if Seagram was planning a bold digital future for Universal, it was keeping its cards very close to its chest as its deal prospectus in November 1998, when 'the buzz surrounding the internet had become impossible to ignore', was defiantly *analogue*.

'The prospectus for the PolyGram purchase did not mention the internet, nor the nascent consumer broadband market,' he wrote. 'It did not mention the personal computer, nor recent advances in audio compression technology. It did not mention the possibility of streaming services, nor the potential for widespread file-sharing. And it did not mention the MP3.'[8]

John Kennedy was chairman of PolyGram UK at the time of the acquisition and was appointed chairman and CEO of Universal Music UK in December 1999.[9] He says he was kept in the dark about the deal machinations until near the end of negotiations, only gathering nuggets of information from newspaper coverage of the rolling rumours. 'I was often reporting to my staff on the basis of what was happening in the *Financial Times*,' he says. 'That's just the way it is. If the company is being taken over, you don't know much about it.'

When the deal was confirmed, and his promotion within the new organisation, Kennedy was reported in *Music Week* as saying that his restructuring plans for the UK would be very different to what Doug Morris was pushing through in the US. 'I don't think it will follow,' he said. 'The strengths of the different labels in the US are different to their strengths internationally.'[10]

He says there was an immediate jumping up through the gears as soon as the merger was approved and the restructuring programme was starting to be put into place. Now the combined companies had a massively increased roster of artists and, with that, a massively increased release schedule.

'What was really exciting about it was we, as PolyGram, had really been a nine-months-of-the-year record company to my mind,' he says. 'We didn't have enough releases for twelve months a year globally. Suddenly, with the merger, we were a fifteen-months-of-the-year record company. Our releases were just fantastic by putting the two together. That made life easier, it made it more exciting and it increased our market share – which was a factor but not as big a factor as it is now.'

Despite the position of market dominance the company found itself in, Kennedy says that the expectation to perform and to grow that dominance was felt immediately.

Because the major label record business was lauded or damned by its performance in every quarter, the pressure was enormous to have not just a steady flow of albums but a steady flow of *blockbuster* albums.

'[If acts] don't deliver a great album, like anybody, we're in trouble,' Kennedy says. 'We're relying on them to a huge extent. Because they were really global artists, the effect on the company worldwide would be tremendous if it was not a great album.'

He feels that PolyGram was vivified by finding itself – under new management and as part of an enlarged entity – with whole new pressures to not just outperform the competition but also for internal labels to be set against each other in a battle for supremacy.

'PolyGram had probably been resting on its laurels a bit,' he says. 'It was time for a bit of disruption within the company. And it ended up not being a bad thing. It's a bad thing that some people lost their jobs, but there was definitely some complacency around. This re-energised the idea of competition internally between the different labels. That worked well.'

The policy of having internal labels compete with each other, for signings as much as for market share, was something Doug Morris particularly championed, believing fear to be a great lubricant for corporate success. 'He had a Darwinian approach to business and he wanted his lieutenants to compete against one another directly,' said Stephen Witt.[11]

Kennedy feels this cut-throat environment pushed executives and A&Rs (who would sign and develop acts) to excel, but it also came at a cost.

'The people who were running A&M, Polydor and Phonogram were fiercely competitive with each other,' he says. 'They would almost rather that Sony or Warner got the act rather than their sister label. You can find an excuse to lose it to Sony or Warner, but amongst your own label, you don't want your [sister labels to beat you]. This is not a collegiate system that you build from that point.'

As head of the UK operation, however, he says whipping up this inter-label rivalry also had to be policed by him to avoid internal bidding wars.

'You don't want them to be bidding against each other, so that you have to manage,' he explains. 'If the hot act comes in, you don't want one of your labels offering £100,000, the next one offering £150,000 and the next one offering £200,000. You don't want that to happen. Otherwise, you want them to be living on the edge of their seat trying to find the next big thing.'

Hip-hop label Def Jam Recordings was 60 per cent owned by PolyGram at the time of the Seagram deal and the *Los Angeles Times* termed it 'currently the hottest record label in the music business.'[12] In early 1999, Seagram moved to buy the remainder of the company.[13] Lyor Cohen was chief executive of Def Jam and following the sale of the final 40 per cent he was promoted to president of the newly combined Island Def Jam Music Group.

Cohen says Def Jam's phenomenal success at the time in hip-hop made it a priority purchase for Seagram.

'When the transaction happened for PolyGram, they realised, Edgar realised and Universal realised, that the largest market share in the North America company wasn't wholly owned,' says Cohen. 'It wasn't Mercury or Motown or Island or A&M, it was little Def Jam. And at the top of the year [1999], we ended up selling the company for a $360 million valuation and $130 million was ours [Cohen and Russell Simmons, Def Jam's co-founder].'

Cohen says Bronfman 'was delightful to work for' and that Doug Morris 'was also delightful to work with.' He was, however, to repeatedly and badly clash with Jimmy Iovine, head of Interscope Records and one of Morris's closest friends inside the company.

'He [Morris] understood how hard it is to find an artist, break an artist, market and promote an artist,' says Cohen. 'He was hugely appreciative, always encouraging and hugely supportive – except when it came to Jimmy Iovine. Before I could blink, he had moved U2 [from Island] to Interscope.'

Cohen believes he was not part of their tight inner circle was seriously disadvantaged as a result.

'Doug Morris and Jimmy Iovine's careers have intertwined,' he says. 'They go back to back with one another. They absolutely love and adore one another, explicitly trust one another. And I was more the outsider. So that's what you do to outsiders.'

He says that he and Iovine would clash over corporate and professional matters.

Lyor says this culture of ruthlessness was a hangover from Morris's days at Warner Music. 'That is his shtick. That's what he did at Warner. Warner was, for years, a very vicious, competitively vicious, place.'

Cohen felt his only option was to respond in kind. 'Every time Jimmy tried to hit me, I would hit him five times harder,' he shrugs.

An armistice of sorts was eventually reached between Iovine and Cohen.

'Jimmy operates in the shadows,' says Cohen. 'He finally asked me to visit him at a hotel room in midtown Manhattan, the St Regis, and he said, "I want to do a truce. Let's just play it cool together".'

I ask Cohen if he accepted the olive branch. 'Yeah, of course,' he says. 'I have no interest in intrigue. It's hard enough being a record guy without worrying about your teammates trying to poach your shit.'

When interviewing Bronfman, I listed Cohen's accusations and asked how he mediated when Cohen and Iovine locked horns.

'Well, if you put Jimmy Iovine and Lyor Cohen in the same company, they're going to compete,' he says. 'The answer to that is to figure out that dynamic and make it positive for you rather than negative for you. And I think Doug did a great job of that.'

(Jimmy Iovine did not respond to multiple requests to be interviewed for this book).

Kennedy says that Bronfman was 'very supportive' when he was promoted to the CEO role at Universal in the UK but adds that Boston Consulting Group adopted a very hands-on approach.

'I remember I went in one day with one page [for a company presentation], and I said, "Right, this is what I'm going to do." And they said, "You can't take that to Edgar Bronfman at his conference." I said, "Why not?" They said, "No, no, no." They took my one page away and converted it into eighty pages. I was just fazed by that! But then when I went to the conference, I just used my one page and said what I was going to do.' He pauses. 'That was a challenge.'

Kennedy admits that in order to hit their cost-saving targets and to reduce the workforce, some cold and heartless measures were being employed inside the company, a corporate barbarity that was deemed acceptable at the time but that would surely cause uproar today.

'I had about five managing directors reporting to me – and this would not be allowed in human resources terms anymore – and I said, "I want you to mark all your people out of 10",' he reveals. 'They came back with their review out of 10. Basically, the people that were marked quite low [were people] we should really have been moving out of the company before this exercise. People had become complacent. There's that General Electric thing where you get rid of the lowest 10 per cent every year. That's pretty brutal because, at some stage, you get to the point where you're letting go off people who are quite good just because they are in the bottom 10 per cent.'

In February 1999, *Music Week* was running details of the cuts at the

UK arm of Universal, noting that five hundred people had been laid off across A&M, Mercury and Geffen at the end of January 'in the most sweeping restructuring ever seen in record industry history.' An unnamed senior executive at Universal was quoted by *Music Week*, loudly outlining their criticisms of the whole process. 'This has been going on a long time, but now they are demolishing everything here,' they said. 'It is all pretty stinky.'[14]

I put the accusation of 'stinky' behaviour over mass redundancies to Kennedy over two decades after the fact. He says that it is simply a consequence, as unfortunate as that is, of modern business.

'If you were going to get rid of one person, you'd have one person who could make that quote,' he says. 'There were people who hadn't been happy when I came in in 1996, for instance. They would have perceived the idea of a lawyer running a record company as not a good development creatively. I would have had my opponents anyhow, especially when you let people go. However you do it, when people lose their jobs and their colleagues that they have worked with for a long time, it's not nice. I wouldn't even disagree with the idea that a merger is going to be "stinky", if that's the word. I wouldn't disagree with it.'

On an organisational level, Universal in the UK shrunk from four labels to three by rolling Universal and Island into one. Mercury was to remain as it was and Polydor would have US repertoire fed into it from Geffen, DreamWorks and Interscope.[15]

Alongside the staff redundancies, speculation was rife that a mass culling was coming and that multiple artists were going to be dropped from the assorted label rosters. The manager of an act signed to a PolyGram label that had sold over a million albums spoke anonymously to *Music Week* about the mounting paranoia they were feeling. 'It would be nice if the senior artists were called and told,' they sniffed, 'but that's the music business for you.'[16]

Doug Morris was quoted in *Music Week* at the end of 1998 as he tried to dampen down rumours of a bloodbath across the Universal labels' rosters, hoping to deflect people away from any negatives by suggesting that Universal was the most artist-friendly company in the business.

'What we're really trying to do is to create something special,' he said. 'The artists are going to be number one, two and three in this company. We have a unique opportunity to create something that is very artist-friendly, backed by the most brilliant entrepreneurial executives we can put in place.'[17]

As soon as the merger was announced, the dropping of artists was a story that crossed over from the trade and business press into the consumer press. Magazines that rarely covered the music industry were now idly speculating about the fate of the acts they regularly wrote about.

Q, for example, reported that Polydor had dropped indie rock band Shed Seven and suggested that both Audioweb and Silver Sun were at risk, adding that the future for several acts on Island hung in the balance. An artist manager hinted that artists were pulling out of contract signings with Universal labels. 'You could sign with people that just won't be there next year,' they said. *Q* even found space in the piece to throw a jibe at Bronfman, calling him someone 'who once wrote a Cher B-side.'[18]

Q did have to print a retraction in the next month's issue, saying that Shed Seven had not been dropped and were, in fact, in the studio working on their next album for Polydor[19] and that it was due later in the year.[20]

Mojo was also speculating on the future of Universal-signed acts. 'If your name's not Elton, U2 or Pavarotti, the next few weeks will be anxious ones,' it said. It added that this consolidation among the majors could conversely benefit independent labels. '[T]he bigger the majors get, the more out of touch they become with the subtleties of the market,' it proposed.

An unnamed industry insider was quoted as saying, 'It's increasingly obvious that the majors don't know how to handle artists apart from throwing vast amounts of money at them. It won't be the end of the world for the acts who get dropped. As so many have discovered, it's an unreal world in there. One minute, you can be discussing a million-pound campaign for your third album. The next, you're out on your ear.'[21]

Duff McKagan, bassist in Guns N' Roses and a solo artist in 1999, was one of many acts to find they were now surplus to requirements in the new Universal Music. His first solo album, *Believe In Me*, came out on Geffen (by then part of MCA) in 1993, and they were sending out promo copies of his next solo album, *Beautiful Disease*, to the media in 1999.

In his autobiography, McKagan recounts going into the Geffen offices in December that year to find that, following the acquisition, there were going to be 'mass layoffs' at the label. His album had been scheduled for release on 5 February 2000. He wrote, 'On my birthday – the day of the album's supposed release – an intern from the label called and left a message on my answering machine to say it wouldn't be released that day or any other day.'

He and the label could not agree terms for him to buy back the album and take it to another record company, so he walked away.[22]

Kennedy claims, in the UK at least, he had no intention of slashing the roster and there was no corporate expectation that he should.

'Everybody told us that we were going to lose artists' releases because of the merger and it was going to be a disaster – and we sort of prepared for that to be the case,' he says. '[But it turned out that] I was not under any pressure to drop any artists at all. I insisted on the A&R budget not being reduced, but I wasn't under any pressure to reduce the A&R budget. We had plenty of money to spend. Maybe we hadn't been spending it as well as we should, but that was never an issue. My one-pager would have said, "It would be a big mistake to reduce the A&R budget." There was never any pressure on that.'

Throughout 1999, Universal was focused on streamlining, restructuring and consolidating its position as the most powerful music company in the world. With regulatory approval behind it, there was a sense of invincibility gripping the company, a belief that it was impervious to external challenges as it left its rivals choking on its dust. Intoxicated with power, it did not anticipate that one of the biggest challenges to the PolyGram/Seagram deal could come from within.

In late June 1999, Herb Alpert and Jerry Moss, founders of the legendary A&M label, filed a $200 million breach-of-contract lawsuit against Universal. A&M was acquired by PolyGram a decade earlier for $500 million and the lawyer acting on behalf of A&M alleged the label was dismantled following the sale of PolyGram. This was a revision of the suit filed by A&M in June 1998 as the Seagram deal was happening.

'The amendment drastically ups the ante in the original suit against PolyGram, which centered on accounting disputes and claimed about $5.6 million for profits owed to the pair [Alpert and Moss] and their share of a Canadian tax settlement,' reported the *Los Angeles Times*. The breach of contract accusation stemmed from a sales clause, dubbed an Integrity Clause, that required PolyGram to sustain A&M as an active label for at least twenty years.[23]

LA Superior Court judge Aurello Munoz cleared the way in August 1999 for the A&M suit against Universal to progress. 'The duo [Alpert and Moss] was also entitled to profits for five years from the sale's 1990 closing, money they say they've never received,' reported *Variety*.[24]

The case rumbled on throughout the rest of 1999. In October, Munoz had come down on the side of Universal who, as *Variety* noted, claimed 'Alpert and Moss were not the proper parties to pursue the claims.'[25]

By December, *Variety* reported that Munoz 'reversed his earlier ruling and granted a motion for reconsideration', which meant Alpert and Moss could 'sue as individuals (instead of on behalf of a trust, which could not claim as much in damages) and show they were damaged by Universal's alleged violation of a unique 'label integrity' clause in their contract.'[26]

The issue of divestments as a byproduct of the merger was also starting to impact by the end of summer 1999. *Billboard* ran a feature entitled 'The Gold Rush That Wasn't', suggesting that Universal would have to offload artists and assets that independent distributors would be offered the chance to take over. It concluded that only a few imprints had gone to independent distributors, noting that Koch International had picked up Eureka Records (previously distributed by Island).[27]

Jim Colson, VP of independent distribution at Distribution North America, was quoted as saying, 'It was kind of interesting. Everyone thought they would drop a lot of labels, but they ended up consolidating lots of labels and doing other things to basically keep everyone in the fold.'[28]

Despite this turbulence, Universal galloped towards a successful first anniversary of the deal being approved. In October, *Billboard* was quoting analysts who were suggesting the company would reach $1 billion in EBITDA (earnings before interest, taxes, depreciation, and amortisation) in fiscal 2000. 'As such, it would be a new benchmark for a company in the music business.'[29]

Universal was hungrier still for even greater success and even better results, setting huge targets and amplifying the pressure on executives to hit them. A European executive, speaking anonymously to *Billboard*, spelt this out in terms heavy with the dark subtext of heads about to roll should anyone dare to fall short of the ramped-up expectations. '[We were told] that those who make [the financial target] will be noticed and appreciated and that those who don't will be noticed,' they said.[30]

The year of 1999 ended with Universal furiously blowing its own trumpet at how successful, brilliant and wonderful it had been.

In the UK, Lucian Grainge was promoted from head of Polydor to deputy chairman, adding responsibility for Universal Island and Mercury to his remit. 'I want Lucian to motivate the team and to be the catalyst of a true music man at the front,' John Kennedy told *Music Week*. He added that he expected Grainge to succeed him as UK chairman in the 'medium-to long-term.'[31]

Grainge said, '(Universal) needs hit records and an executive who can identify hit records and manage creative people. They came to the conclusion that's what I can do.'[32]

Billboard ran a multi-part feature titled 'Universal: One Year Later'[33] in its final issue of 1999 that was so fawning and so effusive that even Universal's corporate communications team might have deemed it somewhat excessive and cloying.

It quoted Doug Morris, who said, 'We are taking a lot of costs out of the system and increasing market share at the same time.'[34] It noted that Universal grew its share of the US albums market for the first nine months of 1998 from 23.6 per cent to 26.9 per cent for the first six months of 1999. The independents saw a marginal increase from 15.7 per cent to 16.3 per cent in the same period. Of the other majors, only BMG saw an increase (11.7 per cent rising to 15 per cent). All the others saw a drop. WEA slipped from 18.4 per cent to 16.3 per cent, Sony dipped from 16.9 per cent to 15.4 per cent and EMI declined the most, going from 13.7 per cent to 10 per cent.

Merrill Lynch analyst Jessica Reif Cohen told *Billboard*, '[Universal's] gain has been almost everybody else's problem. I don't think anybody can argue with their numbers. Market share has gone straight up ever since they combined.'

Universal executives stepped forward to praise the new structure and regime, but they also claimed that the enormous success was making it a benign kingdom. One European executive said, 'It *is* a more human place to work. We don't kid ourselves: If our numbers are bad, we'll be fired anyway, but they are certainly trying to be more human.'

Another major market executive added, 'There was a lot of threatening [at PolyGram]. Here it's nicer. You don't hear the F-word all the time. We still fire people. . . but we do it in a more human way.'

THE SHADOW CREEPS FURTHER: HOW THE OTHER LABELS RESPONDED TO UNIVERSAL'S ROLLING AGGRANDISEMENT

Reducing the number of major labels from six to five was not just a simple transferral of market share that happened in a vacuum. The fact that Universal was now so much bigger than everyone else created a new centre of gravity in the record business and put them all, major and independent, at a growing disadvantage.

Universal had more weight to throw around and could demand better deal terms. This would drive further growth. That growth would come at the cost of everyone else, so the others had to try and buffer themselves and also bulk themselves up. Consolidation impacts everyone and the natural rhythm of consolidation is towards *further* consolidation.

Having missed out on the Seagram deal, EMI was back on the shelf and, as the weakest of the majors in the US (the world's biggest record market), facing the most uncertain future. As PolyGram was being bought by Seagram, EMI was flashing an ankle to anyone it could.

Michael Dornemann, CEO of Bertelsmann Entertainment (owners of BMG), was the first to wink in response. In September 1998, he made it known in a media briefing in New York that his company might be interested in EMI. He said 'for sure' that Bertelsmann would want to buy the company, but only if its share price was lower. *Variety* reported that, at the time, EMI was valued at around $5 billion, but what the magic price would be to get Bertelsmann to make a bid was not made clear.[35]

EMI chairman Colin Southgate had announced around the same time that he was going to step down and that the company was currently seeking a replacement. This arguably took EMI out of the running until his successor was found but that, when they were appointed, EMI buying another major or being bought by another major would be a priority.

Southgate's successor was eventually named in March 1999. Eric Nicoli, head of United Biscuits, would take charge of EMI in July that year. Nicoli was not a total outsider; he'd been a non-executive director at EMI since 1994.

Los Angeles Times journalist Claudia Philips noted that Southgate had 'been criticized for bungling talks that could perhaps have led to a sale of the company to Bertelsmann Music Group, Seagram Co. or News Corp.' and spoke to Nicoli about merger or sales plans, asking if he could get a deal over the line where Southgate had failed.

'We supported Colin in the calls he made,' said a highly diplomatic Nicoli. 'Sometimes he would share approaches with us; sometimes he wouldn't. He was the chairman and chief executive of the company and still is. If people make audacious approaches, they shouldn't be offended if the board doesn't get excited.'

Pressed on the collapse of the Seagram talks, Nicoli suggested they were more rumour than substance.

'I don't believe an offer was ever made,' he claimed. 'There were discussions, and they didn't even nearly reach a conclusion. And Seagram moved on, didn't they? And we wish them luck. The industry and press comment that followed was absolutely inevitable, wasn't it? Because Seagram went on to buy another company, so the speculation was that presumably they could have bought EMI. They never made an offer, so there was never an offer to discuss. It's quite normal for companies in the same business to talk about what they might do together. But it didn't materialize.'

Philips asked Nicoli if it was true that he was explicitly brought in to drive through the sale of EMI. 'That's crap,' insisted an indignant Nicoli. 'I understand why some people would hope that's the case – particularly those who might be interested in buying the company. But I wasn't recruited to sell this company. I was recruited to build this company. And that is my commitment to the board and to the management.'[36]

It would take until 2007 for EMI, after failed talks with multiple suitors, to be sold. Its buyer was outside of music – private equity company Terra Firma. The deal proved utterly disastrous.[37]

Perhaps concerned that the regulatory environment would not, at least not for some time, allow a merging of majors that would create an entity bigger than Universal, other majors took a more piecemeal approach to growth. Rather than pursue a mega-deal, they looked to buy up independent labels.

In January 1999, Warner announced it was acquiring the other 50 per cent of British independent label China Records that it did not already own. Warner had already bought half of the company in 1994, but exercised an option in that deal which came up on New Year's Eve 1998. This enabled it to buy the whole company and add acts such as Morcheeba and The Levellers to its roster.[38]

In August 1999, Sony Italy acquired Italian independent label RTI Records, which sat within Silvio Berlusconi's Mediaset conglomerate. *Billboard* called it 'the last remaining large independent label' in the country, noting that Warner Music Italy had bought the CGD label in 1992 (rebranding it as CGD-East West) as well as Nuova Fonit Cetra in August 1998, while BMG had acquired the Ricordi label in 1994.[39]

Paul Russell was chairman of Sony Music Europe at the time and was heavily involved in the RTI deal, saying it was part of Sony strengthening its foothold in particular European territories by acquiring robust domestic labels.

'We were looking to expand, particularly in Italy,' he says. 'The [general] market was very strong there, but very, very strong in local repertoire. We felt that we needed to strengthen the local repertoire. You could either do that by signing and breaking more Italian artists or via acquiring local companies. That was our policy pretty much everywhere. We were very pro investing in [companies locally].'

He says this strategy originally came out of the UK, notably through a deal with Creation Records in the 1990s.

'I remember saying to our guys, "You look at the charts every week in the UK and 50 per cent of the charts are made up by [labels] other than major labels. Why should we limit ourselves to 50 per cent of the charts?"' recalls Russell. 'One of the things which our companies in Europe needed was bigger and better UK repertoire. Although we maybe only ended up distributing the independent labels that we made deals with in the UK, we had licences for that repertoire across Europe and in the US. That was an extremely successful policy. If there is one thing I'll say, yes, I was the genius who invented that!'

In summer 1999, Warner Music appointed Roger Ames – former president of PolyGram, who left the company when Seagram bought it – as global chairman and CEO. 'Naming of Ames was widely viewed in the industry and by WMG insiders as one that would initially cause the least amount of angst among senior WMG execs,' suggested *Variety*. 'If the nod had gone to one of the label group chiefs, insiders suggested, the others were expected to have revolted.'[40]

Ames had been promoted from his role as president of Warner Music International where he had been since April 1999. Time Warner Chairman Gerald Levin told the *New York Post* that the appointment of Ames was a significant and symbolic one. 'This is the first time in the history of the company where we have put a music person as the CEO of the Warner Music Group,' he said.[41]

Ames told *Music Week* that he would unite the international and US arms of Warner. 'It will be one world rather than two separate worlds,' he said. 'There will be more linkage.'[42]

An extended interview feature in the same issue of *Music Week* could have been mistaken for a report on the actual Second Coming such was its vociferous joy and seemingly endless exultations at Ames's appointment. Calling him both a 'deadly negotiator' and 'notoriously publicity-shy', the piece marked him out as a singular talent, the subtext being that Warner was lucky to get him. It peppered the piece with glowing testimonials from heavyweight industry figures.

'Ames is a maverick – and mavericks are rarely encouraged in the increasingly corporatised world of music,' added *Music Week*. 'Ames's low profile means few know him well. But those who do describe him as an inspirational, unpredictable and even sometimes eccentric individual. No one should underestimate him.'[43]

All of these manoeuvres by the major labels were being keenly watched by the independent labels, who were growing concerned that a culture of consolidation and growth among the biggest labels was going to cost them dearly.

Guy Holmes, founder of Gut Records, was passionately opposed to how the majors, particularly the label heads in the US, carried themselves, especially the skyscraping scale of their egos. 'That level of arrogance, that level of pomposity,' he spits. 'They were wankers.'

The independents knew this was coming and had been preparing themselves for several years. Collectivism and unity were to be their shields and in the UK that manifested itself through the creation of AIM, the Association of Independent Music. In an age of accelerated major label consolidation and with the oncoming possibilities/threats of digital, they needed to speak and act as one (see Chapter 4).

Alison Wenham was to become CEO and chairman of AIM when it launched, but had started out running independent classical label Conifer Records, selling it to BMG in 1993 and staying at the major for five years.[44]

'It was a huge race for market share,' she says of Seagram/PolyGram. 'That moment was just a reality check. The aggregation of market share was driving the majors all through the 1990s.'

She says when she started at AIM that she conducted analysis of label market share going back to 1989 and found surprising results.

'In 1989, at around 4 per cent market share, the largest independent, Virgin, was not very much smaller than the smallest major,' she explains. 'There was a very balanced competitive marketplace with no great behemoths, no great low-hanging fruit. And then Virgin, A&M, Chrysalis, Island, one by one, most of the big indies [were sold]. The reason for that was partly to do with the extraordinary revenues coming from the CD format. The CD basically turned the record industry from a cottage industry into a national, then international, and finally a global industry.'

She adds, 'This feeding frenzy started, and it was going on all through the 1990s. When I looked at my chart again, sometime in the noughties, the largest independent wasn't even 1 per cent. That really shows you how the market had totally changed. And to be in that position in the independent sector was to be up against not just the usual forces of competition, but also the internal forces of getting access to the market in the first place.'

Martin Mills, head of Beggars Banquet, the leading British independent label by the late 1990s, suggests things did not really snap into focus until after the Seagram/PolyGram deal.

'At that point in the consolidation,' he says, 'no one had put two and two together and worked out it was a problem.'

It was only going to become a bigger and bigger problem for the independents as the new millennium began. Seagram/PolyGram for the independents would prove to be akin to the first fleeting glimpse of the shark in *Jaws*. Much worse was to come.

LUDDITES BE DAMNED: THE 'MIXED-SPEED ECONOMY' IN THE RECORD BUSINESS AS DIGITAL ASCENDS

For a business predicated entirely on technology, the music industry has always had an attitude towards new technological developments that could be most generously described as 'mixed.' It absolutely loved new formats that it had created itself – like the LP, developed by Columbia in June 1948[45] and initially known by the cumbersome title of the 'Columbia LP (long playing) Microgroove'[46] – or formats it had been deeply involved in from the off, such as the cassette, the CD and the MiniDisc.

Digital, however, was not something that had a testing and development process like, for example, the DVD, the anointed new format at the end of the 1990s.

Digital was happening wholly without the music industry's permission. The record business could get involved, it could delude itself that it could slow it down or detail it, but digital was happening regardless. It was, by the early 1990s, like gravity. You can, should you so wish, declare war on gravity, but you're not going to win.

The trick, the labels were to find out, was in coexisting with new formats coming from the outside, but that was to prove much easier said than done.

The heads of the biggest music companies in the world in the late 1990s were not exactly Luddites, taking sledgehammers to computers and modems, but neither were they comfortably sitting at the cutting edge of what technology could achieve for both them and their business.

Donna Cohen was one of the earliest people within the record industry to be focusing on the possibilities of digital. She had been working with computer graphics since 1980, describing herself as 'an artist who understood tech.' She moved to Apple to work in its Human Interface Group in 1989. Warner senior executive Stan Cornyn approached her the next year with an intriguing job offer. 'He was given money and he had a little skunkworks group called Warner New Media,' she says. It had a heavy emphasis on CD-ROM.

She says it was extremely hard to get others inside Warner to understand the power of digital, but she would concentrate on slowly converting people.

'The publishing company, Warner Chappell, and the distribution company, WEA, were the most resistant,' she recalls. 'I have images of sitting in those offices talking about the internet and them being very uncomfortable. I remember sitting and trying to educate executives about the internet at the publishing company. They were resistant. There was, like, one person in each label who was a complete "I get it" champion. They were able to just jump in and own it.'

Warner was arguably the most digitally progressive major label in the early and mid 1990s. Todd Steinman was director of online and new media at Warner Bros. Records between 1993 and 1996 before becoming VP of new media and marketing at the label between 1996 and 1999. He claims that Warner Bros. Records was the first record company to be online and that he was the very first person in the record industry to have a role dedicated to the internet.

'The beauty of the music industry is they were willing to experiment in these weird abstract things,' he says of those unimpeded and freewheeling early days, where he was able to operate under the corporate radar a little bit. 'It was this guerrilla-level effort, but I had the ear of some seasoned executives, including the head of creative services who I was reporting to. But it wasn't like I was anywhere near the most important thing in his day. I was probably the least important thing in his day for those couple of years. But it was super interesting.'

His role, initially at least, came under the purview of marketing and he was encouraged to experiment, notably around creating artist websites.

It was the launch of Pathfinder in 1994, an early-days web portal set up by Time Warner for its assorted properties, that changed the temperature inside the company with regard to the internet. 'That was one of the things that got more of the senior execs' attention on the business and it was being taken more seriously,' he says.

Jeremy Silver was VP for new media at EMI between 1995 and 2000, based in Los Angeles but with a global remit.

'There was a mixed-speed economy, you might say,' he explains of the industry's attitude to digital by that point in the decade. 'There were people inside the organisation like me who were, from about 1993, saying that we should be looking at this and doing something about it. Did I see [digital] as a threat? I did! I absolutely could see that this was going to transform the whole game. I didn't think it was something that we could stamp out. I thought this was an opportunity that we had to take and totally transform the shape of our industry.'

He says, however, there were huge levels of vested interest in the record business to keep things as they were, to ensure the staggering revenues from CDs would continue to flow unimpeded.

This meant that whatever ideas, as utopian as they might have been, he had about digital and its transformative power, they were always going to bump up against entrenched thinking and would never really be able to skirt around it.

'There were enough of us around who could see what this [digital future] could look like and could see that there was a whole architecture that could unfold,' he says. 'But what none of us really could quite understand and appreciate was the degree [of vested interest]. When people talk about vested interest, that's a meaningful term. The level of investment that had gone into creating major labels to that point was billions and billions of pounds over a hundred years. That wasn't about to be all swept away overnight. But I thought it should be.'

In his book, *Digital Medieval*, Silver recounts the story of Francois Xavier Nuttall coming to EMI in 1996 with the idea of a digital music service over a cable network in France. Silver met with him and Nuttall, perhaps caught up in the moment, decided to tell the *Financial Times* that EMI was about to partner on his project.

Silver was summoned by a displeased Colin Southgate and told, in no uncertain terms, that no deal would be considered. 'We're not about to license our music to anyone, least of all a bunch of French cable operators,' Southgate told Silver. 'We will never be in the business of making our music digital and degrading its value dramatically, as long as we are continuing to sell CDs. Are you out of your mind?'[47]

Those individuals within record companies who were fired up by the possibilities of digital could find themselves ignored or, worse, belittled and even pitied by their colleagues.

'We had been talking about MP3s and the sharing of content [for a while],' says Ant Cauchi, who joined EMI in London in 1994 and became Parlophone's new media manager by default as he expressed an early interest in the internet. 'I was showing people how I could just download this thing. But people would go, "That's just because you're this geek in the office, so it's not going to be for everyone else." I used to have so many meetings with a lot of people who'd ask, "When's this all going to go away?"'

Also working within EMI UK's nascent digital arm at the time was Eric Winbolt, serving as digital commercial manager there from 1998 and becoming head of digital in 2000.

He says that the most senior people at EMI were focused so much on possible mergers and restructuring that they were tuned out of what was coming digitally. 'If you were on the digital side, you were also seeing something far bigger lurking in the wings. The realisation of the scale of what that was [was very powerful].'

He feels that part of his role was as an ambassador for digital through the company, explaining to other colleagues what changes were afoot, although he often faced indifference or outright denial.

'I can remember going into the office and having arguments with people about whether they were going to have a CD collection in two years, five years, ten years, whatever sort of time interval,' he says. 'There was a bigger issue, like a shadow slightly out of focus, on the periphery, but I don't think most people would have really caught on to that yet. People in digital roles were closer to it and had a grandstand seat, as it were, of what was about to happen. While the corporate stuff was present and very front of house, there was also this rumbling in the background that not everybody was hearing yet.'

He was also focused on spreading the digital gospel to artists and their managers, trying to get them onside as that would mean he and his colleagues could start making digital the heartbeat of their marketing and promotion.

'I had to give this speech multiple times to artists, to managers and to the label itself, to evangelise about the creative opportunities that digital was bringing for the way that we packaged and represented our music,' he says. 'I was pretty excited about it. It genuinely was like being handed an incredible new toolbox, which changed every few months when another opportunity would arise. It was unbroken ground. It wasn't like anybody was saying, "You can't do this because someone else has already done it."' It was all virgin territory.'

There was, suggests Steinman, an age-defined divide within labels around the internet in the mid 1990s.

'There definitely was a chasm,' he says. 'At first the chasm was purely generational and it was because digital was so different from everything that most of the executives, especially the senior executives, were thinking about. There were only about five or six of us in that seat at every label in total. I knew them all. We did share a lot of information. We all talked. I wouldn't say it was "us versus them",' but there was not a lot of camaraderie around what we were doing in the space inside of our own buildings because we were these renegades inside our record labels – and the record labels focused on everything else.'

He says that as the potential of the internet grew incrementally, he was encouraged to be 'an agitator inside the building', testing the limits of what was possible. 'My boss wanted me to tell him what was happening, to really push the boundaries on it and stay ahead of it,' he says.

There was a real sense of battle lines being drawn within the business around digital, with those entranced by it all viewing anyone who was not as effusive as them as being anachronistic or simply in the way. They would also judge companies and individuals based on how digital savvy they were (or were not), suggesting that this was a good barometer for how forward-thinking they were and how ready they were for the digital revolution.

Ben Drury, when working at *Dotmusic*, says, 'I do remember going to meetings with some record labels and they didn't even have the internet.'

Paul Hitchman was working in A&R at Warner Music in London in 1998 and 1999. He suggests that the company, outside of a tiny pocket of people, was characterised by a certain paranoia about digital in general and the internet in particular.

'There was an overriding view, certainly at Warner when I was there, that the internet was a risk,' he says. 'A data breach risk, a content leaking risk, a copyright infringement risk. You had to have special permission to be able to go online. There was an intranet of Warner but you had to have special permission to actually access the internet.'

The socio-cultural impact within the company was that this was something most of the staff should not be engaging with and certainly nothing to concern themselves with.

Scott Cohen of The Orchard makes the point that, for some label executives, the *architecture* of the internet was something that they only understood and experienced in partial terms. They could see its use in certain, and very specific, cases but they had not yet grasped its macro importance.

'With the people running the labels you have to remember that they were still having their emails printed out and placed on their desk as if somebody had sent them a letter,' he laughs. 'This was in the 1990s and into the early 2000s, until the BlackBerry came along. A music executive didn't directly use the internet. They indirectly used it because somebody sent him an email and they printed it out like they got a letter.'

This, Cohen proposes, impacted the overall culture of the company. If the heads were not evangelising about digital, or cautioning about it, then the rest of the company were not treating it as a priority.

'You have heads of labels that are completely out of touch with how things are done – with their own consumers,' he says. 'That's the thing; they're out of touch with the end consumer. There were great people at the majors and great people in the independents, but they just were not the ultimate decision makers. And when you have people at the top who don't understand what the end consumers are doing, they're out of touch and it slows things down.'

Al Teller had been through the major label system and, frustrated by the indifference he was seeing with regard to digital, left it and founded digital-centric label Atomic Pop in 1997.

'At the time, we were an ant on an elephant's butt,' he says of how Atomic Pop fitted into the broader record business. 'I don't think the majors were particularly concerned about us at that time. More importantly, they just weren't paying any attention to where the world was going. The major criticism I have is that. You get so lost in your immediate concerns that you lose sight, if you ever even had insight, of the bigger picture and the longer-term implications for your business model.'

Cliff Fluet was the lawyer for the ESP (Enterprise & Special Projects, known colloquially inside the company as Extra Special Projects) division of Warner Music UK in the late 1990s, handling everything that did not come under the purview of the frontline labels. This included what was nebulously termed 'new media' at the time.

He recalls the atmosphere within the wider company with regard to the internet at the time as 'febrile' and defined by 'a very fear-based opportunity.' He notes that he was seconded to the BPI, the UK record company trade body, for periods of time and says that the organisation was gripped by a 'sense of general paralysis' when it came to online.

'There was a whole, "What's the Warner approach to this? What's the industry approach to this?"' he says of the types of questions he was being asked at the BPI. 'And of course, from an industry perspective, you had very, very, very different views depending on the parent companies of the various entities as well. So you saw it from a micro and a macro perspective. I would say that there was a massive sense of paralysis and a massive sense of fear.'

He suggests that the fundamental problem is that the most senior executives were driven by self-interest and a rewards-based scheme that was built around short-termism and not challenging the status quo. The impact of digital was going to be felt for years and it was going to take many years, even decades, to properly recalibrate the business. For some executives, this was so far into the future as to be little more than science fiction to them.

As a result, there was corporate buck passing on a wholly unprecedented scale.

'Some of [the senior executives at the time] have said to me subsequently, "It wasn't going to be my problem",' says Fluet. 'They saw the time horizon and realised that it wouldn't be their concern. Many of the people in the music industry, it wouldn't be controversial to say, are focused on their bonus in relation to their time horizon.'

Jay Berman had been chairman of the RIAA, the US record label trade association, but had moved to become chairman and CEO of global trade body the IFPI at the start of 1999. He suggests that the record business, at the top level, in 1999, was focused only on sustaining the financial wave that powered the 1990s through the success of the CD. A generation gap was starting to open up in the record business, but the ones who made all the final decisions were being paid handsomely to use the past as a way to block the future.

'It had been a business built around a physical product and that physical product, the latest incarnation of which was the CD, was extraordinarily successful,' he says. 'So the whole concept of where we were [at the time] was to protect that business. This was what the labels were specifically focused on. How do we protect this business?'

He continues, 'It made perfect sense. If you looked at the guys who were in charge of the companies at that point, it was an older generation. For a lot of them there, their compensation packages were tied to physical sales. The initial reaction and response was, first of all, this was not a format over which we had any control.'

Jac Holzman, founder of Elektra Records and a long-standing technophile, felt at the time there was an institutionalised inertia gripping the record business at the highest level and this was holding everything and everyone else back.

'The record executives back in that time were not used to change,' he says. 'Things would happen, there would be a format that would go on for a number of years, there would be increases in sales. They were worried about the accounts more than they were about the music. Let the guys who run the labels worry about that.'

Hilary Rosen, then the president and CEO of the RIAA, distils down the existential crisis facing the old guard of the record business in the 1990s by using a film analogy.

'They saw moving into something completely different as jumping off a cliff,' she says. 'Because there was no way back: like Butch Cassidy and the Sundance Kid, where you basically have to jump into the river below because they're coming for you and pray that you'll live. They just resisted doing that.'

Rob Wells, working as head of digital at BMG in the UK at the time, says there are two ways to look at how ready record companies were for digital in 1999. On a marketing level, he says BMG was well down the road here, but the company had not got to grips with what online would mean as a revenue source.

'[We had artist websites], but we weren't ready for commerce,' he says. '[But being] digital ready in terms of having everything digitised, pipes open, waiting for DSPs to come in and ingest catalogue and all the metadata was accurate? On a scale of one to ten, where ten is flick the switch and deliver, they were probably a two. Consumers were receptive to marketing messages received via email. There was so much engagement with our CD-ROMs. All the new media stuff, that was a ten. Commerce? Were we ready to sell? Fuck, no.'

Raoul Chatterjee, head of sales and new media at Warner Music UK, says that Martin Craig, head of Warner Music International's ESP division, was not being listened to by some senior executives the company and was left to operate in his own bubble. 'Martin was the loudest voice within Warner,' he says. 'We had [some executives] still running the company then who didn't really have a great deal of interest in this stuff. [They were] much more into the music and the art [than the technology].'

He adds, 'They had no appetite whatsoever, in my opinion, back then to really embrace the commercial aspects that the web and digital and new media might bring. The US was different because you had these people like George White at Atlantic Records, who was relatively influential, wanting to do cool shit. New media [in the UK] was an add-on rather than a core requirement. They weren't running to the future; they were walking towards the future.'

Martin Craig, who helped set up the ESP division within Warner International, says it was an uphill struggle for many years for senior management to treat digital and online with the gravitas he felt it deserved and understand that this was going to change their business whether they wanted it to or not.

'The senior people, the established people, did not believe in it at all,' he says. 'The common response was, "Why are people going to listen to music on a computer?" They couldn't get their heads around that [points at my iPhone] being a computer. It wasn't protectionism. It was really not believing that it could happen. I think the industry resisted it, hugely, because they were frightened of it. And then when they realised that you could copy things so easily, they became terrified of it.'

He calls his time at Warner ESP 'by far the most frustrating job I've ever had' because so many of his projects were being derailed by senior management. 'Everything I'd try and do was just blocked, because everyone was frightened.'

Steinman suggests that the culture of experimentation he was encouraged to pursue in the mid 1990s had, by the end of the decade, been superseded by a growing corporate uncertainty, or strategic indecision, across the company as to the best way to navigate the internet.

'It was really just about trying to corral some centre of gravity, but there were no hard lines reporting into Paul [Vidich, Warner's lead on digital] or anybody at the centre at the music group level,' he says. 'Maybe that, in turn, could have been problematic because we couldn't get real consensus. It was hard to get consensus. You had to just sway personalities to try to gain consensus.'

He says there was a mirage of control within Warner by this stage, where the company was convinced it was going to be fully in charge of the direction and the speed of change.

'Slowing [things] down and stopping certain things felt probably a little more like we had more control, but the truth was, there was no control,' he says. 'The control was being pushed from the outside in.'

The situation at Sony was perhaps the most antithetical of any of the majors in 1999. On the one side of the company was its music division and on the other side was its hardware division, focusing on devices like the PlayStation and trying to make the MiniDisc, which launched in 1992, a viable format. In 1999, it was also finalising its first digital music player, the Network Walkman, which launched at the end of that year.

On paper, Sony should have been the major label leading the digital charge. In reality, music and hardware were locked in their own silos and not really talking to each other.

'The only way I can describe it is total non-intervention,' says Sony Music Europe's Paul Russell of the relationship between the two halves of Sony. 'There were the hardware guys who got on and did their business. And we got on and did our business. Obviously, they were making a lot of money from hardware that was maybe hurting our business, or it *was* hurting our business, but that was our problem, not their problem. They had their business to run and it was total non-intervention.'

Patrick Decam, president of Sony Music Benelux and the executive in charge of the company's digital activities across mainland Europe, agrees with Russell. He offers up the story of one meeting he attended by way of illustrating the scale of the disconnect between the two halves of Sony.

'I organised our first meetings with the Sony hardware guy in Holland, near Schiphol, in Badhoevedorp,' he says. 'It was like *Avatar*. You had people from one planet meeting people from another planet – and they were at the same table. I had convinced my bosses that we needed to meet with the tech guys so that the company would not get schizophrenic.'

Decam adds that Sony did see a digital future for itself – not in music but rather in gaming.

'Sony understood what the future could be, of course, but they thought they had the ultimate answer that was the PlayStation,' he says. 'Yes, there would be a digital world. Yes, every sound would be digitised. But customers, in order to listen to music or watch videos, would have to go through the PlayStation. It was a proprietary platform. That was the vision of how Sony would control dematerialisation.'

Darren Hemmings was working in Sony Music's IT department at the time and bluntly states, 'Sony were also irritatingly myopic in that they never, in my time there, managed to actually synergise all the things they owned.'

Neil Cartwright was brought in as head of digital at Sony Music UK in 1996 and says the corporate disconnect between music and hardware was in equal parts ideological and geographical.

'There wasn't a huge amount of communication between Sony hardware and electronics and Sony Music,' he says of the UK situation specifically. 'Sony Corporation were in a huge building in New York. Music, electronics, everything was in this huge skyscraper in New York. I think there was a lot more dialogue there; but Sony Electronics [in the UK] are based in Weybridge![48] I went to a couple of meetings later on, but there was very little coming down [from the heads at Sony for greater integration].'

He adds that many of the label executives at the time were not even considering the internet as part of their long-term strategy and were nonplussed by it.

'There were very few people in senior management who proactively knew what the internet was or what the implications would be over the next twenty years,' says Cartwright. 'In fact, there was probably more scepticism than there was support. But I will give Paul Burger [chairman and CEO of Sony Music UK] credit. He supported it. He's got to be given some credit.'

The necessary generational shift was never going to happen overnight. It was going to take years. For some record company executives, even well into the 2000s they were like corner office Don Quixotes, still tilting at digital windmills.

In 2007, Doug Morris was interviewed by *Wired* and revealed that, even many years into digital's profound impact on the music business, he was still pining for the blue remembered hills of LPs and, at a push, CDs. *Wired*'s Seth Mnookin called Morris 'an old-school music mogul who can barely hide his indifference to technology or his contempt for the download-loving public.'

He vividly painted Morris as someone, even this late into the process, incapable of seeing the bigger picture. 'Morris has never accepted the digital world's ruling ethos that it's better to follow the smartest long-term strategy, even if it means near-term losses,' wrote Mnookin. 'As far as he's concerned, do that and someone, somewhere, is taking advantage of you. Morris wants to be paid now, not in some nebulous future.'

Eight years after Napster, six years after the iPod and four years after the launch of the iTunes Music Store, Morris was happy to admit that he – and, by default, Universal – was still pretty clueless about digital.

'There's no one in the record company that's a technologist,' he asserted. 'That's a misconception writers make all the time, that the record industry missed this. They didn't. They just didn't know what to do. It's like if you were suddenly asked to operate on your dog to remove his kidney. What would you do? [. . .] We didn't know who to hire. I wouldn't be able to recognize a good technology person – anyone with a good bullshit story would have gotten past me.'[49]

Lyor Cohen says he personally tried to gently usher Morris into the digital age in the 1990s, but admits to not being sure just how successful he was.

'Just so you know, I brought Doug Morris his first computer and said, "If you're not going to use it, at least have it on your desk and open it",' he says.

I ask Cohen if his gift was something Morris used.

'He opened it,' he says, letting his words hang portentously in the air for a moment. 'You have to ask him if he used it.'

While Morris was still desperately adrift in 2007, here he offered a telling snapshot of the attitude towards digital that was shared by many senior record company executives in 1999. Many did not understand its long-term implications. Among the handful who did, there was a mounting horror that the old ways that had made them personally very wealthy might no longer be fit for purpose.

CHAPTER 3

The Missionary Zeal of the Converts

(The digital generation try to control how labels are rebuilt from within, albeit slowly)

'A major label has always wanted to control everything,' argued Jeremy Silver in his *Digital Medieval* book. 'That is the mindset [. . .] As the internet grew in importance, the label stance shifted from instinctive denial to bargaining for dominance.'[1]

In the years since 1999, as time telescoped, a particular narrative has ossified around how the record business responded to digital. It was sleepwalking. It was arrogant. It believed itself to be invincible. Digital, it follows, was cold revenge on an industry that not only did not wish to change but also flat-out refused to even contemplate *why* it should change.

This line of argument, however, is ahistorical and refuses to accept the layers of complexity around what was actually happening. Of course there were senior executives who could not operate their own email accounts, who thought anyone using the internet was a 'geek', who just wanted more CDs shipped so they could take home their quarterly bonus.

A few levels down the corporate hierarchy, however, were small but dedicated teams of people absolutely alive to what digital was going to do to the business and, even within strict corporate parameters, trying to prepare everyone for it. These cartographers of the future were growing in both number and influence within companies. The complication, of course, was the speed at which they were allowed to grow.

DIGITAL PREPARATION: WARNER

'The great myth was that the industry didn't know what was coming,' says Cliff Fluet. 'I call bullshit on that.'

Small digital fiefdoms – or digital enclaves, depending on the level of influence they wielded – were slowly becoming established within record companies. Fluet does admit, however, there was a degree of ghettoisation happening around digital.

'Warner ESP was the bucket that anything that we then called new media, because it was new then, fell into,' he says. 'And there was an absolute ban on anyone at a label touching this stuff.'

By operating in a bucket, there was the real possibility that digital was being 'othered' within companies – something that happened *over there* behind closed doors and no one else was allowed to get close to it. Some staff members would be intrigued, but it possibly engendered a certain level of company suspicion that curdled into disdain.

Martin Craig feels, with hindsight, separating out new media was a bad idea.

'It was always a mistake to have a new media division and to have it separate,' he says. 'It needed to be part of everything. To separate it out is a mistake as you ghettoise it and you make it this special thing.'

Fluet recounts the story of a two-day company conference looking at digital and the impact it would have on the traditional – and, in corporate terms, still very powerful – divisions of Warner. A senior marketing executive, testily responding to previous discussions around a future based on instant digital access to music and the oft-quoted idea of the celestial jukebox, addressed the audience.

According to Fluet, 'He said, "OK – non-stop music, genre-specific, personalised, available at any time in any way that someone wants? Ladies and gentlemen, it's called radio. I bid you adieu." And he just walked out of the room!'

Mark Foster was SVP of new media at Warner Music International (based in London) and helped set up the company's new media division. He says part of the division's role was a 'defence strategy' as 'the obsession at the time was primarily focused on defending the CD.' He suggests that this was for two clear reasons: because Warner executives were paid bonuses on CD sales; and Wall Street analysts were heavily focused on growth in the market, of which the CD was the most easily understood success metric.

He also says his division was 'to get on the front foot in terms of the new technologies that were coming in and to 'figure out what e-commerce opportunities were out there such as still selling CDs and using the internet to do it.' He recalls that, as the division was only set up in the final quarter of 1999, it took until 2000 until his calls to start licensing music for digital sale were actually being listened to.

'The first remit was to figure out what was going on and what all these technologies are, how they will affect our business model in terms of piracy, cannibalisation of sales et cetera,' he says. 'It wasn't really until the following year that we started winning the argument that, "If we don't get on the front foot and start issuing licences to some of these people in a very controlled way, they will just eat our lunch. We need to figure out who the players are, what the formats are, how we can generate licensing revenue for these new formats. If MiniDisc isn't going to work, is it going to be the Diamond Rio?"'

There were, however, still plenty of cynical voices in the company that were unmoved by their digital evangelism, says Foster. 'Martin Craig used to walk around the building with his mobile phone and some of the early MP3 players and say, "One day these will be the same device." And everybody would go, "Yeah, right"!'

Craig suggests that this digital distrust was deeply embedded in certain parts of the company, making what he wanted to do – and how he wanted to evolve Warner, both strategically and ideologically – close to impossible. On the one hand, there were people in the company wishing to embrace digital completely; on the other, there were people in the company wishing to erase digital completely. This lack of consensus created a vacuum where little could be achieved.

'I'm not sure there was a Warner stance, to be honest,' he says. 'It was confusing. I remember being summoned by a, let's just say, very senior person who had come in at a very senior level. In a room of his deputies and lieutenants, he said to me, "OK, tell us why what you're doing is going to replace what we do".' To great merriment in the whole room. They were all taking the piss. You're giving them too much credit [in terms of their digital foresight]. They didn't really believe in it.'

Foster says that fear of a loss of control – over distribution, over content, over revenues that was gripping Warner Music International – meant that projects and initiatives were being blocked on a regular basis by the top strata of management.

'We were just playing defence initially,' he suggests. 'Like in cricket, you were just playing your blocking shots. "You can't do that. You can't do that. You can't do that".' Then gradually we were realising that people were going to do this anyway. How could we turn this into a positive rather than just being afraid of our entire business model being blown into fragments.'

Warner Music was headquartered in the US and executives there had the final say on much of what was being done in territories around the world.

Donna Cohen, after having gone to Philips Interactive Media for two years, returned to Warner in 1995 as VP of internet strategy and business development. She says it was the artists who were really pushing the company's recorded music arm to experiment online, but that Warner Chappell, Warner's music publishing arm ('I think they were tech-phobic'), was hugely resistant.

'The publishing companies were scared,' she says. 'The artists really pushed the thing – and the young punks at the record labels. It was not productive. I mean, they were vanity projects, all the artists' websites, all of that. It wasn't really good at driving sales. They were just marketing pieces. We just didn't have the sales piece together.'

At the time, she suggests, there was no deeper online strategy at the company than merely having some websites.

'You knew everybody needed to have one, but you didn't know what [to do with it],' she says. 'There wasn't a lot of strategy behind it. A lot of it was keeping the artists' egos satisfied. The savvy ones needed them. And they wanted big budgets.'

Paul Vidich was promoted to EVP of strategic planning and business development at Warner in May 1999[2] and was running its digital operations and strategy globally. 'I was the least wedded to what I'll call the traditional music approach to the world,' he says.

He suggests that, while he oversaw all digital activities globally, he was somewhat open and flexible. 'It wasn't a fiefdom so much,' he argues. 'All of the digital strategies around the world, including out of London, which was the head of Warner Music International, reported to me. They had a lot of independence, but we set guidelines and parameters under which they would go off and do deals.'

By July 1999, Warner was moving to test the impact of downloads on its business, both as a promotional tool and as a way to drive record sales. Across its three main label groups it was offering free tracks from twenty-three established and developing acts, including Jewel, Sugar Ray, Missy Elliott, Kid Rock, Pretenders, Natalie Cole, matchbox 20 and Paula Cole.

'We will do more [track downloads] in the next ninety days than the [majors] have done collectively up to this point,' Vidich informed *Billboard*.

Warner hired three different research companies to test the effectiveness of the downloads and use that to figure out how much of its future promotions should be around digital.

All the downloads came wrapped in DRM (digital rights management) to limit how they could be stored and came with an assigned dollar value (ranging from $2.99 to $3.49). Even though they were free, Warner said this was done in order to reinforce in the minds of consumers that they have a financial value.

'We are not looking to give anything away,' Dave Mount, chairman of WEA, told *Billboard*. 'In the long run, we are a business about selling, so we want to figure out a way to tie [the downloads] into a sale of some kind.'[3]

Vidich describes 1999 in the record business as 'totally chaotic' but suggests things were not derailed as much as they perhaps could have been. 'We didn't lose all control,' he argues. 'We were on the verge of losing all control. We saw where things would go if they weren't, in some way, controlled.'

DIGITAL PREPARATION: UNIVERSAL

Universal, the year before Seagram bought PolyGram, had set up eLabs, its dedicated digital division.

'Originally the name was Electronic Commerce & Advanced Technology but it got changed to eLabs because of corporate politics,' says Larry Kenswil, who was president of the division from 1997 to 2008. 'There was a lot of political pushing and pulling us to where digital distribution would fall on the organisation chart. It wasn't decided. We were never set up at eLabs as being an operational unit. It was always [to] find out everything, put together business plans and technology plans, and then push it to the operating companies. We wanted it to not look like we were the electronic commerce operational unit; so that's why we changed it to eLabs.'

He suggests around fifty people were working in eLabs by 1999/2000. One of the first things he did at the start of eLabs was to set up a marketing street team of college students and then it moved into what Kenswil calls 'technological vetting' – meeting outside companies pitching services and filtering out the best and most interesting ones to potentially work with. The eLabs team was, he says, a mix of 'techies, marketers and businesspeople', showing the breadth of its remit.

'There was no doubt in our minds that it was the future,' he says of digital. 'No one knew when the future would arrive. Certainly at the labels, there has always been a marketing versus profits push/pull. The marketing people love to give stuff away. That's how, for instance, retail worked. The way you get promotion at retail was to give a lot of free units to retailers, either by way of discount or actual product. The finance people did not want to set up another system where that would be the case. We were very much aware that digital could provide a way to get better price and positioning schemes, which it did.'

He reveals, however, that after the merger, he was running into a very different working environment at PolyGram than he was used to at Universal, especially around digital and online.

'Right after the PolyGram merger [we took] a tour around the world to the main PolyGram offices so the US people could find out what they were up to,' he says. 'We found out PolyGram was a very difficult place to do digital business before the merger. PolyGram was for sale for quite a while, so they were keeping costs down. When we got to these offices, we found very, very little actually going on, because there were so few computers. And the reason there were so few computers is because every PC purchase had to be approved by this worldwide CFO of PolyGram. Which was amazing to us.'

He continues, 'I remember visiting Paris and talking to the person who was doing the PolyGram Paris digital media marketing site. They had to do it from home. They could not connect to it from the office! We were, internationally, under a lot of pressure to build this up. We established people in London in the international unit that oversaw the world outside of North America to speed this along. People went in there and started pushing it.'

Bronfman says that shortly after the PolyGram purchase was cleared by the regulators was when he really started to understand the impact digital would have on his new company. It was not quite buyer's remorse, but there was a definite widening of the eyes at what was coming.

'I became worried as 1999 unfolded that the digital distribution process was potentially going to disrupt us,' he says, noting the chaos that erupted towards the end of that year. 'I certainly felt like I overpaid for PolyGram given what happened twelve to eighteen months later.'

John Kennedy, running Universal in the UK, says the onrush of digital for the record business in 1999 very quickly cast Seagram's purchase of PolyGram in 1998 in a whole new, and much harsher, light.

'[Looking at] the digital picture, Edgar Bronfman, poor old Edgar Bronfman, must look at his vision of buying a record label and just think he was too early, really, in a sense,' he says. 'I'm sure mistakes were made, but just in a sense too early. He bought the company on the basis that he thought the business would build geographically, that markets like India and China would come in, and that's how the business would expand.'

He continues, 'But he did then see the digital truck that was coming straight at us. He brought in a team of people. These were very bright people with tech backgrounds. Were they the Messiah? Did they have the solutions? No, because this was evolving considerably. He was not scared to spend. I don't know that he knew the [imminent digital] problem before he bought the company, but he knew about it very soon after.'

Kennedy says there was clear and immediate pressure on the company to not just manage the shift into digital but to get ahead of it and reimagine Universal for the 21st century.

'To be fair to Edgar, I don't think he knew what he was getting into,' he proposes. 'But the minute he knew what he was facing, he got quite excited about being the record company of the future, if you like. But, of course, he then had pressure from shareholders as well, which he had to balance.'

Talal Shamoon was vice president of InterTrust when it signed a deal with Universal to 'supply the rights management software that will form the basis of its online music sales activities.'[4] He argues Bronfman was a pivotal figure in the record industry adapting to the digital changes happening all around it at the time.

'Bronfman is a real entrepreneur,' says Shamoon. 'He was like, "I don't care what happens to the aeroplane, we're going to fly as fast as we can, we're going to make this happen." He's a true visionary, by the way. Edgar Bronfman doesn't get enough credit in this whole thing. He's often painted as a romantic, rich kid, frustrated. . . bullshit! That guy saw it and he incinerated billions of dollars and made it happen. It wasn't until Universal gained the leverage they gained by buying PolyGram that they could push people around to make them do what they wanted. And he hired the best of the breed. Bronfman is a hero in the story.'

The bit between his teeth, Shamoon continues. 'He didn't have to do any of that. He could have flown around on corporate jets and made money off shitty rum [. . .] If I were a rich kid, I'd live in a penthouse and walk around in a bathrobe all day. I wouldn't bet my family fortune on saving an industry that was beyond saving. Hats off! That's real entrepreneurship.'

Bronfman did, ultimately, see digital as a net positive for the business, but only when it was brought to heel by music companies.

He says, 'The control that was being undermined was principally control of distribution. We were still promoting. We were still doing all the other things that we did uniquely well or uniquely period. But control of distribution was definitely being undermined. And that was going to clearly be problematic. It also, I thought, had tremendous potential – if the industry could harness it.'

The big upheaval, he thought, would be felt at the retail level, but he saw what would replace the physical store as a phenomenal opportunity as consumption moved from the high street to the computer and, eventually, to the mobile phone.

'It was clear to me that this was going to happen, that there was going to be digital distribution and that, ultimately, would overwhelm physical distribution, which in my mind was a wonderful thing,' he says. 'Because you're going from literally hundreds of thousands of retail outlets to eventually billions of telephones. It's a phenomenal increase in distribution, and at no incremental costs. It's just ones and zeroes. You don't have to build a new distribution platform.'

He pauses to contemplate how that was to play out. 'I thought it might be a rough couple of years,' he sighs. 'I didn't realise it would be a rough decade and a half.'

The biggest problem, he believes, is that 'we were a music company, not a tech company', which considerably held it back. He says that the music business needed help and guidance from the tech industry in the late 1990s but feels that was not forthcoming and that they were being intentionally isolated and left to fend for themselves.

'We didn't get any help from the tech industry,' he says. 'I don't know how it would have been different if we had, but, effectively, we were on our own. We just weren't very good at doing what we'd never done before.'

Despite this, he claims he was not felled by pessimism around how the record business would survive. 'First of all, things change over time; they don't change overnight,' he says. 'A lot of people were screaming doom and gloom. I wasn't really that concerned. It may have been gloom, but it wasn't doom.'

DIGITAL PREPARATION: BMG

Jeff Liebenson was VP of legal and business affairs at BMG in 1999, based in New York but overseeing all legal and business affairs staff across fifty-three markets outside of the US.

BMG had set up its online strategic task force, with ten executives involved in it initially, specifically to prepare the company for digital. 'We had representatives from various key markets around the world, with different types of backgrounds and expertise,' he says. 'We all sat and discussed what the right approach to the internet was.'

Younger team members were essential, he argues, for this to work, and he cites Jon Vlassopulos in Hong Kong and Rob Wells in the UK as being absolutely critical.

'It was great for us and gave us a lot of additional perspective because Rob and Jon are as close to having digital natives on the team as we could get,' says Liebenson. 'I learned so much from both of them. It was really valuable to have access to their perspectives. I remember them bringing a lot of things to light because they were just closer to it and more natural with the digital realm.'

Further up the BMG hierarchy, however, there was a much slower embracing of digital.

'There's this phrase that technology moves much faster than the law, so the law is always struggling to keep up,' says Liebenson. 'But parallel to this, technology also often moves faster than management. You have these seasoned managers that came up usually because they earned it. They're excellent at what they do. But when the industry changes underneath them, it provides a lot of surprising elements for everyone. And not everybody is agile enough or curious enough to want to learn new things. They tend to focus on what their strengths were and that brought them their success. Sometimes they get swept away by the new developments instead of getting on board.'

Jon Vlassopulos was director of business development at BMG between 1997 and 1999. He says he ran into obstinacy from certain senior people at the company over what he and his team wanted to do digitally.

'A lot of the music executives who had built their careers in the CD era didn't necessarily want to adopt some new medium that they didn't particularly understand,' he says. 'They'd rather keep things as they were.'

Rob Wells says that his role at BMG in the UK was to ensure that the executive team there quickly learned about this new world and how to work with it. Richard Griffiths was chairman of BMG UK and Wells recounts going to his house every Friday morning for a digital show and tell.

'It was a pre-breakfast meeting, so I'd cycle round to his place in Putney,' says Wells. 'I'd be showing him ripping CDs and even stuff outside of the industry, like looking at weather charts and things like that. We'd talk about what it would mean, about the immediacy of the internet. He was very receptive.'

(In September 2022, I emailed Griffiths to ask him to be interviewed for this book. 'I'm sorry but I don't want to get into that,' he replied.)

People like Wells were important translators within the major record companies as well as being digital evangelists, knowing they had to get the whole company on side. Initially it was a delicate outreach mission.

'People didn't know what we did,' says Wells of the rest of the UK company's attitude towards him. 'I made a point at BMG where I would wander around the floors – publishing, A&R, marketing – I'd be like, "I'm a new media guy. I do digital, look after the internet stuff." And they'd be like, "Oh, could you sort that printer? That printer is a bit fucked".' I would go, "I'm not IT, but let me look at it." I loved it, though. Not being smug, but I think it was knowing what the promise of the space was going to bring. You're looking at all these people that are trading in the plastic business and doing great things with breaking bands, but they had no idea what was coming.'

DIGITAL PREPARATION: SONY

In part through serendipity, Sony was slowly building a digital team from 1995 onwards. Paul Russell, with a Europe-wide remit at the company, worked closely with Patrick Decam who was running Sony Music in Belgium. Decam had a keen interest in technology and Russell felt he could help prepare the company for whatever was coming.

'Patrick and I became really close,' he says. 'It was a bit of a punt when we said to Patrick, "You understand this shit! I don't understand it. Come and help us." He continued to run the Belgium company, but he appointed a deputy and he spent 90 per cent of his time on trying to get this organised and keeping us informed [. . .] He made it his business to understand it and he was a very smart guy.'

Decam says he was a very early adopter here and worked to bring

Sony forward digitally, saying he built Sony Music Belgium's website in 1994, claiming this was the first Sony company website in the West. 'There was no sound, just images and text,' he explains. 'It was a UFO for most of our other colleagues!'

He says that he was playing around with technology, seeing how far he could push it and what things he could do with music.

'With a couple of friends, we managed to import a chip from Asia and we stored thirty seconds of music on it,' he recounts. 'That was the first ever attempt to do that. We put it on a CD jewel box with a little button. When you pushed on the button, you could hear 30 seconds of what was inside the CD. It was inside the package. I presented that to my American boss. He cracked and he said, "Patrick, hide that. You want to kill the industry!" This was way before the Diamond Rio. That triggered in the minds of my bosses the idea that if there was a guy who could maybe try to understand what was happening, maybe it could be me.'

He says that, initially at least, the internet was seen within Sony as purely a marketing tool. He also travelled to Sony offices around the world, showcasing the Sony Music Belgium website and getting them to understand the potential for their own markets.

The speed of digital adoption was, he claims, very different depending on the territory.

'The Germans hired one guy, then we hired some help for him,' he says. 'They were employees of the German company, but they were reporting to me for their functional job. The French were fast on the ball. The Dutch were fast, too. I must say that the Brits were very slow, but they were, in a way, close to the reaction I had seen with my American colleagues. The Americans were extremely sceptical. In fact, to be maybe a bit brutal, they didn't want to hear anything about new technologies or the digital train coming to hit them. We were pretty much on our own for some years. So we could experiment with what the internet was about to bring to us.'

Neil Cartwright says scepticism about the internet ran through Sony in the UK. He was head of eMedia from 1996 and notes that UK head Paul Burger 'recognised that the internet was something that was going to be permanent.'

However, even though the more senior person at the UK company was keen to embrace the internet, this did not trickle down through the rest of the company.

'I used to get a couple of comments from people, "Are you still in a job? What are you still doing here?"' he recalls. 'They thought it was a flash in the pan, a fad that had come along and it would soon pass. That scepticism was inherent for quite a few years.'

Much of his work in the late 1990s was exploring the marketing possibilities of the internet rather than trying to figure out business models related to it.

'A lot of our money was spent on e-cards and the little executables that you would create,' he says. 'They were a big thing at the time. The whole viral thing was starting off in these little executables. I'm sure everyone can remember when they first arrived and you would double click them and suddenly your alarm would go off and your computer would go crazy. There'd be a huge cock on the screen! "Fuck! Fuck! Fuck!" Everyone would be sending this shit around to each other.'

The real proof of concept of viral internet marketing came from an unexpected, and highly scatological, source.

'Chef's 'Chocolate Salty Balls' from *South Park* was number one in January 1999,' he says. 'We were going up against Cliff Richard [with 'Can't Keep This Feeling In']. He used to do his annual Christmas track and 'Chocolate Salty Balls' was going up against him. We produced this little executable with *South Park* characters and Mr. Hankey, the Christmas Poo jumped on Cliff Richard's head so there was this great big shit stain on his head! It got mentioned on [BBC] Radio 1 because we'd sent it to them. I like to think that that was one of the very first virals and it actually achieved a number one record.'

DIGITAL PREPARATION: EMI

At EMI, the company that seemed doomed to always be rumoured to be for sale but not actually sold, digital was something that was increasingly being taken seriously by senior management.

Tony Wadsworth was running Parlophone in the 1990s before taking over EMI UK in 1998. He says it was the arrival of Ant Cauchi, then studying at the Brit School and doing work experience at Parlophone, that alerted him to what was happening digitally and, most shockingly, what it would mean for the company.

'He was the guy that came to me one day with the CD-R saying, 'This has got The Beatles on it," recalls Wadsworth. 'I said, "Where did you get that from?" "I downloaded it.' "What do you mean by that? From where did you download it?" "The internet." So he had to explain all of these terms. I asked, "What track is it?" He said, "All of them!" And that was when I realised things were going to be very different and that this is something I should start taking a real interest in. He was a bright guy, fresh out of the Brit School, but I put him in charge of looking after our so-called new media. The Blur website, which was one of the first pop websites in the UK, was something he initiated. He was in the right place at the right time – with the right brain.'

Cauchi says he was doing work experience in the video department at Parlophone in 1995 when a computer, very different to the grey-screen monitors used within the company at the time, arrived.

'1995 feels like it should be quite modern, but it wasn't very modern,' he says. 'I just read a few magazines like *.net* and I said I'd take it. Suddenly it became my all-encompassing world and I became the internet guy.' He became, more by default than by design, the first digital person at Parlophone in the UK.

He worked closely with artists who wanted to explore the possibilities of the internet, especially in how they could communicate with fans in new ways.

'Paul McCartney loved doing these little videos and you'd upload them,' says Cauchi. 'It would just be him reacting to fans and talking to fans. He realised very early this was a really interesting way of talking to people more directly. Radiohead, of course, were really into that and just took it on in their own way with the launch of [official site] WASTE. Every band we signed, pretty much, came in with their idea of how they wanted to manage their [online] property to talk to fans. They saw it as, I guess, digital fan clubs.'

There was, not by 1999 anyway, any pressure to make online a major driver of revenue within EMI. 'This wasn't about directly selling music,' says Wadsworth. 'At that point it was seen as a marketing tool.'

Cauchi says he might have been given a budget of, at most, £20,000 for digital marketing around a major album. 'To me at the time, because we went from having zero, it felt like a lot of money,' he says. 'At the time when people were spending £200k, £300k, £400k on a video, it was probably a fraction of the money.'

EMI wanted to be seen as digitally progressive and was working on projects and platforms that it felt would express this to both consumers and the wider media.

The first was www.lookon.net, set up by Parlophone in May 1999 as an interactive lifestyle magazine and positioned as 'the biggest overhaul of its web strategy in three years.' *Music Week* reported that it would feature a chat forum alongside articles 'on topics ranging from snowboarding to computer games', with non-music content making up around 10 per cent of its total output.

Ant Cauchi told *Music Week*, 'There is only a certain number of people on the web who want to hear music. By offering other content as well, we believe the site will appeal to a wider audience.' He added, 'It's going to be an online brand that staff here will be able to use as a marketing tool.'[5]

Reflecting, over twenty years later, on what the site was trying to achieve, Cauchi says, 'Parlophone for me was more than just music, it was culture. Food and all the other sub-labels [within EMI] were culturally relevant and culturally driven. It was: how do we become a bit more always-on? My frustration was this. We had a hundred people who are working on a Coldplay album and then the album comes and then they move on to the next thing. But I didn't move on to the next thing. You're still there and you're still trying to keep it going. It was part of that. It was the early days of CRM [customer relationship management]. How do we build a fanbase of people that we can talk to?'

(Coincidentally, in the same issue of *Music Week* that announced the launch of www.lookon.net, a short story appeared with the news that Parlophone had 'beat off stiff competition to sign one of the most sought-after in [the] past six months' bands. That band, photographed by the fountains in Trafalgar Square 'signing' their record deal on a trestle table, was Coldplay.)

The second initiative was based on Virgin Records' existing Media Warehouse and was a way to digitally send content to media, thereby speeding up delivery times and, ultimately, lowering costs and wastage.

'The issue was that we were sending bikes and couriers everywhere with press releases and printed photographs,' says Wadsworth. "Why don't we just make things available on the internet? It'll be so much quicker.'

The ideal proved greater than the reality.

'It was a media assets site,' explains Wadsworth. 'So if you were *Kerrang!* or the *NME* or whoever and you wanted this photograph of an artist, instead of waiting for the bike to come over with it, because that's what happened, you could download it. The problem we found was that none of the magazines had the facilities to download anything! So we were making this great solution for people who weren't ready to use it. That was the thing that held it back. It was ironic that the Fourth Estate were the people calling *us* Luddites.'

In July 1999, EMI became, according to *Music Week*, 'the first UK major to establish a dedicated new media division' and this was 'in recognition of the increasing commercial opportunities presented by the internet.' Fergal Gara was appointed head of the division and was joined by Eric Winbolt and Ant Cauchi.

'Gara says the web is developing at a fast rate and gives labels the ability to do PR, marketing and retailing in one move,' reported *Music Week*. 'He adds it is rapidly extending from being a promotional tool to presenting commercial opportunities.'

Tony Wadsworth added that it would enable EMI to go beyond just experimenting in digital. 'We are in an excellent position to shape our strategy,' he said.[6]

Reflecting on the reasons for this structural change, Wadsworth today says, 'I was trying to make sure that each of the labels were sharing best practice. Things were moving so fast.'

EMI was also enormously enthused about webcasting at the time, despite the resolution being, by today's standards, diabolical and the audience numbers being minuscule. In many ways it was about the media attention around the webcasts rather than the webcasts themselves. They quickly found out that a successful webcast was a poisoned chalice – at least economically.

'At the time, bandwidth was so expensive,' notes Cauchi. 'There was this real concern about audience size. Unless you had an MSN [funding it]. If you were doing it yourself, you were worried about the volume [. . .] Webcasting was brilliant. But it went from "Oh, great, we've got a thousand people watching," to, "I hope we have no more than two thousand." It was thousands and thousands of megabytes.'

It was the artists themselves who helped change the company's attitude to the internet, or, at least, the most commercially successful acts who it was understood had to be listened to (and occasionally have their whims indulged).

'From an EMI point of view, a lot of artists drove it,' says Cauchi. 'Look at Radiohead and the way they turned marketing and interest awareness into commercial awareness. For a lot of bands, Radiohead became a real lead in that era in just doing that. Very few people, especially within labels, just didn't see beyond this being a fad.'

In the US, some of the artists affiliated to EMI were running into some label politics with regard to their digital experiments.

Ian Rogers started an unofficial Beastie Boys website in 1993. It was eventually spotted by the band and their management and he was recruited to work for them and their label, Grand Royal, which was distributed through Capitol Records. Rogers would travel with the band, recording their live sets on MiniDisc from the soundboard and post MP3s online.

'There are some old articles about the fact Capitol did try to shut me down but the band and I just gave them the finger,' he laughs. 'We were like, "Shut up!" It was never really an issue. Then we get this call. They're like, "Oh, you guys need to stop posting the songs online." I remember Mike [D, Beastie Boys] and I looking at each other and going, "What? Are they serious? Do they think we're going to listen to this?" I called them and was like, "No. Forget it. You don't tell us what to do. We're the Beastie Boys. This is what we do." At the time, none of us could figure out why they would even care about the fifty people who might download an MP3.'

Eric Winbolt says that artists getting the potential of the internet and the fact that doing something new would reflect well on them was what helped get the wider message to percolate through the company and help reflect back a certain progressiveness about the company to the outside business world.

'Many artists, probably 90 per cent, would say, "We want to do something no one's ever done before",' he says. 'That was almost baked into the job. I had a much more traditional role in looking after things like search marketing, SEO and building websites, but the real crown jewels were [artists saying], "Dazzle us. Dazzle us with what technology can do." Because if you do that, not only will the artists be delighted and feel they've got kindred spirits who are reflecting their creativity in the way that digital is used to portray them to these new audiences, but it will also send a message to investors and to shareholders and everybody else that these businesses are clued up.'

He says that, as digital's potential was incrementally understood by the company and as it was making it clear it would shape its future, the naysayers inside EMI suddenly became total converts, but this was driven less than by pure faith and more by solipsism.

'It didn't happen until a couple of years later, but when it did, you saw businesses restructure and you suddenly saw that everybody in music wanted "digital" in their job title because it was a survival tactic,' he says.

'Everybody had realised that this had gone from being the icing on the cake to becoming the cake itself.'

MARKETING VERSUS PROMOTION VERSUS REVENUE VERSUS. . . SOMETHING ELSE

Perhaps the biggest conundrum for digital and new media departments within record companies in 1999 was where it all sat with regard to established corporate divisions. It was still too early in digital's uptake for it to really affect A&R (although platforms like Peoplesound, Vitaminic, Mudhut and Musicunsigned were all trying to do just that). People I spoke to in these departments at the time gave tellingly different answers. Some said that, because of the existence of artist and company websites, it fell under the purview of communications and PR. Others said it was treated as an extension of marketing.

Where divisions were really most apparent between companies was in the commercial role of digital: was this a new cost centre that had no commercial targets? Or was it going to be an additional revenue source to run alongside those delicious profits coming from CDs?

Bronfman says the digital policy within Universal in 1999 was explicitly commercial in 1999. 'I saw it as a short-term revenue threat and a long-term revenue opportunity. I did not see it as a promotional opportunity at all.'

Perhaps no one of this era exemplifies the unapologetic push to make digital a money spinner for record companies as much as Jay Samit, who came to EMI as SVP of new media in April 1999.

'So I'm a digital guy,' he says. 'Nowadays that makes sense. Everybody's a digital guy. But I started on the internet in 1978.'

He was, he claims, the first person to put video on a computer and was there in the earliest days of CD-ROM, exploring how music and video games could intertwine, notably a game that licensed music from the Geffen Records roster, which led to him setting up a games division within Universal Studios.

He was introduced to Ken Berry, then EMI Recorded Music CEO in the US, and pitched him about a commercial role within the company.

'I go over to the meeting and Ken apologises that he's got to go to London and doesn't have time to meet with me,' says Samit. 'I don't take no. You'll find this about me. So I said, "I'll ride with you in the limo to the airport, and then they'll take me back." Knowing that I'll get, in LA traffic, a full hour of a CEO's time. I explain what it means. He goes up in the air. I stay up that night and I write a whole business plan of what I believe the label can do and how they can make a ton of money. When he lands he has this. Now I'm the global head of digital.'

He says he was unapologetically commercial from the off, taking a hardline approach to getting content licensing deals done. A significant problem they had was around being able to license music digitally and if consumers could cherry-pick tracks rather than buy a whole album. Until the arrival of the iTunes Music Store in 2003, this was not a mainstream way of consuming music. The underlying complication was that historical recording contracts did not anticipate 'uncoupling' of individual tracks, so this was going to be an issue for emerging à la carte download models.

'So Ken and I are having a conversation,' says Samit. 'And Ken did probably the boldest move of that time period, which we didn't talk about then, which was, "Let's go through and see every artist of the past hundred years that has audited EMI or sued EMI, put them in one pile – the DO NOT TOUCH pile. Everybody else I have permission to put in every deal. If these people and their descendants start cashing the cheques, that's acceptance." We didn't ask for permission. I had a list of ninety-two acts that I couldn't touch. And you know their names!'

He says that, steadily, they were able to convince almost everyone on that list to allow their music to be sold that way. It did, however, take years. Samit says when he left EMI in 2003, that list had fallen to just five acts. 'Five of them wouldn't do it,' he says. 'The Beatles never got off the list in my day.'

(The Beatles eventually licensed their catalogue for download on iTunes in November 2010).[7]

INDIES

CHAPTER 4

Indie-fatigable: the Rearguard Action Against Major Consolidation

(The independents seek to take control of their own destiny)

In September 1998, as Edgar Bronfman Jr was nervously awaiting official regulatory approval to buy PolyGram and turn Universal into the biggest of the (now) five major record companies, news broke that, after a year in the planning, a new trade body for British independent record companies was coming.

It made the front cover of trade publication *Music Week* under the headline 'Indies aim to create new voice.' No one was officially commenting on it, but enough meaty details were present in the piece to suggest inside information was being carefully and strategically fed to *Music Week*.[1]

The body would be called AIM, standing for the Association of Independent Music. Some of the driving forces behind it were still members of the BPI, the British Phonographic Industry, that had been the de facto trade body for British record companies since its launch in 1973.[2] Martin Mills (co-founder of Beggars Banquet, arguably the pre-eminent British independent label of the era) and Derek Green (chairman of China Records) were understood to be leading the charge.

While there was a suggestion that this was very much not 'a breakaway group from the BPI' as the two bodies would continue to coexist, well-placed – albeit anonymous – sources suggested AIM was coming into being to give independents 'better representation in the industry' (subtext: the BPI was singularly failing to represent independents) and that it would give independents 'a stronger, coherent voice' (subtext: the BPI was not giving independents *any* voice). It was suggested that a shortlist of possible names to become the AIM chief executive had been drawn up and an official announcement would come in the next few months.

This was more than just a testing of the water to see how the BPI and the major labels would respond. This was the opening salvo in a new inter-label war, independents pitched against majors. But the independents had been here before, trying to organise themselves into a single voice, and it had apologetically fizzled out. Was it really going to be any different this time?

The punk scene in the UK from 1976 onwards saw a flowering of independent labels,[3] with Rough Trade (which sprang from the West London record shop of the same name) helping to set up The Cartel in 1978 as a cooperative network of British independents to offer distribution for their records.[4] Spartan Records, which also launched in 1978, began offering nationwide distribution to independent labels. A multitude of small and like-minded labels now had collective tools and a collective cause.

Iain McNay, founder of Cherry Red Records, said the independent sector at the time was really based on 'who you happened to meet and then staying in contact.' While the independents were, on paper anyway, competing with each other for acts and audiences, there was a nebulous network and an abstract community linking them. In the early 1980s, McNay said there was a move to create a 'loose association of independent labels' to find areas of common interest and collectively represent them.[5] It was called Umbrella.

'It was designed so that we could meet on a monthly basis and discuss our mutual problems,' explained McNay. 'By then, I had been elected to the BPI Council. The major companies at that stage were completely in control at the BPI. The independents like us, Factory and Rough Trade were having Top 40 success at that time too. Umbrella didn't have a formal structure as such – it was more ad hoc than that. There wasn't an official membership, but a lot of us labels used to meet regularly.'

There was no direct funding for Umbrella or a dedicated team running it and, according to McNay, it eventually petered out in 1991. 'After that,' he said, 'there was a bit of a void.'

Martin Mills says, 'We were never members of Umbrella. Umbrella was very political, very left wing, it didn't have any funding at all. It was quite tied into the revolutionary Rough Trade ethos. It was, I think, too political and not professional enough.'

Throughout the 1990s, an idea was percolating among a small group of British independent labels, most of them based in London. They felt that the independents needed formal representation in the shape of a trade organisation. It could not, however, be Umbrella II. It had to be fully professional.

AIR[6] (the Australian Independent Record Labels Association, which was formed in 1996) offered a template, but the UK was a much bigger market, both domestically and internationally, and had significantly more active independent labels than Australia. Whatever was formed in the UK would have to be able to go toe-to-toe with not just the BPI but also similar national organisations such as the RIAA in the US.

Mills was on the BPI Council alongside Derek Green and Steve Mason, who had acquired Pinnacle Distribution[7] in 1984. As key representatives of the independent sector at the BPI, they felt they were somewhat letting the side down.

'It was independents sitting around the BPI Council realising we weren't doing a very good job for independents by being on the BPI Council,' explains Mills. 'It was the realisation that independents' interests were very different from the majors' interest in many ways.'

Mills, Green and Mason had dinner at a restaurant on Queenstown Road in South London and, according to Mills, 'decided that we should explore the idea of creating an organisation purely for independents'.

A second dinner followed with, Mills estimates, ten people from different labels in attendance. The idea of an independent trade body was met with general enthusiasm.

'Then we had another meeting with about twenty people in it,' continues Mills. 'And then we had another meeting with about fifty people. We expanded the scope of the buy in. By the time we got to the fifty-person meeting, we said to people, 'You're going to have to commit some money to this as well.' We felt that we had to go ahead to do it.'

Andy Cleary, co-founder and director of Jammin Music Group, sat on the BPI board with Mills and says he was party to those early discussions.

'Probably more importantly, we both sat on the PPL[8] board,' he says. 'I think that's where a lot of the necessity for AIM came from. It was the fact that you could see global deals emerging and the BPI weren't really equipped to look after the indies.'

I ask him if the independents were frustrated that the BPI was not properly representing them.

'I wouldn't call it frustration,' he says. 'They didn't really have a mandate to do it. They really were only looking after British interests and we were moving to a global market.'

He says he was not as driven by vitriol to set up AIM as some of the other independents.

'There were a lot of indies that just wanted to form an indie club because they hated the majors,' he says. 'I was never one of them. Sean O'Brien from Telstar was pivotal in those dinners because he definitely had a foot in both camps. He did very well out of the majors with his compilation business. He was one of the very few indies that did. So he was probably as close to anyone that wanted to see it work – the two bodies coexisting and cooperating.'

Guy Holmes, founder of Gut Records, was initially approached by Daniel Miller, founder of Mute Records, who was among the first wave of independents to start to properly discuss the creation of this new trade body. He does not hide his long-standing disdain for the BPI, saying he refused to have his record company ever become a member.

'I thought they were a bunch of wankers,' he says, flatly. 'I wasn't giving them a load of my money [in membership fees]. I generally thought it was a boys' club that was run by people who wanted to shaft us. They kept changing chart rules and eligibility rules and all sorts of bits and pieces. I thought, "I know what your game is".'

Holmes was at the third meeting (he estimates there were eighteen people there) and recalls how it went.

'When the original eighteen of us sat down in a room we went, "Listen. We're being screwed [by the majors]. What can we do?" We had about a 24 per cent or 25 per cent market share for the independents, which they [the majors] really didn't like.'

Holmes says the idea of a new independent-centric trade body that was, in many ways, the diametric opposite of the BPI really appealed to him.

'I went to boarding school and had the shit kicked out of me because I was dyslexic and stupid, so I have a very bad rebellious streak around people I think are authoritative and when people aren't straight and are bullying,' he says. 'I really saw certain members of the BPI as being cunts. You can quote that. I don't really care. There were people that I really had a vehement dislike of. And I thought that they were rigging things in favour of themselves and they were screwing the independents. Their pomposity was beyond any form of decency. I just really hated what they stood for.'

Mills, along with Green and Mason, told the assembled independents that, if this was to have a chance, everyone had to get fully behind it.

'We said, "If we're going to do this, we need a budget which is going to hire someone who's really good and a decent staff. So we've got to be talking about £300,000 or £400,000 to run this organisation. So everyone's going to have to commit to pay their share if we're going to do this at all." The first point was: if we're going to do it, we've got to do it properly.'

Holmes says he was completely sold on both the idea and Mills's idealism. He immediately committed financially. 'I wrote a cheque for ten grand at the time,' he says. 'Martin drove it intellectually. And Martin drove it morally.'

Alison Wenham was to become the first head of AIM. She had set up independent classical label Conifer Records before selling it to BMG.

She says that, long before the creation of AIM, when she was involved in BPI meetings, she noticed a very clear division between the majors and independents in terms of how they pushed through certain agenda points. The majors, she believed, were agreeing their positions in advance to be able to steamroller them through the meetings. As such, the independents' voice was being drowned out.

'I was on the BPI Council at the time,' she says. 'We had great people – really fine, clever people like Martin Mills and Derek Green. But when I sat at that table, I was disquieted by the tenor of the conversation. We would all turn up at this meeting. The majors would turn up at the meeting as well, but it felt to me as though there had been a pre-agreement or something like that between them. I think the bottom line was that we were elected to represent the independent sector and we weren't doing a particularly good job of it. As owner managers we simply didn't have the time or the resources.'

The collective power of the independents was, she feels, being badly under-utilised at the time.

'I felt we were letting our side down rather badly because we were just throwing uncoordinated opinions into the debate,' she says. 'We didn't consult. We didn't reach out to the sector and say, "This is coming onto the agenda and this might affect your business. What do you think?" We didn't do any of that. So we weren't really doing the job that we were elected to do. You could say, "Well there wasn't really a sector to represent." But when you get to the agenda that AIM did put together, which was dramatically different from the BPI's, you can say, "Well, that was an oversight, wasn't it?"'

Wenham believes that the independents were only really consulted and involved in things at the BPI when it suited the agenda of the majors. Independent labels were quoted or referenced occasionally as proof that the BPI represented majors and independents equally – but this was wholly conditional.

Wenham feels the independents were badly manipulated by the majors here. 'There was a rather subtle undercurrent of the moral high ground being best presented through the eyes and voices of the independent sector,' she says. 'I felt that we were wheeled in at appropriate moments, like, for example, the Monopolies & Mergers Commission inquiry into pricing.' (The Monopolies & Mergers Commission inquiry into CD pricing was conducted in 1993/94, and looked at claims CDs were being artificially inflated for the consumer.[9] After eleven months of investigations, the Monopolies & Mergers Commission eventually cleared the record companies of overcharging for CDs[10]).

Wenham says she became part of a BPI-led PR drive to counter the argument that CDs could be sold for a fraction of what they were being priced at. She says, as the head of a classical label, recording costs were enormous, suggesting that getting the Royal Philharmonic Orchestra in to record an album would be around £40,000 in the early 1990s (around £82,000 in 2023).

'I wrote a letter to *The Guardian* and was quite "Mrs Angry From Carshalton". I used the whisky bottle analogy: that [people didn't understand that] you're not pricing the glass bottle, you're pricing what goes inside it. And yet there was this whole very facile, one-dimensional argument that music was overpriced.'

That letter led to her being invited in to meet the BPI, which subsequently led to her being elected to the BPI Council.

'That's how I ended up being one of the main spokespeople for the industry in the Monopolies & Mergers Commission investigation into CD pricing,' she explains. 'It was vital to my company's survival that Gerald Kaufman [who chaired the investigation] did not get his way in his kangaroo court banging on about cheap CDs. However, it did, I think, irreparable damage to the industry because, although we won, the legacy remains – a rip-off industry. But for my own selfish reasons, I had to push back on this notion of a £4.99 price point. During that whole period, I was very, very active for the BPI doing TV, press, radio, whatever. But I did feel a little bit uncomfortable because I knew that it wasn't the whole story. I felt that I was being used as a mouthpiece for a point of view that did not hold water under close inspection.'

She also says that the BPI agenda was dominated by issues around piracy and copyright in the 1990s and it was very much a protectionist stance. It was also, she felt, a reductive stance.

'Through the 1990s, because we were such a mature and successful industry, the role of the BPI was somewhat to keep the government at arm's length,' she explains. 'Wine and dine them and take them to the BRIT Awards, get them to give the best copyright environment and the best anti-piracy environment, but nothing else. Because that was the only thing that was of importance to the biggest companies.'

The independents understood there were wider issues that needed to be discussed but the growing realisation was that the BPI – for historical, organisational and ideological reasons – was not the place to discuss them.

Conifer Records was bought by BMG as the Monopolies & Mergers Commission was happening, but Wenham found that working within the major label system was slowly eating away at her. She was speaking regularly with Beggars Banquet and other labels – among them Warp, Cooking Vinyl and Ministry Of Sound – who were key to the formation of AIM. She was approached to apply for the job at the new organisation.

On 4 November 1998, in the grip of a heavy cold, Wenham began work as AIM's first chief executive, initially from her own house.

'I was at home at my daughter's vanity unit with a phone, a landline, a piece of paper and pen,' she recalls. 'I did everything from founding the company, registering it at Companies House, finding premises and staff and raising money.'

The founding labels were all asked to each contribute £10,000 (treated as a loan to be deducted from their membership fees) to get AIM off the ground, open an office and to start recruiting staff.

'We needed to look and feel like a serious player,' says Wenham. 'Otherwise, we would have been dismissed or ignored as another informal and unstable grouping of disaffected indies. Decisions down the pub and no permanence. I really wanted to wait until we had an office, full-time staff, a registered company, a bank account, a constitution, membership terms and some policy documents. What were we going to stand for?'

Just ten days after Wenham started, *Music Week* reported that around fifty independent labels and distributors were backing this new organisation and that its creation was the eighteen of discussions that had been happening over the previous eighteen months. It was estimated there were 1,500 independent labels in the UK and AIM was seeking to sign up as many of them as possible. The body was defining 'independent' as companies that retained at least a 50 per cent ownership stake (i.e. a major could still buy part of the company but not a controlling stake).[11]

Wenham told *Music Week*, 'There has been overwhelming support among independent companies for the Aim [sic] initiative, a fact which alone points to the need for a stand alone approach.' Martin Mills added, 'We [independents] have 20 per cent of the marketplace, but we haven't acted with 20 per cent.'

The BPI was trying to be hugely diplomatic about the news but could not quite paper over the fact that there was, among certain of its major label members, a mounting sense of outrage that AIM was being willed into existence.

John Deacon, director general of the BPI, was quoted in the same *Music Week* story as saying, 'We feel we have always looked after the small companies in the same way as the large companies, but I fully understand they may feel the need for the independent voice to be recognised.'

Helen Smith had been legal adviser at the BPI and joined AIM as director of legal and business affairs in early 1999. Her appointment was announced in *Music Week* on 6 February 1999 alongside the news that Guy Holmes (Gut Records), Daniel Miller (Mute Records), Steve Mason (Pinnacle) and Andy Cleary (Jammin Music Group) had been appointed to the AIM board, while Martin Mills (Beggars Banquet) was named as vice chairman.[12]

'I had heard it was an organisation representing the independents and it was going to be working on issues that were of particular relevance to them,' says Smith when she first became aware of the nascent AIM. 'That sounded really interesting to me. I felt really motivated by the idea of working for the independents. Then there were, of course, all the individuals setting it up. These were people who were involved in labels that had a significant impact on me as a person. That was personally very motivating.'

There were a lot of political and organisational issues to settle between the BPI and AIM and they were to stretch through most of 1999. It took until June for both organisations to agree a joint formula where AIM would be part-funded by taking a share of the membership contributions made to the BPI by labels that had dual AIM/BPI membership.[13]

Billboard said there was still uncertainty around if AIM 'will be part of the BPI, a separate entity, or something in between.' Martin Mills hinted at the difficulties and tensions behind the scenes as well as making clear the defiant mood among the independents. 'I think the final arrangement will be one that nobody is completely happy with but which everyone can work with,' he said. 'The bottom line for AIM is that the BPI cannot have sovereignty over us. That would defeat the point of us existing.'[14]

The BPI attempted to appear sanguine in its public statements. 'I very much want AIM to be part of the BPI,' said John Deacon. 'The BPI has put forward proposals to AIM as to how we think we can work together.'[15]

A certain, if begrudging, cordiality played out across the pages of the music business trade press during this time, but the closed door talks between the BPI and AIM were often fraught, insistent, angry, exasperated, exasperating and occasionally lurched into blazing brinkmanship.

Wenham says AIM was able to play hardball because 'they [the BPI] had a problem because if they didn't come to a deal with us, the big indies who had supported the formation of AIM would leave.' This meant that large independents who were members of the BPI, and who made significant financial contributions to its running, would terminate their memberships.

'I was completely taken aback by the ferocity with which the BPI greeted the formation of AIM,' says Wenham. 'I thought that it was really rather vain of them to assume that AIM had something to do with them or needed to do something with them or had formed because of them. AIM formed because the independent sector needed to have an unsullied and focused agenda, something which was of no relevance or interest to a major record company. Access to finance, access to local and international markets, knowledge sharing, skills development, and practical support for the day to day issues. We needed to exist. Full stop.'

Helen Smith suggests the BPI did not react well to the news that AIM was going to be established. 'They saw that as an undermining of their position as the sole organisation representing both majors and independents,' she says, adding that one key figure was not convinced. 'I think John Deacon was very upset that AIM was being set up. He was solution-focused and a team person. He wanted unity. He saw unity as very, very important. The founders of AIM felt a distinct voice wasn't contradictory to unity but complementary.'

Wenham says that how the BPI read the establishment of AIM was significantly different to the internal reasons for its establishment.

'Their reaction really was, I thought, quite hysterical,' she says. 'I was terribly regretful that John Deacon might have thought it was a statement about a failure by the BPI. It wasn't at all. If there was a failure at the BPI, it was its board; it wasn't its secretariat. The board at any company creates the strategy. If they had been smart, they could have seen this coming for some time.'

She adds, 'When AIM was formed, yes, it was a Pavlovian response – which I didn't think had merit. I felt that AIM needed to exist. We were no threat to the BPI, we did not set our stall out to say, "Well, those bastards over there let you down, didn't they?" It had nothing to do with that. We simply had a clear focus on a very important and vital sector within the record industry. The independents' role is vital to the industry as it is where all new music, new genres begin. So it was rather astonishing to me that there were strenuous attempts by the BPI to undermine us and me personally.'

(John Deacon politely declined to be interviewed for the book, saying he was now in his eighties and wished to enjoy his retirement.)

Mills calls these initial meetings 'fraught' and adds that they were 'very stressful for Alison personally.' The combative nature of some of these discussions arose from the fact that there was fear around what AIM represented both organisationally and symbolically. 'The BPI saw AIM as a threat and they were very unhappy that we started it,' claims Mills. 'There clearly were common interests, but it was difficult to get into them.'

He adds that the BPI wanted to control the independent label agenda and that its major label members wanted to control the market. AIM represented a breaking apart of both types of control here. 'They wanted control,' he explains. 'What they were very reluctant to lose was control – control over the market.'

There was also a wider existential worry for the BPI, as pinpointed by Mills.

'The problem for the BPI is that, if they don't represent independents, they can't represent the industry,' he says. 'They need to be able to say they represent the small as well as the big. The problem for us is that, in any relationship with them, they tend to want to dominate. It's been a see-saw all the way along.'

AIM was not against fighting fire with fire in these negotiations with the BPI. The person primarily wielding the flame-thrower for AIM was Guy Holmes.

'They were so condescending,' he recalls. 'They came and said to us [patronising tone], "We'll fund you. We'll help you." That shit. I did some of those BPI meetings. They'd pull me in when they wanted somebody to be rude.'

He says the BPI's ultimate goal was to erase AIM completely or, failing that, find ways to control it. 'They would try every piece of manoeuvring and trickery [they could],' he says. 'Alison is not stupid. She was fucking brilliant.'

For Holmes, all AIM was seeking was 'fairness' and to be allowed to compete on equal terms with the majors.

'The entirety of our existence was about fairness and levelling the playing field,' he says. 'And being a part of the discussion about where things were going to go. We could already see the writing on the wall then that the market was in trouble.'

In late June 1999, *Billboard* was reporting that the BPI was asking its 230 record company members to consider changes to its constitution in the light of AIM's establishment. To allow time for consultation around the AIM issues, the BPI took the 'unusual step' of postponing its AGM.[16]

Key BPI and AIM board members had met on 9 June to thrash out a deal, with Wenham calling the talks 'substantive and constructive'. She added, 'I believe [the bodies] should work together. AIM represents the sectional interest of the independent. The BPI represents the national industry. We don't want to have a tussle over membership.'[17]

Wenham claims that meeting was in large part down to the BPI seeking to publicly save face, but it was still not taking AIM as seriously as she believed it should. 'I think that they couldn't help being patronising,' she says. 'I think I was patronised for years. They did not take AIM seriously. Which, believe me, was irrelevant to me.'

Andy Cleary suggests there was 'disbelief initially from a lot of people' within the BPI and the major labels at the emergence of this new independent upstart.

'They were just saying, "Why are you doing this? Why do you need to do it?" There were too many major label guys that hadn't ever been in our shoes and just didn't appreciate the challenges we were going through. Like everything else the majors ever did, they were just so slow.'

It took until late September for all the details to be worked out between AIM and the BPI. *Music Week* called it 'an historic accord which seeks to create a single voice tackling issues common to both major and independent record companies.' Current BPI members who wished to avail of dual membership would pay a joining fee of £100 (+VAT) to AIM and the BPI would pay AIM an undisclosed percentage of AIM members'

BPI subscriptions. Standalone AIM members would pay the joining fee plus 9 per cent of their PPL income annually.[18]

Rob Dickins, BPI chairman, told *Music Week* 'It is necessary for the BPI to function as the industry body that represents everybody. If members felt there was a need for Aim then we had to recognise that.'

Mere days later, speaking at the BPI's (delayed) AGM, Dickins called the AIM/BPI deal 'the dawning of a new era' as their relationship was formalised. He added, 'The way forward that we've mutually agreed is very good for the BPI, [enabling us] to be an industry with – as much as possible – one voice.'[19]

Billboard reported that the BPI 'agreed to change its constitution following pressure from some members to recognize independent members as a separate interest group.' It added that AIM had a membership base of 250 labels, which was twenty more than the BPI had. IFPI chairman Jay Berman, who was a guest speaker at the BPI AGM, called it 'a critical step forward in unifying one of our industry's most important national groups.'[20]

Dickins was, despite other entrenched attitudes within the BPI, seen as generally quite supportive of AIM.

John Kennedy, chairman of Universal Music Group UK at the time as well as being on the BPI board, recalls initially being against the idea of AIM but, as it started to become established and was deep in negotiations with the BPI, Dickins helped change his mind.

'When the idea of AIM came along, I think that we were supposed to fund AIM partly [via the BPI],' he says. 'I wasn't keen on this. I remember Rob Dickins coming to see me on a Friday afternoon, maybe with Martin Mills, or maybe on his own, to explain to me how I had to be a bigger person and be prepared to go along with this, that this was for the good of the industry. When he left the office, I was convinced. He was very, very good.'

(Rob Dickins did not respond to multiple interview requests).

Peter Quicke joined Ninja Tune in 1992 as label manager and says it was not until the formation of AIM that he came alive to the macro issues outside of his office. Ninja Tune was not one of AIM's founding members but was in the next recruitment tier.

'To be honest, at the beginning of 1999, I hardly read any trade press,' he says. 'To me, it was just about keeping the label running, putting out records, finding acts. It was in 1999 that I discovered this world of music politics. That was when it crystallised the need for a collective voice and action. That's what AIM was. I was excited to join. It was a revelation to me.'

Quicke says Ninja Tune had never been a BPI member ('They definitely didn't smell right to us') and he liked that AIM was a David to the BPI's Goliath.

'We definitely always saw ourselves as indies and we were suspicious of the majors,' he says of himself as well as Matt Black and Jonathan More, members of Coldcut and co-founders of Ninja Tune. 'Matt, Jon and I are socialists. The idea of being in a union of the underdogs definitely suited us and we wanted to try and campaign for the ability for small labels to be able to operate and have a level playing field.'

Matt Black was equally enthused about what AIM could mean for independent labels and independent artists.

'I began to understand that, by ourselves, we were just too small to negotiate with these big guys,' he says. 'But with AIM, we were able to actually have a seat at the table. I obviously supported that idea. Unity was strength. Otherwise, if we hadn't managed to do that, and find that cooperative common ground with the other indie labels, we would have been crushed. They would just have eaten us up and spat us out. They were trying to get away with murder, those guys – like proposing much lower rates for independent labels as the majors were on their back saying, "We want the big piece of pie." If we hadn't fought hard, we would just have ended up with mere scraps. We wouldn't have been able to even survive.'

AIM's arrival marked a shift in attitude within the independent record company world. Where previously they felt industry politics were only things the majors or the biggest independents could get involved with, they were starting to understand the importance and the power of collectivity. The fact that the Seagram/PolyGram deal coincided with the formation of AIM only served to sharpen their focus and strengthen their resolve.

Not all independent labels were aligned, however. Simon Williams set up the Fierce Panda label in 1994, a label so defiantly 'indie' that in its early years it would only sign acts to one-off single deals. In his memoirs, published in 2022, he explained why Fierce Panda was not sold on the idea of AIM and independent label collectivism.

'We've never been a member since it launched in 1998, partly because I always thought it was weird being an independent label and joining up with loads of other independent labels, like some mighty *Life of Brian*-esque paradox,' he wrote. 'I realise I am in the minority here, and lots of other independent people really do love independing on other independent people, but nobody said being an outlier was supposed to be sensible or fun either.'[21]

AIM was issuing statements through the year to show that it was more than a trade organisation, that it had a finely tuned commercial remit and that it had more dynamism than the BPI.

In May, it announced it was going to enable its members to sell CDs through the AIM website (musicindie.com). Martin Mills told *Music Week*, 'The attraction of having a central indie music site that can offer both e-commerce and a route to individual sites is incredibly strong.'[22] (It did not happen and Wenham, when I interviewed her, had no memory of the initiative beyond saying that AIM was exploring several options around e-commerce).

In September 1999, it announced plans to open another office in the north of England, possibly in Manchester or Liverpool. Wenham told *Music Week*, 'If we decide to go ahead, it will be relatively simple to do and yet massively effective. This is one country but it seems to be two different nations when it comes to the music business.'[23]

That satellite office never happened. 'I had done a lot of travelling that year to go up and down the country,' explains Wenham on the thinking behind it. 'It felt to me that we did need to have a physical presence there, but we never found the right partner.'

The malevolent shadow of Universal Music Group loomed over 1999, hinting at even more consolidation to come. The majors only made their purest and truest sense when they were huge and in a permanent state of becoming huger. Scale meant power; and power only served to increase the appetite for even greater scale.

The majors were predicated on the belief that the bigger they became the harder it would be to sideline or topple them. Their shield was their size. But the one drawback they did not quite realise about scale on their level was that changing and adapting to external forces takes years rather than weeks. Things were fine when they were party to the coming change and could slowly recalibrate accordingly, as they did with CDs in the 1980s. Things were less fine when the coming change was happening far from their boardrooms and, crucially, without their consent.

There is a commonly quoted analogy in the music business that the major labels are like oil tankers: so enormous they presume themselves to be unassailable, but take a long time to change course slightly or turn around completely. Independents, in contrast, are compared to speed-boats: small but zippy and agile, able to switch course instantly.

Nowhere was this dichotomy more apparent than with the coming of digital. As the majors were concentrating power and control in the old world of physical products, the independents were seeing digital as less of a threat and more of a catalyst for a new type of empowerment for them and, in sharp contrast to the majors, providing them with a tactical head start.

DIGITAL DOMINANCE: THE ONLINE LIFELINE FOR INDEPENDENTS

As both a recording artist and a label owner, Matt Black was in a unique position when digital fully hit the music business. As the earliest of early adopters, he had the prescience to not just know what was coming but also how to best respond to it.

'I got fascinated with computers in the 1970s,' he says. 'I got into the idea that they could be used for creative, and even revolutionary, purposes.' He cites two books, *The Shockwave Rider* by John Brunner in 1975 and *The Selfish Gene* by Richard Dawkins in 1976, as having a transformative impact on him personally as well as on his thinking.

He formed Coldcut in 1986 with Jonathan More and, after seeing a demo of an Amiga computer in Selfridges in London, they started to add computer visuals to what they were creating musically.

'By the beginning of the 1990s when Ninja Tune started, we were already doing quite a lot of digital stuff,' he says. 'As the 1990s got going, and the internet got going, I already had an email address at The WELL, the Whole Earth 'Lectronic Link.[24] Not that I was terribly active, but I thought it was cool to be able to dial into this network.'

Copying some HTML code enabled him to build his first rudimentary website, but it was the serendipity of sharing an office building with an early web marketing company that proved to be the digital Big Bang for Ninja Tune.

'The building we ended up in by London Bridge in Winchester Wharf was a bit of a magnet for some interesting startups,' he says. 'There was this company called Obsolete and they were one of the first web companies in London. They got the gig to do the Levi's website. Levi's paid for a fast link into the building, which was probably only 256k or something, but at the time that was like a lightning-speed connection compared to our dial-ups. They very generously put this at the disposal of the people in the building.'

He found himself part of an early digital community and, sensing an oncoming revolution, wanted to make sure Ninja Tune as a label and the artists signed to Ninja Tune understood the enormity of what was about to happen.

'I've always been like a mad little dog dragging Ninja Tune along on a short lead in the technology race,' he says. 'Sometimes they're like, "Hold on, Matt. Let's just see how this works out first".'

The addition of a forum on the official Ninja Tune site showed the new ways audiences could be reached and nurtured.

'We realised that this was a very good thing that was happening, that there was more interaction and that there was a community of fans [out there],' he says. 'It was exciting.'

He was gripped by the endless possibilities of online and the opportunity for reinvention. 'I bought into the cyberpunk revolutionary fervour of the time as well,' he says. 'We're going to change the world with this stuff. This was how we were going to do it. We were going to break the existing monopolies on stuff. This was a chance for the young upstarts to kick up and perhaps campaign for a fairer world, have more access, less control, the ability for anyone to publish themselves, whether it be music or their opinions, or make films on your desktop.'

Coldcut experimented with CD-ROM technology and worked with Cambridge ART to create the VJamm software for live video mixing to accompany shows. A demo version of VJamm was given away with the CD-ROM version of their *Let Us Replay* album in 1999.[25]

They also set up Pirate TV as an early experiment in webcasting and got Radiohead to perform on it. 'That was probably the biggest internet music event there had been to that date,' says Black. 'I remember that there were about three hundred people listening. Radiohead got quite enthused by the idea that they could stream from their studio and maybe they didn't need to tour again. Of course, real-life touring is good, but that was a moment.'

He acknowledges that this was down as much to luck as it was to their growing interest in digital technologies and the internet.

'We were the right bunch of people in the right place at the right time,' he says. 'It's that thing of being on the wave. If you're too far in front of the wave, it crashes on top of you or you miss it and you can't get going. If you are too far behind, you miss the wave. If you catch it at just the right time, you can stay on it and you can ride it. It was the excitement of doing that. We knew what we wanted to do. And we were doing it.'

Peter Quicke says Ninja Tune being seen as digital pioneers was primarily down to Black. 'Jon was into it,' he says, 'but Matt was obsessed with it.' Their digital evangelism also reflected back well on Ninja Tune and they also saw the benefits commercially.

'It made us seem cool,' says Quicke. 'It was cool. We were very much into working with any internet [company]. There was a lot of scepticism about piracy and downloads and all that nonsense, but we were working with anybody. There was a download site called Wippit. We were on there early. It was amazing. We used to get six hundred quid or eight hundred quid a month from them. At the time, it was really amazing. We didn't have to do anything and then money just [came in]. Obviously now it's totally normal. You get your monthly check from the DSPs, but at the time it seemed weird. And wonderful.'

Al Teller, who had been through the major label system since 1981 before setting up Atomic Pop in 1997, argues that the independents have a willingness to push boundaries built into their DNA. Experimentation, he feels, is the *sine qua non* of independent labels.

'I've always been a huge fan of independent labels from the very beginning of my career,' he says. 'They were always playing on the edges. They were always prepared to experiment with something that the majors were not yet ready to do. So, in many ways, the independents pushed the business along. And as they became successful doing certain kinds of things, those practices would be adapted by the majors.'

This was a core thrust of AIM's early discussions with its members and potential members: that digital was going to be far more opportunity than threat for them.

'We knew that with the world going digital and global, we had to get the indies understanding this quickly,' says Andy Cleary.

Helen Smith adds there was a clear push to get the independents to understand the commercial opportunities that could open up to them. 'The view of the independents was very much pro-change and pro-digital,' she says. 'Let's grow this market and have our own voice.'

Wenham tells a story, possibly apocryphal or possibly intended as a poetic metaphor, about the divergent attitudes between the independents and the majors when it came to digital. It took place at a cross-label event at Midem, the annual international music trade event in Cannes in the south of France in January each year.

'In around 2000, at a large round table meeting of EU officials and music industry representatives, there was a chap from, I think, Universal France who was banging the table, literally, in a really aggressive way, saying the EU had to ban the internet. He was deadly serious. He wanted the internet banned so that we could all go back to the old days. It was at that point that I felt we better get proactive because we saw the internet differently, as an opportunity. It removed gatekeepers and freed up access and, crucially, reach. Whether or not it would amount to a row of beans in terms of revenue wasn't the point. Being the risk-takers in the industry, we were more disposed to experimentation than the majors could afford to be, and we wanted to engage.'

Mills says that Beggars Banquet was reasonably early in its embracing of digital music, saying they were offering their entire catalogue for digital sale globally by the end of the 1990s. 'It was definitely the Wild West,' he says. 'And everyone was trying to work out what to do and whether there was a collective answer there as well.'

Understanding that digital was going to break apart the old distribution model for independent record companies, often based on territory-by-territory deals with distributors or sub-licensing agreements with majors or independents in particular markets, Beggars Banquet saw online distribution as a way to seize autonomy at the earliest stage.

'We decided we wanted to take it out of that system and we wanted to do it digitally for ourselves,' explains Mills. 'We got involved with Consolidated Independent who facilitated distribution. We basically built a business ourselves. It was a crucial part of our development. [The majors losing] control for us was an opportunity because distribution was becoming democratised. It was a huge opportunity.'

Mills believes the independents' jump into digital and the formation of AIM were happening in synchronicity and that they were important proactive developments to ensure that they had a first-mover advantage, before the majors swept in and attempted to forcibly adjust the market to suit their needs and serve their interests.

'It was pretty clear that the majors were getting into a position to be able to force the digital services to pay them more than their share,' he says. 'That was the real impetus. And then that tied into the consolidation thing. It was pretty clear that indies were getting treated as second-class citizens in terms of deals. That was the impetus for a lot of that coming together.'

These were not discussions confined to the closed rooms of trade bodies and the insular world of the music trade press. The independents were also keen to take this message of digital and the internet as a new form of empowerment to the consumer press.

'The Internet is a fantastic democratisation of opportunity in the global market,' Wenham told *Q* magazine in a multi-page feature on label consolidation and the coming online upheaval. 'Indies are acknowledged to be agile, to populate new technologies more quickly than majors and you can be imaginative, sexy and creative on a website, whereas shops have just looked like seas of plastic boxes since CDs came in!'[26]

In the same feature, Tony Crean, creative and marketing director at Independiente, was much more forthright in his views about how differently the independents and the majors were handling things here. 'Just say the words "major record company" and it already sounds antiquated,' he argued. 'They are going to be fucked by the internet. People are going to download from the internet like we used to download from the radio to cassette!'[27]

Alan McGee, co-founder of Creation Records, was initially sceptical about the internet in particular and digital in general, but he had a moment of conversion and became a vociferous evangelist. He also had a sharp enthusiasm for speaking to the consumer music press about whatever idea or artist was occupying his thoughts that particular week.

For example, in 1996 he paid somewhere between £6,000 and £12,000 (accounts vary) to take out a full-page ad in the *NME*, all the better to outline his various thoughts on a Sex Pistols reunion show he had just seen – 'Britpop? More like Shitpop. You're welcome to your mediocrity. The band are our alternative Royal Family.' – adamant that his thoughts needed to be heard as widely as possible.[28]

David Cavanagh, in his magisterial book on Creation, outlined McGee's conversion to digital. Creation had launched its company website in 1995 but it was not regularly updated and was left to atrophy until 1998.

'McGee, more technophobic than Luddite, had not fully recovered from illness when the site had opened, and paid it no attention for the first couple of years,' wrote Cavanagh. "I thought computers were for people like [staff members] James Kyllo and Mark Taylor – super-bright, geeky people,' he says. 'I thought: I'm Alan McGee, I write everything down in a list and I'm not that clever. Then Kate [Holmes, his wife] got a little Apple Mac out and put my name in. She said: "Look at all these things people are saying about you on the internet." I was scrolling down the pages, going: "That's not *true* . . ." After about an hour, I suddenly looked at it and thought: my God, I can work the internet. It was so easy. Then Kate showed me how to log on and log off. The next day, I ordered a computer and for the next six months I hardly left the house.'[29]

McGee was instructing the Creation press department to send him press clippings on technological developments that would impact on the music business. 'I just thought: wait a minute. This is another culture. This is a revolution coming about,' he says.'[30]

With the vigour of a man who regularly declares anything new that he agrees with to be 'the new punk rock', so it was with his internet conversion. In an op-ed for the *NME*, he opined, 'If you're 15 years old and you buy a laptop, your mum doesn't even know how to turn it on, man! That's rock'n'roll!'[31]

He was making similar proclamations in *Music Week* in May 1998. 'There is something afoot and the music industry is not in control of it,' he said. 'It is so behind. The real issue is that there aren't going to be record companies any more [. . .] The music business is on its arse and dying.'

He added, 'Maybe this is the revelation, like punk was, but maybe this time it's about how we go about buying records. Record shops are so unsexy, but turning a computer on isn't, because patents can't do it. Young bands will think it's sexier to download their music on the internet.'[32]

In January 1999, he told the *NME* that the old business would cease to exist in a decade's time. 'I just think that if you run a record company and you're in denial of the internet you'll be blown out of the sea,' he proclaimed. 'This is the biggest change the music business has had in thirty years. In the seventies it was punk rock, in the eighties it was acid house, in the nineties it's the technological revolution. If people don't realise that then maybe they've taken too many drugs. It's the British music industry that's out of step, not me. It's not going to go back to the way it was.'[33]

Creation staff and artists were used to McGee's constant hobby-horsing and Martin Carr of The Boo Radleys witheringly put this latest cause in context. 'It was nothing that we hadn't been hearing for two years,' he told Cavanagh. 'It was just McGee being a bit behind as usual. Except that when he says something, everybody hears it.'[34]

The bit firmly between his teeth, McGee went into full evangelist mode, arguing forcefully that the internet was going to pull the business inside out and he, frankly, could not be happier at the chaos it would cause for the bloated majors.

'They might be all smiley-smiley at the BRITs, but it's an industry in absolute crisis,' he said. 'The people at the top recognise that the internet is going to change the whole way that music is sold to people, and they're getting out now while the going's good.'[35]

As a provocateur and contrarian, McGee was hoping his words would raise the hackles of the majors – despite (or maybe because of) the fact that Sony Music had acquired 49 per cent of Creation in 1992 to prevent it from going bankrupt.[36]

Rob Dickins took the bait ('Alan went further than he needed to go') with regard to his revolutionary theorising about the internet. 'McGee was made a pariah by the industry,' wrote Cavanagh. 'In his speech at the BPI's annual general meeting on 8 July, Dickins called McGee's prophecy 'an absurd, ignorant point made by [someone] who should know better.' And in an echo of Margaret Thatcher's outburst against the 'moaning minnies' who had found fault with society under the Conservatives, *Music Week* labelled McGee a 'doom merchant' whom it would be better off without.'[37]

By 1999, McGee was talking about plans to post recordings of Creation acts' concerts online the day after they happened. Sony, concerned this would negatively affect record sales, told him he was not allowed to do it. They also vetoed his plans that spring to sell albums digitally.

Andy Saunders, director of communications at Creation, explained to Cavanagh how this was handled.

'It was a very tricky situation,' he said. 'I was told I was not allowed to go to war with Sony on this. I had to phrase it in such a way that it became a mutual agreement. I said: 'Look, this is not something that Sony have prevented us from doing. They have merely asked us to put a hold on it until they clarify their global situation.' Which was my way of saying: "They've told us to fuck off".'[38]

Independent labels and independent artists were often at the forefront of digital developments in 1999 and fans of independent-signed acts were also often more digitally progressive than mainstream pop consumers. This is illustrated nowhere more perfectly than in the case of the Best Newcomer Award at the BRITs in January 1999.

It was presumed that Steps, with a multi-platinum debut album in

1998 alongside three Top 10 singles (including a number one), and who were signed to Jive which was part-owned by BMG, would get the award, as the BRITs tended to treat commercial success as the only metric worth bothering with.

On the night of the awards, however, Best Newcomer was awarded to Scottish indie band Belle & Sebastian. They were signed to small independent label Jeepster Records and their highest chart placing was number 12, for 1998's *The Boy With The Arab Strap*.

Steps producer Pete Waterman immediately suspected foul play and there were accusations of vote rigging behind their shock win.

The Best Newcomer award was one of the few awards at the BRITs that was voted for by the public, rather than by music industry professionals. It was opened up to listeners of BBC Radio 1 and they could call or vote online. Steps' fans, it appeared, mostly called in to vote, but Belle & Sebastian's fans had organised themselves online to vote *en masse* through the Radio 1/BRITs website.

Waterman claims the BPI had assured him in advance that Steps would win. When they did not, he demanded an investigation, claiming that 12 per cent of the online votes could be tracked to two addresses in Glasgow (where Belle & Sebastian were based) and Cambridge.[39]

Belle & Sebastian denied any subterfuge and Lisa Anderson, executive producer of the awards, told the *NME* that an investigation had found no evidence of skullduggery. 'Ms Anderson also mentioned that there had been an anomaly in the voting from e-mail addresses at Strathclyde University, however taking into consideration that they were from Belle & Sebastian's home area, they weighted this section of the votes.'[40]

The *NME* noted that the band's website got an average of a hundred thousand visits a week and that this resulted in 20 per cent of their fans voting for them. 'The main reason we believe that this story has run, is that most major record companies see the Internet as a threat to their business, whereas Jeepster positively embrace technology and the opportunities it has to offer,' noted the *NME* in its coverage of the story.

Speaking about it almost a quarter of a century on, Stef D'Andrea, joint owner of Jeepster, said, 'A lot of Belle & Sebastian's fans were fourteen to twenty. The two youngest people at Jeepster at the time were nineteen or twenty years old, and a chap who worked with us called David understood where the internet was going. He had started Sinister List, the band's mailing list, which the fans would join and have these great long chats. So the suggestion came from one of those chat rooms

– why don't we spread the word to all the Belle & Sebastian fans to vote via Radio 1's website.'[41]

In the UK at least, the gulf between the majors and the independents in terms of how they viewed the impact of the internet on their business was laid bare in *Music Week*'s December 1999 feature asking executives and musicians across the board to reflect on the key stories of the past year.

Much of it was people bloviating about how many number one records they were involved with or how many awards they had won. Richard Griffiths, chairman and executive VP Central Europe at BMG, listed his greatest frustration of the year as 'Luddites', but did not expand beyond that single-word answer.

Only two record label people mentioned the internet specifically. They were both from the independent sector.

Alison Wenham said her greatest frustration of the year was, 'Struggling to figure out how the internet will change our industry – and still struggling!' Jeremy Marsh, UK MD of Telstar, said this was, 'People's lack of understanding of the internet.'[42]

It turns out it was musicians who had the most prescient answers. UK garage producers Shanks & Bigfoot, whose track 'Sweet Like Chocolate' was a UK number one that summer, were asked what their low point of the year was. They opened with a rum and ill-advised topical reference ('Gary Glitter's[43] hard drive') but jackknifed into a more serious point. 'No, seriously, the advent of MP3. We're afraid the party's over, guys. Better develop some cheap hobbies now.'

When speaking to those who established AIM, a common phrase used by them all is 'community' – that AIM was more than a trade body, that it was a whole world and a whole worldview, a catalyst and an important point of identification.

'If you build a community, you have strength in numbers and the fear is less,' says Wenham. 'The internet was attractive, but better approached together rather than a spotty, piecemeal and wholly unsuccessful engagement on an individual company basis. Many, many companies would have gone bust because they wouldn't have got paid.'

Out of AIM in the UK sprang a variety of independent trade associations, notably Impala (established in 2000 to represent independents in Europe), A2IM (the American Association of Independent Music, set up in 2005) and WIN (the Worldwide Independent Network, in 2006).

Today WIN lists over thirty different independent trade associations[44] around the world including Associação Brasileira da Música Independente, Association of Independent Music Ireland, Asociación de sellos independientes de Argentina, Associação de Músicos Artistas e Editoras Independentes, Belgian Independent Music Association, Canadian Independent Music Association, Fédération Nationale des Labels et Distributeurs Indépendants, Asociación Gremial Industria Musical Independiente de Chile, Independent Music Coalition Japan, Israeli Federation of Independent Record Producers, Produttori Musicali Indipendenti and Unión Fonográfica Independiente.

Martin Mills suggests, '1999 was absolutely a pivotal year because digital and the common market [in Europe] gave us the opportunity to be global. The success of the experiment in collectivising created a whole different strand to how we operated. Because up to then, we considered the environment and the climate as a given, as something you couldn't change. In forming AIM, we realised that actually we could change it.'

He adds, 'There was a board of fifteen people who were all our friends and peers. More important than anything, I think AIM created a sense of community. That has grown in the last twenty-plus years to a very significant degree, both in the UK and worldwide. There really is an independent community which celebrates each other's successes. I think that's been its primary achievement.'

Andy Cleary says that, with the arrival of digital and the lurch into even greater consolidation by the majors at the end of the 1990s, the need for an organisation like AIM was as inevitable as it was unavoidable. The timing of its arrival could not have been better scripted.

'It would have happened anyway,' he says. 'It just would have – because there were too many smart people around for it not to have happened. It just had to.'

PIRACY

CHAPTER 5

Marauder on the dancefloor: music piracy goes from analogue to digital

(Outsiders try and take control of music circulation)

The naming is, of course, entirely ideological: 'piracy' evokes images of marauding and plundering ships at sea, vicious attackers snatching precious cargo and butchering anyone who stands in their way. The etymology of the word, coming from Old French via Latin via Greek, dates back to the 1200s and means 'attack'/'attacker' (with the root of the word coming from 'trial, attempt, endeavour').[1]

It is, in the music business, a highly charged and politicised word, becoming shorthand for a state of permanent risk from unknown outside forces driven only by their avarice. It is also a highly contested word in the music business, with many arguments against its appropriateness here. The very definition of the term implies that a single, tangible, irreplaceable item has been taken away from its rightful owners.

'As a figure of speech, the term accomplishes a ridiculous conflation,' argues academic Jonathan Sterne. '*Piracy* collapses people who make mix CDs for their friends with kidnappers who operate off the coast of Somalia, among other places. It suggests lawlessness and seems to authorize military or police vigilance against its spread [. . .] Viewed from the litigious wing of the recording industry, piracy is a dangerous, anti-market force.'[2]

What it really means is unauthorised 'copying' or 'duplication', but that does not have the same impact, the same *bite*, as 'piracy.'

In the mid-to-late 1990s, the word started on its journey to a new type of ubiquity. The kind of music piracy that existed before then was suddenly made to seem almost benign, having both physical and geographical limitations and, as such, was contained. Or at least containable.

Piracy shifted sharply from being based around a physical object where audio degradation was an inevitability to developing an unstoppable intangibility where one single source could be endlessly replicated *digitally* without denting or scratching the sonics at all.

The flashpoint moment was the arrival of Napster in the summer of 1999, but there was a much longer and more complex history that brought the music industry to this unimaginable precipice. Napster was not the first means of accessing digital music for free. It was also not the last. But it became a potent and powerful metonym for music piracy happening on an entirely new scale and the inevitable consequence of everything that had come before it.

It might seem fatuous to say it, but piracy (or, more specifically, unauthorised copying) is almost as old as the music industry itself, an inevitability in an age of mechanical reproduction.

History academic Alex Sayf Cummings, in her 2013 book *Democracy Of Sound: Music Piracy & The Remaking of American Copyright in the Twentieth Century*, traces the long history of piracy in music back to 1877.

By the 1890s, rudimentary cylinder and disc piracy was becoming so prevalent that early record companies would stress their *originality* as a sonic selling point. 'Companies emphasized that their recordings were loud and clear because they were 'original', as opposed to the inferior records that unscrupulous competitors made by copying the sounds inscribed on other firms' cylinders and discs.'[3]

Cummings cites the posting of an ad in the first issue of *The Phonoscope* in November 1896 by comedian and recording artist Russell Hunting decrying imitators releasing recordings that were trying to pass themselves off as being by him. This was effectively mimicry with names like 'Frank N Hunting' being used to hoodwink unsuspecting customers.

'He [Hunting] complained that piracy was bad, not because his competitors took advantage of the imaginative element of his story or the skill that went into performing and recording it, but because the unauthorized copy failed to be as loud as the original [. . .] For Hunting, the technical quality of the device mattered more than its creative content.'[4]

The piracy situation was growing so much in the late 1800s that by the turn of the century, Lionel Mapleson, who was illegally recording performances at the Metropolitan Opera House in New York, became known as the Father of Bootlegging. Incredibly he would bring a wax cylinder phonograph, capable of recording up to three minutes of music at a time, into the venue. The major grievance in 1901 when he was doing this, however, was that audience members would become irate that the horn was obscuring their view of the performers on stage.[5]

Legislative measures at the time were criticised as toothless, either being seen as insufficiently robust or simply impossible to enforce. The Copyright Act of 1909[6] in the US, however, had an immediate effect. The Eastern District Court of New York 'handed down one of the first decisions on a clear case of piracy.'[7]

Music academic Barry Kernfeld argues that widespread piracy, as we understand it today, actually began in 1929 with sheet music being illegally duplicated. He writes about a series of raids in April 1930 'on individuals peddling bootleg song sheets on Broadway [New York] between Forty-Second and Forty-Third Streets'. An 80-year-old woman called Sarah Yagoda was among the first arrested.

Paul L. Fischoff of the Music Publishers Protective Association told the judge in the case against Yagoda that it was really the duplicitous operator behind the scenes that they most wanted to bring to justice. 'Your Honour, it is not this who we seek,' he said. 'It is the racketeer making a fortune by having copyrighted song hits printed and sold for 5¢ a copy.' This was becoming an industrialised problem that the music publishers wished to cauterise as swiftly as possible.[8]

Until 1929, the sheet music industry 'was operating a distribution system that was as perfectly controlled as it could possibly be',[9] but access to cheap printing presses blew a hole through that control and sheet music began being 'distributed through unauthorized channels by bootleggers.'[10]

There had been 'a minor epidemic of bootleg song-sheet peddling in Chicago' around 1892/93 but it had been quickly stamped out. It returned, however, in a more virulent form in 1929, reaching such a scale that in September 1929 performance rights organisation ASCAP (the American Society of Composers, Authors & Publishers) submitted a complaint to US District Attorney Charles H. Tuttle about widespread selling of unlicensed sheet music on the streets of New York.[11]

Even Al Capone got embroiled in the song-sheet bootlegging issue as arrests and convictions started to rise in 1930. Capone was compelled to write to ASCAP to outline his 'regret that his name was used by three gunmen who held up a Chicago music publisher', insisting they were not connected with them and ominously suggesting that, if he were to discover who they were, he would mete out appropriate punishment. (Kernfeld says that extensive research was unable to find any direct connection between Capone and song-sheet bootlegging, implying there were certain activities that even he would not touch).[12]

Kernfeld suggests that song-sheet bootlegging effectively evaporated by the early 1940s, in part through prosecutions and in part through the emergence of licensed lyric magazines. They were so immediately popular that, in November 1942, the MPAA announced in its annual report that US publishers were receiving $275,000 annually by licensing lyrics to the three leading song lyric magazines in the market.[13]

This new revenue opportunity snowballed quickly, with *Variety* reporting in March 1944 that music publishers were making $600,000 a year in licensing fees from song sheets. This was a booming market, with one title alone, *Hit Parader* (promising 'popular hit songs from screen, stage, radio'), reportedly selling six hundred thousand copies a month.[14]

(There was a coda to this with the arrival of the Xerox copying machine in 1949 when a new type of sheet-music copying became possible. Kernfeld says lawsuits here were 'extremely rare' compared to mass produced and unlicensed songs sheets and books, saying he could only find reference to two suits filed in relation to education establishments.[15] Such 'invisible' copying was to prove a foreshadowing of home taping two decades later).

This was to become a motif in the industry's fightback against piracy when it morphed into a new form, using heavy legislative measures as a first course of action and then slowly developing a legitimate version of what the pirates were offering. For the music business, it has always been stick first, stick again and then, when the inevitability of it becomes overwhelming, eventually carrot.

It was, by this stage, not just something affecting music publishers. Record labels were starting to panic about unlicensed reproductions of their sound recordings.

Wynant Van Zant Pearce Bradley – 'a colorful and mysterious character who arguably pioneered piracy and the legal hijinks associated with it' – began pirating records for Zon-O-Phone and was sued by the Italian label Fonotipia Records for copyright records that it had licensed to Columbia Records for manufacturing and sale in the US.[16]

By the 1930s, jazz collectors and labels like the Hot Record Society were reissuing obscure records, believing themselves to be performing an important public and cultural duty to help this music reach an appreciative audience.[17] This eventually prompted major labels like Columbia, RCA Victor and Decca to reissue albums themselves that had previously been impossible to find[18], effectively seeing the Hot Record Society and others as having done their market research for them, enabling them to capitalise on swelling public interest in certain artists and genres. They had argued that it was impossible and uneconomic to keep every single title in print,[19] but such wildcatter reissue companies were helping to de-risk this for them.

After the Second World War, however, bootleggers were slipstreaming the likes of the Hot Record Society, which had been licensed reissuers, and putting out unauthorised versions of obscurities.[20] While there was much industry outcry about the growth in 'disk-legging', in 1951 the majors scored an own goal when RCA Victor, through its custom pressing service for small-run batches of records by third parties, was accused by jazz collector magazine *Record Changer* of pressing unlicensed compilations from Victor and Columbia records for a label called, ominously and appositely, Jolly Roger.[21]

The year after the Jolly Roger debacle, the Recording Industry Association of America (RIAA) was established by record companies as their representative trade body. From the off, it had a remit to tackle illicit recordings and lobby for legislative changes to aid its cause. The RIAA was always going to be playing catch-up with technological changes that allowed piracy and bootlegging to shape shift, but it took on a deep symbolism as a more hardline approach to tackle the issue head on.

Jolly Roger and its ilk were eventually superseded by the realisation within organised crime networks that the rock'n'roll explosion could be a huge money spinner for them. This set in motion a new challenge for existing labels, but also a moral argument for them to lean on: that buying unlicensed records was fuelling gangs and crime (apart from, of course, Al Capone).

The initial irony of bootleg operations was that they were showing the value of catalogue to the labels who owned it but were letting atrophy; the double irony was that, in trying to clamp down on them through copyright law, they ended up choking part of the catalogue market. 'It was collecting that led to bootlegging, and bootlegging that led to legal suppression and, eventually, to an expansion of copyright restrictions that would make collecting more difficult,' proposed Cummings.[22]

Pirates and bootleggers were swift to spot legal loopholes and exploit new technologies, meaning the copyright owners had to reactively move to try and contain or eradicate it. This 'cat and mouse game between owners and bootleggers'[23] has remained the background noise, sporadically rising to a metallic screech, for the music business throughout its existence.

(For the purposes of this book, I am looking at piracy purely in terms of unlicensed copying/infringement of music and how it affects publishers and labels. It is not looking at piracy in the context of radio – namely the unlicensed and unregulated broadcasting of music over the airwaves. This dates back to Radio Luxembourg in the mid 1930s[24] but really hit its peak in the 1960s.[25])

Mass piracy and bootlegging was restricted in the first half of the 20th century to people who had, directly or indirectly, access to pressing plants to manufacture discs at scale. The development in 1964, however, of the compact cassette by Philips set a domino effect in motion, drastically reducing the cost of entry into this dark market and also allowing the average person at home to make recordings. It was a slow build for the format, but by 1983 it had overtaken vinyl sales in the US. Its dominance as a licensed format (officially issued titles sold through legitimate retailers) was also echoed in its dominance for unlicensed usage (home taping and also industrialised production of pirate and bootleg titles).[26]

In the Eastern Bloc during the Cold War, bootleg releases became an underground response to a government-mandated banning of Western music (the ultimate in forced scarcity) and, in and of themselves, a powerfully political act of resistance. X-ray plates became impromptu records, with grooves cut into them using customised machinery and played clandestinely at parties. As a result, such records were known colloquially as 'ribs' or 'bones.' The audio quality was often terrible, but it was what these 'records' represented that gave them their true resonance.[27]

In the Western counterculture, bootleg albums (of live shows or studio tracks that had never officially been released) became totemic of a certain and very conditional iconoclasm. They were simultaneously 'sticking it to The Man' but also showing that the owner had tapped into a secret source of music that the average consumer was excluded from; that they had somehow got the source music no one wanted you to hear. Clinton Heylin has been the major chronicler of this movement.[28]

Vinyl production, however, was so expensive and so specialised that there were many barriers preventing pirates and bootleggers from gaining a foothold here for many years.[29] Legitimate and licensed pressing plants tightly controlled manufacturing, but slowly some were persuaded to run off illegal copies as a lucrative sideline, doing so in the hope they would not be caught.

Billboard was reporting in 1951 that fifty thousand bootlegs a week were being pumped out across four plants in the New York metropolitan area. This was all 'under the direction of an unknown man who was utilizing four different aliases and at least as many different bank accounts.' By the late 1950s and early 1960s, the issue was becoming 'rampant', where pressing plants would take orders from labels, over-produce and sell the additional copies through 'illicit channels'.[30]

The pirates and bootleggers were becoming more brazen and the process becoming increasingly normalised. There were reports in 1960 that unlicensed records were being sold in supermarket and drugstore chains in both New York and New Jersey.[31]

Cassette piracy took off in the late 1960s as it was 'simpler and cheaper than phonograph-record' production. 'This punched a huge hole in the recording industry's control of the distribution system,' says Kernfeld. 'Illicit manufacture proliferated.'[32] This issue only escalated in the CD era.

Kernfeld summarises the growth of piracy as a battle between two sides: there are the musicians and music companies who wish to keep their monopoly over songs/recordings and prevent others from exploiting them without paying anything, and there are the individuals who wish to break apart, or ignore completely, that monopoly on music rights and use these songs/recordings as they see fit. He terms this eternal tension as a battle 'over obedience and disobedience.'[33]

Sterne uses a slightly different duality to explain the tension here, proposing that in the digital age (of which more later) it be best understood in terms of the tragic and the heroic thesis of piracy.

'A tragic mode highlights the damage this did to the most powerful players in the recording industry, especially labels that were part of transnational conglomerates,' he argues. 'A heroic version of the story holds up file-sharing as part of a social movement which has fought the major-label monopoly over the distribution of music.'[34]

Piracy is, therefore, the story of a fight over control, with new technologies being used to break apart (or attempt to break apart) long-standing controls.

Kernfeld makes the argument that one piracy format only becomes obsolete when another piracy format supersedes it by proving to be cheaper, more convenient or of better quality – or a combination of all three. The illegal copying of cassettes, he proposes, only ended when the illegal copying of CDs, at an industrial level or at home, became possible.[35] It is important to note, however, that cassette piracy in certain markets, most notably India, carried on well into the 21st century.[36]

In a throwback to the supermarket and drugstores selling illegal records in the 1960s, in 1979/80, US music and entertainment retailer Sam Goody was embroiled in an investigation into the selling of counterfeit cassettes and eight-track tapes. Its president, George Levy, and vice president in charge of procurement, Samuel Stolon, were charged with 'racketeering, interstate transportation of stolen property, and the unauthorized distribution of copyrighted sound recordings.'

The *New York Times* reported, 'Among the singers expected to testify for the prosecution are Billy Joel, Olivia Newton-John and Paul Simon. They are among the singers whose works were allegedly counterfeited, "fraudulently depriving" them of their "rightful royalties and payments".'[37]

The case against Sam Goody went through several twists and turns, including a retrial, but by November 1982, both sides had reached a bargain position. The company pleaded 'no contest' to the charge of having shipped 23,000 counterfeit versions of the *Grease* soundtrack from New York to Minneapolis. The company was fined $10,000 – it was originally facing fines of $350,000 or more – and Stolon was given a one-year prison sentence (later suspended and he was instead put on probation for three years and given two hundred hours of community service).[38]

The RIAA had attempted an outreach programme in the 1970s, encouraging members of the public to inform on known pirates, setting up a 24-hour hotline that people could call to tip off the organisation about the production or the sale of illicit recordings. It was not, by any stretch of the imagination, a roaring success. '[A]n industry spokesman implied that the number got few rings.'[39]

As technology developed and devices shrank in size, copying of music became something that could be done at home. As such, it was largely invisible, not done for profit and impossible to police. The convictions the industry has scored over the years against organised pirates were irrelevant here.

Part of the music industry's response to home taping was to push for levies on the sales of blank tapes and tape recorders. This was, they argued, to help offset perceived lost sales that were due to people at home who were copying records. Markets like France, Germany, the Netherlands, Portugal and Spain adopted variations of legislation covering blank media, but the UK, US and Canada did not.[40]

The UK's response, for example, was to undertake a far-reaching PR campaign launched by record company trade body the BPI in October 1981. Taking a silhouette of a cassette and adding crossbones – a very heavy handed extension of the 'pirate' motif – its black and white ads declared in bellowing upper case: 'HOME TAPING IS KILLING MUSIC – AND IT'S ILLEGAL.'

The BPI was arguing that a £305 million drop in record sales from the year before was primarily down to home taping. 'Technology has overtaken the law in the audio-visual field and chaos has resulted,' it said.

A similar argument was being made in the US in the early 1980s, noted author Stephen Witt. Economist Alan Greenspan had conducted a study based around a severe sales slump that badly battered the record business in 1982. He blamed tape bootlegging for the slump and argued that, even drawing on complex economic modelling around various pricing strategies that could be used to counteract the decline, either lowering or increasing prices of records at retail would be unlikely to fix the drop. 'Instead, Greenspan figured, the only way to reverse the sales slump was through an aggressive campaign of law enforcement against the bootleggers,' wrote Witt.[41]

The BPI at the time of Home Taping Is Killing Music was pushing for new copyright laws as the existing ones were viewed as dangerously outdated and did not cover things like home taping. The UK government rejected plans for a blank media levy, which prompted the BPI to join forces with the Musicians' Union, the MCPS (Mechanical Copyright Protection Society) and MRS (Mechanical Rights Society) on the Home Taping Is Killing Music campaign. Acts backing it included Elton John, Cliff Richard, Gary Numan, Dame Margot Fonteyn and Debbie Harry.[42]

There was a curious contradiction at the heart of what the BPI was doing at the time, noted *Mojo* magazine. 'The organisation protested long and loud about the legality of the home taping of albums, yet Island Records' Chris Blackwell opted to inflame the situation with the 13 February introduction of One Plus One cassettes, a tape that provided a full album of music on one side, leaving the other blank for recording purposes,' it said.[43]

Neil Storey, publicist at Island at the time, says there was 'a huge furore' when the One Plus One series launched and 'the BPI got very sniffy indeed'.[44]

This had come the year after Malcolm McLaren, in a characteristically provocative move, persuaded EMI to release Bow Wow Wow's 'C30, C60, C90, Go!' single on cassette with the B-side left blank for the owner to tape whatever they liked on it. It was perfectly in keeping with the lyrical theme of the song, which celebrated taping songs off the radio and copying records rather than buying them.

This 'paean to home-taping' was apparently 'deemed so dangerous that EMI refused to promote it, fearing it would bring the music industry crashing down.'[45] McLaren claimed that the release drew so much opprobrium that EMI quickly pulled it.[46]

In 1982, the BPI moved to take legal action against a retailer, Ames Records & Tapes shops in Lancashire, England, for hiring out albums for £0.50 each and also selling blank cassettes, implying that the shop was facilitating home taping and profiting from it. The judge in the case did not agree, saying that Ames 'in no way sanctioned or encouraged home tapings from albums hired out by the shop.'[47]

The home taping panic of the 1980s actually has a deeper history. In 1944, *Variety* wrote about the Armour Foundation producing a wire recorder that was planned for consumer launch when the Second World War ended. It could, using a spooled wire that was two miles in length, record up to seven hours of music. This would, *Variety* suggested, result in a 'knock-out blow to recording companies and record sales' but, fortunately for the record business, the market was still focused on phonographs and this wire recorder never took off. Equally, reel-to-reel tapes never gripped the public's imagination in any meaningful way.[48]

The industry may have dodged two bullets here, but it was not going to be bulletproof forever.

In September 1981, the launch of the Amstrad TS55 twin-cassette player caused immense consternation in the UK record industry. Amstrad's founder, Alan Sugar, was developing a tower system home stereo and had spotted a Sharp-branded twin-cassette deck for sale in a high-end music hardware shop in Akihabara, the area of Tokyo famed for its high concentration of electronics retailers. He felt that a low-cost version aimed at the mass market could be a success.

'Bingo!' wrote Sugar in his autobiography. 'On the plane from Tokyo to Taipei, Bob [Watkins, technical and manufacturing director at Amstrad] and I sketched up a tower system with a *double* cassette deck mechanism. One of the cassette mechanisms would be play-only, while the other would be the normal play-and-record type, the idea being that consumers could dub their own tapes.'[49]

Sugar said the Amstrad TS55 'took off like a rocket' when it appeared in stores. He claimed, even though he patently did not invent the twin cassette, that 'every single audio manufacturer in the world [. . .] produced twin cassette audio units as staples' but that Amstrad's head start here meant it 'had a good eighteen-month to two-year run at it.'[50]

Amstrad undertook a huge advertising campaign, with Sugar saying they included an important caveat in the small print. He said, 'I told Malcolm Miller [marketing executive] to take the precaution of putting an asterisk beside the picture of the new TS55 twin cassette tower system with its 'tape to tape' logo and at the bottom of the advert, in large, bold printing, we stated, '*It is illegal to copy copyrighted material. This machine should only be used to copy material you have generated yourself.' If you picture a full-page advert in the *Daily Mirror*, the warning was in bold, black letters about a centimetre high.'[51]

This was 'a cheeky tactic' Sugar admits.

'People would read it and think to themselves, 'Hey, that's a good idea! I can use this machine to copy my mate's Abba cassette.' *That* was the effect the warning had, yet there was I, keeping within the law, whiter than white, telling people that the product should not be used for that purpose. Is that called reverse psychology?'[52]

('IT TAPES TAPES!' barked a print ad for a later standalone Amstrad device, suggesting Amstrad understood implicitly this would be used in ways that were not benign).[53]

Reverse psychology or not, the BPI was quick to respond, arguing this player both encouraged and facilitated piracy, and contacted Amstrad to outline their concerns. 'The first few letters they sent me, I chucked in the bin,' revealed Sugar, before saying the BPI soon 'started to get a bit heavy.'

Tony Willoughby, Amstrad's lawyer, issued a statement to the effect that if the BPI kept 'harassing' the company, he would not wait for them to start legal action and would instead take the preemptive step of going to court to get a declaration that Amstrad was not doing anything wrong. 'In other words, attack is the best form of defence,' wrote a typically truculent Sugar. 'He [Willoughby] said that if he lost this case, he would give up being a lawyer and become a pig farmer. That's how sure he was.'[54]

A new career as a swineherd was shaping up to be Willoughby's fate. 'Well, nine months later, all I could say was, "Oink, oink",' said Sugar.

'The judge ruled for the BPI. I wouldn't have minded, but the BPI hadn't even brought an action against us.'[55]

Tony Grabiner was the barrister representing Amstrad in the case. Sugar claimed that when the judge announced the ruling that sided with the BPI, Grabiner turned to Willoughby and said, 'Don't worry about this – the judge has gone mad. We'll win it on appeal.'[56]

The appeal was eventually escalated to the House of Lords and Amstrad emerged victorious.

The Lords ruled 'the defendant conferred the power to copy but did not grant the right to copy, therefore did not authorise the infringement'.[57] What that in effect meant was that Amstrad could not be held liable (as a contributory infringer) for what its customers did with its hardware.

'It was an historic victory,' crowed Sugar, 'which set a legal precedent – many subsequent disputes over breach of copyright have cited the Amstrad vs. BPI case. From my point of view, though, I could have done without this aggravation.'[58]

Shortly after the BPI's assault on home taping, a landmark ruling in the US happened that was to have huge repercussions for decades. It was specifically about taping video content, but the implications for the music business were also profound.

Sony Corp. of America vs. Universal City, Inc. (known more commonly as the Sony Betamax case) was finally decided by the Supreme Court on 17 January 1984, just one day shy of a year after it initially began. The case hinged on whether or not a video recording device, in this case the Betamax player developed by Sony in the 1970s, used by people at home to record TV shows constituted copyright infringement or if it simply enabled time shifting (i.e. letting people record a broadcast and watch it at a later date or over and over again) and, as such, was classed as fair use.[59]

'[T]he court ruled 5-4 that Sony could manufacture VCRs for people to record copyrighted TV shows for their own use,' summarised Steve Knopper.[60] This helped normalise the idea among the general public that copying for personal use was perfectly fine, regardless of the legal small print. It took a further eight years, however, for private copying exemptions to be specifically applied to music.

The Audio Home Recording Act (AHRA) of October 1992 was an amendment of US copyright law, specifically through the addition of Chapter 10 ('Digital Audio Recording Devices & Media') that allowed people to make copies of albums they had already purchased as long as they did not sell or distribute them.[61] [62]

Steve Knopper noted, however, that a carve-out in the AHRA proved a time bomb whose ticking got louder as the decade progressed. Computer companies demanded an exemption that would allow users to back up their files to a CD-ROM (which were launched in 1985). Computer companies were adamant this had to happen and labels initially resisted but, after listening to their lawyers and lobbyists, eventually accepted it as a compromise that would allow the AHRA legislation to pass.

Computer manufacturers were therefore able to sell machines with in-built recording devices. They did not have to pay a blank media levy and they would not have to limit the number of times files on a computer could be copied.

Marc Finer, marketer for Sony's DAT, says the labels tripped over their own feet by not trying to impose some sort of restrictions here. 'They blew it,' he said. 'Completely.'[63]

THE PERFECT COPY CONUNDRUM: A DIGITAL PIRACY TSUNAMI THREATENS TO ENGULF THE RECORD BUSINESS

The music industry did not realise it at the time, but it was being given a dry run for the hell that was going to erupt later in the 1990s when it encountered DAT (digital audio tape) piracy. Developed in 1987 by Sony, DAT cassettes were primarily used in recording studios as they were smaller than cassettes and had superior audio capabilities, even if they could only be recorded on one side.[64]

They did not take off as a consumer format, but the fact they could make a digital copy – although one that, due to technological restrictions placed on DAT recorders, slightly degraded in audio quality if copied again[65] – was something that gravely concerned the music business.

The music industry was spooked by DAT, fearing it 'would become the home taping device of choice, displacing the widespread but technically inferior analog recorders' and threatened legal action – something manufacturers were fearful would, regardless of the court outcome, tie them up for years.[66]

'They were not met with hugs and flowers but with glares and threats from the labels,' wrote Knopper of the arrival of the format on the industry's radar. He quotes John Briesch, president of Sony's consumer audio-video group, who says of the labels' response, 'They proceeded to claim that DAT would be the end of the world, cause cancer and create global warming.'[67]

In response to mounting worries, CBS Records created Copycode – 'a tiny circuit that would cut notes out of the music if anybody tried to record a CD onto a DAT' – as an early form of digital rights management (DRM). In a meeting in Canada, dubbed The Manoeuvre in Vancouver, Sony's team responded badly to labels trying to force this through and walked out of the meeting. CBS responded by refusing to release music on DAT.

In 1989, however, a compromise was reached at a meeting in Athens, Greece. A widget, called the Serial Copy Management System, would be installed in DAT players that allowed users to copy music once for personal use but would prevent copies of copies from happening. This was offered by Sony in exchange for governments not applying blank media levies. Music publishers rose up in arms and Sony had to capitulate on the levy issue. It all became academic, however, as struggles over how to control the format in the market helped kill any momentum it might have had. DAT became yet more roadkill on the side of the format highway.[68]

All the major trade bodies around the world had anti-piracy teams in place and were primarily focused on closing down illegal pressing plants or prosecuting existing plants that handled legitimate produce but that also pressed up pirate and bootleg releases on the side.

Mike Edwards was director of operations at the IFPI between 1992 and 1999, having previously co-founded independent label Timbuktu Records. 'I was responsible for anti-piracy, licensing, the practical sides of rights and rights administration,' he says. 'Up until 1997, we didn't have an actual active role in piracy. What changed things in 1997 was that CD piracy had become a massive, massive problem.'

In the slipstream of the CD boom of the 1990s came the CD piracy boom. The CD itself was launched in October 1982 in Japan[69] and the first pirate CDs were spotted in 1986.[70] Edwards recalls in 1998 that, in one operation, the IFPI seized over ten million CDs that were being put through a single warehouse in Hong Kong.

'We basically hired our internal police force in 1997,' he says. 'We hired a guy called Ian Grant, who was a detective inspector in the Hong Kong police. 1997 was when Hong Kong was handed back to China and a whole lot of very well-trained law enforcement people were on the job market.'

The anti-piracy team at the IFPI included a forensic expert who could trace unlicensed discs not just back to a factory but to an individual CD stamper because of microscopic blemishes on the CDs. 'We were able to examine the discs and identify which stamper had pressed that disc just by the characteristics of wear over time and little flaws,' says Edwards.

Paul Jessop, chief technology officer at the IFPI at the time, says the international trade body was incredibly advanced in what it was able to do here.

'We set up a CD forensics laboratory, which was, I believe, world-beating,' he says. 'Nobody else was doing anything like it. We were looking at very detailed scratches on moulds to work out which CDs come out of the same pressing plants. We were even planning a bit of forensics on the content of the disc to which versions of the masters were being used.'

Legitimate plants were issued with a SID (source identification) code and that had to be engraved into each stamper to stop it being changed (and therefore showing up on any illegitimate discs they pressed off the books). Inevitably, the more cavalier operators attempted to develop a workaround.

'What we actually found was that the pirate plants were inserting a ring on the stamper that had a fake SID code,' explains Edwards. 'We could say, 'OK, this SID code has been assigned to such and such a plant, but the stamper isn't one of their stampers.' That's how we discovered they were doing that.'

Initially, CD counterfeiters were trying to push their black market product through legitimate plants and either bribing them outright or deceiving them.

'I first brought litigation against a company in Israel that was pressing CDs,' says Edwards. 'They claimed they didn't know what it was, but they were pressing Rolling Stones and Beatles CDs. It was inconceivable that they didn't know what was going on. Then there were plants in the Midwest in the United States and guys from Latin America would come and say, "Here's my cousin's band. I'd like six million CDs pressed up." And it'd be Luis Miguel or some Latin American superstar. The guy in the Midwest couldn't speak Spanish and had never heard of the act. The legit plants were pressing CDs until we sued them.'

Jessop refers to this practice as 'moonlighting' and notes that it was difficult to fully police what the pressing plants were doing.

'The stories were ridiculous,' he says. 'Somebody who would turn up with a suitcase full of cash and CD box design with the lips and tongue [used by The Rolling Stones] and say, "Could you make me fifty thousand of these?" They'd say, "Certainly, sir." There were two different issues here: plants making more of the orders than were authorised and diverting the excess into pirate markets; and plants not taking enough care to check that new orders were legitimate.'

Jollyon Benn joined the UK trade body BPI in September 1997 as its first internet investigations executive, a role he created from scratch. He recalls that, even with all the forensic tools they had at their disposal, securing convictions against labels trading in bootlegs and pirate products was far from straightforward.

'We'd make test purchases and then start the civil process against those labels,' he says. 'It was a bit like the myth of Sisyphus. It felt a bit unrewarding, long-term stuff, quite expensive, very difficult to prove. You were relying on a musicologist to do A/B tests and say, "Yes, this is definitely that particular performance".'

His arrival at the BPI coincided with a serious step change in what music piracy was. Pressed disc piracy may have been an ongoing problem, but there were already the low rumblings of a challenge of an entirely different stripe that would erupt into a previously unimaginable crisis.

Music had been available to download from websites as early as 1994, but it required a great deal of searching and a phenomenal amount of technical knowledge to get this music and to play it back. The arrival of Hotline in 1996, however, was to be the first digital deep sea volcanic eruption for the music business. It was described as 'the first user-friendly file-sharing service' and immediately gripped users with its 'streamline and high-speed system'.[71]

It was created by Australian teenager Adam Hinkley. 'Based on a proprietary file transfer protocol, Hotline allows anybody to turn a computer into a server in less than a minute,' wrote *Salon* in a profile piece in 1999. 'Visitors to that server can upload and download files, chat and post messages to bulletin boards.'[72]

It melded FTP (file transfer protocol), IRC (internet relay chat) and the Usenet distributed discussion system in an addictive blend for people who were already spending large amounts of time online. The sharing and social networking on Hotwire drew around 1.5 million users within three years. It probably would have been bigger but was invite-only, with a $30 donation being optional.

One user, 22-year-old Noah M. Daniels, who was also running a private server offering classical MP3s for download, spoke to *Salon* about its appeal but also about how it was already being infiltrated by groups of people who did not care for its founding principles (a recurring criticism that would be levelled at every subsequent social network).

'Hotline has become primarily a place to download warez [pirated software] or MP3s, but it's also one of the best multi-user chat environments out there,' explained Daniels. 'The difference between Hotline and other virtual communities is that there is a core of users that's always there,' he said. 'Then there are people who treat Hotline as a way to get files that they are looking for, and just don't care about the sense of community. Unfortunately, the latter group is what exploded with the popularity of Hotline.'[73]

It was made up of two constituent parts: Hotline Client (allowing users to set up their own servers); and Hotline Connect (for users wishing to connect to those different servers).

Macworld said, at its peak, users could 'connect to thousands of Hotline servers that suited every imaginable user interest' and that 'a sense of libertarian independence pervades the community.'[74]

There may have been libertarian politics debated on the discussion boards, but that was really a side attraction. 'File sharing was the star of the Hotline show, there is no doubt about it,' noted *Coin Telegraph* in a 2015 article on the service.[75]

It did not last. By 2000, most of the servers were choked with digital tumbleweed and by 2001 Hotline Communications was out of business.[76]

It was arguably John the Baptist to Napster's Jesus (or Napster's Satan, if you are the RIAA) and was quickly overtaken by the arrival of the latter in 1999. But it was, for good and for ill, a pioneering service that paved the way for what was to follow and should not be written out of the story of digital music.

While Hotline was not sued by the RIAA or IFPI, these trade associations were fully awake to the threat of online piracy and were quickly formulating their legal responses.

In early June 1997, the RIAA was already targeting three online sites and charging them with copyright violation. They ran on a reciprocation basis, where users were expected to upload additional music files in exchange for the ones they had downloaded. *Billboard*, which rather quaintly called them 'World Wide Web sites', was reporting that one of the sites in question was receiving 29,000 hits a month. It added that the previous month Oasis's management was threatening legal action against a hundred fan sites that hosted unlicensed song clips, lyrics and photos.[77] Earlier in the year, Sony managed to shut down a fan site hosting clips from *Be Here Now*, the band's upcoming album, that had been downloaded from the Sony Brazil website.[78]

It was estimated that tracks would take an average of five minutes each to download from these sites and that they were 'near CD quality.' Labels were said to be tentatively considering offering music downloads for purchase as a countermeasure.

'The idea is to crack down on an illegal market, but also to create an opportunity and an incentive for a legitimate market,' Hilary Rosen, president and COO of the RIAA, told *Billboard*.[79]

The RIAA claimed the sites were fully aware they were operating illegally and even posted disclaimers they believed would absolve them of any liability. One such disclaimer read: 'All MP3 files on this page are for trial purposes only. If you like what you hear then you will have to go out and buy the CD. Please be aware that it is illegal to use these files beyond their trial purpose.'[80]

The RIAA first noticed sites offering unlicensed music at the start of 1997 and quickly began filing cease and desist letters to the operators.

One of the three sites targeted in the June 1997 action was Fresh Kutz, which was offering over five hundred recordings from acts like The Beatles, Alanis Morissette, Guns N' Roses, Madonna, Led Zeppelin and The Notorious BIG.

'The suits seek a permanent injunction to prevent the operators from putting songs on websites and ordering them to erase all unauthorized copies of recordings,' reported *Billboard*. It suggested the RIAA would seek damages of up to $100,000 for each infringing recording, but noted that the organisation was undertaking an educational campaign at universities to get them to help in tracking down offending sites as well as warning students that they were committing theft.[81]

Labels were increasingly paranoid about albums leaking online ahead of release. So much so that they were taking steps to try and prevent music reviewers being able to share them, which only served to offend and annoy a multitude of music writers. Journalist friends say that in summer 1997, Creation Records was sending out review copies of *Be Here Now* by Oasis in portable cassette players that had been glued shut. This followed EMI doing something similar with Radiohead's appositely titled *OK Computer* a few months earlier.[82]

Online leaks were not exactly new in 1997, with Steve Knopper suggesting one of the earliest online album leak can be traced back to 1993 when Depeche Mode's *Songs Of Faith And Devotion* album suddenly appeared being shared on online chatrooms.[83]

By 1997, however, they were slightly better prepared. They might have been relatively powerless to stop it immediately, but there were people within labels and trade bodies who had their antennae up to the reality of online leaks.

'Being the sort of person I am, I could see that more and more people were getting access to the internet and these communities were building online,' says Jollyon Benn of his early days at the BPI in 1997. 'And people were naturally enough wanting to share their passions, let's say, and that included music.'

He helped set up a working group with representatives from several major labels in the UK and they would meet regularly to share information and ideas, operating as an early warning system for the industry at large.

'They would come along, sit in an office with IFPI reps and say, "What are we doing about this piracy problem?" he explains. 'From that, we then grew across IFPI groups globally and tried to put the alert out to say, "This is something that we think is going to grow. What are you tooled up at the moment for dealing with this?"'

Mike Edwards says he and Benn would do demonstrations for the IFPI's other national groups in different markets, and also for record label executives, to explain to them what digital piracy was and what it would mean for their business.

He says, 'We'd go into an hour-long meeting and say, "OK, we're going to show you what's out there." We'd go and find a bulletin board with a whole list of tracks. We'd start downloading and at the end of an hour-long meeting, we'd say, "OK, now we've got this one track that we've downloaded!" It was really, really slow. When speeds got high enough and compression got good enough, that's when digital piracy became a problem.'

Benn admits things were relatively unsophisticated in the late 1990s, noting that a lot of pre-release sharing of music was happening over IRC and some were private so were hard to infiltrate.

'In terms of getting stuff taken down, you'd always be trying to find the servers where they were hosted and who'd be managing those, tackling it that way,' he says. 'The law itself was rather undeveloped as well.'

He recalls that sites offering music at that time were trying to find loopholes in the law to avoid takedown or prosecution, with some arguing that hypertext links *pointing* to files elsewhere on the internet would absolve them of guilt and allow them to act with impunity.

He says, 'There was this whole thing about them saying, "Well, I'm not liable for this because I'm just basically showing you where it actually is. You have got to go and talk to those people over there that have got the actual file on a server." Pretty quickly we realised that was quite a cynical way of interpreting the law.'

Infringing sites would be identified and contacted. They would either shut down permanently or shut down and reappear relatively quickly. 'It was like playing Whac-A-Mole,' he says. 'People would very quickly set up another account and you'd start all over again. There was no automation.'

Staying on top of all the technological developments was a major challenge for Benn and his opposites at the other trade organisations.

'We were on a very steep learning curve about the architecture of this new internet, how it worked and how it was structured,' he says. 'Things like Who Is [to find out who domain names were registered to] were great for us back then because people would literally register a domain with a real name and their real address. You could simply contact them and say, "What you're doing is infringing copyright and you need to stop." I don't think we were particularly heavy-handed to start with.'

Edwards says when Jay Berman took over at the IFPI in early 1999 they were able to dramatically increase their anti-piracy capabilities, getting a budget they felt was commensurate with the problem they saw multiplying before them.

'I managed to get a million-dollar budget for the building of an automated system for searching, finding and issuing takedown notices,' he says. 'We built that system and we brought in outside technology consultants, who went and looked at what the RIAA were doing manually: a room full of people just searching, finding, verifying, issuing takedowns. That basic system remained in place for over ten years. It was only in the 2010s that the IFPI then reinvested to update it. That million dollars that they invested and that I oversaw was very well spent.'

Berman adds that this was part of a wider organisational recalibration at the IFPI to show it was able to respond to new technologies and the perceived threats that they could bring.

'One of the first things we paid attention to [when I joined] was to create within the IFPI not just an anti-piracy effort but a technology department.'

David Arditi says the RIAA at the time was creating what he termed a 'piracy panic narrative', claiming this was a deadly threat to its very existence and threatened to destroy its revenues.[84]

Alongside railing against an industry-led claim that its revenues are being snatched from it, he takes issue with the politics underpinning the terminology the music industry uses here. He argues that downloading music from the internet is 'not the same thing as stealing' and is, in legal terms, 'not even property theft.' He argues, '[I]t cannot be compared to property theft because when a user downloads music, they are not taking something away from another user. The original user still has the ability to listen to the downloaded music and can still allow others to download their music. File sharers are not stealing music.'[85]

THE DMCA AND TRYING TO ANTICIPATE THE LEGALITIES OF THE DIGITAL FUTURE

The passing of the DMCA (Digital Millennium Copyright Act) in the US in late 1998 was intended to pull copyright law into the internet age. It had to perform a difficult, even impossible, balancing act to try and keep copyright companies and technology companies happy, with both sides at various points praising and criticising aspects of the DMCA.

'The new law was crafted to offer copyright protection to authors, composers, filmmakers and other content creators in the new and quickly evolving digital world, both online and off,' wrote *Wired*. 'The problem, as they saw it, was that it was just too easy to make exact replicas of their works.'[86]

It was also, in part, 'written to protect Internet service providers from unknowingly hosting any illegal activities' noted Trevor Merriden.[87]

Jay Berman was involved in the drafting of the DMCA and explains why he feels it was significant and necessary but also where it was, from the music industry's perspective, limited.

'The previous change in the ground rules was in 1976, which had been a long time coming,' he says. 'You had all of the format changes between 1976 and the late 1980s and the DMCA was an attempt to catch up with those things that were happening at the moment. It always takes place in a political context. It's always a very difficult process. I can remember standing outside, Hilary [Rosen, RIAA] and me talking, wondering if we should agree to this and realising that there were certain political constraints. Did the DMCA give us everything we wanted? The answer was no.'

He says he was fully aware that it could never solve everything the music business wanted but it had to be drafted in a way that could anticipate, as much as possible, technological, societal and legislative changes coming in the future.

'The idea we had in the DMCA was, to the extent that it was politically possible, to try to at least get even with the curve,' he says. 'It's very difficult to get ahead of the curve, but at least we saw the beginnings of things that were happening. And we saw the DMCA as the opportunity to try, for the first time really, to get on the ground floor of vis-à-vis a set of rights. That took a lot of compromises.'

He accepts that squaring the needs/demands of the music industry with the needs/demands of the technology industry was always going to be impossible within the framework of the DMCA, but each side had to fight their corner as much as they could.

'We were very conscious of the fact that we were at the beginning of something,' he says. 'We didn't know what that something was. First of all, we had an incredibly worthy adversary in the consumer electronics guys. They had an enormous amount of clout. I look back at the DMCA and, you know, at that time we did a pretty good job. The problem was that it wasn't designed to last forever. It eventually got overtaken by events.'

WHO DO YOU THINK YOU CD-R?: HOME TAPING GETS SUPERCHARGED

Home taping on cassettes was seen as a problem for the music business, but it was one that was inherently limited; plus there was an in-built degradation in the audio quality. It was, behind closed doors at least, accepted as an unfortunate part of the business.

Pressed disc piracy (both CDs and LPs) was a much bigger problem, especially as it was industrialised and others, not the record companies or the music publishers (or, indeed, the artists), were profiting from it. With CDs, there was 'no significant degradation in sound quality, so long as care was taken in transferring the digital code from one object to the next',[88] but, as the pirate operators generally had to go to pressing plants, there was at least a way of tackling this through raids.

The arrival of CD-R (compact disc-recordable), however, flipped everything the music industry knew on its head. Not only could people at home make perfect digital copies of music (which would not deteriorate if they were copied again and again), pirates could quickly and relatively cheaply set up CD-R copying operations that would operate below the radar.

There were no blemishes from CD stampers that, under a microscope, would reveal where these discs were being manufactured and cause the factories involved to be shut down. They were, in that sense, utterly untraceable. Bedrooms and garages anywhere in the world could become centres of CD-R production and the industry would only ever be able to stop a fraction of them.

At a hi-fi show taking place at a hotel in Heathrow in September 1991, the CD-R was publicly unveiled.[89] It was the release of Hewlett-Packard's HP 4020i, manufactured by Philips and costing $995, that started to make the technology more widely accessible.[90] The CD-RW (CD-rewritable) followed in 1997.[91]

Burning CD-Rs at home was still a complex and erratic process for most people, with *Hi-Fi News & Record Review* reporting in March 1999 that the Easy CD Creator software, developed by Adaptec to link a PC to a CD-ROM burner, was 'very flakey' at launch and 'even now the system is far from ideal.' It added, 'Modern PCs used high speed CD-ROM drives which are very erratic when used to read audio. By far the easiest way to make CD audio recordings is to use a consumer CD-R deck, particularly the Philips CDR 870 and CDR 880 models.'[92]

By May 1999, Memorex was selling eighty-minute CD discs for £1.59 (which was twice the price of seventy-four-minute discs), with reports that the price was going to quickly fall.

Hi-Fi News & Record Review was not convinced that the growing popularity of CD-R was damaging sales for record labels. 'From the record industry's complaints, you would think disc-recording is putting them out of business,' wrote technology columnist Barry Fox. 'But the flashy, glitzy BRIT Awards coincided with the release of figures from the BPI which show sales are up by 11 per cent, with albums up 10 per cent. This bears out the Japanese experience, where home copying has always been a way of life. Copying stimulates interest in music: people buy and copy.'[93]

He did mention in the same column that UK company C-Dilla was claiming to have found a way to stop people from copying CDs to blank discs. 'The music copies but sounds awful,' he wrote.

Peppered through the music trade press in the 1990s were stories of CD plants being raided, notably in Eastern Europe and Asia, and loud proclamations of the millions of illicit discs that had been seized. As the decade progressed, stories about CD-R piracy increased and became as frequently published as stories about pressed disc piracy.

In April 1999, for example, *Billboard* was quoting a report from Santa Clara Consulting that said 650 million blank CD-Rs were sold globally in 1998, with forecasts that this could jump to between 1.5 billion and two billion in 2002. It added that a CD recorder could now be bought for $500 while PC-based CD-R drives cost around $200. It ramped up the piracy fear by noting that companies like CD Cyclone and Mediastore allowed multi-disc copying and added that Microboards had introduced modular CD-R towers in 1998 'that operate at up to four times real time and can duplicate anywhere from two to thirty discs at a time.'[94]

In June 1999, the IFPI was claiming that CD-R piracy was growing in China, France, Germany, Greece, Japan, the US and the Netherlands, calling it 'a new and serious problem', with reports of empty CD jewel boxes being stolen from music retailers in France and the Netherlands (the assertion being they were intended to house CD-R copies of the corresponding pirated albums).[95]

The IFPI added that there were 400 million pirate CD sales in 1998, a 20 per cent increase from 1997, and this cost the industry $4.5 billion that year in perceived lost sales. To hammer home the point about the darkness underpinning this illicit market, it claimed organised crime was behind around three-quarters of piracy.[96]

Patrick Decam, president of Sony Music Benelux in the late 1990s, says this was not just industry scaremongering and that organised crime really was deeply involved in the pirate music market.

'We were told to watch out for our own security,' he says. 'Sony had created a team specialised in anti-gang vigilance. We were supposed to make sure our factories, our stock, our people, our company were not exposed to theft of master tapes or master files piracy. There were criminal gangs who were involved in drug trafficking who were very interested in CDs all of a sudden. They had calculated they would get more profit from a CD than from its equivalent in drugs in weight. There were trucks that were hijacked with the CDs in them.'

Gangsters and other nefarious characters were especially drawn to CD-R piracy because the startup costs were lower than dealing in pressed disc piracy and they could effectively 'franchise' their operations.

'The first place we saw industrial-scale CD-R production was in Italy where the organised crime families were farming it out to homes all over the south of Italy,' says Mike Edwards. 'Little CD replication set-ups and little old women in black would be pumping out millions of CDs collectively. They were then labelled professionally at another location and put onto the market. That became a lot harder to take action against because it was so diverse. And also because it was the Mafia.'

Later in June 1999, it was announced that the music business in the Netherlands would benefit from an additional blank media levy on CD-R to compensate for perceived lost sales. This would swing into effect in September 1999 – following similar legislation in Spain, Austria, Finland and Hungary – and could generate up to six million guilders ($2.8 million) a year that would be distributed to rights holders.[97]

Paul Russell, chairman of Sony Music Europe in 1999, says the issue was becoming widespread in the markets he oversaw, suggesting that CD-R sales were significantly overshadowing legitimate sales. 'There were CD factories in places in Eastern Europe that were churning out ten or twelve million CD-Rs a year,' he says, 'but the local market was 850,000. Kids had access and the CD-Rs were very sexy. Everybody could become a pirate. Also the machines that were being sold were coming down dramatically in price.'

In June 1999, the BPI was reporting that 720,000 pirate CDs had been sold in the UK in 1998, double the number sold in 1997. It highlighted CD-R piracy as a new threat, although *Music Week* pointed out that it appeared to be limited in the UK. 'There are an increasing number of CD-Rs appearing for sale in pubs, local markets and in particular computer fairs,' said Jollyon Benn of the BPI anti-piracy unit. 'The price has really come down because so many people are actively compiling them.' He added that CD-R duplicators are selling for £2,000 meaning that illegal traders could get set up relatively quickly and cheaply.[98]

By August in the US, illegal CD-Rs were being described by *Billboard* as 'the newest pirate pest the RIAA faces.' It reported that seizures of illegal CD-Rs were 155,496 units so far that year, up sharply from 23,858 a year earlier. The piece argued that legitimate plants were refusing suspicious orders so pirates were being forced underground, adding that many CD-R 'factories' were run from home basements. The RIAA was also offering a bounty of $10,000 via its CDReward Program to anyone who could provide them with information on illegal CD-R operations.[99]

In Asia, according to Larry Kenswil, president of eLabs within Universal Music Group between 1997 and 2008, the CD-R problem was even more endemic than it was in Western markets.

'I remember being in Asia at that time and the stores were just full of burned CDs,' he says. 'As a matter of fact, it didn't matter what you're buying, it was all the same price. It was basically the price of the blank CD plus a markup and they put anything you wanted on the CD. It didn't matter.'

Cary Sherman, senior EVP and general counsel of the RIAA, claims CD-R piracy exploded because the record industry was left to fend for itself as the electronics industry did not want to help here.

'CD-R piracy had been something we'd been focusing on since around 1997,' he says. 'Basically it was just a more sophisticated form of home taping. We had been dealing with home taping since the 1980s. We had even gotten *Congress* to enact a piece of legislation because we had finally reached an agreement with the consumer electronics industry on how to handle it. The problem was that the computer industry refused to participate in it. As a result, there was an exception for general purpose computers and, since all CD-R piracy ultimately moved to computers instead of dedicated CD-R devices, the loophole basically obliterated the benefits of that legislation.'

He says, however, that this might have appeared a huge issue at the time, but it was soon going to look like a walk in the park compared to what was coming over the horizon. 'CD-R piracy was small by comparison to what we were facing online,' he says. 'CD-R piracy was one copy at a time, made by an individual or sold to an individual whereas online was one person to a million.'

Retailers were starting to complain that CD-R piracy was badly affecting their bottom line. 'Retailers are voicing increasing concern about the volume of business they are losing to internet piracy and CD-R counterfeiting,' wrote *Music Week* in July 1999. 'Although it is difficult to estimate the true scale of the problem, anecdotal evidence from retailers suggests that the falling cost of CD Writers and blank CD-R media as well as easy access to pirate internet sites means a growing number of people are creating their own CDs rather than buying legitimate copies.'[100]

Jo Walters, who ran the Trading Post record shop in Stroud, despaired at the scale of the impact it was having. 'It has happened gradually over the past six months as word gets round and as the equipment becomes cheaper,' she said. 'But it's not just burning CDs – it's internet sales, too. I know how the greengrocer felt when the supermarket arrived in town. I feel the days are numbered.'[101]

The trauma and pain the record business believed were being caused by CD-R piracy were clearly not being salved by Philips, the company which developed the CD in conjunction with piracy and had moved out of music by selling PolyGram to Seagram in late 1998, trumpeting its early successes in CD-Rs.

On the front page of *Music Week* on 7 August 1999, under the headline 'Philips launches £3m CD-R push', it was reported that Philips was undertaking its biggest ad campaign to promote CD recorder machines. Devices would cost from £240. Philips had launched in the sector in 1997 and was claiming to have a 95 per cent market share of the CD recorders, selling twenty thousand units in 1998. Mark Chatterton, marketing manager for audio products at Philips, told *Music Week*, 'We had a tremendous year in 1998 and this year has gone like a train.' For record labels, they would insist that this was proving to be less a speeding train and more a train-wreck.[102]

Music Week added, 'The BPI says it will be watching Philips' ads closely, although it adds that the biggest threat to the industry is from cottage piracy and not home CD-R units.'[103]

Gavin Robertson was working at PRS/MCPS as new media and research and development manager in the late 1990s and, as such, had to keep abreast of technological developments. He had to be able to translate not just how they worked but also what their implications were in a way that the senior executives at the organisations could grasp.

'I was doing presentations to the board about CD-R piracy,' he says. 'I remember doing a demo where I said I was going to burn this CD while I was presenting. I did it and played it back. The whole room was just horrified! I think that [CD-R piracy] was a much bigger concern initially. You've got to imagine the sheer value of CD sales, which had taken everybody by surprise. So anything that was going to hit that was a problem. And therefore, if something could be deemed as being equivalent to CD, it would be acceptable. And they were never going to accept less than CD value.'

Richard Ogden, SVP of Sony Music Entertainment Europe, highlights an important contradiction in the heart of the company where he worked. Essentially Sony's technology arm was explicitly working against the best interests of its music arm. The bleak irony here was that it was manufacturing and selling hardware that could be used by people in their homes to make unlicensed copies of albums whose copyrights may have been controlled by its recorded music division.

For the music division of Sony, and equally for all the other labels,

CD-R was a malevolent threat to the revenue boom they experienced throughout the 1990s. The good times, it seemed, could come crashing to an end.

'I was working at PolyGram when Philips launched the CD,' he says. 'It had been an absolute gravy train. That ten- or fifteen-year period was an absolute gravy train for the record business. They were making massive profits from the sale of little round plastic discs.'

Now a variation on those same little round plastic discs was threatening to derail the gravy train.

From the industry's perspective, there were some breakthroughs around CD-R piracy towards the end of 1999. *Billboard* noted that online auction site eBay said it was banning the sale of CD-Rs from 17 October, 'citing possible copyright infringement.'[104] In the same issue of *Billboard*, the Italian Anti-Music-Piracy Federation FPM was reported to have 'made a breakthrough in its fight against CD-R piracy' following a raid in a farm in Puglia where police seized 64 CD burners, 4,900 duplicate CDs (of both domestic and international acts) plus 38,000 blank discs. It was hailed as the first raid in Italy to discover a CD-R manufacturing chain.[105]

Like Gremlins fed after midnight and then thrown in a swimming pool, the problem quickly multiplied with the arrival of MP3 CDs and devices that could play them.

CD-Rs held around the same amount of music as a commercially released CD so there was like-for-like copying possible. The MP3 CD, however, was like a TARDIS compared to the standard police box of a CD-R as entire discographies, not just single albums, could be stored on them.

'The content on that one disc was so compressed that you only have to duplicate that one disc and – *boom!* – you could see the exponential impact of something like that,' says Jollyon Benn. 'They were turning up at markets and car boot sales [flea markets]. Then the organised crime networks obviously start to get involved in it as well because there's money and just because of the scummy nature of it, basically. I remember one market up near Skegness [England]. You could see that there were teams that would all pile into vans at the end of the day and cart off the unsold stock and whizz off. They'd be dotted around this huge market there, selling counterfeit CDs but also MP3 compilation CDs.'

Direct action against those profiting from piracy was one thing; but the other half of the equation here was the consumer, and the music industry was moving to warn them against buying illicit CDs and CD-Rs and, more importantly, trying to stop them making their own CD-Rs.

SUM OF A TEACHER, MAN: TRYING TO EDUCATE A NEW GENERATION ABOUT PIRACY

In the early 1990s, the Home Taping Is Killing Music campaign felt anachronistic – a relic of a different era. Besides, the record labels were enjoying rocketing revenues from CDs and, at this stage at least, they were a format that no one at home could copy onto. The average person in the first half of the decade could, of course, copy a CD to a cassette (for their Walkman or to give as a mixtape), but they could not easily copy from a CD to another CD.

Besides, Home Taping Is Killing Music had become something of a joke. People wore T-shirts with the campaign title and the cassette/crossbones on them as an act of irony or defiance – or both. A cassette version of *In God We Trust, Inc.* by The Dead Kennedys in 1981 had one side left empty and proudly displayed this message: 'Home taping is killing record industry profits! We left this side blank so you can help.'[106] On his 1988 album *Workers Playtime*, Billy Bragg added the message 'Capitalism is killing music' and advised that fans 'pay no more than £4.99 for this record.' Other parodies include 'Music Industry Is Killing Music' and 'Home Sewing Is Killing Fashion.'

It felt too open to mockery – too much of an open goal for satirists – to bring the campaign, or a variation of it, back for many years. The rise, however, of CD piracy and, more specifically, CD-R piracy made its PR resurrection an inevitability for an industry panicking about its bottom line.

In 1998, the RIAA initiated the Soundbyting campaign that targeted colleges and universities where a new worry, online piracy, was starting to come through.[107] It was asking musicians to lend their voices to the campaign by writing public letters opposing piracy.

'The artists are free to make up their own quotes, plus the letter offers up some pre-fab suggestions ranging from catch phrases ('Stealing Music Is Wrong. Get real. Get legit'); to pleadings ('. . . Remember, I sing for my supper'); to threats ('The RIAA is making sure that people who break the law are held accountable'),' wrote MTV.[108]

Cary Sherman, EVP/general counsel at the RIAA, was a driving force behind this campaign.

'We launched educational efforts, especially at the universities because that's where the problem was the greatest by far,' he says. 'It was all designed to get them to step up to the plate and stop illegal file-sharing on their campuses. Congress got involved and held hearings on theft that was going on on college campuses and what universities were doing about it. Or not doing about it. It was a multifaceted campaign, from PR to education to threats to everything we could think of to try and bring this thing under control.'

He says the RIAA was fully aware that the problem was always going to be with them and that they were not deluded into thinking they could eradicate the issue completely. 'One thing that is important to understand about efforts to deal with piracy is that you never eliminate it; you can never completely eliminate piracy,' he says. 'We were trying to stop what was a leak from becoming a haemorrhage. If it could just be reduced, if it could be diminished to the point where it wasn't completely destroying the marketplace, that would be a victory.'

Paul Jessop says that Sherman was always leaning towards education over and above litigation and feels that this side of what Sherman was trying to do has been forgotten over the years as the story ossifies around the idea that the RIAA and IFPI were only ever swinging sledgehammers at nuts, regardless of their size. 'Cary's the most anti-litigation lawyer I've ever met,' says Jessop. 'He'd much rather fix it than litigate it. I don't think he gets credit for that.'

In Europe, two major piracy education initiatives were rolled out in markets that, according to labels and trade organisations there, were being significantly hit by CD-R piracy and where legitimate sales were tumbling.

In July, the NVPI, the trade body for record labels in the Netherlands, announced it was undertaking a media 'awareness campaign' to tackle home copying. It claimed that 30 per cent of teenagers in the county traded homemade digital copies of albums and that something needed to be done about it.[109] Its research was far from robust, however, gathering the data from a survey of just under 450 schoolchildren aged 12 to 18.

Despite the anaemic nature of the proffered statistics, the NVPI said it wanted to alert parents of schoolchildren to what was happening behind closed bedroom doors in their homes. The IFPI and the NVPI were drawing what they claimed was an incontrovertible direct line between CD-Rs and a drop in the market for recorded music. They said it had slipped 8 per cent between 1997 and 1998 and suggested that it was already down 20 per cent that year and this was despite a strong Dutch economy.[110]

Just two months later, in early September 1999, Germany was starting a similar education campaign under the banner of Copy Kills Music and with the slogan *Das Ende Vom Lied* (The End Of The Song). The Germany's industry was ramping up the panic by suggesting that thirty thousand jobs in the music business could be at risk and claiming that the loss of income from ten thousand illegally copied albums could kill an emerging act's career.[111]

Millions of fliers would be sent to German schools and the five schools with the highest response rates would be visited by local musicians. Both VH1 and MTV promised to throw their weight behind it and offered free broadcast time to get the industry's message across.

Wolf-D Gramatke, chairman of the IFPI's German group and chairman/CEO of Universal Music Germany, told *Billboard*, 'In Germany, there is more sympathy for the criminals than for the victims. And in this case, we are the victims, as something is being stolen from us, while it is claimed that the criminals are just poor kids. But this is not so. On the other hand we do not want to criminalize our own target group. What we have neglected to do and what we must do now is to create a feeling that people are acting wrongly by copying CDs.'[112]

He added, 'Stealing music cannot be seen as being any better than stealing a pound of butter or sweets. But, funnily enough, that's just what many people think. We have to start by making it clear that it is not cool. We have to go into schools and educate the children. If necessary, we have to say that otherwise the burners will be confiscated by the police.'

The *Das Ende Vom Lied* campaign took to the road between 11 November and 3 December 1999. Over thirty acts (including Smudo, Sabrina Setlur, Mr President and Die 3 Generation) visited schools and addressed children at cinemas about the impact of copying CDs. Bands formed at the schools visited could submit demos to label A&R staff who were on the tour and a music industry internship could also be won.[113]

Jay Berman says that persuading artists to speak out on industry matters was something he initiated when he was at the RIAA and he carried it over to his role at the IFPI. He admits there were some who did not want to be mouthpieces for the business, but others willingly stepped forward. 'Not only did you have to find an artist who was willing to do it, but you had to find the artist's lawyer to say, "Oh, yeah, it's OK for them to do it." That was another element. At the IFPI, we relied a lot on George Martin and Jean-Michel Jarre. Jean-Michel was great. He took the time to find out what the issues were. He took the time to actually physically walk the halls with me.'

Universal Music head Doug Morris had a much simpler solution to this all. Initially he was gung-ho for litigation, but soon realised that the best thing to do was to just find ways to release blockbuster albums. Education was fine, but nothing trumped hits.

'Doug Morris thought throwing the bootleggers in jail was an outstanding idea,' noted Stephen Witt. 'He had, however, learned an entirely different lesson from the tape-trading era. You don't solve the problem of piracy by calling the cops. You solved it by putting out *Thriller*. In Morris's view, it was Michael Jackson's 1982 blockbuster that had really rescued the slumping industry – what had been missing wasn't law enforcement but simply hits.'[114]

Karen Allen was digital music strategist at the RIAA between 1999 and 2002. She says there was also an education push by the organisation *within* the music business about all of these issues that ran concurrently with the consumer-facing initiatives. This involved her attending conferences to represent the RIAA viewpoint as well as comment on key online discussion boards that focused on the music business.

'I was sent to all the conferences,' she says. 'I was put on all the panels. I was the vocal voice of the RIAA on the Pho List.'

Co-founded by Jim Griffin, the Pho List was effectively an early music business social network but also a debating chamber where new ideas could be presented and dissected, often oscillating between praise or condemnation. It could be an invigorating and educational read. It could also be terrifying.

'I was very, very, very active on the Pho List,' says Allen. 'Everybody was on the Pho List, but the people who were vocal on there were the ones who were on the side, so to speak, of the startups and not on the side, so to speak, of the music industry. I was very vocal on that. I was the public-facing digital music person for the RIAA at a time when the RIAA was not very popular!'

She also ran outreach programmes with the various labels in the US to not just put forward the RIAA's views on key and current issues – the subtext being that the label executives should fall in line with them – but also to gather information from the labels, especially from those working in digital, and feed that back to the RIAA so that it was better informed on contemporary matters.

'I would talk to our member companies at least twice a year,' she says. 'I would do the rounds and go to all the digital departments of the majors and the major indies that were involved with us. It was just giving them the update. "I don't know what you hear in the press, but this is what's really going on. This is where we stand on things that we're trying to do." If you wanted to know what was really going on, you'd have to talk to all the VPs of new media.'

In the UK, the fightback against CD-Rs was being led by John Kennedy, CEO and chairman of Universal Music, who used a speech at a Universal conference in London to outline his concerns. He called for, in *Music Week*'s words, 'a high-profile PR offensive against the potential scourge of recordable CDs' during his 'impassioned speech.' Days earlier, the German music business was blaming a 9.8 per cent decline in the first half of the year on CD copying.[115]

Kennedy told *Music Week* that CD copying was becoming normalised and represented a huge threat for the industry. 'When I speak to 18- and 19-year-olds, I find they clearly have no concern at all about CD-R copying and MiniDisc copying,' he said. 'It confirms the stories about campuses where one person buys CDs and copies them for others. They don't think they're doing anything wrong or damaging the artists and songwriters.'

He insisted this was different from cassette piracy, and not just because of the improved audio quality. 'It was not really commercially-based before,' he said, 'but in school campuses and places of work, this has become a commercial exercise.'

Reflecting on that time when I interviewed him in summer 2022, Kennedy suggests his calls for a PR and educational campaign in the UK were a proactive move to try and get the UK ahead of the issue rather than having to play a desperate game of catch-up like in other markets.

'It was more prevalent in Europe than in the UK,' he says of the scale of CD-R piracy. 'At the time, we were suffering from imports, CD-R piracy and digital piracy. It was a storm. Certainly not the perfect storm, but it was a storm.'

Jollyon Benn feels the various PR campaigns around this were ultimately doomed by a problem of terminology and, as such, a muddied message going out to the public.

'In terms of PR, I'd say the industry probably did really struggle on that count, because we couldn't think of any other way of describing the issue it was causing than as theft. Ultimately, it's people not paying for something, but it's not really like theft. It's a really hard concept [to get across].'

TECHNOLOGY MOVES FASTER THAN THE LAW: ETERNALLY PLAYING CATCH-UP WITH THE MACHINES

Even in early 1999, the ground covered by the DMCA, its green shoots only a few months old, was looking more like a corner that the music industry had found itself painted into.

Jay Berman (above) said the DMCA 'eventually got overtaken by events', but the disparity between what was happening here with the law and what was happening there with technology was never wider and more apparent than it was in 1999.

Talking about the draft E-Commerce Directive in Europe, itself based on the DMCA, in January 1999, Berman said, 'We always think we're legislating for the future, and we end up legislating for the present. Then, all of a sudden, as we've completed the present legislation, the future is upon us.'[116]

Martin Bandier, chairman of EMI Music Publishing Worldwide, was arguing a similar line a month later specifically around what he called the 'new frontier' of the internet. 'Like the US in the 1700s,' he said, 'we're trying to come up with a body of legislation to carry us for the next thousand years.'[117]

Throughout 1999, Berman and his contemporaries were calling for tougher legislative measures and greater government help to tackle the growing piracy problem as it mutated across formats and teleported from the physical to the intangible.

'It was pretty traumatic, when you thought about it,' says Berman looking back at that time. 'The initial response was litigation. How do we stop it? That always puts you in a bind, in a way always behind the curve, because the one thing, if you look, is that no matter how hard you try, it's virtually impossible for the law, the law being a set of rules that protect your rights, to stay apace of technology.'

As the enormity of what was happening started to reveal itself to the industry, and the realisation began hitting that the law was rapidly becoming outdated, there was a mounting sense of disquiet across the music business.

'There was a feeling that the industry was under siege,' says Mike Edwards. 'And in big danger.'

Al Teller had been running digital-first label Atomic Pop for two years by this point and he felt that the role of labels was not to pause and wait for legislation to be pushed through. They should, he felt, be the ones to try and find new business models for new times.

'Having been deeply involved with the RIAA and the IFPI [during my time at major labels], I was going to let them deal with the lawsuits,' he says. 'Both of those organisations, particularly the RIAA, at some point became more like a lawyers' group than anything else. The concept of the RIAA [was that] the meetings were supposed to be [run] by the heads of the companies, not by the head of their legal department. So when these meetings degenerated into legal discussions, my attitude was to let them do all the lawsuits they want and they could sue everybody and anybody. We were trying to find a marketplace solution to the problem.'

Alex Sayf Cummings made a bold claim in her book on music piracy. 'Piracy might not kill music, but history may record that it killed the 20th century record industry,' she said.[118] All forms of piracy, from the early 1900s right up to the CD-R, may have appeared as the biggest and deadliest threat imaginable when they first appeared. Yet they were to prove to be mere mosquitoes buzzing around the head of the record business compared to the clomping behemoth of the MP3 that looked like it was going to pancake the record labels under its elephantine feet.

MP3

CHAPTER 6

World War MP3: The Downloadable Insurrection

(The format that mangled control over music's circulation)

The germinal intention of the MP3 was not to set in motion billions of tiny detonations across the record business that, collectively, made it truly believe that the end was nigh. But that is exactly what it did.

The dark irony is that this *compression* of audio files had enormous and widespread repercussions. It was the tiny format with colossal implications.

Indeed, for the record business, the brief was: the smaller the file, the greater the chaos.

The MP3 has a long, twisting history, dating back to 1982, symbolically the same year the CD was developed. As with all software, it was a team effort, but one name has been singled out as the driving force behind what it became: Karlheinz Brandenburg.

'I don't like the title "The Father of MP3",' he told *NPR* in 2011. 'Certainly I was involved all the time from basic research [to] getting it into the market.'[1]

Yet that sobriquet, The Father of MP3, will never leave him.

In the late 1970s, Professor Dieter Seitzer was working on ways to transmit speech quicker and more efficiently over phone lines – both copper lines and over ISDN, which was being seen in scientific circles as the future of telecommunications. Seitzer, in refining his ideas, looked to transmit music files this way, but was denied a patent on it.[2] 'This is impossible,' the German parent examiner apparently told him, 'we can't patent impossible things.'[3]

Brandenburg, one of Seitzer's PhD students, was brought onto the project, alongside a team of between ten and fifteen other audio researchers. His doctoral thesis was focused on audio compression.[4]

Brandenburg says it took until 1986, when computer technology was at a level to make more things possible tied around the discipline of psychoacoustics (essentially understanding and isolating what the human brain hears and does not hear, meaning extraneous elements can be stripped out to help shrink file sizes). Psychoacoustics had been conceived by Eberhard Zwicker ('an obsessive investigator') and Seitzer had been his protégé, passing on this deep interest in the subject to Brandenburg.[5] The world they existed in was small and self-referential.

At this stage, work on the core idea of what was to become the MP3 began in earnest and was when the first patent around this simmering new format was awarded.

Brandenburg gave NPR a neat synopsis of what he was working on. 'Others had the idea that we really should use psychoacoustic use and knowledge about what we hear, what we don't hear – so-called "masking," that sometimes we hear something, sometimes it's masked by other sounds,' he said. 'With this system I gained, on the one hand, efficiency – being able to reduce bitrates for the music, the compressed music – on the other hand, I got the flexibility to adapt better to the properties of the human auditory system.'[6]

In 1987, the Fraunhofer Institute for Digital Media Technology in the Ilmenau Technical University, based in central Germany, 'began researching high-quality low bit-rate audio coding' wrote *Tech Times*. 'It was called the EUREKA project EU147, Digital Audio Broadcasting.'[7]

In January of the following year, an international team called the Moving Picture Experts Group (MPEG for short) was convened following a request by the ISO (International Organization for Standardization) to put out a call for standards in audio encoding. In April 1989, Fraunhofer was granted a patent in Germany for what became the MP3.[8] At the same time, teams at Philips and Bell Labs were also working on similar ideas. In total, fourteen different groups working on the same core idea submitted their technologies to MPEG.[9]

Brandenburg completed his thesis in 1989 and joined Fraunhofer, having been guided there by Seitzer, who oversaw the department and was fired up by the progress he saw Brandenburg making here.[10]

Brandenburg did not, at that stage, have wild ambitions for what he was researching and studying during his PhD. 'In 1988 somebody asked me what will become of this, and I said it could just end up in libraries like so many other PhD theses,' he told the BBC in 2003.[11]

There were two routes that the development of the audio compression could have taken: for audio to be streamed by an end user from a central server, as Seitzer had originally conceived; or for the audio to be transferable to a user's computer where it would be stored locally for playback.[12]

Brandenburg said that his colleague Leonardo Chiariglione had 'the vision that [audio] standards could be useful' and cites him as a key figure here. The original application was around video on CD-ROM, but there was also an audio subgroup within MPEG and they worked through different iterations – Layer I, Layer II, Layer III.

'[M]ost of our ideas went into the modes of compression in MPEG audio. . . which was the most complex one and the one giving best quality at low bitrates – that was called Layer III,' said Brandenburg.[13]

There had been rolling experiments to compress music across a wider variety of genres – except rap. This was because one of the Fraunhofer team, computer programmer Bernhard Grill, apparently disliked the genre. Grill also went beyond music and included recordings of 'fast talkers with difficult accents', as well as bird calls and crowd noises, to really push the limits of the experiments.[14]

Famously, the a cappella version of 'Tom's Diner' by Suzanne Vega became the song everyone wanted to crack in its compressed form. 'The way it's recorded – with Suzanne Vega in the middle and a little bit of ambience and no other instruments – is really a worst case for the system as we had it in 1988,' says Brandenburg. 'Everything else sounded quite OK, and Suzanne Vega's voice was destroyed.'[15] The early stereo encodings of the Vega track apparently 'sounded as if there were rats scratching at the tape.'[16]

Due to hard-drive storage limitations at that point, they could only test twenty seconds of music at a time.[17]

Researchers had also tried to perfect compression of a tricky German accent 'that had plagued audio engineers for years'.[18] 'Tom's Diner', however, became an obsession, the sonic Holy Grail. If they could compress that recording and for it to sound *close* to the version on CD then everything else would fall into place.

Brandenburg claims he listened to the song upwards of a thousand times to perfect the compression without gelding the audio. By 1992, after endless tinkering, it was at a stage where everyone involved was content. But then it just sat there. Its antecedent (MP2) was the one that was picked up on. 'In the early days most people, especially people at the big consumer electronics companies, thought that Layer II is a good compromise,' he explained. 'Layer III is too complicated to be of real use. So the first run of applications went to the Layer II camp.'[19]

The MPEG-1 standard was published in 1993, the MPEG-2 standard was developed in 1994 and then published in 1995.[20] These standards were set at such an early stage in the development of the internet and consumer hardware that the developers' notion of interoperability at the time was very different to what we might now expect. 'They were thinking about hardware boxes that might go in professional studios or in people's homes, and of the portability of content within and across industries,' argued Jonathan Sterne.[21]

As an interesting sidetone, Vega actually visited the Fraunhofer Institute, somewhat bemused by the Fraunhofer PR's claim that she was 'The Mother of the MP3' on her way to meet the 'fathers' of the MP3. The team played her various attempts they had made to compress 'Tom's Dinner' and then – in a *ta-da!* moment – played her the final "clean" version, suggesting it was indistinguishable from the CD version.

Vega was not sold. 'Actually, to my ears it sounds like there is a little more high end in the MP3 version? The MP3 doesn't sound as warm as the original, maybe a tiny bit of bottom end is lost?'[22]

The Fraunhofer team reacted as one might have expected if told that the thing they had devoted years to was not as great as they had thought. Vega, herself, accepted 'there is room for subjectivity in this argument' but diplomatically chose to 'back down' in her criticisms of the audio quality of what she had just been played.[23]

Author Stephen Witt suggested that the early signs were far from encouraging, that the MP3 was looking to be doomed to invisibility or painted into a corner of esoterica as it was the passion project only of 'a team of ignored inventors' whose work was 'a blithe attempt to make a few thousand bucks from a struggling business venture.'[24]

There was a lot at stake here as getting an official endorsement from MPEG 'might mean a fortune in licensing fees' (just as Philips and Sony had made vast fortunes from the CD).[25]

Witt also said the MP3 was almost declared dead in 1995 as it was cowering in the shadow of the MP2. The situation was looking final as the Fraunhofer team was 'running out of state funding' and 'their corporate sponsors were abandoning them'. After four years of trying to push it, Fraunhofer had not managed to sign up any long-term commercial customers for the format. It was looking like it would be nothing more than an academic footnote.[26]

(The first sale of a decoder had actually happened in 1988 to 'a tiny radio station run by missionaries on the remote Micronesian island of Saipan.')[27]

A quirk of fate in 1991 had meant Fraunhofer and the MP3 were forever tied together. MPEG ran a competition for audio compression in Stockholm where entries were 'graded against two audio benchmarks' – including an Ornate Coleman solo, a glockenspiel, a recording of fireworks, a ten-second snippet of castanets and 'Tom's Diner' (which was Fraunhofer's suggestion).

MPEG's team of judges listened to, and meticulously rated, all the submissions and came to their conclusions. It was 'a statistical dead heat' between ASPEC (backed by Fraunhofer, AT&T, France Telecom and others) and another team called MUSICAM (with backing from Philips and Panasonic among others).[28] They were both miles ahead of the other entries. In April 1991, MPEG publicly issued its endorsements. Moving Pictures Experts Group's Audio Layer I was a compression method 'optimised for digital cassette tape that was obsolete practically the moment the press release was distributed.' Audio Layer II (eventually known as MP2) was for MUSICAM. Audio Layer III (eventually known as MP3) was for Brandenburg and Fraunhofer.[29]

This resulted, against MPEG's original unifying intentions, in a war between the formats. MP3 might have been technically superior but MP2 'had name recognition and deeper corporate backing.'[30]

Academic Jonathan Sterne noted, 'Layer II was less complex, and therefore less taxing on computers (a concern in 1992). It was also less susceptible to transmission errors in digital audio broadcasting, but it did not compress data as efficiently as Layer III, which meant that a Layer II file of the same sound quality as a Layer III file was bigger.'[31]

A number of competitions in the next few years had Audio Layer II and Audio Layer III pitted against each other. Audio Layer II was picked for uses such as digital FM radio, DAT, CD-ROM and Video Impact Disc. Audio Layer III was repeatedly overlooked, often dismissed as 'too complicated.'[32] The biggest blow came in early 1995 when Audio Layer II beat out Audio Layer III for the audio track for DVD players.[33] Fraunhofer looked like it was out of the race.

Luck came in the shape of Telos Systems, which became MP3's 'first – and for some time, only – enterprise-scale customer', with the company commissioning hundreds of Zephyrs (MP3 conversion boxes 'the size of VCRs') that could stream MP3 audio in real time.[34] They were then licensed by Telos to the National Hockey League in North America for use in its arenas.[35]

Niels Rump had joined Fraunhofer in 1992 as an intern and became a member of research staff in 1995 before being promoted to business relationship manager in 1997. He was not involved with the development of the MP3 in those early years but was keenly aware of what the engineers were working on.

He was, he admits, not immediately sold on the idea.

He says, 'At that stage, I thought, "What a strange idea of compressing music. We have a wonderful format – the CD. Why would you ever want more than that?" I then started to be reeled in in 1994.'

The MP3 compression technology meant that file sizes were dramatically squeezed down, 'compressing CD-quality sound into a file just one-tenth the size of the original with a marginal loss of fidelity.'[36]

Running parallel with all this, Rump became involved with MODE (Music On Demand), an EU project that was coordinated by Dagfinn Bach. 'That project tried to develop an online music trading system where consumers could buy music,' explains Rump. 'But the crucial point was we wanted to make sure that consumers couldn't just rip off the music and run away with it.'

From here a slow move towards DRM (digital rights management) around files was starting to happen and Rump became the lead developer at the Fraunhofer IIS (Institute for Integrated Circuits) for this DRM system.

Norwegian telco Telenor was involved. 'We started to develop the online platform and the secure wrapper and that was what I was doing,' says Rump. 'The secure wrapper where you needed to have special software to unlock to be able to hear it.'

How Fraunhofer made the MP3 software available worked in a bifurcated way that reflected the type of business model they saw for it. Encoding tools and software (i.e. taking a source song and compressing it) would be expensive as they would be used by large companies; decoding tools and software (i.e. taking the encoded files and allowed them to be converted back into audio that users could listen to) would be cheap. Big businesses would effectively subsidise the end users.

There was a push by Brandenburg to court the home user with this new technology. He got Bernhard Grill to create a PC-based application that could encode and also play back MP3s. This was created in a few months and called the 'Level 3 encoder', or L3Enc for short. The program was small enough to fit on a floppy disc.

'L3Enc represented a new paradigm of distribution,' wrote Witt, 'one in which consumers would create their own MP3 files, then play them from their home PCs.' The arrival in 1993 of the Pentium chip from Intel was pivotal here as it was the first mass-market processor that could play back an MP3 without stalling.[37]

Brandenburg, in a major gamble to boost the MP3's profile, decided to give the L3Enc encoder away for free, putting the file on thousands of discs and tossing them around like confetti at trade shows in 1994 and 1995.[38]

Ricky Adar had founded 'digital jukebox' Cerberus, which was almost bought by Sony in 1994.[39] He met with Brandenburg to discuss the possibilities of the MP3. 'Do you realize what you've done?' Adar presciently asked Brandenburg. 'You've killed the music industry!' Brandenburg was dubious and felt that this was something the record business could work with not against. Adar, who had spent two years locked in futile negotiations with labels to try and get them to license to Cerberus knew the labels would be horrified at what the MP3 represented.[40]

A last roll of the dice came when Brandenburg asked Grill to make an MP3 player that would be bundled with the new Windows 95 PC operating system.[41] The WinPlay3 took a month to write and was, again, small enough to fit on a floppy disc. The story runs that all file formats on Windows 95 had to be truncated to three letters – hence '.mp3'.[42] Someone on the Fraunhofer team said there was 'a window of opportunity to let MPEF Layer III become the internet audio standard.' The christening of '.mp3' would help streamline that process.[43] There was also an unforeseen numeric benefit. MUSICAM also had to truncate its file name to '.MP2.' 'While the two technologies were bitter rivals that had been developed in parallel, the naming scheme implied that the MP3 was somehow the MP2's successor,' noted Witt, 'a misconception that worked in Fraunhofer's favor.'[44]

Sterne added, 'The name served several functions at once. It promoted Fraunhofer's technology; it made uses and applications easier to track; and it concretized the format in the minds of users. An MP3 was a thing, like a .doc or a .pdf. Naming the format helped demystify and make banal digital audio for users: your word processor documents are .docs, your spreadsheets are .xlss, and your music files are MP3s.'[45]

(Sterne also argued that it was surprising that MP3 won out over MP2. 'Given the much greater power and influence of Layer II's backers, we might have expected Layer II to win the day in the marketplace,' he wrote. 'By some measure, it was a wonder that Layer III became a successful commercial format at all, much less a household name.')[46]

WinPlay3 was what was dubbed 'crippleware' (a term that would be unthinkable today). This meant it could play twenty songs and then stop operating. It could only be reactivated if the user paid a registration fee to Fraunhofer in exchange for a serial number. This was not exactly a hugely successful strategy and sales only managed to 'trickle in.'[47] Encoding licences originally cost $125, but by the middle of 1995 this had plummeted to $12.50 and by the end of the year was reduced again to $5. On a dedicated site launched in late 1995, the L3Enc encoder was available for DOS, Linux and Windows – but not Apple as it was deemed to have such a tiny share of the home computer market as to not justify the time and effort needed to create specific L3Enc software.[48]

L3Enc was 'shareware' and offered for free as a way to demonstrate what it could do. Fraunhofer encouraged people downloading it to share with others and, if they really enjoyed using it, to send back a payment, payable by mail or by fax, of eighty-five deutsche marks. It was a stiff. In its lifetime, says Witt, the L3Enc demo generated less than $500.[49]

Winamp was one of the earliest pieces of consumer-facing decoding software to connect with a mass audience. It was set up by Justin Frankel from Arizona, then 19 and described as a 'college dropout and programming genius.' Winamp quickly became 'the first standard for playing MP3s online'.[50]

Brandenburg said, while there were patents around it, they made a conscious decision to not go after freeware authors, although Winamp did eventually pay a patent fee.[51] The US patent for MP3 was granted in November 1996.[52]

1996 was a significant year for the format as it was almost the year it was put to sleep. That was despite it having been licensed by both Microsoft, for an early version of its Windows Media Player, and WorldSpace, for satellite radio broadcasting.

'The overall revenue from these deals was modest – enough to justify the technology's continued existence, but not enough to justify the thousands of man-hours and millions of dollars Fraunhofer had spent in development,' noted Witt. Fraunhofer's plan was to migrate its very small customer base to the second-generation AAC (Advanced Audio Coding) format. It had submitted AAC for standardisation towards the end of 1996, the plan being for it to take over and make the MP3 obsolete.[53]

Indeed, some involved in the development of the MP3 'consider it a technological compromise at best' and preferred the format they were designing to supplant it. '[They] will freely laud the superiority of their AAC [. . .] codec, which was developed after the MPEG-1 standard was set.'[54]

Everything steadily rumbled along. . . until it got hacked. Brandenburg claimed that in 1997 a student in Australia bought the professional-tier L3Enc encoding software. Except they paid for it with a stolen credit card from Taiwan. 'He looked at the software, found that we had used some Microsoft internal application programming interface. . . racked everything up into an archive and wired some Swedish site, [and] put that to a US university FTP site together with a read-me file saying, "This is freeware thanks to Fraunhofer".'[55]

The Internet Underground Music Archive had been set up in 1993 and had initially been using MP2 but switched to MP3 after the 'thanks to Fraunhofer' leak.[56] This helped set the format on a course towards wide adoption by music obsessives online.

There was, however, an even earlier leak in 1992. A demo version of the software had been issued that allowed music files to be converted into MP3. A version was held on a server at the University of Erlangen in Germany but it was hacked by SoloH, the online name of a Dutch hacker, who copied the MP3 code, revised it and then shared it online so other hackers could further tinker with it.[57]

Niels Rump had the job of trying to sell the encoding software, with the demo version intended to give users a tantalising taste for what was possible and then they could ideally be upsold to the premium version. It did not quite run as smoothly as they intended.

'The codec [the coder-decoder] wasn't very good,' says Rump. 'It was deliberately bad because we wanted to sell the code for the good encoder. But we realised that people didn't really care. Bad quality was good enough and, frankly, if you have your normal speakers in your laptop, at least in the late 1990s, quality was pretty crap anyway, so you wouldn't hear much of a difference.'

Sterne wrote that '[t]he term *MP3* entered into wide journalistic use' in 1997.[58] It got its first substantial mention in a major media outlet in May 1997 when *USA Today* wrote about the rise of music piracy on university campuses. It reported that David Weekly, a Stanford University student, had been uploading music files to his own personal web server that ran through the university's system. There were two thousand visiting it daily. The demand was so heavy it was accounting for '80 per cent of

Stanford's outgoing network traffic.'[59] By 1998, its uptake had snowballed to the point where 'MP3' was one of the most-searched-for terms online.[60]

As a foreshadowing of what was to happen over the coming years, attempts to stop it being distributed anywhere online proved impossible and calls for people to not use this stolen software were roundly ignored. 'He gave away our business model,' bemoaned Brandenburg. 'We were completely not amused.'[61]

It was not just Fraunhofer's business model that was at risk of being given away.

Marking the 25th anniversary of the naming of the MP3, I wrote a piece for *The Quietus* in 2020 arguing the MP3 was the single most important format in the music industry's history.

'No other music format since the phonograph in 1877 has had anything even approaching the profound impact that the MP3 has had on the music business,' I proposed. 'All formats before the MP3 were designed specifically to plump up the profitability of the music business; the MP3 ripped it to shreds.'[62]

For good measure, I added, 'The MP3 kicked the legs from under the record industry and then offered it a highly conditional route back to recovery at a fraction of the size of its bloated peak as the 1990s wheezed towards their close.'[63]

The team at Fraunhofer was horrified that their creation could be used to pirate music. They reported some of the hackers of the codec and arranged a meeting with the RIAA, offering up the copy-protectable MP3 as proof they wanted the format to only have legitimate uses. The Fraunhofer team was urging the RIAA to get its member labels to adopt the format and get legal download offerings out in the market.

The RIAA did not bend to Fraunhofer's demands and Witt offers a number of possible explanations as to why. Firstly, to adopt MP3 would have been expensive in terms of licensing royalties and Fraunhofer would have benefited enormously. Secondly, the RIAA could not demand its label members do anything that was deemed commercial as it was up to each of them what they should do. The third theoretical blocker was that studio engineers and others felt the MP3 was sonically lacking and they said it should not be embraced.[64]

Fraunhofer had already spoken to the record industry in the early 1990s to explain what they were doing and what the wider implications would be – namely that anyone using the software could rip a CD into a file so small it could be shared via email or online.

'There was not that much interest at that time,' Bernhard Grill, one of the team at Fraunhofer, told Steve Knopper. 'Oh, there were some meetings, but not with the top hierarchy. They didn't realize how fast the internet would grow. No one saw it coming that fast.'[65]

One such meeting was with the IFPI and its approach was to try and pressurise Fraunhofer into retreating on MP3.

Paul Jessop, chief technology officer at the IFPI, outlines its barely believable shuttle diplomacy displayed on a trip to the Fraunhofer offices that he took with Mike Edwards, director of operations at the IFPI.

'We flew to Germany to talk to Karlheinz and Niels to say, 'You know, this MP3 thing? Just don't. [Laughs] I'm thinking I can't believe we're being this crass! But that's what we'd been told to do. "Go and tell Fraunhofer to withdraw MP3".'

The labels soon blamed the MP3 for its locust effect on their profits, but Brandenburg himself did fantastically from the royalties that came to him as the dominant name that appeared on all the patents for the format. 'His personal economic stake in the MP3 project was enormous,' wrote Witt.[66]

It was widely licensed to dot com companies, software companies, chip manufacturers (for PCs and MP3 players) and more. Names such as Amazon, Apple, Microsoft and Motorola were among the most obvious to license it, but other less obvious names like Airbus, CNN and Mattel also licensed the MP3.[67]

Thomson, with its stake in the format and acting as the licensing representative for Fraunhofer, was heavily pushing it.[68]

Henri Linde, its VP of intellectual property and licensing, was relocated to California in April 1999 to do deals. In the first four years of him working on licensing, he had signed under twenty deals. In the next four, he signed over six hundred.[69]

By the end of 1999, Fraunhofer was reported to be making $100 million annually from licensing the MP3. It would continue to make similar sums every year for at least the next decade. Jonathan Sterne suggested that all the companies with a stake in the MP3 format were seeing a windfall of 'hundreds of millions of euros' every year.[70] [71]

Sterne, writing in 2012, stated that the assorted MP3 patents remained Fraunhofer's main revenue source. 'Their value derives from the MP3 format's ubiquity. But this ubiquity is the result of a confluence of sanctioned and unsanctioned markets.'[72]

*

While the music industry was perhaps not as attuned to what was happening as it could have been, and deluded enough to think this could all be *de*-invented or at least put on ice, nascent internet communities, among them musicians, were becoming increasingly intrigued by this format and what they could do with it.

Rob Lord and Jeff Patterson were studying computer science at the University of California-Santa Cruz. Patterson was also in a band called the Ugly Mugs while Lord was studying psychoacoustics. They had found the MPEG specifications online and taught themselves to encode music as MP2, posting the files on Ugly Mugs internet newsgroups, including one of their songs with the delightful title of 'Cold Turd On A Paper Plate.'[73]

They were soon contacted by people from around the world asking for them to post more music. This led to them starting the Internet Underground Music Archive, where unsigned bands could post MP2 files of their music. '[T]hey had the foresight to stay away from copyrighted music owned by major record labels.'[74]

Lord clearly had incredible prescience and understood completely the implications of all this. Speaking to the *San Jose Mercury News* in 1993, he proclaimed, 'This is going to kill the music industry.'[75]

MP3 was still far from a mainstream idea at this stage because, for the most part, it required high levels of technical know-how to get it to work.

Ian Rogers was working with the Beastie Boys and posting live recordings online for them in the mid-to-late 1990s. He joined Nullsoft, parent company of Winamp, in late 1998.

He outlines the esoteric nature of the technology at the time. 'The thing is, and people forget this, in 1998 if you're like, "Hey, here's an MP3," you also had to be like, "OK, to play this MP3, first of all, you're going to need a sound card." Because your computer didn't come with a sound card. Your sound card didn't come with a speaker. To get music to come out of your computer was hard. To rip a CD, it was from the command line. You ripped the CD from the DOS command line and you had to get the MP3 codec and all this shit.'

Software like Winamp was designed to open up the possibilities of MP3 and digital music to a mass audience without them having to do a computing degree or teach themselves code. It was only in making music in a digital form frictionless that it could hit critical mass. A company like Winamp was not looking to disrupt old business models: it just wanted to open digital music to everyone.

'If you look at what we were interested in, we weren't interested in changing the music business,' says Rogers. 'We didn't care. We just wanted to listen to music. We wanted to help other people listen to music.'

A large part of the record industry's opposition to the MP3 was the fact that it was uncontrollable. Hilary Rosen, president and COO of the RIAA, adds another argument: it was sonically lacking.

'Everybody hated MP3s because MP3s were really terrible audio quality,' she claims. 'It insulted artists, who'd spent hours and hours with their producers in the studio mixing the best quality music they could. Whereas MP3s were so compressed, it took out the highs, it took out the lows, it took out the nuance.'

This may, of course, be historical revisionism because the sound quality on MP3s was not much different from the sound quality on the file formats being offered by other technical partners that were assisting the record industry in its push towards DRM.

Cary Sherman makes the point that the industry was, at this stage, too focused on protection and sonics to really grasp what it was that was drawing consumers to the format.

'At the time that MP3s came along, labels believed – they were wrong – that nobody would pay for an MP3 file instead of a high-quality master on a CD,' he says. 'The quality sucked! The quality was awful. For the record companies, and music people generally, the holy grail was better and better quality: making it sound like you were in the studio with the artists. That's what they thought people wanted. It turns out that people wanted free much more than they wanted quality.'

FROM THE LABORATORY TO SEDITION: THE MP3 BECOMES THE RECORD INDUSTRY'S BÊTE NOIRE

How 'MP3' became shorthand for 'piracy' within the music industry is a long and sinuous story. The fact the record industry was not involved in its development, and hence it stood outside of their control, was obviously a major strike against it. The fact that DRM was not the default setting also caused consternation among those at record labels who understood the wider implications of this technology in the wild.

The matter was confused further by the fact that there was nothing inherently wrong with the underlying technology, but there were enormous fears over how copyrights could be abused by it. So the MP3 was simultaneously good and bad. But, as far as the major label record industry was concerned, this philosophical dichotomy was not even worth engaging with: to them, MP3 was *all bad*.

The industry's view on MP3 was almost immediately curdled on encountering it and the following years saw a mounting war on not just the format but also what the format represented.

By 1998, the MP3 was firmly in the record industry's crosshairs and a propaganda war against it was moving into full swing. Trade titles like *Music Week* and *Billboard* would often refer to it with a prefix like 'controversial file format', essentially parroting the hardline stance espoused by record companies and trade bodies like the RIAA, IFPI and BPI. This was unquestionably an orchestrated smear campaign.

In August 1998, for example, *Music Week* ran a cover story about the introduction of the MPMan, the first MP3 player on the market, and carved out a multitude of caveats in its coverage.

'The MP3 technology it uses for compressing digital files is used almost exclusively for music piracy on the internet,' it wrote. It noted that the IFPI was estimating there were eighty thousand infringing MP3 files online at any one time and this was being used as an argument against MP3 players being made available (more of which below).[76]

The following month, tied to the launch of the Diamond Rio MP3 player, *Music Week* was calling it 'the controversial MP3 technology.'[77] In December 1998, *Billboard* was writing, 'MP3 technology continues to draw fire as the preferred tool of Internet pirates.'[78]

There were some attempts from companies working with digital music to try and rehabilitate the format and accentuate the positives – as long as MP3s themselves could be brought to heel.

Rick Fleischman, Liquid Audio's senior marketing director, told *Billboard* in February 1999, 'We are trying to build a bridge between MP3 and legitimate content providers. We felt like we needed to embrace MP3 in a way that is responsible so we can start to work past the problems because of the stigma associated with it.'[79]

The same month, Bill Woods, marketing communications director at Liquid Audio, told *Music Week*, 'MP3 music has been branded as stolen goods, but it doesn't have to be that way. We are bringing some legitimacy to it.'[80]

This was a point that was reiterated by Cary Sherman the following month in *Billboard* when he said, 'We are trying to salvage a legitimate marketplace before MP3 piracy takes over.'[81]

The digital Cold War played out across the music trade press throughout the late 1990s. It was a fight over semantics, with business publications complicit in pushing the major label agenda here. It also crept into wider technology titles with a whole new type of frenzy being whipped up around the mushrooming number of MP3 sites.

In October 1999, *Wired* reported that the BPI in the UK was 'targeting MP3 sites that suck users into pornography loops.' It expanded on this: 'The BPI said it will specifically target music sites that use pornography as an advertising vehicle, and claimed that music pirates on the Net are "luring users to sites using the names of stars, but then are forcing the user to watch horrific scenes of teenage sex as part of the process of accessing the illegal music for downloading".'[82]

It quoted Emma Fanning of the BPI on the nature of this insidious piracy/pornography crossover. 'It has always been the case that piracy has links with pornographers and organized crime,' she said. 'I am afraid nothing has changed in the internet age. But what is most repellent about this is that it is clearly likely to attract the younger user.'

Wired added the IFPI, which estimated that over a million illegal music MP3 files had been posted online, was filing cease and desist letters against a multitude of site operators.[83]

By November 1999, Jay Samit, SVP of new media at EMI, was underscoring the scale of the problem as the industry saw it. 'A billion songs were downloaded this year without paying anybody,' he told the audience at the Music Biz 2005 industry conference in California.[84]

Ted Hooban, director of digital media at CDnow, countered with the argument that free downloads, as long as the labels and their artists were complicit in making them so, were a catalyst for sales.

'Using free digital downloads as a mechanism for merchandising album releases, we noticed that when we gave away digital downloads for Sugar Ray or Todd Rundgren, we saw upwards of a 100 per cent increase in sales [for those acts] during the promotion,' he said.[85]

Despite the occasional voice like Hooban's, the overwhelming amount of coverage around MP3s in the trade press was not just negative, it was outright scaremongering.

Jay Berman, chairman and CEO of the IFPI, says his stance at the time was that MP3s were a clear and present danger for the global record business. 'I think it was an existential threat because it wasn't just a format change,' he proposes. 'You went from something that was physical, regardless of what it was, to something that was intangible. That was pretty monumental.'

Edgar Bronfman Jr, who had acquired PolyGram in 1998 and, in a single move, turned Universal Music Group into the biggest of the majors, felt MP3's biggest threat was that it was largely circulating without DRM. For an industry predicated on control, a format that was inherently uncontrollable was hugely alarming. He claims this was exacerbated by the fact that there was no digital distribution process in place to paid download services that met with the majors' approval.

'The technology wasn't there,' he says. 'The only technology that existed was the MP3 technology which was, by definition, unprotected. Therefore to license our catalogue to an MP3 distributor, regardless of whether they thought they were collecting royalties or not, was not, we thought, really a good thing.'

Jollyon Benn, internet investigations executive at the BPI in the UK, believes an anti-MP3 stance was being hardwired into much of the record business by this stage. He laughingly references a mocking image, designed to look like a propaganda poster that might have been issued by the RIAA, that was frequently posted online in the early 2000s. Created by ModernHumorist.com, it shows a young man wearing headphones and using an iMac while a satanic figure in Russian military uniform rests a clawed hand on the youth's shoulder and watches what he is doing on screen. 'When you pirate MP3s,' it says, 'you're downloading communism.' A hammer and sickle are included in the artwork for maximum impact.[86]

'There were people in the industry who thought, "MP3s are evil",' says Benn. 'What they meant was just the ubiquity of them. Just the fact that they never degraded in quality through their transmission. They were really genuinely seen as an evil thing because, "We couldn't lock them down! There was no DRM on them! There was no way of monetising them!"'

Mike Edwards says the industry belief that MP3s be 'regarded as an instrument of crime' sometimes flipped over into a type of hysteria previously never encountered by people working in the anti-piracy sector.

'During one of the more frenzied European anti-piracy meetings, one of the national group guys said, "I'm going to go and get the police to arrest anyone they see walking down the street listening to an MP3 player",' he laughs. 'It was that bad. The record industry felt under siege. MP3 was the devil's work.'

Jonathan Sterne has argued that digital piracy has to be understood in different terms from other types of theft. Indeed, he asserts that it is not theft or piracy in the traditional sense that the record business understood it.

'The MP3 is a *nonrivalrous* resource because from a user's standpoint, making a copy of an MP3 for someone else doesn't deprive the original user of its use,' he writes. 'An MP3 costs almost nothing to make and reproduce – once someone has invested in a computer, software, a relatively reliable supply of electricity, and some kind of internet connection (because of these costs, we cannot say that it is truly free even when it is not directly purchased).'

He continued, 'An MP3 is a *nonexcludable* resource because it is impossible to prevent people who haven't paid for it from enjoying its benefits. Borrow a CD, rip it, give it back. Now you and the original owner can both listen to the music. Share your MP3 through a peer-to-peer network and millions of others can listen to the same recording at no direct cost to you, or to them (though even this apparently free transaction requires the initial investments listed above).'[87]

Rump feels that Fraunhofer managed to avoid being tainted by its association with MP3 and, as such, sidestepped the record industry's opprobrium. The format, not the format's developers, took the political hit.

'Despite MP3 being controversial, or being the bad thing, Fraunhofer never really was the bad boy,' he says.

In a battle for hearts and minds, associating MP3s almost exclusively with piracy – which was in turn associated with organised crime, which was in turn associated with nefarious pornographers – was a very deliberate play, the whole intention of which was fixing in people's minds only negative associations with the format.

RIO GRANDSTANDING: TRYING TO DEFUSE THE MP3 PLAYER GRENADE

As MP3s were a string of zeros and ones, they were, for the major labels, an invisible enemy. You could not actually hold them. And if you could not hold them, then it was going to be impossible to crush them.

The arrival of MP3 players, however, gave this intangible threat a tangible form. In Chapter 1, Warner Music lawyer Cliff Fluet described the Diamond Rio as being viewed like a 'grenade' by senior executives at the company. Between 1998 and 1999, the industry attempted to tackle it, convinced that if they could decommission its perceived threat then MP3s themselves would be neutralised.

The first MP3 player to hit the market was the MPMan (or the MPMan F10 to give it its full title). Developed by South Korean company Saehan Information Systems, it was unveiled in March 1998. It had 32MB of Flash storage – 'enough for a handful of songs encoded at 128Kb/s'[88] – and initially sold for $250.

Its arrival in the UK in August 1998 was big enough for it to make the front cover of *Music Week*, but a large proportion of the news story was concerned with highlighting the wider record industry's concerns about it and intoning its uptake, despite the fact it only held an hour of music, could serve only to normalise a growing culture around unlicensed MP3s on the internet.

Nic Garnett, IFPI director general and chief executive, told *Music Week*, 'At this stage the MPMan has to be a major concern and we are looking into the legal situation.'[89]

It was the Rio, however, that was to spark a complex and fraught legal action from the US record industry. Developed by Diamond Multimedia, the Rio PMP300 launched in summer 1998 and retailed for $199, undercutting the MPMan by $26, and came with a CD featuring two hundred licensed tracks from MP3.com and GoodNoise, quaintly described by *Music & Copyright* at the time as an "Internet record company".'[90]

The device's arrival in the UK in September 1998 was met with industry ire. The IFPI called it 'damaging' for the industry, arguing MP3 is basically a pirate format. Mike Edwards, director of operations at the IFPI, told *Music Week*, 'Definitely at this stage it is doing more harm than good. Wherever we find these devices being marketed illegally we will take action.' Given the right to reply, Ken Wirt, Diamond's VP of corporate marketing, countered, 'We're not promoting the illegal use of music. With the Rio, we've included two hundred songs from unsigned artists who want to distribute their music via MP3.'[91]

The major labels felt they had a strong case against the Rio. 'At the time, the RIAA argued that every MP3 file was an illegal copy because of the lack of any "legitimate" MP3 retailers,' wrote David Arditi, 'by that argument, the Rio PMP300 was capable only of playing illegal files.'[92]

In October 1998, the RIAA and AARC (the Alliance of Artists and Recording Companies) secured a TRO (temporary restraining order) against Diamond Multimedia. This was expected to remain in force until a full hearing of the case would happen.

'The RIAA and AARC claim that the Diamond Rio MP3 player violates the 1992 AHRA [Audio Home Recording Act] by encouraging consumers to infringe the copyrights of artists by trafficking in unlicensed music recordings on the Internet,' reported *Music & Copyright*. 'Under the AHRA, manufacturers, importers and distributors of digital audio recording devices have to pay a royalty fee to rights holders and incorporate a Serial Copyright Management System into copying devices to stop the making of second generation copies.'[93]

Diamond argued that the Rio was only a playback device, not a recording device: as such, they proposed, it was not subject to the AHRA.

The RIAA said it had wanted to avoid litigation and to reach a solution with Diamond without going to court.

'This isn't the step we wanted to take,' insisted RIAA president and CEO Hilary Rosen to *Variety*. 'We wanted to have a constructive dialogue. Unfortunately we needed to have that conversation before they shipped the machine. By shipping the product, they are threatening legitimate online distribution.'[94]

Coinciding with the launch of the Rio in the UK in late October, Rosen also spoke to *Music Week* about the ongoing court case and the reasons for it. 'This is not an anti-MP3 action,' she said. 'They (Diamond) are going out to market at a time when the majority of MP3 files on the internet are not legitimate.'[95]

By the following month, however, Diamond had won a reprieve when Judge Audrey Collins of the US Central District Court of California rejected moves by the RIAA and AARC to slap an injunction on sales of the Rio. The RIAA and AARC said they planned to appeal but, meanwhile, the Rio could continue to be sold to the public.[96]

Cary Sherman, senior EVP and general counsel at the RIAA, said, 'We think the judge made an error of law.' He added, 'Everybody has a moral obligation to protect creative works and we want to engage in a dialogue with these companies. We are doing everything we can to move this process along.'[97]

In May 1999, *Music Week* reported that over twenty-five thousand Rio devices had been sold so far that year in the UK, and over 200,000 had been sold globally. It was referred to as 'the controversial product' and the publication noted it was being heavily advertised in the national press, including in *The Times*. Tiny Computers in Surrey was offering it as part of a 'complete entertainment system' for £1,526. That package was made up of a Rio, a computer, a DVD drive, a CD-R and software to make custom CDs.[98]

'THE INTERNET MUSIC REVOLUTION IS HERE. SEE AND HEAR IT FIRST AT TINY' ran the ad in screaming upper case. 'RECORD DIGITAL QUALITY MUSIC FROM THE INTERNET. PLAY BACK ANYWHERE. CREATE YOUR OWN CDS. LATEST MP3 TECHNOLOGY.' *Music Week* noted that the ad carried 'a small disclaimer' saying it was unlawful to record copyrighted material without permission.

The BPI argued it normalised piracy.

Jollyon Benn, the BPI's internet investigations executive at the time, said, 'We are not happy about it, though we are pleased to see they have put a message in there about copyrights.' A Tiny spokesperson responded, 'We are taking advantage of technology that is already there. We are not condoning piracy. If the ad is slightly controversial then that is the way it is sometimes. We've checked it legally and we were happy to go ahead.'[99]

In a plot twist, Diamond Multimedia claimed it did not approve of the Tiny ad. Neil McGuinness, PR manager for Diamond in northern Europe said, 'It's a good ad but unfortunately it wasn't given to us to proofread.' He then added, one imagines with a highly raised eyebrow, 'They probably could have been a wee bit more diplomatic'.[100]

The player was seeping into the public consciousness and was treated in some quarters as a welcome and iconoclastic force. Reviewing the Rio in May 1999, *Q* magazine called it, in what one presumes to be ironic quote marks, 'The New Punk Rock!' and added that it and the rapid multiplication of MP3 sites online had combined to mean 'the music industry has been rudely awakened from its technophobic slumber.'[101]

It was all over for the RIAA and AARC in June 1999 when the 9th US Circuit Court of Appeals ruled in favour of Diamond and insisted that the Rio did not violate the 1992 Audio Home Recording Act (AHRA). 'Because the Rio cannot make copies from transmissions or from digital music media such as CDs and tapes, but instead can make copies only from a computer hard drive, it is not a digital audio recording device,' it said in its ruling on the case.[102]

The appeals court upheld a lower court decision. '[It] found the Rio is not an audio recording device and that its time-shifting and space-shifting functions are legal under fair-use provisions in copyright law, including the Audio Home Recording Act,' reported *Billboard*. The ruling essentially extended the 1981 Betamax decision around fair use exemptions for home recorders.[103]

Diamond pushed the line that this was a victory for the average music fan as it clarified a consumer privilege that the RIAA had long argued did not exist.

'The court has endorsed the point that it is entirely proper for consumers to make copies of digital recordings that they own or have acquired properly,' said Andrew Bridges, one of Diamond's legal team.[104] Dave Watkins, RioPort president, added, 'We always believed the device operated well within the law.'

The RIAA said it was 'looking at the [court's] decision and considering its options but, legally, it had run out of road.[105]

There was a sense of disbelief across parts of the industry that the case, a case they were convinced was inarguable from any position other than their own, did not go their way.

'The Rio case was a bad decision,' insists Mike Edwards today. 'It's always easy to be wise after the event. But it was a bad decision, I thought, from a legal point of view.'

Talal Shamoon, then vice president of InterTrust, says anyone taking a longer view of technology and legal matters may have seen that the industry did not necessarily help itself here.

'The way Diamond got out of jail was using the Betamax verdict,' he says. 'In Betamax there's a thing called time shifting. The court basically said it was fair use. The consumer had the right to time shift. Diamond's defence was based on this idea of space shifting. You bought the disc. Well, you want to listen to it somewhere else. Fair use is not a law. It's not a right. It's a defence. It falls in the "I know it when I see it" category that a judge and a jury can interpret, like intent. It's like, dude, people have been recording music on cassette tape since the 1960s. You never said anything about cassettes. You complained *a little bit*.'

Matt Oppenheim, SVP of business and legal affairs at the RIAA, feels Diamond won 'under an esoteric part of the copyright law' and that the decision to initially bring it under the AHRA was something of a legal gamble with a broader ambition.

'Nobody had ever brought a case under that before,' he says. 'That statute was basically unexplored. So you have this decision that comes out; whether the decision is right or wrong doesn't matter. Even if the industry had won, it would have just led to royalty systems. So it really wasn't going to stop the device from being sold. The idea was to have some way of legitimising the industry.'

Oppenheim says the bigger contextual issue was that portable digital music players were coming into the market at a time where there were no legal download services for people to go to in order to buy legitimate content to put on the devices. (There were legal services in 1998 and 1999, just not any that the majors had licensed their content to).

'Everybody was competing to try to find a way to offer legitimate music online,' he says. 'And everybody had different formats and different codecs and different DRMs. It was completely disjointed. The market wasn't established yet. So we had these devices that were coming out and the concern was that they were going to drive an illegal market. So then the issue was that these devices weren't tied to any kind of legitimate marketplace. So the question we were trying to answer was: how do we stop devices that aren't connected to a legitimate marketplace from being distributed?'

He says that the music industry should have been a partner to these companies – to work with them to help build a legitimate market – but they chose to operate in isolation from the music business.

'In the industry's mind, if you're going to come out with a device, you should be working cooperatively with the industry to figure out how that device is going to work and how we are going to deliver content to it,' he says. 'These companies – Diamond Rio just happened to be the first in line – were coming out with these devices and they were discarding the idea that there should be any cooperation with the industry at all.'

While the RIAA argued that devices like the Rio were coming into a market where no legitimate download services were in place, it actually directly inspired the launch of one such service in the UK.

Jonathan Davis had been working as a marketing manager at Perfecto, DJ Paul Oakenfold's record label in London, and then went on to create the *Back To Mine* compilation series for DMC. He read about the Rio in *Music Week* in 1998 and got a colleague in the US to buy one for him. (They were not on sale in the UK at this point).

'I was probably one of the first people in the UK to have one,' he claims. 'It was just a moment. I was just like, "Oh my god! This is a mind-blowing piece of technology. This feels like a real change in the way that I can carry music around with me".' For me, that was the trigger point to then start talking to other people that I knew in the music business and the technology business. I'd show them this player and talk to them about what that would mean for the future of music and how music was consumed and moved and how people carried it around with them.'

His evangelism was such that he was convinced this was – following on from vinyl, cassette and CD – 'a new medium' for music consumption.

He knew Richard Davies, who was running an internet business in 1998, from his time in the music business and together they began to think of ideas that could stem from the Rio.

'I went to see Richard and we started having a conversation about music and MP3 and hardware players and software and the internet,' he says. 'Then we started looking around for where people could download music in the MP3 format in November 1998 from UK companies. And there really wasn't anywhere to download music.'

This led to them quickly building the idea for Crunch (later to be renamed iCrunch) in January 1999. By March 1999 it was open for business. Inspired by MP3.com and GoodNoise, it sold MP3 downloads for £0.99 each, mainly from independent dance labels to begin with. 'It was the UK's first MP3 download site offering signed artists,' he says. 'That was our point of differentiation.'

He says most people in the British music business at the time were not attuned to download culture and so early talks were part business development and part education, with his Rio becoming totemic for him and a way to quickly articulate the core idea behind Crunch.

'The majority of people that I was visiting in independent labels and major labels didn't know what it was,' he says. 'They'd never had their hands on an MP3 player. So when I was taking them the Diamond Rio and showing it to them, they were having their first experiences with it. We had a UK major label come and visit us to get a demonstration of how to download music from the internet and what an MP3 player was. We were part of early education – on educating colleagues within different labels about what it was and what it could mean for consumers. Some of those conversations went on to become licensing agreements. But many of them, certainly within the major labels, it was just like, "Great, thanks for telling us!" and then [sound effect to suggest they left the room swiftly] zzzoooooom!'

The loss of the case against Diamond and the Rio in 1999 was to prove significant in both the immediate and the long term. '[I]t signals a shift in power between the consumer electronics industry and the recording industry as consumer electronics manufacturers were no longer dependent on agreements with the recording industry to create content to play on their devices,' wrote David Arditi in 2015. 'Whether or not record labels agreed to have their music reproduced in digital files was irrelevant to whether or not music listeners would have music to play on digital devices.'[106]

Hindsight is a cruel master and devices like the MPMan and Rio – and others that followed in their wake like the 30GB Personal Jukebox, which came out of Compaq's Systems Research Center in 1999[107] – are looked upon retrospectively as limited, limiting and clunky, especially when held up against Apple's iPod, which arrived in October 2001. Steve Levy, in his book on the iPod, dismisses its progenitors as clunky and where 'novelty was their main, if not their only, virtue.'[108] He is especially harsh on the MPMan, calling it 'a flash-in-the-pan' but begrudgingly calls the Rio 'a stumpy little box that held only twenty-four songs but was a pioneer nonetheless.'[109]

Indeed, Apple's designers and engineers used the Rio as an example of what *not* to do when they were refining the iPod. 'We would sit around and say, "These things really stink",' said Phil Schiller, head of global marketing at Apple at the time. 'They held about sixteen songs, and you couldn't figure out how to use them.'[110]

(As an interesting historical sidenote about the long gestation period of the iPod, buried in a feature about download standards in April 1999, *Billboard* made a passing reference to an industry rumour that was currently circulating: 'Apple is also researching development for a Macintosh-compatible portable music player, says the source. An Apple spokesman declined to comment on pending availability of these products.' This was two and a half years before the iPod officially launched).[111]

CHAPTER 7

Shaking the Temple's Pillars: MP3.com's Onslaught on the Old Business

(Old control starts to wobble)

It began as a way to promote a nascent search engine but soon became the fly in the record industry's ointment, its latest adversary.

Michael Robertson, living in San Diego at the time, had set up www.filez.com, a search engine for software, in January 1997. By May that year, it was handling seven million search requests a month.[1]

'We were just like any other search engine, only we indexed FTP servers instead of web servers,' he says. 'I used to watch the list of what was the most popular, which a lot of people do. But what was most interesting to me was what was on the bottom of the list that was never on the list before. If you're an entrepreneur, that's the goal. If you miss that, it's too late, it's over.'

A curious category started to appear in his monitoring of search requests: MP3. 'I knew nothing about it,' he explains. 'I was like, 'Oh, it's just random constants and a number.' But I knew that if people were searching for it, it could be a marketing draw for my search engine.'

Filez was based on a pay-per-click business model and Robertson understood that anything that could drive more traffic would likely boost the company's revenues. Curious about this new alphanumeric thing that users were searching for, he looked more deeply into it. It was to be that lightbulb moment every entrepreneur is questing, and praying, for.

He says, 'I remember downloading my first song and going, "Holy smokes! This is incredible." At the time Real Audio was the state of the industry, which was nice. It was technically astounding to be able to send audio – and, of course, video eventually – through the internet, but the fidelity wasn't great. But with MP3, the fidelity was phenomenal. I'm like, 'Wow! This is going to change everything".'

He cannot remember exactly what song he downloaded first to deliver this Damascene moment, but knows it was 'a classic jazz song' – possibly 'Four Play' – as that was what he was interested in.

Smelling a whole new business opportunity, he paid $1,000 to purchase the domain name MP3.com, founding the company with Greg Flores, and started courting musicians. They were mostly, according to music writer Fred Goodman, unknowns and this made the site 'the world's largest repository of garage bands, aspiring professionals, and weekend warriors.' If it was all about scale, it meant that 'the very occasional gem was buried underneath ten tons of junk'. Goodman adds that, as long as MP3.com did not host any of the acts signed to them, the major labels were of the view that it was 'commercially irrelevant' to them.[2]

His blood fired up with the liberating power in the meshing of the internet and the MP3, Robertson wanted to bend the majors to his cause and this set him off on the mission of a zealot. 'I got in my busted up Honda Accord and drove up to Los Angeles to try to convince the record labels that this was the future,' he says.

He met with three different major labels but says, for the most part, 'they were entirely dismissive' of what he was enthusing about, in a large part because it was a new world he believed they could not wrap their heads around as well as being an assault on the very foundations of the record business.

'What I was up there saying was, 'Hey, I know the centre of your music universe right now is a stack of CDs on your oak cabinet. But that's all going to move to the PC. It's all going to be digitised. It's all going to be on demand. You can make your own list of songs and you can send them to friends and control what songs are played and in what order.' All that kind of stuff. It was so funny because the objections were things like, "Well, this is crazy. Most computers don't even come with sound cards." That was one of their objections. Which was true.'

The more the labels shrugged or pushed back, the more Robertson was convinced he was really onto something. 'They couldn't see the future,' he says. 'Which is why entrepreneurs always have an advantage. We see the future.'

In 1998, fizzing with the possibilities, he went out to try and raise money for the company. Silicon Valley was giddily going through the first dot com bubble, although no one yet knew it would burst in early 2000. This was a time when investors were lining up to invest in anything digital. Robertson knew momentum was on his side.

'I was seeing what was happening up in Silicon Valley with a lot of digital music companies,' he says. 'I was watching MP3.com and saying, "Well, we have more users, more traffic, more revenue, more everything than those guys – so it should be easy".'

It was not *exactly* easy. He first met with VCs in San Diego as they were local to him.

'I said I would give them a killer deal,' he explains. 'I'm going to raise $3 million at a $7 million pre-money valuation, which means that they would get 30 per cent. There is pre-money and post-money. All the San Diego VCs said no. I was really irritated because I was seeing what was happening up in Silicon Valley and I knew that my proposal was way below market, that we could raise far more money. But my thinking was that I would go with such a great deal, with such compelling stats, that they'll jump on it.'

Rejection followed rejection. Robertson dug his heels in. He focused on building traffic, seeing that metric as validation that would, eventually, draw investment.

Just before Christmas 1998, he got a phone call. Sequoia Capital had bitten.

'They said, "Are you interested in taking money?" I was like [non-committal voice], "Well, yeah, you know if it was right, but, you know, it's not a huge focus of ours." They said, "Will you come up and do a presentation?" I said, "Yeah, but let me be clear here. We're focused only on growth. We don't have this big glossy presentation that looks like I spent a ton of money on graphic artists." They said, "Don't worry about that. Just come up and just tell us your story".'

The meeting took place in San Francisco on a Monday morning as that was when the company's partners met each week.

Doug Leone had been at Sequoia since 1988 and had seen a lot of pitches in that time.[3] He was the first person at the table to move.

'I saw him pass a note,' says Robertson. 'He'd written something down and I saw it move around the table. It was a big table with twenty guys around it and I'm up there talking. After I got funded, I went to a partner who was on my board and I said, "Hey – what did that note say in that meeting?" He said, 'Oh, it said, "Fund these guys".' Here's where the story gets really crazy. They take me out to lunch right after the meeting and they say, "We're really interested. We're going to give you a term sheet." I said, "Great, super." I fly back to San Diego. When I landed, I had an email. I looked at it and they had already sent me a term sheet.

I told them I wanted $10 million because I knew from watching and from observing that the more money you ask for it, the more seriously they take you.'

He says the $10 million offer was based on a $12 million pre-money valuation for the company. Sequoia also wanted exclusivity and a no-shop clause for sixty days, meaning Robertson could not speak to other companies about investment in that lock-out period.

He considered the offer and decided to play hardball, getting his lawyer to say he would take $10 million, but not on a $12 million valuation. He wanted a *$40 million* valuation. Sequoia wanted control of the board. Robertson said they would only be a minority shareholder. As for the no-shop clause, he said he was going to shop the company to whoever he wanted, even as the Sequoia negotiations were happening.

'My attorney goes, "Michael, you don't really understand. This is Sequoia Capital. This is the premier company that's done Oracle and Apple and HP and Cisco. While there's some movement for negotiation and for terms, they're not going to triple your valuation." And I said, "Fine, then they don't do the deal. They called me. I didn't call them".'

He threatened to leave the law firm unless they put a different attorney in place for this deal. A new attorney was duly appointed and he presented all the points Robertson was inviting on to Sequoia. 'And – *bam!* – we had the deal done in three weeks.'

(It was actually reported at the time that Sequoia invested $11 million in the company. *CNet* called the investment 'a milestone in the evolution of the MP3' but added that it was 'scorned by many in the mainstream recording industry because it is favored by music pirates.'[4])

Robertson says he was able to hold his ground as the data on the service and the user numbers, not quixotic forecasts, proved every claim he was making. The data was, he says, incontestable.

He says, looking back, that he understands why the major labels were so resistant to working with him. The MP3 was like foundation rot in their corporate headquarters.

'This was the heyday of the record label business because it's CDs,' he says. 'You had to pay sixteen or twenty bucks for one or two songs. When I talk with people and they say, "Oh, the record labels were so dumb. Why didn't they see MP3 or the internet?" I remind them that if you were sitting at the boardroom for any of the majors, at that point in history your number one goal is to keep everything exactly as it was. They were making such huge profits. Any change that threatened that, or potentially threatened that, you would oppose. That explains why they were so resistant to MP3 or any technology. When I went up there, and I was talking to record labels I'm like, "Hey, guys, imagine this. Imagine a music store in every person's house. You think you sell a lot of music now? What if there's a music store at every person's house?" And they were like, "Nah – get out of here! That's crazy talk!"'

He says MP3 sat at the intersection of two cultures: the traditional record business and Silicon Valley. That was its blessing and its curse. Silicon Valley loved it for the disruption it would cause; record labels hated it for exactly the same reason. If Robertson was going to pick a side, it would be with the former.

'Those were two separate worlds,' he says. 'They were sort of bumping into each other, but they were not intersecting in any meaningful way. What I mean by that is that Silicon Valley didn't care about the record labels. Did not care one bit. They didn't know how many major record labels there were, couldn't name them. They didn't care about that.'

There was, in many ways, a guerrilla war being waged by MP3.com against the entrenched thinking at the record labels. Unlike others, such as Liquid Audio, who were recruiting staff from the major labels, MP3.com had a HR policy of *not recruiting anyone* from the record business. 'Their instincts were 100 per cent wrong,' insists Robertson. 'Because they didn't understand the internet.'

He did, however, recruit Doug Reece, a writer on digital for *Billboard*, when the Sequoia investment happened, so he was not totally against getting staff from the wider music business establishment.[5]

This strategy, he says, was both beneficial and deleterious. 'We were the only digital music company out there that didn't court the music industry, didn't hire people, didn't hire consultants and worked with the same attorneys,' he says. 'We weren't playing the game of trying to be friends. That put us at great odds.'

He feels it was the right decision to protect what he believed to be the soul of the company. He felt the wind of change was blowing in his favour and that it would eventually force the majors to capitulate.

'I didn't expect to ever work with the major record labels,' he says. 'I didn't need them, as far as I was concerned. I wasn't going to court them. If they were going to work with us, it was going to be on our terms, not theirs. And by the way, they did eventually.'

He says an ongoing frustration was that the major labels did not grasp – or were not set up to handle – that the internet was borderless. The old system of territorial licensing and releasing of music was rendered irrelevant by the internet.

'When they came to me and said, "We can give you the rights to play this song in the USA, but not Canada," I was like, "Get out of here, man! It's the internet! The song goes on MP3.com and it's available to be listened to by everyone in the world or I'm not putting it on." They said, "Yeah, but the way we've done our licence . . ." "Yeah, whatever. That's the old world. Don't care. We'll leave that behind".'

He says MP3.com became the antithesis of the record business and that was going to be its ideological and commercial stance. 'Every decision that we made was the opposite of what they made,' he insists. 'But I knew I was right because we were doing an internet approach. They were doing their old business on the internet; their record label business on the internet.'

This antithetical stance also mapped across to the contracts they offered artists wanting to post their music on the platform. Unlike the majors, who typically offered artists contracts that held them for years and where the label owned all the masters, MP3.com contracts were such that acts, if they were not happy with what they were getting, could walk away when they wanted and take all their recordings with them.

'This was such a dynamic change and it really set the whole tone for how the industry online went,' he says. 'Prior to this, it was all about, "Hey, I'm going to do a deal but I'm going to get your rights at the end. I'm not going to tell you that. I'm going to soft sell that part of it. I'm going to focus on your advance or your tour support or whatever. But at the end of the day, I'm going to get your rights." I said [to artists], "I don't want your rights. We're not going to take any of your rights. Any time I'm not giving you value, you can leave. So if you want to graduate to some other service that's serving you better, go for it." But I knew they wouldn't leave because we had all the fans. That's the bottom line because, with people on the internet: wherever the fans are, that's where all the value is.'

Richard Robbins, COO of MP3.com, was also forthright in his views, insisting that the labels were deluded to think the MP3 was not going to fundamentally change them. 'The revolution has already been won,' he told *Billboard* in March 1999. 'MP3 is not going to ruin the music business, but the nature of the business is changing, and the [music industry] is scared. Internet users will buy what they want to buy, and they'll take for free what you give them.'[6]

In May 1999, MP3.com filed for an IPO (initial public offering) which was the typical route of startups as they looked to raise their profile and put a rocket under their growth potential. (This was often under pressure from early investors who wanted to see a fast return on their investment – often through a dangerously inflated valuation).

'Controversial Web site MP3.com' is how *Billboard* referred to the company in its coverage of the IPO. It reported the company was seeking to raise $115 million and that No Limit Records (home to acts like Master P and Snoop Dogg) would get $2.5 million in stock in exchange for the rights to a number of its recordings. As part of the deal, No Limit acts would be expected to display MP3.com signs at their concerts and participate in the site's chat rooms.[7]

The validation of an IPO helped to legitimise the service – with music publishers at least. In June 1999, ASCAP signed what was classed as a 'comprehensive' licence to allow 'unlimited interactive performances' on MP3.com of ASCAP-cleared copyrights. An ASCAP radio station, featuring music from ASCAP writers, would also be launched on the MP3.com site.[8]

Despite the validation, Hal Bringman, PR for MP3.com, said the IPO was really the end game for the company. '[T]here was no vision after the IPO,' he said. 'Michael Robertson, when they asked him what kind of business he was in, said they were in the IPO business.'[9]

Analyst Mark Mulligan claimed that MP3.com woke up the record industry 'to the immensity of disruptive force the internet could wield' and that it 'took the concept of online music to the mainstream consumer.'[10]

Despite some acceptance from the traditional music business, MP3.com could not stop itself from poking the hornets' nest and making a virtue out of its pariah status.

In the 28 August 1999 issue of *Billboard*, it took out a full page ad for itself. The entire page was a devilish red with a small box in the centre, much like the health notices on a packet of cigarettes. It read, 'WARNING: MP3.com has been found to be addictive. Prolonged use may lead to considerable discovery of new music. If conditions persist, increase dosage.' The only other copy on the page beyond this tongue-in-cheek message was the MP3.com logo and its website address.

This was the company on manoeuvres, like a foreign power televising the testing of its warheads. It was deliberately using the US music industry's own 'bible' to show that it had so much money for its growth that it could afford to spend it on frivolous things like advertising to the very people trying to crush it.[11]

There was sporadic coverage of MP3.com in *Billboard* throughout the remainder of 1999, much of it showing, undoubtedly to the major labels' chagrin, that it was growing, it was doing deals and it was very much not going away.

At the end of October, it was reported that MP3.com's stock had jumped to $46.8125 a share and that it would be providing the source music of thirty tracks from MP3.com artists for *First Wave*, Francis Ford Coppola's new TV show.[12] In the same issue of *Billboard*, it was announced that MP3.com (now referred to as 'Wall Street darling') and new company myplay.com would offer users online storage for files.[13]

Myplay offered users 250MB of free memory (enough storage for sixty-seventy songs) as well as fifty free tracks by acts like Kid Rock, Public Enemy, Chris Rock, Buckcherry and Aimee Mann. MP3.com would offer 50MB of free storage (enough for around an hour of music).

Michael Robertson, hinting at a move from ownership to access that would really gather pace the following decade, told *Billboard*, 'This moves digital music forward by making it live on the Net instead of just on the PC.' This would be a foreshadowing of what MP3.com was planning later in the year with MyMP3.com.

As was the case with almost every VC-backed company at the time, profitability was not the definitive metric of success. Losses were, for a while anyway, happily stacked up as long as user growth was increasing. It would be a maxim Jeff Bezos was to take stratospheric with Amazon, itself slowly moving into music retail in the late 1990s: scale first and worry about profits later.[14]

To that end, MP3.com posting a loss of $19.9 million for the three months ending 30 September was not a cause for concern. Despite this loss being significantly up from the losses of $33,341 reported for the same period in 1998, it was not really seen as anything out of the ordinary or something to be unduly worried about. In the dot com boom, huge losses for startups were expected. It was alleviated somewhat by the fact that revenues were up $276,577 to $4.05 million in the same period.[15]

It would have been out of character for MP3.com not to do something that year to irk the majors. And so it was with the launch of a new feature called Payola. The nomenclature was designed to bring back mortifying memories of the scandals that ripped through the record business in the

1950s and again in the 1980s where labels were accused of bribing radio stations and DJs to play their records.[16]

The Payola feature for MP3.com was somewhat more benign. It was an auction program for artists to bid on 'advertising placement on any of 13 genre Web pages', limiting them to ten slots on each genre page each week.[17]

The wilful goading of the industry by MP3.com did not come out of nowhere and was, in many ways, an act of defiance, an act of resistance, an act of disobedience.

Robertson is adamant there was, at the senior level, record label resistance to MP3.

'All the major record labels, their new artists divisions were all fans of ours,' he claims. 'For sure. But [some] senior execs [were against us] – and I'd probably say senior-execs-slash-legal-department. I would not underestimate the power of the legal department to dictate how record labels are run. [Some executives] were incredibly resistant. Incredibly resistant.'

He says he had booked a booth at a music conference to promote MP3.com but soon got a call to say, sorry, your booth is no longer available. 'They said, "It's not going to work out. We have got to cancel your booth." I was like, "Alright, whatever".'

He says the conference was under 'enormous pressure from the industry not to validate MP3 in any way.' His approach, he says, was to 'go renegade' and attend the event anyway but with everyone in the team wearing T-shirts with a 'Who Invited These Guys?' slogan on the front and walking around handing out flyers about MP3.com.

He claims he was also removed in advance from a conference panel and 'given some "the dog ate my homework" kind of story' as to why he was not allowed to participate. He was allowed, however, to put a CD of acts using MP3.com into the delegate bags as well as a flyer saying 'MP3 is not the devil.' He was also permitted to ask a question after the main panel discussion – the one he was not allowed to sit on the stage for. He had a Barnumesque plan up his sleeve.

'Albhy Galuten is up there,' says Robertson of the panel. 'He's a very famous producer. Speaking to the audience, he said, "There's this technology that lets you encode an audio CD into MP3s that sound great, and then you can email them around." And I yell from the audience, "It's in your bag! It's under everyone's chair." There's three hundred people reaching under their bag and pulling it out!'

He is then permitted to ask his question. He quickly twigged that his pariah status was complete as far as the old record business was concerned. And he revelled in it.

'I get up and I give a little soliloquy, and they start booing!' he laughs. 'The audience started booing. That plus meeting with them, in the early days of driving my beat-up Honda Accord up there [Los Angeles], I knew these guys were never going to work with us. Never, never, never, never. Every second that we invest, every dollar we invest, is going to be wasted. We've got to go to the internet and build from that and let them come to us when we're sufficiently big enough to be meaningful. That was our approach.'

Robertson claims that while certain industry voices were opposed to MP3, some labels divisions were incorporating it into their daily jobs, notably A&R.

'While the official position of the major label was that they were opposed to MP3, every new artists division that they had was all over MP3.com looking for those new artists to sign,' he says. 'The top guys were like, "Our official position is we hate MP3!" All the new artist people would come down to our office. Maroon 5 and a whole generation of artists started on MP3.com and were found by the major record labels on MP3.com because of the success they had.'

He says the company was not territorial about the acts it was helping to break. MP3.com was always going to be their starting point, not their end destination. To Robertson, their success was merely proof of concept for MP3.com.

'We didn't say, "Maroon 5 is ours. You can't have them." We were like, "Hey, go for it. That's a feather in our cap if you sign them to your label. That just shows that what we're doing is reaching people".'

In late 1998, *Music & Copyright* was reporting on MP3.com's claims that major labels were stopping artists from releasing music, for sale or for promotion, on MP3.[18] This helped paint an image of the MP3 and, by default MP3.com, as iconoclastic and dangerous. Maybe even sexy.

'They were throwing lawsuits and they were threatening partners,' claims Robertson of how the major labels were responding to his company. 'If you worked with us, they would really put the hammer on you. So whether you were an artist or whether you were a manager or whether you were a retailer, or a conference, if you worked with MP3.com, they were using their incredible leverage to try to block us.'

Cliff Fluet says that there were very firm orders from the very top at

Warner that MP3 was not to be entertained as a format in any way, shape or form. It was deemed to exist beyond the pale.

'We used to get lots of memos every couple of weeks about what you could or couldn't do,' he says. 'Anything that involved MP3 was banned. Any system that worked on MP3 had to be cleared at all of the upper levels within the business, it had to be cleared by everyone. There really was a bogeyman view of that phrase. And there was a real smackdown on that phrase.'

The more the old industry attacked MP3 and tried to blacklist it, the more validated Robertson felt. If the labels hate it, he reasoned, it had to be good. 'Looking back on it with history, it was obvious now that MP3 was going to win,' he says, 'but it was not obvious at that conference.'

The romance of the entrepreneur is that they have the prescience and the tenacity to deliver to the future to everyone. Any resistance they meet along the way is sparked by fear, ignorance or both. It seems that Robertson fully buys into this deification of the entrepreneurial ideal but accepts that it comes with as many strengths as it does flaws.

'It was exciting, it was fun, it was explosive, it was a great time for me,' he says of his years running MP3.com. 'But it was a real battle. It was a bit lonely, I must say, because I can't stress enough that we were one of the few people that didn't court the labels. We were looked at as the pariah, the outsiders. Luckily for me, I'm a fighter and I'm not swayed by public opinion. If I know and believe one thing, I'm going to go in that direction.'

Jeremy Silver, himself working in digital at EMI in the US at the time, was one of the few senior label executives who – if not officially and publicly, due to industry politics – supported much of what Robertson was doing and proposing. In his book on the digital era in music, Silver talks of Robertson's 'cult following' and how he would go to industry conferences and lay into 'the luddite, fan-unfriendly music industry with a witty and campaigning spirit.' He even goes so far as calling him 'the hero of the MP3 nation.'[19]

Scott Cohen, co-founder of The Orchard, believes Robertson to be a catalyst for enormous change and upheaval in the record business. But because he was so early on much of this and the first out of the trenches, he took most of the bullets.

'Michael Robertson – fuck, the music industry hates him,' says Cohen. 'Because he was just shooting off his mouth, not scared and speaking the truth. He doesn't get enough credit for what he did to change the industry. Before Napster, he was the one that really shook it up.'

Tim Westergren, at the time working on the idea that would become music recommendation and discovery company Pandora, praises Robertson for defiantly swimming against the tide and for looking to shake up the consensus in the record business.

'Michael was taking a sledgehammer to those guys,' he laughs. 'He was fighting and he was constantly poking the bear. Because he owned that site [MP3.com], he became a very influential representative of digital music.'

Westergren does, however, understand why the industry wanted to neutralise the threat of companies like MP3.com.

'There are a lot of folks who, in hindsight, knocked the music industry for not embracing things more quickly,' he says. 'It's so easy to say it in hindsight, but it's hard to not get into a defensive crouch when you're up a tree and someone's at the bottom of the tree with a big saw! I don't know who in that position would have the calmness and patience to say, "Oh, we don't need to do anything. We should encourage that guy to saw faster and we'll find a different tree." That's hard to do.'

Robertson himself feels, absolutely, that something needed to come along and show there was an alternative to the old record business – that the internet was allowing the building of whole new futures. Even if his economic, technological and moral crusade failed, he felt it would be a glorious defeat.

'When people look at why I did MP3.com, specifically about the lawsuits, some people would say we were reckless,' he says. 'To me, if you worked with the record labels, you were just standing on the train track ready to get run over. You had to move fast in a direction and hope it was the right direction! Working with the labels, to me that just felt like standing on the tracks. The record labels were not going to willingly empower another technology company or another retailer in their business. They weren't going to do it.'

GENUINE MUSIC COALITION: THE WORLD OF MP3 TRIES TO VALIDATE ITSELF

In a move to try and legitimise, or at least *destigmatise*, the 'MP3' name, the Genuine Music Coalition (GMC) was set up in January 1999 by just shy of fifty companies in and around digital music distribution, including MP3.com, GoodNoise, Diamond Multimedia, Sub Pop, Rykodisc, Tower Records, Best

Buy and CDnow. Their focus was to promote the MP3 format and counter the wider record industry's attacks on it. It came after the establishment of the MP3 Association in October 1998, led by Diamond Multimedia when firmly in the crosshairs of the RIAA-led litigation against it. It launched with much noise but quickly went quiet.

The GMC was a second swing by those looking to push the positives of MP3 against the major labels' war against it. It was not just a PR exercise. Those signing up had to 'guarantee that music issued by its members' was legitimate. It would also use watermarking developed by Liquid Audio to stem online piracy of tracks.[20]

'The watermark will contain a unique serial number, copyright information and links to the copyright owners Web site(s),' wrote *The Register*. 'In effect this creates yet another downloadable music format, one that's halfway between "pure" MP3 and Liquid Audio's MP3-based Liquid Tracks format.'[21]

Interestingly, given how much Fraunhofer and others were making from licensing of the MP3, the Genuine Music Mark could be encoded in downloads royalty free by GMC members. The files would be compatible with all existing MP3 players. 'The Genuine Music mark is certainly a big step in the right direction to provide better copyright protection for the MP3 format,' said Karlheinz Brandenburg of Fraunhofer.[22]

The Genuine Music Mark was described by the GMC as 'a seal of authenticity' and something which 'provides consumers with confidence that the content they downloaded is authentic'. A logo would appear on music player software to guarantee it was not pirated, acting as a guarantee to consumers.[23]

Given that it launched as the majors were focusing on SDMI (see Chapter 10), it was always going to be doomed to exist on the margins. Those signing up to the GMC fully understood this. As *CNN* noted, 'Coalition members readily admit that this deal will not single-handedly pull the record industry off the fence and into large Internet investments. The only thing that could do that, jokes MP3 CEO Michael Robertson, is "a million zillion dollars".'[24]

The RIAA did, however, politely – but conditionally – welcome its arrival. 'We applaud any effort that helps consumers distinguish between pirate content and legitimate content,' it said in a statement. 'It's a step in the right direction to creating a legitimate online marketplace for promoting and distributing music.'[25]

John Schuch, COO at Sub Pop and one of the GMC members, outlined the tightrope that independent labels were walking here. They wanted to protect their copyright, but equally they understood that consumers were embracing MP3. 'Technology is morally neutral, and I think a lot of energy has been expended in condemning a technology [MP3s] that our customers seem to enjoy,' he told *MTV*. 'But we're also fully cognizant of the copyright issues that the majors are concerned about.'[26]

Rick Fleischman, senior marketing director at Liquid Audio, argued that the GMC and SDMI were effectively singing from the same hymn sheet. Indeed, Liquid Audio was a member of both. 'You can look at this as a building block,' he said. 'Obviously a key element of SDMI is security. For the major labels, to release content on the internet, they want to have some sort of security mechanism in place. What we're talking about here doesn't involve security, it involves authentication.'[27]

Given the majors were panicking throughout 1999 that if security was compromised then so too was their control over the market. For them, authentication was a sop and was never going to trump their eternal desire for the security of control.

I WANT MY MP3: REPOSITIONING THE FORMAT THE RECORD INDUSTRY HATED SO MUCH

Robertson was the most visible, and the most vociferous, supporter of MP3, but there was a groundswell of support for the format happening around him through 1998 and 1999.

In late October 1998, MP3.com was joined by Diamond Multimedia, GoodNoise and digital software companies MusicMatch and Xing Technology to create the self-explanatory MP3 Association. *MTV* reported that they would 'promote the controversial format as the next step in digital-audio distribution' and their goal is 'to educate consumers about the legalities of MP3 use.'[28]

Wired added that the MP3 Association wanted to push legitimate and licensed downloads and 'educate users about music piracy.' Gene Hoffman, CEO of GoodNoise, insisted they wanted to work with the industry. 'The distribution of music to other people is not legal, and artists should be compensated,' he said. 'We want to see what we can do to help the RIAA.'

There would, the body said, be an outreach programme to universities where they would undertake on-campus promotional activities to educate students about music rights and music distribution.[29]

IT'S NOT THE SIZE OF THE THREE-HEADED DOG IN THE FIGHT, BUT THE SIZE OF THE FIGHT IN THE THREE-HEADED DOG: THE TRAILBLAZING EFFORTS OF CERBERUS

One of the earliest movers here was Cerberus Jukebox, set up by Ricky Adar (real name: Richard Faria) in the early 1990s. It had file protection systems in place as well as an online payment system. It approached record labels early to secure licensing deals but, because it was so early, these negotiations were fraught, protracted and incredibly one-sided.

It quickly attracted the attention of Sony Music and, in September 1994, it was reported to be looking to acquire the company, or at least licensing it. That was, of course, contingent on the labels working out exactly how something like this could be licensed.

Steve Hodges, music development manager at Sony UK, told *The Independent*, 'The people who would hook into this over the internet are the same people to whom we are marketing.' He had sent his report on Cerberus to the Sony board, but admitted that Adar and what he was doing had spooked the labels somewhat.[30]

'They are a very bright bunch,' said Hodges. 'Mr Adar knows what he is talking about. He is a sort of techno-punk, quite anarchic, but what they are trying to do is very interesting.'[31]

Adar, however, was not looking to be absorbed into a major label. 'I am not interested in being bought out by a major record company because that would put the digital domain in the same position as today's music business,' he insisted. 'It's imperative that Cerberus remains completely independent.'[32]

The Sony acquisition did not come to pass, but true to his 'techno-punk' and 'anarchic' nature, Adar seemed to enjoy the consternation within labels that he was creating, even going so far as to proclaim himself the Noah-style saviour, rather than the destroyer, of the major labels as the digital floodwaters were rising around them.

'I think some major record labels have been a bit panicky,' he told the *Chicago Tribune* in January 1995. 'But our view is that we're building an ark for the industry. As far as we're concerned, we are giving the artists and record labels a future, one that doesn't involve the development of millions of pirates and people copying songs without any royalties being generated for the artists concerned.'[33]

The business model for Cerberus would be a per-download fee set by labels, with users able to hear snippets before buying. He would also make money, he hoped, by selling promotional/advertising space to labels (calling it 'virtual real estate, really'). Magnanimously, unsigned bands could get this for free, but Cerberus would take a cut of any sales that followed.[34]

The company offered a free music player for users to install on their computers to manage and play back their digital libraries. He did, however, reveal that a track download would take on average twenty minutes. Even this early into the digital music story, Adar had his eyes on a bigger prize than downloading: he was aiming for a streaming-based service. 'In eighteen months, Cerberus will be able to transmit music on-line in real time,' he insisted.[35]

Gavin Robertson, new media and research and development manager at PRS/MCPS in the UK, dealt with Adar, helping him get a pioneering deal in place with music publishers where they and songwriters would get 'mechanicals' (essentially a fee paid for the right to reproduce a piece of music on a sound carrier, be that an LP or a download).

'The first licence MCPS did was for ringtones, basically charging a mechanical for the right to make a copy of a ringtone,' says Robertson by way of set up. 'Every time the telcos or the services sold a ringtone, MCPS got a fee for that. That was one of the first official available licences. All the other licences were custom agreements with specific services. Cerberus was the big one. Although Liquid Audio and Real Networks are remembered as the early ones, Cerberus was a country mile ahead of all of them at that point. Ricky spent a fortune working with MCPS on the first licence. And it was like a telephone directory. Honestly. If you dropped it, it would have broken your foot! It was utterly nuts.'

He continues, 'This is one licence for one company to just make mechanical copies. Basically what they were trying to do was to understand all the problems. Poor Ricky never made much money out of it because he was just too early and the bandwidth couldn't deal with it.'

In May 1997, *Campaign* reported that Cerberus had secured a deal with EMI, possibly with other major labels to follow, and was selling tracks at £0.60 each.[36]

It did get off the ground but its first-mover status was more disadvantage than advantage. The market for buying downloads simply was not there.

Speaking to *Sound On Sound* in February 1999, Adar said, 'The truth of the matter is that we haven't had that many downloads. There is a market on the web – but we don't think it's a market that's going to mature as fast as we'd like.'[37]

A growing wave of musicians were coming out in support of MP3 and the revolution they felt it was ushering in: a revolution of artist empowerment, of breaking the controlling grip of the major labels, of new ways to build audiences.

Chuck D of Public Enemy was leading the vanguard here. The tiny MP3, he said, was going to prove to be the nemesis of the corrupt, controlling and conceited music business.

'They can't stop you from uploading and downloading,' he told the *NME* in January 1999. 'They are running scared. The retail and record companies have scammed the public for years with the CD scandal (*i.e., making something for 50p and selling it for £14 and taking 85–88 per cent of the profits*).'

He added, 'Now with MP3 the chickens are coming home to roost. The industry, as we know it, will flip in the next two years. . . if you can burn your own CD at the crib of the music you like, for $5, why would anybody go to a store to pay $12? Retail, as we know it, is headin' towards the colour of dead.'[38]

In July that year, Chuck D spoke again to the *NME* to expound further on his enthusiasm for what downloading would do to undermine the established music business.

'Downloadable distribution just forces the first two methods, majors and independents, to share the marketplace,' he argued. 'It's a method that helps out the artist and the public, it bites out the middle area of radio, retailer, record labels [. . .] You're gonna have probably a million artists and five hundred thousand labels in five years. I think it's good. I'm like: come one, come all to the download ball.'

He continued, 'People say, "But there's something romantic about going to a record store and looking through all the covers" and I say, "Yeah, because you're from 1968!" You still do the same thing on the computer. Overall it's a good thing for rap music and hip-hop, which is still undernourished as a genre. I can't tell you what it's gonna do for Robbie Williams or Shania Twain, but in my genre, 89 per cent of music is under-serviced to the world, and there's a world appetite for it.'[39]

The same month, he was talking to *Billboard* about why he felt the internet revolution was long overdue and why it would empower artists that had been screwed over by greedy and duplicitous record labels for too long.[40]

He identified two flashpoint moments in the early 1990s. The first was in 1991 when he used the internet to promote a Terminator record.

The second was the sale of 50 per cent of Def Jam to PolyGram for $11 million in November 1994.[41]

'Even though Public Enemy and LL Cool J comprised most of the sales, we didn't receive any piece of that transaction,' he said to *Billboard*. 'I knew that there had to be a better way.'

He argued that the major record labels 'are all run by lawyers and accountants who don't give a fuck about the creative process.' The internet, he suggested, was their day of reckoning. 'They must learn to understand that this is a technology that the public got before they had a chance to control it, as opposed to the other way around.'

He said this meant that, for the labels at least, the 'glory days of 600 per cent profits are over' but he was not worried about his music circulating for free online. 'How can I be mad if ten million people get three of my songs for free?' he asked. 'I have faith that enough people will recognise that artists need income to keep making music.'[42]

Dexter Holland from The Offspring was a flag-waver for MP3s, seeing its rise as an inevitability. The band were making song tracks available via RealJukebox.

'We wanted to do something that allowed us to directly interact with our audience,' he told *Billboard* in May 1999. 'MP3 and the internet have been a real eye-opener for us. . . I guess we really decided to do this after reading that we were the No. 1 most-pirated band on the internet. It's almost as if there's a new global radio station called the internet. This is just a good way to get music across to kids who want to hear it.'[43]

Even though the majors were waging a propaganda war against MP3, some acts signed to major labels were attempting to embrace it – and corporate politics be damned.

In March 1999, Tom Petty put his track 'Free Girl' on MP3.com. Within two weeks, Warner, his record company, asked MP3.com to take it down. It had been downloaded over 150,000 in the first week.[44] Petty retaliated by running a competition on MP3.com asking fans to submit covers of his songs to the site. Warner compromised by allowing Petty's latest album, *Echo,* to be sold via MP3.com (in physical form).[45]

Warner issued a statement in the matter that involved some heavy biting of tongues. 'While we are happy that MP3.com has found a way to work cooperatively with Tom Petty & The Heartbreakers to promote the legitimate sale of their music, Warner Bros. Records Inc. does not endorse the dissemination of its copyrights through any unsecured digitally distributed format.'[46]

Petty joked about the corporate politics behind this in an interview with David Letterman. 'There was a casual elbow in the ribs that "maybe you shouldn't do this, Tom",' he said.[47]

Petty's manager, Tony Dimitriades, commented on the issue in an interview with *Billboard* in June that year. He was ostensibly trying to downplay it but was simultaneously revealing how labels were pulling in one direction here but artists and their managers were pulling in another.

'I wouldn't call it a disagreement with Warner Bros.,' he said. 'The record company's concern is to protect its copyrights. My and Tom's agenda was to do something on the promotional end for the fans.'[48]

This was not to be the only issue of an artist working with MP3.com that Warner was to become embroiled in that year. By some distance, the most high-profile case was with Alanis Morissette having MP3.com sponsor her summer tour of the US promoting her *Supposed Former Infatuation Junkie* album that had been released in late 1998.

'[S]ome labels are faced with the awkward situation of trying to prevent their signed acts from cutting ancillary deals directly with technology and internet companies,' wrote *Billboard*.[49]

Morissette was rumoured to be receiving 'an undetermined financial stake' in MP3.com as part of the sponsorship and Tori Amos, another Warner act, had reportedly been approached to go on the tour.

Maverick, the imprint of Warner that Morissette was signed to, was reported to have held an emergency meeting to figure out how to respond to the move.

Billboard quoted a source close to Morissette as saying, 'The label executives are under an enormous amount of pressure. The A&R people that work directly with artists would love to be doing this, but there are corporate policies that prevent them. . . How bad can it be to experiment with this stuff? Why not try to deal with this consumer phenomenon, which is now at critical mass?'[50]

Albhy Galuten says artists cannot be expected to carry the entire music industry on their shoulders and sometimes business decisions – which this was very clearly – are inherently solipsistic.

'For any other new technology, you make a business decision based on your own business,' he says. 'You could expect Alanis Morissette to say, "This is not good for the record industry in general. If it's good for me, then it's good for me".'

Morissette and her management were treating it all, beyond the not-insignificant issue of stock in MP3.com, as a data-gathering exercise, as they would get email addresses of fans as part of the deal.[51]

'They felt this was an opportunity to embrace the internet,' said Scott Welch, a partner in Atlas/Third Rail Management, the company managing Morissette. 'All of us are in uncharted territory. I think we all are trying to find a way to increase the relationships the artists have with their fans.'[52]

Best Buy also got involved by sponsoring the tour, allowing shoppers in stores to watch a live webcast of performances on the tour.[53]

Paul Vidich was executive VP of Warner Music Group between 1998 and 2004, responsible for its digital strategy and deals. I ask him about the Alanis Morissette/MP3.com deal and how the company responded when the story broke.

He was sanguine about it.

'The artists had a whole different view,' he says of attitudes towards digital experimentation in the closing years of the 1990s. 'The artists were, "We don't care about the future of the industry. What we do is that we care about the future of our next album." You had a lot of artists who were very conflicted about all of this change. Their stuff was being ripped off, but on the other hand, they wanted to see themselves as rebellious.'

Live became something of a focus for MP3.com as it partnered with the William Morris Agency to promote a US college tour, featuring Goo Goo Dolls and Tonic, that would travel around twenty-eight schools from 28 October. There would also be an MP3.com Village at every stop with demos of the service.[54]

In September 1999, TLC partnered with MP3.com to give away their track 'I Need That' on the service. This was part of a wider partnership where MP3.com was also sponsoring their tour. 'It is very important to reach as many people as we can,' said Tionne 'T-Boz' Watkins of the group at a press launch. 'With MP3.com, we can do that all across the world.' MP3.com was also selling advance tickets for the tour and committed to giving $0.10 to the Sickle Cell Disease Association of America every time 'I Need That' was downloaded.[55]

Robertson is less enthused about the TLC deal, suggesting it was more of a statement or positioning piece than anything truly ground-breaking.

He says, 'That one was a little bit more, "Hey, guys, we're here. We can attract interest from the major artists." That one was a little more intentional, in my opinion. It was like, "Hey, guys. We're not going anywhere. We can get the major stage if we want. And the artists know that we have something going on." That one was a little more intentional, I think.'

Later that year, Morissette partnered again with MP3.com to promote her *Unplugged* album. MP3.com offered a streamed version of 'These Are The Thoughts' (the studio version, not the MTV version). An MP3.com spokesman told *Billboard* they had turned down the offer of a different track. 'Maverick and Atlas came to us first with 'Thank U', but they wanted the track to be secured, and that's not what we do,' they said.

Maverick claimed it was unaware of the MP3.com promotion but was offering a DRM-protected download of the song 'Thank U' (but not the version from the MTV *Unplugged* album) to fans pre-ordering the album through a range of retail partners.[56]

Vidich says it is important to remember that within the corporate structure of Warner Music Group there were a series of fiefdoms that sometimes moved collectively, sometimes individually. This meant there was no agreed and explicit policy on how to respond to something like the MP3.com deal with Morissette.

'There was the Warner Brothers label and then you had Maverick and you had Alanis Morissette,' he says. 'If you had five music executives and you asked them their view of what should be done on any individual issue, you'd probably get five different opinions. Because there was no consensus. There were people who wanted to experiment and wanted to take advantage of the technology whose interest wasn't selling the album at hand. There were other people, who may be the head of the label, whose view was, "Well, I can't do it now because, if I do it with you, I have to do it with five others. And then we're going to go down the slippery slope".' He reflects further. 'As you would expect, in a period of rapid change, and chaotic change, there were wildly different views of what was the right thing and wrong thing on individual issues.'

When I interview Robertson in early 2022, I ask him about the Morissette deals and the tailspin they appeared to throw Warner into. He tries to downplay them somewhat.

'Those deals were inconsequential, largely inconsequential, in terms of what they actually did,' he says. 'But they were very consequential because the artists were moving online in spite of the record labels trying to battle against it.'

Then he adds, 'Here's a story. I'm in New York and the guy looks at my bag and it says "MP3.com" and he said, "Hey, that's Alanis Morissette's company!" It was so funny. So I said, "Yeah, you're right." She didn't give us any music. There's no Alanis Morissette songs on MP3.com. We sponsored her tour or something very tangential to music delivery, but you could get a glimmer of what was happening. There were different forces.'

A year after the MP3.com deal, Morissette issued a filing with the Securities & Exchange Commission to sell $1 million of stock in MP3.com.[57]

RUNNERS AND RIDERS: SOME OTHER NOTABLE ARTISTS AND COMPANIES TRYING TO MAKE DOWNLOADS ADD UP IN 1998 AND 1999

- In July 1998, indie act Rialto, signed to China Records, made their track 'Monday Morning 5:19' available as a paid download. 'As the official Chart Information Network (CIN) does not recognise internet sales, there is no chance of the single making the Top 40,' noted the BBC. John Benedict, MD of China, said, 'We as an independent record company are not always in a position to market a single to a level where it is going to be received high in the charts. Because first of all it requires a very large budget and it requires a very substantial level of media and retail support.'[58]
- At the very end of 1999, Tony Wilson (co-founder of Factory Records and organiser of the annual In The City conference in the UK) launched his latest venture, a download store called Music33. The premise was simple: tracks would be sold for £0.33 because people are, Wilson argued, 'fed up with trawling around record shops to find albums which have three good tracks and they're the singles anyway.' The economics were that everything would be split three ways: the site would take 11p from the sale, as would the artists and the record label.[59] (He appeared to have overlooked the publisher/songwriter in this equation, something MCPS were quick to point out (as noted elsewhere in this chapter).) It was not to be, but in typically Wilsonian terms he would have defended it as follows: 'It was a *beautiful* failure, darling.'
- In May 1999, Neil Burrows of Superior Quality Recordings (and manager of indie band The Bluetones) set up an online store selling not just CDs but also MP3s. He told *Music Week* it was designed to have 'the feel of a real record shop' with virtual record racks and something called a 'demo

dump bin' (presumably somewhere for new acts seeking a record deal to submit tracks). Burrows said he was inspired to set up the store after nine thousand of the fifteen thousand UK sales for The Bluetones' single '4-Day Weekend' came via their own site.[60]

MECHANICAL ENGINEERING: PUBLISHERS TRY TO DEFINE THEIR SHARE OF THE INCIPIENT DOWNLOAD MARKET

While much of the digital activity was being driven by, or being held back by, the record labels, the music publishers were keen not to get left behind or badly short-changed here.

In early November 1999, the Mechanical-Copyright Protection Society (MCPS) in the UK – which collects royalties and protects rights for its music publisher, songwriter and composer members – announced it was going to set a mechanical rate for downloads. Its board had 'agreed in principle' that a rate of 10p per download in the UK (for tracks up to five minutes in length) would be applied, increasing by 2p for every additional minute. This was a very different model to the one applied to physical discs, where mechanicals were calculated at 8.5 per cent of the dealer price. It would apply with immediate effect and run until September 2000.[61]

A spokesman for MCPS told *Music Week*, 'There is no precedent here. The board felt it had to put down a marker on a value it believed was right.' Tony Wilson, clearly concerned about the impact on his nascent Music33 download service, said the rate was higher than the average currently for songs delivered in physical form. 'If that's the case then they're ripping off the public,' he said. 'It's disgraceful.'[62]

It was deemed a big enough story to warrant an op-ed from Ajax Scott, *Music Week*'s editor. 'Has MCPS got its sums right?' the headline to his column asked. 'Calculating a new rate where there is no precedent is fiendishly difficult, so MCPS has opted to rip up the rulebook and set a flat fee rather than basing its charges on a percentage of dealer price as currently happens,' he wrote. 'Having done this the issue simply becomes one of where to pitch that flat rate. And it is this that is likely to cause such a fuss in some quarters.'[63]

He calculated that on a 12-track album with a dealer price of £9, a mechanical rate of 8.5 per cent would work out at 6.4p per track. 'The difference between this and the proposed 10p for downloads may not seem like much, but when you think of the hundreds of thousands of tracks that it is predicted will be downloaded in the UK within a few years, the gap becomes far more significant.'[64]

It did not take long for the labels to respond. The independent labels, specifically. AIM, the trade body for the independents, demanded that the MCPS scrap the 10p rate. Alison Wenham, head of AIM, said, 'The whole of 1999 has been about the coming of e-commerce. In that context, I find it extraordinary that no industry discussion has been going on about this.' Chris Martin, director of business affairs at MCPS, countered, 'Before you start talking about something like this you have to have some idea of where you want to be. The technology for this market is not analogous to what is happening at the moment.'[65]

Mainland European societies were also, according to *Music Week*, considering pushing through a rate of €0.20 (equal to 13p) per track, with a sixth of that money covering performance income. *Music Week* added, 'The US Government has set a digital download rate of $0.071 (4.4p) per track or $0.0135 (1p) per minute – less than the MCPS's proposed UK rate – depending on which is the greater.'[66]

Sarah Faulder, chief executive of the Music Publishers' Association, had a letter published in the 23 October 1999 issue of *Music Week* on the matter. Naturally, she and her organisation backed the 10p rate.

'In the internet age, record companies will increasingly be in the rights business, just as publishers are,' she wrote. 'Songwriters, composers and publishers have fought hard over the years to be rewarded for their creative work. It is in all our interests that they should continue to be so rewarded.'[67]

She argued that, because consumers were likely to download individual tracks rather than whole albums, publishers and songwriters needed to be protected. 'The concept of the 10- or 12-track album may not survive,' she said. 'There are implications for all content providers, including record companies who will themselves want to set a realistic royalty on their valuable masters downloaded by the on-line [sic] retailer.'[68]

Faulder concluded, 'A flat rate offers a simple and robust way of establishing that value and rewarding creators – while leaving plenty of room for consumers to benefit from reduced distribution and manufacturing costs.'[69]

Gavin Robertson, new media and research and development manager at PRS/MCPS in the UK, was heavily involved in the trial mechanical rate for downloads. The labels argued there should at least be parity with the rates paid on physical records, but Robertson says the publishers saw it a different way.

'The argument at the time was there was no manufacturing cost, therefore there was a larger chunk of the pie,' he explains. 'And it was an opening gambit. Why not? Publishers have always been underpaid [compared to the labels] – they would argue. But that was the opening gambit. This was the publishers' chance to set their stall in the new world.'

As director of legal and business affairs at AIM, Helen Smith was helping outline the independent labels' opposition to the MCPS rate. 'There were two factors here,' she says. 'One was the process. Should the publishing of digital music be licensed the same way as physical product, or should there be a direct licence? And the second was the rate. What was the rationale for having a higher rate? It's interesting because those arguments have been resurfacing again [in late 2022, when we speak]. There's still a demand for more from the publishing community who have done a great job getting better value.'

Smith says AIM tried to discuss the matter with the MCPS and its publisher members, but got nowhere. 'One of the options at the time was for labels to take care of licensing as in the physical world,' she says, 'but it was clear that the publishers decided they didn't actually want that.'

She argues that this was a power play by the publishers, via the MCPS, with the politics here being heightened because labels were not consulted in the process. 'That is about control,' she says. 'To be in control of a massive, or what would be a massive, area of the business. And rewriting the calculations. Grabbing the calculator back!'

Robertson says that the MCPS was taking the brunt of the criticism of the rate, but explains that the organisation was only implementing what its members had wanted.

'The 10p rate had to be approved by the MCPS board, which was all the publishers,' he says. 'They were hiding behind this to an extent because they were all part of the same majors [as the labels]. So let's not imagine MCPS would just go in [solo], making these decisions themselves.'

Smith, and many of AIM's label members, were certain this rate was bad for the nascent download sector because, facing a reduction in their margins, labels might not push into digital as forcefully as they could or should. 'We didn't want to have a chilling effect on the development of the market, that's for sure,' she argues.

It was not just the (independent) labels rising up to oppose it: some of the download services were too.

'I had a very public argument with Tony Wilson at [music business conference] In The City,' recalls Robertson. 'He was launching a service called Music33 where he was trying to sell everything for 33p. It was the RPM of vinyl and Tony thought that was a good price. I was on the panel and said, 'Well if it's 10 pence, your pricing is not going to work, is it?' I said something along the lines of, "You just want MCPS licences to suit your logo!" We caught up afterwards and were really good friends from then on! We had a very good relationship.'

Other early download services in the UK in late 1999 were initially more amenable to the 10p rate – or they were certainly less bellicose than Music33. 'We were less worried about whether it was 10p or 8p or 7p,' says Jonathan Davis, co-founder of Crunch. 'We were just happy that we could actually get a licence. We could proceed legitimately. The negotiations can always follow, right? And they do. But we just thought saw it as a great legitimiser – that an organisation like the MCPS, on behalf of all their members, was coming to the table and was enabling [the launch] not saying, "You can't have anything".'

This position shifted slightly the following year. Liam McNeive, lawyer for Crunch, starts digging into his files when we speak and pulls out a letter dated 12 June 2000. 'It was saying we're happy to pay mechanical royalties on downloads once an agreed scheme is established,' he says, summarising the contents of the letter. 'And we said we supported the position of AIM on it. We had a lot of interaction with Alison Wenham. We basically aligned ourselves with AIM. AIM was very much our world. The membership of AIM was our constituency.'

Andy Cleary, co-founder and director of Jammin Music Group, was on the AIM board at the time this rate was introduced by MCPS. He says it was, in many ways, unsurprising that they went as high on the rate as they did, but he says he has to respect how the organisation was fighting the corner of its publisher members.

'Name me a format when the MCPS didn't go in high!' he says, laughing. 'To be fair, they'd done a good job for the members. That was just them looking after the publishers. They tended to win those digital battles over the record industry, actually. I thought they looked after their members better than the BPI or AIM did back then.'

The 10p rate was never carved in stone, insists Robertson. It was always intended as a *starting point* rather than an immutable position. It was really a pathfinding mission. 'The thing was at the time that nobody really knew where it was going and how it was going to work,' he says. 'There was a real concern you were going to end up with a percentage of nothing. So why not start with a fixed fee and then see where the discussions are going on? As you go there and have a wider discussion [there would be issues]. And let's face it, the labels, AIM, the BPI, PPL, nobody knew any more than the MCPS did at the time. So it was, "Here's the starting point".'

The MCPS, he argues, felt it had to make a play otherwise everything would be numbed by inertia. 'It went on for so long that they said, "Look, let's just do this because we've got to make some sort of decision." The 10p rate didn't really hang around for long, but it certainly got the discussion going!'

That discussion is still ongoing. The 10p download rate was merely the opening salvo in a war between labels and publishers over how the spoils of the digital boom should be carved up. It remains a burning issue today. And will remain so for a long time into the future.

CHAPTER 8

Trading Standards: Building a Paid Download Business

(A licensed attempt to claw back control)

The major labels were like worker bees in a global hive of money, duty bound to protect the CD queen at all costs.

They could not envisage a world where the CD was not the centre: or, if they could envisage it, they probably would have wished to instantly scrub such a horrifying image from their minds. Replacing the highly profitable and high-margin 12-track CD with individual downloads was not a business model that filled them with much confidence.

There were, however, some who had been through the major label system who felt that downloads were not just *another* option: they were the *only* option.

Al Teller was both a technologist and a record label executive, putting him in a unique position at a unique moment in the record industry's evolution.

He left his role as chairman and CEO of MCA in November 1995 and started a venture that was funded by investment banker Bruce Wasserstein's company that, within a week of being announced, was sold to Alliance Distribution.

'Part of what I wanted to accomplish with this venture was to be very aggressive on the digital front,' says Teller. 'I had long been advocating that the transition, or the coming, of the internet, in a serious fashion, particularly in the form of the World Wide Web, was going to impact the music industry in an extraordinarily profound way – in a way that nothing previous had done to it. And unless the industry was aggressive in learning about it, adopting it, being aggressive and being at the forefront of that transition, we would ultimately get pushed around by forces outside the business. Which is exactly what happened.'

He says he felt like Cassandra during his later years at MCA, his warnings about the coming digital revolution being disbelieved or, worse, going unheeded.

He adds that while he was at MCA he was made aware of a new company being set up in Seattle in 1994 called Progressive Networks who were experimenting with streaming music over the internet. In 1995, he went to meet them and, over the course of a day, sketched out the terms for a major investment into the nascent company by MCA.

'A cornerstone of our thinking was that we were going to launch a digital label and start concentrating on the digital side of music,' he says. 'That deal did not happen because they got a better offer financially from a Wall Street firm. So we never made that deal. But that company, Progressive Networks, changed its name to RealNetworks. RealNetworks, when it went public, I think had a maximum public valuation somewhere around $9 billion.'

He pauses in contemplation. 'Just step back for a moment and think how differently the intersection of music and the internet would have unfolded had the deal with Progressive Networks by MCA taken place. We would have been at the forefront of this revolution.'

Frustrated at this missed opportunity and convinced that digital was the future, he set up Atomic Pop in early 1997, but it did not publicly launch until February 1999. Within a month, it was drawing five thousand visitors a day to its website, even before a full advertising and marketing campaign had been put in place.[1] It had $5 million in initial funding from private investors.

'We plan to break artists online and migrate a number of record company functionalities online,' he told the *Los Angeles Times* in an interview in early 1999. 'Because we will be Web-centric, our cost structure is going to be radically different than that of the major record labels. We intend to create a very different financial landscape that will be appealing to artists.'[2]

The Atomic Pop model was based around licensing the digital rights for a range of artists' music and then selling it online as downloads.

'We were also going to create the support mechanisms to enable an artist to develop themselves,' Teller says. 'If they went on tour, we would send someone on the bus with a little video camera to just record things and we would put it up on the website. Sort of a fairly early kind of YouTube thing. We would make sure that we were populating various chat boards with stories about the artists that we were involved with.'

He says they wanted to make the matter of ownership of their masters 'a non-issue' as it was something artists were always concerned about. 'We said, "When you're in business with us, here's our deal. If you don't want to be in business with us, we wish you the best".'

The deals would run for a year and, if both sides were happy, they'd roll over for another year. If the artist wasn't happy, they could walk. Paying large advances was not part of the Atomic Pop model, with Teller describing it as 'a cooperative venture' between label and artist, where profits were split down the middle and the artist always retained ownership of their masters or digital rights.

'It was a very attractive proposition and, from my perspective, I didn't want to put up unnecessary roadblocks to be able to attract artists to Atomic Pop,' says Teller. 'I thought by eliminating the ownership issue, that was a key step in that direction.'

He says there was a vacuum in the business at that moment as record deals typically covered physical goods but digital rights had often not yet been negotiated. Atomic Pop was going to focus on the digital rights and build a download market around them. Getting physical rights was not a requirement but, if they became available, Atomic Pop wanted first refusal to do a deal for them.

I ask Teller if he felt like he was betraying the major label system he had been in since the late 1960s (and holding senior executive posts there since the early 1980s).

'I never felt like a traitor!' he snorts. 'I felt like I was simply following the natural consequences of the evolution of business models.'

He signed up a range of acts to work with Atomic Pop, the most high profile being Chuck D of Public Enemy, someone who was fully signed up to the digital revolution, especially because it would ideally break apart the old stronghold of the majors.

'Chuck never messed around!' say Teller, laughing. 'Conceptually, we thought alike in many, many ways, but I didn't think it was particularly helpful to be as incendiary about it. Some of those comments [from Chuck] were quite incendiary and we'd get the kind of knee-jerk reaction you'd expect from folks who did not hold that point of view. You'd get people digging in their heels on both sides of it, as opposed to sitting around a table and coming up with a thoughtful manner in which to move forward.'

Atomic Pop put out *There's A Poison Goin' On*, Public Enemy's seventh studio album, in July 1999.

Chuck D spoke to *Billboard* about it and did not hold back when he considered the damage a move like this could cause the old business.

'If the majors could sell Brillo pads with a slice of cheese, they would do it; they give less [of] a fuck about the music,' he said. 'This gets music across to the people, and the business is irrelevant. I am happy to be a contributor to the bomb. The three Rs [radio, retail, and record companies] aren't fucking with me anymore.'[3]

Atomic Pop did give Chuck D an advance for signing with it as he had what Teller calls 'name power' that would help raise the profile of the new company. He says he cannot remember the exact amount, but that it was 'actually quite modest' and 'a fraction of what he could have got from a traditional record company.'

As part of the marketing for *There's A Poison Goin' On*, Atomic Pop and Public Enemy would release a cappella versions of the tracks from the albums as MP3s and ask fans to remix them, with the five best getting a full release. This kind of thing would have had the major labels in 1999 clutching their pearls.[4]

Billboard kept a close eye on the Public Enemy album and reported that it had sold 3,624 units in a week, noting tartly this was not enough to get into the *Billboard* 200. It was available as a download for $8 and on CD for $10 from the Atomic Pop site before the full 20 July release. The week after the full release, downloads went up to $12 and CDs to $11.88 from the Atomic Pop site.[5]

Teller told the publication, 'We are pleased with the results and the awareness we have for the record. We were perfectly content with first-week sales [at retail]. Don't forget, this is still being positioned at retail, and we haven't taken a track to radio yet. We have a long-term marketing plan. It will be methodical and steady in support of a very good album.'[6]

Music retailer Trans World refused to carry the album in protest at Atomic Pop giving itself the early exclusive. Jim Litwak, EVP of Trans World, sniffily told *Billboard*, 'If you want to do an exclusive and not make us a partner, go in good health.'[7]

In October 1999, Atomic Pop also licensed the digital rights for the entire 4AD catalogue as both MP3 and Liquid Audio downloads. The label was home to acts like Pixies, Throwing Muses, Cocteau Twins and Lush. It went through Beggars Banquet. 'I was very excited about that,' says Teller. 'Trust me, I really wanted the Beggars catalogue. I loved their taste. They had great music taste.'

Martin Mills, heads of Beggars Banquet, says this chimed with what the company was looking to do with its music digitally. 'We were trying to get our whole catalogue out and available everywhere,' he says. 'It was a big funded deal so 4AD was exclusive to Atomic Pop for a while.'

The timing of the deal was telling as Atomic Pop had just secured $10 million from internet investment firm Rare Medium Group.[8]

In November 1999, Robin Wilson (formerly of Gin Blossoms and then of Gas Giants) spoke to *Billboard* about the reasons for working with Atomic Pop and how it represented an alternative to the majors. 'The biggest break in our career was when Interscope dropped us after the merger,' he said. 'We bumped into Atomic Pop, which had a clean roster and a new business model that gave us total control over our product and a new way to work our record. For the first time ever, we're going to release a record without any debt, and we don't have to sell nearly as many records to make money.'[9]

The following month, Ice T spoke at the Webnoize conference about putting his *7th Deadly Sin* album out via Atomic Pop and ramped up this notion of artist empowerment through digital. 'My record might not sell as much as on one of the majors, but it was a sacrifice for me to learn the game,' he said. 'It taught me about the internet, and [now] I'm in a position to make power moves.'[10]

Speaking at the same conference, guitarist and David Bowie collaborator Reeves Gabrels spoke about putting out his album *Ulysses (della note)* as an exclusive download.

'What I'm trying to find out, and hoping to be proven right about, is that we don't really need major labels for the music,' he said. 'We don't even need a tangible form [of music]. We need to become comfortable with music existing as an intangible item, just like when musicians play it.'

More interestingly, however, he spoke about the financial terms of releasing music this way. The album retailed at $9.99 for the download and he got 80 per cent of that. If he was on a standard label deal, his share would have been around 10 per cent.[11]

Revolutions do not come cheap. A *Forbes* profile of Atomic Pop in early 2000 reported that the company had revenues of $2 million but was still a loss-making enterprise. 'Looking ahead, [Teller] hopes to build Atomic Pop into more than just a record label,' said *Forbes*. 'The Web site offers the online equivalent of radio and TV programming, as well as videogames. The idea is to lure listeners with freebie music samples and then sell music to them, by download or CD, from both Atomic Pop acts and other bands.'[12]

Atomic Pop did not last the distance – it officially closed in September 2000[13] – but it was a signpost to the future, where digital was more important than physical and artists got a larger share of the spoils. Perhaps it was too early and perhaps it was too utopian in its approach to the business, but as a foreshadowing of what was to follow, the significance of this short-lived digital-first label cannot be underestimated.

Launched in early 1998, the role of eMusic in also heralding a new type of music consumption cannot be underestimated. It debuted as GoodNoise but officially changed its name to eMusic in June 1999.[14]

By the time of the name change, it had deals with 60 independent labels and was selling album downloads as MP3s in the US for $8.99 each and individual tracks for $0.99.[15] [16]

CEO Gene Hoffman used the media attention around the name change to insist that the MP3 could be a force for good and should not be seen as a dirty word. 'The MP3 news to date has led people to believe it's this pirate thing,' he told *ZDNet*. 'Our message now is, it's not only compelling, attractive, and available at a good price, but you can also get it in a commercial way that's easy, safe and clean.'[17]

Gene Rossman, president of eMusic, told *Billboard*, 'Revenues from digital [music] distribution aren't that high. . . but it does help [the labels'] off-line sales. What was a nascent market is now building significantly. We see a lot more customers every day. . . It's an opportunity to find a lot of cool independent music in one place. The independents have a chance to make a name for themselves with the public. You may end up seeing people being customer-loyal to independent music. You'll see more mainstream customers interested in the independent marketplace.'[18]

Jeff Price, president and co-owner of New York independent label spinART, stated that his company turned to eMusic after 'frustrating' distribution deals with Sony and Giant Records: 'We were the first record label to put its catalogue up for sale in the MP3 platform,' he claimed.[19]

He added that a track from the *New World Record* album by Poster Children was downloaded twenty thousand times in two and a half weeks. 'Is it ultimately helping our physical sales?' he asked. 'It feels like it. I don't need a warehouse. I don't need to deal with returns or COD or terms. . . [the internet] totally levels the playing field, because it cuts the majors off at the knees.'[20]

Also heavily backing the eMusic model was Rykodisc who had made 175 album tracks available on the service in February 1999. Lars Murray, director of new media at Rykodisc, told *Billboard*, 'The idea was, "We gotta get in the game." We had to get beyond, "Who's afraid of big, bad MP3?". . . The idea was to engage the marketplace.'[21]

At the tellingly named MP3 Summit conference in mid June 1999, M-80 Interactive Marketing executive Dave Neupert told delegates, 'MP3 is the best marketing tool the music industry has ever had, and the majors are not taking advantage of it. You can create a fanbase and market directly to them.'[22]

At the same event, eMusic revealed it had sales of $20,000 in the previous quarter. This might not seem like a volume that would turn the record industry on its head, but this was up from a mere $400 in the previous quarter.[23]

The company did, however, have a bolder expansion plan in mind. The month after the MP3 Summit, eMusic announced that it had acquired the Jewel-Paula-Ronn label's master recordings, comprising over eight thousand R&B, rock'n'roll and gospel tracks from the 1960s onwards. The deal would, of course, see the music released as MP3 downloads, but eMusic would also release the music on physical formats through traditional retailers. *Billboard* claimed this would make it possibly 'the first Net-dedicated firm to diversify into brick-and-mortar marketing.'[24]

Through 1999, it kept expanding, signing up another six independent labels – JetSet Records, Parasol Records, Monolyth Record Group, Sonic Unyon, Lounge Records, and PopSmear – in July, bringing its total to eighty-five.[25]

The growing licensing deals, however, stood in stark contrast to the company's mounting losses as it tried to get a foothold in a market that was still so heavily dominated by the CD.

In August 1999, eMusic reported a net loss of $10.8 million for the fourth fiscal quarter, four times the loss it had reported in the third quarter. Revenues may have been up 141 per cent over the same period, but they topped out at just $51,000. For the full fiscal year, the company had $92,000 in revenue, but had racked up $15.12 million in losses. While these may appear shocking numbers, they were far from atypical for companies in the midst of the first dot com boom. Huge losses were normalised as part and parcel of being on a path to growth.[26]

In August 1999, eMusic partnered with AOL to sell downloads via its Spinner, Winamp and ICQ services. *CNN Money* reported at the time of the deal that eMusic had a catalogue of twenty thousand tracks.[27] AOL had acquired Spinner and Nullsoft in June that year for an estimated $400 million in stock.[28]

In September that year, it was working with They Might Be Giants to release their *Long Tall Weekend* album as MP3 downloads. The band had left Elektra (part of Warner Music Group) in 1997 and had been one of the first acts to really see the power of online as a way to nurture a fanbase. It was hailed as eMusic's biggest-selling album to date, but no official sales numbers were made public. Interestingly, the band were saying at the time that there were no plans to release the album on physical formats – that it would be a digital-only release.[29]

They Might Be Giants were the most downloaded band (based on legal sales) in 1999, according to eMusic.[30] True to their word, the album has still not had a physical release.

Major labels acts started to be drawn to eMusic as a way to gain a certain kind of digital credibility and to be seen as embracing the future. British rock band Bush, signed to Interscope (part of Universal Music Group), released 'The Chemicals Between Us' as the lead single from their third album, *The Science Of Things*, on 8 September via eMusic. It was available as an MP3 and a RealAudio download.[31]

In November 1999, covering the first fiscal quarter, the company announced that revenues were up 255 per cent to $180,000 but net losses had grown from $10.8 million to $13.5 million in the same period.[32]

Despite the mounting losses, the company moved in late November to purchase Cductive, which had been running since 1996. It was selling downloads, all from around 150 independent labels, for $0.99 as well as allowing users to create their own compilation CDs. It was a stock-for-stock deal that valued Cductive at $38 million.[33] [34]

The thrill of expansion now gripping it, eMusic also acquired music site Tunes.com and subsidiary sites RollingStone.com and DownBeatJazz.com at the end of November. *MTV* reported that the stock-for-stock deal valued at $130 million. It also added that eMusic had grown its catalogue significantly to offer music from five hundred independent record labels.[35]

It ended the year with another significant exclusive, getting the *James Brown For The Millennium & Forever* album, selling it for $8.99 for the complete album or $0.99 per track.[36]

In the UK, heavily inspired by GoodNoise (before its name change), Crunch wanted to take the à la carte MP3 download model and bring it to the UK, working on a flat rate of £0.99 per track, which was based entirely on the $0.99 price per track GoodNoise charged in the US.

'When we launched, MP3 felt like it was the *de facto* format that consumers wanted to use,' says Jonathan Davis, one of the founders of Crunch. 'It was easier to use, quite frankly. All the other formats like WMA [Windows Media Audio] and Liquid Audio, the DRM just added layers of complexity. MP3 was just much simpler and easier. I could download it, I could move it to my device, I could move it to any number of devices I wanted, I could move it to a range of different players. It was just an easier format for consumers.'

The earliest labels to license their content to Crunch were independent dance labels, in part because of Davis's background in the dance industry but also because they were typically based around singles and were often technophiles. Those dance labels included Nuphonic, Wall Of Sound, Pussyfoot, Soma and Ultimate Dilemma. The majors, however, were not willing to even consider licensing their catalogues as MP3 downloads.

'The reason why MP3 was such a disrupter is, ultimately, control,' suggests Davis. 'Between the major labels, the bigger independent labels and the major retailers – let's not forget the retailers in this question – those parties had a very nice business, very profitable and they were in control of it. The high street back in 1999 was a completely different place from the high street in 2023.'

He says that MP3 felt like a direct assault on the control the major labels believed was the very foundation of their businesses. 'It was always about control, but MP3 was the spark, the fire, the fuse, the ignition point,' proposes Davis. 'If it was a line of gunpowder, it was fizzing into all the different parts of the ecosystem – and making people go, "Whoa!"'

He does not, he says, blame the majors for being so resistant to the format. It worked against what they regarded as their core business interests and so they did not want to be seen to be embracing or condoning something they were certain threatened them and their CD-powered profitability.

He says, 'It's very easy to sit there and go, "Oh, yeah, they're all idiots." But they're not. And they weren't. I think it's important not to completely bash them. If you're the CEO of a $100 million business, you have got a responsibility to try to build or maintain or stop that business shrinking.'

As dance labels were typically trading in singles, Davis says they viewed downloading as additive to their business. The majors, however, used singles to sell albums. Their business was predicated almost entirely on the high margins from sales of albums on CD. Consumers being able to buy individual tracks for £0.99 and not but an album for £13 was regarded as digital Semtex being placed under their future.

'For the labels that we were working with, it wasn't a concern,' says Davis of the Crunch retail proposition. 'I think if you were in a major label, you were absolutely concerned about the disintermediation and the disaggregation of the album. Singles were a loss leader. But for the labels that we were working with, that wasn't a point of resistance.'

Richard Davies, the other co-founder of Crunch, says the pricing was anathema to the majors. 'They clearly didn't want to touch us with a bargepole,' he says, laughing. 'My memory of [meetings with majors] was that they showed us the door pretty quickly! They really were not supportive of downloads at all, in any regard – free or paid. They were pretty short conversations.'

Liam McNeive was working at the time in what he terms 'the extremely nascent world of internet-related law' with a major client in the shape of AOL. He joined as the lawyer for the company and also helped open up investment opportunities.

McNeive says, 'I know that Jonathan and Richard spent a lot of time talking to contacts in major labels. Obviously, for Crunch it would provide a real imprimatur for the business if Warner or Universal or whatever were to sanction the use of Crunch for their content. There was a sort of paralysis, an industry paralysis. They had CDs come along and a complete bonanza that allowed them to sell records they'd already sold to people, only in the CD format. And now along comes this thing which they just cannot put their arms around at all. Is it a threat? Is it an opportunity? Of course it was both, but they saw the threat more than the opportunity. So they were paralysed. Not that, logically speaking, they should have said to a tiny little business like ours, "Here's all our content. Go and sell it for us." But they weren't about to.'

By November 1999, the company had four thousand users who had registered their credit cards with its online payment system.[37]

Given it was directly influenced by GoodNoise, it was somewhat fitting that eMusic (as it became known) was one of the early investors in Crunch. The company raised over £4 million in total during its short life, with GoodNoise being one of the earliest investors.

Davies says the GoodNoise/eMusic investment gave it a 25 per cent share in Crunch.

McNeive says the idea of having a global store meant record companies could now retail to consumers that were previously unreachable. 'We genuinely thought that if you were putting highly desirable, often UK-based, dance and indie content online, and people who couldn't otherwise get to a record shop in Tierra del Fuego wanted that stuff, then they'd be prepared to pay £0.99 to download a track. It didn't seem like a preposterous proposition.'

He pauses and then expands on the challenge they had not seen coming. 'The trouble is, as everyone knows, you need to have unbelievably desirable content for anybody to change their behaviour in such a way as to do something nobody had done before, which is put their credit card online and pay £0.99 for a piece of music. Especially with the length of time it would take to download a track, it was always going to be a bit of a challenge.'

Via McNeive, the company also brought in David Phillips, president and managing director of AOL UK, as CEO of Crunch in January 2000. AOL also took a shareholder investment in the company.[38]

'He helped us in terms of fundraising and he helped us with visibility,' says Davies. 'We suddenly had someone who was very well connected in that world to put us on the map a bit. And he brought with him, quite quickly afterwards, some quite serious investment from [a financial holding company].'

Even with significant investment in Crunch, it was to be a short-lived operation.

'Back then with the mania that was going on [in the investment world], it was fear of missing out – FOMO,' says McNeive of the investment frenzy of the time. 'People who had a few bob would bung it into any old startup that looked like it might have a chance of planting a flag in a particular sector. And for a brief time, a very brief time, we were one of those vehicles.'

That hype cycle came with its own problems as investors were putting pressure on the company to accelerate their growth, primarily because they wanted to cash out at the peak of the dot com bubble.

The team at Crunch feel they were too focused on short-term growth rather than long-term sustainability.

'We, I think rather foolishly now looking back, thought we could just run before we could walk,' says Davies. 'We tried to open up in too many territories before we'd really got the offering completely right. We were running offices and staff all over the world. And then the money ran out and the dot com bubble burst. It's the age old story of a business going under or having to be sold in a fire sale. Because we had overstretched ourselves and we couldn't pay the wage bill.'

Crunch also had to change its name to iCrunch following a trademark dispute with a chain of gyms in the US called Crunch. By this stage, it was rapidly running out of money and the company was acquired by Music Choice in April 2001. It went for a fraction of the price they were hoping for when it was originally taking off. Davies says he managed to cash out 'to the tune of a few grand.' Reflecting back on it now, he says the idea was simply too early for what the market could support.

'I think we had a great concept, but we were too early,' he sighs. 'There's sometimes nothing wrong with being too early as long as you can stay the course to enable the market to come to you. We just didn't enable that to happen. We were growing too quickly. It was unsustainable. And we got found out. My biggest regret is not having played it a bit safer and stayed in the game to be a player of some description within that sector. It's a harsh lesson to learn. It's one that I've taken with me since with subsequent businesses I've set up. I wouldn't take that route again of large-scale investment, burning as fast as you can to grow a business before you really established what the model is.'

McNeive says Crunch was not just early, it was 'stupidly early', but reveals that it came close to a glorious and lucrative exit strategy. In December 1999, he got an unsolicited call from a lawyer representing a large banking company in the US.

'They said, "We are looking into the world of online music. We are interested in commencing discussions with Crunch about acquiring the company." I went, "What?" I gulped before I said this, "Roughly what are you thinking of in terms of price? Do you have a ballpark figure?" "Well, we are thinking of a figure in the region of a hundred million." And I didn't bother asking him if he meant dollars or pounds. I was already spasming. I probably squeaked slightly [strained voice], "Well, I'd imagined we could see our way to [discussing that]." Because of the silence on my end, which was just shock, he said, "But that would be a starting point." He thought my silence signified that I was unimpressed! We had that conversation and I said, "Let's continue discussions".'

Timing was against them, as early in 2000 investors started to express growing concern about digital companies and by March the dot com bubble had burst.

Reflecting on the multi-million buyout that never was, McNeive is surprisingly sanguine. 'That,' he says, 'is when I knew the world had gone absolutely fucking crazy.'

While eMusic, Atomic Pop and Crunch were trying to pull the record business into a digital future, their emphasis on MP3s was only ever going to get the backs of the majors up. MP3 was a swear word as far as they were concerned. MP3 represented a loss of control at a hugely important juncture in the industry's history. MP3 was also, as far as many at the majors could make out, merely a synonym for piracy. They, for the most part, recoiled violently from it, hissing like vampires suddenly exposed to daylight.

They did not want to devote any time to figuring out if MP3 could benefit them. Rather they were looking at where MP3s – or, more specifically, MP3s of music by *their artists* – were mainly being made available online and moving to cut off the circulation lest the entire bloodstream of the record business be poisoned.

CHAPTER 9

Internet Disservice Providers: the Majors Declare War on Web Providers, Search Engines and Civilians

(Eradicating threats as an attempt to re-seize control)

By 1999, the record industry was reasonably well versed in how it was addressing online piracy.

Cary Sherman joined the RIAA in May 1997 and argues this was a critical period. '1997 is the year that MP3 became part of the public consciousness,' he says. 'By June of 1997, we were sending demand letters to FTP sites to take down music hosted on them.'

This coincided with the passing of the NET (No Electronic Theft) Act into US federal law in December that year.[1] In effect, it allowed for criminal prosecutions for copyright infringement, even if the person or individual involved was not directly benefiting financially from said infringement of copyright. Under it, federal copyright law's definition of 'financial gain' was updated 'to include the receipt of anything of value, including the receipt of other copyrighted works.'[2]

By 1999, the whole process to tackle music piracy online was being accelerated globally.

At Midem, the annual international music industry conference in Cannes, France, in January 1999, Sherman spoke about how the RIAA was targeting pirate music sites, suggesting it would work closely with search engines to stop them pointing users to sites hosting or linking to unlicensed music.

'Music on the Internet is playing a leading role in a drama that is playing out before our eyes,' said Sherman. 'Intellectual property and technology are at a crossroads [. . .] Technology has the potential to profoundly expand the presence of art in our world, to deliver music in a series of expanding circles where creators are supported for their work and inspired to create more and greater works of art.'[3]

The following month, search engine Lycos announced it would co-operate with the RIAA over its establishment of 'the world's largest searchable database [of] MP3 audio files on the web' hosted at mp3.lycos.com. It was initially not going to distinguish between legitimate and illegitimate files, but this was quickly pounced on by the RIAA. Sherman stated that Lycos 'have committed to work with us to develop procedures to eliminate infringing sites from their directory.' Lycos added that it would comply with DMCA (Digital Millennium Copyright Act) requirements to remove infringing content when alerted to its existence.[4]

Lycos general manager Robert Frasca said that mp3.lycos.com had five hundred thousand indexed files and that this was 'ten times bigger than anything that's out there.' He added that MP3 searches are often in the company's top five searches. '[Y]ou can't overlook what your users are looking for,' he said.[5]

Frasca admitted there were serious limitations to what they could currently do. 'We have no human way to figure out what's pirated and what's not,' he said. '[We will] embrace watermarking technology once it's out there and filter the [results] so that once you run the search, you'll see what is watermarked. . . first and fast'.[6]

Jollyon Benn says his role at BPI at the time involved going out to meet various ISPs and putting forward the BPI's case. 'We'd invite them along for a cup of tea and a few little presentations about what internet piracy looks like,' he says. 'We just wanted them to be aware of it, basically.'

It was, he recalls, incredibly difficult to get the ISPs to properly hear them out and to respond to their concerns. 'It kind of fell on deaf ears in a way because I don't think the ISPs could get their heads around being in that space as a business,' he says. "They thought, 'Well, we're a telecoms company. We plug wires into walls and people can talk to each other." It was a bit frustrating.'

Labels and trade bodies had to go on a recruitment drive to bring in people who understood the new and emerging technologies and how to address the threats (as well as the opportunities) they presented.

'The record companies and the IFPI groups and the RIAA didn't have the in-house expertise,' says Edwards. 'Hiring Paul Jessop in 1997 was the first step in us getting that expertise. And then Jeremy Banks on the enforcement side. We didn't really know what it was. We had no idea where it could go. All we knew is that it was already eroding the markets.'

A major IFPI-led operation targeting FAST Search & Transfer began in late March 1999, described as 'the first action against an internet search engine company.'[7] The IFPI claimed FAST, which had only launched in February 1999, was directing users to pirate sites and *Billboard* called it 'a groundbreaking attempt by the international record industry to control piracy over the internet.'

On 24 March, the IFPI had asked the public prosecutor in Norway to bring criminal proceedings against FAST, arguing that it contravened Norwegian copyright law.

'One source within the public prosecution service says that internet-based music piracy is simply too small a crime for prosecutors to be interested,' reported *Billboard*. 'The source adds, "There is also another issue. We are here to protect Norwegian citizens, and this is more of an international manner. If it's a cause for concern for the music industry, let them take this case to Britain or America".'[8]

Mike Edwards, director of operations at the IFPI, told *Billboard*, 'FAST has developed a search engine software that encourages massive systematic copyright piracy by searching all MP3 files worldwide and then storing all the direct links to those files in a database. It involves software that continually scans the internet for new MP3 files, monitors the availability of each MP3 server, and updates, hour by hour, the database of links.'[9]

Jay Berman, the head of the IFPI, claimed, 'Right now we're facing a terrible combination. We have a major piracy problem with physical product, and, at the same time, what we have with FAST is a virtually all-pirate atmosphere which in some respects prevents us from doing legitimate business.'[10]

The Norwegian prosecution service said it could take between six and nine months for them to decide if they were going to take action.[11]

In July that year, FAST[12] claimed it had reached a settlement with the IFPI over the removal of unlicensed MP3s. This was news to the IFPI who denied any such agreement had been reached.[13]

In October, the IFPI was taking action against 'hundreds of infringing sites' in over twenty different countries. It was a two-pronged assault – targeting individuals uploading infringing content and going after ISPs who might be hosting infringing sites. The IFPI estimated there were around one million unlicensed music files online at any one time. Echoing the education programmes outlined in Chapter 5 the IFPI was signing up musicians to join its rolling Action For Legal Music On The Internet campaign.[14]

Matt Oppenheim, SVP of business and legal affairs at the IFPI between 1997 and 2004, suggests that targeting search engines was a difficult legal strategy compared to going after file-sharing services directly. 'The idea of going against a search engine was a much harder case legally than going against a system that really was built for the single purpose of distributing unlicensed music,' he says. 'So legally, it was target, target, target. It was much easier than compared to search engines.'

By November, the RIAA was trying to persuade university campuses to fight their corner, especially regarding the worst student offenders who were turning them into hotbeds for piracy.

'The RIAA recently contacted the University of South Carolina Spartanburg about a student who had turned his PC into a jukebox and was selling pirated MP3s,' reported *Wired*. 'Since the music was copyrighted, the RIAA was reportedly ready to take the student and the university to court.'[15]

Frank Creighton, senior vice president and director of anti-piracy at the RIAA, said the body was not threatening a lawsuit and would rather address this all in a spirit of cooperation. 'We request simply that they remove the material,' he said. 'We leave it to the university to decide what action to take.'[16]

This is not to say that hardline action was not being taken by the RIAA. In the same report, *Wired* noted, 'On 8 November, severnty-one students' internet access was taken away at Carnegie Mellon University for alleged illegal MP3 use. In August, University of Oregon student Jeffrey Levy was convicted of MP3 piracy for storing files on his school's servers. He could face up to three years in prison and a US$250,000 fine.'[17]

It was not all label-led legal action here, with The Artist (the name Prince was operating under at the time) suing a variety of websites in early 1999. One of the sites he went after, uptown.se, was a fan site based in Sweden, who he accused of violating his copyright when using an unauthorised photograph of him online and in print. He also pursued several other sites for selling bootlegs of his music and offering other recordings for free.[18]

Arguably the most significant, and unquestionably the most controversial, anti-piracy move in 1999 was the suing of a Swedish teenager.

In late September 1999, IFPI Sweden moved to sue Tommy Olsson, then aged 17. This was viewed very much as a test case and one that would, so the IFPI hoped, set a powerful precedent. However, the judge in the ruling on 15 September at the District Court in Skövde said it should be thrown out and Olsson was acquitted.[19]

The judge said the site did not constitute the 'primary infringement' that the IFPI alleged. Lars Gustafson, managing director of IFPI Sweden, was unbowed, telling *Billboard*, 'Even [though] we lost, it gives us good guidance for the next one.' He added that the IFPI 'doesn't want to jump on all the kids in Sweden' but would work with police and prosecution authorities to tackle the problem.[20]

'Olsson's lawyer said the case against his client had no merit since Olsson was simply disseminating information – the location of the files – not the files themselves,' reported *The Register*. 'However, the IFPI (or, rather, its Swedish wing) claims that Olsson's site does indirectly infringe the copyright held by the owners of the original music tracks.'[21]

The importance of Sweden as a test case market was significant. It had the highest level of internet penetration per capita in the world in 1999 and IFPI Sweden said it had closed down a thousand locally operated sites that offered access to unlicensed music in the previous eighteen months.[22] 'Digital piracy was particularly acute in Scandinavia,' says Edwards. 'It was a massive problem. They had piracy rates of over 90 per cent.'

IFPI Sweden said that it had noticed Olsson's site six months earlier during routine online checks where around three hundred music files were being offered. They sent him an email telling him to stop (although at this stage they did not know his identity). He did not reply, but IFPI Sweden saw that he had switched the site's address so they informed the police.[23]

Billboard reported, 'Because Olsson had not actually copied or distributed any files, said the court, the case should be dismissed.'[24]

Paul Russell, chairman of Sony Music Europe at the time, says he was against the local office of the IFPI taking action against Olsson. 'It was just stupid,' he says. 'I remember talking to the guy who ran our Swedish company saying, "What are these people doing? This has got to be the worst possible publicity you could imagine".'

He adds, 'I think that the Swedes were particularly sensitive and wanted to be aggressive, but were getting no help from the government. So they figured that picking on some student was a way of getting the government off its backside to give them some help.'

Generally independent labels were opposed to the IFPI action against

Olsson, regarding it as unnecessarily heavy handed, akin to dropping a hydrogen bomb to crack a nut.

'Our view was that you couldn't do that,' says Martin Mills of Beggars Banquet. 'Fighting our customers because of technology was not the right way to go.'

Helen Smith, director of legal and business affairs at AIM, remains certain it was the wrong strategy to pursue. 'That was awful,' she says of the court case. 'That was really unacceptable. Nobody had a problem with suing services. No one objected to that. The problem was suing kids.'

On the collective view of the independents on this she says, 'That type of litigation and the narrative around those court cases is something we didn't think was helpful. Obviously it is also a question of tactics in terms of picking your targets. It was how the litigation was handled and the story around it. Perhaps more so than complete opposition to the idea of litigation. This idea of suing music fans was a point of disagreement. We said, "No litigation".'

Peter Quicke, label manager at Ninja Tune, says he was horrified by IFPI Sweden's hardline stance here. 'The idea of it is just nonsense,' he sighs. 'You can see why it's a matter of principle and a matter of upholding legal principle, but that is just fucking ridiculous.'

In the early 2000s, this targeting of individuals was ramped up dramatically and the outcry was immediate. Lessons from the Olsson case, especially the horrifying PR fallout, had clearly not been learned.[25]

PANIC OVER THE NORMALISATION OF 'FREE'

Following on from Jay Samit's claim in November 1999 that over a billion tracks had been downloaded so far that year without being paid for, the following month Mike Edwards, director of operations at the IFPI, spoke at the Online Music Distribution conference in London and claimed there was a worrying and growing trend among music consumers. 'Free' music was becoming normalised.

'A large percentage of consumers have now got used to the idea that music can be obtained for nothing on the internet,' he said in his keynote speech. He quoted from MP3.com/Music Dish research that found 33 per cent of respondents would stop downloading if forced to pay for it.[26]

Jonathan Davis from Crunch, on a panel at the same conference, said,

'Some music will go for free on the internet, some people will give it free as a reward, but quality music should not be given away for free.' The challenge, he argued, would be 'to attach a value to music.'[27]

In a different news story in the same issue of *Billboard* reporting on the Online Music Distribution conference, a story ran based on National Retail Security Survey data which claimed the consumer object that was most attractive to shoplifters was the CD. The record labels must have increasingly felt they were being attacked from all sides.[28] Indeed, Edwards argues, 'There was a sense of siege amongst the music industry at that time.'

John Kennedy, CEO and chairman of Universal Music in the UK, says the problem for the labels was that there was nowhere for consumers to buy their music online. 'People weren't opposed to the MP3 format; people were opposed to free,' he argues. 'If somebody told us, as it came to pass, you can get the MP3 format and your artists and your songwriters can be paid properly for this, that's fine.'

The majors did eventually give up on their hardline stance on DRM and opposition to MP3. But the reason why no one could legitimately buy the majors' music digitally in 1999 was because it was not available *anywhere* in *any format*.

A legitimate market did emerge eventually, supercharged by the arrival of the iTunes Music Store in 2003 in the US (2004 in Europe), but the majors were enormously hesitant to license their music for download until there was a congruence of various factors, notably CD sales falling below a certain level and Steve Jobs of Apple convincing them to license to iTunes.

IT WAS A STEPPING-STONE FORMAT: NOTHING MORE

For all the claims that 'MP3' was replacing 'sex' as the most searched-for term online in the late 1990s, and for all the attempts to turn the format into a folk devil, the MP3 had a relatively short time in the spotlight. Even if it did burn brighter than any spotlight.

In my piece for *The Quietus* on the 25th anniversary of the MP3, I dated what I termed its Iconoclastic Years as running from 1999 to 2003 and that was followed by what I called The Co-option & Pyrrhic Victory Years, running between 2003 and 2007. 'The MP3 was the last gasp for the notion of ownership before giving way to access,' I wrote. 'But it was a kind of ghost ownership as the MP3 was not something you could display on a shelf.'[29]

As streaming started to go mainstream, MP3s started to feel like a relic of a lost world.

Jim Griffin, digital consultant and digital evangelist, says this was always going to be its fate: it could only ever be a bridging format into a world of on-demand streaming access on smartphones. He says he was arguing this very point in the late 1990s when most people in the music business were only just hearing about MP3. He says he loudly sounded the death knell for the format at a conference in California organised by MP3.com and Michael Robertson.

'I went to his conference in San Diego and people had kind of tied me into this downloads thing,' says Griffin. 'I gave a speech where I said, "Look, enjoy your downloads now. Pretty soon they won't mean anything to you." And people started booing! They threw things at the stage! Somebody yelled out the back of the hall, "There's a clock on the wall, but you got a wristwatch!" I mean, seriously. They were *angry*. I said to them, "The future is about the just-in-time arrival of customised digits, not their download. Not you having them and holding them and managing them".'

He continues, 'People were pissed off. When I drove home, in some ways I looked in the rearview mirror to see if people were following me to my house because they were so angry! Wow. Telling them that it wasn't going to be about downloads, this infuriated people.'

He argues that, for a period of time, MP3s gave the consumer a new sense of power. It might have been a fleeting approximation of power, chimerical even, but it was always going to slip away from them.

'To people who loved downloads, it was a part of their physicality, that they wanted to download music and to have it and control it,' says Griffin. 'It was a battle for control of the music and the fans fancied that they had won. So the idea that they wouldn't even be downloading it soon, this shook them up. I went there certain that it was true and they were equally certain that I was giving them shit. It turned out to be the truest thing I ever said.'

FREE FOR ALL: THE EARLY PIRATE SITES

In his book on the rise of online piracy, Stephen Witt outlines the clandestine growth of sites in the second half of the 1990s entirely devoted to getting pre-release music and leaking it, with members of assorted groups competing for the kudos of being the best leaker. He distils the story via the activities of Dell Glover who worked at a Universal-owned CD pressing plant in North Carolina and how he was involved in smuggling CDs out of the plant.

He was introduced to The Warez Scene (or, more simply, The Scene) where software was pirated but so was everything else – from games and fonts to photos and pornography.

One member of The Scene hid behind the onscreen name NetFraCk, who Witt terms the 'first industrial-scale MP3 pirate.' NetFraCk used the Fraunhofer L3Ens encoder and set up, in Witt's words, 'the world's first ever digital music piracy group.' It was called Compress 'Da Audio (or CDA, a play on the .cda filename extension that Windows used for compact discs containing audio).

The story is precisely dated to 10 August 1996 as that was when CDA released to IRC (Internet Relay Chat) 'Until It Sleeps' by Metallica – the world's first 'officially' pirated MP3. News of it spread like wildfire on the internet and soon other pirating crews were scrambling to release pirated music online.[30] The sharing system was still relatively primitive as the Metallica track was actually stored as a compressed RAR file and split across four 3.5' floppy discs that were sent out through the mail.[31]

Among the pirating crew were Rabid Neurosis (RNS), and they were battling among themselves for supremacy.[32]

Even before the Metallica leak, however, Usenet, a computer network communication system dating back to 1979, was 'awash with pirated music files' by late 1995.[33]

A new acronymic group, DAC (Digital Audio Crew) emerged just after the Metallica leak and sought to dramatically up the ante. They posted a tutorial on ripping tracks to MP3 on Usenet and linked to Fraunhofer's FTP site, handling out the serial number required to unlock the encoder.[34]

By 1997, the players here had long moved on from floppy discs and were availing of university campus servers to supercharge what they were doing. Being the first to leak music became an Olympic sport. Lurking on IRC were two teenagers, Shawn Fanning and Sean Parker, who started to talk about a better, an infinitely faster, way to get music online. Springing out of their frustrations with this covert world, Fanning started to write the eighty thousand lines of code on his Dell notebook that would bring everyone the dream solution. He named it after his IRC and hacker handle: Napster.[35] [36]

STANDARDS

CHAPTER 10

It's Fun to Stay at the S-D-M-I: Counting Angels on Pinheads

(Trying to control the shape, direction and shareability of music downloads)

A theological conceit in the 17th century – attributed variously to Thomas Aquinas[1] and William Chillingworth[2] – posed this question: how many angels can dance on the head of a pin?

Back then, it was asked in part to mock mediaeval scholars as it would tie their minds in knots. In the modern age, it is a way, albeit an archaic way, to explain how enormous amounts of time can be frittered away debating a topic that is often doomed to futility and invariably of no actual use or practical value to anyone.

Throughout 1999, some in the record business became obsessed with not just the counting of angels on pinheads but also what the pin standard should be and how DRM (digital rights management) could lock the angels to a single pinhead and not allow them to be transferred to any other pinheads.

The Secure Digital Music Initiative (SDMI) began as a way to try and tame the intangible, quickly became an obsession for those involved, found itself in a political crossfire where consensus between vested interests was only ever going to be a mirage, watched helplessly as technologies and the public overtook it and, finally, spluttered out of life, dissolving first into inertia and finally into apathy.

As with so much in 1999, SDMI was about the major labels trying to exert their control on music formats, on technology and on audiences. It can be seen as not just the response to the MP3 but also its diametric opposite.

At heart, it was about trying to create standards for music downloads, like a digital update of the Red Book standard for the CD, covering its technical specifications (including not just the agreed sonic standard but also how much audio it could hold and how many tracks it could be divided into).[3]

In effect, anyone wanting to make a CD player or a CD disc would have to meet these standards and, in order to carry the Compact Disc logo, pay Sony and Philips, as creators of the format, a royalty. This was not insignificant income. *The New York Times* reported in 2001, 'Analysts say Philips receives about 1.8 cents in royalties for every CD sold, and the Sony Corporation 1.2 cents; the companies [. . .] also share license payments of about 2.5 percent from makers of CD players and related equipment.'[4]

Work on SDMI officially began in December 1998 with, as music business writer Phil Hardy put it, 'the aim of creating a secure online system for the digital distribution of music' and the whole operation was 'in response to the threat posed by the unregulated open MP3 standard.'[5]

SDMI was made up, on the music business side, of the five major record labels, the IFPI, the RIAA, some independent labels, music publishers (major and independent) and songwriter rights organisations. They were joined by technology companies (both software and hardware, including Microsoft, Intel, Sony, IBM, Toshiba, Panasonic and Texas Instruments), distributors and retailers. Membership cost $10,000 a year, but this went up to $50,000 a year for companies on the SDMI steering committee.[6]

Tellingly, Apple was not involved in SDMI. Steve Jobs, Apple's co-founder, had only just returned to the company in 1997 after having been exiled and was working hard to disprove F. Scott Fitzgerald's thesis that there are no second acts in American lives.

In 1998, Apple launched the iMac, which completely revitalised the company. In the period during which SDMI was playing out, Jobs and his team were working on a piece of music ripping and management software (iTunes) as well as a portable music player (iPod) that launched in relatively quick succession in 2001 and they were joined in 2003 by the iTunes Music Store, making Apple the new centre of gravity for the digital music business. Apple did not want to be sidetracked by the trivialities of SDMI. It was not interested in counting angels on anyone else's pinheads.

Diamond Multimedia, the great pariah of the record business due to the development of the Rio, was also not a member. Nor was Michael Robertson of MP3.com. The memo about keeping your friends close and your enemies closer clearly did not reach the steering committee at SDMI.

From the off, it felt like an accursed exercise given the exponential growth of MP3s online. Yet the record industry, or at least the major labels, had to be seen to be doing *something*. As Jeremy Silver, then vice president of new media at EMI Recorded Music Worldwide, put it in his *Digital Medieval* book, 'The MP3 horse may have bolted, but that wouldn't stop the RIAA seeking to build a whole new stable.'[7]

If the industry was hoping to eradicate or supersede the MP3, its thinking was that it needed an insider, someone who really understood what the MP3 was, where it came from and what it was capable of.

In Leonardo Chiariglione, they believed they had found the perfect person to lead the SDMI discussions and to develop the standard they felt would not only save them from MP3 but also return the record business to a position of total control once again.

Chiariglione grew up in Turin, Italy, and studied electronic engineering at university, going so far as to complete a PhD on the subject in the 1970s. A polyglot, he worked at Telecom Italia's corporate research centre, so had incredible technical experience and could work with teams from around the world. Most significantly, he helped set up the Moving Picture Experts Group (MPEG) in 1988 and was part of the team that approved the MPEG-1 standard which contained the MP3.

Bingo.

Cary Sherman, senior EVP and general counsel of the RIAA, was the driving force behind SDMI from the music industry's perspective, and he says that Chiariglione was approached to run SDMI for very clear practical and political reasons.

'He was not someone looking to revolutionise the music industry or the motion picture industry,' says Sherman of Chiariglione. 'He was just trying to create standards. We had a lot of sympathy from grownups who understood that this could be a problem and if there was a way to get the benefits of this interoperable technology along with security that the industries could agree on, they were all for it. That's why getting him was a way of lending a lot of credibility to the standard and the effort of SDMI.'

Wooed by the RIAA and sensing an interesting challenge ahead of him, Chiariglione accepted the role.

'The MPEG group had developed the MPEG-1 audio standard that included layer one, layer two, layer three – the last being known as MP3,' he explains. 'And because MP3 was clearly – even though that was not in our intention! – destabilising the music business, they probably thought that I could be a good candidate for doing this work.'

Telecom Italia allowed him to go on secondment in order to take the role at SDMI. He firmly believed that music was merely the first type of content passing through the digital wringer and that other media, notably video, would be next, making what SDMI was hoping to achieve all the more pressing and pertinent. The learnings from music could be filtered back to his bosses at Telecom Italia.

I ask him what SDMI hoped to achieve at its beginning.

'What they wanted to have was a framework that specified the watermarking layer so, through that, they could "manage distribution",' he says.

Like Chiariglione, Niels Rump was seen as another 'insider', having worked at the Fraunhofer Institute on the expansion of the MP3. He joined software development company Intertrust in 1999 and soon after was appointed as chair of the functional requirements working group at SDMI.

'SDMI was a very, very political organisation,' he says. 'Each of the working groups had a chair and two co-chairs: one from the rights holders; and one from the device manufacturers. We tried to develop the functional requirements for a music delivery system that met the requirements of the technology sector as well as the requirements of the rights holders – the labels as well as publishers and the collective management organisations.'

Jay Berman, chairman and CEO of the IFPI, believes that SDMI helped to focus the record business on trying to achieve a single solution rather than having everything confused and diluted though self-interest as each company searched for a digital standard for themselves.

'Each one of the majors undertook its own initiative to create technology departments and for a long time, they each went about that in their own way,' he says. 'So some reached out to Microsoft, some reached out to Liquid Audio. It was kind of a free for all.'

One of the enduring problems for the major label record business was that it had to dance around issues of collusion and to not be seen – publicly, anyway – to be deciding industry-wide policies that could be seen as an outright abuse of their market position.

As the SDMI process was starting off, the major labels in the US were facing a huge investigation into CD price-fixing. The Federal Trade Commission (FTC) undertook a two-year investigation into the matter and in May 2000 it concluded that the majors were complicit in price-fixing discussions and tactics.

'[It] found the companies used illegal marketing agreements to end a price war, inflate the prices of compact discs and sharply restrict the ability of retailers to offer discounts,' wrote *The New York Times* at the conclusion of the FTC investigation. 'The officials estimated that consumers were overcharged by $500 million over the last four years.'[8]

This investigation was buzzing around the heads of the majors as SDMI was getting off the ground. Talal Shamoon, then VP of corporate development and technology initiatives at Intertrust, was a key figure in the SDMI process and said everyone from the major label side was self-consciously treading very carefully and hoping similar accusations to those around CD price-fixing would not be levelled at them.

'They do this thing where they say, "We need a common spec and, for antitrust reasons, it's got to be through an open forum",' he says. 'So they created SDMI. That's the part in *2001: A Space Odyssey* where the lights are going fast and everybody goes batshit! And that was the beginning of 1999 being the pivotal year.'

Paul Jessop, chief technology officer at the IFPI at the time, says everyone involved in SDMI was acutely sensitive to accusations of collusion and this made all the meetings complex and underscored with enormous jeopardy. This slowed things down and it also compromised both what could be done and how it could be done.

'You had the entire music industry in the room,' he explains. 'The music industry, the CE [consumer electronics] industry and the IT industry all in a room trying to reach agreements on things – the very definition of an antitrust violation unless it's done properly. To do it properly requires that you create processes and you follow certain steps. Those steps prolong things that make it difficult to progress. It really inhibited our ability to cut deals.'

There was a kind of shuttle diplomacy happening *within* the meetings to ensure that no antitrust laws were being broken or even coming close to being violated.

'I was in the room at SDMI trying to get all the record companies on board for standards and then go back into the room with the IT companies and the CE companies and say, "Here's our proposal, this is how we want to move things",' says Matt Oppenheim, then the SVP of business and legal affairs at the RIAA. 'I was trying to build a consensus both within my room and then with the other industries. That was my job. Our companies definitely had competing views, but all those competing views were just shades of the same colour. Then you go into the other room and they were definitely not even shades of the same colour – you were fighting a totally different colour.'

Jay Samit, SVP of new media at EMI, believes the antitrust worries ensured that everyone involved was left to drown in red tape and any progress that could have been made was pulled down with them.

'Here is what my take was on SDMI,' he says. 'Nerds in the bowels of these big companies that had never been let out of the basement to see the light of day, every month get to travel to exotic cities around the world for a week. These people are never going to stop and agree and do something. They're having too much fun. So after the first couple, I'm like, "This is a waste. I'm doing my own thing." What I then had to learn was antitrust laws. I obviously know my counterparts at all the labels. I'm allowed to talk to them about certain things but not other things – legally. How do I get them into the deals that I'm going into so that these startups have a chance? If you just have one-fifth of the world's music, you're going to die.'

Sherman says the court action against the Diamond Rio in 1998 was, in part, an attempt to clear a path for the success of SDMI. To that end, the history of SDMI cannot be explained wholly without the contextual shadow of the Rio.

'The Diamond Rio, by coming out before we had developed the standard, basically undermined the possibility of SDMI ever succeeding because everybody would have to rush into the marketplace with competing players and it would be very difficult for everyone involved,' he argues. 'The idea was that there would be interoperability. It would be good for the tech industry because every platform would work with every other platform. And it would be good for the music industry because we would have security so that people could engage in legitimate commerce without having piracy destroy the legitimate marketplace.'

Just as SDMI was convening its first meetings of 1999, the Genuine Music Coalition had been launched, made up of labels (including Sub Pop and Rykodisc), artists, producers, device manufacturers (including Diamond Multimedia) and digital music retailers (including GoodNoise and MP3.com), all committed to watermarking files, using Liquid Audio technology, as a way to 'thwart piracy.'[9]

Wired reported, 'The Genuine Music mark will be encoded in the sound file and provided royalty-free to coalition members. The marked Liquid Audio and MP3 files will be open and compatible with all existing MP3 players, as well as portable players such as Diamond's Rio. However,

Liquid Audio will not – as previously reported – release the watermarking technology as an open source.'[10]

The major labels were conspicuous by their absence and the RIAA responded airily that this was not a viable alternative to SDMI and that it would be the key focus in 1999 of the trade body and its (major) label members.

THE LONG ROAD TO SETTING THE STANDARD

The whole SDMI process had to be opened up to proposals so that technology companies could pitch their solutions, the members of SDMI could assess them and a standard could be arrived at.

Sherman, reflecting back on the story of SDMI, suggests that all involved knew it was going to be an incredibly difficult uphill trek and that success was not guaranteed. (This is despite those involved regularly telling the music trade press at the time that this was the single most important thing the industry was doing in 1999 and that failure could never be countenanced).

'It was obviously a very, very difficult sell to get people who loved technology to limit that technology in any way,' he says. 'We understood that from the get go. But we were faced with asking, "What's the solution here?" And there was no solution. You couldn't bring enough lawsuits; you couldn't collect enough damages. You couldn't get injunctions. What really were the options?'

He continues, 'We hired a consulting firm to take a look at this entire situation and come up with the strategy. And the only strategy was to buy in the consumer electronics and IT industries to a solution that would be better for business for the creators as well as business for technology companies. If it failed, it was not going to be a surprise. If it succeeded, it would have been amazing. So it was worth the effort.'

He says that eventually two hundred companies became members of SDMI, showing a cross-industry willingness to reach some kind of consensus. 'It wasn't as though this was a half-hearted effort that a handful of companies participated in,' he insists. 'We had everybody.'

Chiariglione says that everyone involved in SDMI ultimately wanted to reach the same destination; the issue was deciding which technology was the right one to get them there.

'If you say you want to go to Mars and I want to go to Venus then it's hard to find convergence,' he says. 'But everybody wanted to go to Mars. The point was: would we use a rocket with a central propulsive system or another one? The priority was we wanted to go to Mars, but the receptacle containing the humans, in terms of its shape and size, was dependent on functional specifications and functional requirements. Based on this we called for companies to explain how we would solve that.'

Chiariglione says an important thing to remember throughout all the SDMI discussions is to never conflate 'DRM' with 'protection' as they are very different things.

'DRM – people think this is protection, but it is management, actually,' he says. 'Watermarking is a management system.'

I ask Chiariglione how he and his team assessed the submissions they were sent and how they filtered down to the ones that they felt had a hope of success.

'We wanted something robust,' he says. 'If you receive ten proposals, and one gives you, say, a robustness of seven, but no one gives you more than that, so what are going to do? Either you take the seven or you say, "I give up because I didn't get what I wanted." We wanted a watermark, we wanted it to be robust and we were going to choose the most robust of all.'

Jeremy Silver called SDMI an 'audacious project' and noted that Chiariglione 'presided over the SDMI proceedings like a papal emissary.'[11]

When news of the establishment of SDMI was made public, it pushed utopian notions of security and an industry dedicated to building a new download business model, one far away from the deceitful and disloyal MP3, by working in glorious harmony with the technology and software sectors.

Berman called it 'a critically important initiative' and instantly dismissed the option of licensing MP3 for the initiative. 'Under current circumstances there are no measures of security in MP3,' he told *Music Week*.[12]

He did accept that there had been some tardiness in the music industry's part in fully addressing this, with an estimated eighty thousand unlicensed MP3s already circulating online.

'The move is partly in response to the threat posed by the unregulated open MP3 standard, which the US record industry association RIAA and international record industry association IFPI believe enables widespread music piracy on the internet,' reported *Music & Copyright* in January 1999, parroting the industry's line about the evils of MP3s. 'SDMI also hopes that the new system will protect copyrighted music in all existing and emerging digital formats and create inter-operable products by harmonising different delivery methods and storage media such as high-density discs.'[13]

The major labels had placed themselves at the centre of the SDMI efforts, but some of the larger music publishers were not as gung-ho as their record company opposites, sniffily dismissing the whole thing as 'little more than a PR exercise' as it was being debated at the Midem industry conference in January 1999.[14]

Sherman was presenting the initiative as nothing less than a declaration of war on MP3. 'We are trying to salvage a legitimate marketplace before MP3 piracy takes over,' is how he explained SDMI's goals to *Billboard* in March 1999. He added, 'This is an effort that needs to be undertaken immediately due to extreme market pressures. . . For the longer term, we are trying to create an infrastructure for new forms of consumer transactions of music in a standardised way.'[15]

Rick Fleischman, senior marketing director at Liquid Audio, said the emphasis lay in shifting consumer behaviour before it became entrenched around the MP3 as the default format for music online. 'The challenge is to come up with something as easy to use as MP3,' he said. 'If consumers don't like it, then the SDMI effort is all for naught. It is very encouraging that the SDMI is moving quickly and establishing firm deadlines. . . A critical thing to watch out for is whether or not the [SDMI Foundation] is meeting its goals in a deliverable time frame.'[16]

Richard Robbins, COO of MP3.com, countered that SDMI was a desperate act of futility.[17]

The system would be based around the watermarking of digital files, with two types of watermarks being used. A strong one would survive the compression of the audio into a digital file whereas the weak one would be erased by the compression. Any SDMI-compliant device would then seek out both strong and weak watermarks. If it could only find the former, it would know the file was a copy and the file would, theoretically at least, be rendered unplayable.[18]

SDMI had set itself a goal of having compatible devices and services in the market before Christmas that year. The PR angle being pushed was that record companies were forward-thinking and proactive entities, keen to make a net positive impact on digital music online.

'To comply with SDMI membership criteria, companies must be involved in providing digital music security, have made strategic financial investments that affect the music industry or be highly visible in the music market,' noted *Music & Copyright*.[19]

Developments were starting to accelerate by April 1999, with thirty-five companies having already presented their proposed solutions to the SDMI team. *Billboard* reported that Microsoft badly fumbled its pitch for its new audio format to become the SDMI standard.

'Microsoft is having a difficult time convincing music labels to embrace its forthcoming MS Audio 4.0 technology,' it wrote. 'In fact, some record companies have banned their new-media executives from supplying Microsoft with content.'[20]

There was a sense of stasis in the record business about backing any new audio format until SDMI had given its stamp of approval, hence Microsoft being left dangling. One anonymous executive told *Billboard*, 'Microsoft has misjudged the industry. They seem to think that "if you build it, they will come," but that isn't necessarily how the music industry works. Still, Microsoft has an unlimited amount of capital to push this through.'[21]

Chiariglione insists that the politics between record labels and technology companies were generally cordial and not as fraught as some reports suggested. They had, he accepts, goals that did not always align, but he claims there was more consensus that there was dissensus.

'It was clear that the mess the music industry [was in] and the music market at that time were unbearable,' he says of the labels' desire to get things moving as quickly as possible. 'Of course, the record companies wanted to have their content protected and the manufacturers at that time – Philips, Sony, Toshiba, Panasonic – were all involved. Everybody wanted to have a solution so that they could make devices so that everybody could do business right. It was, overall, a collaborative spirit. Of course, when you make a decision that will have an impact on your business, then you react. But the technical issues were solvable.'

Shamoon's take on it all suggests this is perhaps all historical revisionism.

'SDMI's politics make the politics of the Middle East look like a kindergarten,' he exclaims. 'Look at the Middle East. Every major power has their own proxies. The proxies fight the other proxies on behalf of the major powers. The proxies fight within themselves. The major powers fight within themselves. They switch sides all the time. That was child's play compared to what was happening at SDMI.'

*

By late May, following a three-day SDMI meeting in London at the start of that month, more developments were being announced, with SDMI's team keen to show that swift progress was being made. The five major labels had confirmed they would add watermarking to future CDs as all CDs to date had been issued without any form of DRM or digital protection. SDMI also said that measures would be put in place to watermark licensed music downloads and render unauthorised downloads unplayable.

Shamoon says he ended up becoming the chairman of SDMI almost by accident because of his expertise around watermarking.

'One of my colleagues, Jack Lacy, was the head of the original working group at SDMI that specified what the portable device was going to look like,' he says. 'They needed to pick a watermark and, in true Forrest Gump style, I turned out to be the only guy in the room who knew anything about watermarking because that was my research expertise back before I ran away from the science zoo and became a business guy. My company didn't do watermarking, so I was neutral. They wanted to use the same watermark technology that had been used for DVD-Audio.'

The goals of the major labels within SDMI were, however, clashing with the goals of device manufacturers. 'Some consumer electronics companies are concerned that the moves will conflict with their plans to offer MP3-compatible devices,' said *Billboard*.[22]

In June 1999, cyber rights advocacy group the Electronic Frontier Foundation (EFF) made its opposition to SDMI clear by setting up CAFE (the Consortium for Audiovisual Free Expression), disdaining SDMI as an assault on free speech.

'Online music fans should not be forced to relinquish important rights like fair use and free speech because others fear they will abuse those rights,' claimed Tara Lemmey, executive director of the EFF at the launch of CAFE. 'EFF supports the development of an open digital-audio architecture that respects the public's long standing legal rights under copyright and international standards of free expression.'[23]

CAFE did little to shake SDMI. It powered ahead unaffected.

In June 1999, *Music & Copyright* reported that there would be a two-stage approach for the rollout of SDMI's ambitions. The first fully SDMI-approved music devices were expected to be sold by December, but watermarked CDs and downloads would be released by August.

Given the growing use of, and increasingly widespread availability of MP3s, there would be an armistice of sorts through a transition period. The initial wave of players would support MP3s, but a trigger in the devices could, when pulled, mean only SDMI-compliant files were playable.

Further details of the bifurcated launch strategy for SDMI were soon unveiled. Phase 1, moving into effect before the end of 1999, would see screening technology integrated into SDMI-compliant digital players (software and hardware) with their ability to play unprotected MP3 being unaffected during the first stage. Phase 2 would screen all tracks and block unauthorised ones, although no date had been set for it at this stage.[24]

Chiariglione told *Billboard*, 'You will be able to play your MP3 files on the portable devices of today, but at a certain point in time, which might happen quite soon, the record companies will start embedding some signals into the future content so that it can become playable only on SDMI devices.'[25]

The timing of a second phase to the project was the subject of much discussion – effectively only enabling SDMI-compliant files to play on SDMI-approved devices – with the argument being this could only kick in when the number of SDMI-compliant music files available online vastly outnumbered the unlicensed (generally MP3) ones online and there were enough consumers to make it viable. Go too early (and without the interim breadcrumbing of MP3 compatibility) and users would not be tempted to upgrade to the download services and hardware that SDMI had officially approved.[26]

In July, *Billboard* wrote that a flurry of portable digital music devices from brands such as Thomson, Samsung and Creative Labs would be hitting the market in September following news that a standard specification had been adopted at an SDMI meeting in June and ratified at another meeting the following month.[27]

'Two years ago, the technology sector laughed at us for thinking there was going to be a way to deliver music to consumers online with any degree of security,' declared Hilary Rosen, president/CEO of the RIAA. 'This is a huge step.'[28]

More details on Phase 2 were finally made public, specifically that within the next eighteen months, users would be forced to upgrade their devices in order to play new and copy-protected music because any pirated or unauthorised music would be screened out by devices. No CDs manufactured before Phase 2 began would be watermarked, meaning tens of millions of unprotected files could theoretically be available online.

'The ceding of this point was a difficult but necessary one to move the process forward, according to participants,' noted *Billboard*.[29]

Rosen admitted there was no technological solution for legacy CDs already in the market, but there was an enforcement one. 'I have the authorization to be as vigorous as ever in enforcement [against online piracy],' she cautioned.

Sherman added, 'What we have with this is the start of a new legitimate market for music, and that is exactly what we had hoped for.'[30]

The bombast and certainty around SDMI that ran through the summer had, however, started to ebb away by the autumn. In a *Billboard* piece about upcoming device launches from Diamond, Sony, Sanyo, Creative Labs and Lyra, it was announced that ARIS Technologies would provide the watermarking for the initial rollout of SDMI-compatible devices. This was deflated somewhat by an admission that SDMI-compatible devices would almost certainly not be ready for sale by Christmas, thereby missing the biggest sales and consumer adoption window of the year.[31]

Chiariglione tried to put a positive spin on it by emphasising that they were 'very happy with the progress that has been made on this', while Rosen, speaking on a panel at the Wall Street Journal Technology Summit in Washington at the end of September, said it was not something to get unduly stressed about because 'the market is very young' and that 'Christmas should not be held as a marker' for the success, or otherwise, of SDMI.[32]

Rosen's quixotic optimism here, despite all the evidence to the contrary, puts one in mind of the scene in *This Is Spinal Tap* where manager Ian Faith tries to reassure the band that a cancelled show in Boston was not a sign of a drastic slump in their popularity. 'I wouldn't worry about it,' he says. 'It's not a big college town.'

Berman was, in the same issue of *Billboard*, keenly accentuating positives where he could find them, calling the SDMI programme 'the single most important initiative ever undertaken by the recording industry.'[33]

The numerous speed bumps and missed targets started to echo that deathless Douglas Adams quote: 'I love deadlines. I like the whooshing sound they make as they fly by.'

Chiariglione claims he was not unduly worried about things slightly slipping behind schedule as 1999 rolled on. 'I love deadlines; we always pushed people to agree on deadlines,' he says. 'But you cannot put people in jail because they did not work to a deadline!'

Things, however, were beginning to pick up pace again by the end of the year.

Standards for Phase 2 had been discussed at an SDMI meeting in Hawaii, a detail that only served to further fuel suspicions that SDMI was little more than a run of foreign excursions with some meetings tacked on. Those involved in SDMI were self-aware enough to joke about these perceived mini-breaks they were going on.

'I've still got the T-shirt somewhere – the SDMI World Tour T-shirt,' laughs Paul Jessop, chief technology officer at the IFPI at the time. 'We met all over the place, like in Japan and in Hawaii. Hawaii was the least offensive one of all! Hawaii in late November is incredibly cheap, because it's after the summer but before the winter. And for the Japanese it's a short flight for them. It's a short flight from the West Coast. And who doesn't want to go to Hawaii?'

The SDMI meetings that he attended were, according to Jollyon Benn, internet investigations executive at the BPI, not exactly invigorating. 'Jesus, they were dull!' he wails.

While some might have scoffed at these trips, the clock was against them and they had to show that results were being achieved, regardless of the location of the meetings.

'[T]he task of clearing up the internet of infringing files. . . [has]. . . become a more pressing one,' noted *Billboard*, before providing more details on the specifications for the next wave of portable devices and how they would filter out 'demonstrably pirated' and unlicensed digital music files.[34]

Copies of files would be limited to four, one on the host device (i.e. the PC) and three on portable devices; music copied in this format would not be able to be transferred online; and content could not be transferred to a second host device. On top of this, music created and released after Phase 2 began would have an embedded signal (termed a 'flag') promoting users to upgrade to the new software and would not be able to receive any new music files until they did.[35]

SONY-DINGER'S CAT: WHY ONE MAJOR LABEL DID AND DIDN'T BACK SDMI

As noted in Chapter 2, there was often a yawning disconnect between the music and the hardware divisions of Sony. But Sony Music was deeply involved in SDMI's attempts to get a single digital music standard and the electronics arm of the company was simultaneously working on its bespoke MagicGate copy-protection technology under the auspices of SDMI. It was a rare example of two Sony divisions actually working towards a common goal.

MagicGate was developed in lockstep with Sony's Memory Stick Walkman. The company had revolutionised portable music with the original cassette Walkman, originally launched in 1979 but really seen as a totemic device of the 1980s. Its Discman portable CD player was also a hit in the 1980s and 1990s. It was hoping that it could repeat its success for a third time in the new digital world.

Announced in September 1999, the Memory Stick Walkman would go on sale on 21 December that year, initially in Sony's home market of Japan. It would draw on Sony's ATRAC3 audio compression technology instead of MP3.[36] A US launch would follow in January 2000 where it would retail for $399 and hold up to eighty minutes of music.[37]

UNMAGICAL THINKING: BREAKING THE SDMI SPELL

The hubristic bubble the SDMI team were operating in became all too apparent when they decided to make the SDMI watermarking software public. So confident were they that they had a watertight watermarking solution, they released four preselected music samples in September 2000 and challenged hackers to try and crack them within three weeks, stripping the files of their watermarking. If they could break the unbreakable in three weeks they would win $10,000.

'One song in the pair had two versions – a version with a watermark and a version without,' wrote Paul Goldstein about the challenge. 'The other song came in a single version with the identical watermark. The challenge was to make a copy of this second song, but with the watermark removed.'[38]

They were told to submit their entries to an 'oracle' on the SDMI site and they would be assessed by the team there, approving any that managed to remove the watermark but without deteriorating the audio quality of the file.

An estimated 450 hackers rose to the challenge and a team, led by Edward Felten at Princeton University, did exactly what SDMI was convinced was impossible. It was in part driven by Felten wanting to teach the SDMI an important lesson: no software or watermark was unbreakable.

'There's a phenomenon that some technologists call "magical thinking", that technology can do anything if you work hard enough,' he said. '[T]here seemed to be a lot of magical thinking in the music industry about SDMI.'[39]

Felten and his team claimed victory in having cracked all four watermarks, saying their submissions had been verified by the SDMI 'oracle.' Chiariglione disputed this, saying the quality of the audio had not been determined.

Felten reportedly refused to sign the confidentiality agreement tied to the challenge and therefore could not claim the prize money.[40] He did, however, wish to publish how they hacked it and was immediately met with legal threats from the RIAA's lawyers. Felten did not back down. Instead he sued the RIAA, calling the presentation of the hack a form of free speech that needed to be robustly defended. The RIAA capitulated quietly and Felten presented his paper on the hack at the USENIX conference in Washington, D.C. in August 2001.[41] [42]

The damage, however, had been done. SDMI had been professionally and publicly ridiculed, its weaknesses exposed for all to see.

ONE DEFLATION UNDER A GROOVE: THE SLOW PUNCTURE OF SDMI

Steve Knopper, in his 2009 book *Appetite For Self-Destruction*, listed SDMI as one of 'Big Music's Big Mistakes' as the digital age was dawning. He witheringly noted that they met 'thirty-two times over almost three years, at expensive hotels in exotic places.' He estimated that SDMI cost somewhere between $5 million and $10 million to run for its short life. He noted that the 'SDMI-compliant' logo, intended for retailers and device manufacturers to proudly display they were signed up to SDMI, cost $200,000. The feeling that SDMI was a money pit could not be avoided.[43]

Shamoon says it quickly became ludicrous and excessive. 'Everybody showed up with their own hyper-expensive lawyers,' he says. 'The thing took on a life of its own. The people attending SDMI became friends and started to enjoy showing up every two weeks or every month. They got bored of showing up at the LAX Marriott, so the locations got fancier and fancier.'

He offers an exhaustive list of all the problems with SDMI and why he believes it was a doomed operation. It is a lengthy and hugely entertaining quote that is worth running in full to really capture the disbelief and exasperation that gripped him as he recounted what happened and looked to summarise the many flaws.

> They got the guy [Leonardo Chiariglione] who created MP3, as MP3 came out of MPEG. Think of it: it's almost like capturing a strategic chess piece from the other side. You get the guy who built the standard that created MP3. The guy was unassailable, ostensibly, because he was neutral and had these ideas of technology and free love and everybody was on a level playing field. You get him to be the executive director of SDMI. He [eventually] took a backseat and they allowed them to have this guy Jack Lacy who he kind of liked, who'd been at AT&T and had joined us as part of the exodus from AT&T to run the first portable device working group.
>
> Then I took over the watermarking group. Most of my job was just managing the politics between the different players. There were three constituencies. There were the IT companies. There was the consumer electronics constituency. And there were 3.1 protagonists there. Sony, who was the really cool, beautiful kid; Panasonic who could do what Sony could do without the glow, but had some muscle; and Toshiba, as back then Toshiba was a player. Toshiba was firmly in the Intel and Microsoft camp, Panasonic played both tables. Sony was Sony and had the sense of manifest destiny: the Walkman, Akio Morita, Sony Music, Columbia. Sony is royalty in that game. And then there was the gallery. The gallery was all these new Silicon Valley startups that were looking for funding, looking for their IPOs, looking to get their technology licensed to IT companies and CE [consumer electronics] companies. And then the labels via the RIAA. You literally had every major IT company, every major consumer electronics company and every record label in the room. You couldn't eat a croissant at the break table without having an antitrust lawyer tell you how many bites you could take! And you certainly couldn't discuss how much that croissant cost!

Rump says that SDMI was too stop-start to really be able to get momentum going and to deliver on its promises, a situation exacerbated by the partisan nature of some of the participants. 'It's the only organisation that I know of where nearly every plenary we had, where we had meetings, we had to stop the discussions because one of the two groups wanted to go away, have a huddle, have a discussion amongst themselves and come back to the main room,' he says. 'Typically, this is all done in the open, not within SDMI. So it was a very, very political discussion.'

Knopper accepted that SDMI did manage to produce a copyright encryption standard, albeit a 'flawed' one, that was developed by ARIS Technologies. 'By this time, it was obvious to frustrated panellists that SDMI was at best unworkable, and most likely doomed,' he wrote.[44]

Chiariglione claims that he was always insistent throughout the process that watermarking on its own was never going to be enough. 'Just defining the watermark was insufficient,' he says. 'I remember that I said, "We need to define the format for audio compression." I wanted to have a complete form – not just the watermark. Unless you get something that is really transportable, the format is useless. Having the user conditions embedded in the watermark, saying what they could and could not do, that is something they did not want.'

He pauses and then announces, 'At that moment, I understood that the SDMI project would fail. The reason why I accepted that is not so much because it was a solution for the music industry, for which I was hired of course, but because it was a solution that would influence other media as well. It could have been a watershed moment, but it was not.'

He claims that a major weakness throughout the SDMI process was that the record labels, the software companies and the hardware manufacturers did not fully grasp the value of a standard that would work across all music downloads.

'I am a standards man,' Chiariglione says. 'I think that a standard should be done thoroughly. If you define standards for a piece then you may satisfy the people who are concerned with protection of content but you will not satisfy other people. The CD worked because they decided that the CD was formatted in this way [and the various parts agreed upon]. You cannot say, "This bit is free, Sony can do it in this way." That doesn't work and shows a lack of understanding of the fundamental point [of standards].'

He adds, 'A standard is a standard. A standard with options will fail. It will always fail. Standards are not a case of either you use it or you go to jail. Adoption of a standard should be a free decision. A free decision based on business reasons.'

He feels it was all a huge, and tragic, missed opportunity for the music business.

'If we had defined this protected music format, I think that that would have made a difference,' he asserts. 'There would have been a single format that was protected and that was accepted. It doesn't mean that the format would have been bulletproof. Nothing is bulletproof. This protected format would have been something transparent to the user. If things are not transparent in the media domain, then nothing works.'

Larry Kenswil, president of eLab (a division of Universal Music Group) from 1997 to 2008, rolls his eyes when I raise the topic of SDMI, saying he preferred not to attend the meetings and instead sent his digital lieutenant Albhy Galuten to report back on any important developments.

'God, they were awful!' he laughs. 'They were just terrible meetings to have to sit through. Often they were in airport hotels around the world. Albhy was the one who did the grunt work on that, going to every meeting, whereas I was sitting back and looking at the results and directing him as to which way the company wanted to go.'

For him, SDMI was akin to painting the Golden Gate Bridge: an eternal task that was destined to never be finished to anyone's satisfaction, especially as there were so many different parties involved all expecting slightly different results.

'It would take years to do these negotiations and the tech people were coming up with technical solutions, and the business people were putting their requirements on that, especially for copyright protection,' he says. 'All those discussions just took so long that the technology advancements would overtake it. And if you did come to a decision, it would be archaic within a year. That became obvious. And it is one of the reasons why SDMI was one of the last attempts at doing that. [A key] problem was the length of time it took [to deal with the] competing interests of everyone in the room.'

Rump believes that the labels effectively defenestrated themselves (and SDMI) by focusing on DRM proposals that would be delivered at some abstract time in the future. All the while they continued to release millions of CDs each year without any copy protection. It was like double-locking your front door while simultaneously unbricking every wall in your house.

He says, 'I do remember talking to former colleagues at Fraunhofer who said, "What's the point of protecting all these MP3s? As long as the record companies put out their masters to consumers, what's the point in protecting things?"'

Jessop says this was a point he was repeatedly raising in SDMI meetings and that the labels really needed to address it. 'It was fairly clear that unprotected content would proliferate,' he says. 'The line I was taking was that unprotected content will proliferate anyway because you are still putting it out on CD.'

That said, Rump claims that he always held faith that, with a good wind behind it, SDMI could actually work.

'I never felt it was doomed,' he argues. 'But I certainly remember it was hard going and it was a slugfest that you needed to work through. But there are technical solutions. For most technical problems, there are technical solutions. I still thought that we could find technical solutions to it. I was wrong!'

Like the theory of praxis, Rump feels SDMI making mistakes and not really achieving anything was actually a good thing in the end. Searching for the silver lining in the cloud, he suggests it allowed the business to learn from its mistakes and recalibrate its thinking.

'SDMI turned out to be a cul-de-sac,' he says. 'I don't see that as a problem. You need to go down those cul-de-sacs to realise that they don't lead anywhere and then find a better way.'

Several people involved in SDMI told me that meetings became serendipitous opportunities for participants to discuss among themselves matters that lay outside of the purview of SDMI itself.

Yet even if people spent more time on SDMI-related matters rather than extracurricular dealmaking, it was never going to make SDMI work and 'save' the music business from the threat of digital piracy and music being freely circulated online.

'It was a ball, but the bottom line is that for the whole year-and-a-half of SDMI you had a patient that was terminally ill, and you were throwing every flavour of chemotherapy into that body on a wing and a prayer, but the cancer was just moving way too fast,' says Talal Shamoon. 'And the only way the cancer was stopped was literally through luck and through the liberal application of even more chemotherapy outside in the court system.'

Things started to quieten down for SDMI through 2000, with *The Register* writing in January 2001 that Chiariglione was leaving his post in the coming months and that SDMI had 'almost nothing to show for its efforts but broken deadlines' and that 'it was always the music industry's puppet.'[45]

SDMI officially ran out of road in April 2002 and was disbanded. Rob Glaser, CEO of RealNetworks, did not mourn its passing. 'It ended up dying a gristly, painful death,' he said. 'It was an incompetently run pipe dream. They were trying to do something technologically that technology wasn't able to do. And as a result, they lost control.'[46]

On the technology theme, Oppenheim suggests that the whole thing imploded because the software faction fundamentally did not want it to succeed. That was because it ran counter to many of the philosophical beliefs that Silicon Valley was founded upon – namely the endlessly repeated mantra that 'information wants to be free', a rallying cry and belief system that dates back to the first Hackers Conference in 1984 in California.

'The CE [consumer electronics] industry was willing to sit down and work on things and they knew how to do that with us,' he says. 'It would have been a hard negotiation but we probably would have worked it out. The IT industry had not been engaged in those kinds of dialogues historically, either with the CE industry or with the music industry. Their view of the world was, "We're going to go in alone. Content should be free. We don't want to have to do deals." They really tanked SDMI because they didn't want any standards. They wanted to draw this process out as long as possible. They were in the room so they could do individual deals, but they weren't in the room in order to enable a broader functional marketplace.'

Jay Samit is bluntly dismissive of the entire project. 'They were doing this SDMI thing and just wasted money and time,' he scoffs. 'They didn't know what they were doing.'

Equally, former Geffen executive and co-founder of the Pho List Jim Griffin says he was absolutely certain it was a dead duck from the off and did not want to waste his time on it.

'I knew that it would be a failure,' he snorts. 'I never attended a single meeting. The people who were doing it were complete idiots. In digital at that time, if IBM was behind something, I knew it was going to fail. You just knew it was going to fail, because it would be heavy iron, it would be a corporate system, it would not relate to the kinds of people that we were reaching out to.'

Paul Vidich, executive VP of Warner Music Group, says that any optimism that might have formed around the *idea* of SDMI quickly evaporated for him as soon as the actual *process* behind SDMI began, especially when he realised how slowly it was going to move.

'In the very first meeting, it was clear to me that it was never going to succeed,' he says. 'The problem was in a mass situation like that you have all these competing interests. You're operating in what I'll call tectonic time as opposed to real time. Real time was what was happening in the marketplace. Tectonic time was the two, three, four years that it typically took for a standards body to agree on a standard, get it adopted, and then put out the licensing protocols. Those two things were completely at odds with each other.'

Jeff Liebenson, VP of legal and business affairs at BMG International, feels that the very structure of the record business was such that SDMI was always going to be a fool's errand. Too many competing voices effectively dropping bombs on what should be common ground. It is a problem cursed to repeat itself eternally.

'As we've seen, through various generations of efforts to reach industry consensus on what would appear to be key things, like SDMI where you need industry-wide cooperation, it's incredibly hard to get it,' he says. 'And every effort seems to require innumerable meetings and the expenditure of huge amounts of money – and then ultimately no results. The industry is so internally competitive, which usually is a good thing, but it makes it very hard to achieve any of those larger shared goals that could have been positive.'

For Scott Campbell, founder and MD of MediaSpec, there was a towering irony behind it all. The more the majors tried to push for controlled and controllable digital formats, the more attractive formats like MP3 became to the consumer.

'What was happening in SDMI was that these power groups weren't going to agree on anything,' he says. 'If you get a bunch of lawyers in the room from different groups, they're all, "This is my bit here." They are all fighting for the window seat and trying to get the ball back. So it was a disaster. It's unfortunate because it had the right intention; but the reality was the market demand for the MP3 thing just grew and grew and grew. It was popular [with users] because of its banned aspect and the illegality of it!'

It was all a matter of uncontrollable greed and desperate overreaching according to Scott Cohen, co-founder of distribution company The Orchard. He references back to the enormous royalty windfall that Sony and Philips got from the CD and says those jostling to get their standard adopted by SDMI were like cartoon characters with dollar signs for eyes.

It will come as no surprise that Michael Robertson of MP3.com thought SDMI, and the push for DRM, was patently ludicrous. He was so fundamentally opposed to it that he tried to take it down, or at least cause serious structural damage.

'I was enemy number one because, if you go back and look at the archives on MP3.com, I leaked documents on SDMI and all those initiatives,' he says. 'I sabotaged all of them because I thought they were insane. I thought that DRM was horrible for the industry and it was a huge step back for consumers. I wanted an operability environment where every piece of audio worked with every other audio. I didn't endear myself to them! I wasn't shy about it. You can go on MP3.com and you can read the articles. Most of them I wrote. In those early days, I was saying that DRM was not the right strategy. It just wasn't.'

His dander now firmly up, he continues, 'I was stridently opposed to DRM. I thought it was dumb. I thought it was counter to everything I stood for and we weren't going to support it. Period. Did not care who they were.'

He reveals that the major labels tried to get his company to embrace DRM by dangling their content in front of him. He was not going to compromise. 'Some of the major record labels came down to us and said, "Hey, we want to do something with DRM?" We were like, "Get out of here! We won't do it." It was too cumbersome and bulky for the users and the songs would expire and they wouldn't play everywhere. It was such a mess. We were just not going to play. We're not going to do it. I'm sure that did not endear me to the record labels, but it endeared me to the music fans. To me, that was a more important constituency than the major record labels.'

Sherman remains convinced that SDMI was not the total disaster that some now see it as and that it actually produced some unexpected positives, although they did not reveal themselves until years later.

'SDMI turned out to have a hidden benefit that none of us thought about at the time,' he says. 'It brought together every person in the world – in the music industry and in industries if they were involved in creative works – into one place that talked about the issues. Everybody got to know everybody else. All those people travelled the world to attend meetings that we personally organised every two weeks or once a month. Everybody knew everybody else and later on all those people, when they moved companies, they would go from one job to another job in another sector of the industry, because of the contacts that they formed at SDMI.'

He continues, 'It was, in a way, an incubator for figuring out how this business might work, whether or not the standard-setting part failed, it was a huge success in terms of bringing together all these people in order to, in the future, build a business out of this whole new music technology and digital downloads and streaming business.'

Paul Jessop is sanguine about it all, which is quite something given how deeply involved he was with SDMI for the duration of its short life as a project. Given all the (often conflicting) interests of the assorted parties involved, he feels it was a miracle anything actually happened. Its collapse was foreordained.

'SDMI was remarkable in that it happened,' he says. 'It was remarkable in that there was cooperation between these warring factions. It ultimately stalled because it's an unsolvable problem. Even so, there was still a residual, vestigial hope that we would actually get something that was so good that it would displace piracy because it would be more convenient.'

Shamoon argues that the real legacy of SDMI was that it could be held up as evidence of the music industry trying to embrace a digital future. This was something it was desperate to project outwards when in the full grip of litigation against serial uploaders in the great file-sharing wars that defined the opening years of the new millennium.

'One of the roles SDMI played politically was when consumers complained in Congress – because there were congressional hearings [about the legal action against file-sharers]. Initially, it was like [Cleetus voice], "What are you doing to help my constituents acquire music over this new thing called the internet?" Suing 16-year-olds wasn't a very good answer in a congressional hearing. "We're building a standard to create devices. We're working with the greatest technology companies in the world to deliver a quality experience." That's a great answer. So SDMI played a role in lobbying, as well as a role in getting the technology industry lined up to sing from the same book with, what I think was a romantic and noble ideal – to really deliver to consumers a new format.'

Berman agrees that SDMI was the other side of the coin from litigation for the record industry as the 1990s ended. Litigation would only go so far and the industry had to be seen to be backing and building legal alternatives to file-sharing sites, albeit ones that seemed to prize DRM over consumer experiences.

'We were very much in uncharted waters in that respect,' he says. 'We had a mandate to sue. But we didn't have, other than SDMI, an industry-wide mandate to [address it]. The only way that you can actually fight something like this is to create a legitimate alternative. That was a business decision that each one of the majors had to come to on its own. So there was a disconnect between what we were able to do and what might have been actually practically effective.'

He adds, 'It was a monumental struggle. The way to fight this and to give you the tools with which to fight it, to create something that we want to protect and that there is a way for the consumer to take advantage of: that took an inordinate amount of time.'

Shamoon feels SDMI was never going to work. There were too many political issues ping-ponging between the participants for real progress to be made, plus it was always going to be playing catch-up with both technology and consumers. It was trying to bottle lightning in a container made from tissue paper.

'There's the old Otto von Bismarck line about the two things you should never watch being made – laws and sausage,' he says. 'SDMI and all the litigation around that was literally the law version of that quote. You know what? I don't regret it. I don't think anyone regrets that the thing collapsed. It could have never succeeded in hindsight. It was far too ambitious and far too complex against the backdrop of one of the most major disruptive events in the history of technology. Like a thousand-legged beast with 16 brains, there was just no way it was going to work.'

DRM-MONGERING: AN INDUSTRY DIVIDED ON COPY PROTECTION IN THE DIGITAL AGE

The record industry was largely split on the matter of DRM along the lines of majors and independents. DRM was a core component of what SDMI was trying to achieve and the major labels, publicly at least, were insistent that DRM was the panacea and the only way forward to build a legitimate music downloads marketplace.

The independents, however, were taking an entirely different stance: DRM as a form of control was fundamentally anti-consumer and not something most of them wanted to be seen to be condoning, let alone imposing.

Alison Wenham, chair and CEO of independent label trade body AIM, feels the obsession around DRM by the majors was 'a great big PR own goal' and something that dogged the record business for years.

'As if we didn't need another PR own goal after the 'rip-off industry' accusations,' she says. 'The PR of the industry has suffered over the past twenty years due to our own actions. It was all self-inflicted.'

Helen Smith, AIM's director of legal and business affairs, concurs.

'The negative PR that came out of DRM, that was just awful,' she says. 'It was an awful time to be associated with those types of obsessive control. It was not something that really sustained the reputation. All those things they had heard about the music business were absolutely true. We were concerned about bad PR for the music sector. At the same time, obviously, we also wanted to be sure that music wasn't getting ripped off. It was a tricky issue to navigate.'

At Beggars Banquet, the company was seeking to have a more nuanced take on it all, trying to figure out why the majors were pushing in the direction they were. Martin Mills, head of Beggars, says they weighed up all the options and ultimately sided with what they thought was the most consumer- and artist-friendly approach.

'We were a bit torn on it,' he says of the DRM debates. 'We liked the idea of being adventurous with new formats, but at the same time we were concerned about the value of our rights. We were quite tempted by locked-down files, but at the same time we realised it didn't really suit our business, it didn't really suit our artists. We were never as committed to locked files as the majors were.'

Other independents tried dipping a toe in the waters of DRM but soon realised that it was just putting up unnecessary barriers for consumers and risked detonating a legal download market before it even had a chance of getting off the ground.

'You didn't want to penalise the people who did buy your records by making it harder for them to play them,' says Peter Quicke, label manager at Ninja Tune. 'We probably did try a few DRM things just because they were new technologies, so we would have experimented with them. It didn't seem like a very sensible idea, to be honest. We did a few CD albums which had some sort of DRM on them as well. But you're penalising the people who do actually buy your records by giving them a product that's basically harder to use.'

Paul Hitchman, who left Warner Music Group in the UK in 1999 to co-found Playlouder, says DRM was not just a PR disaster; it actually put giant barricades in the path of the entire digital music business.

'It was the DRM and the fantasy of SDMI [that held things back],' he says. 'I don't think anyone in the music industry understood it. And they were being sold snake oil by [certain voices in the industry] – that they could bottle and own the water, rather than the water being free flowing from the tap, Jim Griffin-style. If there hadn't been any independent sector, the majors would have been even tougher on locking stuff down.'

Quoted in Mark Mulligan's 2015 book *Awakening: The Music Industry In The Digital Age*, Cliff Fluet, then in the legal team at Warner Music in the UK, said, 'SDMI was born out of an absolute belief that the internet was simply a 'new format' that could be controlled.'[47]

Mulligan himself wrote, 'SDMI's uncomfortable mix of lofty ideals and cynical business aspirations were never the best recipe for success [. . .] SDMI's preoccupation with control acted as a blinker on its strategic vision, stymying its ability to both see and address the bigger picture.'[48]

Ian Rogers, then at Nullsoft the parent company of Winamp, calls DRM 'a red herring from the very fucking beginning' and says it was only ever about the self-entitled major labels aggressively trying to exert control over the internet or, more specifically, exert control over music on the internet.

'DRM was the most idiotic part of this entire story,' he says. 'The record labels, they had control, they wanted to keep control and they didn't understand the internet was going to represent a revolution of information. It's easy to say now, but it was obvious in 1996 – and there were so many people who were in denial [then] that the internet would be a revolution of information. It wasn't about MP3. It was about the lack of DRM.'

Some at the majors were possibly even more dismissive of DRM, but this was not something they could express publicly. Elizabeth Brooks was working in A&R at Sony Music in 1999 but left her job there to join Napster as its first VP of marketing.

'There were billions spent on DRM,' she sighs. 'It was madness. It didn't make sense. Like the horse wasn't out in the barn; the horse was long gone and frolicking in the fields of easily available music.'

There were other DRM naysayers at the majors at the time who were trying to, internally at least, push for a slightly more flexible approach.

'There were definitely people on the DRM side,' says one source at a major label, of the internal debates around this issue. 'They were the anchor going, "No, you can't do that. You have to lock it and you can't rip it." There was definitely that DRM crew, but most of us in that group were trying to push things forward. We were going, "Come on, guys. No one's ever going to get into this if it's too full of friction." It was the digitisation of the format and the freedom of it. But there were people still talking about security.'

Charles Grimsdale, founder of digital music distribution company OD2, says years were lost with the major-led delusion about the healing waters of DRM. 'With hindsight,' he proposes, 'if only the labels had just said, "Look, we're not going to concern ourselves with rights management technology. It's going to be an arms race forever – and that's one we're never going to win. We need to make it as easy as possible for consumers to buy music".'

Some high street retailers also regarded DRM as suffocating their nascent efforts to get their own download services off the ground, incredulous that labels wanted to impose digital restrictions on downloads while simultaneously selling unprotected CDs in physical retail outlets.

'We were very frustrated that the music industry was not putting the customer first,' says Simon Wright, MD of Virgin Retail UK in 1998 and 1999. 'They were putting protection of their copyright first. Which is understandable, don't get me wrong. I'm not suggesting they cut loose with that. But the customer wanted to download. The whole industry at that point should have been quicker to understand the consumer demand, not the technology risk.'

STARTUPS

CHAPTER 11

The Startup Shakedown: Containing and Restraining the New

(Trying to control the next generation of music services by bleeding them dry)

1999 was not just the year the global record industry peaked, it was also the year the dot com boom reached its apex. No one, of course, knew this at the time. But common sense had dangerously slipped its moorings that year. *Ridiculous* business plans were flying around Silicon Valley that were making *ludicrous* claims for the impact of whatever new digital service it happened to be.

Profitability was rarely mentioned; indeed, it was often deemed irrelevant. The only word that mattered was 'scale.' Get enough users and *somehow* it would all come good.

Retrospectively, this has been termed the Bezos Strategy, after Jeff Bezos who founded Amazon in 1994 as a humble online bookstore and for years was running at a loss and any profits were ploughed back into driving growth.[1] The goal of turning Amazon into the 'everything store' eventually paid off handsomely for Bezos. In June 2023, *Forbes* ranked Bezos as the third richest person in the world, with a net worth of $143.3 billion.[2]

But for every Bezos in the late 1990s, there were a thousand founders persuading investors and VCs to put millions – tens of millions, *hundreds* of millions – into their idea. They all promised the world and an IPO to die for, but ended up merely ripping through various stages of investment like a forest fire and leaving behind them nothing but ash and tears.

'In the second half of the 1990s, there were a lot of music ideas that got funded,' says Tim Westergren, then working on the idea that would eventually become Pandora. 'I mean, a lot. Maybe not compared to other sectors, but there are many – MP3.com and MyPlay and Uplister. There were a lot of them.'

The huge sums of money being thrown around in 1999, running concurrently with a staggering lack of due diligence and quality control, suggested an investor sector freewheeling out of control, drunk on its own perceived genius and assured that every dollar it invested in a new company would quickly get ten – even a hundred – back in a short period of time. The magic terms 'IPO' or 'acquisition' were all they needed to hear to keep the delusion in the air.

'Around that time you started to realise that there was no gravity anymore, that objects were floating around you,' says Jim Griffin, former Geffen Records executive and music business consultant. 'You'd think, "Really? I'm not on Planet Earth anymore?" You started to wonder if any of your business instincts mattered at all. Because the economy was moving hundreds of millions of dollars on hunches and bets and technologies that seemed crazy. They weren't crazy, but it definitely made you question everything you knew.'

In the UK, things were not as accelerated as they were in the US, primarily because most of the heavy-hitting VCs were in Silicon Valley. The same dynamics, albeit on a smaller scale, were playing out there, however.

Ben Drury was working at *Dotmusic*, a well-funded startup (for the UK, at least) in the late 1990s and saw firsthand the unhinged thinking and the *laissez-faire* approach to business models that characterised the times.

'In hindsight, 1999 was this great moment of huge euphoria around the world with tech and dot com stuff,' he says. 'We had companies with no revenue going public for hundreds of millions. But at the same time, for the music industry, they were on the cusp of doom. The world was on the cusp of this euphoric, brave new world of tech. But the smart people in the music business realised, "Oh my God – we're on the precipice of disaster here".'

The smart people in the music business, he says, were very much the minority. 'For most people, they just wouldn't even have been thinking about this tidal wave coming,' he sighs. 'It was just, "Let's party!"'

Helen Smith, director of legal and business affairs at AIM, says that there was a clear policy from the majors to nullify any new companies that threatened their supremacy or could force them to recalibrate their comfortable and lucrative business model that had taken them thus far.

'Squeeze them for money and not really be a threat,' is how she defines their approach to startups. 'There was this kind of approach, with regard to technological development, to dismantle, to ignore, to discredit. And then when that doesn't work, you buy them. You buy them and then you just let them die.'

In Chapter 1, I looked at how the dot com boom represented a brewing storm for the music business. The watchword for many of these companies charging out of (mainly) California was 'disruption': disrupting businesses and disrupting business models were the two most important things in the startup catechism.

The bible at the time was a book by businessman and Harvard professor Clayton Christensen that was published in 1997. In *The Innovator's Dilemma*, Christensen argued that successful businesses risk failure and calamity if they do not embrace new markets and models that might kick the legs from under their core operations and profit centres – even if they do not meet their short-term growth targets. The trick – the innovator's dilemma at the heart of the book – was in launching new companies that could build a business specifically around the very technologies that threatened to disrupt them.

'Disruptive technologies bring to a market a very different value proposition than had been available before,' he wrote. 'Generally, disruptive technologies underperform established products in mainstream markets. But they have other features that a new fringe (and generally new) customers value. Products based on disruptive technologies are typically cheaper, simpler, smaller, and, frequently, more convenient to use.'[3]

He added, 'Disruptive technologies typically enable new markets to emerge. There is strong evidence showing that companies entering these emerging markets early have significant first-move advantages over later entrants. And yet, as these companies succeed and grow larger, it becomes progressively more difficult for them to enter the even newer small markets destined to become the large ones of the future.'[4]

The dilemma Christensen outlined was a painful one for companies that were complacently luxuriating in their market dominance, believing it would last forever. The bigger they became, the harder it became to adapt to changes bubbling up outside of their control.

'[A]s companies become larger and more successful, it becomes even more difficult to enter emerging markets early enough,' he proposed. 'Because growing companies need to add increasingly large chunks of new revenue each year just to maintain their desired rate of growth, it becomes less and less possible that small markets can be viable as vehicles through which to find these chunks of revenue.'[5]

*

The record industry was far from oblivious to the mushrooming number of upstarts looking to turn their business on its head and rip its future up in front of its eyes. They could declare war through litigation (Diamond Multimedia) or use black ops to smear, to defame and to undermine (MP3.com). But an increasingly preferred strategy was to pounce on these services, suck them dry of funding, squeeze them for equity and lock them in development hell-style licensing negotiations so that they ran out of time, money or patience – or often all three. This ensured they never launched, or, if they did, they were almost always immediately moribund.

There was something deeply *vampiric* about it all.

One company, more than any other, symbolised the great major label startup shakedown of the late 1990s in digital music. It stands as a warning from history: it is the preeminent music dot com morality tale.

Musicmaker.com began in 1996 in Reston, Virginia, a forty-three-hour drive to San Francisco across the width of the US. It had a straightforward idea: let consumers build their own compilation CDs. It would license recordings from the labels and charge users $9.95 for the first five songs on their bespoke compilation and then $1 per track after that, up to a run time of seventy minutes.[6]

In February 1999, the company announced it would start selling MP3 downloads, offering twenty thousand individual tracks and 2,500 albums. Individual tracks would cost $1. This expansion of its offering was read at the time as a deft move by Musicmaker, concurrently offering both physical and digital consumption options for consumers. The news came off the back of a deal with independent label Platinum Entertainment which licensed its catalogue to Musicmaker on an exclusive basis, including tracks from Dionne Warwick, The Beach Boys and George Clinton. Platinum Entertainment also had an equity stake in the company.[7]

Bob Bernardi, chairman and CEO of Musicmaker, told *Billboard*, 'We are combining the technology with a legitimate music source. Most labels would really like to support MP3, but there have been copyright issues. This is a way for them to get some comfort.'[8]

By March 1999, it had licensed just 150,000 tracks for burning to compilation CDs, initially only from independent labels, which it sorted digitally at its fulfilment centre in Reston where, responding to online customer orders, it would burn the tracks to CD and print a label with the compilation title the purchaser had given it. There was even an option to print album artwork uploaded by the customer.[9]

It might sound terribly quaint today in an age of Spotify and Apple Music playlists that are assembled in minutes and shared in seconds, but this was pretty revolutionary in the 1990s. The record labels tightly controlled the completions business with major brands like *Now That's What I Call Music*, Ministry Of Sound's *The Annual* and a thousand tawdry thematic compilation ideas (driving songs, best punk songs ever, love songs, drinking songs and so on).

The majors were initially hesitant to license to Musicmaker for two main reasons: one, it could pose a threat to their own compilations business; and two, the music could be easily leaked online. Musicmaker agreed to watermark the tracks, using watermarks developed by ARIS Technologies, but this was not enough to get the majors to willingly sign up. As the five majors controlled the bulk of the market – around 80 per cent in the US, according to *The Washington Post*[10] – the venture was always going to be severely compromised.

Compilation albums live and die on hits – and the major labels over-indexed in hits. So without all five majors signed up, Musicmaker would not have a hope of being a mainstream service.

It did, however, have a strong executive team with a background in record labels. President and co-chief executive Devarajan S. Puthukarai was president of Warner Music Media; vice chairman Irwin H. Steinberg had been chairman of PolyGram Records between 1975 and 1982; and marketing vice president William Crowley had worked at Warner Music Enterprises and PolyGram.[11]

By March 1999, the company was haemorrhaging money and had worked through $7 million of its funding, boasting sales of a mere $74,000 in 1998. It needed licensing deals in place with the majors, it needed to raise its profile and it needed to start making money. *Fast.*

In June 1999, Musicmaker thought it had been thrown a lifeline by EMI. That lifeline, however, turned out to be a noose.

EMI agreed to sign an exclusive five-year licensing deal with Musicmaker where it would make five hundred thousand of its tracks available for custom CDs and for download through the Musicmaker service. As a condition of the deal, its first with a major, Musicmaker had to give over 50 per cent share of the company to EMI, although there was no cash element to the deal.[12] Jay Samit, EMI's SVP of new media, also joined the Musicmaker board as part of the deal.

'This is one of a number of opportunities for EMI to generate additional income from our extensive back catalog,' Samit told *Billboard*. 'This agreement will also benefit consumers, who will be able to enjoy music in a new way by creating the albums they have always dreamed of owning.'[13]

Raju Puthukarai, president of Musicmaker.com, said in a statement, 'We are pleased that our first relationship with a major music company is with EMI Recorded Music. We believe that the EMI partnership, combined with our exclusive marketing agreements with Columbia House and others, will ensure that Musicmaker.com becomes a leader in the digital distribution field. We are confident this is going to be an agreeable and fruitful relationship.'[14]

This was, on paper at least, a landmark deal for Musicmaker, giving it a new kind of industry legitimacy and allowing it to build on its existing deals with Columbia House, the mail-order music club set up by Sony Music and Warner Music Group, and AOL's Spinner.com.[15]

Musicmaker had planned to file for an IPO in February 1999, something that could have raised $30 million for the company. It dramatically pulled the brakes on it in April pending talks with a major label: that label, of course, turning out to be EMI. Bob Bernardi, chairman and chief executive of Musicmaker, told the *Los Angeles Times* that, with the EMI deal in the bag, the IPO would be back on and likely to happen at the end of the month.[16]

The IPO took slightly longer than Bernardi estimated, with it actually happening in early July. Shares were originally priced at $14, doubling to a high of $28.13 at the peak of first-day trading before closing the day at $24. This gave the company a stock market value of over $600 million.[17]

'As part of its agreement with EMI, the Net company will have to pay down about $17 million in debt annually for the next five years,' noted *Wired* in the immediate wake of the IPO. 'The company also plans to spend a substantial portion of the proceeds from its IPO to license material from other top labels.'[18]

The Washington Post was reasonably effusive about the Musicmaker IPO. 'Usually, the decision to delay an initial public offering bodes badly for the company going public,' it wrote. 'But exactly the opposite may be the case for musicmaker.com.'[19]

Musicmaker said it sold 5.3 million shares and it emerged in coverage of the IPO that Virgin Holdings Inc, a division of EMI Recorded Music, actually held the music company's half.[20]

Today it might seem flabbergasting that a digital music company would hand over 50 per cent of its equity to just one of the major labels – and in 1999 there were five of them, with EMI the third biggest – as this would drastically dilute the equity the founders and initial investors would be left with. It would also mean the other majors and independents would be left with slim pickings if they were insisting on equity stakes. Yet that was the conundrum Musicmaker found itself facing.

It was a serious roll of the dice: get EMI signed up and hopefully the other majors fall in line. In order to do that, however, it needed to license some catalogue as a statement of intent and this was the extreme cost of getting one of the majors on side.

Westergren says that licensing was always the trump card the labels held and there was a huge amount of initial naiveté among music-centric startups about just how complicated, painful and expensive licensing discussions, especially with the majors, could be. There was a brief window where such startups thought they would be able to have smooth and productive licensing discussions with rights owners. And then reality bit. *Hard.*

'At that point, I think there was not an awareness of the problem of licensing,' he says of the second half of the decade, a time when startups could almost operate under the radar. 'There were a bunch of ideas that ultimately had to reckon with licensing. In the beginning, they were building cool products and no one was paying too much attention to them from the music industry. And then, one by one, they ran into that problem where they started to have to get rights, or they got large enough that the labels cared.'

Jay Samit became president of digital distribution at EMI in 1999, having joined from Universal Studios. He says he had an explicit, and unapologetic, commercial remit straight out of the gates. He was there, he insists, to do deals and to make money.

He says there was added pressure on him as EMI was going through a particularly tough time in the US – it had historically been weak in recorded music's biggest market – and he felt the onus was on him to open up whole new revenue opportunities for the company.

He also says he spotted a huge opportunity with digital startups before his parallels at the other majors had. This was going to be, to use the business argot of the time, an easy win that could stabilise and save the whole company.

'We were laying off tens of thousands of people,' Samit says. 'We're having meetings about shutting down Blue Note and Angel. Horrible stuff. Nobody else in the industry would license any of these [digital startup] bozos anything because they didn't have the rights.'

He says he was going to reposition EMI as open to deals as a digitally savvy music company. He was going to explicitly court the world of startups and quickly bring in money for EMI.

'I got the word out: "If you got cash, you're ahead of the line, I'll get you a deal. If you don't have cash, and your business model has one thread of a chance, I'll take equity in your company in exchange for giving you a licence".'

While most of the deals were being run out of the US, the desire to present EMI as *the* digital record company was also happening within the UK arm of the company.

'We wanted to show that we were putting our arms around this technology and not to be cowed by it or threatened by it,' says Eric Winbolt, digital commercial manager at EMI UK between 1998 and 2000. 'This was a fantastic opportunity. There's a whole new toolbox emerging and we are going to demonstrate [we can use it]. That was a part of the job, to be out in the weeds figuring out what was actually going on and bringing it back to see how we could best take advantage of it. It was our job to be A&R for technology.'

As a strategy, brazen as it was from Samit, it worked – and the results were pretty much instantaneous.

'The first year, we made $100 million – that doesn't have to get shared with artists – just off of equity deals,' Samit tells me. 'I did that the second year as well. So suddenly, I have a seat at the grown-ups' table. I'm not like I was at Universal, the nerd boy that nobody cares about.'

He says he had the ear and the trust of Ken Berry, president and CEO of EMI Recorded Music, who was running the company's US operations. This allowed him to push forward with his digital commercialisation plans. 'Ken is a great guy,' Samit says. 'I give all the credit to him. When I said I wasn't a music guy, he said, "We've got ten thousand music guys. What we don't have is a future." So I could barge in with, "Here's my crazy idea." He'd tell me why it sucks. And then I'd go back. It was a really great relationship.'

EMI might have been keen to look like it was open to doing digital deals, but there was a much darker strategy at play.

Jeremy Silver, vice president of new media at EMI Recorded Music Worldwide at the time of the Musicmaker deal, wrote in his *Digital*

Medieval book, published in 2013, about the enormous pressure on digital executives in that era to bring in millions of dollars each quarter through licensing 'regardless of, or sometimes because of, the questionable sustainability of the businesses paying out.'[21] Another conundrum was around the vast amounts of data coming out of these new digital services.

'Suddenly the data associated with digital transactions was clear and unambiguous and very powerful,' Silver tells me. 'Record companies – for years! – had traded on dodgy numbers. That was potentially an enormous value to this data, but there was also a terrible downside to data that labels were very worried about and that business affairs people were very worried about. That [downside] was the degree to which artists would understand the true degree of sales.'

He explains further, 'What [the lawyers] were afraid of was wholesale renegotiation of artists' contracts triggered by data transparency. In those early days, our instructions from our business affairs people were that we didn't want to know the data and we didn't want to see it. The lawyers were in a state of trauma!'

Ben Drury suggests this was an annihilation policy that some labels were engaged in at the time.

'I heard this expression – "engage, embrace, extinguish",' he says. 'The three Es. That was a deliberate strategy [from the majors] with all this stuff. It was, "We are not going to ignore it, we are going to learn about it, we'll show interest and embrace it and then we're going to extinguish it".'

In their defence, some who worked at the majors at this time also said there was a huge amount of vanity and entitlement coming from startups, convinced they were the future and that the old guard of the record business should prostrate themselves before their inherent genius.

'Some startups were arrogant and they came in with this idea of reinventing the music industry, but with very little understanding of what the music industry actually was or what it actually takes to develop an artist,' says one digital executive at a major label. 'Those kinds of startups probably meant that certain elements of the music industry adopted a more defensive stance than they needed to – because it became quite confrontational.'

Braggadocio and conceitedness became a feature, rather than a bug, in many startups at the time. As they were raising huge sums of investment, they could start to see themselves as avatars for the future as well as being invincible: that world-changing success was their destiny. The music business is powered by ego and so running into a whole new generation of companies and founders who were even more pompous and self-regarding than they were was never going to sit well with record label executives. A culture clash was inevitable.

'There was a bit of the arrogance of Silicon Valley at the time that "we know better and we know more about your business than you do",' says Westergren, who saw a lot of it firsthand. 'It just became oil and water.'

Despite the onerous terms of the deals being proffered by EMI – often sweetened with the 'promise' of getting catalogue from huge EMI acts like The Beatles, Queen and Janet Jackson – a multitude of startups signed up. '[F]or the labels, it was like taking candy from children,' noted Silver.[22]

Silver tells me that he and Jay Samit had seen Musicmaker's IPO document in advance and, realising the company could raise a lot of money through it, persuaded them to temporarily park the IPO in exchange for a licensing deal with EMI. The logic being that having EMI's catalogue in place before going into an IPO would dramatically bulk up the potential value of the company.

'We licensed our entire catalogue to them,' he says. 'They were the first company that EMI ever licensed its entire catalogue to.' Even The Beatles? 'No, [EMI's biggest acts] never got into any of those deals.'

Musicmaker agreed to EMI's demands. 'The label then proceeded to pull off one of the most excessive music deals in the history of the first dot com bubble,' wrote Silver in his book.[23]

In taking 50 per cent equity, EMI fully understood that Musicmaker would not have enough equity left to offer the other majors parity in exchange for a licensing deal. With only one of the majors' catalogues on offer, this paltry consumer offering was expected to wither and die, leaving EMI to walk off with millions, none of which would be accountable to its artists. It was a three-card Monte on a monumental scale.

Silver says that the July IPO was all EMI really cared about. On the day of the IPO, it cashed out the bulk of its shares and walked away with, after tax, $80 million profit. '[Jay] Samit became EMI's dot com hero and went on to mastermind a number of similarly rapacious deals,' wrote Silver.[24]

Reflecting on the IPO and EMI's unprecedented windfall at the distance of over two decades, Silver says, 'On the one hand, there's a nice plan to pull a plum out of the pie to say, "Here it is, look, this is more money than we've made from any other deal ever." It was a classic.

Absolute classic. Or an absolute anomaly depending on how you think about it. But it was head and shoulders above any of the other deals that we did.'

EMI also requested that Musicmaker digitise its catalogue for it.

'The technical state of readiness that EMI was in was nowhere,' reveals Silver. 'The day after we signed the [Musicmaker] deal, my office in the Capitol Tower was filling up with boxes of CDs that had to be sent over to Musicmaker [for them to digitise]. But we did get copies of those digitised files.'

In November 1999, when EMI, as a publicly listed company, pushed its numbers for the first half of the year, it revealed it had made £24.8 million from its licensing deal with Musicmaker.[25]

EMI was keen to push the line that it was a digital-forward company, interested in working with companies rather than working against them.

'These are not business opportunities that necessarily we could generate internally, so we are making relationships with [Web companies],' he told *Billboard*. 'Downloading as a big business is still probably some years away, but that doesn't mean that new media can't have a material impact on the financial performance of music companies in 1999 and the year 2000.'[26]

As proof of EMI's digital openness, Berry said the company was speaking with thirty internet partners and others associated with the music business. 'Not every single business will work,' he accepted. 'We think we will have a lot of success in identifying business strategies and partners that we can really bring success, but there is some big pioneering work going on right here.'[27]

EMI pulled off a similar equity deal with software company Liquid Audio in June 1999. As part of a non-exclusive deal, Liquid Audio would encode EMI's catalogue for download and EMI would in exchange get 'an unspecified amount of Liquid Audio stock' when the company did its IPO later that month.[28]

The Liquid Audio IPO went ahead as planned and it raised $63 million, with 4.2 million shares being offered.[29] Shares were initially priced at $15 each, reaching a high of $48 and ending the first day of trading at $36.56. The *Wall Street Journal* called the IPO 'a big success.'[30]

One well-placed source says this strategy was built into their company's business DNA as soon as it realised that Silicon Valley represented a potential revenue bonanza on an unprecedented level.

'The message was very simple,' they say. 'It was, "Let's do as many deals as we can with these startups and let's think about licensing as much of our content as we can".'

They talk matter of factly about the focus on Silicon Valley that was growing inside their company, and at others, as the dot com boom became, for a short time at least, a lottery ticket that seemed each week to have the winner numbers.

'We formulated this model early on – and today it seems fairly obvious, but at the time was entering into quite difficult territory for the company – which was content for equity,' they explain. 'Did we also get advances? Oh, yes! They weren't happy [to give over equity], but the race was so competitive at the beginning and we were really interested in licensing services and finding services that we could license at scale.'

Winbolt says in 1999 and the early 2000s there was 'an absolute feeding frenzy around the financing of startups' that the labels were keen to make the most of. 'There were revenues to be had, either licensing catalogue to them in exchange for cash or equity or whatever else it might be.'

BMG, despite being the smallest of the majors, could also be aggressive in its dealmaking with startups.

'The market power was pretty limited,' says Rob Wells, head of digital at BMG in the UK, 'but I remember that the crew of folks running the operation side of the US business back then were definitely in that party in terms of jamming new and well-funded startups for cash and equity. Hands in the air, I'm a little guilty of doing the same sort of thing as well when I got to Universal.' (Wells joined Universal Music Group in 2000, rising to become president of global digital business between 2010 and 2015).

EMI was commonly seen at the time as the most ruthless (or the most prescient, depending on your viewpoint) of the five majors with regard to equity. The other majors, certainly their offices in the US who were leading many of the global deals, expected a lot but were not, at least not yet, quite as hardline about it as EMI.

'We would try to get equity in companies that we were going to support with the use of the technologies that we were getting equity for,' says Larry Kenswil, president of Universal Music Group's eLabs division between 1997 and 2008. 'But we would pay for the equity at a fair market value. What we would always avoid would be promising content in return for equity, because that would essentially mean we had to deal with the fact that artists should be getting a piece of that if we were trading that content for equity; essentially we'd be bypassing the licensing cash that we could also get. We didn't start getting bigger advances until later, much after 1999. If someone came in and wanted to write us a cheque, whether we believed in them [and their business model] or not, we would certainly entertain it.'

Kenswil says that equity was an assurance, as far as the labels were concerned, that they were not going to have another MTV situation on their hands.

(It has become industry folklore that the original deals the labels signed with MTV in the early 1980s, essentially giving the nascent company videos for free as they believed it counted as promotion, was their biggest corporate own goal ever as it turned MTV into a powerhouse and the labels became utterly reliant on it. It is often held up as the kind of colossal mistake that should never be made again).

'That was definitely in the front of a lot of our minds,' Kenswil says. 'On the other hand, MTV was also in the minds of a lot of the labels and marketing people because they saw massive sales growth as a result of MTV. They really didn't care too much about the fact that Viacom [who bought MTV in 1985[31]] suddenly had a multi-billion dollar company as a result, because that's not how labels were measured. They were measured by sales.'

He continues, 'Up above the labels, the finance people, the corporate people, and the head of our company, Doug Morris, were all wary of ever creating another company because we had let them go with our content and give us a small amount of money in return for massive equity in a business. We were very aware of that.'

It is important to note that, certainly in 1999, the independent labels were not as thirsty for equity as the majors were. They were also not in a strong market position to expect equity as a non-negotiable point in licensing deals. They did, however, often demand large advances.

'There was a lot of investment money kicking around and we were fortunate to raise some of it,' says Jonathan Davis who had launched the Crunch download service in 1999. 'We did end up paying independent labels some substantial advances. We didn't give them equity, but we did pay them substantial advances in return for exclusivity.'

One well-placed executive in the UK with a digital remit at the time says the independents were more than happy to accept substantial advances in lieu of equity. Their feeling was, the executive says, that advances were a joyously unexpected windfall and they were often utterly unworried about whether or not the services paying out the advances would make it to market. This was especially true of the services targeting the independents as they knew that trying to get major label catalogue would be too fraught, unnecessarily complicated and ridiculously expensive. As such, they would position their service as being all about the ground-breaking music they romantically claimed the independents had the monopoly on.

The service with the deepest pockets at the time was arguably eMusic (formerly GoodNoise until it changed its name in June 1999).

'There were loads of these advances going around,' says the anonymous executive. 'Basically, all people wanted was to say they were licensed and the VCs would give them money. Part of the reason the dot com bubble burst was because the infrastructure couldn't deal with it. So it didn't matter how good your ideas were: there was no infrastructure to actually deal with it.'

Peter Quicke, label manager at independent label Ninja Tune, refers to this era as 'a sort of mad Wild West' where, at the height of the dot com boom, 'there was tons of money flying around.'

He notes, however, that much of this money sluicing around was entirely speculative. 'Digital rights actually weren't worth very much at that point,' he says. 'People weren't buying many MP3s and there was no streaming.'

Quicke says some services were seeking to license on an exclusive basis. Normally this would be something labels wouldn't do, but given the fact the download market was so nascent as to almost be non-existent, Ninja Tune was not discounting such offers.

'We were talking to a company called Cductive who did CD burning and they also did downloads,' he says. 'They made an offer for our digital rights. [Independent label trade body] AIM was cautioning, quite rightly, that you should be careful about signing away your digital rights. But it seemed to me that no one was buying MP3s, so it was madness for them to be paying for them. Paying big chunks of money. So it seemed like a really sensible idea to take a load of money from venture capitalists for short-term rights on something that wasn't really worth anything. We started talking to Cductive and then eMusic were bidding against Cductive so we ended up getting a huge advance. Which at the time was really fucking bonkers because no one was buying MP3s. I guess we were leveraging the bit of hype we did have after Coldcut and Mr Scruff, so we actually did sign our rights for three years to eMusic. And we bought this building that we're in now [in Kennington, South London], using that money as a deposit.'

He adds, 'It was such a weird time. The whole thing was weird. We didn't want to sign our exclusive digital rights to anybody. That was counterintuitive. But, because the amount of money was so silly, and the rights so short and not worth very much, it seemed like a sensible thing to do. I think in the context of being a label and trying to continue doing what we were doing and supporting artists and paying our rent, we basically funnelled some of that venture capital money into releasing the records that we released [over the next few years].'

Jim Griffin argues that the desperate grab for equity by the majors was a reckless game of short-termism that was always going to end badly for everyone involved. Countless companies would pile up as roadkill on the side of the internet as labels became convinced that they were digital kingmakers who could dictate the speed and direction of change. It was all, Griffin believes, a grand collective delusion.

'The people at EMI, they were not disruptors,' he spits. 'They were defenders of the status quo. They were like the guys who were definitely harassing [new companies]. They knew where the whiff of digital was. And they would go wait there and ambush whoever was hanging around.'

An IPO alone is not enough to make a business a success. If anything, it merely piles even more pressure on a company. Musicmaker might have had a deal, albeit an astonishingly one-sided deal, with EMI, but profitability was still something of a pipe dream.

In September, it reported a net loss in Q2 of $3.6 million, up sharply from a loss of $830,215 in Q2 1998.[32] It was still out signing deals, however. That month it also secured a five-year deal with Zomba, whose acts included Backstreet Boys and Britney Spears, for use in its customised CD compilation business. Zomba also received an equity stake in Musicmaker, but the amount was not disclosed.[33]

At the end of September, it signed a deal with Pete Townshend to offer tracks from his *Live: A Benefit For Maryville Academy* album ahead of its physical release. Steve Devick, president of CEO Platinum Entertainment, Townshend's label, said, 'I think retail understands that downloads are a good promotional tool. They can only help.'[34] It also signed an exclusive five-year deal with TVT Records, whose catalogue included tracks by Nine Inch Nails, Sevendust and XTC.[35]

Perhaps its biggest commercial deal of the year came in October when it signed a deal, estimated at $20 million, to sell compilations and downloads via AOL.com, Netscape Netcenter and ICQ (all sites owned by America Online). This followed the AOL/Spinner.com deal. Over three years, Musicmaker would pay over $18 million to American Online but share in the profits of products sold via its online brands. Making up the $20 million was American Online being given a $2 million equity stake in Musicmaker.[36]

Musicmaker limped on through 2000, but its fate was already sealed, having given away too much equity to attract the other majors or to give the company a fighting chance to be profitable.

In September 2000, Robert Bernardi resigned as chairman of the board.[37] Days later, the company announced a one-for-ten reverse stock split. 'The move is intended to raise the company's per-share price, which has been hovering at just under a dollar on the Nasdaq exchange for more than a month,' wrote *Hits Daily Double*. 'If a stock stays below one dollar for more than ninety days, the exchange can remove the company's listing.'[38]

Then in January 2001, it closed down its website and its board were recommending to shareholders to vote to dissolve the company and to liquidate its assets.

'We've done everything possible we could have to give the consumer their music their way,' said Mark Fowler, the company's CFO. 'We tried, and now we think that the best value we can get for the shareholder is to liquidate and distribute the proceeds.'[39]

Its assets included $32 million in cash and cash equivalents but in the first nine months of 2000 it had lost $44.7 million based on revenues of $5.2 million.[40]

'We were in this for the business,' said Fowler. 'We wanted to be either the next CD or the next 8-track.' With gallows humour, he added, 'It looks like right now we're kind of stuck in the 8-track mode.'[41]

BCG Strategic Investors, an investment firm with a majority stake in the company, filed a letter with the Securities & Exchange Commission in early January 2001, asking the company's shareholders to give it control in order to liquidate the Musicmaker assets. Musicmaker's chairman, Devarajan S. Puthukarai, was urging shareholders to rebuff BCG.[42]

It was an ignoble, if sadly all-too-predictable, end for the company. It was not the only digital music company to crash and burn in this period, but it is the one that most illustrates how the short-term avarice of the labels killed the long-term potential of companies.

THE ONUS BONUS: THE RIDICULOUS STRESS ON STARTUPS TO IPO

There was enormous pressure, and mounting expectations, in the late 1990s for companies to IPO. It was seen as a form of validation for the company and a growth strategy for investors.

Paul Hitchman had left Warner Music in the UK in 1999 and was setting up music site and music platform Playlouder. He says that an IPO was often not just the first goal for a startup, it was the *only* goal.

'If you go back to 1999, the model was an entrepreneurial opportunistic one of startup, IPO, exit,' he says. 'That was the model. I don't think anyone thought they were building a viable business. Maybe Michael Robertson [of MP3.com] did. There were maybe one or two people who were perhaps on track to build a viable business. For many, many entrepreneurs at that time, it was a question of trying to raise some money and then having these investors breathing down your neck trying to get their exit.'

Any IPO is a gamble: go too early and you risk undervaluing the company; leave it too late and any shares you offer are little more than junk. Michael Robertson says he was gripped by a rumbling fear in 1999 that the market was about to peak and that he had to push through the MP3.com IPO as quickly as possible. If he did not, he fretted, everything was going to crash down around him.

Paul Ouyang had previously worked at Tickets.com and had also been through the IPO process before.[43] He became CFO of MP3.com in early 1999 and Robertson tasked him with taking the company to the IPO stage by the summer.

Robertson recalls, 'I said [to him], "Great. You're hired. Get to work!" Because I was seeing what was happening with the internet bubble and I'm like, "We've got to get out there and get our IPO done as soon as possible because I don't know how long the enthusiasm will last." We were a legitimate company. There were a lot of companies out there that had no revenue, had no users, had no business. They were so speculative. We weren't one of those. But nonetheless, I knew that when the tide turns, it takes down everybody. Or it would make it hard for anybody.'

Robertson says, 'I worked my ass off for three and a half weeks', having eighty-six meetings in that time of a road show that was pitching MP3.com. 'I'm talking to bankers and I knew they would not get the internet,' he recalls. 'So if you talk about too much internet-y stuff, you are just going to lose them.'

To sell the idea of MP3.com to the banking world, Robertson created the DAM [Digital Automated Music] on-demand CD-burning system to place the business in the realm of the physical world for investors who might have been web-sceptical or simply unaware of how any of this worked.

'It was a very tongue in cheek name,' says Robertson. 'But what it allowed artists to do on MP3.com was they could upload their songs. They had to give us one [track] for free to give away. That was the deal. "I'm not going to charge you for hosting or bandwidth or any of the stuff that people are charging for in the late 1990s. I'll give you a free web presence, but you have got to give me at least one song to give away for free." By the way, they gave me four on average. [With DAM], they could upload all the songs from their CD and create a virtual CD and sell it. And when they sold it, we would manufacture it in real time. We would send it out and give them half the money. We gave this for free to every artist, no upfront costs, no setup costs, they got to set the price of the CD, but a minimum of $5. They could set the price at fifteen bucks, twenty bucks, ten bucks, whatever you wanted. They would get half and we would get half. And we would do all the work. The reason I tell you that is because when I did that road show, I knew that that would impress the investors.'

At the end of May 1999, MP3.com filed for its IPO with the Securities & Exchange Commission, hoping to raise $115 million. *Billboard* reported, 'In an unprecedented move, MP3 might give early customers of the site stock options in the company, according to a source.'[44]

No Limit Records, with acts like Master P and Snoop Dogg, was reported to have received $2.5 million in MP3.com stock in exchange for licensing the rights to a number of its recordings. As part of the deal, No Limit acts would be expected to display MP3.com signs at concerts and have its artists participate in the site's chat rooms. Some other MP3.com acts could also get support slots at shows by No Limit acts.[45]

MP3.com initially planned to offer nine million shares but increased this to 12.3 million shares just before the IPO.[46] It raised $344.4 million, with the 12.3 million shares selling at $28 each. This was higher than the $24–$26 range that had been set by underwriter Credit Suisse First Boston Corp. The IPO gave the company a market valuation of $1.86 billion.[47] CNN Money called it 'a smashing debut.'[48]

(A historically interesting side note to the MP3.com IPO was that it forced the Security & Exchange Commission to change its rules regarding the number of friends and family who can participate in an IPO. Under the friends and family provisions in 1999, only US citizens could apply, but MP3.com opened it to any artists who had uploaded any music to the service. In total, 18,000 people qualified. Thereafter, the Security & Exchange Commission imposed a cap on the number of friends and family who could qualify).[49]

These halcyon and fecund days, from EMI's side at least, were never going to last forever. Plus there were going to be long-term consequences to what they were doing. What was happening then would seriously damage the reputation of the labels for years and for them to be disdainfully viewed by Silicon Valley companies and VCs as myopic, avaricious and conniving.

'Jay was running around the world making deals left, right and centre – but what he was also leaving was a trail of unfulfilled promises on the other side,' says Silver. 'We ran really, really fast down the road. But the point was that we ran really fast down the road by claiming that we got it, by claiming that we were liberal, that we were advanced, that we were progressive in our thinking, that we were going to change. Maybe I'm being unrealistic or I was naive. But certainly at the time, I felt like, "No. Actually that's complete hypocrisy. That is a story being told way ahead of where the business actually was." The business wasn't any more progressive, or interested in investing in its own infrastructure changing, than any of the other majors were.'

He adds, 'It was a smart move, to make some quick money, but it didn't reflect well on the industry in the end. And in a way, it sowed some seeds of distrust, which you can still see today between technology and business.'

'That was a short-term view,' says Paul Vidich, EVP of strategic planning and business development at Warner Music, of how EMI's strategy here was very different to his company's strategy. 'That was not solving an industry problem. He was creating a profit pool that he would then get bonused on. I didn't see my job as that. Whatever money was going to be made by advances, that would go to the labels. I wasn't really looking for equity in small companies that were going to disappear. My job was trying to figure out an industry solution, something that would be the equivalent of the CD for the next generation. That meant finding the right technical solutions and the right technology partners.'

For Silver, the ruthlessness of the startup shakedown happening within EMI, and the ripple effect it was having across the other majors, had been niggling at him for several months through 1999. Eventually he had to choose between the music business and the startup world. He chose the latter, joining playlisting company Uplister in 2000 as its EVP.

'The most significant thing for me in 1999 was that that was the year in which I had to make a decision about whether to leave EMI and go and join a startup or not,' he says of his career crossroads. 'It was a really difficult decision. So much was going on. The level of innovation was huge.'

Commercially it may have made more sense to stay in the label system and to rinse and repeat what the company expected of him; ethically and professionally, however, he knew that was unsustainable for him and for the business as a whole.

Silver looks at the Musicmaker deal as symbolic of a spreading corporate rot within the company where the mercenary was prized over and above trying to build the record industry a digital future by working with, not against, the new wave of services starting to come through.

'The other reason for doing the [Musicmaker] deal was that we made loads of money out of it and they also digitised our catalogue for us,' he says. 'Was it a good deal? It was and it wasn't. The company didn't survive and the reputation of EMI as a sharp operator at that point [was damaged]. It was a legendarily sharp deal that took advantage of the imbalance in the relationship between the tech companies and the content owners.'

He feels there was a dangerous myopia in the record industry at the time, powered by a smugness and a phobia of the future. Startups were there to be sucked dry, gelded and discarded so that the record business would not have to look internally and think about changing itself. It thought it could control the future by killing a series of startups, convinced anything new was poison rather than nourishment.

'I don't think anybody at that point looking at this really believed that we were going to fall off a cliff,' he says of the industry's arrogance and hubris as the 1990s came to a close. 'No one believed that. No one saw that coming really. And that was the challenge. What they saw was, on the contrary, an opportunity to make more money out of these investors who had the money tree. The investors had grown a money tree and we figured out how to shake it.'

He felt the record companies had a duty of care to themselves as much as to startups to get new ideas into the marketplace, but its default setting was to exploit and derail everything it saw coming along the tracks.

'If your motivation is that you actually want to change, if you actually want to transform things, then you would be more systematic, you would be more selective and you would follow through on the deal that you were doing in terms of providing your part of the equation in order to create more integration,' he says. 'Whether that was a build or buy scenario in terms of what these businesses were doing and how their functionality could serve a new model or not, those were things that in subsequent years did work their way through.'

There was a conversion moment for the majors with regard to digital startups, but not until into the 2000s.

'Of course, the labels became more acquisitive and the nature of those deals changed because they started to see that these third-party companies could provide infrastructure, services and functionality that the business itself didn't currently have,' says Silver. 'That was a great way of achieving it. And that was a much more constructive mentality. But at that early stage, when this model of funding was just bouncing around as being a massive opportunity, there wasn't any systematic thinking. That was the frustration for any of us who really were thinking further ahead.'

There was clearly a professional and commercial schism opening up between Silver and Samit and that was never going to be workable.

'Things fall apart; the center cannot hold,' as W. B. Yeats put it in *The Second Coming*.

'Jay taught me a huge amount, even though I found him impossible to work with,' sighs Silver. 'I learned more about how to use chutzpah in business from him than anybody else I've ever worked with. But I was utterly frustrated. Because I wasn't interested in just doing exploitive deals that ripped off investors, which was what I felt we were doing.'

Samit, however, has a very different reading of the end of their professional relationship. 'I fired Jeremy,' he claims. Silver says he was actively seeking new opportunities and left under his own steam.

'I feel bad about that,' continues Samit. 'Good guy. Good guy. His remit and what I wanted to do weren't the same thing, looking back. His job was to pay attention to what was going on in digital. And I came home with the line, "No – we have got to start businesses." He was a misfit, but he was a good guy.'

OFFERING SERVICES AT LEAST A FIGHTING CHANCE AND THE CONSEQUENCES OF MAJOR LABEL PILLAGING

It would be historically inaccurate to paint a picture that implied everyone at the (primarily major) labels was hellbent on bulldozing through every new startup that popped up on their radar, concerned only with ransacking them for equity, forcing them to IPO and then squeezing every last drop of equity out of them to the point where they were financially desiccated and commercially unviable.

There were many who, in 1999 at least, were more focused on being a doula for founders, enabling them to bring their startups to full term and for them to emerge, bouncing and healthy, into the world.

'My attitude when I met these companies was that I would try and get the licences,' says Neil Cartwright, head of eMedia at Sony Music in the UK between 1996 and 2004. 'I always felt that these companies were innovating and, by giving them licences, we would find which service was the one that appealed to consumers. Rather naively, because it turns out that people at other record labels were just charging advances. It was really whoever could afford the advances.'

The notion of suffocating startups at birth, just after you forced them to pay out huge advances and hand over great clumps of equity, was something that Edgar Bronfman Jr claims Universal opposed as he says the company understood the damage such an approach could cause.

'I don't see Whac-A-Mole as a strategy,' he says of other labels trying to spay new digital companies. 'The notion that you're going to suffocate one and then suffocate the next one. . . it's nonsense, right? These things are happening. They're popping up all over [the place]. If you're not going to realise that this is a fundamental change in the way life is going to be going forward, you're crazy.'

At Warner, one digital executive there claims the company policy could, retrospectively at least, be classified as doing the opposite of what EMI's digital team was doing.

'Whatever money was going to be made by advances, that would go to the labels,' says Paul Vidich, EVP of strategic planning and business development at Warner Music. 'I wasn't really looking for equity in small companies that were going to disappear. My job was trying to figure out an industry solution, something that would be the equivalent of the CD for the next generation. That meant finding the right technical solutions and the right technology partners.'

This is something a colleague of Vidich's agrees with. Mark Foster, SVP of new media at Warner Music International, also points out there were so many companies pinging up on their radar that it would have been impossible to have some nefarious scheme or conspiracy in place to raze them after gutting them for money.

'Because things were happening so fast, we couldn't possibly keep up,' he says. 'We were just busy, trying to keep track of everything, all the changes that were happening, the new technologies that were coming in on the scene. We knew that there'd have to be a shakeout at some point where some of them would succeed and some of them would fail. A lot of our job was trying to identify which ones would be the winners and which ones would be the losers. And obviously, you couldn't possibly tell. We didn't know which ones were going to succeed.'

He continues, 'It was never an explicit thing at Warner, certainly not at Warner International. Certainly Paul [Vidich] and I never talked about that. We never talked about, "Let's squeeze all the life out of these people before they can get up to scale." I think we were genuinely much more curious to figure out which technologies were going to get traction in the market and, therefore, who we wanted to partner with, rather than squeezing them until they bled to death.'

A kind of lawlessness was gripping parts of the record business in 1999 with regard to treating startups as things to asset strip as quickly as possible. This was all seen as a financial jamboree and a free for all, like winning the coin toss over and over again. By early 2000, however, the good times were going to hit the wall and shatter into a billion pieces following the dot com crash.

By the end of 1999, the record business had an *atrocious* reputation in Silicon Valley for its smash and grab strategy. Then suddenly the whole startup world was in free fall just as the new millennium was getting started. These two factors combined to put all startups, but especially music startups, through the wringer.

In late 1999, Chris Barton was working on the idea that became music-recognition service Shazam and by summer of 2000 he was looking to raise investment. The dot com Disneyland that sparkled alluringly when he came up with the idea had become a wasteland in the space of a matter of months.

'Compared to the dot com bubble, it was the absolute reverse of plenty of venture capital money,' he says. 'That was probably the hardest time to raise money in venture capital history.'

He says the thing that saved Shazam in those dark early days of raising money was that the music lawyers he brought to advise him said that music recognition would not need a licence from the labels or publishers. Shazam was going to avoid the licensing hell that toppled so many digital music companies before it.

'That legal advice honestly saved the company,' he says. 'If we had needed music licences, honestly, it would have taken so many years to get there. We all know how different that is. And not just so many years, but probably crazy amounts of money. That we didn't have. We almost went bankrupt as it was during those years. Looking back, I would say that that was so fortunate for Shazam.'

The company did try to launch a product called Song Mail, where someone could send a thirty-second clip of a track they had identified on their phone to a friend. Shazam opened licensing talks with labels, but soon realised it was going to be too costly and too complicated to launch. Song Mail was mothballed.

'It was not like Napster,' says Barton. 'It was just listening to a song over a phone call. And it was only thirty seconds of a song. It was pretty non-threatening, but it was pretty darn challenging to get any sort of licence for music at the time.'

He says that in the dark dot com bust, and with mounting digital piracy fears, that followed the days of plenty, labels were so paranoid that licensing became too onerous and too expensive for most startups.

'I don't think they [the labels] really saw this as an opportunity that was going to open up their future or anything like that,' says Barton of the Song Mail idea. 'I remember it being surprising and frustrating as an entrepreneur. If you look at all the digital music startups, there were almost none that were just more purely beneficial to the music industry than Shazam at the time. It was literally just a thing where you find a song that you like, discover the artists, find out who it is and then, of course, the chance of you buying it is heightened. So Shazam had zero cannibalisation. It was purely just fostering the discovery of artists.'

He says that even having angel investors like Colin Southgate (executive chairman of EMI until early 1999) and John Preston (chairman of BMG between 1989 and 1998) involved, as well as Jeremy Silver as an advisor, getting fruitful conversation with record labels at the time was proving impossible.

'Record labels had this built-in history of working around advances,' he says. 'So they took that same history of advances and then they applied it in this new modern age of digital startups. As an analogy, it'd be like me joining a startup. Let's say they hire me to join the startup. Let's say I made $100,000 a year and then I tell the startup, "OK, but I want the first five years all upfront, so give me $500,000 now." If everyone did that the startup wouldn't be able to hire people. You can see why advances don't make sense for a startup. The startup is, by definition, cash strapped.'

He says the whole model was built on unstable foundations as it rewarded short-term benefits at the cost of long-term improvements for everyone. The aggressive label culture of hitting targets to unlock huge bonuses severely damaged the business, but those who got the bonuses were not going to be around to survey the slow-motion wreckage they caused.

'You may not even be at the label two years from now, so you want to get all that cash now so you can get your giant bonus right away,' says Barton. 'I'm not blaming anyone. This is the way the music industry was built. There's a reason they existed; and they were systemically built into the culture of record labels. Literally the compensation structure of executives incentivised the requirement for advances. That really was not ideal for agreeing deals as with all startups.'

Shazam did, however, have the fairy tale ending that so many other digital startups of the time were denied. It stayed the distance, with the arrival of the iPhone in 2007 and the App Store in 2008 dramatically boosting it. Then in December 2017, it was reported that Apple was looking to acquire Shazam,[50] finally closing the deal in September 2018.[51] It did not make the purchase price public, but multiple sources say it sold for $400 million.[52]

There was a schizophrenic approach to *new* music companies coming through: screwing them over and taking all their money; or carefully rearing them and hopefully creating a new ecosystem for everyone.

There was a tension between some parts of the record industry seeing the new generation of digital music services as inherently utopian and other parts seeing it as dystopian and only out to steal the labels' power by making them subservient to a new Silicon Valley superstate. None of these services were, however, bringing in any revenues of note. Not yet, anyway. Sure, there was money in advances and equity if the spellbinding

IPO could be manifested. But the digital services were not profit centres in their own rights.

By far the labels' biggest commercial partners in 1999 were the retailers – the shops that sold the billions of records that provided the lion's share of their income.

The CD boom of the 1990s was fantastic for labels and retailers, but there was always a tension between them about who was really in control and who should profit the most. This love/hate relationship worked fine. . . until it stopped working.

1999 was to prove a flashpoint year for music retail. It was the peak year for global record sales, but there was a growing worry that the glory days were, if not ending completely, certainly about to be paused. The tussle over control between labels and retailers, these harsh politics of 'us and them', was going to erupt in 1999 in ways that no one could have predicted even a few years earlier.

Labels and retailers were not just battling between themselves for control: they were battling against outside forces for their very survival.

RETAIL

CHAPTER 12

Retail/re-model: the High Street on High Alert

(The battle for control of the consumer)

It is not exactly a chicken/egg conundrum in that record shops are only *slightly* younger than record labels. They had to come second, but only just. Claiming to be the oldest *surviving* record shop in the world, Spillers Records in Cardiff, Wales, opened in 1894.[1] D'Amato Records in Malta, however, lays claim to being even older, dating back to 1885.[2]

The longest-*running* record label is Columbia Records, now Part of Sony Music Entertainment, which was incorporated as the Columbia Phonograph Company in January 1889.[3] The Edison Speaking Phonograph Company pre-dates it, however, launching on 24 January 1878.[4] Businessman Jesse Lippincott became 'sole licensee of the American Graphophone Company [. . .] by purchasing the Edison Phonograph Company from Edison' and he set up the North American Phonograph Company on 14 July 1888.

The first HMV shop dates back to 1921, opened on London's Oxford Street by Edward Elgar.[5] It was followed by other major retail brands such as Fnac in France in 1954,[6] Tower Records in 1960[7] and the first Virgin Records shop, which launched above a shoe shop located on what founder Richard Branson called 'the cheaper end of Oxford Street' in central London in 1971.[8] It had sprung from Virgin Mail Order Records, which had launched the previous year.[9] The first Megastore, in what was to become a rapidly expanding chain through the 1980s and 1990s, opened on Oxford Street in 1979.[10]

The CD boom in the late 1980s and 1990s saw record companies and record shops awash with money like never before. With great profits came a desire for *even greater* profits, so major retail brands like HMV and Virgin were heavily focused on expansion through the decade. They were opening more (and bigger) outlets in established markets and breaking into new ones.

As in almost all areas of retail, phenomenal growth for supplier and retailer happening in lockstep was not a cause for joint celebrations. Record labels and record chains were caught in a relationship of mutual hatred, mutual distrust and mutual dependency. Each side believed it was the important one in the equation and each side believed the other was only where it was because of them. 'We made you!' they would roar at each other. 'Without us, you are nothing.'

The beauty and curse of this stand-off was that both sides were right and wrong in almost exactly equal measure.

Record shops were getting bigger and bigger throughout the 1990s, a decade where size was always hysterically prized over and above quality. Chains would boast of the square footage of their latest store opening, occupying prime real estate locations in the major metropoles of the world, sending out the message that they were the very epicentre, both commercially and culturally, of the cities they deigned to be in.

Investment in a new city centre store was not a small undertaking, with retailers having to sign long-term leases that would lock them to the location for decades. They would have to pay high rent to the landlord and often had that rent increasing on a sliding scale as the term of the lease progressed. The upfront investment costs were phenomenal, not least fitting out and branding each new shop like it was a Versailles of CDs. These costs would only get higher.

It was not a game for the faint-hearted, but the spoils, when they came, were too great, too delicious and too irresistible. They were there for the taking.

Brian McLaughlin was MD of HMV Europe in 1999 as well as chairman of BARD, the British Association of Record Dealers, the trade body for record retailers in the UK. He was unquestionably the most powerful person in music retail in the UK, probably also in Europe.

He started at HMV in 1968 as an assistant at its branch in Portsmouth on the south coast of England.[11] He worked his way up, becoming MD of HMV UK in 1987 and expanding his purview to become MD of HMV Europe in 1996.[12] He had seen music retail grow and new formats, first the cassette and then the CD, take music sales to new heights.

He was a lifer. Music retail was in his blood. What Brian McLaughlin did not know about music retail was, patently, not worth knowing.

Growth begets more growth and McLaughlin put HMV through accelerated growth when he took over as UK MD. 'My remit from 1987, and I think it was right, was to expand the chain,' he says. 'That's what we continued to do in 1999.'

He was inspired by the Next chain of clothing retailers, applying their nationwide high-street expansion strategy to music sales. Next began life as J Hepworth & Son ('Gentleman's Tailors') in 1864 in Leeds, England. In 1981, it acquired Kendalls rainwear shops and rebranded as Next, focusing initially on women's fashion. In February 1982, Next opened its first womenswear store and by July had seventy stores in the UK. It moved into men's fashion in 1984 and homeware the following year. In 1987, the year McLaughlin took over as MD of HMV, Next had moved into childrenswear and had launched the Next Directory, its home shopping catalogue.[13]

Next had become a retail powerhouse in the 1980s and McLaughlin saw it as a model for music retail's future.

'I did quite a lot of research on them back in 1987,' he says. 'I looked at their formula, I looked at their culture and I looked at their expansion. I thought: this is something that the public has fallen in love with. What few stores we had opened in those early days, the public had fallen in love with HMV. So that in itself was the main driver for us to continue expanding. I actually don't think I'm being dishonest by saying that I don't think we had a loss-making store in the whole time that I was there.'

Even before digital first sent tremors and then shockwaves through high-street retail, prior to upending it completely, HMV was facing its own existential crisis in the 1990s. In the UK, business was fantastic. There was, however, growing pressure to repeat the trick around the world.

'All the profits were still coming from the bricks and mortar,' says McLaughlin. 'We obviously did have some business analysts looking at the future for us and they did a lot of good work. But I think that at that stage, in 1999, it was too early [to have a solid digital operation].'

He says the corporate pressure to expand HMV internationally was slowly revealing itself to be a disaster in waiting. All the profits from the UK were being diverted to support HMV's loss-making international operations and this, claims McLaughlin, meant the company did not have the necessary funds at hand to make a prescient investment in its digital future. This was at a time when digital profits were purely hypothetical.

Stuart McAllister took over as chairman and CEO of HMV Group (as it was renamed then) in 1987, just as McLaughlin ascended to the UK MD role. His focus was on bringing the HMV brand to new markets, notably North America and Japan.[14] (McAllister died in 2000).

McLaughlin says the accelerated expansion outside of the UK being pushed by McAllister was the wrong strategy.

'That was something that I was totally and utterly against, because, from a shareholder point of view, I couldn't see where the value was going to come from when we didn't have the management to transfer to these other countries,' he says. 'Even in the US, although Tower were very profitable, they had their own management issues as well. For us to be able to transfer management to Japan, Singapore, Hong Kong, Australia and America, it was really insane at that time.'

Even though he was against the idea he, for reasons of corporate politics, bit his tongue. 'Basically, I could only keep my job at HMV UK by trying not to oppose this strategy,' he says. 'I knew where the line would be drawn. So I had to, by and large, just go along with that. Up to a point.'

The US, the world's biggest music market, became a financial sinkhole for HMV from 1990, when it opened its first store in New York City[15], onwards.

'The US lost most of the money,' McLaughlin reveals. 'There's no way that, for example, you go into New York, as we did, and open two massive superstores on the same day in poor locations with rents that were twenty-five-year leases that increased annually with margins from the record companies in the US that were totally inferior to what we'd have earned in the UK. The financial model itself didn't work from the beginning.'

He says he tried to argue the business case against a major US expansion, but was overruled.

'I said, "Look, the margins are tight enough as it is in the UK. This is what you're going to be facing in the US. And you're also going to be facing rents the likes of which you've never seen before." In the UK, there might be twenty-five-year leases, but they would only be reviewed every five years. I think the two massive, extortionate leases we took on in New York, they were reviewed annually, and upwards only! Let's say, for example, you were fortunate enough to put 5 per cent on your sales growth for the year, that 5 per cent would be swallowed up with the new rent, which meant that eventually you could never, ever make a profit.'

He says that when he took over the international business at HMV he, after having gone on several fact-finding missions to the US, decided to pull the plug.

'In my first twelve months, I closed it all down,' he says matter-of-factly. 'The whole lot. That was purely and simply so that we could get our bottom line to look a lot healthier because all we were doing was seeing the efforts of the UK's staff and management being sucked out of the business. You wouldn't mind if it was being invested wisely; but it was not invested wisely. You could say, "Well, you didn't give it long enough. You should have given it a chance." It had long enough. The business model didn't work.'

The HMV retreat from the US did not, however, happen until 2004 when it closed its last store there.[16] By then, however, it was too late. The low rumblings of change/disaster being afoot in 1999 had become a sickening roar by 2004.

Gennaro Castaldo joined HMV UK in 1985 as head of press and PR and remained there until 2013. He suggests that HMV's enormous strength in music retail in the 1990s was actually one of its biggest weaknesses. Not only could it not see the digital change coming, it simply *could not comprehend* that this highly lucrative business could be taken from it.

'I wouldn't say that anyone was fast asleep,' he says of the digital changes coming in 1999. 'I think it's just they couldn't envisage a world that was so incredibly different to what they had at the time. Certainly from a retail point of view, because of the generation of people that were working and running the organisation at the head offices, who lived and breathed music, it was all about recorded music in physical form or the in-store experience. Online had started to take off, but it was more of a value-based judgement: why would anyone want to get their music in some way other than through their local indie shop or HMV? It wasn't that anyone was lazy or complacent or asleep. They just couldn't conceive of what was to come.'

This emphasis on, even reverence towards, the physical at retail was heightened in the 1990s CD boom and, even if there were signs it could start to plateau as the decade neared its end, the arrival of the DVD in 1997 promised another bonanza.[17]

'DVD came along and rather distracted everyone because it was a huge earner,' says Castaldo. 'Even if music was starting to maybe lose some of its lustre and [market] share, there was this other shiny thing that kept the sales going. DVD was like this huge adrenaline rush of additional sales. It felt like, "Yes, there might be problems [coming from digital] but there are all these amazing extra sales or demand." Going forward, the company was still growing, our sales were still growing 10 per cent or 15 per cent year-on-year.'

He adds, 'HMV were pioneers and they wanted to be the first. They were the first to grab the CD. They were the first to grab the DVD. They always felt something else would come along. So, yes, there would be problems bubbling here and there, but there always seemed to be something bigger that presented a larger opportunity. I think that distracted you from these little existential threats. You either didn't add them all up to realise how serious they were; or you thought you could ride it out and you were just too big as a brand to be threatened by it.'

It was going to be jam today, tomorrow and next week.

Castaldo recalls two key events, a matter of weeks apart, in 1997 that would have, on the surface of it, suggested the CD was just going to keep selling and that music retailers were going to be in clover forever.

On 21 August, Oasis released *Be Here Now*, their third album. Such was the escalating hype around it, so comprehensively had reality slipped its moorings, that the album was released on a Thursday when the normal release day for new records in the UK was a Monday. *Be Here Now* immediately became the fastest-selling album in UK chart history, with 696,000 copies being sold in just *three days*. It was a major news story, with camera crews interviewing the fans queuing up to buy an album that was birthed in a hubristic miasma of cocaine but which quickly revealed itself to be an overblown monstrosity.[18]

On 13 September, Elton John released 'Candle In The Wind 1997', his tribute to Diana, Princess Of Wales, which he had sung at her funeral a week earlier. The single was technically a double-A-side, along with 'Something About The Way You Look Tonight', but no one seemed to care about the other track. It sold 658,000 copies in its first week, with news footage at the time showing shoppers grabbing *armfuls* of the CD single. In its second week, it sold 1.54 million copies. It kept on selling. With over 4.9 million sales to date, it is, by some distance, the most successful single in UK chart history.[19]

'The real heyday was *Be Here Now*,' says Castaldo. 'That was probably a pinnacle because I organised the HMV special openings in the morning. At 8 a.m. there were about eighty shops around the chain that all had the most incredible queues with TV down there for the shutters going up. It was a real sense of an event. That was probably, for me, the peak moment because it conflated with the cultural interest in Britpop.'

Of the Elton John single, he says, 'That was [released on] a Saturday morning and there was hysteria. People were literally grabbing it. That was just trying to achieve some kind of emotional connection to the moment through music. Music's always had a remarkable power, but that was never shown more than in that instance, I think.'

These two blockbuster music moments in 1997, one album and one single, were seen at the time as merely staging posts in the CD's endless ascent. No one knew at the time that they collectively represented a commercial peak that was never going to be repeated.

THE PERPETUAL GROWTH LOOP: MORE SHOPS = MORE CUSTOMERS = MORE PROFIT = MORE MONEY TO OPEN MORE SHOPS

In business, greater profits and larger margins are homilies at the altar of growth. A company not growing is a company dying. For retail in the 1990s, the CD was delivering growth like never before and the arrival of the DVD was another lubricant for wider growth opportunities.

For the retailers, it looked like they had been handed the greatest growth loop of their lives. 'A growth loop is a flywheel of user acquisition and retention that fuels growth,' explains research and consulting firm Gartner. 'It's a system that, when complete, can be used as input for another system and so on, creating an ever-growing loop.'[20]

The natural reaction to booming sales was to open more shops to sell more products to more people in more places.

By 1999, the major retailers were wildly aggressive in their expansion plans.

In January 1999, Virgin Megastore announced it was closing its branch by Marble Arch in London. It had opened in 1985, but the company stressed this was not a retreat from the market; rather it was merely looking for a replacement location. '[T]he retailer has vowed to increase its trading space significantly in central London over the next two years,' wrote *Music Week*. In the same news story, it was reported that HMV was closing down its Oxford Street store, the first it ever opened back in

1921, but would replace it with a store 'virtually opposite' the historic site in the second half of 1999.[21]

Simon Wright, MD of Virgin Retail in the UK, claimed the Marble Arch closure was simply down to the fact the building could not be adapted to meet changing consumer demands. 'While we obviously regret having to close the Marble Arch store, it is essential to continually look for ways to improve the service we offer to our customers,' he told *Music Week*.[22]

Music retail in 1999 was obsessed with the four Bs: bigger, bolder, brasher, better.

In early summer, Virgin made good on its expansion commitment by announcing it was opening a new store in Piccadilly Circus in central London. It was the retailer driving its tanks onto the lawns of both HMV and Tower Records, who also had major outlets in the area.

'The shop will be located [. . .] opposite HMV and just across from Tower's flagship 30,000sq ft site,' wrote *Music Week*. 'At 20,000sq ft, it will be the second biggest store in the Virgin chain and slightly bigger than its HMV neighbour.'[23]

A bullish Wright said Virgin had been biding its time to get the right site. This was as much about expansion as it was about *making a statement* about expansion. Wright suggested the new store, which was scheduled to open in September, could drive sales of between £40 million and £50 million a year. *Music Week* noted the new store would have eight shop windows while its neighbouring HMV only had three, the subtext being these windows would bring in huge revenues from labels keen to promote their latest releases. Tower in Piccadilly, however, had fifteen windows so was better placed to mop up the biggest share of record label promotional expenditure.[24]

Virgin was also expanding nationally, with a 25,000 square foot store opening in Glasgow and a major outlet in Middlesbrough due to open the month after the Piccadilly opening. Tower Records, leaning on the 'a rising tide raises all boats' platitude, said that competition was healthy. 'This will make Piccadilly even more of a mecca for music fans,' insisted Andy Lown, SVP and director of operations for Tower in Europe. HMV was a lot more acidic in its comment to *Music Week*. 'It's on the south side of Piccadilly Circus where there is a busy road to cross and barriers blocking off a lot of the pavement,' sniffed an HMV spokesperson as they moved to bat away competition worries.[25]

A fortnight later, HMV was trumpeting its own expansion plans at its AGM in Brighton. It was committing £20 million to 'its biggest UK expansion programme to date' that could see up to sixteen new stores opened. Already confirmed were outlets in Gloucester, Blackburn, Glasgow and Reading, alongside the relocation of its Bond Street store in London. 'To support the expansion programme, HMV plans what it claims will be the largest marketing spend in its history to highlight its sales activities and the launch of new formats,' wrote *Music Week*. It also said it was planning to offer its full catalogue of 350,000 titles for sale (physically) via its website by the end of the year (more of which below).[26]

In August, Our Price announced that it too was expanding, planning to open ten more stores by the end of the year to add to the 230 stores it already operated in the UK. Deeper in the story in *Billboard* on the expansion was an indication about the macro cost for such accelerated expansion. Virgin Entertainment Group, the owners of the Our Price chain, was said to be looking to dispose of Our Price through a management buyout. Discussions around this had been happening since late 1998.[27]

There was a lot of subtext here, but it would suggest that Virgin was choosing to focus on its dominant retail brand, and its brand with the biggest stores, rather than a 'secondary' brand like Our Price, which typically operated much smaller stores. Big was everything.

Virgin Entertainment Group was not cutting back on spending to boost its Virgin Megastore brand, having rebranded all ninety-three of its UK stores and committing £3.2 million on a major advertising campaign, including its first UK TV advertising, from 22 November 1999 into January 2000.[28]

With all of these new stores opening or expanding in 1999, the UK record business was ludicrously bullish about Q4 that year, its biggest period for sales due to the Christmas gifting market, and how that momentum would carry over into 2000.

'Get set for new Millennium blast off,' roared *Music Week* on the cover of its 11 September 1999 issue. 'The music industry is shaping up for a spectacular start to the new millennium with potentially one of the strongest first quarter line-ups in years,' it said, citing new albums from acts like The Corrs, the Spice Girls, U2 and Oasis all expected in Q1 2000.[29]

OBSESSING OVER PHYSICAL MEANT BLOCKING OUT DIGITAL

As was the case at record labels, in 1999 the major retailers were also heavily focused on protecting the CD. This is what brought them their profits but also what, to their mind, gave them power over the record companies. Where else could they sell their new releases and who else would stock their catalogue titles?

Getting stock into a major retailer was only part of the equation. The priority, certainly for the major labels, was getting prime positioning in the shops. This was as much about pushing their latest releases as it was showboating in front of the other majors that, for this week at least, they could afford prime positioning in the key retail outlets. Prominent racking in stores was desired, but the biggest prize, the biggest display of deep pockets and unfettered ambition, was taking over the window displays. This was the prime real estate in the biggest record shops.

'Getting into an HMV window was the be all and end all,' says Castaldo. 'And I guess it was the same at Virgin and Tower. That was how you communicated with your customers and you'd run some co-op ads and it would drive people to buy the single on a Monday and come to get the album on a Friday or a Saturday. It delivered 90 per cent, if not more, of that week's sales.'

It was often little more than a pissing contest between labels, the cost of which went onto the marketing cost for that week's priority artist, so it left them deeper in debt to the labels as their recoupable costs were ratcheted up.

There was also a pissing contest playing out between the retailers themselves, notably between HMV, Virgin Megastore and Tower Records.

'They just didn't see a future that didn't involve the high street, so it was about expanding, growing, reaching into new places,' says Castaldo about this period of accelerated expansion. 'They were getting into book retailing. It was just about land grabs wherever they could. Really they were storing up all sorts of problems for themselves because they were getting prime locations. This wasn't some second- or third-rate site that was cheap and cheerful. It was a prime location with big rents. With big rents came big rates. The costs were very high. Taking on more staff. It was just assumed that you could just keep growing and growing.'

McLaughlin spells out just how high the stakes were when a retailer like HMV committed to opening or expanding stores. He also feels the record labels did not (publicly) appreciate the roll of the dice retailers were making here.

'Every time we opened a new HMV store, and I showed [the labels] the data to prove it, we grew the market for music and video in that town,' he says. 'They knew this privately, by the way, but for them to admit it to me would mean that they would see the doors opening and that I would be in asking for far too much money. Our margins did improve over a period of time, but that was only because we put our hard-earned cash into the expansion programme.'

He adds, 'The overall issue for us was that we put it in front of [the labels]. I didn't hide and I said I would share every piece of financial information. Here are the last twelve leases I've just taken out on these stores and they're twenty-five-year leases, and these leases are ours for twenty-five years. I can't tear the piece of paper up and say, "Thanks very much for leasing the shop out but it's not working, so here's the lease back." They would say, "There's eighteen years remaining on the lease, so you just have to pay up that eighteen years if that'd be OK." Let's take the new store on Oxford Street: the rent was £2.7 million or £2.8 million a year times twenty-five years. That was the commitment that we were making. I don't think that the record companies ever put up that level of money just to sign an unknown band.'

Glen Ward was president and CEO of Virgin Entertainment Group between 1998 and 2005 and was leading the expansion of Virgin Megastore in North America. He says the economics of opening new stores was always tricky and that retailers also had to engage in rolling contractual debates with labels that could seriously impinge on their margins. This was as true in the UK, where he had worked for both Our Price and HMV, as it was in the US.

'Something that we did in the States, and certainly in the UK, was we went onto main high streets,' he says. 'Going on high streets in the UK is expensive. So you had to be flexible and versatile in your offering and the margins that were required to sustain that. So there were endless debates with record companies about deal terms.'

The 'superstore' model was the natural consequence of the growth-at-all-costs strategy and was imported into the UK from the US, a country obsessed with scale. Multi-story outlets were opened from the late 1980s onwards, not just in the capital as a statement of intent – and as a symbol of vaulting corporate ambition – but also in secondary and tertiary cities around the UK.

'When Brian came in, he could see that there were superstores starting to happen,' says Castaldo. 'Obviously, [Richard] Branson was doing the same thing with Virgin Megastore. Brian and some of his people went to America and they could see this is the future and were going to export it back to the UK. We opened, at the time, the world's largest record store in Oxford Circus, which had up to 50,000 square feet. Fair enough, there was the Megastore on the corner of Tottenham Court Road [central London]. But suddenly we had 20,000 square foot stores in Southampton, in Manchester, in Birmingham and wherever.'

With the major retailers so invested in high-street dominance through high-street expansion, they were making clear and definite bets on the future of music retail being the ongoing sale of CDs. There would be token online offerings (see below), but bigger and bigger and more and more city centre stores was the core of their future strategy.

They were not oblivious to what was happening online and how music files were being swapped, or occasionally purchased, across the internet. The fact, however, was that the major labels, the biggest suppliers for the retailers, were not yet licensing their catalogues for download suggests to the retail brands that nothing was going to change for a long time. It was going to be business as usual.

'They didn't have the knowledge or the expertise to really understand either the full opportunities or the threats digital, in whatever form it came, whether illegal or legal, might present,' says Castaldo of the executive tiers running the biggest retailers in 1999. 'It's easy to say that now with hindsight, but living it at that time, you wouldn't have seen it in the same way.'

This, of course, placed them in a highly vulnerable position, although no one quite understood at the time quite how vulnerable.

'If you think about Oxford Street and Regent Street, you had two HMVs and a massive Virgin Megastore – and Tower in Piccadilly as well,' says Jonathan Davis, co-founder of Crunch download service. 'These were like citadels of the CDs. That was the height of the CD era. For those organisations, whether it be the major labels or the major retailers, which started to include the supermarkets as well, the MP3 was a threat and a major change in the way that consumers wanted to and were able to consume music. It was highly disruptive for anyone whose business was based on manufacturing an item, getting it to a store or selling it to a customer in the store.'

These 'citadels of the CDs' were perhaps deemed to be too big to fail.

The retailers had invested heavily in them and they were not about to change their business models.

As Albhy Galuten, working at Universal Music Group's eLabs division in 1999, says of the industry as a whole as it approached this new crossroads, 'We were not ready to swap analogue dollars for digital pennies.'

Scott Cohen, co-founder of The Orchard, makes a similar point about the need for businesses to ring fence their core revenue source and protect it for as long as possible.

'You're making 99 per cent of your revenue from one format,' he says. 'You can't just go, "Ah, fuck it. Let's just go all digital. Never do it again." Even in today's world physical's 20 per cent of the business. That's twenty years on. On one level, people said, "Oh, they're slow and they're stupid." Hmmm, not really. They're making all their money from one thing. Yes, they did miss certain opportunities to take advantage of it. These are mistakes that are not happening now. Everyone's into Web3 and the metaverse. It's early, early days and no one knows what's going to happen yet, but everyone's in. That attitude didn't exist in 1999.'

The focus for retailers in the late 1990s had to be on maximising revenue from every single square foot they operated. How they did that was very similar to what Doug Morris was doing within Universal Music Group. Rather than have all the labels within Universal compete with the other majors for collective market share, he encouraged labels to compete internally for individual market share. It fostered a culture of intense competition which, in turn, fostered a culture of ruthlessness.

The retailers, notably HMV, were following a similar logic. But they went one step further. It wasn't just one HMV store versus the rest around the country; it was one department versus the rest *in the same building*.

'What HMV did brilliantly was to create competition, not from other retailers, but amongst itself,' reveals Castaldo. 'So it was floor against floor, shop against shop, region against region, nation against nation.'

A business plan on paper is very different from a business plan in practice because of the human factor. Pitch heads of stores and even heads of departments against each and it could get violent. Literally.

'We did it either brilliantly or badly, depending on your point of view,' says Castaldo. 'It almost started to get out of hand because, one year, there was a conference and there was actually a fight between Northern managers and Southern managers. The irony was that they weren't necessarily from the North or the South. That just happened to be where they managed [stores]. They could be from the South, but based in Leeds. Such was the intense level of competition that it was almost spilling over in a slightly unhealthy way. But it was an incredible dynamic that fueled [HMV].'

Simon Wright was MD of Virgin Retail UK in 1998 and 1999 and says he was not from a pure music background and this gave him a perspective and an objectivity that perhaps the other senior executives in music retail lacked. Before taking on the Virgin Retail UK job, he had been CFO at Virgin Entertainment Group Worldwide and before that he was finance director of entertainment at UK chain WHSmith.

'I'm not like Brian McLaughlin or Russell Solomon [founder of Tower Records] or someone like that, who I would have dealings with,' he suggests. 'Their whole careers have been about music. I was actually an accountant.'

He says that retailers had a strong 1990s, but this was a very volatile and delicate sector of the market they were operating in. They were entirely dependent on record companies putting out records that people wanted to buy. This was not like other fast-moving consumer goods such as pasta, soft drinks, detergent or biscuits that would not really change and where sales would be reasonably predictable, albeit with occasional seasonal readjustments.

'Unlike most retailers, we didn't determine what product we sold,' Wright says. 'The music companies and the artists produce stuff and we sell it. If we had a bad year, it was because of bad releases. We couldn't suddenly say, "Come up with better releases!" Most retailers have some control over what they sell and how they sell it. In music retail, you're very much at the mercy of the record companies and the artists.'

This made the relationship between retailers and record labels both tricky and tense. When albums sold well, everyone was covered in glory and shared the spoils. When they did not sell, one side was keen to blame the other for not doing their job properly.

Wright says that retailers were actually in a particularly precarious position, despite what the labels and the public might have thought.

'We used to have to be really careful how we talked about margins,' he suggests. 'If I said to Joe Bloggs in the street that we make 30 per cent margin or 50 per cent profit, they would think that was good. But the person in the street didn't know that our rent on average was 10 per cent, staff costs on average were 12 per cent of sales and all the other stuff.'

He also says there was bleed in their profits from shoplifting that also had to be factored into their overall profitability. CDs were a highly desirable consumer item and, as such, theft was a reality of music retail. He recounts speaking at a conference and explaining the impact it had and how it effectively had to be accepted as part of selling music in the physical world.

'I said, "Do you know what our theft in physical terms is? It's about 2 per cent of our sales. Our global sales are £1.5 billion. Do the math. That's a lot of money. We could stop it. A rhetorical question. Why don't we stop it? The way we stop it is to not sell anything; just close our doors and not sell anything".'

Most of the focus here has been on the UK, but it sits as illustrative of wider retail dynamics across the globe. The UK arguably had the most advanced and dynamic music retailing market in the world in the late 1990s and while it copied some things from the US, it also influenced many things in the US and beyond.

LOVE, HATE, SALES

In a codependent relationship, there is a mutual need that gets curdled by mounting dysfunction. Power balances shift, communication can break down, boundaries are ignored, power plays happen, self-esteem is badly damaged, toxicity can become the norm. The parties in the codependent relationship typically divide into the caretaker (also known as the giver or the enabler) and the taker.[30]

Music retailers and record labels, at various times, believed themselves to be the caretaker and the other to be the taker. They were both right and both wrong. In the 1990s, this love/hate relationship between record companies and music retailers was at its most pronounced, in part because there was so much at stake.

Speaking to people from retail and people from record labels about this period in their shared history, there was a large amount of unresolved tension coming through in how they discussed the other side (and many of them very much saw it as a case of 'sides' that had to be taken). There was some simmering passive-aggression in what some said as well as some outright score-settling that others wanted to achieve. Cutting through what many of them said is that they often felt the other 'side' either did not appreciate them or was hellbent on screwing them over.

At the heart of it was the issue of control: who had it, who was abusing it, how that control could be evened out or snatched back completely.

'At that time, certainly the likes of HMV and Brian McLaughlin thought of themselves as the equal of labels,' says Castaldo. 'They didn't see it as some submissive role because they make all the music and we just meekly sell it. "We are as important in the food chain as anyone else and what we say goes and our views are just as valid as anyone else's." Retail was that powerful. It commanded a lot of the high street, a lot of the sales. The labels and others knew that, unless you got your positioning in the shops and the windows and the racking and chart walls and all that stuff, you just wouldn't necessarily get the numbers to get into the charts. They had a sense of their own worth and they weren't scared to say that.'

Glen Ward asserts that, in this relationship, it was the retailers who were the weakest and the labels often abused their position of dominance. The labels, he believes, existed in a state of constant paranoia that the control they had was always at risk.

'It would have been nice to have control, but as retailers we didn't have that control,' he claims. 'It might have only ever come with the new album releases and the ability to put things front and centre, but the record companies had a lot of control. And historically that had been built up – purposely or otherwise. "Control" is exactly the word for the record companies. The fear of losing control, or not knowing the rules of the new game readily enough, meant a lot of disruption over that period of time. They were an intermediary between the artists and the fans in the first place, but they had control.'

One source at a retailer says that a lot of this tension was grandstanding, a form of corporate pantomime that was vicious at the time but confined to the boardrooms where meetings between retail and label executives took place. Other times, however, it could erupt publicly.

'The funny thing was [a senior retail executive] would invite label heads all to his birthday party and they'd all be friends and the next day they'd be absolutely deadly enemies again,' they say. 'I remember [the head of one label] and [senior retailer] screaming at each other at some awards show. They were swearing at each other. "You're bullying me!" "Fuck you!" When I think back on it, it was very funny.'

Wright says these tensions could reach breaking point when new deal terms were being discussed or labels were invoicing for stock supply.

He claims some major label heads were good to deal with as they understood the value of keeping good relations with retailers. Other label heads, however, saw it almost as a professional responsibility to lock horns with retailers over anything and everything.

'I would put record company executives into two boxes,' Wright says. 'There were those that realised that they're running a business with a customer and they realised they're in an ecosystem. And then there are those [who didn't]. I found dealing with certain people that retailers were seen as a necessary evil. "Oh, God, we have to deal with the retailers. We're in business to make great records".'

On the record company side, Jay Samit, SVP of new media at EMI, calls it 'a marriage of convenience' between labels and retailers, but then makes a clarifying point. 'Both sides,' he says bluntly, 'hate each other.'

For Jeff Liebenson, VP of legal and business affairs for BMG International, there was a complex financial relationship, and set of dependencies, that meant labels often had to bite their tongues as they could not risk going nuclear on retailers. This pulled the brakes on many discussions that prevented a rolling, if occasionally begrudging, armistice flipping over into a declaration of war.

'We were very aware that traditional retail was where we conducted the vast bulk of our business,' he explains. 'I think it was obvious from the very beginning that online was not the favourite approach of the traditional retailers. Our eggs were in the traditional retail basket and would likely remain that way for quite some time. We wanted to make progress but we didn't want to bite the hand that fed us.'

Tasked with building a digital business at EMI, Jeremy Silver says the long-standing relationship with retailers, and the enduring political tensions around this relationship, meant that he was severely compromised in terms of what he could do. Digital deals and initiatives that risked upsetting powerful retailers were not just frowned upon within labels at the most senior level, they were actively discouraged.

'The focus of money making in the business, primarily, was still the traditional way and was still retail,' he says of that period. 'The biggest problem was that we couldn't move without pissing off retail. That was this thing that kept holding everything back and that everyone was terrified of. Why would you compromise your current revenue stream for a high-risk new revenue stream that was yet to be proven? In any kind of accounting perspective, looking at it from a financial perspective, it was very difficult for people to get past that. I'm not criticising anybody for that because I think that is [still] a fundamental challenge today.'

Having run both CBS and MCA in the US, Al Teller has a long history of navigating label/retailer tensions. By 1999, he was running Atomic Pop, a digital-first label, and far enough outside of the major label system to view it all as occasionally childish and often self-destructive.

He feels, as any label person of the time would, that retailers were wholly reliant on record companies for their stock and for putting product on the market that large numbers of people wanted to buy. He feels that the retailers never fully appreciated this and, as such, he has little sympathy for their position or how they conducted themselves in business dealings.

'As far as I'm concerned, the retailers were, by and large, equivalent to third-world countries in the sense that they were dependent upon the generosity of record companies for their economic survival,' he insists. 'If you added up all the advertising funds we gave them, the promotional funds, having to pay for every poster on the wall, for every poster in a window, [having them] dictating terms that were obnoxiously excessive – we supported those people. There were numerous times that retailers would make demands that I would tell our head of sales, "Not a chance. We're not going to do it".'

He says the animosity between labels and retailers has a long history and stresses that label heads have equally long memories. 'In the early days of the CD, they came in long boxes,' he says. 'The long box was there for one reason and one reason only: you could put two of them side by side in an old-fashioned LP bin. The retailers refused to reconfigure their stores unless the record companies [paid for it]. I remember my sales head coming in and saying, "So and so will take the CDs without the long box but we're going to have to pay for reconfiguring their store." I said, "Forget about it." Here was always my bottom line: if they don't want to take our records, they don't have to take our records.'

He feels that much of this braggadocio from retailers was hollow rhetoric because they relied on hits to keep the lights on. If they cut off one source of hits, they were cutting off a major part of their income.

'At the end of the day, kids, the consumers, want the music – and if you are an obstacle to them getting the music, you're in trouble,' argues Teller. 'So if you're a big retailer and you're huffing and puffing and trying to bully the record company, for one reason or another, you're depriving your customers of the music they want. Good luck to you.'

A senior label executive says that the retailers would occasionally engage in underhand tactics in order to improve their profitability – and that came at the expense of the labels.

'One retailer had a returns allowance of 5 per cent,' they say of the policy that allowed retailers to send back a share of stock if they had over-ordered. 'If they needed more than 5 per cent, they usually put CDs on the radiators so they could return them back as faulty goods.'

Characteristic of his background as a lawyer, John Kennedy, chairman of Universal Music Group UK, was much more of a diplomat in his dealings with the retailers. He would always negotiate a deal that was as favourable to Universal as possible, but he was less interested in engaging in, point-scoring, showboating and unnecessarily aggressive behaviour towards retailers. He believed this helped no one. Plenty of label executives over the years craved and actively cultivated a reputation built on fear and intimidation. Kennedy was not one of them.

'A number of my colleagues would treat retailers as the enemy,' he says. 'I think I particularly embraced retailers as our partners, even to the point of some people taking the mick out of me for calling them "partners" because nobody had done that before. But to me they were an essential partner.'

So much of the war of words between labels and retailers was performative, claims Paul Russell, chairman of Sony Music Europe. In many ways, it was a game that was expected to play out and business to carry on as normal: a sport of sorts.

'Let's deal with the UK first of all,' he says. 'The politics were not as spiky as maybe you've been led to believe. They needed us and we needed them. I'd like to think that in the UK there were very good relationships between Sony and the major retailers and some of the smaller independents. They had their point of view and we had our point of view, but at the end of the day 40 per cent of the UK business is done in September, October, November and December – or really October, November and December. They wanted our TV advertising. They wanted our major releases. And we wanted their help, their windows and so on. Because that's when they made 40 per cent of their businesses as well. Everything could be saber-rattled around between January and September and then everybody would just say, "Hey, fuck that! We've got Christmas to run!" That was probably true all over Europe.'

That may have been true for Russell, but speaking to several label and retail executives, even at the distance of two decades, there was still a lot of unresolved animosity between some of them. They, to put it frankly, still *loathed* each other. For some, the fighting might have been a kind of corporate cosplay; for others, it was deadly serious.

A lot of the bad blood between labels and retailers was that certain label heads found it impossible to admit that good retail was as crucial to the success of a record as good marketing and good A&R.

'You couldn't have a big album without HMV, without Our Price, without Woolworths,' says Martin Craig, head of the ESP division within Warner International. 'But if you were head of A&R, or if you were MD of a label, you didn't want to know that. Because, as far as you were concerned, it sold because it was brilliant. Because you'd made these brilliant albums and it would just sell.'

The greatest retailing tensions, because they delivered the bulk of big-selling titles, were around the major labels. The independents were, for the most part, outside of the crossfire and very happy to let the major labels and the major retailers slug it out between themselves.

'That is one of the good things about being a small company: you don't make a big enough dent in anybody's boat,' notes Alison Wenham, chair/chief executive of AIM. 'It really was a battle going on between the majors and the retailers. It was absurd. Absolutely absurd.'

SINGLE LIFE: THE US KILLS IT OFF BUT THE UK SEES A BOOM IN THE 1990S

Since the mid-to-late 1960s, the dominant currency, both creatively and commercially, of the record business was the album. In 1968, production of albums in the UK exceeded production of singles for the first time, with the album making up 80 per cent of revenues in the US.[31]

The album became how recording contracts were measured out and it was where the greatest profits could be mined. Singles, in many cases, were only there to advertise albums. In the most egregious cases, the single was the only song worth listening to on an album.

With the CD increasing the retail price of the album while shrinking its size physically, it became a whole new kind of profit centre for labels and retailers. They could be sold for more and they took up less space in record shops. Any business would have been delirious with joy to land on something where, the smaller you made it, the more you could charge for it and the more it would sell.

The story of the single in the 1990s, however, is dramatically different in the US and the UK. Like a twist on the aphorism commonly attributed to George Bernard Shaw (its true origins are uncertain and disputed) about America and England being two countries separated by a common language, as far as the single went in the 1990s, the US and UK were two countries separated by a common format.

Perhaps it is down to the fact the single resonates more in the UK than the US. The first UK chart started in 1952[32] and was steadfastly based on sales from record shops whereas the US chart, dating back to one in *Billboard* in the 1940s, was, for many years, a curious melange of sales, radio plays and jukebox spins. It may also be partly down to the UK having national radio stations (notably BBC Radio 1 since 1967) and national music chart shows (notably *Top Of The Pops* between 1964 and 2005) in a way the US did not that made the charts part of the national psyche.

In the US, the CD single was seen initially as another way to squeeze revenue out of consumers. In 1988, there were sales of 1.6 million CD singles, rising to 66.7 million in 1997, making it, by some distance, the dominant format for singles. 'As the majors began to turn their attention to CD singles they soon noted that the cost of their manufacture and distribution was virtually the same as that of CD albums,' noted Phil Hardy. 'And so began the long process of withdrawal from the physical singles market.'[33]

CD single sales in the US dropped from 109.7 million in 1998 to 83.6 million in 1999. Fearful that CD singles were cannibalising the highly lucrative CD album business (and perhaps fearful that albums with only one good single were going to be exposed as the scam they were), the majors suffocated the format.[34]

'[T]he decline of singles was linked to the cost of producing a single versus the cost of producing an album,' noted David Arditi. A CD costs between $1 and $2 to manufacture regardless of how much music was on the disc. Singles sold for around $6.98 (with the retailer taking up to 30 per cent of that) and albums sold for between $16.98 and $18.98. As such, the labels considered the CD single to be not only not worth the effort because of the slim margins it offered but also to be potentially undermining album sales.[35]

The labels in the US felt they had pulled off a masterstroke here. If consumers wanted that hit song that was on heavy rotation on radio and MTV, the only way they could get it was to buy the album. Their timing, however, was atrocious. The killing of the CD single coincided with the rise of online file-sharing. Now the fan did have a choice, as Steve Knopper noted. They could buy the album and be good consumers like the labels expected them to be. Or they could download it for free.[36] You, as Americans are so fond of saying, do the math.

Indeed, Knopper lists killing the single as one of Big Music's Big Mistakes during this era. Knopper quotes from an op-ed in *Billboard* in 1997 by Canadian producer and songwriter Terry McManus which he holds up as incredibly prescient. 'When it stopped making vinyl singles and offered nothing to replace them,' argued McManus, 'the [North American music] industry stopped a whole generation from picking up the record-buying habit.'[37]

The US labels either did not read what McManus was warning against in his op-ed or they simply did not care: they were going to consign the CD single to the dustbin of history. It was to prove to be the kind of victory that even Pyrrhus of Epirus would openly mock.

'The moment that America stopped selling singles and started forcing people to buy albums, with ten or twelve tracks on it, one of which was any good and ten or eleven which were not good, was the moment everyone in America went, "Fuck you, we're going to download",' says Guy Holmes, founder of UK independent label Gut Records. 'The Americans, in my opinion, by refusing to sell singles and forcing people to have to spend $15 on an album which was invariably not good enough, destroyed the trust of the record-buying public.'

The romanticised notion of the album, a carefully crafted suite or concept that had to be listened to from soup to nuts, began in classical and jazz and had infiltrated the rock and pop markets by the middle of the 1960s. The album became regarded as an *artistic statement* while simultaneously existing as a highly lucrative commercial unit.

The record business being the record business, this simply became something to exploit and manipulate so much that creative ideals were jettisoned in favour of commercial angles.

'There are some albums that are just a collection of tracks and don't really deserve to be albums, other than it's a marketing conceit to put them on one album,' says Edgar Bronfman Jr, owner of Universal Music Group at the time. 'On the other hand, there were people like Pink Floyd [and albums like] *Tommy* by The Who – now that's an album. Yes, there were a few tracks played from it, but that was an album. This has separated the wheat from the chaff between real album artists and singles artists who are releasing albums at the same time.'

I ask Bronfman if he feels that, by the late 1990s, the record business was guilty of debasing the album as an artistic endeavour in favour of ruthlessly exploiting it as a commercial enterprise, over-charging for a product where, to invert the old industry maxim, it was all filler and no killer. Unsurprisingly, he disagrees.

'It's complete bullshit!' he says. 'And the reason I say that is that the assumption behind that comment is that if we'd been pricing our stuff fairly, this [people turning to online piracy] would not have happened. It's idiotic. I don't know. . . Maybe some albums were too expensive. But to think that had they been less expensive, this wouldn't have happened? It's insane.'

Eileen Richardson, the first CEO of Napster, disagrees and says the ruthlessness of major record labels, where art was routinely trampled underfoot by commerce, was *precisely* why consumers turned to file-sharing. They had been ripped off, she claims, for decades and believed that the recording artists had been ripped off too. Now, however, they could do something about it. Their decision to download illegally was not just shaped by commercial concerns, what they were doing was an act of resistance; it was *political*.

'Seventeen dollars [for a CD] and a dollar goes to the artist after their expenses?' she asks. 'And $16 goes to these assholes [at record labels]? What I would say always was, "Why would you spend $17 on a Britney Spears CD and get only two songs that you like? Wouldn't you prefer to spend $17 and get 17 songs that you like? They might not be artists that the fricking music industry think you might like, but there are artists that you can find on your own based on your preferences".'

Before she joined Napster in late 1999, Elizabeth Brooks was working as an A&R within Sony Music. She insists the album model was horrifically shattered by label greed and it became more broken as the 1990s progressed.

'People were starving and it wasn't a fan-friendly structure,' she says. 'And the price of a CD versus people's incomes had something like tripled in ten years. It was madness and I'd seen this from the label end of how we priced records. You were constantly fighting when you introduced a new artist and dropped the price so that people could actually afford to take a chance on a new record. Things like that. It would be a battle royale to introduce new pricing. I was at a developmental label at Sony and there was a fight that we went through on every single release. We put a Fiona Apple record out and they might have charged $18 for it. $18 for someone you've never heard of? It doesn't work.'

Linked to this, she says, was the eradication of the single in the US market, meaning consumers were expected to buy an album to get the song that had initially piqued their interest.

'There was no sampling, there was no access, there was a vastly overpriced CD market, insanely tightly playlisted radio,' she says of the majors' iron grip on both promotion and the market. 'Everything was restricted and all of a sudden this source of music just opened up for you. Anything and everything you can imagine.'

In the US at this time, the record labels were under investigation amid allegations of price fixing, something they were found guilty of in May 2000 (see Chapter 10). This was interconnected with the desire to nullify the single if it would drive album sales. Sell more albums and charge even more for them was the sort of freewheeling business thinking gripping the industry in the US.

Things were more *tactical* in Europe, according to one senior executive at a major label in the 1990s. Before the introduction of the single currency (the euro) in the majority of the EU member states in 1999, each European country had its own currency.[38] The fluctuation of national currencies was something that presented challenges to companies operating across the European continent and made operational forecasting difficult.

The album was the record industry's major profit centre and clearly labels were keen to push as many sales as possible and to keep raising prices as long as the market could sustain it. In mainland Europe, that meant 'price harmonisation' and in the US that meant a pincer movement of price fixing and decommissioning the single to drive even more sales of the increasingly more expensive CD album.

In the UK, however, it was a very different scenario and the single was proving to be a commercial and financial juggernaut that could happily coexist with the album. Indeed, they were often locked in a beautifully symbiotic relationship.

In the 1980s, multi-formatting in the UK singles market became the fan-fleecing default setting of too many pop acts. Acts would not just put out singles on cassette and both 7' and 12' vinyl, they would also add in 10' singles, picture discs, singles with a range of different sleeves, singles boasting 'exclusive' tracks and more. This was all to mobilise a fanbase to buy as many copies as possible in order to catapult the single up the charts in its first week. It was a brazen marketing tactic that soon became an arms race.

In response to this format-driven greed, new chart rules were put in place in 1991 whereby only five nominated formats would count towards the UK chart. More egregious label bending of the rules inevitably followed and the number of eligible formats was reduced again in 1994 to three.[39]

The net result of this was to introduce the 'double CD single' strategy (the same lead track and two other tracks, be they new songs, remixes, live versions or demos on each CD). In marketing, this became normalised and played on unquestioning fan loyalty to help game chart positions.

CD singles were initially treated as a loss leader for an album in the UK. Labels there, unlike their counterparts in the US, were not as worried about a high-performing single eating into more lucrative album sales. Of course, some single buyers might not go on to buy the album, but enough of them did to ensure that singles and albums sales could run in parallel.

There are plenty of anecdotes from the time of record label sales representatives doing deals with retailers where they would sell them one single at the agreed PPD (published price to dealer) that had been negotiated in advance and then 'gifting' them five singles to do with what they pleased.

The PPD had implications for mechanical rates paid to songwriters/publishers and the royalties paid to recording artists as they were based on a negotiated percentage of the PPD. But if records were given away, and classified as promotion, there was no publishing royalty due. (There were, and still are, caps on the free goods that could be royalty-free based on what was classed as 'reasonable' – itself a highly subjective term).

Hypothetically, if the PPD of a CD single was £2.25 and the retailer was 'expected' to sell a new single for £2 on release week to help its sales, they would lose money on every sale. But if the PPD was £2.25 and they were given five 'free' singles for every one they 'bought', they could sell them all at £2 each, potentially generating £12 in sales but only paying the label £2.25.

Such creative discounting was endemic in the British music business. Record companies lowered the risk of introducing a new act or single into the market and retailers could enjoy pure profit on the brace of singles they got 'free' from labels as part of deal.

For established hits, when something was really in demand, retailers could comfortably charge £3.99 for a CD single. The long-game strategy with discounting was to knock singles out cheaply at the start to get the act into the charts then, if the song was a hit, retailers would increase the price of that single or any subsequent single – as long as the act and their music was in demand. Speculate to accumulate, runs the business adage. Here it was: discount to disseminate.

Except in 1999, labels started salivating at the success of the single in the UK and felt they should cost more. A lot more. The market would, they felt, accept this and so they began looking into disposing of discounting.

In January 1999, *Music Week* ran a news story taking stock of single sales for the whole of 1998. It found that previously heavily marketed singles would enter the charts high and drop out of the charts just as quickly; but in 1998 a new solidity was starting to define the performance of singles in the chart.

'After a year in which more titles took turns at number one than ever before – thirty-one of them, including two which first topped the chart in 1997 – it seems a little odd to suggest that the singles chart showed a new stability in 1998,' it wrote. 'But that's exactly what it did, because most or those chart toppers hung around long enough to sell in large quantities, even if their reigns were on the short side.'

It added, 'While the number of singles to pass through the Top 75 slumped from an all-time high of 1,127 in 1997 to a five-year low of 1,052 last year, a growing amount of hits were shifting in prodigious quantities, with CIN figures indicating that twenty of them sold more than half a million copies in the year – an unprecedented number.'[40]

This was the first early warning sign that something was about to change.

The second sign came in February, with major labels suggesting the scattergun strategy of the past was over. Things were going to be more focused (read: profitable) from now on.

'Record companies are now releasing fewer singles and putting more into the ones they do release,' Jeremy Marsh, music division president of BMG, announced to *Music Week*. 'That is because the cost of entry for a single is so high and the competition so fierce. There are only so many records you can get on a playlist or into Woolworths.'[41]

A new confidence – or, depending on your view, a new arrogance – was defining how the majors were going approaching the singles market.

'There is no crying wolf in this company,' swaggered Lucian Grainge, MD of Polydor, part of Universal Music Group. 'Everything we're releasing between now and June is aim and fire.'[42]

There was the smell of new revenue possibilities in the air. The majors, their nostrils agape, swung into action.

Sony Music moved first. At the start of March, it announced it was imposing a 'free-product ceiling' on major releases from Manic Street Preachers, George Michael and B*Witched. It would mean, according to *Music Week*, that 'only a set number of units will be available under Sony's usual deal arrangement for pre-release retail orders.'[43]

Music Week cited Britney Spears' recent '. . . Baby One More Time' single as marking a crisis point of sorts. It was initially sold at £1.99 and sold just under 464,000 units in its first week. The argument being it was such a nailed-on hit that it would have still sold phenomenally at twice the price.[44] It was to go on to become the biggest-selling single in the UK that year.[45]

'Anything to try and get out of this crazy low-price situation is welcome,' an unnamed senior label executive was quoted as saying. 'It isn't doing anybody any good. It's devaluing our product.'[46]

In April, *Music Week* reported on a wider pan-label trend it had recently spotted. Rather than launch singles at £1.99 on release week, prices were rising to £2.99 (New Radicals, Mr Ozio, Cher, Eminem, Robbie Williams) and even going as high as £3.99 (Martine McCutcheon, Phats & Small, Boyzone).

'Virgin Records' decision to launch McCutcheon's debut single at full price is part of the company's long-term policy which has also included several Spice Girls singles selling at £3.99 in their first week,' it noted.[47]

Mike McMahon, EMI sales director, spoke about the previous two Robbie Williams singles selling for £2.99 and said EMI looked at all singles on a case-by-case basis. If there was sufficient consumer demand, he said, it would move for a price increase. 'We're in a market where the norm has become £1.99 so customers expect singles to be £1.99,' he said.[48]

The *Music Week* story also noted that Sony had taken 'limited steps to place a ceiling on the amount of free product given away for key £1.99 releases', suggesting a bigger recalibration to come.[49]

Brian McLaughlin recalls that he broadly supported the labels seeking to increase the price of singles in the UK. 'You have got to remember that the industry went from giving them away to then trying to pull it all back in and get a reasonable margin for a single,' he says. 'America couldn't understand what the hell we were doing putting singles out, but the UK was a thriving business for singles.'

Tony Wadsworth, head of EMI's recorded music arm in the UK, says that by 1999, in particular genres in the UK, singles were becoming so successful and so profitable that they were creating their own centre of gravity. A hit single could sell so much that a tie-in album was a beautiful dividend rather than an economic necessity.

'It was repertoire-driven,' he says. 'If you look at the top-selling singles in 1999, this was the boom time of Vengaboys and big dance pop singles. They sold shitloads. That was the sale itself. In fact, you didn't depend on selling albums off the back of them. Sometimes you might, but that would be a nice surprise bonus. They were singles for the sake of singles. That wasn't happening that much in the years immediately before that. Before then, singles were predominately loss leaders to help sell albums.'

(Of the biggest singles in the UK in 1999, Vengaboys were only at number 15. Britney Spears was number one and the rest of the Top 20 included the likes of Eiffel 65, ATB, Shanks & Bigfoot, S Club 7 and Steps. The one anomaly was the artist at number three in the year's chart: Cliff Richard with 'The Millennium Prayer'.)[50]

Wadsworth admits discounting would have been the norm for a new act to help them get a foothold in the charts. 'For instance, a brand new artist release such as the very first Coldplay single [on Parlophone], where nobody would have ever heard of them, I would imagine that we were giving that away, or selling it for next to nothing,' he says.

With singles flipping in the UK from loss leaders to profit centres, it was only natural that the labels would start to quickly phase out discounting as this was a market ripe for the milking.

'It was a singles boom,' says Wadsworth of 1999. 'So if there is a singles boom, you don't discount the singles that are in demand. If there's a massive demand for something, then you maximise the price.' (In an age of budget airlines and Uber, this is commonly known today as 'surge pricing' or 'dynamic pricing', discounting to stimulate demand and then strategically upping prices as that demand increases).

John Kennedy says Universal was doing very well out of singles by 1999 and this was why it was keen to end widespread discounting and to stop having a sliding scale where prices only went up if and when the single had already proven its chart and commercial worth. Rather than lean on surge pricing, Kennedy said Universal wanted to have the confidence to go in, from the off, with a price at the top of the market.

'There was supposed to be a model whereby you started on £1.99 to set it off, you moved it up to £2.99 and then £3.99,' he says. 'I observed, when I came in, that some of my MDs were not moving off £1.99 anymore and they'd come in and say, "We think we can do a million copies of this." I said, "Let's hope we don't because you're going to lose money on them if we don't move it up to £2.99 and then £3.99." It seemed inconceivable now that you could sell a single for £3.99, but we were doing very well on it.'

I ask him about the discounting arms race that had erupted during the 1990s and if that was down to a label obsession with market share rather than a sustainable business model for breaking and developing artists.

'Market share at the cost of profitability is no good at all,' he says. 'You want the combination of the two.'

He argues that the pricing of singles at £3.99 was absolutely something the consumer would accept at the time and that it did not necessarily kick the legs out from under the album. All filler no killer albums were an A&R conundrum that had wider economic consequences.

'You can discount a record to try and launch an artist's career,' suggests Kennedy. 'You maybe even discount for the first track off an album by an established artist; but, at the end of the day, record companies are in it for profitability. The public was OK with these singles at £3.99. The bigger problem, which Doug Morris used to talk about quite a bit, was when you were trying to sell an album at a much higher price and that only had one [good] track on it.'

Andy Cleary, co-founder and director of Jammin Music Group, says this heavy discounting of singles in the UK was really only a game the major labels could play. Independent labels, he says, could not afford to deliberately lose money on releases in the vague hope that it would all come good several months, or years, down the line.

'It just wasn't worth having a hit anymore,' he says of the period in the early and mid 1990s when singles were being sold for as little as £0.99 in the UK. 'If you were one of those indies that were trying to compete in the pop crossover market – and we used to do it one single at a time – you just couldn't do that anymore.'

The record labels and the specialist music retailers obviously both benefited enormously from rising prices for singles and albums. Bigger record sales with bigger profit margins were what they craved.

Labels made money outside of CD sales (such as through radio play, licensing, synchronisation) as did retail brands like HMV and Virgin Megastore (expanding into books, DVDs, games, consumer electronics). But the bulk of their business and their brand hinged around the CD. Selling records as loss leaders was only a short-term strategy to break a new record or a new act and then prices would rise when the demand was there. Also, if music is your major product, if you loss-lead on all music, you very quickly will find out that you have no business.

In the late 1990s, however, two different kinds of retailers started to see selling loss-leadings CDs not just as a way to break acts but, more importantly, as a way to build their non-music operations. In entering a Faustian pact with what seemed to be exciting new retail partners, the record companies were not only damning themselves, but they were also damning the specialist retailers who had been their most loyal, if occasionally combative, partners for the entirety of the 20th century.

If they thought they fully understood the economics of loss-leading profits, the record labels were, by their own actions, about to get a brutal and bruising education from online retailers and supermarkets.

CHAPTER 13

Loss-lead Us Not into Temptation: How Supermarkets and Online Retailers Pushed the CD Business to the Brink

(Trying to force control at the checkout)

On paper, it made all the sense in the world. Having more retail outlets would mean greater access to the market and, logically, more sales.

Except. . .

Labels might have fought on and off with the likes of HMV, Tower and Virgin Megastore, but they shared a common goal. Music was their lifeblood and they all wanted to sell more of it. There was an understanding here that what benefited one side benefited the other. If more records were sold, everyone won. And if no records were sold, everyone was out of business.

The shift from dealing with specialist retailers to dealing with specialist and generalist retailers meant a business change and a mindset change for labels. Online retailers and supermarkets moved to a different rhythm, they had different metrics for success, they had different economies of scale. Music was important to them, sure, but it was not the be-all and end-all. If anything, it was there to entice new consumers and get them to buy other stuff, non-music stuff, that had a higher retail price point and much greater margins.

If labels thought dealing with them would give them an advantage over their specialist retail partners, they were going to have a rude awakening. Rather than give them more control, wider control, it was going to take what control they had, squeeze it, strip it back and nullify it.

Phil Hardy dates the rise of the supermarkets in the UK as a serious music retailing force to 1996. By 2009, they accounted for just under a quarter (23.6 per cent) of all record sales in the UK. '[They] successfully sought to pay less for soundcarriers just as they had successfully brought down the wholesale prices of a wide range of goods from baked beans to milk and electrical products,' he noted.[1]

Raoul Chatterjee, of Warner ESP in the UK, concurs that 1996 was the key moment for the ascendency of the supermarkets, arguing it was largely down to the arrival of a new pop phenomenon and the release of their debut album in November that year.

'It was around the Spice Girls era that supermarkets really dived into CDs as they could see how mainstream CDs were,' he says. 'It was a footfall driver and an opportunity to keep people coming back into the shops regularly.'

The impact of the generalist retailer was felt in the US several years before it started to reshape the British music retail sector. Best Buy was the most powerful and the most aggressive here, taking the 'stack 'em high, sell 'em cheap' mantra to a whole new, and much more disquieting, level.

Best Buy started selling CDs across its stores in 1986, early in the format's life, and by the middle of the 1990s it was stocking between forty thousand and sixty thousand titles in its outlets. Despite massively undercutting almost all other retailers, Best Buy insisted it was making money on music sales. Alongside Walmart, Best Buy was dramatically changing music retail in the US. In 1996, the two retailers collectively accounted for 154 million of the 616 million records sold in the US that year. They were enormously powerful and able to dictate terms to the record labels.[2]

Steve Knopper noted that Best Buy would charge labels between $40,000 and $50,000 to promote their releases in its in-house ads and rack them properly in its stores. This was in sharp contrast to Tower, which took a more editorial approach, promoting records its staff and managers liked rather than records it was being paid to promote.[3]

In 1994, noted Phil Hardy, Best Buy was selling new release CDs with a list price of $16 for as little as $10 each and many other titles for under $12 each.[4] For chart albums, this was drastically undermining the specialist retailers who were incapable of competing against those prices. The weaker the likes of Musicland and Tower became, the more powerful the likes of Best Buy became. It brought a whole new level of viciousness to a retail vicious cycle.

Ian Rogers was working at Nullsoft in 1999 and would go on to become CEO and then executive chairman at Topspin Media, helping musicians sell music and merchandise online. He says the labels did not think through what they were doing when courting big box retail. They thought they had a delightful new pet when in reality they had just invited a crocodile into their house.

'If you're selling a CD to Best Buy for $7.49 with a retail price of $13.50 or $13.99 or whatever it is, and they're selling it for $6.99, you're dead,' he says. 'At the moment that you hand your business over to somebody who doesn't actually care about your business, you're fucked. So the moment that Best Buy can loss-lead your product to sell washing machines, you're fucked.'

The majors in the US responded to the endemic discounting by ushering in the MAP (minimum advertised price) scheme. '[It had] the aim of keeping prices high, making discounting more difficult and helping traditional retailers, which had also started to cut prices.' As part of the MAP scheme, if retailers kept prices at a certain level, labels would commit to a certain level of advertising support.[5]

Jason Olim of online retailer CDnow wrote in 1998 that MAP was a tool used by the labels to 'control what it regards as self-destructive competition.' This was designed in part to pull the brakes on excessive discounting by non-specialist retailers. '[R]ecord companies take the position that if you sell music at too low a price, you destroy the integrity and value of the product,' he said. 'If the record label says that it's worth $16.99, how can you then sell an album for $8.59?'[6]

The labels were *deadly serious* about not allowing CDs to be pushed down to rock bottom prices by retailers who had no long-term interest in music or, more precisely, no interest in the long-term survival of record companies.

'The threat was that if a retailer refused to maintain prices, either openly or covertly, a record company might stop doing business with it,' explained Hardy. 'However, for non-specialist retailers for whom music was more important in footfall than in revenue terms, this threat was an irritation at most in view of the volume they represented.'[7]

This attempt to stabilise the market ended up blowing up in the labels' faces. MAP was cited in the Federal Trade Commission's (FTC) investigation into price fixing. It concluded in May 2000 that US consumers had had to pay an extra $480 million for records over the past three years. The labels reached a settlement but without admitting guilt here. It was all a terrible disaster for them.[8]

The FTC insisted that the MAP programme be discontinued for at least seven years. 'These settlements will eliminate these policies and should help restore much-needed competition to the retail music market, consisting of $15 billion in annual sales' said FTC chairman Robert Pitofsky. 'Today's news should be sweet music to the ears of all CD purchasers.'[9]

Debates around discounting and the devaluing of music became louder and more complex as the year progressed. While labels could point to supermarkets and blame them for pushing down prices, they were also involved in giving away music themselves.

In early September 1999, Universal was offering up CDs valued at £4 million as part of a promotion with condiments company Crosse & Blackwell. The company was offering CDs under the title *A Taste Of The UK Music Scene* and targeting it at music fans aged 20–24. A £1 million press, radio and outdoor advertising campaign would back the initiative, with Universal claiming it was its biggest 'premium promotion' to date in the UK. Simon Miller, head of premiums and branded albums at Universal Incentive & Creative Marketing, said, 'There is no question that this will help us to sell more records. We will have a presence in stores where we sell CDs.'[10]

Of course, it is entirely up to record companies if they want to charge for music or give it away, but this was all sending out mixed messages to consumers. 'That cheap music is bad, but this cheap music is good,' ran the doublethink.

At EMI's sales conference later that same month, Tony Wadsworth used his address to rail against the undervaluing of music. He said that CDs in 1999 were lower in real terms to the consumer than in 1989.

'It breaks my heart to see the album of the millennium, *Sgt. Pepper*, being sold at £9.99 more often than not and it confuses the hell out of customers who don't understand why legendary albums such as *Sgt. Pepper* or *Dark Side Of The Moon* aren't more expensive than other albums,' he said. 'It perpetuates the myth that most CDs are overpriced and that's no good for any of us.'[11] He added, 'We need to find new ways of selling music, especially catalogue, not just using price as the main tool.'[12]

I ask Wadsworth about this speech and he had remarkable recall about the wider context of the speech as well as revealing the subtext to it that was not spelt out explicitly on the day. More than anything, his speech was in defence of the specialist retailers.

'This was because Asda and Woolworths had their tanks all over HMV, Our Price and Virgin's lawns,' he says of the move by generalist retailers into selling albums. 'This was about the shift in the retail picture. The fact that these non-music retailers, like Woolworths, were starting to use music as a loss leader. That's specifically what that was all about.'

He also explains that labels were, beyond speeches brimming with allusion, really quite powerless to do anything to stop this price war from erupting further. He worried that it was sending out a message to consumers that labels had been gleefully swindling them for decades. It was also putting in motion a dangerous game of brinkmanship with the specialist retailers.

'We weren't legally able to set the retail price,' he says. 'That is down to the retailer. *We* may have been giving bigger discounts to retailers on the newer artists we were trying to break, but in-store, the grocers – such as Asda, Tesco and Sainsbury's – were selling the blockbuster classic albums at a very low price. We were making the full margin, but they were using CDs as loss leaders to drive in-store traffic to sell more of their higher margin fruit and veg. Inevitably then the music retailers would come back and say, "Where's our discount?" Then it became a fight to shore up the discount line, which was being eroded rapidly! But that was all driven by the actions of the grocers.'

Adding discounted fuel to the pricing fire, UK supermarket chain Asda announced in October that year the launch of a price comparison website for CDs. Using the same strategy as it had for groceries, it would directly compare the price it was selling hit albums for against the retail price its competitors were selling the same albums for. It was, as far as the record companies could make out, a dangerous race to the bottom.

'They're not going to have a different philosophy on the web than the High Street,' bemoaned Mike McMahon, EMI's sales director. 'It's all about low prices permanently and their web prices will be similar.'[13]

A week later, Asda revealed it was going to start selling CDs online as part of its Value Mad scheme.[14]

Then at the end of November, just as the critical Christmas gifting market for CDs was about to take off, chemist chain Boots revealed what *Music Week* termed 'an aggressive discount campaign' where single CD albums would sell for £9.99 and cassettes for £7.99.[15]

Warner sales director Jeff Beard called it 'ridiculous' and added, 'It's going to start a price war without a doubt.' Neil Boote, Our Price commercial director, was livid and said his near-namesake Boots should be 'excommunicated' from the industry.[16]

Meanwhile, Simon Wright of Virgin Entertainment, told *Music Week*:

'I don't understand why everybody discounts at Christmas. There's volume to be had and everyone's on the High Street so some discounting takes place, but there's also more demand.'[17]

I raise this particular issue with Wright and ask him for more clarification on Virgin's position at the time.

'The music industry was odd in this respect,' he says. 'The products with the most demand were given the biggest discount. The same applies at Christmas. Big demand for whatever are the top albums and it's because people are using music to create traffic. They don't expect to make any money out of it. Asda or Boots are not going to live or die over the music industry. They lose nothing by discounting heavily. What they do is get a lot of people coming into Boots instead of going somewhere else. They would literally go below cost. They would sell at a loss. We just couldn't do that.'

Returning to the inferno with yet more kerosene, Asda announced at the end of November 1999 that it was going to adopt a pricing model similar to that used in the US, where CDs were typically cheaper than in the UK. It was fitting in a way as Asda had been acquired that August by Walmart. It was going to cut the cost of its chart albums by £1 to £11.99.[18]

Music Week picked a handful of big albums (Steps, Queen, Shania Twain, Westlife, 5ive) and compared pricing at Asda, Woolworths, HMV and Virgin. Asda's new uniform price of £11.99 stood out sharply against the £12.99, £13.99 or £14.49 its rivals were typically charging.[19]

David Inglis, GM at Asda, revealed this price drop was just the start. 'This is not a throwaway measure,' he told *Music Week*. 'We want to be working with record companies to see if we can collectively reduce prices. We firmly believe we can increase volume by coming to the magic price point of £9.99.'[20]

Supermarket chain Morrisons did not want to be left out. The week before Christmas, its gift to the record business was to announce it was going to undercut Asda by as much as 20 per cent on select albums, selling major titles for £9.99 each. Incredibly, and one presumes with a straight face, the company denied this was a loss-leader move.

With these moves by Asda, Morrisons and Boots, the labels could only watch with growing disbelief, horror and apoplexy.

Wright says that Virgin Megastore was left with no other choice but to heavily discount and bring its prices more in line with what the supermarkets were charging – or certainly for the top 40 or 20 titles that the supermarket chains tended to focus on.

He does, however, say the labels were complicit in this downward pressure on pricing.

'Supermarkets were smashing the prices right down,' he says. 'We had no choice but to compete. And the record companies were not doing anything to help out. They loved the volume coming out of the supermarket.'

He argues it was an economic impossibility for a retailer like Virgin Megastore to match the supermarkets exactly on everything they sold.

'Our average margin would be in the low 30s [per cent],' he says. 'That's before all our costs: staff, rent, everything. When we did that kind of deal, the margins on that would be under 10 per cent. If you allocated your rent to every sale, we were losing money. On everything we sold then, we were losing money. If we could get the overall sales up high enough, then it was OK. Fundamentally, music is a valuable medium. We were flogging off CDs like it was bread or a pint of milk, but yet the costs of delivering that to the market were much, much higher.'

Guy Holmes is unequivocal in his belief that courting the supermarkets, sacrificing volume for profitability, was an industry mistake of staggering proportions.

'The supermarkets did untold damage to the music business,' he says. 'Untold damage. But we enabled them. We all did that. We all shot ourselves in the foot. All of us. I was as guilty as the next man, unfortunately.'

This was not just a storm in an industry-shaped tea cup, with the issue spreading into the consumer music press. In its September 1999 issue, *Q* ran a two-page feature on how supermarkets had taken over the charts. It noted that the phenomenal buying power of the biggest supermarket chains had meant that they could drastically undercut specialist music retailers.

'In musical terms, the influence of supermarkets is already being felt with the emergence of what the music industry is calling "the Asda artist",' noted *Q*. 'This new generation of huge-selling MOR chart acts – The Corrs, Lighthouse Family, Texas and Celine Dion – are all favoured by the supermarkets. Their music is played in-store and the artists are racking up sales as a result. Indeed, there's a growing consensus that it's only by selling successfully in supermarkets that an artist can now push their sales to multi-platinum levels. Jamiroquai's jump from selling around three hundred thousand copies of their second album *Return Of The Space Cowboy*, to the million mark attained by their third, *Travelling Without*

Moving, was widely credited to the group's new-found appeal among supermarket trolley pushers.'[21]

It added that in the US there was not just a pricing issue but a lyrical one. Walmart, it said, was driving a retail conservatism and refused to stock albums with a parental advisory sticker, leaving acts with a conundrum. Keep the lyrics as they are and stay true to their artistic vision? Or issue a 'clean' version and get placement in one of the most powerful retailers in the country?[22]

Record producer and head of the PWL label Pete Waterman argued that it was all an inevitability. 'People want their goods cheaper and this is the result,' he told *Q*. 'I'd love to go back to the old days but I'll be Peter Pan before it happens.'[23]

Q glumly concluded, 'Where less commercial acts could once find a way into the mainstream, they may become marginalised simply because their single or album isn't the first choice of an EUK buyer [Entertainment UK, the supply and distribution arm of Woolworths]. With an increasingly narrow choice of music making it onto the supermarket shelves, the result is just a handful of acts ending up in the shopping trolley and, ultimately, in the charts.'[24]

If the labels in the UK spent 1999 fretting about the impact of non-traditional retailers pushing down the price of new albums, in North America there was brewing concern about second-hand CDs badly curdling things for the new CD market.

It first erupted in Canada in January 1999 when the major labels expressed their displeasure at the sixteen-store A&B Sound chain in Alberta and British Columbia selling used CDs. A&B Sound responded saying that others were doing it and, besides, its second-hand titles were all five or six years old and thus were not undercutting new releases (where labels made the bulk of their revenue).

Brian Robertson, president of the Canadian Recording Industry Association, told *Billboard*, 'The sale of used CDs is a predatory practice. It erodes the disposable income of first-line product and returns nothing to the industry in the way of royalties or margins. The victims are legitimate retailers, artists, songwriters, and record companies. There's nothing illegal about selling used CDs, but legitimate retailers should be concerned with solving the problem [rather] than compounding it.'

Jason Sniderman, VP of Roblan Distributors, was a lot less diplomatic than Robertson. 'It's,' he said, 'a despicable practice.'[25]

The following month, the hundred-store chain CD Plus, headquartered in Toronto, announced it was going to start selling used CDs in twenty-three of its stores. Again, the major labels were far from happy about the situation.[26]

The issue soon crossed the border.

In July, *Billboard* reported that both Tower Records and Musicland were experimenting with selling used CDs in their stores, following the lead of Warehouse Entertainment who first did it in 1992.

Stan Goman, EVP/COO of Tower in West Sacramento, pointed the finger of blame at the record labels, accusing them of pushing retailers into it. 'The labels have almost forced us into this, first with their defective-CD policies and then with their walking away from the singles business,' he said. 'Kids can't afford $17.98 for a catalog CD.' Tower had five stores trading in used CDs and the company aimed to increase this to ten by the end of the year.[27]

It was also stemming from retailers' concerns about the rise of online retailers of CDs. Mike Dreese, CEO of Newbury Comics, told *Billboard*, 'If that begins to cannibalize sales, we need a business that will give us some control over our destiny.' He spelt out the commercial reasons for doing so. Used CDs, he estimated, could equal up to 8 per cent of the company's business and the gross margin on a used CD sale was over 50 per cent compared to a margin of around 38 per cent on a new CD.[28]

Supermarkets and big box retailers were known forces by 1999. Labels may have dangerously underestimated the power they had indirectly handed them in the pursuit of greater sales, a power that would be used against them, but they at least understood the basics of their brand power, their models of economies of scale, their politics of discounting and their growing customer insight teams.

A whole other type of retailer was emerging, however, in the 1990s that had no precedent as far as the music business was concerned. They were untested and unknown entities that were operating away from the high street. They only had stores on websites. None of the earliest operations had grown from existing brands. Who, wondered the record labels, would go to a computer, open up a website, put in their credit card details and order a CD from a warehouse in the middle of nowhere and wait for it to be posted to them? Record labels understood mail order from record club catalogues, as shown in the case of Columbia House (owned by Time Warner and Sony Corp.). But the *internet*?

Record shops, they insisted, were much more than just shops: they were communities; they were whole worlds of discovery; they were places where musical and personal connections were made. Why would anyone give that up for the bland anonymity of buying something *from a URL*?

Scott Cohen asserts that the single most important name in this whole story was not Amazon, which was expanding from book sales to CD sales at the end of the 1990s. Rather it was a company founded by twin brothers in their parents' basement in Ambler, a borough on the edge of Philadelphia. 'It became,' says Cohen, 'this massive online CD business.'

Jason Olim and Matthew Olim set up CDnow in 1994, opening for business on 1 August that year.

In his 1998 book on the origins of the company, Jason wrote about the founding angles/myths around CDnow.

One was related to him borrowing a copy of Miles Davis's *Kind Of Blue* from a friend, loving it and trying to find more music by Davis in Tower Records in Boston but not knowing which albums to pick as they were divorced of context by just sitting on the racks and he could not hear them in advance. There had to be a better way, he thought. 'Thus began an individual obsession that would eventually lead to a corporate obsession: the desire to create a better music store [. . .] Nobody seemed to be working on the perfect music store as I envisioned it.'[29]

The other part of the mythology was based on him and his brother being twins, a fact they relatedly exploited to help garner early press coverage, using the shorthand 'twib' [a portmanteau of 'twin brothers'] to explain the USP of the company founders.[30]

The core idea of CDnow was to mesh a music distributor's catalogue listing all the music they carried along with a database of music reviews. That meant the user could see *everything* that could be bought running contextually alongside reviews recommending *which albums were worth buying*. CDnow would merely be the interface, having wholesalers drop-ship CDs for them (so they had no storage or fulfilment issues) and it would take a cut of the sale.[31] 'My idea was that the store would be an order-taking business,' wrote Olim, 'not a shipping business.'[32]

Its ascent was, in relative terms, rapid. Despite no one, not even their friends, buying anything on the first day, the company grossed $387 in its first month, making a gross profit of $14. In its second month, it grossed $5,000. In October 1994, it grossed $20,000 and in January 1995 it grossed $100,000. Each year was a massive step on from the previous year. The company took in $2 million in 1995, $6.4 million in 1996, $16 million in 1997 and $22 million in the first six months of 1998.[33]

CDnow was not the only company thinking along these lines at the time. There was Music Boulevard, which launched in 1995 and had managed to clear thirty-second sound samples as well as hosting reviews and artist biographies. It also had *Music Wire*, described as 'the Web's first daily music magazine, edited and written by Music Boulevard's staff of professional music journalists.'[34] There was CDConnection, which claimed to be selling CDs online since 1990.[35] There was also MusicNet (not the same MusicNet that was set up in 2001 by AOL Time Warner, Bertelsmann, EMI and RealNetworks to sell music downloads).[36] Plus there was CDEurope, mostly focused on selling imported CDs.[37]

'We weren't the first music store on the Net,' wrote Olim. '[W]e were, at best, the fourth.'[38]

Olim was worried most about MusicNet as he first became aware of it via a two-page ad in *Wired*, a promotional luxury CDnow could not afford. It was selling CDs cheaper than they were. Olim was, however, relieved to find MusicNet only had 'a section of a couple of hundred CDs' and, as such, 'wasn't a viable consumer proposition' as far as he was concerned.[39]

The playing field was not left wide open too long for these upstarts, with Tower Records, which was founded in 1960, starting to sell music online in early 1995.[40]

CDnow launched by referring to itself as 'The Internet Music Store' and, with over a hundred thousand titles for sale, 'the largest music store in the world.' What might seem tardy by today's standards, but which was considered lightning fast in the mid 1990s, it claimed it 'delivers most orders within five business days, standard.'[41]

The Olim twins felt the inclusion of song clips was the magic ingredient and a catalyst for CD sales, but the RIAA felt differently. It wanted to charge CDnow a clip licensing fee, which CDnow said was 'a toll that doesn't exist in the real world' as most real world record stores at the time had listening posts that let customers hear albums before purchasing them. 'Those music samples help sell the music; nobody steals a thirty-second music clip instead of buying an album, after all,' argued Olim in 1998. 'The RIAA is trying to take advantage of the new technologies to create a new set of rights which are unfair to online companies and which will undermine the ability of the retail music business to move into the online world.'[42]

In seeking early investment, Olim said they made a mistake of asking for 'about half a million dollars' initially, upping it soon after to $1 million. '[B]ut that's not enough for most venture capital companies,' he revealed. 'If that's all you need, they figure, there's not that much potential there.'[43]

In August 1997, however, they were supercharged with an investment of $10 million from companies including Grouch Capital Group and Keystone Venture Capital.[44] This was the vote of confidence the company needed to not just expand but also to move towards an IPO.

CDnow launched its IPO in February 1998, raising $65.6 million. In its Securities & Exchange Commission filing, its site had grown from 12,000 average daily visits in January 1996 to 132,000 visits in December 1997. *CNet* reported it had net sales of $17.4 million in 1997, up from $6.3 million the year before. It did, however, post a net loss of $10.7 million for 1997, up from a net loss of $1.8 million for 1996.[45]

(Olim claimed in his book that the IPO raised $75 million.)[46]

In October 1998, *CNN Money* was reporting that CDnow was planning to merge with N2K, which operated Music Boulevard. Together they would have a customer base of 1.2 million.[47] The merger was confirmed in March 1999, with the new entity operating under the name CDnow/N2K.[48]

'CDNow completed its US$522 million acquisition of N2K on Wednesday,' reported *Wired*. 'Now,' it added tartly, 'all the company has to do is cut spending, turn a profit, and make its name synonymous with music.'[49]

As was typical for the era, such retailers were enormous money pits. At the time of the merger, the *Wall Street Journal* noted that CDnow/N2K were looking to significantly reduce customer acquisition costs. For each new customer they were attracting, it was costing them $50.[50]

If CDnow had helped start the online CD sales revolution, it had quickly lost ground to Amazon, which had only entered the CD business in June 1998. 'But it was a household name, and it took only six months to outpace CDNow and become the No. 1 music seller on the Web,' said *Wired*.[51]

CNN Money noted in its coverage of the CDnow/N2K merger that this new combined company could seriously threaten the upstart that was Amazon.com, which had driven music sales of $33 million in the previous quarter. 'We'll have a better music store than any music store separately,' claimed Jon Diamond, chairman of CDnow/N2K. 'It will be better than either site individually.'[52]

Jason Olim, chief executive, was much more hubristic when speaking to *Wired*. 'People point to Amazon as the company that seems to be able to put anyone out of business,' he puffed, 'but they haven't put anyone out of business that I know of.'[53]

Oddly, Olim had a slightly different line when his book was published a year earlier.

'I wish we could have put more money – a lot more – into advertising,' he wrote. 'Until Amazon.com came along and outspent us, we were *the* online commerce story, very much in the spotlight, getting as much press as anyone. If we could have spent more money on advertising we could have pushed ourselves even further into the spotlight, and perhaps made ourselves a true media darling. But it simply wasn't an option. We couldn't spend more money on advertising because we didn't have more money.'[54]

In the same book, Olim got the name of the founder of Amazon wrong, calling him Jim Bezos rather than Jeff Bezos.[55] He also wrote the following words, which history has not been kind to. 'We believe that although it may do well across the board, it won't be able to dominate the music business because it won't be focused enough. Nonetheless, Amazon is a good company. . . and we watch it closely.'[56]

If CDnow was not exactly top of mind of the labels when it launched, it had certainly appeared on the radar of some artists. In an interview with *Forbes* in June 1999, Jon Diamond claimed that both David Bowie and Mick Jagger were investors in his company and that they were in discussions with other artists and their managers to look at ways to sell directly to fans through their platform.[57]

Diamond admitted in the interview that CDnow/N2K was not yet profitable but claimed they were unworried about the rapid ascent of Amazon and that there was a place for both in the market. (This is a failsafe platitude that executives reach for when asked anything about competition).

'[T]he two companies have different philosophies,' he insisted. 'I've had discussions with [Amazon.com CEO] Jeff Bezos over the years about their strategy and they've always wanted to build the Wal-Mart of the internet. And that's what their brand is. We are the music channel on the internet. That's what our brand is. And that's what our goal is: To be the music entertainment brand on the internet.'[58]

The Amazon model was to prioritise scale and worry about profitability later, when all the competition had been driven to the wall. Not every dot com company had the resources to take this approach and for many the end goal was to be acquired by a bigger player. In July 1999, the big payday for CDnow/N2K looked like it was arriving when Columbia House (a Sony/Time Warner company) announced it wanted to acquire the company. This was in large part to give it an established name in online retail, something it was desperate to get a head start in.

The terms of the deal were not disclosed, but it fell apart in March 2000.[59]

In July 2000, however, Bertelsmann (owners of the BMG label) agreed to pay $117 million for the company and make it a wholly owned subsidiary.[60]

The new retailer that was to last the distance – stretching far beyond 1999 and dominating and redefining online retail like no other for music and *everything else* – launched in 1994 initially to sell books but was moving into CD sales by 1998.[61]

Amazon quickly closed ground on the leading online retailers of CDs at the time, with music becoming an expanding area for them. A survey by Media Metrix found that four of the ten leading shopping sites in the US in December 1998 were selling music. CDnow, at number eight in the chart, had 2.69 million unique visitors that month, but it was 'high-flying' Amazon that was starting to attract media attention: across all product categories it sold, Amazon had 9.13 million unique visitors in December 1998. Columbia House just about scraped into the top 10 with 2.45 million visitors.[62]

Billboard suggested that most of Amazon's visitors 'were probably book customers', but added that, due to its size, it had already become the biggest online seller of CDs in Q3 1998, just months after it started offering music.[63]

The emphasis on physical sales was only the start for Amazon, with the company announcing in April that it was going to start to sell music downloads in the coming month. It would not give any more details other than the downloads would come with some form of DRM. It was betting heavily on music, with seventeen full-time music editors on the payroll and a bank of two hundred music writer freelancers.[64]

In the previous month, Media Metrix had announced that Amazon (9.3 million monthly visitors) and RealNetworks (8.4 million monthly visitors) were the two leading music sites in the US. *Billboard* cited the addition of music to its offering as a key factor behind the sharp growth in Amazon traffic.[65]

In his book on the history of Amazon, Brad Stone noted that Amazon initially struggled to get music and film/TV companies to supply it directly, instead having to rely on intermediary distributors. '[They] gave Amazon an initial boost and then allowed it to credibly make its case directly to the big media companies.'[66]

Sensing new ways to grow the market, it did not take the major labels too long to start to supply Amazon directly. The labels thought it was going to give them an exciting new retail partner to keep the established music retailers on their toes; they did not quite understand that they were replacing one long in the tooth name with a much more ruthless upstart. Retailers such as Tower were like Margo Channing in *All About Eve* and the labels were complicit in expediting the rise of Eve Harrington.

In May, EMI Recorded Music North America signed a one-year non-exclusive deal with Amazon whereby its most popular sites would link to Amazon for the purchasing of select albums, DVDs and merchandise items. It was part of Amazon's 'associates program', the presumption being that EMI would get an affiliate sales cut on all sales.

Jeremy Silver, VP of new media for EMI North America, said, 'The real advantage here is that we get a lot of information about buying habits from one vendor for twelve months. We're in favour of supporting all types of retail, and our choice is to maintain relationships with lots of different online and bricks-and-mortar stores.'[67]

Amazon, the retail fox now deep inside the music industry hen house, moved swiftly to have its name deeply associated with music, all facilitated by labels, artists and managers in awe of this whole new retail experience, focusing on the short-term benefits and letting someone else worry about the long-term consequences.

In early May 1999, Amazon ran a promotion for *Mirrorball* by Sarah McLachlan, offering it with two free downloads. Amazon had approached her directly.[68] At the start of the following month, Amazon became the exclusive retailer for Cowboy Junkies' *Rarities B-Sides & Slow, Sad Waltzes* album that was released via the band's own Latent Recordings label. Amazon had the exclusive from 1 June until 31 August, after which it went to other online retailers and bricks-and-mortar stores.[69]

Not everyone was delighted by the rapid rise of Amazon and in 1999 its tax arrangements were increasingly being put under the microscope (a situation that carries on today).

At the ICSC (International Council of Shopping Centers) Convention in Las Vegas looking at the rise of online retail, the issue of Amazon and how it was finding ways to sidestep sales taxes was a hot-button issue. Utah governor Michael Leavitt 'attacked sales-tax inequities' in the conference's opening meeting, explaining how he had bought goods on Amazon and compared them to a local store with a website. '[Utah state] law states if a retailer has a physical presence in the state, it must collect sales tax on its Web sites, too,' he said. 'Amazon was cheaper because of ignoring sales tax.'[70]

Glen Ward says this was a snowballing issue for major retailers like Virgin Megastore at the time. 'The chart albums were loss leaders to get people through the door and tempted with the full-price product,' he suggests. 'Similarly online, you were competing with Amazon who weren't charging sales tax at the time. You were always being undercut by Amazon – and that grew and grew. That was the joy of the internet.'

Amazon was still losing money all through this time, but it was focused on gaining market share wherever and however it could. Its net sales were up 171 per cent to $314.4 million in the second fiscal quarter in 1999 and its customer accounts in June 1999 were 10.7 million, up from 3.3 million a year earlier. Even so, it reported a $138 million net loss in the second fiscal quarter.[71]

In August, Amazon, calling itself 'the Internet's No. 1 music retailer', announced it was offering tracks from a range of Warner Music Group acts (including Emmylou Harris, Linda Ronstadt, Stereolab, Natalie Cole and Genesis) for free download.[72] Greg Hunt, Amazon's digital download product manager, told *Billboard*, 'Offering the free downloads have proved [sic] to be incredibly effective in selling albums. And while it's obvious there are a variety of retailers out there doing the same thing, we're trying to show the labels that we do the best job.'[73]

The EMI deal in May was part of a charm offensive by Amazon and other majors soon started to swoon. In September, Universal Music & Video Distribution became the second major to start selling direct to Amazon.

Amazon was obviously keen for these direct deals to lower its cost of purchase, but there was a concern that the majors could nurture Amazon and CDnow to be the heavyweights of online retail and undercut their own moves to sell online. *Billboard* did note at the time that Sony and Warner were looking to, via Columbia House, acquire CDnow so this could have repercussions for any deal, or lack of deal, with Amazon akin to the ones EMI and Universal had secured.[74]

As Amazon grew, it was keen to not just undercut existing retailers but also to protect itself from any form of attack from any retailers, new or old. In November 1999, it filed a lawsuit against Barnes & Noble over its patented 1-Click online purchasing technology, something it viewed as key to its rapid ascent and a major factor behind consumers' repeat purchases.[75] The case was not settled until March 2002.[76]

Its losses kept mounting in 1999. It might have had sales of $356 million in Q3, more than doubling the $154 million in sales in Q3 1998, but its operating loss for the period was $79 million, up from $21 million for the same quarter a year earlier.[77] Sales in Q4 were $676 million, up sharply from $253 million in Q4 1998. The losses increased, totalling $185 million in Q4 compared to $22 million in Q4 1998.[78] For anyone else, these numbers would have caused panic. For the apostles of Bezosology, however, everything was going swimmingly.

The US labels were equal parts excited and terrified by the rise of Amazon in 1998 and 1999, but in the UK the focus in this period was on another booming online retailer, with Amazon being something that was more typically mentioned in passing.

Music Week – if we can take it as a metonym, or at least a weathervane, for the British music business – was paying much more attention in 1999 to Boxman, a Swedish online retailer, than it was to Amazon, primarily because it had more of a foothold in the British music market.

Boxman made it to the front page of *Music Week*, albeit at the bottom of the page, on its 13 March 1999 edition. It was mentioned alongside Amazon as one of the companies about to shake up British music retail, but Boxman was the real focus of the piece. It had, *Music Week* noted, captured 90 per cent of all online music retail in Scandinavia (and 5 per cent of all music retail) since it launched fifteen months earlier and its investors included pop stars Ace Of Bass and Roxette. It was suggested that it would sell chart CDs for £10 each (but charge an extra £1 post and package). Joe Wilson, MD of Boxman UK, told the title, 'We expect to retail at about 20 per cent cheaper than the average High Street retail price.'[79]

Intrigued by the rise of these new online retailers, *Music Week* ran a comparative analysis in June 1999, looking at the average price and delivery speeds of a range of players here including Boxman, Ent Express, Amazon, Audiostreet, Capital Radio, HMV, iMVS and CDnow. It picked five albums, both chart and catalogue titles, and looked at the shopping experience through each retailer. 'US retailer Amazon came out cheapest on price alone, with a CD costing an average of £9.23, followed by Scandinavian-based music store Boxman at £9.49,' it said.[80]

The study found that it, depending on the retailer, could take between seven and twenty minutes to place an order and that delivery speed ranged anywhere from two days to eight weeks.

It added that some legal issues needed to be raised with regard to how some of these brands operated, asking if they were breaking parallel import legislation when mailing US-manufactured discs from the US while the other retailers were sourcing their products from Europe.

In November, *Music Week* returned to the issue and did an audit of the major online music retailers and assessed them based on how broad their catalogues were as well as providing a brief history and synopsis of each. HMV had 250,000 titles and Virgin Megastore had 260,000 titles, while Tower Europe had 850,000. For the online-only brands, Amazon had 120,000 music titles (and 10,000 soundclips), CDnow had 500,000 titles and Boxman had 600,000.[81]

Boxman merged with British company iMVS in July 1999, hoping to create a new online retailing powerhouse.[82] By October 2000, however, Boxman was scrambling to raise £30 million to stay in business after its planned April IPO, where it was hoping to raise $435 million,[83] was pulled. In light of this, it suspended its website.[84] Later that month it was seeking voluntary liquidation.[85] In the final week of October 2000, all 120 of its staff were laid off.[86]

Boxman was, in many ways, the stalking horse company to Amazon in 1999 and 2000. It perhaps suffered as it was European and could not get a foothold in the US (or access the kind of VC money that Amazon could). It also exposed the difference between the dot com world in Europe and the dot com world in the West Coast of the US. The US was the epicentre as far as digital companies went at the end of the 1990s. That was to change in the 2000s, notably with Spotify, but at this stage if you were not in America where the centre of gravity was, you were going to drift off into (cyber)space and never be seen or heard of again.

In May 2023, Amazon had a market cap of $1.095 *trillion*.

RETAIL RECLAIMED: LABELS TOY WITH SELLING MUSIC THEMSELVES

As record companies started to encourage the rise of new retailers, thinking this would keep the old retailers in their place, they did not realise they were simply surrendering even more power and control.

They were perhaps intoxicated with the belief that if some kids in their parents' garage in the boondocks of Philadelphia could set up shop online or if some *nerd* based in Seattle could sell CDs alongside books then they – these bold captains of industry and tenacious arbiters of art – could use the internet to sell music themselves.

Record labels were typically one step removed from the customer. They generally relied on the retailer to bring in the customer for their product. Of course, there were things like Warner and Sony's Columbia House in the US or PolyGram's Britannia Music Club, but in the fast-moving world of the internet, mail-order clubs felt like bringing a Matchbox car to the Grand Prix.

(It is important to note that HMV had been owned by EMI until 1986, when the latter merged with Thorn.[87] That was when HMV Music Retailing[88] became a separate division. There was a management buyout of EMI's HMV operations in 1998, but EMI retained a 43 per cent stake in the retailer).[89]

The labels desperately wanted to have a direct relationship with the consumer in the way that the retailer did. Previously it was logistically complex and financially prohibitive to run chains of shops in the high street, but online meant they could potentially reach more people much quicker and for less financial outlay.

The arrival of the internet presented them with a double opportunity: they could sell music on physical formats online; and they could sell music in digital formats online. Crucially, they also felt they could control the speed at which consumers would transition from physical to digital.

The Madison Project came to the record labels via IBM in 1997. In coming through IBM it meant, as Jeremy Silver noted, that the labels could sidestep any worries about antitrust issues. 'The industry had to avoid any perception that it might be acting as a cartel,' he wrote. 'Yet to create a platform on this scale, they had to work together. The only legal solution was for IBM to run the whole thing, and for the labels to be individual and separate participants.'[90]

There was a worry that a move like this would raise the hackles of the major retailers like Tower Records and Best Buy, but the labels assured themselves that this was not a replacement for them; it was an addition to them. Still they ploughed on.

Just as Seagram was settling in as the new owner of PolyGram and working on its masterplan for Universal Music Group, news of the Madison Project was making the front page of *Billboard* in its final issue of 1998. The headline 'Labels Striving For Security In The Digital Future' splintered into a triptych of sub-headlines: one on industry panic over MP3; one on SDMI as a potential solution to that panic; and one on the Madison Project.

A vague launch date was set for Madison in the first half of 1999 and it was being tested in 'hundreds of homes' in San Diego whereby people could pick from an initial catalogue of two hundred titles to download (in this case, as it was a trial, they would not be charged). Their behaviour and the technology enabling it would be monitored 'to ensure that music gets from one place to another in a secure manner.'

San Diego was selected as the test market as it was the only city in the US that was 'capable of handling broad-band [sic] digital transmission technology.' As such, there was encryption and watermarking to stop illegal copies circulating. The *Billboard* story explained that prices would be roughly equivalent to what albums would cost in the shops and there would be no 'decoupling' of individual tracks from albums. Users would not be able to make their own compilations. A single back end would be overseen by one of the participating majors, but at this early stage who that would be was not made public. Sources told *Billboard* that downloading a full album should take between three and six minutes.[91]

Scott Campbell's company Virtually Atomic was involved in developing the codec for the Madison Project and he saw its inner workings up close. He also understood that the labels were viewing this as a potential power play in the earliest days of digital music delivery and consumption.

'The Madison Project was about being able to download music over the internet and burn it onto a CD,' he explains. 'It was about being able to take a song from the cloud, in today's language. You don't store it on your computer, it just comes straight down and onto the CDs. It was in a cache, I guess you could say, and then it would get burned onto your CD. And afterwards it would just be on the CD and you'd now got this over the internet. The labels liked it because it played within their frame of control.'

By February 1999, the number of users in the trial in San Diego had been raised to a thousand (as had the number of albums they could access), but details of how it would all work remained scant. 'It's not yet clear whether the trial will involve dedicated set-top box hardware or generic PCs hooked into the network through cable modems,' wrote *The Register*.[92]

Forbes was sceptical of the whole undertaking, witheringly writing in

February 1999 that, despite 'all of the sound and fury displayed by IBM', it looked likely 'the Madison Project could merely be a footnote in the historic metamorphosis of the recording industry.'[93] So it proved to be.

Even though the labels shared a common goal, namely bringing digital distribution of music to heel, consensus was to be a chimaera. Their natural instinct was: a) to distrust each other; and b) to want to get one over on each other. Jeremy Silver noted that, just as one would expect when trapping cats in a sack, there was inevitable turmoil and disagreement between the participants.

'Sometimes Sony and Warner seemed to be in complete agreement about the way forward, working hard to bring the other three companies in line,' he recalled. 'At other times, the two lead majors seemed to be pulling in completely opposite directions. IBM executives spoke a completely different technical and business language from the music companies. They swore a lot less and made fewer jokes.'[94]

Indecision reigned and budgets were broken before the inevitable happened. 'Despite intense efforts on all parts,' noted Silver, 'towards the end of 1999, the Madison Project eventually subsided under the weight of its own internal complexity.'[95]

Reflecting on it all several years later, Silver tells me that the Madison Project was an explicit attempt by the labels to push traditional retailers to the margins and have the labels grab control of the customer relationship.

'That was intended as the industry's answer to the [rise of digital] technology,' he says. 'It was intended to lock out the retailers from the business and to create direct relationships with consumers, with no retail involvement. And it was intended to be a closed system; so making use of internet-type technology, but not using the internet in order to have a secure end-to-end solution. Warner in particular was very active in developing this. It was very secret because they were terrified they would upset the retailers, although ultimately they did share it with them and tried to let them in as the thing started to crumble. But of course it was ponderous, it was slow, people had their misgivings, they didn't necessarily believe that this was a meaningful solution, there were varying degrees of senior management buy-in.'

Brian McLaughlin claims that all through this period he and the rest of the management team at HMV knew exactly what the labels were trying to do – which was to undermine their business and try to fully control the relationship with the music consumer.

'Their long-term strategy was to cut the retailer out,' he says. 'This thing that was coming looked to them to be the solution to people like me and other retailers.'

He claims the labels refused to discuss any digital plans with them, something which only amplified their fears and convinced them that duplicity was afoot.

'If there was a big new release, they would have pinpointed HMV to do 35 per cent or 40 per cent of the sales of that album,' he says of the way business was done in the 1990s. 'They'd already had that in their marketing plan. So their marketing monies would have gone straight into HMV. There would have been a six-week campaign through HMV to maximise it and to get that album to number one. That's how we used to work with each other. In this particular case it was, "Whatever we're going to do, we're not telling you." There was no way that they were going to include us in what they saw was a way of excluding us eventually.'

There was the public presentation of unity between the majors in the Madison Project (and SDMI), but they were also spreading their bets and developing offerings that they would have majority ownership of and, therefore, greater control over. The unity of Madison was, in some ways, a smokescreen to disguise the solipsism that self-interest really powered the majors. If anyone ever needed to understand how the major labels really worked side by side, they only had to read the final paragraph of George Orwell's *Animal Farm*.

Warner and Sony had Columbia House and during this time BMG aligned with Universal on Get Music. It was announced at a press event in April 1999 where Edgar Bronfman Jr from Universal and Thomas Middelhoff, group chairman of BMG, were both in attendance, suggesting this was a priority project for the two majors.

'The formation of GetMusic.com arguably was something of a milestone in the music industry's painful crawl into the Internet age,' noted *CNN* in its coverage.[96] The site would promote the labels' acts and sell their CDs.

Initially, it was going to launch in the US and then, if it got a good enough wind behind it, it would expand internationally.

In August 1999, Andrew Nibley was named president and CEO of Get Music. Tellingly, he was not a music person, coming from Reuters where he co-founded Reuters NewMedia in 1994.[97] This was a statement hire, expressing the idea that the labels involved were thinking outside of the narrow and self-referential domain of the record business.

'This is not just a music retail play,' Nibley told *Billboard*. 'It's about content and community; it's about linking recording artists to fans; it's about building unique content for music lovers. I have a lot of background in intellectual property and content.' He refused to reveal how much money the two majors were ploughing into Get Music beyond saying that the 'investment is substantial.'[98]

'We had the famous three Cs – content, commerce, and community,' says Jon Vlassopulos, director of business development at BMG, about where the project was pointed. 'When I went to New York in August 1999 to work for Get Music, this was the same time that MTV.com was coming to market. It was a consumer play, the first of its kind for the labels. There was a whole initiative at Bertelsmann, broadly speaking, about how we could adopt digital – if it should be in a new division and then you keep the traditional business in a separate division. At Viacom there was MTV and MTVi. We were considering Bertelsmann's new digital ventures separate to our traditional media ventures. There were lots of corporate meetings and debates about it. Generally the feeling from a lot of the new digital executives like myself and my colleagues was that it should all be eventually integrated in the future and it would all be part of one corporate entity. This ended up happening across all industries as digital became the basis of marketing, creative, sales et cetera.'

At its peak, Get Music had around 150 people working on it, headquartered in Chelsea in the West Side of Manhattan.

'We had a whole content team and studio,' says Vlassopulos. 'We were producing original programming and artist interviews. We had all the original curation and playlists and then we had the community and the commerce. That era was fun as there was a collective energy to do things differently. We were definitely ahead of the times.'

Jeff Liebenson, VP of legal and business affairs at BMG International, says there was a spirit of experimentation within BMG at the time and Get Music was very much part of that push.

'A lot of people wanted to disintermediate traditional retail and establish the rights holders as their own retailer and to develop brand equity in our retail store,' he says of the industry thinking of the era. 'That was a big push, to centralise everything and feed it through one overarching global retail store. Many of the people at BMG in the US were pushing for that. They wanted one store with different genre looks and feels. It would really be one store, but there would be one that had a hip-hop look and another that had a country music look and a pop look and a rock look et cetera. On the international side, we were thinking we should have a more diverse approach.'

He notes the limitations of all the utopian thinking at the time: that a label had what marketers would call limited brand recognition and weak brand affinity with consumers.

'The brand wasn't the record label,' says Liebenson. 'No one goes to a record label's website to obtain music. That isn't the brand that the majority of the fans are familiar with. It's nice in theory to build up brand equity, but we thought it was much more realistic to go with our strength, which was the artists as the brands and drive traffic to the artists' sites and drive activity there.'

This was not the only joint venture that Universal and BMG were working on at the time. In December 1999, amid much fanfare, they announced a whole other undertaking, codenamed Nigel, that was expected to launch in early 2000. Where Get Music was focused on CDs, Nigel would focus on downloads.

Nigel took its name from XTC's 1979 hit 'Making Plans For Nigel', but others sneered that it was actually named after Nigel Tufnell, the gormless lead guitarist in fictional rock band Spinal Tap who was obsessed with amplifiers that went up to 11 rather than the standard 10 ('It's one louder') and being endlessly foiled in his dream of perfecting the folding wine glass.

Edgar Bronfman Jr addressed the PaineWebber investment conference in New York on 6 December and announced that tests would begin within 10 days to check if the 'fundamental technology works.' *Billboard* claimed sources close to the project were insistent there was no set start date for the test. The sources added that no downloads will be charged for in the initial tests. Instead they would be offered for free or as part of an added-value promotion. Pricing of downloads was expected to happen by April or May, with Bronfman adding that by Q4 2000 a 'more robust' version of Nigel (dubbed 'Nigel 2.0') would be rolled out. 'More artists than we needed signed up to be part of the experiment,' he claimed, but declined to name them.[99]

Other partners beyond Universal and BMG included Matsushita Electric Industrial (who would make players for the downloaded music), AT&T (providing the downloading technology) and InterTrust Technologies (providing the DRM).

Bronfman added that this was part of a wider digital investment by

Universal, where the company's spending in the area that year was expected to top $75 million.[100]

Talal Shamoon, vice president of InterTrust at the time, summarises how the majors were trying to do things together, in factions and individually, and how this amounted to a kind of erratic uncertainty or capriciousness, shaped in equal parts by politics, panic and paranoia.

'The Sony guys, they had one foot in each camp because they're being pushed very hard by Tokyo,' he says. 'I guess EMI was experimenting, but they were very dilettante-ish about the whole thing. Like the guy who walks into the casino and just puts a bet on every table. The math says you average to zero at that point. That was the EMI story at that point. EMI shot their wad in the 1970s and 1980s. They accumulated some great catalogues and then they just went into pure decadence. When PolyGram got bought by Universal, they just didn't have enough scale, records-wise, to hold their own and management has started to fall into pure decadence. Universal was the main driver, so we built this system.'

Larry Kenswil, president of Universal Music Group's eLabs division, suggests the retailers, despite what Jeremy Silver and others claim was the end goal with the Madison Project, were overly paranoid about being circumvented here as they had failed to understand the prohibitive costs involved here meant labels were not suddenly going to offer all their music digitally.

'The one thing that generally people don't get is the amount of back end work it took to convert to digital distribution,' he says. 'It wasn't like these files were sitting around in a format that could be just put online. We had to create a digital vault, convert all the tracks, hundreds of thousands of tracks, that we hadn't released – never mind back catalogue that had gone out of release – into that format and then store it in the digital vault and then create ways of pushing it from the vault to the retailers. We did not want to eliminate retail; we didn't want to go into just selling it for ourselves.'

He also says that the idea of a Universal Music download store was never going to take off, primarily because it would only have Universal-signed acts. It might have been the biggest label in the marketplace, but *it alone was not the marketplace*.

'We knew that a Universal Music store, even if we had a third of the market share, was not going to succeed,' he argues. 'You needed everything. You needed to have stores that constantly added to its inventory so that if someone went back to it after a week it wouldn't be the exact same stuff that was being offered for sale; there would be lots of new stuff as well as newly released catalogue stuff. All that required everything to go into the digital vault, which cost a lot of money and took a lot of time figuring out how to do it.'

Inevitably there are conflicting opinions on what was happening at this period and if record labels were actually trying to negate the retailers who had helped power the phenomenal 1990s they collectively experienced in terms of booming CD sales.

For Liebenson, there was a level of impatience among the labels with regard to getting a presence in the emerging digital market and a feeling that, while they were moving conditionally and hesitantly towards a digital future, the retailers were defined by an inertia here.

'Traditional retail was not especially supportive of anything that had the word "digital" in it,' he says. 'It's inevitable that there would be tension between rights holders who saw a possible future online and physical retailers who would naturally resist it. It's a delicate dance for the record industry in how to navigate that because they're biting the hand that has fed them for a long time.'

Martin Mills, head of Beggars Banquet, says that, on paper, record companies becoming digital retailers was highly attractive, but the reality and the practicalities mitigated against it.

'That has often felt appealing, but it's never quite felt viable,' he says. He gives more context when he suggests that the independents let the majors try it first and for them to prove the futility of it. 'I think we realised from the example of the majors that rights owners don't make good retailers,' he says. 'If there were an independent one, you'd have additional problems, like who's in and who's out or what the musical identity would be. There were just so many problems with doing it that we never got around to it.'

The majors were, according to Glen Ward of Virgin Megastore, 'starting to get out of their lane' at this stage, mesmerised by the idea that they could give retail a real go. Ego and the temptation to seize the power the retailers held proved too much to resist.

'The control element was becoming a bit fraught and threatening,' he suggests. 'So they stepped out of their lane and started talking about doing their own downloading services and releasing stuff pre-physical release. For me, it's always been that you ignore your customers at your peril. Our customers were the end consumer, the paying fan of the artist who buys the music; whereas for the record companies, we were their customer. They lost sight of that very early on. It was a case of, "No, we don't hate you. You're in the supply chain. You're in the way. But we'll leap over that".'

He feels there was, for a moment, mass amnesia about where the skills of labels lay and where the skills of retailers lay.

'Just because you can doesn't mean you should,' he says of the labels' doomed attempts to encroach on his turf. 'It's an understanding of what your business is. I understood the end consumer. I knew how to present my stores. I knew how to present online. Whereas the record companies, their ability should have been to spot the talent, nurture the talent and cut out the cumbersome management side of things. All of us were kidding ourselves. We didn't realise we were just in the middle between the artists and the fans. Ultimately, that's what's happened in the subsequent twenty years. It is all about going straight from artists to fans.'

Simon Wright is firmly of the belief that the labels were not conversant enough with the intricacies of retail anyway as to make this point moot. (The subsequent disasters of Pressplay and MusicNet, the majors' attempts to create pre-iTunes download services in the early 2000s, bears this out).

'Fundamentally, the customer thought of the artist or title, not the record company,' he says of why this could never fly. 'You are always going to handicap your demand. It was very difficult at that time. Record companies were all announcing this, but you can imagine what's going on in a boardroom in Universal or whatever. Your John Kennedys [Universal] and Paul Burgers [Sony] would be going, "Shit! We better do something. Put our own digital offer together!" It was a natural corporate reaction to something that was seemingly moving very fast.'

Tony Wadsworth says that what has been forgotten here is that, despite the temptation of going it alone, the labels did not forsake the retailers and, when sales started to decline from 2000 onwards, companies like EMI went above and beyond to help the retailers, not try to shunt them ever further to the margins.

'Once the decline in physical sales started in the 2000s, we went out of our way to over-service physical retailers, particularly independent retailers,' he says. 'They were getting discount deals that were not a million miles away from the discount deals of the multiples. Because we wanted them to stay in business. We didn't want record retail to fall to pieces.'

He also stresses that not only did the record companies misunderstand how to do digital retail correctly, so too did the traditional retailers. They were all deluded in thinking they had the answers when in fact the answers were going to come from technology companies.

'Everybody was trying to do different things, all desperately trying to come up with something that was going to end up being the new model or part of the answer for the future,' he argues. 'When, in fact, none of us were retailers, really, as major record companies. So how would we know? We were not technology companies. So guess what. Eventually the answer comes through a technology retail company [Apple with iTunes]. The cavalry was coming around the corner.'

Ultimately, everything happening here, a lot of it springing from fear and panic, was a manifestation of the long-standing politics of power in the music industry – namely who had control and who wanted to take it from them. Ward also insists the retailers were not as all-powerful as they were presumed to be at the time and that, really, the labels had more control than they liked to admit to.

He proposes that the defining motif of the record industry's history was its desperation to get control and to retail control.

'You can go through history, the payola scandal and such like, where the record company used to have control of that radio airplay, but they realised they didn't want to do it, gave it to somebody else and then payola crept in.'

This attempt to circumvent retailers, doomed as it was, was simply the latest incarnation of that record company addiction to control. The craving for control was in its DNA. Even if grasping for control caused it great harm, the record industry at the time could not help itself from making that desperate grasp. It was to be, once again, a hard lesson learned.

CHAPTER 14

Out of Site, Out of Mind: the URL Land Grab

(Control.com)

Record companies offer recording contracts to artists premised entirely on exclusivity. The artist signs to them for X years or Y albums and they are precluded from recording for anyone else. Sometimes it is a matter of pride to be affiliated to a particular label (Bob Dylan still has his concerts begin with him being introduced as 'Columbia recording artist, Bob Dylan'); other times the label is seen as a gilded cage.

In the days of plenty, labels were content enough to just tie acts to a recording deal and make their money that way. Motown in the 1960s would take a cut of touring and other sources of income from acts, but by the 1990s that was incredibly rare. (In the early 2000s, when CD sales slumped, the arrival of the 360-degree or multiple-rights deal saw labels, inspired by the Motown model as well as being panicked, seek to have a share in non-recording activities like music publishing, live and merchandise).

The growth of the internet in the 1990s raised a whole new concern for labels about if they or the artist should own something that might not bring in money directly but was deemed to have a huge (albeit intangible) value.

The first website as we understand it today dates back to 6 August 1991. It was created by British computer scientist Tim Berners-Lee for the European Organization for Nuclear Research (CERN) and contained information about the World Wide Web Project.[1]

Setting up a website was mainly confined to government, research and academia to begin with, but soon brands realised this could be a promotional platform for them and maybe, at some point, an actual shop window.

In the music industry, some prescient, and tech-savvy, artists grasped the importance of this early and understood that a website not only gave them a footprint online, but it could also become a communication channel as well as a new form of power. Some of this happened without the label's involvement – and sometimes even without the label's knowledge – but by the end of the 1990s these websites were deemed important enough for record companies to want to take control of them and not leave them purely to be run (and controlled) by artists and their managers.

The flashpoint came in late April 1999 when Sony Music started to introduce new contracts whereby new artists signing to it would have to give it ownership of their website. Artist managers and artist lawyers were, naturally, horrified.

It made the front page of *Music Week* at the start of May 1999.

'The initiative which reflects the growing importance of the internet as a promotional tool and ultimately as a means of selling music, marks an attempt to clarify a murky contractual area,' it wrote.

The ultimate goal was for the label to take a 'significant cut' of revenue, such as the sale of merchandise, through artist websites. Sony also, according to a draft contract leaked to *Music Week*, wanted to own the data around each site.[2]

The initiative was driven out of Sony's HQ in New York and was understood to be a contested clause that was delaying the signing of contracts with new artists, notably with pop act A1. 'This could become a deal-breaker,' claimed one source, but others suggested new acts might be prepared to lose some rights in order to get a contract. No other major label had yet, as far as *Music Week* understood, introduced such clauses to their artist contracts.[3]

Tank from Furtive Management, who looked after Reef, said, 'We have always kept active control of our website. For us the internet is about being independent and it should be independent.' Lawyer Sarah Stennet, of Spraggon Stennet Brabyn, added, 'It's like taking over the artist's fan club. Sony's angle is that the artists will be better off, but in layman's terms it's an encroachment of artist's rights. The principle of the internet is to open up opportunities or artists and that's exciting, but Sony seems to want to take that away.'[4]

The story rumbled on into the pages of the following week's issue of *Music Week*, although it had moved from the front page to page 9. 'At this stage there is still little indication how widespread the practice will become among Sony-signed artists, let alone whether any other company will attempt to mirror its move, but there is no doubting the importance of the issues it raises,' noted the publication.[5]

Marc Geiger (co-CEO of Artistdirect, which sold merchandise for The Rolling Stones and the Beastie Boys) said, 'We believe this is the single most important issue today. It's not digital distribution. There are new revenue streams, new information streams and new media channels opening up. The issue is who owns and controls those channels.'[6]

One artist manager added, 'What Sony is saying is that it wants a percentage of every ticket sold through the website, which takes away money from the artist.'[7]

Nick Moore of the International Managers' Forum said he was not so concerned about the move by Sony, suggesting it was more a token move rather than part of some clear strategy. 'I don't see the big artists like Jamiroquai or Manics [Manic Street Preachers] signing [website ownership] away,' he said. 'Sony is the first and if the other majors move on it, it'll be a huge issue. But to be honest, I don't think a lot of them have the expertise.' He ended on a line that intended to suggest that the labels were one of the least internet-savvy parts of the music business so they would not really know what to do with artist websites if they got them. 'A lot of labels won't even let their staff use the internet or have them connected,' he snorted.[8]

The story erupted in the US the following month, with *Billboard* asking what, exactly, was at stake and what, exactly, labels were looking to seize ownership of. 'Artists have traditionally been treated badly by the record companies when new technology arrives,' said James Fisher, general secretary of the International Managers' Forum, with the body having already met with key artist managers to discuss what they should do next.[9]

Billboard also noted that this was all coming as a surprise to established artists. Sophie B. Hawkins said, 'Companies want so much already. I would never give away my publishing, the right to control my fan club, or control of what goes on the internet about me.' She added, however, that Sony had been helpful with marketing and she wished to work closely with them. 'I would never go behind Sony's back and not clear things I plan to do, like post samples of my music,' she said.[10]

Dexter Holland of The Offspring, chimed in on the issue. 'I'm not an industry guy but I can say that I don't like anything that limits our freedom as a band,' he said. 'I enjoy having our own Web site and having control over it, just like we have control of our music and imagery on T-shirts.'[11]

Robert Rosenblum of legal firm Greenberg Traurig, said, 'It's a complicated issue. In most agreements, the artists own the rights to their performing name. But the labels might be able to present a compelling argument that they have a right to protect their investment online.'[12]

The argument coming out of the labels in defence of this move to own artist websites was that, in most cases, they had paid to build and host the sites so it naturally followed they should have an interest in those sites.

Neil Cartwright, head of digital at Sony Music UK, says that most artists in the late 1990s were not that bothered about having, let alone owning, their own website. 'They didn't know what websites were for a start,' he says. 'Actually, having worked with a few artists recently, I'm not sure if that's actually changed! I don't think the artists care. Why should they? They are musicians.'

Websites in 1999 were incredibly expensive to build, often costing thousands of pounds or dollars to get the most rudimentary site up and running. Because so few companies had the requisite coding skills to create websites, and long before self-serve web-building platforms became widely available, there was a brief window of time where web companies could pluck numbers out of the sky and add them to invoices. For a short period of time, it was a licence to print money for web development companies.

Just how expensive were websites in 1999? To answer a question with another question: how long is a string of 1s and 0s?

Raoul Chatterjee, part of the Warner ESP team in the UK, says that it was not uncommon for a website at the time to cost £10,000. Acts, because they increasingly saw websites as an extension of their identity, did not want a site that looked cheap in the same way they did not want a promo video that looked cheap. As such, website costs quickly spiralled.

'Often those that had a good visual identity would really want a cool website to go with it,' says Chatterjee, noting that they were initially more concerned about what their website would say about them rather than how their website could be used to more efficiently drive sales. 'It was more about the visualisation of the artist's story than it was about the hardcore CRM, marketing and the opportunity to build up the fan database.'

Neil Cartwright offers an example of the costs involved at the upper end. Thunderbugs were a girl group signed to Epic, part of Sony, with the twist being they played their own instruments (an idea that pop group Busted would run with a few years later). *The Independent*, writing about the group in August 1999, pinned them down as one of the occasional acts that labels spend terrifying amounts of money on. It suggested Epic paid the most it ever had in its history to sign a new act and that Thunderbugs had been put through 'Eighteen months of pre-launch grooming.'[13]

Major labels occasionally get into a situation where they have spent so much money developing an act that they just have to keep spending. Thunderbugs were not just a money pit; they were a series of money pits stretching over the horizon. Money, mostly out of fear rather than necessity, had become no object. Their debut single, 'Friends Forever', managed to make it to number five in the UK charts in September 1999.[14] The second single, 'It's About Time You Were Mine', only got as high as number 43.

'They flopped, but not before we'd spent £25,000 on the most expensive website we'd ever done,' says Cartwright. 'We built this huge site in Flash based on an airport lounge. It was incredible. But the band were dropped before we even released the website! We spent twenty-five grand on this website that never ever saw the light of day. Extraordinary!'

Thunderbugs were symptomatic of the times. Singles in the UK could be incredibly lucrative and, awash with money, major labels were not shy about spending and spending and spending to try and make something hit.

Cartwright says that Sony would have been the driving force between the Thunderbugs website, adding the £25,000 to the band's growing, and recoupable, debt. If they were going to throw bales of cash at the act, Sony wanted to own what it was spending money on.

'I thought, and still do, that the website is a critical part of an artist's marketing, sales, promotion, ticketing, whatever you like,' says Cartwright. 'Those were very early days. In 1999, there was no real talk of that. We used to register the artist URLs, primarily because the artists didn't do it. That was one of the first things that we did when we signed an artist – assign the URL. Artists weren't really thinking about their website. Very few were. Travis were one band who were using their website a lot. George Michael was another good example. But there were very, very few artists who knew what the website was or even gave a shit.'

He says that Sony UK head Paul Burger was insistent at the time that each new signing should have a website, but was not so concerned that they were a cost base rather than a revenue source. 'Paul Burger saw the internet as part of communication,' says Cartwright. 'It definitely had a marketing role, but certainly there were no revenue expectations back then at all.'

As a lawyer within Warner Music UK, Cliff Fluet says part of his brief was ensuring a range of URLs were registered for Warner artists and the company saw them as something to own and, crucially, to protect.

'I remember making a web company's Christmas when I gave them a list of three hundred artists who were on the live roster and to please go away and secure these domain names,' he says. 'There was a genuine sense that ownership of the URL was as important as securing the trademark to all of our label identities et cetera. There was very much a sense that the top level domain name was going to be one of the most important assets that we would need going forward.'

In 1999, it was newer acts who were under the most pressure to hand over the running, and the ownership, of their website to their record company. Albhy Galuten, then working at eLabs within Universal, summarises the debates around if the label or the artist should own the website and, more importantly, who had the most power to make the final decision.

'You could make the argument that the U2 website should be [run through] Universal Music – so www.umusic.com/u2, or whatever band it was,' he says. 'So even if the band went somewhere else, they didn't have to maintain it. You always had a URL that you would print on the back of a CD and it would always point to something that was good. It would make this guarantee that this website would always be up. So if U2 went from Universal to another label, to Warner or something, the website would stay good and you could track it and have business people follow it. Whereas bands, of course, wanted to control their own websites. This was the beginning of bands wanting to garner their own control and have control over what was going on. They would want their own website so they could control their own destiny. This was a non-trivial battle.'

The importance of owning URLs and domain names for musicians became explicit in 1999 through a number of high-profile court cases around alleged cybersquatting. This is defined as 'unauthorized registration and use of internet domain names that are identical or similar to trademarks, service marks, company names, or personal names.'[15]

In October that year, lawyers acting on behalf of Led Zeppelin requested that Robert Siciliano hand over the LedZeppelin.com domain name, which he had registered five years earlier as he was 'Boston's biggest Led Zeppelin fan.'[16] Around the same time, lawyers for Don Henley and Eagles were filing trademark infringement suits against Mark Elsis over the registration of specific domain names (don-henley.net, don-henley.org, donhenly.org, theendoftheinnocence.com and e-a-g-l-e-s.com). They even offered to buy the domain names from him.[17] The following month, lawyers for Dwight Yoakam were targeting Sharon Anchak over two domain names (dwightsite.com and dwightyoakam.com) on similar grounds.[18]

This was to continue to be an issue for several years, but 1999 was when many major acts woke up to the pressing importance of not only controlling a domain name but also controlling all the data around it.

The policy at EMI at the time around artist websites hinged around the simple argument that the label was incurring the cost of building them so the label should own them.

'Once the power of artist websites and digital databases became apparent, there was a battle which began to be fought over ownership of these sites,' says Tony Wadsworth, in charge of EMI UK at the time. 'I think we probably assumed we own everything, because we paid for everything! Yet artists and their managers very quickly made it clear that that wasn't the way they saw it. There was too much value to be derived from other income streams, for which the website and databases were key. This was new territory and led to discussions, which are still being had, about the record label's contribution to these other income streams, and under what circumstances costs and revenue might be shared.'

Web properties were more developed in the US than they were in the UK in 1999, but Jeremy Silver argues 'only a small number of band managers' really understood where any of this could go in the future.

'Everybody saw there was novelty value in it and everybody saw this is where some marketing expense was going on so they should get in on this,' he says. 'But not that many of them had really figured out strategically what this really meant for the band and the brand. That sense that the band is the brand, not the label, was still a really weird one. There was a sort of naiveté about that. If they had been a bit savvier and smarter, they might have registered the domain name, owned that and then told the label to build the site on the domain name. That would have been a smart thing to do. It's obvious to us today, but it wasn't then.'

At BMG, the view on websites was that they were honey pots for data. Compared to today, the analytics then were rudimentary but the label quickly understood that they could gather basic details about fans, notably their email addresses, and start to market directly to them. It was this aspect of artist websites that BMG and others saw as the most valuable and that the retailers saw as the most damaging to them.

Head of digital at BMG in 1999 was Rob Wells. He started out in the company gathering and processing consumer data that came from CD inserts and flyers handed out at shows. Initially, it was a physical mailing list, where cards would be posted out to fans who had signed up to a particular act's list, but it was slowly becoming digital.

'This was about ownership of the consumer,' he says. 'The retailers were doing everything they could at the time to retain control of that relationship. And the labels were like, "These people are fans of our acts".'

Take That, who had split in 1996, were held up by BMG as the prime example of a database helping to power an act's success. Wells says, at its peak, the Take That mailing list ran to 350,000 names and was used to promote not just Take That but also to cross-promote other pop acts on assorted BMG labels.

'We also did a lot of research,' says Wells. 'We'd send out these questionnaires once a year – deep questions – and we'd incentivise them, whether it was a meet and greet or signed merchandise or gold discs or whatever. In the late 1990s, we started to take the consumer databases and link the mailshot to a CD-ROM area on a database called Interact. So the later versions of 5ive singles and Westlife singles would actually have the consumer database included on the CD-ROM. You'd send the mailshot and above your name on the mailshot was your unique ID. You'd buy the single, drop it in a CD-ROM drive and you'd get to see the new video. Then there was a hidden area that, if you entered your code, you'd be greeted personally.'

This was nothing short of a revolution for record labels. 'It was like magic to the marketing people,' says Wells. 'You had a return path from the mailing list to purchase. Then you could print off a signed picture with your name on it. "Hey, Eamonn, we love you. You're a great fan of 5ive. Thanks for buying our new single. Lots of love." We won awards for this shit!'

Wells admits that he actually made a cameo in some of the CD-ROMs sent out for data gathering. 'I dressed up as this mad professor – Professor

Pat Pending', he laughs. 'I was pointing to areas on the screen and clickable functions would turn up where they could answer questions about their musical tastes, what they thought about the band's styling or the name or the new video. It was fully interactive. The thing that really appealed to us inside the direct marketing team was that the more of these things we sent out, the more engaged the fanbase was. They became part of the process. It was phenomenal.'

He says that around 1996 and 1997, mainly as a way to reduce overheads, they began migrating from posting out cards to fans to doing direct marketing via email. This is where the retailers began to rub the throbbing veins in their temples as it started to become clear the labels were going to take ownership of the customer relationship that had been theirs for decades.

'The rights owners never had that direct link with the consumer,' says Wells. 'They'd never had that. That's what they always strove to have. That's why my first job was in direct marketing, because BMG had bought a company to try and knit that relationship with the consumer. From direct contact and direct marketing comes direct selling. The retailers were resisting that. There's always been – whether it was retailers or broadcasters or collecting societies or DSPs – that barrier between the rights owners and the consumer. And there always will be. That will always remain. There's always been that tension. There has always been that sense of, "Those fuckers are trying to steal our shit or take our margin." Personally I think that's commercially very healthy.'

There was a major stand-off in the 1990s between EMI and HMV over these inserts in CDs. The label wanted to build customer databases and this was the quickest way to do so at scale. The retailers tried everything they could to stop them from doing so.

'Some retailers threatened that, whenever they got them, they were going to take them out and put them in the bin,' recalls Wadsworth. 'They thought we were planning to steal their customers!'

This accelerated when labels started asking for not just postal addresses for fans but also their email addresses, although Wadsworth says the retailers were being unnecessarily precious here. 'They were probably worried about the fact that that email could say, "Don't bother going to HMV to buy this. Come to us". That wasn't on the agenda. Certainly not at the time. We had no direct sale option at all.'

The initial response from the retailers was to simply have the inserts removed when each batch of new stock arrived.

'We used to take all the cards out so they couldn't have the names of the customers so they wouldn't go direct,' confirms Stuart Rowe, general manager of direct and e-commerce for HMV Europe in 1999.

Wadsworth suggests it really only became a wedge issue between labels and retailers right at the end of the 1990s. This was because email marketing was starting to show its power. Consumers could now be targeted cheaply, immediately and at scale by labels in a way that was physically and financially impossible at the start of the decade.

'The postcard insert thing had actually been going on since much earlier in the 1990s and without too much aggro,' he says. 'It wasn't right at the very beginning that they started taking the postcards out.'

Brian McLaughlin claims he tried to reason with EMI over this matter, insisting that HMV's concerns at the time were genuine.

'I asked Tony Wadsworth for a meeting,' he recalls. 'I said, "Tony, where's this going? The relationship up until now is that you make the product and then you sell it to us. We then handle the customer and sell it to the customer. We manage the customer for you – hence why we have got 250 stores." Tony was quite surprised that I was upset about this, because he said, "Why do you feel threatened by this when this is just the way the world is going? Everything now is about copyright. The future, Brian, is about the ownership of copyright. That's what it is. And we own it." So I said, "Well up until now you haven't wanted to, you know, because you've never had a vehicle to own it other than through us. And don't forget that EMI opened the first HMV store many years ago." That's how they saw, years ago, how they were going to not only manufacture it but they were also going to retail it.'

Wadsworth disputes this version of events.

'I was surprised at their upset, but we just felt that targeted communications through databases, some of which were built through retail card inserts, was an effective and efficient way of marketing,' he says. 'There was no plan at that point for direct-to-consumer selling. We valued the retail relationship too much. Especially the specialists like HMV – much more than with the supermarkets who only stocked a limited range. The cards were meant solely for driving sales, which would go through retail.'

John Kennedy says he has enormous sympathy with the retailers and understood completely why HMV in particular was taking such a hard line on inserts.

'That was very bright of Brian McLaughlin,' he says. 'He didn't want to surrender his relationship with his customer. Why would he? HMV had a very loyal following. He would actually perceive that as not market research but trying to have a direct relationship with his customer. He may have been right.'

This dispute between the labels and retailers would reverberate into the 2000s, but this was not the only way the record companies were trying to build direct relationships with the consumer.

In the late 1990s, labels were also excited about a whole new type of direct communication with fans – the webcast. Despite the crackly and tiny image on the screen as well as the juddering feed due to a slow connection speed, there was experimentation with streaming concerts live to people watching on their computers at home, at work or at university.

The spin-off from this was the web chat where artists would go online and hope that lots of fans were logged in and asking them questions. It did not always follow that the fans showed up, often because the chat was badly marketed or the fans did not have easy access to the internet.

Wells recounts a story of one web chat going fist-chewingly wrong. 'I'm not going to give you the artist's name,' he insists. 'But there was an online web chat and I was moderating it. Basically, no one had come in. I ended up on one machine logging on with twelve different identities in the chat room and I was basically sat opposite this artist running this chat as twelve different fans. I was going for an hour. It was exhausting. I remember I was sweating profusely. He was asking me questions. He's like, "Wow! This guy sounds like he's even in the room!" I was like, "Yeah! Crazy how knowledgeable this bloke is!" And I was there typing questions.'

RANCH DRESSING: UNIVERSAL EXECUTIVES BUILD A FARM-THEMED WEBSITE IN HONOUR OF THEMSELVES

In *Citizen Kane*, Orson Welles used the construction of the ostentatious Xanadu, lifting its name from *Kubla Khan* by Samuel Taylor Coleridge, to mock the untrammelled vanity of newspaper baron William Randolph Hearst for building Hearst Castle. This was a palace of the ego, the kind of thing the braggart reaches for to save wear and tear on their vocal cords.

The antecedents stretch back through every palace and temple commissioned by a king or emperor to stand as a permanent monument to their self-proclaimed greatness. Record executives perhaps acted like kings or emperors, but they knew deep down that they were nothing of the sort.

In the record business of the 1990s, the proof of ultimate power was having unlimited access to the corporate jet as well as occupying the corner office. These were outward projections of success, a marker in the sand separating the top executive from everyone else in the company. The internet, however, offered a new kind of ego boost to the record company executive who had it all. Every other head of a major label had a private jet and a corner office. They were the old metrics of success. But did they have a website named after them?

The white elephant that was Jimmy & Doug's Farm Club probably began with noble intentions, but by the time the two people it was named after – Doug Morris, the head of Universal Music, and Jimmy Iovine, the head of Interscope Records – got their hands on it, it arguably became something very different indeed.

It was announced in late November 1999 and was presented as an act of great altruism, as well as a sign of the biggest record company in the world adapting to an emerging new world. Like courtiers cowering under the wickedness of a child tyrant, one can only presume that no one at Universal had the courage to point out the gaping flaw in its nomenclature: outside of the tight confines of the record business, *no one knew who the hell Jimmy and Doug were.*

The basic premise was that it would allow unsigned acts to upload tracks (along with one photo and a short biography) to a website for evaluation by ten label talent scouts. The best acts discovered this way would get a contract with Interscope. Iovine told *Billboard*, 'We're also arranging for major artists to listen to the material and post their thoughts [. . .] It's an excellent way of diving into the enormous pool of talent out there. Plus, it allows us to gauge the interest of the general public [. . .] The bottom line is that we're reorganizing the need to broaden our reach and style as a label. Times are changing and we're committed to doing more than keeping up. We're committed to being ahead of the curve.'[19]

Each week, the three best acts would be selected to put on live performances that would be voted on. Typical of the era, a soft drinks brand was brought in as a sponsor, in this case Sprite.

The talent search show would live online as well as having a weekly one-hour show on USA Network, screening just after the World Wrestling Federation's *Raw/War Zone* show, which attracted around 6.6 million viewers. It would also be cross-promoted on MTV.[20]

It opened for entries on 1 December and stated there would be a full launch in February 2000. Edgar Bronfman Jr, president and CEO of Seagram, talked it up and said it would generate 'revenue streams that no other music companies have.'[21]

Iovine described the concept to the *New York Post* in December 1999, '[It is] a place that would be like Carnaby Street in the sixties and Haight Ashbury – New York's Greenwich Village – a place where people want to go [. . .] A hybrid, an Internet company, record label and TV show – all in one,' he said.[22]

To try and attract the audiences they were after, it could not just feature unsigned (read: unknown) musicians. It had to have big names. Universal ensured that the biggest names on its roster would show up. Acts performing or being interviewed on the show during its short life included U2, Limp Bizkit and No Doubt.[23] Fred Goodman, in his biography of Edgar Bronfman Jr, says the show really just became a showcase for Universal's already massive acts. '[V]ery little of the show's airtime was given to unknown bands,' he wrote.[24]

Perhaps chastened by the fact that it only lasted fifteen months, screening its last edition in June 2001, its co-founder, reflecting back on it in 2015, admitted the scale of the solipsism at play in its naming. 'I don't know why we called it Jimmy and Doug's Farm Club,' said Doug Morris. 'We were egomaniacs!'

A reported $25 million had been sunk into it, equal to $1.6 million for each month it lasted. That could have bought almost two Gulfstream GIV jets in 1999.[25] Or it could have bought significant Manhattan real estate to turn into the world's biggest corner office.

MARILLIONNAIRES' CLUB: THE BAND GOING IT ALONE ONLINE

It started with a tour of the US in 1997. A tour the band could not afford to put on but which the band's fans, already alive to the power of the internet, decided they could help underwrite. From there spawned a whole new type of cottage industry for acts who had been through the major label system but which were no longer deemed profitable enough to remain in the major label system.

British prog rock band Marillion formed in 1979 and signed with EMI, putting out their debut single in 1982. They built steadily and in 1985 released 'Kayleigh', a number two hit in the UK and the album it came from, *Misplaced Childhood*, went to number one. They had a solid run of Top 40 singles hits until 1994, barring 'Uninvited Guest' in 1989, which only got to number 53. By 1997, the decline had set in and they were dropped by EMI, although their last single for the label, 'Beautiful', had managed to get to number 29 and their last studio album, 1995's *Afraid Of Sunlight*, had got to number 16 on the British charts.[26]

Mark Kelly, the band's keyboard player and one of its co-writers, says they knew the jig was up in 1997, calling it their 'worst year as a band in terms of earnings.' Their peak years for record sales and touring were 1985 and 1986, but 'then it was downhill from there really'. They knew the end was coming for several years.

'You could literally chart the album sales,' he says. '*Misplaced Childhood* was two million sales, *Clutching At Straws* was one million sales, [lead singer] Fish left, *Seasons End* was 650,000 sales, *Holidays In Eden* was 450,000 sales. We were at 300,000, possibly 250,000, by the time we did *Afraid Of Sunlight* – and that was the point the record company [EMI] dropped us.'

It's a chart trajectory familiar to many bands. The years of struggle, the hits and then a slow but steady slide into what *Smash Hits* magazine in the 1980s tartly termed 'the dumper.'[27]

That could have been it for the band, doomed to play the nostalgia circuit to ever-diminishing returns, eking out a living and refusing, despite all the evidence to the contrary, to give up on their dreams. As Les McQueen, the tragicomic former member of 1970s rock band Crème Brulee in dark comedy series *The League Of Gentlemen,* would say: 'It's a shit business.'

Marillion soldiered on, signing to Castle Communications and releasing *This Strange Engine* in 1997 and *Radiation* the following year. 'We did an album a year just to keep our heads above water,' says Kelly. 'It was getting to the point where we were struggling to keep churning albums out once a year and touring, really just keeping the wolf from the door. That's how it felt.'

Several years before this, however, an online fan community, mainly in the US, was building around the band. The members were aware of it but Kelly was the one who paid closest attention ('lurking in the background'). Fans were repeatedly asking when the band would tour the US again and Kelly posted on the Freaks community that they had been dropped by EMI, there was no label to give them tour support and, anyway, they always lost money on US tours. Jeff Pelletier, a long-time fan of the band, asked how much they would need to fund a tour. Kelly, spitballing, suggested between $50,000 and $60,000. Pelletier proposed that the fans pay in advance for tickets. Within a few weeks they had raised $18,000, with another fan opening a bank account to hold the money. The target was hit and the tour went ahead.

'We did this tour,' explains Kelly. 'We got lots of publicity around the story of the "tour fund", as they called it. It was probably one of the earliest examples of fan crowdfunding.'

From that sprung a wider idea that, circumventing the need for a record label, they could fund new albums like this, the first being *Anoraknophobia,* which was released in 2001, but which the band started fan funding in 1999, getting fans to order it in advance and using the money raised to pay for the recording, mastering, pressing and distribution.

'It made me realise [several things],' says Kelly. 'One, I was very interested in the internet, probably more so than anybody else in the band and realised that there was a lot of potential there. We had contact with these fans. It made me realise that actually, if they would do this, with no promise of anything apart from the possibility of a tour – we weren't giving them free tickets or anything. It was charity, I suppose. I had already had the idea that we should be pushing the internet, we should be pushing online because that was the future. It was obvious that was the way things were going.'

The band understood early on the power of data, something that the internet was starting to deliver back to musicians. They placed their website at the centre of everything they were doing, even calling their 1999 album *marillion.com*. 'It seems stupid now, but people didn't really know about the internet,' says Kelly. 'I said, "Let's call the album *marillion.com*. It'll make people realise that we have a website".'

The band, however, did not originally own the www.marillion.com URL, initially having to make do with MarillionOnline.com. That infinitely more desirable domain name was owned and operated by Jeroen Schipper, a fan based in the Netherlands.

'At some point, I asked Jeroen, "Can we please have Marillion.com?"' says Kelly. 'And he finally gave it to us. That wasn't a problem for us. [At the time] the record companies wanted to own that real estate because it was a shop window, wasn't it?'

The album *marillion.com* was the band's final release as part of a three-album deal with Castle, but they knew they did not want to stay on the label. They understood that they could use this album to help set themselves up as fully independent.

'I'd heard that the shops were removing the CD inserts because they didn't want it to go online,' he says. 'It was a real backlash. We had two plans, really. One was to ditch our record company. They wanted us to re-sign, but I had my eye on the future, thinking, "We're not going back to this company once we finish this album." We weren't happy with them. I said, "OK, we're going to call the album *marillion.com*. We're going to print this mail back card in the artwork, so they can't remove it, and then start collecting names and addresses." Most people didn't have email addresses, to be fair. We had a chap working [on it] for us called Erik Nielsen.'

Nielsen, an American, was a fan of the band and had met them when he responded to a request from the band on a Usenet newsgroup, alt.music.marillion, looking for a US-based keyboard tech to join their US tour as they were in a bind. Nielsen joined the tour and bonded with Kelly around music but also what was happening on the internet.

'Erik was my partner in crime, I suppose,' says Kelly. 'Because he understood it. He got it. We were the ones that were driving the band in this direction. Erik came from a background where he was involved in databases and he worked at a hospital, managing their online database. He was very much like, "Guys, you need to get a database. We need to start collecting [names], find out who our fans are." That was the start of that.'

Nielsen had taught himself HTML and helped the band set up their website, evangelising about how it could become not just a fan community but a way for the band to make more money from records than they ever did under a label contract.

'By January or February 1998, I had the whole system up and running and we were taking the first online orders,' says Nielsen. 'They would come through as emails, I would then compile stuff together and send them off to the studio engineer in the UK and he would literally take the ten CDs down to the post office and put them over the counter. At which point, we went, "Well we have to do better than this".'

Nielsen moved to the UK and despite some, what he euphemistically terms, 'visa issues', started working full time for the band and helped them take greater control of their online presence (as multiple fan groups existed in different countries and the band wanted to unify them and take control of them in a centralised way).

'We had a bunch of fan clubs in different countries around the world and they all had their own databases, which they jealously guarded,' says Kelly. 'We wanted to prise these databases away from them without demanding that they give them to us. We said that we could do a Christmas CD, give it away for free and we could send it to all the fan club members. In order for us to do that, we had to ask the fan clubs to give us their database of addresses so we could send the free CD to their members.'

The band offered things like a bonus disc of unreleased material for free as a way to gather fan emails and build an operational database, eventually taking over the fulfilment of CDs and merchandise themselves.

In March 1999, the band worked with EMI who had remastered and reissued the *Clutching At Straws* and *Afraid Of Sunlight* albums where hidden tracks could be accessed through a special code on the enhanced CD versions of the albums. The fans, to get the bonus tracks, had to fill in a questionnaire on the band's website in order to be emailed the access code. 'Reply cards are reasonably effective if they are freepost, but people will be more inclined to fill in questionnaires due to the hidden tracks,' Nigel Reeve, product manager at EMI's catalogue division, told *Music Week*.[28]

It was deemed a success, with EMI reporting in July that year that sales of Marillion's catalogue titles had tripled and their website traffic was up 25 per cent. In the first three days of the initiative, over five hundred fan names and email addresses were added to the band's database. This rose to one thousand in the first week and three thousand within eight weeks.

Marillion, noted *Music Week*, were not the only act experimenting here, saying that BMG had sent a CD-ROM to twenty thousand fans on new pop act Mero which had different possible singles and video clips. Over twelve thousand fans responded.[29] It was not as successful as Marillion's fan engagement as Mero managed just one single, 'It Must Be Love' in March 2000, that only made it to number 33 on the UK chart before they were dropped.[30]

EMI/Parlophone was also testing the waters with one of its biggest acts that July, emailing a multimedia presentation to Blur fans to promote their single 'Coffee & TV.' 'The eSingle, which compresses 16Mb of graphics, video and sound into an easily e-mailable size, features a sample of the band's video, artwork from the CD, a competition to win tickets to the T In The Park event on July 10 where Blur are playing, and a link to the band's website,' explained *Music Week*.[31]

It was sent to seventeen thousand names on the Blur database or it could be downloaded from their website. Parlophone senior marketing manager Sue Lacey said, 'We were very conscious that people who got normal e-mails only got a boring bit of text whereas normal mail-outs have postcards or other add-ons. This eSingle makes it more interactive and exciting for the receiver.'[32]

Things behind the scenes with the Marillion enhanced CDs did not run quite as smoothly as the trade press coverage suggests.

'I remember what an absolute nightmare that was because, if you didn't have QuickTime installed, it wouldn't run,' reveals Nielsen. 'Because we were marillion.com, loads of people were emailing us even though it was EMI's product. We had to get EMI to generate a universal access code so that people who couldn't access it [could]. They were getting really pissed off and abusing us by email. "Just use this code. Shut up! It's the universal access code. If you're contacting us you already know who we are, we already know who you are. Just use this one".'

Nielsen claims that the labels the band were involved with, EMI and Castle, were not too concerned about their data-gathering exercises and happy to let them get on with it.

'We never had any issue because, not stretching my arm too much to pat ourselves on the back, no one else was doing the level that we were doing,' he says. 'If Sony or EMI or Castle or whoever said, "We want control over this", we'd say, "Quite frankly, fuck off! You can't do what we're doing. We're doing this directly. We're selling our own merchandise." I don't think that was ever a question. I think everyone understood that that's what we were doing.'

Tony Wadsworth confirms that the EMI stance at the time would have been to let an act out of contract with the company do whatever they could to keep their career going. 'Marillion wouldn't have been a worry internally because with Marillion, I think it's fair to say, by that time they were past their first flush of album-selling success.'

The band built on this and invested heavily – £25,000 according to Nielsen – to build an e-commerce platform so that fans could order directly from the band. 'At the time everything was so prohibitively expensive,' he says. 'It was a dark cavern of uncertainty. The tech heads got it and no one else really did.'

He says that it was a slow grind, but in ten years the band grew their database from eight thousand people to around 130,000 people, enabling them to become truly self-sufficient.

Radiohead may have stolen all their headlines in 2007 when they released *In Rainbows*, their first album after the conclusion of their contract with EMI, as a pay-what-you-want download and a premium box set[33], but it was Marillion, another ex-EMI act, who had paved the way for them almost a decade earlier.

What Marillion were doing online in the late 1990s remains the backbone of what they continue to do now. Their 20th studio album, *An Hour Before It's Dark*, was released in March 2022 and was funded once again through fan pre-orders. Normally when a band is dropped by a major label, that hastens their demise. Marillion, however, showed that another option was out there. This was, in a large part, because they viewed online as being a revenue source from the off.

'I certainly saw it as a commercial thing right from the start,' says Kelly. 'I didn't get that whole, "Oh, the internet is just for marketing, make everything available for free and you'll make money in other ways." I just didn't see how that was going to work as a business model.'

It was more than the serendipity of being in the right place at the right time just as the internet was starting to go mainstream. It was equally about spotting new opportunities and taking the leap into the unknown – to take control of their career in a way that was never possible before.

'The internet could take some of the credit for the band's revival of fortunes,' says Kelly. 'We have gone from playing small venues in London back up to the Royal Albert Hall. We went through a bad period. The lowest point was around 1997 and then from then onwards, with the crowdfunding thing and with the special editions of the album and all the rest of it, that really cemented the fanbase back in and brought new people in. We weren't prepared to admit that we would have to stop. But I think we could see the writing on the wall. And if it hadn't been for the internet, that's where we would have ended up.'

O-KIOSK COMPUTER: THE SHORT-LIVED ATTEMPT TO LET CONSUMERS BURN THEIR OWN CDS

Musicmaker, as covered in Chapter 11, initially began as a mail-order service where consumers would build their own compilation CDs online and then the company would burn them, add artwork and post them out.

By 1999, however, its IPO added new pressures to the company to flip from a loss-making enterprise to a whole new model for consumption. With EMI a major owner of the company, and with mounting worries among retailers that labels were conniving to undermine their business, the kind of ideas that happen two hours into a meeting – when the coffee and pastries have run out and fatigue is mounting – started to migrate from a scrawled note in a jotter into the real world.

Like the pepped-up high school kids in a saccharine 1950s movie, all dazzling teeth and glossy hair, someone somewhere had the bold idea of putting the show on *right here*.

Rather than have a customer wait several days for their customised CD to arrive in the post, surely the whole thing could be expedited by allowing them to walk into a record shop and make their compilation disc there and then. Something you could order online was now something you could walk to a shop to get. Such was the counterintuitive logic of the music business grappling with the internet in 1999.

Musicmaker was not, however, the first to make this move.

In May 1997, Swiss company CD World Corporation (CDWC) announced it had licensed 350,000 tracks for compilations created through its Music Points vending machines in the US, launching the service in September that year through its Music Network subsidiary. Positioned in record shops, shopping malls and other public places, people could use the Music Points machines to create CDs with a running time of up to 45 minutes, costing between $18 and $24 per disc. It would only offer music that was at least three years old.[34]

Even CDWC was not the first, with *Music & Copyright* noting that Blockbuster had attempted something similar in 1993 in a joint venture with IBM (called New Leaf Entertainment), but it died because the majors refused to license their music digitally for it.[35] And back in 1987 Personics Corporation was letting users build their own 12–15-track compilations on cassette.[36]

CDnow, still early into its life but at least trying to anticipate where the next wave of disruption would come from, acquired customised CD company SuperSonic Boom in June 1998. It had launched in January 1997 but analysts were not impressed by what it was trying to do.

'The business that SuperSonic Boom is in is not one that the music business is the least bit interested in,' Mark Hardie of Forrester Research told *CNet*. 'When you talk to music industry people about SuperSonic Boom, they just laugh.'[37]

In July 1998, Cerberus was brought in by fashion brand Levi's to install its Virtual Record Store hardware in over three hundred of its clothing stores in Europe, Africa and the Middle East. This followed a trial in June in the Regent Street branch of Levi's in central London. The compilation CDs were being sold for an introductory price of £4.99 in Levi's stores and 10-track compilations for £10 on the online version of Virtual Record Store.

'We see some unusual choices,' Cerberus founder Ricky Adar told the BBC. 'We've had people combining Classical with Rock music, next to House, but there seems to be some theme running between these songs that they like [. . .] With the way that we distribute music, there is no stock, no warehouse and no shipping. Because it's the most efficient way for the music industry to operate, we've halved the price of CDs at stores and we're actually returning more money back to the writer and more money back to the record label.'[38]

Making compilations CDs was clearly back in vogue for startups and investors in 1998 and 1999. In April 1999, Warner Music announced it was working with CustomDisc to allow users to make their own 12-track customised compilations, initially testing it with the Warner jazz catalogue. The *Best Of Smooth Jazz* compilations could be created from a section of just 50 tracks, somewhat limiting the scope of what the resulting CDs could be. There was, however, a prize of a trip to the Catalina Island Jazz Festival for whoever could create 'the most innovative custom discs.'[39]

By September, CustomDisc was boasting of a catalogue of two hundred thousand licensed tracks and was partnering with BMG Direct to let BMG Music Club customers make their own compilations.[40] Then in November, CustomDisc signed a five-year deal with the Sub Pop label to make compilations featuring acts on its roster that included Nirvana, Mudhoney and Afghan Whigs.[41]

In June 1999, Sony announced it was going to bring download kiosks to the high street in early 2000 in the UK in a deal with Digital On-Demand. The grand idea behind it was that consumers, if they could not find a deep catalogue title in the shop, could simply walk over to the kiosk, type in the album name, burn the CD, print out the artwork, pay and walk out of the shop with the album – all in a matter of minutes. *Music Week* also noted that the WHSmith chain was also running trials to burn computer games to CD-ROM in two stores, but it had no plans to offer music this way.[42]

Sony was, however, taking the idea to the US first, having licensed catalogue of four thousand titles for the kiosks that would be installed in retail outlets including Trans World and Virgin Megastore (starting in its Columbus, Ohio store) from July. The kiosks could burn CDs and print liner notes and album art 'in a matter of minutes', noted *Billboard,* and the discs are double encrypted so as to be 'secure.' The selling point to retailers was that it would allow them to participate in digital but in a way that protected their core product (i.e. physical discs). *Billboard* added that there were plans to add DVD-Audio burning later in the year as well as MiniDisc titles. Participating stores would be connected to Digital On-Demand via a high-speed internet connection with the music being sent over it. Customers would then plug their portable devices into the kiosk, so long as they were SDMI-complaint.[43]

Not wishing to be left behind in this kiosk cattle run, HMV announced in July 1999 that it too would have in-store kiosks, although details were scant. *Music Week* said it was part of a JV with two unnamed partners, but that one of them was a major label and other majors were being approached for licensing. The music would be delivered over a secure network, presumably because of piracy worries. The kiosks were expected to clank into action before the end of the year.[44]

By August, Musicland Stores and Wherehouse Entertainment in the US were signed up to trial in-store kiosks after agreeing a deal with Digital On-Demand's Red Dot Network. *Billboard* suggested that five stores from each chain would be involved in the trial, with between three and five thousand titles from EMI and Sony on offer. Digital On-Demand was also said to be in advanced discussions with Universal and BMG to offer their music this way.[45]

'Sony clearly sees the kiosk as an alternative distribution stream for back catalogue,' noted *Music & Copyright* in its July 1999 round up of what was happening here. Runners and riders, according to the publication, included Digital On-Demand, PersonalDisc, V-Sinc (in Japan) and Cerberus Central.[46]

It also reported that the Japanese market was focusing more heavily on MiniDisc than CDs.

'Japanese technology company V-Sinc has developed a kiosk system, Music Press on Demand (Music POD), which creates custom MDs at a fraction of the normal retail price,' it wrote. 'The company aims to capitalise on the large, growing Japanese MD market, which comprised 85m discs and 2m players in 1998. There is an installed base of over 12m MD players in the country. Music POD discs come with lyric card stickers.

As part of an initial trial, at least 30 Music POD terminals have so far been placed at record stores, shopping centres and convenience stores across Japan, including the newly launched record store Muteki Records in Tokyo. The company expects to install 1,500 kiosks by the end of the year and six thousand by the end of 2000.'[47]

Possibly biding its time, it took until October for Musicmaker to announce its in-store plans, although precise details were thin on the ground. Multiple retail partners would be involved but Musicmaker would not name names. It did, however, reveal that compilation albums would take between five and seven minutes to create and an hour of music could also be sideloaded onto portable digital music players. Depending on the number of tracks, it would cost between $9.95 and (a frankly mind-boggling) $24.95.[48]

Looking back, from the safe distance of almost a quarter of a century, it seems incredible that anyone thought this was a good idea, that it would be a huge draw for consumers and that it would instantly solve the catalogue storage issue – what *Wired*'s Chris Anderson would term 'the long tail' a few years later[49] – by making even the most niche titles available digitally.

But hindsight is not just 20/20; it is also unbearably smug.

Even so, those involved with kiosks at the time say that they would often have to bite their tongues and toe the corporate line. The record business, both labels and retailers, had to be seen to be doing *something*. The quality of that something was not up for debate at the time: the very existence of it was seen as enough.

EMI, through its Musicmaker deal, had significant skin in the game and its public statements at the time suggested a company wholly convinced by the idea and assured of its success. Most of it was being directed out of the US, but the UK arm – very much in keeping with the British default setting of weary cynicism – was significantly less gung-ho about the idea than their American colleagues.

'I thought it was really clunky and doomed to failure,' says Tony Wadsworth. 'Why were we spending time doing this? I am sure HMV hated it, too.'

Those slightly down the corporate pecking order say they were scornful of the idea at the time but let their seniors run with it, in part because they did not want to get involved and have the inevitable disaster reflect back on them.

'It seemed like it was adding a colossal amount of friction to the process to me,' says Eric Winbolt, digital commercial manager at EMI in the UK in 1999. 'You had to go to a kiosk when actually the whole future of this was that distribution was going to be through your machine at home. So why on earth [would you use this]?'

Neil Cartwright snickers when I ask him about Sony's involvement in kiosks. 'Yeah, we licensed them,' he laughs. 'That's because people just thought the CD was going to be with us forever.'

Not everyone, however, was rattling with contempt when remembering this short-lived retail experiment (or folly, depending on your stance).

Andy Cleary, co-founder and director of independent label Jammin Music Group, feels they were something of a misfire but thinks the idea behind them as a stepping stone technology was solid. 'It's weird how those kiosks never really got a good head of steam up because they were almost a natural conduit from the old world to the new one,' he argues.

Liam McNeive, lawyer for download service Crunch, had a direct involvement with one major retailer's temporary use of kiosks. 'We had a Crunch kiosk in HMV,' he says. 'I thought, "Jesus, this is amazing." We had all these tiny little label [catalogues] that you could turn into a CD in HMV. I almost feel like I'm hallucinating remembering it.'

The retailers, who were hosting these kiosks in their huge stores, have a multitude of views on what they represented and what they say about the record business in 1999.

Glen Ward feels that it was a potentially good idea but that it missed its incredibly narrow window of opportunity as technology and consumer expectations had already moved on by the time the first kiosks were being installed in retail stores.

'It wasn't a huge business,' he says of their contribution to Virgin Megastore's balance sheet in the US. 'I think that by then people were playing a bit of catch-up. So there was CD burning going on. But it was soon surpassed by the technology and the ability to get things online.'

Ward's colleague Simon Wright says he does not want to rewrite history by claiming at the time to have had the prescience to know that kiosks were never going to work.

'There was making playlists, which I thought was gimmicky,' he says. 'However, if you wanted an album and it was not in the shop – the shops weren't big enough to stock it – we have a CD burning facility where we could not only burn the CD, but we could also print the cover. That meant we could have the whole catalogue but not actually stock the physical CD. You wanted an album, we'd burn it and it'd look just like the one you would have bought, we'd print the cover, slip it into the CD case and there's your copy of the album. We tried that. That lasted a year because things were moving so rapidly.'

At HMV, there was something of a vested interest to be seen to be trying to make it work, but even its head of PR struggled to get a positive spin on it.

'HMV had it in its Oxford Street store but it looked gimmicky,' says Gennaro Castaldo. 'We got a bit of press but it just didn't achieve the scale that you would need it to. People didn't really understand it. You're talking to people who just want to buy Take That singles or Led Zeppelin albums.'

If it was to be a bridge between the old physical world and the new digital world, the executive at HMV tasked with navigating that very transition felt the whole kiosk idea was asinine and preposterous.

'I was involved with it, but I didn't really want much to do that [work with kiosks], to be perfectly honest, because I thought it was a nonsense,' says Stuart Rowe. 'Operationally, they were just awful. You just looked at it and thought [exasperated voice], "Really?" There were people making money left, right and centre from weird ideas where stupid investors would just pile in during the dot com boom. It would have been cheaper and easier to buy that long tail from a mail order outfit that had a big warehouse somewhere. I hated it. I thought it was rubbish.'

The kiosks were quietly retired and the focus instead went on trying to build retailer brands online for both physical records and downloads. Kiosks were a curious, even ludicrous, footnote in this transition period. They will be remembered mainly as a gewgaw temporarily distracting everyone from where the real work that needed to happen.

RETAIL RECONFIGURATION: THE CONDITIONAL RESPONSE TO DIGITAL

Just as the labels could not jackknife from producing CDs to offering their entire catalogues as downloads, so the retailers could not jettison the proven CD overnight in favour of the nebulous promise of digital. They were going to experiment, of course, but they were going to experiment *partially* and, more importantly, *slowly*.

There were several examples of this throughout 1999, but it often felt performative rather than a bold leap into the future.

In February, for example, HMV partnered with a2b, a division of AT&T to offer a free download of a track by Squeeze from their album *Domino*. The track was available via hmv.co.uk, but so too was a voucher to get £1 off the album if you bought it in an HMV store or on its website. On the surface it seemed like an embracing of digital, but really it was about driving physical. In that sense, it was a metonym for how the traditional music retailers were positioning themselves throughout the year.[50]

In April, HMV in the UK was offering, in collaboration with Yahoo!, free internet connections via a free CD it was giving out in its stores. It included a discount on certain albums, such as Blur's *13* for £9.99 (which was £4 cheaper than in the high street stores). Stuart Rowe told *Music Week*, 'It's an extra incentive for people to take up the offer. We'll see how it goes. We want to create awareness, bring music buyers on the internet and into our site.'[51]

By November, HMV was trying to make its dual strategy of 'bricks and clicks' (i.e. selling CDs online but in a way that did not undermine its high street operations) add up. In a special supplement on online retailing, Rowe explained the vision to *Music Week*.

'There is synergy to be had between the net and the High Street,' he said. 'Our strength is in our offline brand. The customer who shops in the High Street will also trust our brand online. We will have tighter integration between our traditional stores and new technology features in the coming years. At the moment we're looking at in-store kiosks very seriously, especially with our smaller stores, where the range of stock is limited.'[52]

The big-name retailers, in part in the grip of experimentation and in part in the grip of desperation, were trying all manner of things to crack open new ways to sell physical records in 1999.

In November in the UK, Tower Records unveiled something called Tower Satellite, which it said was still at the development stage. *Music Week* explained, 'Tower is planning to tap into new markets by launching what it claims is a groundbreaking internet-based retail concept for scores of non-traditional sites such as libraries, schools, universities, trains and aeroplanes.'[53]

Andy Lown, Tower SVP and MD, added a flourish of extra detail. 'Say you are on your way to New York,' he hypothesised. 'You browse the Tower website, order a CD for your girlfriend and it will be delivered to your hotel before you land. Online is the mothership for exposing the

Tower brand and developing new initiatives.' This was clearly going to be a lifesaver for the multitude of, presumably male, consumers who could only express their emotions through the purchasing of CDs.[54]

Tower was also testing same-day delivery in London from its website in December. 'Anyone can have a million different titles and although great value CDs will always be an issue this is about giving more value to customers in other ways,' said Lown who then, inevitably, stressed that, of course, online and the high street could merrily coexist.[55]

Later the same month, Virgin Megastores Direct spotted that mobile could become a sales driver and, keeping it in the family, partnered with Virgin Mobile to let consumers order CDs via their phone. 'Users can listen to up to a minute of a song from ten new albums each week introduced by Radio One presenter Steve Lamacq and can press a button at any time to order the title from Virgin Megastores Direct,' noted *Music Week*.[56]

In the run-up to Christmas and in a moment of bleak symbolism, Our Price announced it was going to give away CDs to promote its 'fully-transactional internet site.' People could enter a pop and general knowledge quiz on the retailer's site. Each week, whoever had the highest score would win a hundred albums and the overall winner at the end of the campaign would win a thousand albums. Our Price was spending £2 million on the promotion, in part to make up for lost time here. Neil Boote, commercial director at Our Price, said, 'We are relatively late into the e-commerce field so can avoid mistakes made by our competitors by launching too early. This promotion acts as an incentive for people to find out more about Our Price, while allowing us to create an e-mail database.'[57]

Throughout the year, the traditional retailers were insistent that they would comfortably manage this transition stage and that the high street was going nowhere. To paraphrase Mandy Rice-Davies[58] in the Profumo case in 1963: 'Well, they would say that, wouldn't they?'

Brian McLaughlin, MD of HMV Europe and chairman of BARD, estimated that online would account for between 5 per cent and 15 per cent of retail in the next decade and he was bullish that record shops would remain at the centre of the business. 'So where is the other 85 per cent of the business going to be done?' he rhetorically asked *Billboard*. 'I presume it will be done through the record stores.'[59]

He added, 'The record shop is now more of a destination store, more of a magnet for fun and excitement. It's not just a question of shoving records in a browser and hoping people just fall in the door. We've got to work very hard to provide a more entertaining and vibrant atmosphere. That may involve technology being part of that, with online facilities available to people in the store.'

McLaughlin suggested that three types of store would survive: 1) 'big stores, with a wide range of product'; 2) 'specialist genre stores'; and 3) 'stores in a convenient location that cater to local requirements.'

He also used his interview with *Billboard* to land blows on the record labels that he felt were going behind the backs of the retailers, retailers that had been so supportive and loyal for so many years, by trying to move into retail themselves.

'One of the things that concerns me most is where the record companies sit,' he said. 'I don't think that the record companies anywhere in the world have handled this particularly well. We recognize that behind the scenes they're working to try and get themselves a share of the Internet business. That is totally transparent noise, even though most of them actually deny it. . . As far as I'm concerned, good luck to them.'

He was adamant that traditional retailers (like HMV, Virgin and Tower) and new online retailers (such as Amazon and CDnow) would make a better fist of retail, in whatever form it was going to take, than the labels ever could.

'They don't have experience in dealing with this business,' he insisted. 'They've never had any experience in dealing with the customer. What would concern me is – as the copyright owners, what are they going to do with this newfound retail arm? Am I going to be treated fairly? Is there going to be a level playing field when this product is released? Is it going to be released to me on the same day as it's released to their own retail customers?'

McLaughlin was somewhat sceptical about e-commerce but made a bold prediction for where it was going to go. 'This thing is not necessarily going to end up online,' he said. 'A number of us – not just record retailers but other retailers in Britain – believe e-commerce is going to end up through the TV.'[60]

Stuart Rowe says that the tensions between traditional retail and the labels at this time were explicitly and acidly playing out across the pages of the music trade press, but there were also, behind the scenes at the major retailers, bitter turf wars being fought.

As the person leading HMV's digital strategy, he says he found himself in the crosshairs repeatedly.

He helped launch HMV's first e-commerce website, building on the existing HMV Direct, which was initially a mail order offering. As it was initially a small operation, there was not much thought put into stock control. They used the retailer's flagship London store as their stockroom for a while until things became politically untenable.

'We used the Oxford Circus store as the warehouse to replenish the sales that were going through the website,' he says. 'That was really unpopular internally. Really, really unpopular.'

How unpopular?

'We were fulfilling stock from the store which was messing up the stock positions at the store itself,' reveals Rowe. 'That actually culminated in one of my guys having a fight with one of the store guys in a pub on a Friday night.'

He says the HMV website quickly became profitable, saying its turnover was 'in the millions', putting that in context by suggesting that the Oxford Street store would turn over around £30 million in a year. 'The website very quickly became the equivalent of a very good store,' he says. 'And I think that suited everybody.'

To try and avoid more Friday night punch-ups in the pub, Rowe was on a diplomatic mission to ease the rest of the company into digital retail. Speaking at sales conferences to store managers, many of whom had been in the business since before the CD launched, he had to be careful not to spook them and to underline their continuing importance to the company.

He says, 'All the speeches at the store manager conferences were reassuring, but also saying, "Look, we are pioneers and we are at the cutting edge of what we're doing. We're taking the time and we're not just going to crash and burn the whole market. We're going to be sensible pioneers of something that will happen in the future." That was really the way that was done.'

The biggest challenge was around pricing. The economics of online retail were very different to high street retail. There were warehousing and fulfilment overheads, but they were not buckling under the weight of city centre store rents and large staffing bills. A retailer like HMV had to pitch its online prices to compete with the likes of CDnow and Amazon, which were already significantly undercutting not just the bricks-and-mortar music specialists but also the supermarkets. There was enormous downward pressure on pricing and no online retailer could ignore this.

'I had to price the HMV websites in line with what was going on online,' says Rowe. 'That caused a lot of friction internally. Particularly where some of the HMV own brand or exclusive product was being put up there and we were making decisions on the fly as to how to price it. So if you had an exclusive box set and then we had it cheaper on online competitor stores then, understandably, the product director would go, "Why the hell are you doing that?" I'd say, "The disparity between our exclusive version and the normal version is so big that it just looks ridiculous, so we won't sell any – so we can discount it." There was quite a lot of friction around that.'

The expansion of HMV online at this time was, according to Brian McLaughlin, ultimately little more than 'a bit of window dressing' and felt like a token gesture rather than a signpost to a new and very different future. 'The view was that we had to be seen to be in this new world that was coming,' he tells me. 'But I don't really think that it added up, in reality, to very much.'

In sharp contrast, Simon Wright says that Virgin was taking it all extremely seriously. The entire digital agenda was being set by Virgin founder Richard Branson.

'Richard is very good at thinking ahead, and he is invariably right, even though he doesn't know why he's right,' says Wright. 'He is very good at thinking like a customer. He'd already seen the writing on the wall. He would have said something like, "Well, surely as the internet gets bigger and bigger and people are listening to their music or playing games or watching films [online], what are we going to do with the stores?" And I would have said to him, "Well, we have the most diverse stores. Our competitors are more entrenched in music than we are. Our stores are more like lifestyle stores, albeit over 50 per cent of our sales are music." Don't get me wrong, we were very dependent on music.'

He suggests that the zeitgeist was crackling with indicators of transformation in 1999 and that it would have been a corporate dereliction of duty to have ignored or dismissed this.

'Different retailers, different record companies and artists were all experimenting to some degree, dipping their first toe in the water,' he says. 'You couldn't fail to know that something was going to change that year.'

He adds, '[Branson] was starting to ask questions in 1998 and 1999. Just at a very basic level. But he was seeing things happening across various industries to do with the internet. He was very quickly going, '2 + 2 – this is a problem.' When you're in it, you don't see it as the same problem.'

Glen Ward had launched HMV Direct in 1996 but left the company in 1998 to join Virgin Megastore and bring the brand into the US, opening the first stores there in April 1999. He regards that year as a pivotal one for the music business and retail. 'From a retail perspective, things were in a state of flux,' he says. 'It was just realising that, as with any business, nothing's immune from innovation.'

He says the trick was always in balancing the needs of the high street side of the company with the ambitions of the online arm, having them synchronise with each other but not cannibalise each other.

'We always tried to maintain – or at least I did when I was running the store business and the online – that they weren't to be mutually exclusive,' he says. 'We were trying desperately to overlap and there was the experience of the physical store, which people still enjoyed, and there was the opportunity and the 24-hour nature of being able to shop online. But we always tried to incorporate one without the other. So we had digital listening devices that we developed in conjunction with Microsoft which could scan any CD in the store and [let you] listen to anything, going back to the glory days of listening. But then there was burning a CD in store, all legit and licensed. But online, we were very swift to embrace the premise that you should utilise the technology to help with discovery of music. That was very much fundamental in our specialist nature.'

Reflecting on it today, Ward says that he never felt threatened by the emerging technologies ('It was just change – nothing is immune from innovation'), but perhaps wishes they had done more to move with the times.

'It was a real rollercoaster, but we should have embraced it more,' he suggests. 'I tried desperately with the online offerings and physical stores, the interface with the stores, to embrace that. I always fought that corner. There was a recognition that there was more to music than just music.'

Wadsworth says there was a huge amount of denial going on among many of the more established retailers about the need to evolve and the speed at which they should evolve.

'I could understand that nervousness, but I did feel that there was a lot of Luddism going on with them,' he says. 'I do remember, even as late as 2000 and 2001, having conversations with some of the heads of those retail chains, who were saying, "You don't think this digital thing's going to catch on, do you?" We knew that, of course, it was going to be the next big way of consuming music, in whatever way it came. Who knew how it was going to come? But they were in denial. They really thought that there was a way of heading this off at the pass.'

One way the retailers considered heading this upheaval off at the pass was to try and get the record companies to slow down, or even halt, their transition into digital. To force them to listen, the retailers decided to declare, or least heavily intoned, all-out war with the labels.

WITHDRAWAL SYMPTOMS: RETAILERS THREATEN TO DUMP MUSIC ENTIRELY (OR DO THEY?)

It was always going to happen. As the love/hate relationship between record labels and retailers tilted further from the former and more towards the latter, cracks were going to appear, threats were going to be made and bluffs were going to be called.

There was no single, seismic moment, but rather a series of events that snowballed and reached the point where retailers, partly in all seriousness and partly as a negotiation tactic, threatened to pull out of music entirely.

The labels, sensing disaster on the horizon, moved to mitigate as much of the oncoming problems as they could. Some of their measures were tokenistic, but others were intended to bring stability and end the hostilities.

The first major flashpoint of 1999 was around *Synkronized*, the fourth studio album from Jamiroquai. It was coming off the back of 1996's international hit album *Travelling Without Moving* and, as such, was a priority for both Sony Music and the retailers. It was released via the Work Group imprint in the US, but in late May, Sony Music Distribution moved to delay internet sales of the album on physical formats amid concerns that it would damage opening sales in traditional record shops internationally.

'Sony is concerned that online sales could hurt brick-and-mortar sales outside the States and has requested that e-commerce sites not ship the album until after its international street date,' wrote *Billboard*. A source from Valley Media, the online fulfilment distributor, told the publication: 'We've received a flurry of calls from Sony about the Jamiroquai release and Sony's reasoning is that they don't want to endanger the regional markets.'

Other online retailers, including CDnow and Amazon, were contacted by Sony, who insisted they delay international shipments.[61]

'We have a policy against exporting product outside of the US, and we don't condone it,' Danny Yarbrough, chairman of Sony Music Distribution, told *Billboard*. 'We always request that all retailers not ship overseas. These are not new policies.'[62]

Normally records were released on different days in different markets, but for major albums there was a push to have a single international release date. The aptly named *Synkronized* was originally planned for 14 June for release, but the US promotion for the album was scheduled for the week before and could not be moved. There were suggestions of veiled threats from Sony that if any online retailers broke the release date (i.e. shipped early) they would be subject to future releases from the label being shipped to them late. Ship this early, ran the threat, and you will have to ship everything else late as we will stop you getting stock in time.[63]

This was symptomatic of a business that was used to operating on a territory-by-territory basis struggling to navigate into a world that was now, to all intents and purposes, borderless – and doing so in a way that did not infuriate long-standing retail partners. It was an issue that was only going to become more pronounced.

As part of an international peace accord, EMI was trying different things in different markets to show the retailers that, yes, they valued them and, yes, they would continue to support them even as online (both physical and digital) sales grew. There was, however, a major release by a major artist on EMI coming later in the year that would blow apart all the good will that the company was trying to build up with retailers. The next chapter will pick that apart in much greater detail.

In late August, Capitol Records (part of EMI North America) announced that its plans to release the new album by country superstar Garth Brooks as a download had been scrapped. It was an unusual album as it was Brooks masquerading as a fictional alternative rock musician called Chris Gaines. Even so, as an album by one of the biggest solo acts in the world, EMI had huge expectations for it.

The marketing angle would have been that this was the first album by a major league country star to get a simultaneous download release, indicating that both EMI and Brooks were agents for change and digitally progressive.

Pat Quigley, the president of Capitol Records Nashville, said there were several reasons for pulling *Garth Brooks In. . . The Life Of Chris Gaines* as a download. He claimed the digital distributors were not interested in doing it. One source said the distributors did not want to rush to set it up for a 24 August release.

Quigley told *Billboard*, 'I believe that you can create a lot of awareness through having the album downloaded. But instead of this being a Garth story, it came back to me that the software companies were hoping to make this a downloading story.'[64]

He claimed some of the distributors wanted to piggyback on the marketing budget for the album to help establish the downloading format. '[I]t came back to me that while merchants were thankful to be included as a site where the download could be obtained, they weren't really gung-ho to do it,' he said. 'Garth Brooks will only work through the retailers. For all the companies trying to bypass the retailer, this will put pressure on any record company to make the digital download an extension of their retail distribution and not an alternative distribution. We are a brick-and-mortar-driven business. For Garth and me, that will always be so.'[65]

Jay Samit, SVP of new media at EMI, says this was in part down to Brooks not renegotiating his contract with the label to allow for digital sales of his music. He says there were a handful of major EMI acts on a list that he was unable to get onto digital services during his tenure at the company – and Brooks was one of them.

'Garth Brooks was one of those artists that I never got off the list,' he says. 'One of the big five. He had no interest in trying to understand that world. When people would get on my case and call him names, I'd say, "You go in a room and come out forty-five minutes later with something three minutes long that earns you $40 million. Then you can have an opinion. He's a genius at what he does. He's not supposed to understand what we do".'

He then reveals there was another issue, a more tonsorial issue, behind the brakes being pulled on the album download idea. He says, 'The one part of the Chris Gaines thing – and I sat in meetings with Garth – that he didn't think through in his creative idea was that he would have to tour wearing that wig.[66] He's a big guy. There's no way you're disguising who you are. This isn't like Clark Kent's magic glasses where you can't recognise he's Superman. And that was the end of the Chris Gaines thing.'

(In 2014, Brooks set up the GhostTunes services to start to sell his music directly as downloads rather than go through Apple's iTunes Music Store or a similar third-party service.[67] It barely lasted two years and was folded into Amazon Music.[68] Brooks has still not licensed his music for streaming and so his catalogue remains unavailable on services such as Spotify and Apple Music.)

EMI made a peace offering of sorts to the retailers later in the year, but some within the company suggest this was more a last-ditch attempt to drive sales of a career misstep album.

(The album did go to number two on the US charts and is registered as double Platinum, with Platinum status being awarded by the RIAA for sales of one million.[69] His previous album, 1997's *Sevens*, was released under his own name. It went to number one in the US and was certified Diamond by the RIAA, meaning it had sold over ten million copies. Other albums, notably 1990's *No Fences* and 1991's *Ropin' The Wind* were also certified Diamond.[70] The Chris Gaines album significantly under-performed compared to many of his earlier releases).

In late November, just as the crucial Christmas gifting period was kicking in, EMI was offering retailers a $3 rebate on all Chris Gaines CDs.

'In exchange for the rebate, retailers have been asked to lower the price of the Capitol album and give a good positioning in stores,' wrote *Billboard*. The promotion was set to run from 14 November to 9 January. Pat Quigley claimed it was just a 'price promotion' and not an act of desperation. 'It's not to pump up Garth's numbers,' he insisted. 'It's just not what we promised retailers in profit. I'm trying to help them sell enough units at full margin so they can still make their Christmas profit on Garth and tell their stockholders Capitol's a good partner.'[71]

Billboard spoke to sources who claimed that three million copies of the album had been shipped in the US but noted that sales tracking company SoundScan was reporting that just 663,000 had been sold so far. The album was listed at $17.98, but *Billboard* wrote that Capitol wanted retailers to mark it down as low as possible, rack it at the front of the store and have signage for it.[72]

In the UK, despite butting heads with the likes of HMV on a regular basis, EMI was keen to return to something even vaguely resembling unanimity in its dealings with the high street brands. Part of this was to launch a password-protected website called Pulse365.com to offer to a range of partners, but particularly retailers, up-to-date information on its marketing and promotion plans.

EMI told *Billboard* in early October that it would be updated '24 hours a day, seven days a week as marketing and promotional plans develop.'[73] The idea was credited to Tony Wadsworth, EMI UK & Ireland's chairman and CEO. It would, reported *Music Week*, provide details 'on everything from advertising strategies for projects to artist TV appearances simply by typing in a password.'[74]

Wadsworth reportedly had the idea because retailers were always complaining they had not been told what was going on. He also wanted to show how labels could start to think progressively around the internet. Delivering his keynote at EMI's sales conference in London in September 1999, he said, 'There's so much time spent talking about the protection of copyrights which is crucial, but it makes record companies sound extremely negative when it comes to the internet. In fact, nothing but good can come out of it.'[75]

Reflecting back on it now, Wadsworth suggests Pulse365 would have been a sop to the retailers, a way to placate them while not detailing EMI's wider digital goals.

'Setting up the new media division and Pulse365 would not have been unconnected,' he says. 'My head of sales, Mike McMahon, would have been coming to me saying, "We're getting so much flak from retail over all this new media stuff." And so I said, "OK, tell you what, I'll put you in charge of it. And Fergal Gara [head of the new media team] can report to you." So there was a central new media division with a very strong reporting line to the sales division. That was a defensive move by me to make sure that anything we did in marketing new media didn't harm our core business at the time – physical sales through conventional retailers.'

It was an unstable and uncertain armistice that was barely holding at points during the year, with threats of boycotts being thrown about by retailers. This was a deep and far-reaching battle for control over the present and the future of retail, with skirmishes occasionally tipping over into heavy threats of nuclear war.

In the Netherlands in early 1999, major retail chain Free Record Shop felt that the record labels were not doing enough to act on 'CD cloning' (i.e. consumers burning CD-Rs), a major problem in the country as covered in Chapter 5. The chain said it would boycott labels' products if they did not act swiftly and decisively here, giving them a deadline of 1 April to outline their plan of action with regard to CD burners being openly and cheaply available.[76]

Jaan Da Silva, the general manager of the Free Record Shop chain, told *Billboard* that he had gone to industry trade event Midem earlier in the year to lobby labels and the IFPI about this. Dutch record label trade body the NVPI said it agreed with him about the scale of the problem but felt the April deadline did not leave them enough time to formulate a plan. He said he would be happy if they engaged and wanted to extend the deadline, just as long as they appeared to be doing something. Otherwise he would seek to source stock from outside the Netherlands.[77]

This was more of a benign threat against the labels, really something to spur them into action, but things took a heavier turn later in the year in the UK with the two leading specialist music retailers firing multiple shots across the bows of the record companies.

In late September, Brian McLaughlin used his speech at the BARD AGM in London to wheel out some heavy artillery. He was angered by the moves by labels to offer albums digitally before they were available in stores. If they went heavy on this, McLaughlin said he would have no qualms about boycotting the labels and artists involved.

'It is unlikely we would stock it or the back catalogue of the artist in question,' he said, adding that 'feeling is running extremely high' and '[r]ecord retailers in the UK are not going to stand for it.'[78]

He added, 'We're obviously responsive to the huge opportunities offered by e-commerce – indeed, all the leading retailers have invested considerable resources in launching their own promotional and transactional sites – but we do seek a level playing field in making music available to everyone at the same time.'[79]

His rabble-rousing speech was triggered by the actions of one label and one artist in one country in particular (covered in the next chapter). It was intended to stand as a stern warning against other labels and other artists trying something similar. 'While I recognise that this is a US initiative and can't be downloaded by fans in the UK, we must be alert to more record companies attempting similar ventures, and possibly paying no regard to the relationship between suppliers and retailers in the UK,' he said.[80]

In December, Richard Branson stepped forward and warned the record business that if it failed to properly commit to high street music retail – and to make clear its plans for online and downloads – then he would have no other option but to withdraw from selling music at Virgin Megastore shops around the UK.

'Virgin Group chairman Richard Branson has issued a stark ultimatum to record companies: tell us your retail plans, or we'll focus our business elsewhere,' reported *Music Week*. 'Branson is pressing for a top-level summit on the future of music retailing, saying his company and other music dealers urgently need to know the direction in which the music industry believes retailing is heading – or he will switch investment to other "more profitable retail areas".'[81]

Branson said, 'All these record companies are meeting behind closed doors, working out the future as they see it, whether it's the internet, cutting out record shops, downloading or whatever, but without involving music retailers in the discussions [. . .] If the industry doesn't want music stores in the future we need to know. We can and will turn the stores over to selling other products if it's the only way to survive. If the industry wants to work with us, it should be telling us.'[82]

Those 'other products' would include something Virgin was heavily backing already. 'If we don't get the support of the record industry either we turn them over completely to all mobile phones or at least devote more space to them,' Branson warned.[83]

The threats were deemed serious enough by *Music Week* to warrant an editorial on them.

'Should we believe a word that Richard Branson says?' asked *Music Week* editor Ajax Scott. 'His knack for headline-grabbing publicity stunts sometimes makes it hard to take them seriously. But he meant every word of a speech in Glasgow last week, by all accounts [. . .] It is worth remembering that Branson's music retail business is different from that of rivals like HMV. It is just one part of a portfolio that stretches from planes and trains to clothes and financial services. Although the music was the foundation on which his empire was built, it is no longer at its heart.'[84]

He added, 'But there is more behind his words than opportunism. Pricing and concerns about the internet are worrying every retailer in the land, not to mention record companies. And the pain is compounded by the fact that there simply isn't a broad enough sweep of big sellers at the moment to guarantee a steady flow of people into record stores. Retail rivals might welcome a tactical retreat by Virgin. But the business as a whole needs it like a hole in the head.'

There can be a lot of spiky and angry words tossed around in the heat of the moment, where brash statements play out across the pages of the music trade press, but they are often just part of a game of PR that both sides know the other is willingly and complicitly engaged in. And then there can be wrathful words that are intended as aerial bombardments, where the rage is real and not pantomime.

With more than two decades' distance, I spoke to labels and retailers about this scrimmage happening through 1999, reaching its bitter crescendo just before Christmas – the most important time of the year for labels and retailers – to ask them how things got to this stage and if the threats being tossed so frequently around were real or if they just amounted to so much bluster, bloviation and bravado.

Brian McLaughlin does not say how far he was prepared to push it, but he suggests that 1999 was a tipping point year for relationships between the heads of the major retailers and the heads of the major labels. He felt that, ultimately, the labels badly undervalued the retailers and so the threats he was issuing at the BARD AGM could perhaps be understood as an attempt to get the labels to understand how valuable retail was to them.

'There were some very professional chairmen and managing directors of these companies,' he says. 'They were all different in their own way, but they were all bonded together by the one thing that was, "I don't want us giving him – HMV – any more money than we have to because it'll just never end." I don't really think that we were treated fairly in relation to how much investment and how much risk we put into the pot.'

I ask Simon Wright if the apparent fulminations of Richard Branson in December 1999 were just posturing for political gain or if he was seriously considering pulling out of music completely.

'It was somewhere in between,' suggests Wright. 'We were not going to shut stores immediately. But he would definitely have stopped investing.'

Stuart Rowe says the threats from HMV to boycott releases and pull out of music if labels were prioritising digital over the high street were 'deadly serious' at the time, estimating that Virgin Megastore and HMV convectively controlled around 30 per cent or 35 per cent of the music retail sector in the UK at the time. Losing them would have been a disaster to the labels, and the retailers knew it.

'They were unbelievably powerful – and that power [is something that] Brian used. One of the reasons why they loved him and hated him at the same time was because he was taking all the marketing income, opening more stores and therefore getting more market share and getting more power over them. So he was deadly serious about that. And so was Branson at the time. They were going round to each one of them and saying, "Here's the new Robbie Williams. It'll go to number one. How many do you want?" "Oh, we'll buy 300.' 'What do you mean 300? You're pissing us around!" That power was used in normal negotiations, actually, but also around this as well. Brian was really a tough and courageous MD. He was absolutely up for a fight.'

The threats were real, says Cliff Fluet, and they were taken very seriously within Warner Music. It was, however, less about making music available digitally than it was about making music available digitally on a *specific format.*

He says, 'I saw memos from the retailers that said, "If you put any of your repertoire on MP3, at 5 p.m. on Friday all your materials will be removed from our store."'

The biggest names in physical retail were, according to Fluet, applying enormous pressure on the labels not to deviate from a formula that had the high street at the centre of everything they did. 'Physical retailers were holding a gun to the puppy's head,' he says.

There was, suggests Raoul Chatterjee, a lot of diplomacy being deployed by the digital teams within labels to ensure they did not do anything that would send the retailers into a rage.

'I was in the new media world, but I also certainly had lots of scars on my shins from working with retailers,' he says. 'I knew the challenges intimately because I was right in amongst it with the sales team. I was in every single internal meeting and the regular planning meetings with the retailers about how their businesses were going.'

There were occasionally explicit commands during record company meetings to not risk anything that would upset or infuriate the traditional retailers. Richard Ogden, SVP of Sony Music Entertainment Europe, says, 'The thrust of one meeting that I remember being in was, "What's Brian McLaughlin going to do? What's he going to say? Is he going to penalise us heavily if we start selling digital music? We have to stop it happening, not facilitate it happening." I don't remember there being any controversy about online retail. The only question was selling music digitally without a box and without a disc. That was a no-no. And the people making it a no-no were the bricks-and-mortar retailers.'

In the US, retailers were punishing labels and companies that were doing a lot more than tentatively dipping a toe into the digital waters. Atomic Pop, as a label that had digital at its core but still released records on physical formats, found itself at the sharp end of the matter according to Al Teller, its founder.

'There were some retailers who actually said they would not stock our physical goods because we were cannibalising their business by virtue of the downloads,' he says. 'Here was always my bottom line: if they don't want to take our records, they don't have to take our records. Good luck to them. Just good luck to them. We had the same pressure put on us by [big retailers] at times that if we didn't give them an exclusive or a better deal or whatever, they were not going to take a record. My attitude was always, "They don't have to buy the record".'

Intonations of retailer boycotts were, claims John Kennedy, so frequent as to be yawningly unexceptional. In the cut and thrust of business, it was something the heads of the biggest retailers would reach for if they felt things were not going their way.

'Threatening to pull our records off the shelf wasn't something that happened in 1999 – it happened every year!' he says, laughing. 'Woolworths were huge at the time and every time Woolworths got a new buyer, they'd ask for a meeting, and they'd come into my office and I'd give him a cup of tea. I'd say, "I know what you're going to tell me." "What do you mean?" "I know what you're going to tell me. Can I have a guess? You're going to tell me that, if I don't give you bigger discounts, you're going to take all my records off the shelves." That disarmed them a bit because they thought they were coming with something new. We just had to live with this all the time.'

Kennedy implies that the threats might have been delivered loudly by the retailers, but they ultimately rang hollow. 'One of the great things about the music industry is we have more unique product than lots of other industries,' he says. 'You could get a vacuum cleaner from different places, but you can't get the Shania Twain album from anywhere other than us. So that puts us in quite a strong place. I asked one of them [from Woolworths] what they did before this. They said, "Well, I was in charge of garden furniture worldwide." And I said, "I bet you can go to your garden furniture suppliers in the UK and say you'll get it from Korea if they don't give you a better price. You can't do that with us".'

Even though they would not admit it publicly, the retailers were not so concerned about labels putting out catalogue titles digitally. They were always a stocking issue in the stores anyway and a deep catalogue title might only sell a handful of copies a year, but retailers felt compelled to carry them as it made them look encyclopaedic. The bulk of their business was from the Top 40 sales and new releases were their lifeblood.

One major artist, however, was fully in the grip of the digital revolution, completely enthused by the boundless possibilities of the internet and utterly unconcerned about the internecine warfare (or the threat of it) between labels and retailers. Their digital evangelism was something they wanted to shift from the abstract and put fully into practice. If digital was the future, then this most restless and inquisitive of artists had to lead by example, as they had done so many times over the previous three decades.

For the release of their 22nd studio album, they were going to sell it digitally two weeks before it could be bought physically in the shops.

David Bowie could sense the *coup d'état* coming and wanted to storm the barricades first. And damn the consequences.

BOWIE

CHAPTER 15

Cyberspace Oddity: David Bowie's *hours* . . . Album Causes Retail Uproar

('Grind control. . .')

It is far from his best album, and certainly not even his best album of the 1990s, but *Hours. . .* is David Bowie's most significant album of the decade. Not because of the music on it, but rather because of how it was released.

As covered in the previous chapter, the plan to release the *Garth Brooks In. . . The Life Of Chris Gaines* album digitally was pulled at the eleventh hour by EMI/Capitol Records Nashville. It, however, was going to have its digital release synchronise with its physical release.

Where Bowie was bucking convention was that his would be the first by a major artist on a major label to be released as a download *before* it was released physically. The download would be available to purchase through digital retailers and the singer's own website on 21 September and would then be available on CD in traditional retail outlets on 5 October.

This was only for the US release of the album. Its international release would be a lot more conventional.

Writing about it in August, *Rolling Stone* called it a 'cyber-coup', saying it was a continuation of Bowie's fascination with releasing music online, which he started by offering the 'Telling Lies' single online in 1997. He had enthusiastically embraced webcasting as well as creating his own ISP with BowieNet (see Chapter 1).[1]

'I couldn't be more pleased to have the opportunity of moving the music industry closer to the process of making digital downloads available as the norm and not the exception,' is how Bowie explained it in a statement on the album's release.[2]

With his record company mindful of the fiery politics around MP3 and the ongoing efforts of SDMI, the album would only be downloadable as Liquid Audio or Windows Media files, with an emphasis on DRM.

Bowie understood this was much more symbolic than it was commercial, tempering expectations by saying that sales would be low – but this would be a staging post into the future.

'We are all aware that broadband opportunities are not yet available to the overwhelming majority of people, and therefore expect the success of this experiment to be measured in hundreds and not thousands of downloads,' he said. 'However, just as color television broadcasts and film content on home video tapes were required first steps to cause their industries to expand consumer use, I am hopeful that this small step will lead to larger leaps by myself and others ultimately giving consumers greater choices and easier access to the music they enjoy.'[3]

There had been experimentation with streaming albums, as opposed to singles, ahead of, or at the time of, their physical release. It was not just independents leading the way here, with the major labels occasionally rolling up their sleeves and proving, despite what the naysayers claimed, that they were not total Luddites or busy collapsing under 'anticipatory anxiety.'

In early 1998, Virgin Records/EMI had made Massive Attack's *Mezzanine* available for streaming in full online at the same time as its physical release, albeit previewing it track-by-track over several weeks.[4] At the time, the BPI in the UK cautioned against this, suggesting that such streaming experiments could increase the possibility of streamed albums being pirated by tech-savvy individuals and burned to CD.[5]

This did not stop other major labels or their acts from experimenting occasionally here. Both Def Leppard and Red Hot Chili Peppers, who shared a management company in Q Prime, were making their latest albums, respectively *Euphoria* and *Californication*, available to stream in full on 4 June 1999, four days before the records would be in the shops.[6]

'As with any internet promotion, we were concerned about security,' said Bob Merlis of Warner Bros., the Red Hot Chili Peppers' label. 'But we felt good about this since it was not downloadable. Getting airplay is getting airplay, you just have to define air.'[7]

The Bowie album, especially for an artist so interested in new technologies and also so keenly aware of harnessing the power of media interest in him to his own ends, was designed from the ground up to be a significant step forward from what others had tried in the recent past.

In 1999, Bowie was interviewed by Jeremy Paxman for the BBC's *Newsnight* show where he talked about his career, his art and, most invigoratingly for him, the internet. The sixteen-minute interview is still available on the BBC website and is frequently shared, especially since Bowie's death in January 2016, as evidence of his startling prescience with regard to the impact the internet would have on art, politics and society.

'I don't think we've even seen the tip of the iceberg,' he told a wearily cynical Paxman. 'I think the potential of what the internet is going to do to society, both good and bad, is unimaginable. I think we're actually on the cusp of something exhilarating and terrifying.'[8]

Paxman, in his arch way, suggested it was just 'a tool', which saw Bowie spring into action. 'No, it's not,' he said. 'No. No – it's an *alien life form*!'

He went on to say that the internet would completely change the dynamics of consumption. 'The actual context and the state of content is going to be so different to anything that we can really envisage at the moment, where the interplay between the user and the provider will be so in simpatico it's going to crush our ideas of what mediums are all about,' he said.[9]

Paxman, off camera at this point, presumably pulled a face. But Bowie was proven right again and again. He was not the first person to say any of these things: many of his points had already been kicking around the discussion threads on the Pho List (see Chapter 5) for a number of years. But, as he had done so many times in his career, Bowie was synthesising ideas from the margins and delivering them to the mainstream. He did not come up with many of these arguments, but he was a catalyst for them reaching a much wider audience.

Perhaps there was hesitancy about giving the plans for *Hours. . .* away too early, or else the plans themselves were changing frequently, but in mid August 1999 *Music Week* in the UK ran a capsule-sized news story with the headline 'Net gets first taste of Bowie LP.' It was suggested that a teaser campaign, featuring short clips from the album, would be the main marketing and promotion angle.

'David Bowie is to preview tracks from his forthcoming album *Hours. . .* on the web prior to its retail release by Virgin in October,' it wrote. 'Starting this Friday (August 13), Bowie will be posting forty-five-second snippets of each of the album's ten tracks at weekly intervals. He will also gradually reveal the album's artwork, unveiling three sections at a time on the web every few days. The campaign can be found at: www.davidbowie.com.' That was the full news coverage in *Music Week* at the time.[10]

Early the following month, *Music Week* was given more details about the release. Perhaps because it was primarily a US story and *Music Week* was a UK publication, it was still treated as a NIB (a 'news in brief') story.

'Virgin Records is releasing David Bowie's new album, *Hours. . .*, on the internet two weeks before it goes on sale at retail,' it said. 'The album and an extra track will be available via retail websites from September 21 at a slightly lower price than the ultimate retail price when the title becomes available in-store on October 4.'[11]

There was no mention of the consequence of this move or how it threatened to upend the already delicate *entente cordiale* between record labels and retailers.

Being a US publication, and this being a US-only digital release, *Billboard* devoted considerably more column inches to dissecting the story and trying to anticipate its implications.

In its 11 September issue, *Billboard* ran a lengthy piece under the headline 'Virgin Pulls Out All Stops For Bowie Set.' It was described as 'a complex marketing plan that heavily utilizes the Internet and advanced technology', noting that fifty different retail partners in the US would be involved and they could set their own price, although it was expected to sell for around the same price as the CD when it became available. The download version would be bolstered with an extra track, but it would only be available for the two-week window before the album would be available physically.[12]

Choosing his words diplomatically, Andrew Pollock, VP of marketing for HMV North America, told *Billboard*, 'Obviously we prefer to stick with more traditional methods. But this is the wave of the future, and we all need to start preparing for that [. . .] More than anything, it seems like a good way of generating some public interest in the project, which is fine.'[13]

Billboard implied that Capitol Nashville's plans, albeit subsequently scrapped, for the Chris Gaines/Garth Brooks album were going to be 'via similar means.' This implied the album could have been available as a download first but without actually confirming if that was the case.

Jay Samit, SVP of new media at EMI Recorded Music, told *Billboard*,

'This is an experiment that we believe is a foreshadowing of the future. Digital distribution is going to be part of the process of releasing music within the next couple of years. It's a thrill for us to start out with an artist who has tremendous vision about technology.'[14]

Bowie himself provided a comment to *Billboard* on what this all meant. '[Digital distribution is] a major part of the future for the music business,' he said. 'In general, the internet is gradually changing the face of the industry. Every day there are remarkable new options available. I find the exploration of these new avenues endlessly fascinating [. . .] It's a wonderful way of giving something special to the fans as well as testing the waters for the project. Ideally, the previews will whet many an appetite for the new album.'[15]

He called the teaser campaign, mentioned above, a 'musical striptease', where paying members of BowieNet were given forty-five-second snippets of songs and glimpses of sections of the sleeve artwork for two months before release.

Billboard noted that Bowie would not tour the album, but there would be substantial online and offline marketing, with Bowie making a series of high-profile appearances on TV shows to push the album. 'We're covering the full spectrum of possibilities for this project,' said Nancy Berry, vice chairman of Virgin Media Group. 'David has a tremendous amount of energy and drive. Clearly this project is very important to him.'[16]

Alan Edwards, Bowie's PR in the UK, questions the subsequent narrative that this was all completely stage managed by Bowie and that EMI/Virgin simply had to acquiesce to his demands. 'I'm not sure that the decision to issue *Hours. . .* via download was his,' he says. 'Certainly there would have been conversations with Virgin Records.'

In the 25 September issue of *Billboard*, Virgin took out a full-page ad for the Bowie album, stressing how digitally pioneering it was while also highlighting his key media appearances as he promoted it (including the Much Music Award, *Saturday Night Live* and VH1, where he would be Artist Of The Month for October).

'With this album, David Bowie becomes the first major recording artist to team with a major record label and retail to make available an entire album via download at over fifty retail sites, with a bonus track, for two weeks starting September 21,' said the ad. Then in slightly smaller, almost apologetic, font below it said, 'Album in stores October 5.'[17]

As part of the marketing ahead of the *Hours. . .* album, Bowie ran a competition asking fans to collaborate on the track 'What's Really

Happening', which was posted in demo form online. Fans were asked to help finish the lyrics.

Confusingly Bowie claimed there were over two hundred thousand entries but Bowie's own official site said eighty thousand people sent in lyrics. Alex Grant, a 20-year-old fan from Ohio, won and the recording of the song was streamed online using a 360-degree camera.[18]

Grant received a songwriting credit on the song alongside Bowie and Reeves Gabrels. It was described on Bowie's website as 'the first true cyber-song.' Bowie added, 'The most gratifying part of the evening for me was being able to encourage Alex and his pal Larry to sing on the song that he, Alex, had written. It was a cool way to finish the session off.'[19]

The album was only available in the US in its digital incarnation before the CD release, but British retailers were concerned this was the start of something disruptive that could undermine their business.

Brian McLaughlin, chairman of music retailer trade body BARD and MD of HMV Europe, addressed the Bowie campaign and album release specifically at BARD's AGM in London on 23 September. He insisted that UK labels must 'make their international affiliates aware of the potentially disrupting effects such internet initiatives will have if they can be accessed in this country.'

He added, 'Retail has always been about giving the fans the greatest possible access to music and the internet obviously widened our scope in achieving these ambitions. This exciting development, however, must be managed to the benefit of all the parties, including not only the retailers, the artists and record companies, but also the consumer.'[20]

While there were lots of heavy hints about a retailer boycott of labels or artists if they tried something similar to the Bowie album in the UK, much of this could be put down to posturing. In the Netherlands, however, one leading retailer chose action over words.

Free Record Shop had already been calling for labels to do more about CD-R piracy (see Chapter 14), but when Bowie's album was made available as a download in the US before the CD release, it responded swiftly by claiming it would pull all his albums from the shelves of its shops.[21]

Jaan Da Silva, the commercial director of Free Record Shop, tried to be sanguine about it while still stressing that he believed labels were going against the interests of retailers. 'When someone just misses that one Miles Davis title, it's a perfect solution,' he said of the benefits of downloading. 'But if you put a new CD on the internet two weeks earlier than in the store, you make the store old-fashioned.'[22]

Alan Edwards says the album release 'created a lot of reaction, especially amongst retailers who were unhappy with the situation', but he does not recall any serious threats by UK retailers to pull the Bowie catalogue from their shelves.

This, perhaps, was down to some strategic damage limitation by Bowie and his PR team.

'Things were smoothed over with HMV through Gennaro [Castaldo, HMV PR] and helped by Julian Stockton in our office,' explains Edwards. 'David went and did an in-store signing session at HMV. I don't remember it creating that much controversy at the time, to be honest. If Bowie albums were removed from the shelves we weren't made aware.'

He adds, 'It was a moment of transition in the music industry and media opinion was that this was the long-awaited changing of the guard. Rod Stewart, The Who, Fleetwood Mac, [Mick] Jagger and, of course, Bowie were deemed "old" and attention shifted to Oasis, Blur, Robbie Williams, the Spice Girls et cetera. It was very much an end of the century vibe. The internet was the harbinger of change.'

In the US, it was not just the traditional physical retailers who felt they were being sidelined or undermined. A feature in the 12 November issue of *Billboard* examined the issue and the growing calls for parity between online and the high street in terms of music sales.

Some operating in the digital space claimed they were not originally included in Virgin's plans for the Bowie album and, like the squeaky wheel getting the grease, had to demand they were involved. Alayna Hill, co-owner of Record Archive in Rochester, New York, said, 'I wasn't asked to participate in the Bowie download until I complained. Whoever is brainstorming these comprehensive marketing campaigns, you have to offer it to everyone.'[23]

Meanwhile, Carl Singmaster, president of Manifest, used his interview to bewail the fact that releasing an album as a download two weeks ahead of the physical disc is "driving customers to online and teaching them stores are not cool and [are] passé". He added, 'That is foolhardy, because no matter what they do for the internet, the bulk of sales will come from retail for the foreseeable future.'[24]

Bowie was not the only digital pioneer in the crosshairs. Atomic Pop was accused of regularly selling downloads at under the wholesale price offered to physical retailers. Newbury Comics in Boston termed such practices 'obnoxious.' Retailers also worried that adding extra tracks to the download version of an album sent a message to fans that the CD was an incomplete or truncated version of the album.[25]

With tempers already frayed and a code red about to be declared, Bowie himself looked at the rage gripping the retail community and thought it could be cranked up a lot higher. Speaking to *USA Today*, he intoned that the end of the record shop (and, admittedly, the end of the record company) as it was understood in 1999 was coming. . . and it was coming fast.

'Mark my words. . . we are not going back to record companies and through shops,' he said, with *Billboard* quoting from the *USA Today* piece. 'Within five years it will have moved so spectacularly that no one will recognize the music business.'[26]

In his Retail Track column in the 13 November issue of *Billboard*, Ed Christman suggested that Bowie was making bold predictions that could not support their own weight, given that downloading was still incredibly niche. He wrote that EMI/Virgin had revealed that *Hours. . .* had sold just 989 downloads in its two-week exclusivity period. In its first week in bricks-and-mortar stores in the US, it sold 29,000 copies (and had thus far sold 56,000 physical copies). That would have put download sales, even with all the media attention, at under 2 per cent of total album sales.

'EMI and Virgin executives, like Atlantic executives before them, should not be embarrassed by the number of downloads the Bowie album generated,' wrote Christman. 'And like Atlantic, EMI and Virgin did a great job getting the word out about the availability of the download. But at the end of the day, the number of people *willing to pay* for music in the download format right now appears to be in the 1,000–2,000 range. And I would even question that number.'[27]

I interviewed Jay Samit in April 2022 about the Bowie album release and he reflected on it almost a quarter of a century on. 'Bowie was very forward thinking and excellent to work with,' he says. 'The one regret, which luckily nobody picked up on time, was that the album was called *Hours. . .* – and this is pre-broadband – which is exactly how long it took to download an album back then!'

Christman went on to speculate that a substantial chunk of those 989 download sales came from curious people in the music industry, as opposed to general consumers, who were merely 'checking out this newfangled downloading thingamajig.'

Christman then admitted that the whole process of downloading music had flummoxed him. 'I confess I tried, but I couldn't even figure out how to download the player, so never even got the chance to try to download the music,' he said.[28]

He did, however, accept that it was still incredibly early days for downloading music and that this Bowie album and other track download initiatives would help the industry get a feel for where and how things would move in the coming years.

Richard Cottrell, president/CEO of EMI Music Distribution, said, 'This was a first, and everyone was learning. Bowie was about creating press attention and working with retail so that the retailers would maintain the consumer link. But tremendous progress was made as a result of this.' He then added, 'To do it properly, you need about four weeks, now that the mechanism is in place. This galvanized retailers to get their digital-download facilities set up.'[29]

According to EMI, 23.9 per cent of consumers buying the Bowie album as a download needed technical assistance, but the label said that it was actually expecting that number to be higher.[30]

The *Billboard* piece also claimed that, while the download was supposed to be restricted to the US, some consumers in the UK and Japan were still able to buy it on its first day of digital release. EMI insisted this was down to a 'technology encoding error' but stressed it had been quickly fixed and the territorial restrictions in the software were set up again.[31]

Charly Prevost, VP of retail marketing and promotion at Liquid Audio, claimed the download really had a shelf life of a week and that the majority of sales happened in the first two days. Credit cards were not billed until the download was completed, with Prevost saying that 'if they got tired and wanted to discontinue the download', they had a 48-hour window to cancel and not be charged.

'If your phone rang at that time, if you were using a mixed line, you had to start the whole process all over,' recalls Samit of the technical challenges of releasing a major album this early in the life of the internet. 'Tons of press, not a lot of people actually knew how to download an album.'

The full story behind why Virgin Records in the US did this was because, despite being owned by EMI since 1992,[32] Virgin was run as its own fiefdom and did not answer to EMI head office in the way, for example, Parlophone did. It had the muscle of a major behind it, but it had the operational structure of an independent.

'Virgin, organisationally, was a separate company,' explains Tony Wadsworth, head of EMI in the UK in 1999. 'They only became part of my responsibilities in 2001. They were still owned by EMI, but it was two separate companies. Paul Conroy was running Virgin and I was running EMI. We had different sales forces. It was at arm's length.'

I ask him if EMI in the UK would have considered releasing a major album in this way. 'Our reaction would have been that it was just not worth antagonising physical retail,' he says.

I then ask him if he was having to field irate calls from Virgin Megastore and HMV over what was happening in the US. 'Not in reaction to the David Bowie thing, no,' he says. 'I think that probably was targeted straight at Virgin who were doing it. But it was very clear from retail that anything like that would be met with a robust response.'

Stuart Rowe, general manager of direct and e-commerce for HMV Europe, suggests that a major label would not have attempted this in the UK in 1999 and that the US was picked because the retailers there would not have pushed back against it as strongly as retailers in other markets would have.

'I believe that they picked various countries to do these digital downloading tests where the retailers were weak,' he proposes. 'Think about America. You had Tower Records; they were a shambles. You had Blockbuster who did a lot of music, they weren't very well run and very decentralised. I firmly believe they did it in the markets where retail was not particularly strong. Then Brian [McLaughlin] just got up [in the UK] and said, "No, we're not having it." HMV could just literally say, "Right, take all of EMI off the front of the stores." Then suddenly they're no longer in the charts.'

He adds, 'That tells you the difference between the UK retailers and the US retailers. They just weren't as good. They weren't as commercial. They weren't as on it. That would never have happened in the UK. Never.'

The response of Virgin Megastore in the UK at the time *had* this happened there would have been to vigorously oppose it, claims Simon Wright, MD of Virgin Retail UK. He says, 'My reaction at the time would have been, "No, you can't do this. This is a major album release. You cannot sell it through a separate channel and go round the retailer. It's just not on".'

He says, speaking in 2022, that his reaction now would have been somewhat different and suggests that those up in arms over what Bowie had done were only exposing their myopia.

'I think that David Bowie understood his customer,' he says. 'That's what was going on there. He was catering to his customer demand. And he was the one with the foresight. If the record industry had had the mindset of David Bowie, it may have been able to ride this whole period much better.'

He expands on this point. 'When you're in the thick of it, you don't see it that way – because you don't know,' he says. 'The prevailing view would have been, "How dare you do this?" As a point of principle. "How dare you put out a major album through a channel that we cannot leverage?" There are a number of areas where you could contrast what the opinion is now in retrospect versus what the attitude was at the time. That's a very good example.'

In the US, there had been enormous secrecy around it and only a small group of executives were in the circle of trust, tinkering with every part of the release before making it public.

Jeremy Silver, vice president of new media at EMI, says the project was being led by Nancy Berry, vice chairman of Virgin Media Group as previously mentioned, and Ken Berry, president of EMI Recorded Music, and everything was conducted in secrecy to avoid the story leaking early.

'The feeling internally was hugely nervous,' says Silver. 'This was a very closely kept project. It had huge ramifications, but everyone was really, really nervous about it. This was after Bowie Bonds[33] so, in terms of his vision of what you could do with all of this stuff, this was just another instalment of it. We were all super excited. I've still got a signed poster at home of the *Hours. . .* album. It felt like a moment. But the atmosphere inside Virgin was, "Oh my god! What are we doing to our relationships here?"'

The major retailers were far from overjoyed at the Bowie album being released this way, fearing it would merely be the first of a thousand nails in their coffin.

They felt that a prioritising of downloading by labels, still an utterly untested market at scale, was a *de*prioritising of retailers by labels. Every uprising starts with the firing of a single bullet and the retailers felt this was the first assassination attempt on them.

'I'm loath to say it, being a huge Bowie fan, but it was upsetting business-wise,' says Glen Ward, president and CEO of Virgin Entertainment Group and busy trying to establish a beachhead for the Virgin Megastore brand in the US in 1999. 'I could see why he was doing it – just pushing the boundaries, [taking] the opportunity to raise awareness. But from a business perspective, it was irksome to say the least. It was compounded with future releases of that nature. There were exclusives with U2 albums that were put out in Best Buy before they were sold in our store. That was the thin end of the wedge.'

Silver says he is certain a flurry of enraged calls from the retailers would have been made to the most senior people at Virgin. 'It was absolutely seen as being, "OK, guys, this is a step in the wrong direction." Because the cosiness of the relationship, particularly with the retail outlets, was so intense. The view internally was, "This is not going to do anything. What are you doing? You're totally sabotaging our relationship. And for what?"'

I tell him the 989 sales figure.

'I didn't know those numbers until you told me, but it doesn't surprise me,' he says. 'Because of course the market didn't exist. It was still years before it was going to mean something, which was absolutely what made it so extraordinary. Bowie, who was very personally involved in driving that, had that as a vision.'

The response of the other majors, however, suggests that EMI was willing to risk upsetting and sidelining the retailers, but they were not going to be as bold or as brazen. The retailers may have feared that EMI was bursting open the door, but none of the other majors were prepared to follow EMI through it. Not yet. And not for a long time.

'I wasn't very happy to see EMI do that,' says Edgar Bronfman Jr on Universal Music's reaction to it all. Then he says, like a canary in the mineshaft, it quickly became apparent that this was not a good model for the other majors to try and replicate in 1999.

'It actually turned out well because it was so disastrous,' claims Bronfman Jr 'Nobody paid for the album digitally. I think it taught the industry, "Hey, this is not the way to go, which is just to put artists' stuff out there and let people steal it. That's not going to help anybody."'

He feels that only one party benefited from this, but only in their parts of their business *beyond* record sales.

'David Bowie, ultimately as David Bowie Inc, might have done well with that because maybe he was selling out concerts or doing more merch or whatever it was,' suggests Bronfman. 'But the record company, which was spending the money to get that publicity for him, was actually losing money. That just doesn't make any sense. It may well have been a good thing for David Bowie. I met him once, but I certainly didn't know him and I never had a conversation with him about it. But it certainly wasn't good for the record company or for the record industry.'

I ask Bronfman Jr if he communicated internally that the labels within Universal were absolutely not to try and slipstream Bowie or EMI by trying something similar.

'Yeah,' is his immediate response.

The position of Warner Music on it all was less gung-ho according to Paul Vidich, EVP of strategic planning and business development there. He views the Bowie download album as perhaps more of a marketing wheeze rather than a grand technological masterplan for the future. He also says that he had different objectives than his counterparts at EMI and, as such, he would not have tried something similar, with or without EMI getting there first.

'It was a promotional effort,' he says. '"What can we do to bring attention to this?" That's all it was. For every album that's coming out, it is like, "How can we raise the bar on visibility?" It had nothing to do with technology. It used technology, but it was all about creating awareness for the album. That wasn't my job. My job wasn't to create awareness. That was the label's [job]. Jay [Samit] had a slightly different job than I had, because he was also digital marketing. Jay's a great marketer. That was his thing. But that wasn't my job. And, ultimately, it didn't make any difference one way or the other. It was lost in the noise.'

It was not just down to labels having a hard and fast rule on this, says Paul Russell, chairman of Sony Music Europe. He suggests that sometimes corporate policy has to bend to the will of a major artist. That can be a major artist in terms of their vast global sales or a major artist in terms of the reputation and admiration they garner from their contemporaries as well as the generations of artists who have come after them.

'You've introduced into the plot artists and also artist managers,' he says by way of set up. 'And the artists being much more acute, maybe than some of the labels, say, "Hey. This is a good way to kick off the release of my album by releasing it first digitally." And the manager supporting the artists, or vice versa, was pressuring the labels to do things. Obviously, if you've got a very successful artist, you want to be friends with them and to do what you think is going to keep the relationship solid, rather than what is going to please necessarily the retailers or the RIAA or anybody else.'

Cliff Fluet, head of business affairs for the Central Division of Warner

Music UK, agrees and says that the persuasive power of a megastar like David Bowie can never be underestimated in situations like this.

'There was a sense of, "Whoa! These guys are taking it to the market",' he says of the response inside Warner to the EMI/Bowie deal. 'I suspect they had a massive issue because they had possibly one of their biggest and most critically acclaimed artists, who had complete commercial freedom, forcing their hand. I'm not sure other artists could have gotten away with that.'

Warner, of course, would have had a few acts like that in 1999 but, fortunately for them, they had not come up with the idea before Bowie did. Even so, Fluet claims, it was made explicit to senior staff that a copycat release would not be entertained.

'It was absolutely clear,' says Fluet of the internal messaging on this within Warner. 'There was no way we could go anywhere near this.'

Within the major labels, keeping the most significant (culturally and commercially) artists happy will always trump keeping the retailers happy.

Mark Foster, SVP of new media at Warner Music International, says the Bowie release would have pitted several departments within a major label against each other. Some departments, out of self-interest, would have seen the attention it would have brought to the artist and label, reflecting well on them all as fearless pioneers. Other departments, out of self-preservation, would have opposed it as only doing lasting damage to their business and their place within it.

'The marketing people will have wanted to look at the promotional opportunities: it's a first; it gets lots of headlines; no publicity is bad publicity; all that kind of stuff,' he says. 'The sales people will have wanted to protect the relationship with the retailers. The powers that be will have wanted to protect the revenue streams of physical formats.'

He says that his division would have been caught between these conflicting dynamics and forced to think and operate like a UN peace-keeping envoy.

'We in new media would be caught in the middle of all of that going, "How can we be all things to all people? How do we keep our marketing people and, therefore the artists, happy because they're doing cool stuff? How can we keep our sales people and retailers happy by not cannibalising their physical sales? And how can we not let these other technologies and innovations cannibalise our entire business model?" We would be trying to figure out the best place to position ourselves.'

Matt Black, one half of Coldcut and co-founder of the Ninja Tune label, was an early adopter of digital and a flag-waver for the possibilities of the internet. Even he, however, has sympathy for the traditional retailers who took this all as a huge betrayal.

'You hop onto something like that and you get a lot of press because you're the first person doing it, so you can see why people did that,' he says before adding a significant caveat. 'If I was a record shop selling vinyl, a Bowie fan probably working my ass off to try and promote that album, I would have been quite pissed off.'

There was, after the fact, a lot of focus on the download sales – or lack of them – of the Bowie album, as if that was the only way to understand it.

'Really low numbers,' says Glen Ward when I remind him of the 989 sales in its opening week. 'But it held the front pages. And it wasn't that great of an album!'

Bowie had correctly predicted that sales would be in the 'hundreds and not thousands of downloads.' As such, the digital release of *Hours. . .* needs to be understood as a test for artists, labels and retailers as much as it was a test for consumers.

Things had not moved on that much the following year when some other artists looked to replicate what Bowie had done in 1999.

By summer 2000, Ian Rogers had left Nullsoft and was president of new media at Grand Royal, the label the Beastie Boys had set up within Capitol Records in 1992. Rogers says the label was rebooted in 2000 and in September that year it released *Relationship Of Command*, the third studio album by post-hardcore band At The Drive-In. It was released physically and digitally on the same day, but the digital sales were, even for a band with a web-savvy audience, disastrously underwhelming. Rogers blames the restrictive format it was, for political reasons, released on. DRM was, he feels, the single biggest barrier to consumer adoption at this time.

'It was a Windows Media format release,' he sighs. 'I think we sold nineteen or twenty copies. In 2000, nobody wanted to buy a DRM file. But to us it was important that, of course, you're going to release them at the same time. And I really feel for the Liquid Audios of the time who built a way to do this legally and monetise it but couldn't access any catalogue. Our approach at Nullsoft was: we don't care. We serve the customer. We just don't care about that end of the value chain.'

According to research from Computer Industry Almanac, there were

147 million people globally who accessed the internet at least once a week in 1998. That was more than double the 61 million people accessing the internet weekly in 1996.[34] A study by Strategis Group in November 1999, just over a month after the release of *Hours. . .*, claimed there were now a hundred million adults in the US using the internet, but suggested the bulk of activity was sending emails, followed by more general surfing.[35]

Being online was one thing, but there was still enormous hesitancy in 1999 for people to *pay* for content online. This was partly due to a presumption that everything online should be free, but it was mainly down to anxiety about handing over bank details to website operators. The Bowie album release needs to be contextualised as happening at a time when using the internet, let alone buying products on the internet, was not a quotidian activity.

Samit argues that, just as he did musically through his career, this was a case of Bowie signposting the future and convincing other artists of the importance of taking risks. This was more about setting the music business and musicians on a new path than it was about instant commercial results. It was also about showing proof of concept to the VC world, with Bowie bestowing a new level of credibility and approval on the very idea of buying music in digital form.

'You have to remember that for the audience doing that, it isn't just about consumers,' he says. 'It's about educating other artists. It's about making sure that Silicon Valley wants to put money behind these digital music companies so that they continue to fund this experimentation. There's a whole lot of other audiences and that was very effective.'

From the vantage point of 2024, the threats, the recriminations and the panic surrounding an album being sold as a download in 1999 might seem like a broadcast from another (backwards) world, never mind another time. Even the notion of *downloading* music in an age of instant access with streaming seems positively archaic.

Yet this album and how it was released was a defiant line in the sand. It represented a generational schism, a breaking apart of the old way of doing things and a bold leap into a future that was still to be written.

In this most eventful, turbulent and singular year, *Hours. . .* became a litmus test for the music industry. Do you want to just skip to tomorrow today? Or do you want to keep living in yesterday until it suffocates you?

It might have only sold 989 copies digitally and the retailers might have had, much to their chagrin, to wait two weeks to get CDs to sell.

It might not have been in the top 100 albums sold in the US that year.[36]

It might appear towards the bottom, or *right at the very bottom,* when music critics rank the albums in Bowie's discography.[37] [38] [39]

Yet, as far as the music industry in 1999 goes, it was the most symbolic and significant album released that year. It is a metonym for the battles and aspirations that ripped through the year. Like a piece of great art, it might have taken others years to catch up with what it was doing, but they got there. Eventually.

In the meantime, the retailers and the record labels were trying everything in their power to find more ways to sell music on even more physical formats.

David Bowie and *Hours. . .* might have been pointing everyone towards the future, but, just as in the closing sentence of F. Scott Fitzgerald's *The Great Gatsby,* most of them were being borne back ceaselessly into the past. Yet the current they were rowing against was all of their own making.

PHYSICAL

CHAPTER 16

Let's Get Physical (Again)

(The attempt to control physical formats by. . . just creating more of them)

For record companies and for music retailers, their joint dilemma, as per Clayton Christensen's book,[1] was migrating from the lucrative CD market into the nascent legal download market.

Labels had hoped that they could control the speed of this transition, but major events were to drastically overtake them in 1999 (as covered in more detail in the following chapter). They could not terminate such a profitable market in the shape of the CD, but equally they could not afford to fall behind in terms of figuring out what music downloads could do for them.

In 1999, based on US figures, the story of the record market was almost entirely the story of the CD. Of $14.6 billion sales that year, $12.8 billion came from the CD album, $1.1 billion came from the cassette, $376.7 million came from music video, $222.4 million came from the CD single and $31.8 million came from vinyl (LPs and EPs).

A decade earlier, the US market was worth $6.6 billion, of which $3.3 billion came from cassette albums and $2.6 billion came from CD, with vinyl (LPs, EPs and singles) accounting for $336.7 million, cassette singles amounting to $194.6 million and music video making up $115.4 million. The story was similar across many other major markets.

The CD was, in many ways, a magical product during the 1990s. It not only grew its share of sound carrier total revenues from 39.3 per cent in 1989 to 87.9 per cent in 1999, it also *more than doubled* the size of the total sound carrier market in that period.[2]

No one would want to willingly, and quickly, kill a product like that.

Rather than strategically inch away from the CD into the download, the labels spent a huge amount of their time, effort and resources in 1999 not on transition but on trying to expand the physical sound carrier even further. This was not about the slow evolution from one format to another; this was about adding even more physical formats to their repertoire.

As the owner of the biggest record company in the world, Edgar Bronfman Jr had not realised that Seagram's acquisition of PolyGram at the end of 1998 was actually a purchase happening in the penultimate year of the CD's sharp sales uptick. He – and many, many others – naturally presumed that the CD would keep growing. Sure, it might start to slow down *a bit* after such a surge through the 1990s, but there was plenty of life in the format yet. Right?

As reality started to nip in early 1999 – a nip that quickly became a snap, then a bite and then a mauling – the record business started to understand that change was happening and it was a change they could not stop or even control the speed of.

'Seagram had paid $10.6 billion for PolyGram,' Bronfman says. 'We had to get a return on that investment. Number one. Number two, digital didn't replace CDs for another fifteen years in terms of growth. So there was no question that CDs not only should continue, but had to continue. Right? That's not to say, though, that in retrospect, we couldn't have tried harder to build a digital business. But it was very difficult to do given that the CD was a perfect digital master and that there was no way to impose protection on it. It was very, very hard to see that through.'

The CD had been in development since the late 1970s and was created by Philips, owners of PolyGram, and Sony Corp, which did not get into the music business in a major way until 1987 when it bought CBS Records that year for $2 billion.[3]

There were clear antitrust laws that precluded the major labels from discussing issues like pricing and exclusivity together. Larry Kenswil, president of Universal Music Group's eLabs division (and before that head of legal and business affairs at Universal), says there were no restrictions on the majors discussing new format developments together. This was to be a recurring motif though the 1990s. 'There were a lot of meetings on format creation, because the old way of doing things was still the way of doing things when it came down to that,' he says.

There was, however, jockeying to have patent rights on new formats as they were incredibly lucrative if a format took off. The CD, for example, was an astonishing money spinner for Philips and Sony as they got a royalty on every disc pressed with the CD logo and every CD player manufactured.

'Essentially you put together a bunch of rights holders, patent rights holders, and develop a format based on those patents and then divide up the patent rights according to who owned the patent,' explains Kenswil. 'Sony owned Sony Music and that was certainly Sony's way of doing things. That's how Panasonic did things. As a result, there were these long, long discussions about the future of the physical formats.'

He says the discussions around DVD-Audio, offering improved sonics, was something the labels focused a lot of their attention on in the late 1990s.

'The companies with the patent rights were vying to get their patents into the formats,' he says. 'Warner was very good at this. They would have a patent for a small little feature and they'd managed to get those features into the formats so it would be part of the patent pool. DVD-Audio looked to us to be a great transition format because people were putting DVD players in their home. We were assured by the electronics companies that there was no reason why every DVD player couldn't also be a DVD-Audio player. Well, it turned out that there was some kind of reason, because that's not what happened!'

Hardware pricing (see below) was the major hurdle for consumer adoption. It was only when CD player prices fell in the late 1980s that consumers started to invest in them and the CD became the dominant format in the 1990s.

Even so, the labels were convinced that the conjuring trick of the CD – getting people to buy their record collection again, this time at a higher unit price – could happen again. They did not want to make the CD obsolete, but they did want to grow the sound carrier market even more through multi-formatting. As Paul Vidich, EVP of strategic planning and business development at Warner Music, says of the time, 'The big money was on the CD and what was going to replace the CD.'

There was therefore a dual dynamic going in the 1990s whereby: the majors wanted new physical formats to slipstream and augment the CD boom; and they also wanted to have a stake in the potential patent windfall that would come with the development of a successful new audio format.

Below are the new physical formats that the record industry, sometimes in isolation and sometimes in lockstep, were trying to get off the ground towards the close of the 1990s, with particular emphasis on what was happening around these formats in 1999.

MINIDISC

Originally launched by Sony in September 1992, the MiniDisc was positioned as a combination of the CD (high audio quality, convenient, portable) and the cassette (recordable), but struggled to make a significant impact. Arguably it came too soon after the mainstream adoption of the CD started to happen. In its first year, Sony only sold fifty thousand MiniDisc player/recorders.[4] The hardware was beyond the budget of its core youth audience, with the MZ-1 MiniDisc player/recorder costing $750 (equal to $1,621 today).[5]

MiniDiscs and MiniDisc players were not so much stuck on the shelves as nailed to them. The consumer disinterest was astounding. Research by Sony found that 75 per cent of Americans had never even heard of the format, so it attempted to shake them out of their ignorance by, somewhat pompously and presumptively, declaring 1998 to be The Year Of The MiniDisc, throwing a $30 million marketing budget at it and making cheaper players, as low as $250, available.[6]

There was the additional problem that the other majors were not as enthused about the format as Sony Corp was and were not racing to put music out on MiniDisc and pay royalties to the parent company of one of their rivals.

Even within Sony, there was a church/state division over the format. The hardware arm was pushing it heavily, but the music (or 'software') arm was not as enthused.

The Sony Music label in the UK was headquartered on Great Marlborough Street in London, running parallel with Oxford Street, so was positioned in the middle of the busiest shopping area in the UK. Sony felt this was too good an opportunity and so opened a MiniDisc shop at street level on its business premises in late 1999.

Neil Cartwright, head of digital at Sony Music UK, visibly cringes when recalling this retail white elephant and how the company was trying to get it off the ground.

'I used to work at MiniDisc shop on Great Marlborough Street,' he says, shaking his head at the memory. 'We used to sell five MiniDiscs a week. It was never going anywhere. But, of course, Sony were really backing that over solid state hard drives. They just didn't want to invest money in downloading because they wanted everything on MiniDisc.'

He says the core problem was that there was no real communication between the hardware arm of Sony and the music arm – so follies like a MiniDisc shop would happen.

Darren Hemmings, in Sony Music's IT department at the time, calls it 'an absolute joke' and describes with mounting disbelief how it was being operated by the company. 'They put in a MiniDisc store downstairs between our bit and Sony PlayStation. A couple of floors were European Sony people. Between them, they put in this ridiculous MiniDisc shop. Literally they hired a guy to just stand there. It wasn't just that he didn't sell anything – there was *no* footfall. It's just like being put in an empty room and being told, "Stand over there. That's your job." It didn't even have much stock. There were about fifty things on sale. It wasn't like fucking HMV! An absolute waste of time and money. It was hysterical.'

Throughout 1999 there was a slow re-emphasis on the MiniDisc, and not just from Sony. In April, Suede released 'Electricity', the lead single from their fourth album, *Head Music*, as a MiniDisc. This was presented as the first single to be released on the format.[7] The band were signed to independent label Nude, but it had an international licensing deal with Sony Music at the time.

Slowly support for MiniDisc spidered out from Sony. In July, the 43rd edition of the hugely successful *Now That's What I Call Music* compilation series came out on the MiniDisc format, with Virgin/EMI (owners of the brand) saying an initial shipment of two thousand units had gone out and there had quickly been a re-order of five hundred units. Baby steps.[8]

The biggest development for the format came in September 1999 when Warner Music announced it was now backing it and would be releasing a number of major frontline and catalogue titles on MiniDisc. The company had tentatively embraced MiniDisc back in 1993, but soon abandoned it. Mark Foster, marketing vice president at Warner Music Europe, told *Music Week* about the company's change of mind. 'We've been looking at the market which seems to have progressed somewhat to become a small but significant format in the UK.'[9]

Albums by priority Warner acts that included The Corrs, Simply Red and Shola Ama – as well as catalogue titles like Alanis Morissette's first two albums for the label and Madonna's *Immaculate Collection* greatest hits – were scheduled for release on MiniDisc in November, presumably as part of a Christmas gifting push.[10]

Billboard claimed in July that year that a MiniDisc 'revival' was happening in markets outside of Japan, the format's heartland, suggesting it was 'becoming a viable medium for selling albums', although it admitted this was mainly restricted to 'such niche markets as home recording and sound contracting.'

The piece quoted BPI data that said ninety thousand units of the format had been shipped in Q1 1999 and shipments in 1998 were 250,000 units. It added that EMI had started toying with the format properly in 1997 and had put out 32 titles on MiniDisc in the previous 12 months. Steve Davis, director of catalogue development at EMI, told *Billboard*, 'It only makes sense on the big releases.'[11]

In the same issue of *Billboard*, there was a report on MiniDisc in Japan, noting, no doubt to the consternation of the majors, that the primary reason it had taken off in the world's second-biggest music market was that it was the 'home-recording medium of choice' there.[12]

'Warner actually decided to press MiniDiscs at their plant in Alsdorf in Germany,' says Mark Foster. 'There was a limited release of strong catalogue sellers onto MiniDisc towards the end of that year. It didn't really go anywhere as a project. That was all part of the defensive mindset about how we could protect the formats that we already know and understand and that we can measure in terms of units sold and, therefore, forecast profitability and so on. That was going on the whole year.'

Despite the renewed emphasis on MiniDisc in late 1999, it was already feeling like an anachronism.

MUSIC DVD

As covered in Chapter 12, DVD became, according to Gennaro Castaldo, head of press and PR at HMV, a 'huge adrenaline rush of additional sales' from 1997 onwards, perhaps distracting retailers and labels from any market saturation issues with the CD.

As the DVD format took off, labels were keen to make music DVDs an important sub-category, seeing them as a new way to monetise music videos (historically a huge cost that was written off as a marketing and promotion expense) as well as creating opportunities for concert films and documentaries. There had been some success with music-centric VHS cassettes in the 1980s and 1990s, but the improved audio, better visuals and greater functionality on music DVD was, on paper anyway, brimming with market potential.

There was growing confidence around the format as 1999 progressed.

In June, IRMA (the International Recording Media Association) was forecasting that twelve million DVD video discs would be produced in Europe in 1999 and this would grow to 485 million by 2003. Charles Van Horn, IRMA's EVP, pointed to successful music DVDs from acts like Janet Jackson, Eagles, Fleetwood Mac and The Rolling Stones as clear indicators that this was a format set to explode. He noted that music video sales in the US were up 45.9 per cent to 27.2 million units in 1998 and DVDs were 2 per cent of that. 'The DVD media is on its way to becoming global as it rolls out throughout Europe and the world,' he said.[13]

Gripped by the potential of music DVDs, *Music Week* ran a special pull-out supplement on the format in its 4 September issue. It noted that fifty different DVD players were available on the market, with some selling for £300. (Note: this was significantly more expensive than the Diamond Rio MP3 player). The players at the highest end of the market, however, could cost as much as £700 (such as Sony's DVP-7700). It was presented as a replacement cycle for VHS akin to the replacement cycle driven by the CD throughout the decade.[14]

The forecast was that DVDs would go truly mainstream at Christmas 1999. Labels were gleefully embracing the format. Independent label One Little Indian[15] made a DVD single for Björk's 'All Is Full Of Love' along with its Chris Cunningham-directed video. It sold for between £7.99 and £8.99 and was the first chart-eligible DVD single in the UK.

The bulk of the major DVDs lined up for Christmas 1999 were movies, but *Music Week* said that *Yellow Submarine*, The Beatles' animated film from 1968, was '[u]ndoubtedly the most important music release of the season', forecasting UK sales of 25,000.

Other music titles, generally a mix of concerts and video collections, were expected from major acts such as Robbie Williams, Ricky Martin, Celine Dion, George Michael, Will Smith, Charlotte Church, Pink Floyd (*The Wall*), Madonna (*The Immaculate Collection*), Sex Pistols and The Rolling Stones.[16]

In July, the DVD Video Group was projecting that one million music DVDs would be sold in 1999 in the US, doubling the number sold in 1998, with *Hell Freezes Over* by Eagles cited as the biggest seller so far that year. It added that music DVDs made up 10 per cent of the three thousand DVD titles currently available.[17]

DVDs powered ahead for the next few years, peaking in 2005, with sales of $16.3 billion in the US alone that year.[18]

SUPER AUDIO CD/DVD-AUDIO

Not quite a format death match on the level of VHS/Betamax in the late 1970s and early 1980s, the music industry was still dealing with two competing CD formats that effectively offered the same thing: high-resolution audio and surround sound (as well as longer play time).

Hoping for a repeat of the success of the CD, Sony and Philips developed the Super Audio CD (SACD) and launched it in 1999. The standard SACD required a dedicated SACD player, but the hybrid SACD, intended as a stepping-stone format, could also be read by a standard CD player, with the hope that it would eventually replace the CD.[19]

DVD-Audio (DVD-A), meanwhile, did not launch until 2000 but had its standard published in early 1999, meaning labels were preparing releases for the format that year. It was developed by the DVD Forum (previously known as the DVD Consortium when it was founded in 1995, but it changed its name in 1996), which comprised a range of hardware, software and media companies, including Hitachi, Panasonic, Mitsubishi, WarnerMedia, Toshiba and the Walt Disney Company.

Sony trumpeted the launch of SACD in September 1999, releasing an initial fifteen albums in the formats such as Miles Davis's *A Kind Of Blue* and Mariah Carey's *Number Ones*. The initial wave of players were targeted at what were dubbed 'Hi-Fi enthusiasts' and the player from Sony cost a staggering £3,000 (equal to £5,361 in 2023).[20]

Sony was the only label backing the format on its launch, with albums selling for around $24.95 each in the US. Sony Corp president/CEO Nobuyuki Idei was pushing the sonic improvements when launching the format. 'SACD is not a replacement for the CD; it is a sound-enhancement,' he insisted.[21]

Larry Kenswil recalls the damp squib nature of DVD-A on launch. He says, 'I remember going into the stores and asking, "Do you have any DVD-Audio players?" And the salesman would go, "What's that?" Even though they had them on the shelves. That format ended up being a disappointment. They didn't [even] record.'

Despite the hyperbole around its launch, some in the US record business were hugely underwhelmed and cynical about it all. 'We think SACD is a nonevent,' an unnamed major label executive told *Billboard*. 'We don't see consumers buying hardware at that price, and we certainly don't see them buying hardware when there will be such a modest offering of product in the marketplace.'[22]

Paul Vidich says there was not so much concern about a format war cancelling out each of these brave new formats. He saw it as appeasing consumers who wanted better audio quality just at the very moment where the MP3 represented a triumph of convenience over sonics. He admits, however, the idea, regardless of the format, was simply too early for the market.

'Sony had SACD and we [Warner] were the big proponents of DVD-Audio,' he says. 'Our view was maybe that we'll split the market and there are going to be people who love high-end audio, and they will buy a new disc called the DVD-Audio or the SACD – and that will complement what's going on with the low-fidelity MP3s. It didn't actually play out like that. Although, interestingly now the world is coming back to high-fidelity in different ways.'

INTERVIEW CDS

At the peak of any market, there is a desperate tendency towards gimmickry to try and stand out. This can be retrospectively read as a last-ditch attempt to milk the market before it starts to crater. The music industry, however, thrives on novelty, so ideas like 'interview CDs' were greeted with a straight face on launch.

Interview CDs were exactly that: an interview with some pop stars on a CD.

Concorde International Artists (whose roster included pop acts Steps, B*Witched and Boyzone) had set up Unique Projects London to release official interview CDs with acts like Boyzone, 5ive and Hanson. Steps would have the honour of being the first act on its release schedule, with their interview CD selling for £5.99.[23]

A Boyzone one was next, to tie in with their greatest hits album, *By Request*, and was created in conjunction with Polydor, their record label. It replicated the album artwork, boasted an exclusive interview and the CD-ROM element had merchandise links, tour dates and relevant website links.

The idea was developed by Richard Smith, formerly an agent at Concorde, to negate unofficial interview discs that were apparently flooding the market. 'We're now offering artists the chance to combat this unofficial trade in their success and at the same time put the profits back into their own pocket,' he told *Music Week*.[24]

The company has pressed up thirty thousand copies of the Boyzone disc and would be promoting it with a half-page ad in British tabloid newspaper *The Sun*.

The format did not take off and I could not find any follow-up pieces about it in *Music Week* that year. The Boyzone interview CD (with a run time of an hour) was available on Discogs in summer 2023, ranging in price from €2.95 to €25.[25] The Steps interview disc, perhaps because it only had a run time of forty minutes, had sold for between £0.99 and £4.99 on Discogs.[26]

SHAPE CDS

Perhaps the peak gimmick of the CD era, shape CDs were, for the most fleeting of moments, presented as the future of the format.

Shape CD, understanding the importance of a clear name that could also work as a trademark, was the company behind them and had been creating them since April 1997 from its base in Florida. In early 1999, however, *Billboard* gave them significant coverage.[27]

The idea behind the offering was the company would take artwork from labels and 'sculpt the CD to fit the artwork.' Possible listed shapes included a guitar body, backstage passes and logos.

Rod Lowenstein, company president, said, 'So one shaped CD gives a consumer a unique souvenir with both a perceptual and practical value, sometimes with unreleased tracks or an interview with the artist. It also gives a promoter a controlled access device, because CDs already have well-developed anti-counterfeiting technology. And it brings people into the store after the show to buy the record. That's a lot more mileage than you get out of a conventional CD.'[28]

The *Billboard* story noted there was a 'jigsaw' option so fans would have to buy multiple versions to get them to slot together. According to the piece, BMG had bought ten million units in the shape of Elvis in 1998 to mark twenty years since he died (even though he died in 1977).

In a triumph of form over function, the consequence of creating them meant that the disc radius would be reduced, thereby paring down how many minutes of music a disc could hold. Given they were rarely circular, they would be unplayable on CD players in cars or on computer drives.

Lowenstein, however, was not going to let that dampen his enthusiasm for the product. 'The possibilities are almost as endless as the shapes themselves,' he insisted. 'It can revolutionize the backstage pass industry, for instance, which is becoming a bigger part of record promotion. It can project brand awareness in a way that a mouse pad or a keychain can't, because it also offers value-added in the form of content. It's not a pet rock.'[29]

One might be tempted to respond: it's *barely* a pet rock.

IMPROVED CD MASTERING

Audio experts, music producers and studio engineers had long argued that the first wave of catalogue albums remastered for CD were done cheaply, done quickly and done haphazardly. Little care and attention had been paid to the process, presuming that the shift to a new format would be enough to make old albums 'sound' new again. This was not always the case. (Several senior label executives and heads of catalogue I have spoken to over the years have all described the early remastering for CD as 'shoddy', 'slapdash', 'abysmal' and worse).

By 1999, the record business was prepared to admit it could have done a better job in the early 1980s of transferring existing albums to this sparkly new format. A reparation programme – of having another swing at remastering albums, not refunding consumers who had bought substandard releases – was slowly, sometimes begrudgingly, underway.

Jeff Jones, SVP of Sony Legacy, the major's catalogue arm, said, 'Existing catalog, when it was reissued the first time on CD, now sonically suffers, based on the technology we have at hand and also based on the fact that CDs were created quickly and moved into the marketplace quickly in order to facilitate a demand for product.'

Billboard praised Rykodisc,[30] which was founded in 1983, for bringing a new kind of quality control to reissues in 1989 and 1990 when it remastered the David Bowie catalogue from his years on RCA. 'The upgraded CDs won raves from the press and fans alike,' said the publication. It also praised reissue labels like Rhino Records[31] and Sundazed Music for helping raise the bar here.[32]

Sundazed owner Bob Irwin had worked with Legacy on a run of reissues of albums by The Byrds. This provided a template for the major to follow in all its subsequent remasters. 'The CDs that were on the market sounded like crap; they were done in the earliest days, they were done from inferior sources,' he said of a 1990 Byrds box set that fired up his desire to remaster their recordings properly. 'The whole catalog needed addressing.'[33]

Jones added, 'It's a way for us to make sure that our records sound as good as possible and the packages are as complete as they can be, and hopefully reintroduce them to the marketplace, to resell those records to fans and to turn new fans on to those artists by the publicity and product placement that we get.'[34]

Was this a way of finally fixing the crimes of the past? Or was this just another way to try and persuade fans to buy their record collection again (again)?

Given how many times classic albums have been repackaged and remastered (with 5.1 surround sound and/or Dolby Atmos mixes the connoisseur's choice today) in the intervening years, the latter would seem to be the answer.

CASSETTES

In 1973, cassette sales in the US generated $76 million in revenue, equal to 3.8 per cent of the total recorded music business in the country. Its imperial period as a format began in 1980 when it generated $705 million, making up 19.1 per cent of the market and overtaking the 8-track for the first time.[35]

Its standout years were 1983 (when it overtook the LP to account for 47.8 per cent of the US market) and 1985 (when it controlled 55.3 per cent of the market). The CD slowly ate into its dominance, though, and by 1991 was the market leader with 55.4 per cent of the business compared to cassette's 38.5 per cent).[36] In 1998, the cassette had fallen so far that it made up just 10.4 per cent of the US market while the CD held 83.3 per cent.

A plan was afoot, however, to pull the cassette out of its death spiral and grow its market share again. In a year when it was becoming more and more obvious by the day that the record business's future was, whether it liked it or not, going to be digital, a band of US retailers thought this was the opportune moment to start a campaign to save the cassette.

In early July, NARM (the National Association of Recording Merchandisers), IRMA (the International Recording Media Association) and the Audio Cassette Coalition revealed their masterplan.

'Smart Music Retailers Say. . . We've Got Cassettes!' (or 'We've Got Cassettes!' for short) was the name of the initiative. It was actually a revival of a 1997 campaign by IRMA ('Where'd Ya Hide The Cassettes?') that *Billboard* claimed had 'significantly slowed the decline of prerecorded cassette album sales.'[37] (Spoiler: sales kept dropping, but it is unclear just how much more they would have dropped without that campaign.)

The new cassette SOS campaign was scheduled to run for sixteen weeks, with industry experts and retailers extolling the virtues of the format in a series of advertisements. The point of the campaign was really to persuade labels to keep manufacturing and promoting cassette releases as well as for retailers to keep pushing them.

'The audiocassette format is still robust and viable,' said Charles Van Horn, EVP of IRMA. 'It is also extremely profitable and promotable. Some retailers have somehow gotten the wrong message that record labels aren't supporting the format and consumers are shying away from cassette listening. That's anything but the case.'

Billboard itself ran full-page ads for the campaign through the rest of the year. The bright yellow ads featured industry and retail executives expressing how important cassettes were, stressing statistics like 70 per cent of cars still having a cassette player, 97 per cent of music buyers still owning cassette players, one in six record sales being on cassette and so on.

There were plenty of people lining up to give testimonials.

'Cassettes should be the paperbacks of the business,' said Stan Goman, EVP and COO of Tower Retail Operations. 'They're so great because they're disposable. Just grab a handful and take them out on the road.'[38]

'Right now cassette fever is at its peak,' claimed a perhaps over-generous Terry Currier, president of Music Millennium in Portland, Oregon. 'Our customers are praising us because we've got cassettes. They keep coming back to buy more.'[39]

Terry Woodward, president of Disc Jockey Music in Owensboro, Kentucky, who operated 118 stores in 36 states, had this to say: 'Sure, our cassette business is down but it's still incredibly sizable. Why should I give up $20 million worth of business? That's how many prerecorded cassettes I sell in my stores every year.'[40]

George Daniels, CEO and founder of George's Music Room in Chicago, Illinois, chimed in: 'I'm a consumer-driven retailer. If the consumer wants it, I'm going to sell it. And the consumer still wants the music cassette. Industry and technology are moving quickly. It's too easy to get caught up in all the hype. No matter what – we better always listen to our customers.'[41]

John Grandoni, VP of purchasing at National Record Mart, a chain of 181 stores, was sure of the cassette's survival. 'Cassettes will play a large part in our merchandising mix for years to come,' he said. 'Sales overall are 12 percent of our total dollar volume. Although cassette sales are declining, the rate of decline is also declining.'[42]

Dick Odette, SVP of music merchandising at Musicland Group (who oversaw the purchasing for 1,325 specialty retail stores under the Sam Goody, Suncoast, Media Play and On Cue umbrellas in forty-nine states) joined the pro-cassette chorus. 'Cassettes remain an important part of our business,' he said. 'Sales remain particularly strong in many genres of music. We fully support cassettes and plan to continue to carry this convenient format for a long time.'[43]

I remind Glen Ward, president and CEO of Virgin Entertainment Group and based in the US in 1999, of the existence of cassette SOS campaign. He rolls his eyes.

'You can imagine that meeting where somebody comes in from the marketing department,' he sighs. '"We should put cassettes back up!" The blind leading the blind.'

Simon Wright, MD of Virgin Retail UK, is equally dismissive of these attempts to keep the cassette afloat. 'In a way, that's symptomatic of this underlying problem that the record companies had,' he says. '"If I keep pushing you cassettes, even though you as the customer are telling me you don't want cassettes anymore, I'm going to keep telling you that you do.' It's slightly misunderstanding the power of marketing".'

On and on the testimonials kept rolling in the campaign ads through the rest of 1999, but all the efforts and the good will behind 'We've Got Cassettes!' had little-to-no impact.

Cassette's share of the market in 1999 was 7.3 per cent (down from 10.4 per cent in 1998). It kept slipping: dropping down to 4.4 per cent in 2000; then 2.6 per cent in 2001; 1.7 per cent in 2002; and 0.9 per cent in 2003. After that point, the RIAA stopped including cassette sales in its figures.[44]

NAPSTER

CHAPTER 17

Free Form: the Inevitable Chaos Unlocked by Napster

(Record label control is blown to smithereens by a teenager)

No one involved in Napster at the start expected it to do *this*.

They felt it could *change* things, most notably around music discovery. They thought it could maybe even *improve* things for artists and music fans.

None of the people working on, or later for, Napster anticipated it would hurl a multi-billion dollar business into the biggest existential crisis in its history, forcing it to stand witness to a premonition of its own death, like John Baxter glimpsing his own funeral gondola cutting through the waters of a Venetian canal in *Don't Look Now*.

The fact it arrived just as the millennium was ending has imbued it with incredible symbolism. To draw on another cinematic reference, it was being painted like Major T. J. 'King' Kong in *Dr. Strangelove*, a man riding a nuclear warhead ('HI THERE!') as if it were a bucking bronco, whooping and hollering through his sharp plummet and the annihilation of everyone in the record business.

Joseph Menn, in his 2003 book *All The Rave: The Rise And Fall Of Shawn Fanning's Napster*, has written the definitive account of Napster, from its quixotic beginnings, initially as a concept in 1998 and then as a piece of software in 1999, to its dismal collapse in 2002.[1] (The Napster assets and name have been sold and re-sold several times in the intervening years. For the purposes of this book I am referring to Napster in its original 1999–2002 incarnation).

The Napster story has been fleshed out further in the chapter devoted to the service in Adam Fisher's 2018 thoroughgoing oral history of Silicon Valley.[2]

Between them, Menn and Fisher have told Napster's inside story as well as it is ever likely to be told. It would be foolhardy for me to even attempt to improve on these two pivotal texts.

My focus here is specifically on what happened when Napster first pinged up on the record industry's radar in summer 1999 and how events snowballed to the point where legal action was launched against the service by December that year.

Napster was, in many ways, an inevitability for the record business, the malfunctioning fireworks at the end of its most successful decade and a portent for the incredible pain that labels and recording artists would be put through for at least the first decade and a half of the new millennium.

Hollywood screenwriters would look at the timing of Napster's arrival – and how it grabbed so many loose threads that were already happening, weaving them into a dagger that it then thrust into the heart of the record business in the closing days of the century, representing the ultimate in pre-millennium tension – and feel that it was a little too much on the nose, a little too neat, to ever be believable.

But that is exactly how it happened. It was the shock and awe moment that kiboshed what the record companies had presumed would be a never-ending party.

Napster was the brutal hangover for the 20th century record business and it had crashed through the room while the party was still in full flight.

A VERY QUICK POTTED – AND PARTIAL – HISTORY OF HOW NAPSTER CAME TO BE

Shawn Fanning, 'the quiet young man at the heart of the company',[3] was born in 1980 and grew up in Rockland, Massachusetts, just south of Boston. He had a tough upbringing and money was far from plentiful. His parents were both very young when his mother became pregnant with him and his father split soon after. His mother later married Raymond Verrier, a truck driver, but they had a combustible relationship and Shawn and his other siblings spent time in a foster home when he was 12.

Shawn played guitar and baseball, with his interest in the latter being viewed by his mother as his ticket out of a low-income life, believing he could get to college on a sports scholarship. His uncle John Fanning, his mother's brother, became a mentor to him and bought Shawn an Apple Macintosh, unwittingly lighting the blue torch paper that would make computers Shawn's defining passion. His uncle John was a divisive figure but he controlled the biggest stake in Napster (70 per cent, leaving Shawn 30 per cent), an issue that would cause endless headaches throughout the short life of the company.

John had set up Chess.net, an internet venture to allow people (as the name suggests) to play chess online and Shawn got involved, learning to program and refine the code behind it. From there, his skills quickly evolved, but his mind was detonated when he discovered that he could access MP3 files on IRC (Internet Relay Chat).[4]

He also discovered the hacker community online, joining an IRC channel called w00w00. Among the people he met there in 1996 was Sean Parker, whose own career and future success is intertwined with the history of Napster. That said, several people I spoke to, both Napster staffers and active names on w00w00, insist Parker was nowhere near as central to the development of Napster as he has retrospectively claimed. Jordan Ritter, also active on w00w00, was a much more important figure in the Napster story, they insist.

Ritter was no fan of Parker, regarding him disdainfully as an arriviste. Ritter claimed they 'barely ever interacted' and that 'Parker plainly was a groupie' who 'wanted to be part of this elite, underworld group of hackers.' He adds, witheringly, 'But he could never make the cut, which was hard for him, because we were the outcasts. We were the social outcasts. How the fuck do you get rejected by the outcasts?'[5]

In autumn 1998, Fanning enrolled at Boston's Northeastern University. He had originally wanted to get into Carnegie Mellon but had not been accepted. Northeastern was to be where the idea for what became Napster began to coalesce. Fanning and Parker were also active on another IRC channel called dweebs and this is where Parker claims the plan to take Fanning's idea – a streamlined way for people in the university to share music files with each other – and turn it into a business really began.

It was in part inspired by Fanning observing the online activities of his roommate who had 'an appetite for obscure rap music that he was feeding with MP3s.'[6] His roommate was, however, hugely frustrated by the online experience as sites offering MP3s were typically unreliable, quickly outdated and increasingly packed with dead links.[7] Fanning knew he could create something better.

'It was rooted out of frustration not only with MP3.com, Lycos, and Scour.net, but also to create a music community,' Fanning told *ZDNet* of the multiple catalysts for the idea. 'There really was nothing like it at the time. We had good ideas for implementation, so we proceeded. I think it was an excellent solution to the reliability issues with existing search engines.'[8]

Parker claimed Fanning 'had very little business acumen' and 'just wanted to code.'[9] Parker would quickly present himself as the business and marketing brains behind the operation. He also insisted that Napster, or something like it, was always going to happen as it was symptomatic of what was bubbling away online. '[I]f you grew up online, you knew that in a matter of years everyone would be sharing MP3s,' he said.[10]

Ian Rogers was working at Nullsoft when the idea for Napster was percolating. He was active on the IRC channels where Shawn Fanning hung out and they would occasionally chat. He claims that Sean Parker did not appear on his radar in these early days of Napster. 'I never heard Sean Parker's name once until the 2000s,' he says.

The IRC model, where a username appeared on screen when a user was logged on and then disappeared when they logged out, was the germ of the idea for how Napster would look and work. 'His plan was to set up a central server, where users would connect, see their log-on names, and view the titles of MP3s they were storing in folders on their hard drives,' explained author Steve Knopper of what Fanning was looking to achieve here. 'The trick was that the central server contained only information on usernames and MP3 text information. The actual file sharing took place between individual users' computers.'[11]

Tech journalist Trevor Merriden offered this synopsis of how Napster worked. 'Fanning's dream was that if people were willing to share their files on a list that everyone could access, then that list could be updated each time a person logged on or off that computer,' he wrote. 'The computer would therefore always have an up-to-date list of the files people were willing to share [. . .] MP3 files do not pass through the centralized server. The transfer is made directly from computer to computer, known as 'peer-to-peer.' Napster cannot index files based on their content. Instead, such files can only be located and organised based on file names.'[12]

What was to become a huge legal focus later on was something Napster thought would absolve it of any trouble from the record business. They were, of course, proven to be desperately, painfully wrong.

'Only Napster's index and directory reside on a central server; the files are actually transferred via various Windows protocols directly from user to user,' noted *Time* in its 2000 cover profile of the company and Shawn Fanning. 'That means that no copyrighted material is ever in Napster's possession.'[13]

The Napster software effectively turned every computer running it into both a client and a server. As academics Laura Robinson and David Halle noted, 'Napster claimed a completely new way of distributing music online, taking the hassle out of searching for MP3s and allowing users to chat, play MP3 files from within Napster, and use a hot list to keep track of favorites.'[14]

Fanning became so obsessed with the idea that he dropped out of college in January 1999 to devote his time and effort to getting Napster off the ground.[15]

'The idea had become too big,' wrote *Time* of this crossroads moment for Fanning. 'It possessed him. He never went back to his dorm room, leaving behind his clothes, books and bedding. He took his computer with him, of course [. . .] It was the first major program Fanning had ever written.'[16]

The bulk of the program reportedly ran to eighty thousand lines of code.[17] It was claimed the entire source code for Napster was written by Fanning over a very intense three months.[18] According to *Time*, 'He worked feverishly because he was sure someone else had the same idea, that any day now some software company or media conglomerate would be unveiling a version of the same application, and then Fanning's big idea wouldn't be his anymore.'[19]

Parker saw dollar signs and began working his connections in the investor world.[20] The business plan, as much as teenagers with no experience in the startup world could nail a business plan, was a 'user play' to get to ten million active users and then sell them ancillary products such as concert tickets and merchandise.[21]

Fanning tentatively showed around thirty friends, mostly people he knew on chat rooms, the rudimentary version of Napster in early 1999. This was despite some people on the IRC chat rooms he occupied saying it was a towering act of futility, a grand folly, or both. 'It's a selfish world,' claimed one voice on there, 'and nobody wants to share.'[22] Of course, that was *exactly* what everyone wanted to do.

(The Napster name was drawn from Fanning's online username, which in turn was based on a childhood nickname about his 'nappy'[23] hairstyle.[24] Its working title, however, was the much more self-descriptive MusicShare.[25] That became the name for the underlying software).

'Ingenuity requires three things: adversity, scarcity, and necessity,' is how Ritter explained the conditional factors behind the seismic impact of Napster. 'And when those three things happen, you invent new things.'[26]

Word about Napster spread quickly among the community and soon the application had been downloaded 15,000 times.[27]

Several seasoned investors kicked the tyres of Napster but, on 'consulting their lawyers, their common sense, or both', walked away.[28] Draper Atlantic, a venture capital firm, looked like it could be the first to bite, offering $500,000 on the condition that Ben Lilienthal, who had sold his web email company Nascent Technologies in early 1999 and who had put Napster on Draper Atlantic's radar, be installed as CEO. John Fanning wanted more. Talks dragged on for several weeks and John Fanning increased his demands, topping out at $1 million. He kept pushing so much that he eventually pushed Draper Atlantic to breaking point. They walked away.[29]

The first major investor turned out to be Yosi Amram, who already knew John Fanning, having invested $100,000 in Chess.net. This was money, it was becoming abundantly clear by summer 1999, that Amram was not going to get back. But Napster intrigued him, although he wavered at first about the involvement of John Fanning given their strained history at Chess.net.[30]

By August, however, he was veering toward investing. 'He agreed to put money in on three conditions,' wrote Menn. 'First, Amram would name the CEO. Second, he and the CEO would form the majority of a three-person board, and therefore be able to outvote [John] Fanning if need be. And third, the company would move to northern California, where Amram could keep an eye on it.'[31]

John Fanning, running out of time and options, agreed. Amram invested $250,000 over the Labour Day weekend (5–6 September) for 1.25 million shares.[32] Amram also brought in tech entrepreneur Bill Bales who invested $100,000 and became VP of business development at Napster.[33]

The investment made, Shawn Fanning and Sean Parker packed up their things and moved to San Mateo, 20 miles south of San Francisco. Amram was already scouting out a possible CEO to help grow the company, but primarily to bring in serious investor money.

Some in the company were firm in their belief that selling ancillaries like tickets was not a proper business plan and that they should look to charge some kind of monthly subscription. Others were advocating for a per-song download fee.[34] Even without this clear plan, the momentum behind the company was unavoidable.

By October, Napster had 150,000 registered users and 22,000 simultaneous users.[35] There were claims that 3.5 million files a day were being exchanged through the service.[36] That month, it was reported by *Business Week* that Napster alone was accounting for 10 per cent of the bandwidth at Oregon State University. It swiftly banned the service, less on copyright grounds and more on grounds of costs and logistics.[37]

That same month, Napster raised a further $2 million in a new round of VC funding.[38]

With this injection of cash, the company began quickly hiring staff as it started to rapidly grow, with claims that people were cold emailing the company every day just to volunteer as the tech-centric buzz was so powerful they just wanted to be involved somehow.[39]

The fact that Napster featured in download.com's Download Spotlight around this time helped to accelerate things further. This was, as Fanning told *ZDNet* in early 2000, 'the point at which I realized it had serious potential' and that this was going to be more, much more, than just something for people using IRC or spending all their time in their university dorm. 'It was very early, and we were still like beta or alpha stage, and so we started receiving a ton of downloads,' said Fanning. 'The server became overloaded, and that's when I realized that this had a huge market.'[40]

Napster was ready to take off. It was going to rocket into the big time. But the music industry was already fully aware of what it was doing and starting to formulate its response.

DO YOU KNOW THE WAY TO. . . SAN MATEO? THE BIG LEAGUE BECKONS

The move to San Mateo is when the Napster story quickly moved up several gears. Early investors were on board and the priorities now were to build the team, refine the product and raise more money. And to keep the record business at arm's length for as long as possible.

Amram brought in Eileen Richardson as the first CEO of Napster in

September 1999. She was a digital evangelist but also someone who was highly critical of the established record business. Napster had someone who got what it was about and also someone who would not roll over when the major labels and the RIAA, their representative body, started to circle their wagons and plan how they could bring the whole thing crashing down.

Richardson had been deeply involved in the VC world since 1989, based initially in Boston. She moved to Chicago to set up her own VC firm, but really wanted to be in Silicon Valley just as the dot com boom was happening.

'I would go back to Chicago and I would be so excited saying, "The internet is going to change the world!" she tells me. 'My partners, who were older gentlemen who came from the phone industry, would say, "Eileen, you don't know what you're talking about. This is a wave. We have more experience than you and know that waves come and go and the internet is just a wave." I remember thinking to myself, "Well you might think so, but I don't! "So I left".'

She had been involved in Firefly, a company dealing with collaborative filtering and recommendations, gaining crucial experience that was going to feed straight into Napster. It was also going to fire her up about the potential of Napster to radically change how acts were discovered, ideally breaking them out of an unhealthy dependency on the major labels.

In his 1998 book on the dot com boom, Michael Wolff wrote about it as a standout service at the time. 'Firefly has been applying various data-matching technologies to musical tastes,' he explained. 'For example, a person X, represented by a digital marker, might indicate an interest in the rock group Jane's Addiction and theoretical physics and could therefore be matched with Y, a person whose digital marker indicates similar preferences.'[41]

What Firefly was doing was 'being widely hailed as the next big thing in e-commerce, because it exploited the interactivity of the internet to offer customers something that offline stores couldn't match.' So argued writer John Cassidy in his book about the first dot com years. It was such a good idea, he noted, that Amazon created its own version in March 1997 to supercharge its book recommendations.[42]

Richardson explains in more homespun terms why Firefly was the lightbulb moment for her.

'I was a single mom with two little kids,' she says. 'I was stuck at home pretty much all the time, but with this technology you could rate musical artists and then it would tell you about new artists that you didn't know about. So you were discovering new music on the internet. I thought that was world changing. It changed my life, that's for sure!'

She led the investment in the company but admits that they were too early and that Amazon quickly eclipsed them. It was a missed opportunity but, she told herself, there would be a way to correct that. Napster, she soon realised, was that most rare of things: a second swing at the prize.

She already knew Amram and he called her and insisted she download this new piece of software called Napster. She did and every neuron in her brain went up to full wattage.

'I remember thinking, "Oh my gosh! I have never seen anything like this in my life",' she says. 'I called him [Amram] the next morning and was like [excited voice], "You're right! This is amazing! Let's do it! Let's go for it!" So I put some money in myself. He had put some money in. He said, "I love what was going on and I think there is something here, but it is being run right now by Shawn's uncle [John]. But I would put money in if you took over".'

She joined the company and started work immediately, fired up by what Napster could be. 'My role was to raise money, figure out business models, hire executives and make a lot of noise about Napster so that we could make something of ourselves,' she says. 'What you do in venture [capital] is you hire people, you find money, you figure out business models. So I was going to be the startup CEO for the first year or so. It was never like I was supposed to be the CEO full time. It was really just to get things going. I am good at building buzz.'

She recalls meeting 'the Shawns' (or 'the Seans') as she called Fanning and Parker, just when they arrived in San Mateo. Only in meeting them in person did it really hit her just how *young* they were.

She says, 'I remember them coming and walking down the hallway and saying, "Oh, it's so great you guys are here. I'm so thrilled. Go rent a car and get a hotel and then meet me back here in the morning." They just stared at me, "We don't have a credit card. We can't rent a car. We're 19." And I was like, "Holy shit!" I didn't even think of that. Why would you think of that? We ended up going over to the hotel and signing them in. We eventually ended up getting them a car.'

David Kent was brought in early to Napster as its director of new technology, becoming the ninth employee in the company. The generational contrast between the people *building* Napster and the people *running*

Napster could not have been sharper. 'When I was first approached, I had a very strange interview,' he says. 'These were underage 16-to-19-year-old kids, asking me to be their manager. And they wanted to be rescued from management because they felt that the management and the executive interference, especially from institutional investors, was ruining the prospects for their invention.'

I ask Richardson if she felt an obligation, given the callowness of the creators of Napster, to be 'the adult in the room' and guide them, and the equally young team of developers they were bringing in, through the startup and VC worlds. 'For me, that's not a big deal because I was a baseball coach for a boys' team for years on end,' she says. 'I've been a single mother for over 30 years now. It just comes naturally. I love taking care of people.'

The company was heavily bootstrapped in those early days. Richardson claims that during her tenure there, the company did not spend more than $2 million and that she, Fanning and Parker were all on identical (and relatively modest for Silicon Valley) salaries. 'For me that was poverty level!' she laughs. 'For them, it was a lot of money for a 19-year-old.' She wears her frugality like a badge of honour. 'I'm pretty proud of that because that was during a time when everybody in Silicon Valley was throwing millions of dollars at everything,' she says.

I ask her if she felt it was a risky company to get involved with given that music files, *copyrighted* music files, were being traded in their millions via Napster. She was assured it was just like Sony/Betamax (see Chapter 5) and that everything would be fine.

'The only legal anything we had was a memo from a law firm that said, "This technology is just like the VHS tape",' she says. 'So that was it.' She adds, 'Nobody could understand that [emphasising each word] *we didn't have a server where there was music.*'

COUNTDOWN TO APOCALYPSE: THE RECORD INDUSTRY IS IMMEDIATELY PUT ON SCRAMBLE MODE

Napster might have thought, might even have desperately believed, that having no server was its cloak of visibility as far as the law was concerned. The RIAA, and the major labels it represented, thought otherwise.

As covered in Chapter 5, national and international trade bodies like the RIAA, BPI and IFPI were keenly attuned to online developments, especially around anything it perceived as being built around piracy. Or even classed as 'pirate adjacent.' As such, Napster very quickly pinged up on their radars, and the anti-piracy teams in these different organisations were swiftly sharing intelligence between themselves.

I ask Mike Edwards, director of operations at the IFPI, when he first became aware of Napster. 'Immediately,' he says. 'In June. As soon as it was launched. It came to everyone's attention straight away.'

I ask what their response to it was. 'There was absolutely no doubt – as soon as we became aware of it, and we became aware of it immediately – that it needed to be litigated,' says Edwards. 'It was an existential threat to the music business. We were in constant contact with the RIAA. I'm not sure whether it was them who called me or me who called them and said, "Hey, have you seen this?" We were on it instantly.'

Ian Rogers claims it was him who tipped off the RIAA about it.

'I was the person who told the RIAA about Napster,' he tells me, but it was not, he insists, because he hated them or their service, although he does admit he installed it and then quickly uninstalled it as he thought 'it wasn't a great piece of software.' He says the reason was because he wanted a definitive response from the RIAA on its legality; if they were going to let it pass, then Nullsoft could change how it operated.

'The person I spoke to [at the RIAA] had never heard of it before,' he says. 'My call was like, "Are you gonna let this Napster thing live? Because if so, we're going to make a better piece of software. If not, OK. I don't want to compete with it".'

He adds, 'I wasn't like, "Hey, let me rat this guy out." I was like, "Hey, have you guys seen this? Are you guys going to let this be?" Because as Nullsoft, we thought this was a killer feature. "If you guys are going to let this go, then we have to build it. We have to compete with this." It's ultimately why we made Gnutella, which is another chapter of the story.'

Rogers thinks it *may* have been Karen Allen, digital music strategist at the RIAA, who he called, but cannot be 100 per cent positive. I ask Allen and she says she does not have 'clear memory' of how she, or the RIAA, were first alerted to its existence. She was certain, however, that it could not be allowed to go unchallenged.

'We took it very seriously,' she says. 'It was a very clear violation of copyrights. Very much uncontained – and very much growing and spreading. Who wouldn't want a bunch of free stuff? Especially college students. When you are at college and high school, music is super important for your life. Who wouldn't want a big fat pile of free music?'

She continues, 'We saw the massive potential of it. And it was something that had to be urgently addressed.'

The RIAA legal team was immediately made aware of Napster and started working out how to tackle this and what the first contact with Napster should be.

Allen does note, however, that no one at this early stage really understood just how big, just how significant, Napster was going to be. 'I think everybody was taken aback,' she says. 'I think Napster themselves were taken aback. I don't think even Napster thought it would be that good. I think they were surprised and definitely in over their heads. When Shawn [Fanning] built it, I don't even think he thought it would be this big. I think he was just screwing around.'

It was, claims Cary Sherman, senior EVP and general counsel of the RIAA, in April 1999 that the organisation was first made aware of Napster. That would have been when an early version of the software was circulating, mainly among like-minded people in IRC channels.

'I used to organise my emails by different subjects so I could keep track of things,' he tells me. 'I remember I created a sub-folder called 'Napster' that was part of some other folder – because it was just one more little thing! [Laughing] Turns out it deserved its own computer system, not just its own folder! At the time, I created a sub-folder and it just grew and grew and grew.'

Sherman's close colleague, Hilary Rosen, president and COO of the RIAA, stated she became aware of Napster in summer 1999. 'My head of antipiracy came into my office, pulls up Napster and says, "Pick a song," and I think I picked something current that week and there it is!' she said. 'We were astonished. It was so beautiful and simple. And we thought, *This is incredibly cool – but it's obviously illegal.*'[43]

As owner of Universal Music, the biggest of the five major labels, Edgar Bronfman Jr was the most powerful person in the record business. He also had the most to lose. Napster was, for him, a threat that had to be expeditiously stamped out.

'It came up on my radar probably in the summer,' he says. 'I don't remember exactly, but pretty quickly. My first reaction was probably something along the lines of, "Oh, shit!"'

He reveals that Napster was not just going to be fought on a legal level, it was also going to be fought on an investment level. If he could get the ear of senior VCs, he could persuade them to starve Napster of the investment money it was desperately seeking to raise: not just to expand its operations, but also to keep its head above water.

'I'm not going to name them, but there was one prominent Silicon Valley venture capital firm and their managing partner called me and said they were looking at making an investment in Napster,' Bronfman tells me. 'What did I think? I said, "Listen, I just spent $10 billion buying PolyGram. So you have to know that we're going to come after Napster, we're going to come after you, we're going to do anything and everything we can to shut this down. Because they're taking our property. They are stealing our property. And we're not going to stand for it".' He pauses for dramatic effect. 'They didn't invest.'

There was, according to Darren Hemmings, then running the IT desk at Sony Music in London, a bitter irony at the heart of how some in the company responded to news on Napster. While the legal teams and senior executives were formulating a plan of action on how to stop this most egregious of services from spreading, others slightly down the pecking order were seeing it as a tremendous free for all. Literally.

'The hilarity was that this thing was public enemy number one, an absolute disgrace, blah, blah, blah,' he says. 'I was younger and a lot more carefree in those days, but we basically had a laptop running Napster in the IT department. And if you wanted free shit, you came down and saw us and we'd hook you up. We'd have people from Columbia Records coming down and asking if we can sort them out for copies [of big albums] because all this stuff was rampant on Napster. On the one hand, you probably had the executives at the very top saying, "This is a scourge and we absolutely have to rub it out." Then you had all the product managers going, "You got the latest Radiohead, mate?" It was ludicrous.'

The reason why IT suddenly became this hub of illicit behaviour was because all the other staff members' computers were locked down and they were not able to easily install any software or applications on them.

'There's no fucking way someone there was going to understand how to get around that to install something,' says Hemmings. 'They were not technical people; they were music people. Hence we were the only people that had the power to do it and therefore we became quite popular because we could hook people up with all the good stuff.'

Suddenly everyone started looking at the IT team in a new light. 'If you work in a music company, you're the nerd in the IT department who's largely ignored and broadly hated,' suggests Hemmings. 'Because in any IT department, all you invite is hate because, if everything works, no one's coming down and going "Well done, mate. Everything's working great." It's just when shit breaks and then it's your fault.'

While some staff at the labels were stuffing hard drives with unlicensed MP3s, their most senior bosses were starting to contact Napster, playing good cop in the hope that Napster would buckle and they would not have to resort to bad cop.

SHUTTLE DIPLOMACY: TRYING TO BRING NAPSTER TO HEEL WITHOUT UNLEASHING THE LAWYERS. . . AT LEAST NOT YET

In his 1925 poem *The Hollow Men*, T. S. Eliot wrote, 'This is the way the world ends / Not with a bang but with a whimper.'

For the RIAA in working out how to initially tackle The Napster Issue, the approach was very much the bang as a last resort. Initial conversations were not exactly whimper-like, but it was not going to go in studs up. At least not to begin with.

There was a pincer movement happening. Digital executives from different major labels would individually open dialogue with Napster in the hope that this might spook them or shift things along quickly enough so as to come to some sort of agreement where Napster would seek licences and go legit. In the background, however, the RIAA and the lawyers at the majors were preparing their legal assault, perhaps hoping it would be a case of 'if' rather than 'when' it was needed.

Larry Kenswil was president of Universal Music's eLabs division and before that was working in business and legal affairs at the company. As such, he had a very rounded understanding, both technologically and legally, of what was at stake here.

'In 1999, we met with Shawn Fanning – and Sean Parker, I think, was there – to discuss where we could all go with this,' he says. 'The fact is the Napster people were having real problems figuring out how to make money out of it as well. They had no way of making money out of it the way it was established.'

He continues, 'We could never find a business model that worked for both sides. We tried a lot to do that. They wanted to essentially charge $5 a month for access to the technology and then you could do whatever you wanted with it. We saw that as too low a price point. Even if it was

$10 a month, we were still, at that point, very worried about it. It was unprecedented for us to support that. That made it difficult to do a deal. We tried a lot to do a deal but they just couldn't see that they had any business at anything more than $5 a month because of the peer-to-peer systems.'

Kenswil's colleague, music producer and technologist Albhy Galuten, says he understood just how high the stakes were here with regard to digital in general, not just Napster, and it was his job to explain that back to the rest of the company.

'To those people who understood it, it was an existential threat,' he says. 'To those people in management who didn't really understand the risks, they said, "Oh, you know, this is just another flash in the pan. This will come and go. People don't want to do that. They like having physical objects." To those people, it didn't seem like an existential threat, but certainly to us in eLabs, it was an existential threat.'

He adds, 'It was the beginning of the realisation, which a lot of senior executives didn't necessarily get: that once you have digital goods, and not physical goods, then distribution becomes frictionless. Maybe there was a little bit of friction due to bandwidth limitations, but we all knew that was going away, we knew the rate at which bandwidth was increasing, so there was no friction to distribution. If you allow people to share their goods without any restrictions, that would decimate the whole business.'

EMI's digital executives, described by the *Los Angeles Times* as 'industry doves', met with Bill Bales, VP of business development at Napster, in late 1999 'to explore possible alliances.' At the meeting, held at the Capitol Records tower in Hollywood, Jay Samit and Ted Cohen of EMI asked him what the business plan was. 'Bales explained that Napster didn't have a model yet – it was just letting people get music for free [. . .] Bales said he would get back to Samit once Napster worked out a business plan. He never did.'[44]

In an oral history of Napster in *Fortune*, Samit tells a very similar story, but suggests the meeting was with Shawn Fanning and Sean Parker, not Bill Bales. 'Shawn and Sean came in, and they didn't have a model,' he said. 'Their model was: Somebody other than them makes money. Somebody has to pay. I said, "Come back, and tell me how someone is going to get paid." And they never came back.'[45]

The details might differ as the story starts to flip into deep mythologising, but the core fact remains: Napster had not thought through the business model at this stage. Or, if it had, it was not telling the labels.

The labels suspected, and a source within Napster confirmed this to me, that these meetings were all pantomime and it was all a delaying tactic until Napster could get enough users to put it in what it believed would be an unassailable negotiating position.

'For us, all we wanted to do is move to one million users as soon as we could because we felt like that was a point where there's no turning back,' they say.

All of these initial conversations were happening in the US and it was made explicit to labels and trade bodies outside of the US that they were not to get involved. As is so often the way in international politics, the Americans were adamant they could, and should, police it all on behalf of everyone else. Some senior executives were happy, even relieved, that this was something they could leave to their counterparts in the US.

'Initially, it wasn't in our patch – it was in the Americans' patch,' says Paul Russell, chairman of Sony Music Europe. 'It was the RIAA's and the Americans' problem. There was nothing we could do about it in Europe. Apart from saying, "This could be a problem," there wasn't anything we could do.'

His colleague Patrick Decam, president of Sony Music Benelux, says there was an explicit diktat within the company that anyone outside of the US was to stay out of it.

'For us, it was evil,' he said of the threat of Napster. 'What I remember is that we could not talk to the Napster guys. They were like devils. We would have to refer any incident to New York. That's the thing about the Americans: they couldn't care [about Europe] for so long and then, all of a sudden, they wanted to control almost everything.'

Even Jollyon Benn, internet investigations executive at the BPI in the UK, was willingly keeping himself at some distance from what was happening in the US. Despite, by its very definition, Napster being a *borderless* service, he regarded it as a US-centric problem.

'With Napster, the Americans got out of the starting blocks quickly on that [so we let them run with it],' he says. 'People would ask you all the time, "What are you doing about Napster?" "What are we doing about bloody Napster? This American guy created this American entity. The Americans are dealing with it".'

One senior label executive in the UK says that, despite the stonewalling, the labels were sincere in their attempts to reach a deal with Napster, with this being the route they preferred over and above litigation. 'Did record companies want to do deals with Napster?' they ask. 'I think they probably did. Because they were doing deals with pretty much every other company.'

A KILLER NAP': WAS NAPSTER KILLING NASCENT LEGAL SERVICES BEFORE THEY EVEN HAD A CHANCE?

The major labels were obsessing over SDMI (see Chapter 10) and the Madison Project (see Chapter 13) as Napster hit, but there were a multitude of licensed music download services already in the market, notably Atomic Pop, GoodNoise/eMusic and Crunch (see Chapter 8). They were almost exclusively trading in music released on independent labels and trying to get a foothold in the market for paid downloads despite the seemingly insurmountable dominance of the CD.

These were services that had gone through the pain of licensing negotiations and had often paid out significant advances to get labels on side. Suddenly here was a service that had not licensed anything, had not paid advances to labels but that had *everything* and was offering it *for free*.

Those operating the nascent legal services were equal parts appalled and petrified.

'It didn't align to our values as an organisation,' says Jonathan Davis, co-founder of Crunch. 'Because we were in the business of selling music and enabling artists to make a living from music. It didn't feel like Napster was aligned to that! Certainly not when they came to market. It felt that Napster was more aligned to the values of the internet. Which was fair. It just wasn't the same value base that we were coming from.'

Richard Davies, the other co-founder of Crunch, expresses his thoughts in somewhat blunter terms. 'I remember being pretty pissed off,' he says. 'And I wasn't the only one, obviously. I think we were pretty powerless to do anything.'

Al Teller of Atomic Pop describes Napster as 'a serious body blow' to what he was trying to achieve with his company at the time, notably how quickly it was being adopted, especially among students, a core audience for a company like Atomic Pop.

'This was like a wildfire that was totally out of control,' he says. 'We suffered enormously for it. I remember speaking to my partners in this venture and said, "I'm not sure we're going to be able to overcome this in the timeframe that we need to do so. If we wanted to throw X tens of millions of dollars more into this at this moment in time, or another $100 million into it, or whatever the number would be, we could live our way through this while this gets sorted out, but it's going to take time to get sorted out. There are legal ramifications here".'

He glumly adds, 'Knowing the way the legal process works, especially when it comes to copyright infringement, my conclusion was that it was a bridge too far.'

Surprisingly, the major retailers were not, certainly not in 1999, cast into a pit of despair over Napster when it first arrived. They were still operating under the presumption (or, depending on your view, the delusion) that people would continue to buy a lot of CDs in their shops. Napster was a worry, but they were perhaps not as worried as the labels were at this early stage in the Napster story.

'I definitely was uncomfortable about it, for sure,' says Simon Wright, MD of Virgin Retail UK. 'I never really saw it for what it was going to become at that stage. But on the other hand, I never had this kind of paranoia in me that a lot of the music industry had. I hadn't come from that [world]. I was a straight business guy. It's easy to say in hindsight, but, no, at the time, it was disturbing, but very difficult to predict the effect of it. Very difficult.'

Stuart Rowe, general manager of direct and e-commerce for HMV Europe in 1999, says the initial response on hearing about Napster was to leave it to the record labels and their legal teams.

'I don't think we actually felt threatened,' he says of how retailers were responding to early news of Napster. 'Also don't forget at the time, in 1999 and 2000, HMV was a money-making machine. There was a level of arrogance about the whole thing: that nobody could touch us; that we were better than anybody else; that we were tougher retailers; that we knew what we were doing. We just thought we were invincible, really.'

As head of PR at HMV, Gennaro Castaldo says information on Napster would have been circulating within the company, but the problem was that many in retail thought any form of digital music consumption was patently ludicrous and they could not fathom why anyone would want their music that way.

'If you go to retail land, they're like, "Well, these aren't serious music buyers. If you were into music, you'd want to come and buy the album. Why would anyone bother to do this download thing? You don't even own it." Partly there wasn't enough information to know how much it was starting to leak out of the industry, but also, it wasn't taken fully seriously because it was like, "Well is it really a thing?"'

He adds, "They still felt, 'We've got the HMV brand. We've got the Virgin brand. These are global, iconic brands. Surely, in the new world, it's just a question of finding our role and we'll just carry on thank you very much".'

For Wright, Napster in 1999 was something that was happening in the peripheral vision of the retailers, not front and centre. It was something they were aware of, but their efforts and energies were focused elsewhere. They had more immediately pressing issues to deal with. Napster could wait. Couldn't it?

'When I came into the office in the morning, I was much more worried about how Asda and Boots were doing than I would be about what Napster were doing,' he says. 'Because this was happening that day. We knew we weren't losing that much from Napster. Yet.'

THE QUIET CHEERLEADERS: THOSE INSIDE LABELS WHO SAW NAPSTER AS A SPRINGBOARD TO THE FUTURE RATHER THAN THE RECORD INDUSTRY'S UNDERTAKER

There were, generally, two schools of thought within the major labels about Napster. One was public censure; the other, only whispered to trusted colleagues, was that maybe, just maybe, there was something the record business could learn from this.

'Personally, I thought it was a very exciting development,' says Martin Craig, head of Warner International's ESP division, summarising the duality that Napster represented. 'The industry was terrified of it.'

At the heart of this duality was what Napster represented for the future of copyright and what Napster represented for the future of music service software.

As Neils Rump, formerly of Fraunhofer but at Intertrust in 1999 where he was specifically focused on SDMI, puts it: 'I thought, "Hey, that's cool technology." The idea of spreading it wide is quite good. But I could also see the legal implications and the unenviable task for the rights holders to suddenly need to sue, or feeling the need to sue, consumers. Because in the end, if you're running a Napster node, you're a consumer. The whole concept of consumers becoming publishers, which we take for granted today with Facebook and Twitter, [Napster] was one of the first places where that happened. And that opened some cans of worms. I'm not sure that I was aware of them back then. But certainly, it was a cool technology. Immoral maybe, but it's cool technology.'

As co-founder of distribution company The Orchard, one might have presumed that Scott Cohen was horrified and terrified that Napster was a triple-threat that not only undermined labels and digital retailers but also negated the need for distribution companies. He says he was not remotely worried and was actually fired up by the future it pointed towards. 'I was excited by it,' he says. 'We had already been thinking of all these models; we were just waiting for it. We never thought it was a threat to our business either. We [publicly] said we never considered it a threat.'

Independent labels were already aflame with the potential of digital to redress legacy market imbalances and allow them to compete more equally with the majors.

'We weren't, as a label, massively anti-Napster,' says Peter Quicke, head of Ninja Tune and an AIM board member. 'The fact that people could get our records on Napster in a way seemed like quite a good thing. It was just part of the future. We wouldn't actively encourage it, but we certainly weren't getting upset about it. Because it just seemed pointless, like trying to make water flow uphill.'

Also on the AIM board at the time was Guy Holmes, founder of Gut Records. He says he was initially worried about Napster but changed his mind when talking to other AIM members, most significantly Martin Mills, head of Beggars Banquet. He also saw it as marking a major step change in consumer expectations around music.

'What we looked at and what we understood very early with Napster was that the public was telling us what they wanted,' he says. 'What we saw was that all the record labels went, "Fuck you! We're going to sue you." But what we all saw, or a bunch of us saw, was, "Hang on. This is the future. This is where it's all going to go." And Martin in particular saw it with absolute clarity. The first conversation I had with Martin was like, "They're stealing all our music!" And Martin went, "Actually. . ." and explained it. 'Oh!' Bang! It was an awakening moment. I was like, "Actually, no, they're not stealing our music. They're showing us where music can go and how it can grow".'

Holmes feels that you can draw a straight line between the majors in the US killing off the single (to further boost CD album sales) and Napster.

'That drove people to Napster,' he insists. 'And getting people to pay $15 for nine songs they don't want. There's two good tracks, probably. I'm being generous. That's going to drive kids out of bed to do something different. Because kids don't have $15 to spare. They've got $5 or $6 or $7 to buy a track. But more importantly, kids generally use a single track from a single artist as a voyage of discovery. Children are our bread and butter. They don't have a ton of disposable income. And if you mistreat them, which I believe the music business did, then they're going to do something else. And they did. Martin was preeminent in his thinking. He was utterly brilliant, because he went, "We're heading back to a singles market".'

Paul Hitchman, having just left Warner Music to set up music site Playlouder in late 1999, had a similarly swift 180-degree turn on Napster, switching from panic to passion. 'I heard about Napster and I thought, "Oh, shit! This is going to undermine everyone's business model." That was when I first heard of it, and from then trying to get my head around it. And then, of course, getting quite excited about what this meant in terms of disruption. Once I got over the fact that it was going to undermine everyone's business model, I thought the disruption would lead to new opportunities.'

Inside the majors, a generational schism had slowly been rumbling over digital in general, but Napster sharply expedited this.

Rob Wells, head of digital at BMG in the UK, was initially told about Napster by a US colleague who happened to be in London for meetings. Intrigued, he installed it on his computer and started to experiment. Fired up by the technological possibilities, but aware of the commercial concerns, he used a Friday morning senior management meeting to demo it to his bosses hoping they would see, beyond the 'free music' worry, what he saw in it.

'I remember that day I demonstrated Napster to that team,' he says. 'I was really excited. It was game-changing. Somebody's actually built a platform where people can consume music over the internet. I wasn't naive, I knew it was illegal. I was like, "This is the shape of things to come." I remember standing in front of all these people, probably fifty folks just all standing around in the open boardroom, and I booted up the Napster client. I just typed in a track name and there was this cascade of results that just fell down the screen. Brilliant. And I turned around and was like, "Ta-da!" The room was deadly silent and you could just hear the processing. Then one of the lawyers went, "We are *so* fucked!"

Then everyone was, "Aaarrrggghhhh!" And I was like, "No, no, no! You're missing the point! This is going to be fucking amazing! You've got to understand this!"All hell broke loose.'

It was, says Eric Winbolt, digital commercial manager at EMI UK, 'an epiphany' when he saw Napster for the first time, having been tipped off about it by a developer who worked on projects for him. Developers, he says, tended to know about things long before record companies did. 'On one hand, you're thinking that this is terrifying, because not only can all of this content be redistributed, but it's really easy to add more and replicate it,' he says. 'It was a complete fracturing of the realisation that, on the customer side, there's no putting this back in the bottle because this is amazing.'

Napster was, for Jeremy Silver, vice president of new media at EMI Recorded Music Worldwide, a dramatic and shocking coupling of everything he had spent years *enthusing about* with everything he had spent years *warning against*. He says he saw Napster for the first time in summer 1999 and felt immediately that it was everything the Madison Project was trying to be. In that sense, it was a roadmap for the future.

'Those of us that were on the front edge of the digital piece went, "Yeah, this is it! This is what it should be",' he says. 'But at the same time, we said, "This is all the world's music for free. This is the catastrophe that we've been telling you is coming." It was the two things at the same moment.'

He adds, 'That's why our jaws were dropping because we looked in and went, "This is so cool. This has got to be the way we do things." In the selfsame moment, we were going, "This is the entire world's music for free. We are fucked!" Those two feelings at the same time were absolutely summarised in this paradox.'

It was, in that sense, Schrödinger's cat for the record business. Or rather Schrödinger's Nap'.

'It was super exciting,' recalls Silver. 'None of us could talk about anything else. We didn't know where to put ourselves. We knew, on the technology side, that there was something really powerful here. If we could incorporate this and we could find a way of putting the business model behind this, then this was just dynamite. But we also knew, and it was microseconds later, the legal affairs team and the weight of the RIAA was just not going to let this survive. In a way, it didn't matter.'

At the majors, there were some senior executives who were either excited by Napster or not caught in the same panic spin as their most powerful colleagues.

'I was an early supporter of Napster, believing it was going to be a new way to break up-and-coming artists, that Napster fans would be the type interested in different and unusual musicians,' wrote Island Records founder Chris Blackwell in his 2022 memoirs. 'The industry was panicking, thinking that music online was going to mean music would be free, but I was thinking of Napster as a new service that wouldn't mean people stopped buying music. I might have been right, I might have been wrong, but it was a time when, really, who knew what was going on. My instinct was to support something new and disruptive, even if it took me further and further away from what I knew.'[46]

Todd Steinman, VP of new media and marketing at Warner Bros. Records in 1999, says it was almost immediately obvious to him that Napster represented an abrupt new generation gap appearing before the record industry's eyes in real time.

He says, 'I remember downloading it and just thinking, "This is Hotline without the password. How is this possible?" Boom! Every file that I could type in was on there. Then a couple of days later, I was doing a guest lecture for a UCLA class of music students. I pulled [Napster] up and almost all of them knew about it. I was like, "OK, this is the latest thing. Who here has played with it?" Almost every hand went up! I asked, "When did you get turned on to it?" "Two days ago!" "Yesterday!" I knew there was a groundswell that was upon us. That was a super memorable moment. OK, this thing is going to be the catalyst to drive the business. I thought they were going to get big enough to potentially commercialise it and become more like [what became] the first iTunes and put price tags on it and control their own destiny versus staying free forever.'

As president of the Island Def Jam Music Group in 1999, one might have expected Lyor Cohen to have to toe the line as set by Edgar Bronfman Jr and Doug Morris, respectively the owner and the head of Universal Music Group. Not so. 'I thought it was awesome,' Cohen tells me when I raise the topic of Napster. 'I thought that Napster was more of an opportunity for more flow of music.'

He insists that the issue of 'free' music on Napster did not unduly worry him. 'A lot of things were free to certain groups of tastemakers,' he says. 'And if I built an audience, I was always able to monetise it. I wasn't worried about them getting everything and me getting nothing because that never made any sense to me. Maybe it's because of my naiveté, but I always felt like there was no way that they would end up with everything and me with nothing.'

Former Geffen Records digital executive Jim Griffin was certain Napster was a splinter moment in history. 'Napster was the beginning of the end,' he says. 'Napster was proof that they [the major labels] had no control.'

He thinks, almost certainly, he would have heard about it on the Pho List very soon after it started to become publicly available. I ask him what he thought of it the first time he used it. 'I thought it was extraordinary,' he says. 'I thought: this is amazing.'

He tells me that senior people in the record business, who were never the most tech-savvy people at the time, would call him and ask him to come to their homes, install Napster on their computers and show them how to use it. He claims some even offered him $1,000 to drop everything and come to their homes immediately and give them a crash course in all things Napster.

'Inevitably, they would look at the screen and they would stare,' he says of how they reacted when he did install Napster on their computers. 'Then they would say, "Oh there it is! There's the demo tape from John Denver. I haven't seen that in a decade or two decades! This is fantastic! I can see what I've been looking for and I lost." They would be exclaiming, "The things I can find here are not the stuff I see on the shelf at Tower." That's when I knew it was going to be successful: because it was transformative. It wasn't about disrupting how you would get something off the shelf at Tower. It was about things that you would never expect to find there.'

It was the dramatic broadening out of available music catalogues (even music that had never been officially released) that showed some labels executives just how much they had to catch up with in their own licensing efforts. It was also, or at least it should have been, a jolting of the industry out of its apathy and its greed, putting the consumer more at the centre of things.

'Suddenly it changed the entire debate,' says Paul Vidich, executive VP of Warner Music Group. 'Consumers love music. They had been frustrated by the fact that they had to buy an album when they may have only wanted one or two songs. They didn't see that as a good consumer experience. They also found that if you went to any given store, the number of SKUs [stock keeping units] on a big store might be 15,000, but on the typical store, it'd be two or three thousand. It was often the case that you couldn't find what you wanted. They had new releases, but no catalogue. Suddenly, what Napster offered was this incredibly convenient experience. You could get whatever you wanted – out of stock, out of inventory – and it would be available to you.'

He says the Napster interface was 'kleugy' (glitchy) and download speeds for most users were still incredibly slow. Even so, it was a dramatic break from the past that the record labels, whether or not they wanted to, had to respond to.

'What it showed was that there was great consumer demand for that sort of experience,' he says. 'That was the thing that I think really changed people's perspective to, "We better do this quickly because it's clear that the consumers are voting here by their adoption of Napster".'

Vidich believes that the arrival of Napster was, in many ways, an inevitability and that the only people in the record business who were overwhelmed by it had clearly not been reading the key business book of the time.

'I wouldn't say it was terrifying,' he says, adding that when Roger Ames became chairman and chief executive of Warner Music Group in August 1999, he made all the senior executives read Clayton Christensen's *The Innovator's Dilemma*.

'He himself was a disrupter,' says Vidich of Ames. 'The message of that book was, "If you're going to take advantage of disruption, you have to throw out your old way of doing business and you've got to look at new ways of doing business." I was a guy who absolutely believed in that. Roger was a great advocate for what we ultimately proposed with Apple [and iTunes], which was to give them a better consumer experience than Napster. If it's a better consumer experience, they will pay for it. The thing that music executives didn't really, totally take in is that consumers don't buy music; they buy the experience. That's why the Walkman was so powerful. You bought music you could listen to while you're walking or in the car.'

Like a spin on Voltaire's line about religion – 'If God did not exist, it would be necessary to invent Him' – there was a curious predictability tied up in Napster in the sense that something similar would have eventually stepped forward and captured the public's imagination. It was fusing together multiple trends already happening online and finding a way to supercharge the experience and remove all the friction from it. Shawn Fanning's timing, the real secret ingredient here, was impeccable.

'There was a degree of fatalism,' sighs a senior record industry source. 'Somebody was going to do something like this.'

The increasing buzz around Napster in summer 1999 was enough for Elizabeth Brooks, then working as an A&R at Sony Music, to want to join it. She says she was introduced to it 'by a friend of a friend who was 16' and was so blown away that she cold emailed the company asking if they needed anyone with record company experience. That led to a call from Eileen Richardson, a meeting in San Mateo and the offer of a job to become Napster's first head of marketing. 'I was literally an outreach,' she says. 'I was like, "This company looks cool. I want to work there".'

She joined in November 1999 and believed she had just been parachuted into the most important company of the age.

'I saw unicorns,' she says. 'I thought this was the business I knew could change the lives and the experiences of music lovers. That I was confident of. I had a passionate and firm belief, as we all did, that we could build a billion-dollar business. Which we could have. And there's so many things that went wrong. They didn't go wrong mostly in 1999. Most of them went wrong in 2000.'

I ask her if she ever felt that going to Napster was an act of betrayal to her erstwhile colleagues at a major label who were suddenly left in the blast zone.

'I was young and I was still kind of punk rock, so I had some disregard, I think, for authority,' she says. 'I felt care for artists in terms of copyright, but I probably subscribed very much to the fact – in my head, it was a fact – that the record labels weren't exactly taking great care of artists and artists weren't making very much money from their recordings. So I didn't see it as artist damaging at the time. And interestingly, most artists didn't either. There weren't that many artists who were anti-Napster. Most artists were pretty much like, "Oh, I think we can work with you and do something interesting".'

Within weeks of Brooks joining and starting to work on a marketing strategy for the company, Napster was sued.

BEEN COURT STEALING: THE RIAA LAUNCHES LEGAL ACTION AGAINST NAPSTER

'Out there in some garage is an entrepreneur who's forging a bullet with your company's name on it,' warned Harvard Business School professor Gary Hamel in the September 1999 issue of *Harvard Business Review*. 'You've got one option: you have to shoot first.'[47]

As the digital heads at the major labels tried to placate things and sought to find a way for Napster to continue, but as a licensed and legitimate service, the RIAA was also trying to get some sort of resolution with the service without having to resort to the nuclear option.

'In September, we reached out to Napster,' says Cary Sherman. 'We said, "You are unlicensed. We'd like to work with you. We'd like to figure out how you can get licences so that you can operate legitimately. You've got a fascinating technology that has all sorts of potential, but you can't do what you're doing." And they gave us the slow roll. [Sarcastically] "Oh, yeah, we'd love to talk to you." They kept delaying and delaying. Their strategy was to accumulate as many eyeballs – or ears, I guess – as they possibly could so that they would have leverage in negotiations and they would become unstoppable and they could succeed in attracting more and more capital investors and so forth. Once we realised that they were not seriously willing to talk to us and were just stonewalling us [that's when we started legal action].'

A lot of Eileen Richardson's dealings in the early stages were with Hilary Rosen. They did not always, it is fair to say, get on swimmingly.

'I had a meeting with Hilary Rosen, who was running it at that time, and I had been tipped off by some music superstars that that is what was happening,' says Richardson. 'They were going from artist to artist saying, "Look what Napster can do. It is going to ruin your business." Hilary and I talked and I said, "Listen, I'm from tech, you're from the music industry. Here is what you don't understand. We are not giving away free music. We are letting people talk about music as they share it one-on-one." That is called social media today, but back then it was chatting about music.'

Richardson tells me she was at Napster around ninety days before the phone calls and the first letters from the RIAA started arriving. 'Then it got heated,' she says. 'I worked my ass off from poverty to finally have a nice house in a nice area. And now all of a sudden they sue the company.'

In their various conversations, Rosen made it clear to Richardson that she did not agree with Napster's interpretation of what Napster was about. 'She said, "You're infringing copyrights." I was like, "How can we be infringing copyrights if we don't own any of the music? We're a platform for people to talk to each other".'

Richardson continues, 'Hilary Rosen was talking to the wrong person, man. I was bam, bam, bam, bam! I told her, "The horse has left the barn.

So you can either get on it and or you can try to do whatever you're going to do. We do not have to shut anything down until you tell me what copyright law you think I'm breaking." And she didn't have an answer for that. So she said [in a terse voice], "Just open up the *Billboard* Top 200 and use that list." I'm like, "I'm not doing it. You do it." That's when Metallica [in May 2000] came with all the printed out documents of, "Here's where you broke our copyright." That's how they did it. And they did it on paper! They were trying to prove something, you know. I always hated Metallica.'

Elizabeth Brooks was in several of the meetings Richardson talks about and says they were not as pugilistic and dramatic as perhaps they have been retrospective painted as. She intones that the opprobrium was only trowelled on when it came to public statements.

'Our conversations with Hilary Rosen were really civilised,' insists Brooks. 'The conversations behind the scenes were always [civilised]. This was a banner time for Silicon Valley. Things are booming.'

Chuck D of Public Enemy, a huge digital advocate and someone who long campaigned against the iniquities of a market dominated by a handful of major labels, described Hilary Rosen as 'a lioness protecting the asses of five cowards.'[48]

He did not miss an opportunity to praise Napster for its assault on what he saw as the 'old' business that was trying to stop progress.

'I applauded what Shawn Fanning was doing 185 per cent,' he said. 'It was a cause. I thought he was the one-man Beatles. I thought what he had done with Napster was one of the most revolutionary things ever done in music, period. 'Til this day. And I wanted to support that. I wanted to be somewhere around that.'[49]

Richardson still insists that Napster was a direct attack on the greed and the scoundrelism of major label contracts with its artists. This is why, she says, the RIAA and its members were gunning for Napster.

Rosen, in an interview with *Salon* in May 2000, took issue with that line of argument. 'I do get a particular laugh out of technology entrepreneurs who try and say that the record industry has screwed artists over the years,' she said. 'But what is it, now it's their turn?'[50]

In early October 1999, Napster had an estimated 150,000 registered users. By July 2000, it had twenty million.[51]

Brooks says that ratcheting up user numbers was a priority for Napster at the time. 'Growth was mark one, for sure, and goal one, because it's still a pretty common way to build a company,' she says. 'Get users as fast as you can and then you go find a way to monetise your company. It's still a practice and it's been repeated many times.'

Matt Oppenheim, SVP of business and legal affairs at the RIAA, says that the RIAA, in preparing its case, brought in technologists to go deep into the inner workings of Napster to fully understand what it did, how it did it and what this all meant for copyright laws.

'You sit down and you break down exactly every step of what was happening within the system in order for the music to be distributed,' he says. 'When you did that, and understood how it was working, you said, "Oh, wait a minute. They're playing a central role here. But for their involvement, the music can't be distributed." But to do that, we had to bring on board expert technologists to help us understand it. We did that and we were guided by some very smart guys who helped us to understand the technology and then built our lawsuit around what was happening.'

Rosen argued that Napster themselves, despite their arguments about personal use and references back to the Sony/Betamax case in 1983/1984, soon became aware that their legal position was not as solid as they had previously presumed it to be.

'Once they got some copyright legal advice, they realized that the contributory infringement claim was the one that they were liable for, not direct infringement, since they weren't the ones uploading the music,' she said. 'They had created a software program that contributed to infringement.'[52]

In mid November, the news broke on *Webnoize* that the RIAA was planning to sue Napster. *Wired* confirmed the story, quoting an RIAA source who claimed that 'virtually all file traffic is unauthorized' on the service.[53]

The RIAA's suit was formally filed on 6 December in San Francisco's US District Court.

Billboard, in its only significant piece of coverage on Napster in all of 1999 in its print magazine, covered the start of the court case, but it was relegated to p. 8 of the issue dated 18 December and ran below a story on piracy in Hong Kong.

It quoted the RIAA as saying that Napster was "a haven for music piracy on an unprecedented scale." It added, 'The suit [. . .] charges Napster with contributory and vicarious infringement of copyright and related state laws. It seeks penalties of up to $10,000 per infringement [. . .] Napster is the first company the RIAA has sued for allegedly trafficking in authorized music. Napster posts a copyright policy disclaimer on its site saying if informed about possible infringement, it will 'disable access or remove the allegedly infringing material' but adds, 'It is the user's sole responsibility to comply with all federal and state laws".'[54]

(At this stage, it appears Napster was, for the record business at least, a US-centric issue. For example, UK trade publication *Music Week* made no major mentions of Napster in 1999).

RIAA spokesperson Lydia Pelliccia told *Wired* at the time, 'We spent many days sampling the Napster community, and found that virtually all file traffic is unauthorized [. . .] Unfortunately our urgent requests for a meeting were not taken seriously. We really had no other option but to file litigation.'[55]

Eileen Richardson had been expecting the suit and felt that this would 'put Napster on the world map' with the kind of media attention that was impossible to buy.[56]

Sherman insists that a lawsuit was genuinely the last resort and that all the way through they were urging Napster to strike a deal with the labels that would benefit everyone.

'It is often said that, in the music industry, litigation is just another form of negotiation,' he says. 'We brought that litigation because we'd had enough of being stonewalled and the sooner we could establish that this was illegal under existing law [the better]. There were going to be other people trying to set up Napster lookalikes. It was very important for us to establish that this was illegal. And nobody would believe it was illegal until we had a court ruling to that effect. We decided we needed to go ahead with litigation, even though negotiations had not yet failed. I don't recall if they had really begun in earnest at that point. But the point is that if you sue to establish that one way or another then something's going to happen here. And then let's see if a deal can be struck while that litigation is pending. I think negotiations were going on for a long period of time while we were doing that.'

Oppenheim says the RIAA tried repeatedly to help shepherd Napster towards a legal and licensed incarnation.

'I was pretty confident we were going to win,' he tells me. 'Our goal was not to shut Napster down. It really wasn't. We tried every possible way to settle that case where Napster would convert to a legitimate model. My approach was carrot and stick. The carrot being, "Look, what you built here can have a genuine business model to it if you work with us to create a legitimate service." There was no business model. Napster wasn't making any money. So that was the carrot. The stick was, "If you don't work with us, you're out of business! We will win. You will be gone. But that's not our goal." Yet everybody likes to view that period of time by saying, "Oh, the music industry executives were dinosaurs. They had their heads in the sand. They were trying to avoid the technology".'

Oppenheim does reveal, however, that an extremely unlikely figure stepped forward after the lawsuit began and offered their services to help the RIAA defeat Napster.

'I'll never forget Rudy Giuliani [got involved],' he says. 'This is fresh off him being mayor [of New York]. And he had been the US Attorney for New York. He was a very different persona then than he is now. He comes in to pitch the industry, to the RIAA, that his team can come in and fix this and solve it. [Chuckles] I'm sitting in the meeting. Hilary [Rosen] is there, Cary [Sherman] is there, a lot of other senior people are there, and Giuliani's giving his pitch. I'm sitting there relatively quietly, listening to his pitch. Finally, after a while, I interrupted him and I said, "Has anybody on your team ever litigated a copyright case?" And he looked at me and he said [sternly], "That doesn't matter!" I said, "So do you know the basis of the case that's been filed? What would your strategy be that's different from what our strategy is?" [Sternly] "We will figure that, all of that, out!" [Laughs] It was hilarious.'

Legal action against Napster, argues Paul Vidich, was 'a way of buying time' for the record industry to try and figure out the licensed solutions that could ultimately replace Napster. Legal action was also essential, he argues, to send out a clear message that the labels were not going to roll over and accept whatever Silicon Valley was throwing at them.

'You needed to sue for several reasons,' he proposes. 'You needed to sue in order to establish your seriousness. And you needed to sue in order to figure out how the law is pertained in the technical environment of the internet.'

For Edgar Bronfman Jr, the long game was using litigation as a form of leverage for negotiation with Napster rather than litigation purely as a swift route to erase Napster.

'In other words, if we couldn't compromise, then we were going to have to shut them down,' he says. 'But the only thing that brought them to the table was the fear that they would lose that litigation.'

Lyor Cohen is one of the few senior label executives at a major at the time to say publicly that he felt the litigation route was a mistake. 'I don't think they would have done it now in hindsight,' he says.

I ask him what his response was when he heard the RIAA was filing a suit against Napster.

'Disappointment, but I didn't spend much time on it. It was not my primary focus. I think they got vilified very quickly. It was hard to stand on their side. It was like in the 1600s in the witch hunts. You didn't know, but you were scared to death. That this was a way to stop this party. This great party that many people were enjoying.'

I ask him what he feels the industry should have done differently here with regard to Napster. 'Instead of fearmongering, they could have taken the time to really understand what Napster represented,' he says. 'Played more offensive than defensive ball.'

Elizabeth Brooks says that the lawsuit, in many ways, played directly into Napster's hands and that she, as their new head of marketing, was not going to pass up the opportunity to try and ridicule the labels and to position Napster as battling against the backwards behaviour and inequities of the major labels.

'We were David against Goliath,' she says of the marketing angle she very deliberately took. 'And you know what? It was true. We were the little, plucky upstart changing the world. It wasn't a difficult story to tell. True stories are always the best ones in marketing. They're the most powerful.'

Part of this goading of the majors took the form of a T-shirt with the Napster logo and a strap-line on the back saying 'thanks for sharing.'

'Provocation is generally really successful in marketing,' she says when I mention the T-shirts. 'It was cheeky. It was very cheeky.'

This helped inform how Napster presented itself to the world, showing a bold defiance even when mired in legal action.

'It was fun to be at Napster,' says Brooks. 'We weren't smug ever because we were always in imminent danger of losing our business at every moment! But we were passionate believers in what we did. And we were confident. You can't build something like that without some level of confidence. So something like "thanks for sharing" was very, very us. It was probably the first tagline I ever wrote. I'm, still to this day, quite proud of it! The T-shirts are impossible to find.'

BUSINESS, SUITS: THE IMPLICATIONS OF THE LEGAL ASSAULT ON NAPSTER

The lawsuit against Napster was never going to be resolved overnight. It was going to be painful, precarious and protracted. What it did, and the RIAA was fully aware that this would happen, was to draw incredible attention to Napster. This was the kind of media coverage that no company could buy. User numbers immediately shot up.

'We were closing in on a million [users], we got sued and our servers just lit up like a Christmas tree,' says Brooks. 'Which we had expected and were, to some extent, prepared for.'

Napster was now the hottest digital company in the world and it became an avatar for growing opposition to the major labels, bloodying the noses of people in the culture industries. Napster was an iconoclast. Napster was quickly becoming *deified*.

'People didn't know about Napster, and the labels – and the publishers – made this huge brouhaha about suing us,' says Brooks. 'This is really where I think there was a miscalculation as there was a public that was just starved for access to music and starved for information about music and starved of the sense of connecting to other people via music.'

The growing celebrity, or infamy, of Napster may have been a boon to those tasked with getting its name out there, but the software and development team actually building and running it saw the erupting media circus as an unwelcome distraction from their real work. David Kent was the one who saw this most on a daily basis due to his close involvement with the core development team.

'In a sense, although I think it's an unfortunate description, all management is paternalistic,' he says. 'I would say that these youngsters from this generation, being newly introduced to the industry, were indifferent with regard to the emotional rollercoaster. They didn't care much for the fact that they were a phenomenon and had attained celebrity. They didn't care much for the fact that they were being demonised, shut down and possibly threatened. They just wanted to get on with the game.'

He also says his team were not being distracted by the record industry's legal threats as they dismissively regarded the labels, and music copyright, as just being irritating things that were in the way of what it was they wanted to achieve.

'We just wanted to get on with it,' he insists. 'If the music industry didn't like it, and if entertainment law was in the way, then get out of the way! These kids were bitten by it, almost like being addicted to a game. They wanted to code. They wanted to play with their product. That was their motivation.'

In her marketing strategies, Brooks took the famous Oscar Wilde line to heart: 'There is only one thing in life worse than being talked about, and that is not being talked about.' Napster did not want to control what the media wrote about it; Napster just wanted the media to write about it. There were, Brooks says, only two things they wanted in any media coverage: the URL being printed; and the phrase 'free music' being used.

'It certainly gave us our first push towards just immense, immense growth,' says Brooks. 'And immense growth was what we needed to become a better product for our users. The more people, the more music, the more access, the faster the downloads because it's a peer-to-peer construct; so the more people that are online, the faster you get your song.'

This digital media paradox – of trying to stamp something out but only serving to draw more attention to it – finally got a name in 2003. But Napster was The Streisand Effect four years before The Streisand Effect.

The service was heavily targeting indie and alternative music fans as they already thought the major labels were the devil. Napster, in presenting itself as the poor victim being crushed under the wheels of the majors, simply proved everything these people already thought about the majors.

Eileen Richardson says Napster 'felt like a good fight to me', breaking the iron grip the majors had on the market and how tightly they gatekept it. 'I felt like I was fighting for the little guy, for the musical artists who had to pump gas for a living, but was very talented, but those damn record label people just didn't choose them,' she argues.

Kent says that Napster's creator was driven by a desire to empower artists in new ways. 'There wasn't a single bone in his body that did not want to support and enhance artists' revenue,' he says of Shawn Fanning. 'I understand that it was in violation of entertainment law. That's the ruling. That's the precedent. OK. But there wasn't a single shred of animosity or exploitation toward artists themselves. The record labels obviously want to own everything the artist does. And Napster was a way to provide some egalitarianism about what artists did outside of their contract. That's what they dreaded the most.'

John Kennedy, head of Universal Music in the UK, politely and inevitably disagrees with Richardson and Kent on the point that Napster was somehow liberating artists from the tyranny of the majors – majors who were sending smoke signals from the past that railed against the future.

'Oh my god!' he exclaims. 'That doesn't stand up at all. That's one of those naive things that were happening at the time. I would have been lobbied, I'm sure, within the company by my own executives saying that we were not embracing Napster enough.'

He continues, 'If it's the soundbite – "Did Napster make us reinvent our own business?" – then absolutely. But its own business wasn't very good. How long could they have kept going on with their own business? I don't know. Did they make us focus to find a solution? Absolutely.'

On the audience level, Napster completely reconfigured expectations around how music could now be accessed and consumed. The days of music fans having to wait until they could get their hands on a physical disc, from a shop or through the post, were over.

Quoted in Mark Mulligan's 2015 book, *Awakening: The Music Industry In The Digital Age*, Ken Berry (who was then chief content officer at Spotify) said, 'Napster was instant access at the speed of light, it created a generation of music fans accustomed to speed of light consumption.'[57]

Karen Allen suggests that the binary thinking around Napster and the record business was too reductive and that painting one side as the altruistic hero and the other as the manifestation of cruelty gets you nowhere.

'I think they handled it about as well as could be expected, given how early everything was,' she says of the RIAA's legal action. 'I understand their reaction. Both sides were right and both sides were very unreasonable at the same time.'

She expands on this point. 'Napster was right about needing a new form of distribution – and the internet being a very powerful way of that [being achieved]. They were very right about what we now call community and social being a huge part of that. They were never going to get the deal they needed to get to be successful from the record labels. Because the labels were still living in [a world of] $2.99 for a 45 rpm single or $2.99 for a cassingle. They were still living in that world and they were nowhere near doing the $0.99 per track deal that they eventually did with iTunes. They were years from that.'

Napster, argues Cary Sherman, had to be made an example of as there was a wider push from Silicon Valley to try and erase copyrights, the very copyrights the record business was entirely predicated on. This was not, he proposes, just about Napster: Napster was merely the symptom of something wider, something far more disquieting for the record business.

'The Silicon Valley community at that point in time – and still to today, but they are more willing to make concessions to not ride roughshod over creative rights – was all about disruption,' he says. 'The greater the disruption, the happier they were.'

Or, as Jeremy Silver put it, 'Napster unleashed music from corporate control and spawned a whole new generation of ideas about how to access music [. . .] Its launch issued the single greatest challenge ever to the viability of the music industry.'[58]

Talal Shamoon, then VP of corporate development and technology initiatives at Intertrust, spells out in harsh terms what he believes Napster meant. 'Napster was the third leg of the catastrophe, which was that, all of a sudden, any grip you had on isolating the value chain was gone,' he says. 'Millions of machines around the planet could anonymously share with each other.'

This was piracy on a wholly different scale to what had passed before. It made previous forms of piracy almost seem benign. Hence the multiple sledgehammers making up the legal response in December 1999.

'They went after people who had cassette sweatshops,' says Shamoon. 'They'd take *Sgt. Pepper,* make a thousand cassettes and sell them on the street. That was old school piracy. But they didn't go after teenagers making cassette copies giving them out. [Nerd voice] "Here's a mixtape. Please love me." CD came along and CD ripping and all that kind of stuff – and they kind of didn't complain. It wasn't until Napster, which jacked that thing full of nuclear-powered steroids, that they really started to squawk. So they had to put the genie in the bottle. And it was an incredibly expensive, hyper-sophisticated set of legal challenges to what was going on. They had to stop it. And they did. 1999 was the year it all broke. 1999 was the year that all the litigation broke out.'

Sherman says that the majors labels and the RIAA knew implicitly that this court action was going to have to be taken to the end, as bitter as that would be for whomever lost. There was not, he believes, going to be an easy armistice. 'We expected it to be a litigation that we'd have to go to the end with. We were not expecting to settle. Napster was a critical victory in many respects. Public relations is one of them. But establishing the legal principle was vitally important. The fact that we had to fight a second generation of cases [against the likes of KaZaA and Grokster] was just an indication that the first arguments were right.'

It is to be expected that Jay Berman, former chairman of the RIAA and CEO of the IFPI in 1999, agrees unreservedly with Sherman's arguments about the need to set a precedent. Berman also accepts that this was never going to be perfect litigation. It was not going to be neat and tidy. There would, inevitably, be sharp edges and unwelcome repercussions.

'At that moment in time, we had to make decisions,' he says. 'There might have been some that were, in retrospect, not the best cases to bring. But we were in a bind. And we did need to try to establish, in every place that we could, the sense and the reality, that not only was this illegal, but it was incredibly harmful.'

Berman says that Napster was an excruciating, but necessary, wake-up call to the record industry. 'I think the lesson that we would have learned at the RIAA and IFPI was that the only alternative, while you could bring litigation and you could win, was to create a legitimate [service],' he says. 'It was a sense of something coming apart. There was a sense that we needed to infuse the traditional record business with a large dose of technology and people who understood what this was about. And that we needed to do something more than just litigate. Unfortunately, it took a while for those things to materialise.'

One unexpected benefit of Napster was that it broke an impasse with certain artists who were digging their heels in and refusing to renegotiate their recording contracts to allow for the selling of their music as downloads.

'I would spend the night printing out how many pages of screenshots of how many of an artist's songs were available and how many times the same song was up there,' says Jay Samit, president of digital distribution at EMI. 'That was to show them, "You can do my deal. Maybe we'll make money, maybe we don't. Or you can just let this go on and I guarantee that you will never see another dime." Very, very effective. To put it in 2020 terms, "I know you hate needles. I know needles are painful and scary. But here's these people dying of a pandemic. Let me give you a shot." For a few artists that didn't go into digital, it really wasn't about digital; it was about other things in their lives.'

Alison Wenham, head of AIM, who would go on and get the independent labels to try to work out a deal with Napster, feels that it was more than a massive missed opportunity: it was a derailing of the future.

'You could argue that the shuttering of Napster put the whole development of music online back years, and also created much tougher adversaries such as KaZaA and LimeWire' she says. 'I believe it did.'

Jordan Ritter argued that Napster was not a carefully thought out idea with a clear political goal of taking an existing, if stuck in its ways, business and flipping it on its head just to prove that it could. 'You know,' he said, 'we didn't show up with some business model to disrupt the music industry, we did some cool shit that took off and here we are, right? We're just a bunch of punk-ass kids!'[59]

For Sean Parker, it absolutely was driven by politics – or certainly driven by the politics of *some* of the people on the inside. 'There is some truth to the idea that Napster was much less of a company and more of a revolution,' he said. 'Despite all the potential liability, nobody really had anything to lose. Half the company were a bunch of radicals who were not there for the job. They understood that it was a social revolution, a cultural revolution.'[60]

If Napster was a fork in the road for the record industry, the person who created it felt that the record industry, obsessing over copyrights, missed the critical point: that technology had dramatically changed their relationship with their consumer and they could no longer behave the way they had, where everything was on their terms, for the entirety of their existence up to that point.

'It definitely forced the major media companies to have to adapt to something that was clearly providing a better user experience than what they were offering,' Shawn Fanning told *SF Gate* in 2009. '[I]t's adapt or die. As industries change and new technologies come out, you're forced to look at it from the standpoint of what's best for the consumer, what will the consumer want? And through the Internet age, which was the big thing they didn't fully grasp, in the end, the user is always going to win.'[61]

Richardson tells me that she always knew Napster was doomed. But the fight against the RIAA became its primary, and soon its defining, purpose. She says, 'Shawn and I had a debrief a couple of years later and we both decided that we were the first and that we were going to be made an example of – no matter what. Period. End of story. You can say that you wished you did this or that you wished you did that, but we were too early and we were going to be the ones to suffer.'

Ritter described it in much more dramatic, much more heroic, terms. 'Napster had to end,' he said, 'because that's what happens at the end of every revolution. They gather up the leaders, they line them up against the wall, and they fucking shoot them.'[62]

When we speak, Richardson was founder and CEO of Downtown Streets Team, a homelessness charity in Palo Alto. She ran it for seventeen years but stepped down in 2022. She sees that work as a continuation of what Napster was – ideologically, at least – about.

'I am all about the little guy,' she says. 'That is why I am working with homeless folks now. It felt like a movement. It was a movement. And it was super exciting, for sure.'

Napster was, for the record labels, akin to a memento mori, the skull placed on the bookshelf by a metaphysical poet to remind them of their own mortality.

'It reflected,' muses Jay Berman, 'the fact that you had completely lost control.'

ENDINGS

CHAPTER 18

Repercussions and Concussions: the Aftermath of 1999

(Control becomes chimerical)

1999 saw the start of the death of the old music business as well as the start of the birth of the new music business.

There was never going to be a clear and identifiable changeover from one into the other. The two coexisted for several years, often uneasily. Ahead lay a long decline in revenues as the CD, that magic spell that made the 1990s so lucrative for record labels and retailers, steadily slipped out of favour while digital, still too young and too unformed, was never going to make up the shortfall.

New companies, new technologies and new business models were coming, but the transition from the old way of doing things to the new way of doing things was going to be as protracted as it was painful.

The move into the CD in the 1980s and the 1990s was additive. The move from the realm of physical into the realm of digital was going to be, for the next decade and a half, reductive. Many, many loose ends had still to be tied up.

WHO WANTS TO CLIVE FOREVER? THE FIRST GIANT FALLS

Many revolutions are defined by a symbolic slaying: someone who embodies the past is run through with a sword, dragged to the gallows, defenestrated or sent into exile.

For the record business in 1999, there was perhaps no bigger avatar of the Good Old Days than Clive Davis. He *was* the record business.

Starting out as a lawyer, he joined Columbia Records as administrative vice president and general manager in 1965, taking over as president in 1967. His shock firing in 1973 came 'amid allegations of misuse of funds and providing drugs to artists and disk jockeys.'[1] Davis addressed all this, and protested his innocence, at length in his 2012 memoirs. 'Once the charges of payola and drugola, as it came to be called, began to be hurled, the media spun out of control,' he wrote.[2] He added, 'The expense-account issue was a cover-up for my assumed drug and payola crimes. It was the worst sort of damning by false association, which did not make it any easier to live with.'[3]

He quickly bounced back and launched Arista Records in 1974. Through the late 1960s until the late 1990s, he worked with many of the biggest names in the record business. He was obsessed with hits and hit artists. His strike rate was staggering.

Davis was a lifer. He could have retired decades ago, but he loved the chase, he lived for the next hit, bigger still than the last one. Perhaps his crowning glory was helping turn Whitney Houston into one of the biggest solo artists of all time. If global success for Whitney was all he achieved, that would have been more than enough; but he worked with many, many artists and on many, many records that went supernova.

As a result, the power this 'flashy self-promoter and music industry legend'[4] wielded was phenomenal. Everyone – label executives, managers, artists – stopped what they were doing when Clive Davis called.

But in 1999 there was a feeling within BMG, whose parent company Bertelsmann had bought Davis's stock in Arista in 1979,[5] that maybe Davis was done, that he had overstayed his welcome. Much of this was driven by BMG.[6] [7]

A senior source within BMG, speaking anonymously, gives the background.

'Strauss Zelnick [president and CEO of BMG Entertainment] was magnificent at press,' they say. 'And he was going around saying, "We own pop music." The reality was that most of the pop music was at Arista. And everyone said, "Wait a minute, Clive Davis owns pop music." For various reasons Strauss wanted to get Clive out of there. So he moved him aside.'

Davis himself had no idea his ousting was coming until it was actually happening. He recounts how it unfolded in his 2012 memoirs (not to be confused with his 1974[8] memoirs). On 28 October 1999, he was called to a dinner meeting at French restaurant Lutèce in Manhattan by the chairman of BMG, Michael Dornemann.

Davis presents it as an ambush, presuming he was going to discuss future plans for Arista or maybe hammering out the terms of his contract, which was due for renewal in mid-2000. Given Santana's *Supernatural* album, which he had shepherded, was about to go to number one in the US, Davis presumed the dinner was going to be 'something of a victory lap.' Arista was also about to post its highest profits in its history. 'The days ahead looked promising indeed,' he wrote.[9]

Except. . . Dornemann reminded him that BMG had a retirement age of 60 and Davis was by then 67 and special dispensations had been made to allow him to stay. Dornemann outlined his plan. Davis would stop running Arista and become 'chairman of worldwide A&R for BMG and all its labels.'[10] The new president of Arista would be Antonio 'LA' Reid.[11] Davis said he 'went numb' at the announcement and had been 'blindsided.'[12]

Reeling from the news, Davis reportedly told Dornemann and Zelnick, 'There is no one inside or outside of the company who can succeed me.'[13]

Davis walked out of the restaurant and called Allen Grubman, his personal attorney, to formulate a plan. Details leaked to the press and a war of words inevitably erupted. Acts like Aretha Franklin, Patti Smith and Carly Simon came out in his defence. Other label executives expressed their outrage, perhaps fearing that their own positions were now shaky.

Davis said that by the end of the year he could feel 'my negotiating position within Bertelsmann getting stronger and stronger.'[14]

Davis had made it clear in December 1999 that he had 'no plans whatsoever to retire.' He added with a flourish, 'I am absolutely at the peak of my powers.'[15]

Meanwhile Zelnick said, 'I have a responsibility to make decisions based on what's right for the company, and that includes making sure we have an appropriate succession plan in place at Arista.'[16]

The source at BMG adds extra colour to the music business fallout. 'There was a huge industry reaction,' they say. 'Artists like Whitney Houston were out taking full page ads in *Billboard* complaining about it. Everyone was like, "You can't do this to Clive!" It really came back very hard.'

Things dragged on into 2000 and Davis eventually managed to find a way to stay within Bertelsmann, despite what he saw as a grand betrayal. He would leave Arista, but Bertelsmann would provide financial backing to help set up a new label within BMG that Davis would own 50 per cent of. J Records (Davis's middle name is Jay) opened for business on 15 August 2000.[17]

It was not just a huge financial blow to appease Davis; it was equally costly to bring in his replacement at Arista. 'Strauss brought LA Reid in to run Arista,' says the BMG insider. 'But to do that he had to buy LA Reid out of La Face Records, which was usually successful – TLC, Toni Braxton et cetera. That was expensive to buy that out. The cost of pushing Clive out was enormous. Then in November 2000, Strauss resigned from his post at BMG. That was two years after ascending to the top job. All of that shit hit the fan in 1999.'

Such high-stakes politicking and corporate manoeuvring in 1999 and 2000 felt like a relic of a bygone age. This was perhaps the last gasp of that old way of doing business – of trying to drive out the powerful but having to pay large sums of money to do so. The major labels were soon to find out that the bottomless funds they could draw on to indulge their whims or magically eradicate their problems actually did have a bottom.

The days of plenty were looking like they were now over. There would be no bountiful harvest if all the crops had failed.

WHAT HAPPENED NEXT?

The following is an attempt to briefly tie up many of the loose ends in the key developments that began or that reached their apex in 1999. Some of these stories played out in a matter of months, some took years, and some are still unfolding. As such, the following section should be read merely as appendices.

Napster: The legal battle against Napster dragged on until 2002, having gone through multiple twists and turns. In February 2001, the courts ruled that it 'knowingly encourages and assists its users to infringe the record companies' copyrights.'[18] Napster scrambled to reimagine itself within the parameters of the law, signing a deal with UK independent labels, via trade body AIM, in June 2001 as part of a plan to relaunch as a paid service.[19] A subscription price was never agreed on, but it was reported that it could have ranged between $4.99 a month and $15 a month.[20]

Napster eventually ran out of road in 2002 and filed for bankruptcy in June that year.[21] It was bought by Roxio in November 2002[22] and relaunched as a licensed service.

Bertelsmann had invested $85 million in Napster in November 2000[23] to try and make it a legitimate operation, but the company was sued for that investment by the other majors, who argued that it prolonged Napster's life and exacerbated mass copyright infringements. Universal

Music Group settled for $60 million from Bertelsmann in September 2006.[24] EMI settled in March 2007 for an undisclosed sum.[25] Warner Music Group received a $110 million settlement in April 2007.[26]

Napster was sold again to Best Buy in September 2008[27] and then sold again to rival streaming service Rhapsody in October 2011.[28] It was sold again to virtual reality firm MelodyVR when it acquired Rhapsody in August 2020.[29] If that was not enough, it was sold again to Hivemind and Algorand in May 2022, who planned to turn it into a Web3 operation.[30]

Tim Westergren, who was setting up Pandora in 1999, says the reputational damage Napster caused in the world of music startups, where suspicion and distrust became the default setting of labels and publishers, was immeasurable. 'Napster cast a big shadow, for sure,' he says. 'It took us seven or eight years to repair [things and] to be seen as an ally.'

In the immediate wake of Napster came a flurry of services like Gnutella, KaZaA, LimeWire and Audiogalaxy, all of which the labels tried to stamp out. The arrival of BitTorrent in 2001 supercharged everything, meaning enormous files including whole films and TV series, not just three minutes of music on MP3, could be easily and quickly shared online.

Various trade bodies, notably the RIAA in the US and the BPI in the UK, started legal action against serial uploaders on peer-to-peer services, also trying to get ISPs to throttle download speeds of persistent offenders – or disconnect their accounts. The RIAA also sued heavy downloaders, doubling down even when the operation proved to be the worst public relations disaster in its existence.

Piracy online continues today, but the shift from ownership-based models (i.e. downloading files) to access-based models (i.e. streaming) means digital piracy is nowhere near the issue it was in the early 2000s.

MP3.com: Founder Michael Robertson evolved the service into MyMP3.com/Beam-It, essentially a locker service where users could access music they technically owned on CD via the company's servers. The major labels sued in early 2000, arguing that it was unlicensed and, as such, violated their copyrights.[31]

Hilary Rosen of the RIAA wrote to Robertson and said, 'Simply put, it is not legal to compile a vast database of our members' sound recordings with no permission and no license. Obviously, you are not free to take protected works simply because you want them.'[32]

MP3.com was, in many ways, a sitting duck – a well-funded service that was brimming with cash before the crash in 2000. 'MP3.com, because of the dot com boom, had a ton of money,' says Matt Oppenheim, SVP of business and legal affairs at the RIAA. 'So every company who had been infringed sued them, because everybody wanted a piece of that pie.'

The RIAA won the case in April 2000.[33] Author John Alderman called it 'the largest copyright violation in history.'[34] In June, MP3.com settled with Warner and BMG, and the following month it settled with EMI.[35] In August 2000, it settled with Sony.[36] And in November 2000, it was ordered to pay $53.4 million in damages to Universal.[37] In a surprise move, Universal acquired MP3.com in May 2001 for $372 million.[38]

Oppenheim suggests that the company, regardless of the legalities, was pointing towards a different type of access-based consumption and made it clear to the labels that they needed to be ready for it. 'It forced all the companies to start to digitise all of their records in mass, which they had never done before,' he argues. 'These mass infringement lawsuits forced the companies to start to organise their records in mass.'

The major labels: In January 2000, AOL bought Time Warner (home to Warner Music) for $182 billion.[39] The timing was terrible given the dot com crash happened mere weeks later. They demerged in 2009.[40]

French media and utility group Vivendi acquired Seagram, including Universal Music Group, in June 2000.[41] In January 2011, a Paris court convicted Edgar Bronfman Jr of insider trading during his time as vice chairman of Vivendi between 2000 and 2002. The same court convicted Jean-Marie Messier, former Vivendi chief executive, of misleading investors.[42]

A planned EMI/BMG merger was called off in 2001.[43] Various attempts in the early 2000s by Warner and EMI to merge fell apart.[44]

Edgar Bronfman Jr returned to the major label sector by leading a consortium to buy Warner Music in 2003.[45] Sony and BMG moved to merge as a 50/50 JV in 2003.[46] The merger was cleared by the regulators in 2004.[47]

EMI was acquired by private equity company Terra Firma in 2007 for £4.2 billion, but it lost control of the company in 2011. The bulk of EMI was sold to Universal Music, with Warner Music taking the Parlophone label (but not The Beatles' catalogue).[48]

In 2008, Sony bought out Bertelsmann's 50 per cent share of Sony BMG, renaming the company Sony Music Entertainment.[49]

In 2011, Access Industries, led by Len Blavatnik, bought Warner Music Group for $3.3 billion.[50]

Universal Music launched its IPO on the Euronext Amsterdam in September 2021, with trading on the first day giving it a valuation of $53 billion.[51] There are now three major labels who, between them, control 70 per cent of the global record business.[52]

Major labels' digital services: Project Nigel was quietly scrapped in early 2000. The majors split into two camps to develop rival services. Pressplay was created by Universal and Sony in 2001 and lasted until 2003; MusicNet was backed by Warner, BMG, EMI and RealNetworks in 2001 but did not fare much better. High prices, cumbersome DRM, terrible interfaces and an initial lack of cross-licensing of catalogues all helped to sink these two attempts by the majors to become digital-forward retailers.

Retailers: CDnow was bought by Bertelsmann for $117 million in July 2000.[53] Tower Records went into liquidation in 2006.[54] Virgin Megastore was taken over by Zavvi in 2007 in the UK and all its stores rebranded as Zavvi stores.[55] That operation collapsed in 2009.[56] The Megastore brand continued in the US, but rolling store closures meant it was reduced to five outlets by 2019 before the plug was pulled.[57]

Dot coms: The dot com bubble burst in March 2000 and investment dried up overnight.[58] Eileen Richardson says this was a hammer blow to Napster just as it was its most vulnerable, with the RIAA-led legal action against it ramping up. 'The dot com crash came in the exact middle of our fundraising,' she says. 'I had the sweetest deal on the planet lined up. All of a sudden everybody was getting scared.'

Jonathan Davis, co-founder of the Crunch download service, concurs. 'In March and the subsequent months, it became very, very, very challenging to raise money,' he says. 'The environment for raising money [evaporated].'

All new services struggled to get off the ground for many years afterwards, with music being one of the most badly affected areas. It did not help that, as record sales were cratering, music was seen by VCs as too high risk a category to invest in.

Al Teller, founder of Atomic Pop, suggests that services like his were doomed anyway, simply because the market and the infrastructure they needed to succeed was not there. . . yet.

'If I were to broadly categorise the effort, I would say we were just a bit too early,' he tells me. 'I'm a tough enough critic of myself to say that being too early is just another way of being wrong.'

SDMI: Hailed at the time as the single most important thing in the record business, SDMI rolled on into 2000 but was increasingly dismissed as a damp squib. Leonardo Chiariglione stepped down in early 2001.[59] Soon after, SDMI was quietly mothballed.

Physical product: Despite the much ballyhooed 'renaissance' in vinyl and even the cassette (which is really just a form of merchandise now rather than a format), the recording music market is overwhelmingly digital. *Ownership*, which got a temporary shot in the arm with the iTunes Music Store, has ceded almost completely to *access*.

In the US, as reported by the RIAA, streaming accounted for 84 per cent of the market in 2022.[60] Physical sales (rolling together CDs, LPs and cassettes) were 11 per cent. Downloads were a mere 3 per cent. (The remaining 2 per cent was synchronisation income.)

On a global level in 2022, as reported by the IFPI (using a slightly different calculation from that used by the RIAA), streaming was 67 per cent of the world market, physical was 17.5 per cent while downloads 'and other digital' were 3.6 per cent. The remainder was made up of performance rights (9.4 per cent) and synchronisation (2.4 per cent).[61]

Big tech takes over music: Apple launched the iTunes ripping and music management software in January 2001[62] and followed this with the iPod in October 2001. The arrival of the iTunes Music Store in 2003 in the US (and 2004 in Europe) helped make Apple the most powerful player in digital music.[63] The company held tightly to downloads for years but eventually launched Apple Music, its subscription service, in June 2015.[64]

Spotify launched in Europe in 2008[65] and expanded to the US in 2011.[66] Inspired by Napster, the founding idea was to come up with a better offering than the many pirate sites that existed at the time. It is a 'freemium' service where songs are technically 'free' to play but are intercut with ads, while a monthly subscription gives users much greater functionality (ad-free and unlimited listening, ability to cache music for offline play and so on). As of April 2023, Spotify had 515 million monthly active users, of which 210 million were premium subscribers.[67] It is the biggest source of revenue for recorded music in the world (although it has been regularly attacked by publishers and artists for not paying them enough). In order to land deals with labels, Spotify offered all the major labels and the independents (via international independent label collective Merlin) equity in it. The echoes of Musicmaker endured. Spotify had a direct listing on the New York Stock Exchange in April 2018, giving it a market value of $29.5 billion.[68] This listing allowed shareholders to cash out if they so wished. Sony sold around half of its equity in May 2018 for $750 million.[69] Merlin, on behalf of its members, cashed in its shares the same month for an estimated $125 million.[70] Warner cashed in its stake for $504 million in August 2018.[71]

As of late 2023, Universal had not sold any of its Spotify stock.

YouTube launched in 2005 and was acquired by Google in October 2006 for $1.65 billion.[72] It is, by some distance, the most popular music service in the world in terms of users, even if music is only part of its video offering. It is primarily supported through ad revenue, but also launched a Premium subscription tier as well as a dedicated YouTube Music subscription tier. Between them, they had eighty million paying subscribers as of November 2022 but did not break out how many subscribers each subscription offering has.[73]

Amazon evolved beyond selling books and CDs to become the 'everything store' founder Jeff Bezos always imagined it to be. It offers a number of different music services now, including a limited streaming catalogue as part of its broader Prime subscription as well as the full Amazon Music Unlimited, which competes with Spotify and Apple Music.

There are a variety of other international and local music services around the world including Deezer, Tidal, SoundCloud, Pandora (in the US), MelOn (South Korea), JioSaavn and Gaana (both India), Anghami (Middle East and North Africa), Boomplay (multiple African countries), and KuGou Music, QQ Music and NetEase Music (all China).

Record sales fall for a decade and a half: The closing half of the 1990s were the peak years for the record business, with revenues hovering between $38.1 billion and $39.7 billion. By 2000, however, the cracks were appearing and there was a steady slide in revenues, as reported by the IFPI. Even trying to plump up the numbers by adding in performance rights income and synchronisation income, it was still looking like a death spiral. It took until 2015 for growth to slowly start to return. In 2022, the IFPI reported the trade value for the global record business was $26.2 billion.[74] While growth of any sort is always welcome, these numbers are still a long way off from 1999, before control shattered in the hands of the record business.

FINAL THOUGHTS: WHAT 1999 MEANT FOR THE PEOPLE WHO WERE THERE

Having interviewed many people for this book, I put the same final question – 'What do you think 1999 represented or meant to the music business?' – to all of them.

Below are the most interesting, thoughtful or entertaining answers I received.

'It was the year it became apparent that technologies were going to forever change the industry and, truthfully, to the music industry's detriment. At least up through 2007.' – *Edgar Bronfman Jr, head of Seagram, the owners of Universal Music*

'It was a seminal year in the sense that CD sales were still very high and we were still making a lot of money from CDs. But the writing was on the wall that digital was going to completely undermine that business model and those revenues for a very long time to come. 1999 was the year Napster launched and grew by impossible numbers through the course of that year and beyond. And it showed that the law was not up to the task. We had to litigate these cases. We couldn't just send a demand letter and they'd go, "Oh, they got us. We'll have to shut down." We had to litigate those cases from start to finish in order to establish the most basic of principles of how copyright applied in this new business. 1999 was the end of the good times for physical and the beginning of the worst of times for digital.' – *Cary Sherman, senior EVP and general counsel at the RIAA*

'There were two kinds of reactions. Some of my colleagues believe that control was [essential] and therefore we would have to wait until all these fads disappeared, all these new technologies would become old and without having really harmed us. Or we had to face reality and become major actors in this new era. It was not just that the record company fucked up. There were inside tensions, battles and arguments. It was not how people like to think: that we were those stupid guys all along. It is just that we had built rosters, we had millions of contracts with clauses that protected us: not fully, but in some ways.' – *Patrick Decam, president of Sony Music Benelux*

'[The industry had to eat] a little humble pie. It may not taste nice, but it's probably good for you. There was a generational shift in the people who were running the companies so that they weren't so much tied to the past and they had an ability to look and say, "You know what, we need to figure out how to adjust to this".' – *Jay Berman, chairman and CEO of the IFPI*

'I asked the Beastie Boys about the decline of the music business and [Adam] Yauch's comment – he kind of turned sideways and thought about it – was, "Couldn't happen to a nicer bunch of people." Here's what happened, though. I think an important part of the story is how all of these bad decisions really came back to haunt the music business. I agreed with Adam. I felt no pity. I feel sorry for artists, but the industry did this to themselves. The artists did not do this.' – *Ian Rogers, webmaster at Nullsoft (and former webmaster for BeastieBoys.com)*

'We didn't have the solution. 2000 was going to be about working on the solution. It wasn't going to be done from the UK. It was going to be done globally. At least we knew that senior management was taking this seriously. I wasn't going to be begging for the money needed to do these things. But it wasn't money at this stage, it was lightbulb moments that were needed.' – *John Kennedy, chairman and CEO of Universal Music UK*

'We'd already laid quite a lot of seeds and mycelium down in the next decade to show that it was the right thing to do. That growth was just going to become more and more exponential. Which is what's happened.' – *Matt Black, one half of Coldcut and co-owner of Ninja Tune*

'It seemed like maybe the whole thing would disappear. Maybe the record industry would ultimately disappear.' – *Peter Quicke, label manager at Ninja Tune*

'There were a lot of structures and we modelled them, and they were all net positive for the record industry if you believed that the CD would die. If you did not believe the CD would die, it was a completely different calculus and, unfortunately, we couldn't shift that perception in the end. At all. The thing I heard the most was, "I can't do this because of Tower Records. I can't do this because of my relationship with retail. I can't blow up my relationship with retail." And three years later, Tower Records is out of business.' – *Elizabeth Brooks, vice president of marketing at Napster*

'There were definitely progressive voices and forces, and they started to get the upper hand over time. The old guard either didn't understand it or didn't want it. They were trying to cash in their last chips before the end, as they saw it. You could just sense that changing of the guard over time. It took a long time – eleven or twelve years.' – *Paul Hitchman, co-founder of Playlouder*

'We helped create Impala along with European independent record companies so that we could argue our case in Brussels. Because we knew our case would have to be argued. It really was the beginning of this consolidation down from several majors to three. What AIM was doing was building a community that had never really felt like a community. Our shoulders were broad and our vision was clear. I would not have agreed to join AIM if I did not absolutely believe in the need for it to exist – today or any day.' – *Alison Wenham, chairman and CEO of AIM*

'You are sitting on the cusp of a revolution that nobody really understands, that nobody's really been through yet. A business that basically defined the 20th century starts to break apart in the 21st.' – *Eric Winbolt, digital commercial manager at EMI*

'I called it Tarzan Economics. Because they [the major labels] were clinging to a vine that kept them off the jungle floor. They were not going to let go of that until they had the next one in their hand. I was certain that the next one was there for them, and that they would eventually let go of the old one.' – *Jim Griffin, digital consultant and co-founder of the Pho List*

'That year was a pivotal year because it was the year in which the promise of technology, in the hands of maverick companies, demonstrated to consumers that there were some very attractive ways of buying, or acquiring, and enjoying music. They were not in the hands of the music industry or its traditional technology partners. That forced the industry to act and react. It was all the actions and reactions that were initiated in 1999 – SDMI, and others – that ultimately led to what I think was the pivotal event in the new millennium, which was the deal that we signed with Apple [for iTunes]. It couldn't have happened if there hadn't been all of the conflict that developed in 1999.' – *Paul Vidich, EVP of strategic planning and business development at Warner Music*

'When you're inside an environment that has been established for as long as [the record business] had been established, the relationships in the value chain were as strong and historic and as personal, going back through people's entire careers. This idea that the whole thing could be dislodged and entirely new players could come in and totally steal chunks of the market and that entire aspects of your business would just disappear – whether it's retail or whether it's manufacturing, they would just vanish – people couldn't see that. It's very, very hard to see that. I felt like I had some vision of where it was going, but I didn't, in my wildest dreams, think that all of those massive pieces of business would just disappear. I don't think any of us thought that.' – *Jeremy Silver, vice president of new media at EMI Recorded Music Worldwide*

'[Napster] would take away their arrogance of what they [the major labels] thought they did, which was to produce albums and to find the stars themselves that nobody else could. I do think it was probably hard for them. But we had the consumers talking to us, obviously, by using the service; and we had the artists talking to us as well. So there was no longer a need for the record industry, as it were.' – *Eileen Richardson, CEO of Napster*

'If you look at all the companies that were in the emerging digital marketplace around 1999 and what was going on, the majority of the technology companies don't exist anymore. You know who did survive? The record companies. Because ultimately the record companies have the content. And the content is what's important.' – *Matt Oppenheim, SVP of business and legal affairs at the RIAA*

'There was real innovation coming out of the US. And then it went really wonky, in 2000 and 2001, when they started suing people. All the fucking wheels fell off.' – *Rob Wells, head of digital at BMG in the UK*

As the mists cleared from 1999, as people got enough distance from it to be much more objective in their assessments, the enormity of what happened that year started to snap into focus.

For the record business, 1999 was arguably the single most important year in its existence. A *lot* happened that year. That year saw the crashing together of a multitude of forces and the industry is still living with the consequences, still picking through the rubble.

It was an exciting year, it was an exhilarating year, it was a terrifying year and it was a destructive year.

But it was a *necessary* year.

The record industry – plump on profits, haughtily believing it was destined for even greater power and wealth – would never have changed unless it was forced to. The record industry is an amazing industry, but for too long it was an insular industry and it was an arrogant industry.

It is still an insular industry and it is still an arrogant industry, but hopefully the hard lessons learned in 1999 have made it less insular and less arrogant.

One can only hope.

For the record business, 1999 is *the* historic moment, *the* harsh schism, where its presumption of control proved to be desperately deluded. It got badly battered, bloodied and bruised.

There was a lot of collateral damage, making it face up to the unimaginable and the inconceivable: control is always conditional and control is always transient.

Global record sales by retail value (the next 20 years)

2000 – $36.9 billion (down 4.5% in current dollar terms)
2001 – $33.7 billion (down 8.9% in current dollar terms)
2002 – $31 billion (down 7.9% in current dollar terms)
2003 – $32 billion (down 7.6% in constant dollar terms)
2004 – $33.6 billion (down 1.3% in constant dollar terms)
2005 – $32.3 billion (down 3.7% in current dollar terms)
2006 – $31.8 billion in retail value and $19.5 billion in trade value

For 2006, there is reporting in terms of trade value and retail value, after which point the IFPI starts reporting in trade value numbers. The argument for this happening was that, because the business was going digital (iTunes Music Store had launched in 2003 in the US and 2004 in Europe), it was impossible to track retail prices; plus the growth of various revenue streams in digital was all about trade licensing. Following an IFPI council vote, the switch in reporting happened.

2007 – $19.4 billion
2008 – $18.4 billion
2009 – $16.2 billion
2010 – $15.9 billion
2011 – $16.6 billion
2012 – $16.5 billion
2013 – $15 billion
2014 – $14.97 billion
2015 – $15 billion
2016 – $15.7 billion
2017 – $17.3 billion
2018 – $19.1 billion
2019 – $20.2 billion

Sources: IFPI data as reported by *Music & Copyright, The Guardian, Music Ally, Billboard, Forbes, Music Week* and *Music Business Worldwide.*

(Note: in 2001, the IFPI started adding performance rights income to help bump the overall revenue numbers up. Then in 2010, it started including synchronisation revenues. So the decline from 2001 onwards was actually worse than the IFPI numbers suggest. For example, in 2001, $0.6 billion in performance rights income was added to the total; in 2006, $1 billion in performance rights income was added to the total; in 2015, $2 billion in performance rights income and $0.4 billion in synchronisation revenues were added to the total.)

Dramatis Personae

List of all primary interviews for the book (with their job titles/roles in 1999)

Allen, Karen – digital music strategist at the RIAA
Barton, Chris – founder and CEO of Shazam
Benn, Jollyon – internet investigations executive at the BPI
Berman, Jay – chairman and CEO of the IFPI
Black, Matt – one half of Coldcut and co-owner of Ninja Tune
Bronfman Jr, Edgar – CEO of Seagram (owners of Universal Music Group)
Brooks, Elizabeth – vice president of marketing at Napster
Campbell, Scott – founder and MD of MediaSpec
Cartwright, Neil – head of digital at Sony Music UK
Castaldo, Gennaro – head of press and PR at HMV
Cauchi, Ant – new media manager at Parlophone (part of EMI)
Chatterjee, Raoul – head of sales and new media at Warner Music UK
Chiariglione, Leonardo – executive director of SDMI
Cleary, Andy – co-founder/director of Jammin Music Group and AIM board member
Cohen, Donna – VP of internet strategy and business development at Warner Music
Cohen, Lyor – president of Island Def Jam Music Group (part of Universal Music Group)
Cohen, Scott – co-founder of The Orchard
Craig, Martin – head of Warner Music International's ESP division
Davies, Richard – co-founder of Crunch
Davis, Jonathan – co-founder of Crunch
Decam, Patrick – president of Sony Music Benelux

Drury, Ben – producer at *Dotmusic*
Edwards, Alan – founder of Outside Organisation and PR for David Bowie
Edwards, Mike – director of operations at the IFPI
Fluet, Cliff – business affairs manager for the Central Division of Warner Music UK
Foster, Mark – SVP of new media at Warner Music International
Galuten, Albhy – music producer and SVP at eLabs, part of Universal Music Group
Griffin, Jim – digital consultant and co-founder of the Pho List
Grimsdale, Charles – founder of OD2
Hemmings, Darren – in IT department at Sony Music UK
Hitchman, Paul – co-founder of Playlouder
Holmes, Guy – founder of Gut and AIM board member
Holzman, Jac – founder of Elektra Records
Jessop, Paul – chief technology officer at the IFPI
Kelly, Mark – keyboardist and co-writer in Marillion
Kennedy, John – chairman and CEO of Universal Music UK
Kenswil, Larry – president of the eLabs division of Universal Music Group
Kent, David – director of new technology at Napster
Liebenson, Jeff – VP of legal and business affairs at BMG International
McLaughlin, Brian – MD of HMV Europe and chairman of BARD
McNeive, Liam – lawyer for Crunch
Mills, Martin – head of Beggars Banquet and vice chairman of AIM board
Nielsen, Erik – working on digital and online retail for Marillion
Ogden, Richard – SVP of Sony Music Europe
Oppenheim, Matt – SVP of business and legal affairs at the RIAA
Quicke, Peter – label manager at Ninja Tune
Richardson, Eileen – CEO of Napster
Robertson, Gavin – new media and research and development manager at PRS/MCPS
Robertson, Michael – founder and CEO of MP3.com
Rogers, Ian – webmaster at Nullsoft
Rosen, Hilary – president and COO of the RIAA
Rowe, Stuart – general manager of direct and e-commerce for HMV Europe
Rump, Niels – manager multimedia and standardisation at InterTrust
Russell, Paul – chairman of Sony Music Europe

Samit, Jay – SVP of new media at EMI
Shamoon, Talal – vice president of InterTrust
Sherman, Cary – senior EVP and general counsel at the RIAA
Silver, Jeremy – vice president of new media at EMI Recorded Music Worldwide
Smith, Helen – director of legal and business affairs at AIM
Steinman, Todd – VP of new media and marketing at Warner Bros. Records
Teller, Al – founder of Atomic Pop
Vidich, Paul – EVP of strategic planning and business development at Warner Music
Vlassopulos, Jon – director of business development at BMG
Ward, Glen – president and CEO of Virgin Entertainment Group
Wadsworth, Tony – president of EMI Records UK
Wells, Rob – head of digital at BMG UK
Wenham, Alison – CEO and chairman of AIM
Westergren, Tim – then working on what was to become Pandora (he became founder and CEO of the company in 2000)
Winbolt, Eric – digital commercial manager at EMI UK
Wright, Simon – MD of Virgin Retail UK

Acknowledgements

Third time's a charm. Maybe.

First of all, endless thanks and boundless gratitude to the Omnibus Cinematic Universe – namely David Barraclough, Claire Browne, Greg Morton, David Stock, Dave Holley, Debs Geddes and Lucy Beevor. Thanks for letting me type more words (*too many* words), for ensuring those words do not get me in trouble and for promoting the end result.

Next up: all the people who spoke to me (or who helped get me people to speak to) for the book, all of them gracefully humouring my excavations of their past lives and decisions. Thank you for giving me your time. And sorry if going back in time was in any way traumatic.

The background research, the very foundations of this book, would have been impossible, or extremely shaky, were it not for the *incredible* archives in the British Library. That is where I spent days and days and days mining the pages of old business and consumer magazines to help shape the scope of what vexatious people would term 'the narrative' while adding innumerable splashes of colour throughout. The British Library is a palace of brilliance.

My previous book was actually written during lockdown. This book only *felt* like it was written under lockdown. Friends and family were the shafts of light reaching into the Deadline Bunker ensuring I did not, physically and emotionally, become too anaemic.

So great levels of gratitude to: Alex Papasimakopoulou, exceptional holiday coordinator and owner of Skye, Greece's most unhinged animal; Andrew and Lili for 'representing' N16; Louise Haywood-Schiefer for pizza-based cultural excursions (or for cultural-based pizza excursions), plus thanks for the occasional cameo from Vaughn (aka V-Unit), my great pal and London's leading transport/vehicle enthusiast and 'cold' denier; Laura Snapes for both i.e. and e.g.; Anna Derbyshire, Laura Barton and innocent victims everywhere for vitriolic catharsis; Shtum for proving that the internet does not have to descend into bloodshed if people occasionally hold different opinions; Marty Robb, Izzy and 'the weanes'; Stuart Dredge for being a paragon of calmness and patience and therefore my antithesis; Cathy & Darren Brown for moonrats and all things yeordis; Julie, James, Holly (H'Arneau), Nikki, Clod, Jen and the rest of the SVP 'Massive' for far too many dinners.

Equal levels of gratitude to family: Big Annie and Big Eddie for ongoing parental brilliance; Ciara and Mel for Edinburgh-centric excellence; Declan, Eliska and Victoria; Kathleen; Rosie & Denise. And all the rest. Plus all the others in the 'other' family: Harry, Elizabeth, Ingrid, Don, Claire and Gillian. And Ruth.

Financial and professional gratitude to all the publications I contribute to for a) giving me work and b) understanding why, when I was buried in this book, I could not do work for them. Given this book is now done, feel free to give me lots of work.

I also got to hang out with a lot of excellent dogs during the time I was working on this book. That means Brodie, Lucky, Barney (The Hairy Worm), Chico (Chunko), Charlie (Chazza), Millie and Monty (Captain Piddle). Dogs are brilliant.

Imagine all the thanks and love listed above. Picture it. Hold it in your head. Consider its overpowering enormity. That's only a *fraction* of the thanks and love due to Sonja for everything she has to put up with normally (which was only exacerbated x25 million when I was tip-tapping every single word in this book). 'I have a book to write, you know,' is a phrase that will haunt her for years to come. I guess the best behaviour won out in the end. Nineteen (19) hearts.

In memory of Niki Shisler.

Notes

CHAPTER 1

1 Mikuláš Teich and Roy Porter, *Fin de siècle and its legacy*, 1990, p. 1.
2 Ibid., p. 3.
3 Jeffrey C. Alexander, *Fin de Siècle Social Theory: Relativism, Reduction, and the Problem of Reason*, 1995, p. 4.
4 Fritz Weber, 'Heroes, Meadows and Machinery: Fin-de-Siècle Music', in Mikuláš Teich and Roy Porter (eds), *Fin de siècle and its legacy*, 1990, pp. 10–11.
5 Alice Teichova, 'A Legacy of Fin de Siècle Capitalism: The Giant Company', in Mikuláš Teich and Roy Porter (eds), *Fin de siècle and its legacy*, 1990, pp. 10–11.
6 Ibid., p. 10.
7 Ibid., p. 11.
8 https://historyofinformation.com/detail.php?entryid=1189
9 https://ultimateclassicrock.com/the-first-compact-disc-released/
10 https://www.bl.uk/collection-items/sony-cd-player-1983
11 David Hepworth, *Abbey Road: The Inside Story Of The World's Most Famous Recording Studio*, 2023, pp. 272–73.
12 https://www.rollingstone.com/music/music-news/capitol-to-release-beatles-cds-100764/
13 https://www.bbc.co.uk/archive/emi-and-compact-discs/zmwjbdm
14 Phil Hardy, *Download! How The Internet Transformed The Record Business*, 2012, p. 1.
15 Ibid., p. 3.
16 Ibid., p. 7.
17 Ibid., p. 5.
18 Steve Knopper, *Appetite For Self-Destruction: The Spectacular Crash Of The Record Industry In The Digital Age*, 2009, p. 14.
19 Ibid., pp. 23, 25.

20 Ibid., p. 32.
21 https://researchrepository.wvu.edu/cgi/viewcontent.cgi?article=1262&context=wvlr
22 Steve Knopper, *Appetite For Self-Destruction: The Spectacular Crash Of The Record Industry In The Digital Age*, 2009, p. 32.
23 Stephen Witt, *How Music Got Free: The Inventor, The Mogul, And The Thief*, 2016, p. 79.
24 Fred Goodman, *Fortune's Fool: Edgar Bronfman Jr., Warner Music, And An Industry In Crisis*, 2010, p. 35.
25 Ibid., p. 48.
26 David Hepworth, *Abbey Road: The Inside Story Of The World's Most Famous Recording Studio*, 2023, pp. 289–90.
27 Quote taken from an author interview with Rosen for a feature on the iPod for *The Guardian* in 2021.
28 Ibid.
29 https://computerhistory.org/blog/who-named-silicon-valley/?key=who-named-silicon-valley
30 Adam Fisher, *Valley Of Genius: The Uncensored History Of Silicon Valley (As Told By The Hackers, Founders, And Freaks Who Made It Boom)*, 2018, p. 1.
31 https://www.sfgate.com/sfhistory/article/San-Francisco-1855-1856-incorporation-Gold-Rush-12958094.php
32 Quoted in Adam Fisher, *Valley Of Genius: The Uncensored History Of Silicon Valley (As Told By The Hackers, Founders, And Freaks Who Made It Boom)*, 2018, p. 4.
33 https://www.wired.com/story/inside-story-of-pong-excerpt/
34 Adam Fisher, *Valley Of Genius: The Uncensored History Of Silicon Valley (As Told By The Hackers, Founders, And Freaks Who Made It Boom)*, 2018, p. 27.
35 Quoted in Adam Fisher, *Valley Of Genius: The Uncensored History Of Silicon Valley (As Told By The Hackers, Founders, And Freaks Who Made It Boom)*, 2018, p. 103.
36 Roger Lowenstein, *Origins Of The Crash: The Great Bubble And Its Undoing*, 2004, p. 14.
37 Ibid., p. 17.
38 When a private company first begins to sell shares of stock to members of the public rather than corporate investors.
39 John Cassidy, *dot.con: The Greatest Story Ever Sold*, 2002, p. 29.
40 Ibid., p. 6.
41 Ibid., p. 85.
42 Roger Lowenstein, *Origins Of The Crash: The Great Bubble And Its Undoing*, 2004, p. 101.

43 Ibid., p. 110.
44 John Cassidy, *dot.con: The Greatest Story Ever Sold*, 2002, pp. 236–37.
45 Ibid., p. 117.
46 Ibid., p. 125.
47 Ibid., p. 220.
48 Michael Wolff, *Burn Rate: How I Survived The Gold Rush Years On The Internet*, 1998, p. 26.
49 https://www.npr.org/2021/08/06/1025554426/a-look-back-at-the-very-first-website-ever-launched-30-years-later
50 John Cassidy, *dot.con: The Greatest Story Ever Sold*, 2002, p. 22.
51 Michael Wolff, *Burn Rate: How I Survived The Gold Rush Years On The Internet*, 1998, p. 119.
52 Ibid., p. 149.
53 https://www.theatlantic.com/technology/archive/2017/04/a-search-for-the-zombie-websites-of-1995/523848/
54 https://www.internetlivestats.com/total-number-of-websites/
55 Ibid., p. 44.
56 https://www.vice.com/en/article/6vapxr/go-aerosmith-how-head-first-became-the-first-song-available-for-digital-download-20-years-ago-today
57 https://www.cnet.com/tech/services-and-software/liquid-audio-vies-to-provide-music/
58 John Alderman, *Sonic Boom: Napster, P2P And The Future Of Music*, 2002, p. 44.
59 http://edition.cnn.com/SHOWBIZ/9709/10/columbia.single.sale/index.html
60 Jeremy Silver, *Digital Medieval: The First Twenty Years Of Music On The Web . . . And The Next Twenty*, 2013, p. 30.
61 https://www.soundonsound.com/people/todd-rundgren
62 https://www.mtv.com/news/7kn3q7/extra-extra-subscribe-to-todd-rundgren
63 https://www.wired.com/1998/10/the-individualists-music-model/
64 https://twitter.com/princemuseum/status/893152171209969665
65 https://princeonlinemuseum.com/timeline/1-800-new-funk/
66 https://www.forbes.com/global/1998/0921/0112050s6.html?sh=b-da936d34af8
67 https://www.theguardian.com/technology/2016/jan/11/david-bowie-bowienet-isp-internet
68 https://arstechnica.com/information-technology/2016/01/david-bowies-isp-as-remembered-by-the-guy-who-helped-create-bowienet/
69 Ibid.

70 https://www.forbes.com/global/1998/0921/0112050s6.html?sh=b-da936d34af8
71 https://www.britannica.com/topic/radio
72 https://www.loc.gov/collections/edison-company-motion-pictures-and-sound-recordings/articles-and-essays/history-of-edison-sound-recordings/history-of-the-cylinder-phonograph/
73 https://blog.electrohome.com/history-record-player/
74 https://www.historyofinformation.com/detail.php?id=719
75 https://www.bl.uk/collection-items/decca-portable-gramophone-1919
76 https://flashbak.com/the-1924-mikiphone-was-the-worlds-first-pocket-record-player-428477/
77 https://www.liverpoolmuseums.org.uk/records
78 https://designmuseum.org/discover-design/all-design-objects/sony-walkman
79 https://www.smithsonianmag.com/innovation/walkman-invention-40-years-ago-launched-cultural-revolution-180972552/
80 https://www.hifinews.com/content/sony-discman-d-50-mkii
81 https://www.minidisc.wiki/equipment/sony/portable/mz-1
82 https://www.sony.com/en/SonyInfo/News/Press_Archive/199907/99-059/
83 Jeremy Silver, *Digital Medieval: The First Twenty Years Of Music On The Web. . . And The Next Twenty*, 2013, p. 44.
84 Ibid., pp. 44–45.
85 https://www.theregister.com/2008/03/10/ft_first_mp3_player/
86 https://www.theregister.com/2008/03/10/ft_first_mp3_player/
87 Steve Knopper, *Appetite For Self-Destruction: The Spectacular Crash Of The Record Industry In The Digital Age*, 2009, p. 166.
88 Ibid.
89 'MP3 player comes to UK as US legal fight begins', *Music Week*, 24 October 1998, p. 6.
90 'IFPI warns over danger from second MP3 player', *Music Week*, 26 September 1998, p. 3.
91 Ibid.
92 'RIAA calls for online music discussion', *Music Week*, 7 November 1998, p. 5.
93 https://variety.com/1999/digital/news/it-s-a-rio-win-for-diamond-1117503116/
94 Steven Levy, *The Perfect Thing: How the iPod Shuffles Commerce, Culture, and Coolness*, 2006, p. 13.
95 Steve Knopper, *Appetite For Self-Destruction: The Spectacular Crash Of The Record Industry In The Digital Age*, 2009, p. 166.

96 https://www.nytimes.com/1981/04/30/obituaries/jules-c-stein-85-founder-of-mca-dies.html

97 https://apnews.com/article/0a3b82c3c508b4c98e74993e47d52eb2

98 https://www.latimes.com/archives/la-xpm-1995-04-10-mn-53050-story.html

99 Rod McQueen, *The Icarus Factor: The Rise And Fall Of Edgar Bronfman Jr.*, 2004, p. 135.

100 https://www.washingtonpost.com/archive/business/1995/07/06/time-warner-theft-allegations-prompted-firing/6cc5e40f-e298-4c65-8fee-faaf9aad39c0/

101 Fred Goodman, *Fortune's Fool: Edgar Bronfman Jr., Warner Music, And An Industry In Crisis*, 2010, p. 81.

102 Rod McQueen, *The Icarus Factor: The Rise And Fall Of Edgar Bronfman Jr.*, 2004, p. 137.

103 https://apnews.com/article/f58d09c8a428ebfe8539a2a4091baa2c

104 Rod McQueen, *The Icarus Factor: The Rise And Fall Of Edgar Bronfman Jr.*, 2004, p. 138.

105 Fred Goodman, *Fortune's Fool: Edgar Bronfman Jr., Warner Music, And An Industry In Crisis*, 2010, p. 86.

106 Ibid., p. 140.

107 Fred Goodman, *Fortune's Fool: Edgar Bronfman Jr., Warner Music, And An Industry In Crisis*, 2010, p. 43.

108 Ibid., p. 143.

109 https://www.upi.com/Archives/1996/02/20/Thorn-EMI-unveils-profits-and-demerger/3616824792400/

110 Fred Goodman, *Fortune's Fool: Edgar Bronfman Jr., Warner Music, And An Industry In Crisis*, 2010, p. 92.

111 Ibid., p. 93.

112 'Regulatory restrictions and a high price are problems for a would-be EMI buyer', *Music & Copyright*, 6 May 1998, pp. 1, 13.

113 Ibid.

114 Phil Hardy, *Download! How The Internet Transformed The Record Business*, 2012, p. 45.

115 Fred Goodman, *Fortune's Fool: Edgar Bronfman Jr., Warner Music, And An Industry In Crisis*, 2010, p. 94.

116 https://variety.com/1998/biz/news/edgar-faces-music-1117469937/

117 https://www.roh.org.uk/news/remembering-sir-colin-southgate

118 Phil Hardy, *Download! How The Internet Transformed The Record Business*, 2012, p. 47.

119 https://www.latimes.com/archives/la-xpm-1989-07-28-fi-294-story.html

120 https://apnews.com/article/9bbac79ac79c17ddcda46316966efea9
121 'Who is stalking EMI', *Music Week*, 9 May 1998, p. 7.
122 'Weeling and dealing on the rumour mill', *Music Week*, 23 May 1998, p. 5.
123 'Seagram turns from EMI to PolyGram', *Music & Copyright*, 20 May 1998, pp. 5, 14.
124 'Seagram faced clear field as rivals withdrew', *Music Week*, 30 May 1998, p. 4.
125 https://www.latimes.com/archives/la-xpm-1998-may-22-mn-52474-story.html
126 'Executives sign deal of a lifetime', *Music Week*, 30 May 1998, p. 4.
127 'Gloomy outlook for EMI as potential suitors fade away', *Music Week*, 30 May 1998, p. 5.
128 'Takeover gives Seagram 25% of global music sales', *Music Week*, 30 May 1998, p. 5.
129 https://www.latimes.com/archives/la-xpm-1998-may-22-fi-52563-story.html
130 "Charmer' Bronfman woos PolyGram's top executives', *Music Week*, 6 June 1998, p. 5.
131 'Poly/Uni Exec Setup Still Cloudy: EC To Eye Merger's Effects On Euro Mkt', *Billboard*, 6 June 1998, pp. 1, 92.
132 Phil Hardy, *Download! How The Internet Transformed The Record Business*, 2012, p. 61.
133 https://ec.europa.eu/competition/mergers/cases/decisions/m1219_en.pdf
134 Ibid.
135 'EMI Group Touts Its Independence', *Billboard*, 6 June 1998, pp. 3, 95.
136 Fred Goodman, *Fortune's Fool: Edgar Bronfman Jr., Warner Music, And An Industry In Crisis*, 2010, p. 97.
137 'A New Universal Emerges As A Global Force: Morris Team Puts Plans Into Action', *Billboard*, 19 December 1998, pp. 1, 75.
138 'Morris unveils global blueprint', *Music Week*, 19 December 1998, p. 1.
139 Rod McQueen, *The Icarus Factor: The Rise And Fall Of Edgar Bronfman Jr.*, 2004, p. 198.
140 'Bronfman predicts growth in Universal music profits', *Music Week*, 26 December, p. 3.
141 Steve Knopper, *Appetite For Self-Destruction: The Spectacular Crash Of The Record Industry In The Digital Age*, 2009, p. 65.
142 https://time.com/5752129/y2k-bug-history/
143 https://edition.cnn.com/ALLPOLITICS/1998/07/14/clinton.y2k/
144 'Indie retailers voice concern over scrapping of Eros system', *Music Week*, 6 February 1999, p. 3.

145 'Retail gets wired for business', *Music Week*, 13 March 1999, pp. 23–24.

146 https://www.theguardian.com/commentisfree/2019/dec/31/millennium-bug-face-fears-y2k-it-systems

CHAPTER 2

1 Fred Goodman, *Fortune's Fool: Edgar Bronfman Jr., Warner Music, And An Industry In Crisis*, 2010, pp. 134–35.

2 "UniGram': The Euro Outlook', *Billboard*, 27 June 1998, pp. 1, 89.

3 Rod McQueen, *The Icarus Factor: The Rise And Fall Of Edgar Bronfman Jr.*, 2004, p. 199.

4 Ibid.

5 Ibid., p. 213.

6 Roger Lowenstein, *Origins Of The Crash: The Great Bubble And Its Undoing*, 2004, pp. 72–73.

7 https://www.theguardian.com/music/2022/dec/13/a-second-woman-files-sexual-assault-lawsuit-against-atlantic-records-executives

8 Stephen Witt, *How Music Got Free: The Inventor, The Mogul, And The Thief*, 2016, p. 85.

9 https://variety.com/1998/music/news/music-will-boot-3-000-1117489335/

10 'Kennedy hosts merger summit', *Music Week*, 21 November 1998, p. 1.

11 Stephen Witt, *How Music Got Free: The Inventor, The Mogul, And The Thief*, 2016, p. 112.

12 https://www.latimes.com/archives/la-xpm-1999-feb-19-fi-9496-story.html

13 https://www.latimes.com/archives/la-xpm-1999-feb-26-fi-11869-story.html

14 'Universal: 'We're all upset, but it's business as usual", *Music Week*, 6 February 1999, p. 1.

15 'Universal plan sees four become three', *Music Week*, 23 January 1999, p. 1.

16 'Managers kept in dark as acts' future hangs in balance', *Music Week*, 12 December 1998, p. 1.

17 'Morris unveils global blueprint', *Music Week*, 19 December 1998, p. 1.

18 'The Biggest Record Industry Upheaval In The World . . . Ever!', *Q*, February 1999, p. 14.

19 'Shed Seven: An Apology', *Q*, March 1999, p. 20.

20 No Shed Seven album was released in 1999. Their next album, *Truth Be Told*, came in May 2001. It was released by Artful Records, not Polydor.

21 'Make mine a large one', *Mojo*, March 1999, p. 13.

22 Duff McKagan, *It's So Easy (And Other Lies)*, 2012, pp. 296–97.

23 https://www.latimes.com/archives/la-xpm-1999-jun-30-fi-51533-story.html

24 https://variety.com/1999/biz/news/a-m-duo-can-sue-u-music-1117750529/

25 https://variety.com/1999/music/news/a-m-duo-back-in-biz-1117758588/

26 Ibid.

27 'The Gold Rush That Wasn't', *Billboard*, 25 September 1999, pp. 1, 99.

28 Ibid.

29 'International Business Is Universal's Engine', *Billboard*, 2 October 1999, pp. 1, 114.

30 Ibid.

31 In 2005, Grainge became chairman and CEO of Universal Music Group International. Six years later, he became chairman and CEO of the entire company. In March 2023, he signed a new contract that would keep him as chairman and CEO until at least May 2028.

32 'Grainge steps up for Universal deputy role', *Music Week*, 18 December 1999, p. 1.

33 'Universal: One Year Later', *Billboard*, 25 December 1999, pp. 1, 78–79.

34 Ibid.

35 https://variety.com/1998/music/news/bertelsmann-eyes-emi-buy-if-price-falls-1117480768/

36 https://www.latimes.com/archives/la-xpm-1999-mar-12-fi-16436-story.html

37 Eamonn Forde, *The Final Days Of EMI: Selling The Pig*, 2019.

38 'Warner takes control at China', *Music Week*, 16 January 1999, p. 1.

39 'Sony Italy Buys Last Large Indie', *Billboard*, 24 July 1999, pp. 54, 74.

40 https://variety.com/1999/music/news/warner-music-reins-to-ames-1117750429/

41 https://nypost.com/1999/08/22/time-warners-music-man-roger-ames-is-facing-a-daunting-task-in-tuning-up-the-bottom-line/

42 'Ames to unite Warner as global powerhouse', *Music Week*, 28 August 1999, p. 1.

43 'Low-profile Ames storms back as a truly world class music player', *Music Week*, 28 August 1999, p. 10.

44 https://www.musicbusinessworldwide.com/people/alison-wenham/

45 https://blogs.loc.gov/now-see-hear/2019/04/inside-the-archival-box-the-first-long-playing-disc/

46 https://www.theguardian.com/music/2023/jun/21/columbia-records-introduce-first-vinyl-lp-1948

47 Jeremy Silver, *Digital Medieval: The First Twenty Years Of Music On The Web . . . And The Next Twenty*, 2013, p. 75.

48 Weybridge is around 17 miles south-west of central London, where Sony Music UK was based in 1999.
49 https://www.wired.com/2007/11/mf-morris/

CHAPTER 3

1 Jeremy Silver, *Digital Medieval: The First Twenty Years Of Music On The Web . . . And The Next Twenty*, 2013, p. 41.
2 https://variety.com/1999/music/news/warner-music-ups-vidich-1117502228/
3 'Warner Music To Test Sales Impact Of Downloads', *Billboard*, 17 July 1999, pp. 1, 117.
4 https://www.theregister.com/1999/05/04/universal_signs_intertrust/
5 'Parlophone revamps website to embrace life-style features', *Music Week*, 8 May 1999, p. 5.
6 'EMI moves forward with new media division', *Music Week*, 17 July 1999, p. 1.
7 https://www.apple.com/uk/newsroom/2010/11/16The-Beatles-Now-on-iTunes/

CHAPTER 4

1 'Indies aim to create new voice', *Music Week*, 19 September 1999, p. 1.
2 The BPI was originally mandated to 'discuss matters of common interest and represent the British record industry in negotiations with Government departments, relevant unions and other interested parties and to promote the welfare and interests of the British record industry' – https://www.brits.co.uk/about-us/bpi
3 Richard King, *How Soon Is Now?: The Madmen And Mavericks Who Made Independent Music 1975–2005*, 2012; Gareth Murphy, *Cowboys And Indies: The Epic History Of The Record Industry*, 2014.
4 Neil Taylor, *Document And Eyewitness: An Intimate History Of Rough Trade*, 2010.
5 Quotes from *AIM '99 | '09* – a 24-page brochure created by AIM in 2009 to mark its 10th anniversary and given out free to its members. Disclaimer: I wrote and edited it. I also worked at AIM between 1999 and 2001.
6 https://air.org.au/about-air/
7 https://www.billboard.com/music/music-news/mbo-at-uk-distributor-pinnacle-1313997/
8 PPL (Phonographic Performance Limited) is a collecting society focused on the collective rights management of sound recordings. Since 1934, it

has 'been licensing the use of recorded music in the UK' – https://www.ppluk.com/what-we-do/

9 https://www.independent.co.uk/news/monopolies-commission-to-investigate-price-of-cds-2321889.html

10 https://www.independent.co.uk/news/uk/cost-of-a-cd-deemed-fair-monopoly-inquiry-clears-record-firms-of-overcharging-russell-hotten-looks-at-the-arguments-that-proved-decisive-1424692.html

11 'Wenham takes aim for indies', *Music Week*, 14 November 1998, p. 1.

12 'Indie big guns line up as Aim's board takes shape', *Music Week*, 6 February 1999, p. 6.

13 'Aim and BPI set to agree subs deal', *Music Week*, 19 June 1999, p. 1.

14 'U.K. Indie Group AIM Seeking To Define Relationship With BPI', *Billboard*, 10 April 1999, pp. 1, 85.

15 Ibid.

16 'U.K.'s BPI, AIM Discuss Relations', *Billboard*, 26 June 1999, p. 6.

17 Ibid.

18 'BPI and Aim strike breakthrough deal', *Music Week*, 25 September 1999, p. 1.

19 'Dickins hails 'new era' as BPI approves Aim link-up', *Music Week*, 2 October 1999, p. 3.

20 'BPI Is Reshaping Itself: Move Formalizes Relationship With AIM', *Billboard*, 2 October 1999, pp. 12, 112.

21 Simon Williams, *Pandamonium!: How Not To Run A Record Label*, 2022, p. 253.

22 'Indies back Aim's online sales plan', *Music Week*, 29 May 1999, p. 1.

23 'Aim considers Northern office', *Music Week*, 4 September 1999, p. 3.

24 Starting in 1985, The WELL began as a dial-up bulletin board system and quickly helped create an early online community – https://www.britannica.com/topic/The-WELL-Internet-community

25 http://pressbeta.ninjatune.net/article.php?id=166

26 'Going Down, Sir?', *Q*, September 1999, pp. 64–70.

27 Ibid.

28 https://www.nme.com/features/music-interviews/sex-pistols-glen-matlock-david-bowie-malcolm-mclaren-danny-boyle-3001103

29 David Cavanagh, *The Creation Records Story: My Magpie Eyes Are Hungry For The Prize*, 2001, p. 725.

30 Ibid., p. 726.

31 Ibid., p. 729.

32 'McGee in wake-up call to industry on its 'arse'', *Music Week*, 30 May 1998, p. 3.

33 'The Record Company Is Dead: Long Live The Internet', *NME*, 9 January 1999, pp. 6–7.

34 David Cavanagh, *The Creation Records Story: My Magpie Eyes Are Hungry For The Prize*, 2001, p. 729.

35 Ibid.

36 https://www.piasgroup.net/blog/to-this-day-im-still-not-allowed-in-the-sony-building/

37 David Cavanagh, *The Creation Records Story: My Magpie Eyes Are Hungry For The Prize*, 2001, p. 730.

38 Ibid., p. 740.

39 https://www.nme.com/news/music/belle-and-sebastian-107-1394914

40 https://www.nme.com/news/music/belle-and-sebastian-105-1394843

41 Michael Cragg, *Reach For The Stars: 1996–2006: Fame, Fallout & Pop's Final Party*, 2023, p. 137.

42 That was the year – in their own words', *Music Week*, 18 December 1999, pp. 24–28.

43 The disgraced glam rock star was sentenced to four months in prison in November 1999 after admitting to 54 charges of making indecent photographs of children under 16. The images were discovered two years earlier when he took his laptop in to be repaired at a branch of PC World in Bristol. – https://www.theguardian.com/uk/1999/nov/12/simonjeffery1

44 https://winformusic.org/members/

CHAPTER 5

1 https://www.visualthesaurus.com/cm/wordroutes/plundering-the-history-of-pirate/

2 Jonathan Sterne, *MP3: The Meaning Of A Format*, 2012, pp. 187-188.

3 Alex Sayf Cummings, *Democracy Of Sound: Music Piracy & The Remaking Of American Copyright In The Twentieth Century*, 2013, p. 15.

4 Ibid., p. 17.

5 Ibid., p. 75.

6 https://www.copyright.gov/history/1909act.pdf

7 Alex Sayf Cummings, *Democracy Of Sound: Music Piracy & The Remaking Of American Copyright In The Twentieth Century*, 2013, p. 29.

8 Barry Kernfeld, *Pop Music Piracy: Disobedient Music Distribution Since 1929*, 2011, p. 1.

9 Ibid., p. 17.

10 Ibid., p. 25.

11 Ibid., p. 26.

12 Ibid., p. 33.

13 Ibid., p. 45.
14 Ibid., p. 51.
15 Ibid., p. 88.
16 Alex Sayf Cummings, *Democracy Of Sound: Music Piracy & The Remaking Of American Copyright In The Twentieth Century*, 2013, p. 30.
17 Ibid., p. 44.
18 Ibid., p. 52.
19 Ibid., p. 74.
20 Ibid., p. 53.
21 Ibid., p. 55.
22 Ibid., p. 62.
23 Barry Kernfeld, *Pop Music Piracy: Disobedient Music Distribution Since 1929*, 2011, p. 29.
24 Ibid., p. 96.
25 Stephen Hebditch, *London's Pirate Pioneers: The Illegal Broadcasters Who Changed British Radio*, 2015; Adrian Johns, *Death Of A Pirate: British Radio & The Making Of The Information Age*, 2012; Stuart Henry & Mike Von Joel, *Pirate Radio: Then & Now*, 1984; Ray Clark, *Radio Caroline: The True Story Of The Boat That Rocked*, 2019.
26 Alex Sayf Cummings, *Democracy Of Sound: Music Piracy & The Remaking Of American Copyright In The Twentieth Century*, 2013, pp. 84–85.
27 Ibid., p. 93.
28 Clinton Heylin, *The Great White Wonders: A History Of Rock Bootlegs*, 1995.
29 Barry Kernfeld, *Pop Music Piracy: Disobedient Music Distribution Since 1929*, 2011, p. 128.
30 Ibid., p. 134.
31 Ibid., p. 139.
32 Ibid., p. 141.
33 Ibid., p. 2.
34 Jonathan Sterne, *MP3: The Meaning Of A Format*, 2012, pp. 27–28.
35 Barry Kernfeld, *Pop Music Piracy: Disobedient Music Distribution Since 1929*, 2011, p. 126.
36 https://timesofindia.indiatimes.com/city/kolkata/pirated-cassettes-worth-rs-75-lakh-seized/articleshow/16912079.cms
37 https://www.nytimes.com/1981/03/01/nyregion/sam-goody-company-accused-as-pirate.html
38 Barry Kernfeld, *Pop Music Piracy: Disobedient Music Distribution Since 1929*, 2011, pp. 169–70.
39 Alex Sayf Cummings, *Democracy Of Sound: Music Piracy & The Remaking Of American Copyright In The Twentieth Century*, 2013, p. 140.

40 Barry Kernfeld, *Pop Music Piracy: Disobedient Music Distribution Since 1929*, 2011, pp. 161.
41 Stephen Witt, *How Music Got Free: The Inventor, The Mogul, And The Thief*, 2016, p. 83.
42 Richard Evans, *Listening To The Music the Machines Make: Inventing Electronic Pop 1978 to 1983*, 2022.
43 https://www.mojo4music.com/time-machine/1980s/mojo-time-machine-home-taping-is-killing-music/
44 Ibid.
45 https://www.theguardian.com/music/2009/may/30/cassette-tapes-revival-indie-labels
46 https://www.mojo4music.com/time-machine/1980s/mojo-time-machine-home-taping-is-killing-music/
47 https://www.mojo4music.com/time-machine/1980s/mojo-time-machine-home-taping-is-killing-music/
48 Barry Kernfeld, *Pop Music Piracy: Disobedient Music Distribution Since 1929*, 2011, pp. 147, 150.
49 Alan Sugar, *What You See Is What You Get: My Autobiography*, 2011, p. 229.
50 Ibid.
51 Ibid., p. 230.
52 Ibid.
53 https://cpcrulez.fr/people-cpc-amstrad_hits_tape_copy_row.htm
54 Alan Sugar, *What You See Is What You Get: My Autobiography*, 2011, p. 230.
55 Ibid.
56 Ibid.
57 https://www.theguardian.com/music/2013/aug/30/cassette-store-day-music-tapes
58 Alan Sugar, *What You See Is What You Get: My Autobiography*, 2011, pp. 230–31.
59 'Fair use is an affirmative defense that can be raised in response to claims by a copyright owner that a person is infringing a copyright,' notes the Copyright Alliance. 'Fair use permits a party to use a copyrighted work without the copyright owner's permission for purposes such as criticism, comment, news reporting, teaching, scholarship, or research.' – https://copyrightalliance.org/faqs/what-is-fair-use
60 Steve Knopper, *Appetite For Self-Destruction: The Spectacular Crash Of The Record Industry In The Digital Age*, 2009, p. 136.
61 Ibid.
62 https://www.copyright.gov/title17/92chap10.html

63 Steve Knopper, *Appetite For Self-Destruction: The Spectacular Crash Of The Record Industry In The Digital Age*, 2009, p. 78.
64 https://siarchives.si.edu/sites/default/files/pdfs/digitalAudioTapesPreservation2010_0.pdf
65 David Arditi, *iTake-Over: The Recording Industry In The Streaming Era*, 2015, p. 53.
66 Paul Goldstein, *Copyright's Highway: From Gutenberg To The Celestial Jukebox*, 2003, p. 129.
67 Steve Knopper, *Appetite For Self-Destruction: The Spectacular Crash Of The Record Industry In The Digital Age*, 2009, p. 76.
68 Ibid., p. 77.
69 https://www.cnet.com/tech/home-entertainment/it-was-30-years-ago-today-the-cd-began-to-play/
70 'In Quad We Trust: Hi-Fi Fads And Flops 1952–'92, *NME*, 9 May 1992, pp. 46–47.
71 https://core.ac.uk/download/pdf/144227071.pdf
72 https://www.salon.com/1999/02/24/feature_225/
73 Ibid.
74 https://www.macworld.com/article/220650/hotline-revisited.html
75 https://cointelegraph.com/news/how-an-australian-teen-nearly-created-a-decentralized-reddit-in-1997
76 https://www.macworld.com/article/220650/hotline-revisited.html
77 'Downloading Songs Subject Of RIAA Suit', *Billboard*, 21 June 1997, pp. 3, 83.
78 John Alderman, *Sonic Boom: Napster, P2P And The Future Of Music*, 2002, p. 85.
79 'Downloading Songs Subject Of RIAA Suit', *Billboard*, 21 June 1997, pp. 3, 83.
80 Ibid.
81 Ibid.
82 https://pitchfork.com/features/ok-computer-at-20/10039-what-it-felt-like-to-review-ok-computer-when-it-first-came-out/
83 Steve Knopper, *Appetite For Self-Destruction: The Spectacular Crash Of The Record Industry In The Digital Age*, 2009, p. 114.
84 David Arditi, *iTake-Over: The Recording Industry In The Streaming Era*, 2015, p. xvii.
85 Ibid., p. xxiii.
86 https://www.wired.com/2008/10/oct-28-1998-president-signs-new-copyright-law-2/

87 Trevor Merriden, *Irresistible Forces: The Business Legacy Of Napster & The Growth Of The Underground Internet*, 2001, p. 58.
88 Barry Kernfeld, *Pop Music Piracy: Disobedient Music Distribution Since 1929*, 2011, p. 182.
89 'In Quad We Trust: Hi-Fi Fads And Flops 1952-'92, *NME*, 9 May 1992, pp. 46–47.
90 https://www.computerhistory.org/storageengine/consumer-cd-r-drive-priced-below-1000/
91 https://www.philips.com/a-w/research/technologies/cd/cd-family.htm
92 Barry Fox, 'Technology', *Hi-Fi News & Record Review*, March 1999, p. 19.
93 Ibid., p. 27.
94 'CD-R Enjoys Massive Growth In A Wide Range Of Markets', *Billboard*, 3 April 1999, p. 52.
95 'Anti-Piracy Effort Urged: IFPI's Berman Wants More Enforcement', *Billboard*, 19 June 1999, p. 8.
96 Ibid.
97 'Dutch Music Biz Scores Added Blank-Disc Tax', *Billboard*, 26 June 1999, p. 6.
98 'BPI warns of new threat from CD-R compilations', *Music Week*, 26 June 1999, p. 3.
99 'RIAA Targets Illegal CD-Rs', *Billboard*, 28 August 1999, pp. 12, 108.
100 'Dealers feel pinch as CD-R piracy kicks in', *Music Week*, 31 July 1999, p. 4.
101 Ibid.
102 'Philips launches £3m CD-R push', *Music Week*, 7 August 1999, p. 1.
103 Ibid.
104 'EBay Bans CD-Rs: Auctioneer Tackling Piracy', *Billboard*, 2 October 1999, pp. 12, 112.
105 'Newsline . . .', *Billboard*, 2 October 1999, p. 82.
106 Alex Sayf Cummings, *Democracy Of Sound: Music Piracy & The Remaking Of American Copyright In The Twentieth Century*, 2013, p. 202.
107 https://www.salon.com/1998/10/28/feature_264/
108 https://www.mtv.com/news/e2ciiu/riaa-granted-rio-mp3-injunction-soundbyting-campaign-leaked
109 'Dutch Biz Plans Anti-Copy Blitz', *Billboard*, 10 July 1999, p. 51 and p. 63.
110 Ibid.
111 'German Biz Targets Kid Copiers', *Billboard*, 4 September 1999, p. 65 and p. 70.
112 Ibid.
113 'Newsline. . .', *Billboard*, 27 November 1999, p. 62.

114 Stephen Witt, *How Music Got Free: The Inventor, The Mogul, And The Thief*, 2016, p. 84.

115 'Kennedy in CD copying call to arms', *Music Week*, 4 September 1999, p. 1.

116 'Big Issues Await Berman In His New IFPI Post', *Billboard*, 9 January 1999, pp. 6, 78.

117 'EU Authors' Bodies Seek Net Standard', *Billboard*, 6 February 1999, pp. 1, 76.

118 Alex Sayf Cummings, *Democracy Of Sound: Music Piracy & The Remaking Of American Copyright In The Twentieth Century*, 2013, p. 218.

CHAPTER 6

1 https://www.npr.org/sections/therecord/2011/03/23/134622940/the-mp3-a-history-of-innovation-and-betrayal

2 Steve Knopper, *Appetite For Self-Destruction: The Spectacular Crash Of The Record Industry In The Digital Age*, 2009, p. 116.

3 https://www.npr.org/sections/therecord/2011/03/23/134622940/the-mp3-a-history-of-innovation-and-betrayal

4 Steve Knopper, *Appetite For Self-Destruction: The Spectacular Crash Of The Record Industry In The Digital Age*, 2009, p. 116.

5 Stephen Witt, *How Music Got Free: The Inventor, The Mogul, And The Thief*, 2016, p. 7.

6 https://www.npr.org/sections/therecord/2011/03/23/134622940/the-mp3-a-history-of-innovation-and-betrayal

7 https://www.techtimes.com/articles/207213/20170513/the-mp3-is-dead-heres-a-brief-history-of-mp3.htm

8 Ibid.

9 Steve Knopper, *Appetite For Self-Destruction: The Spectacular Crash Of The Record Industry In The Digital Age*, 2009, p. 118.

10 Stephen Witt, *How Music Got Free: The Inventor, The Mogul, And The Thief*, 2016, p. 12.

11 http://news.bbc.co.uk/1/hi/technology/3059775.stm

12 Stephen Witt, *How Music Got Free: The Inventor, The Mogul, And The Thief*, 2016, p. 13.

13 https://www.npr.org/sections/therecord/2011/03/23/134622940/the-mp3-a-history-of-innovation-and-betrayal

14 Stephen Witt, *How Music Got Free: The Inventor, The Mogul, And The Thief*, 2016, p. 15.

15 https://www.npr.org/sections/therecord/2011/03/23/134622940/the-mp3-a-history-of-innovation-and-betrayal

16 Stephen Witt, *How Music Got Free: The Inventor, The Mogul, And The Thief*, 2016, p. 16.
17 Steve Knopper, *Appetite For Self-Destruction: The Spectacular Crash Of The Record Industry In The Digital Age*, 2009, p. 117.
18 Stephen Witt, *How Music Got Free: The Inventor, The Mogul, And The Thief*, 2016, p. 16.
19 https://www.npr.org/sections/therecord/2011/03/23/134622940/the-mp3-a-history-of-innovation-and-betrayal
20 https://www.techtimes.com/articles/207213/20170513/the-mp3-is-dead-heres-a-brief-history-of-mp3.htm
21 Jonathan Sterne, *MP3: The Meaning Of A Format*, 2012, p. 137.
22 Quoted in Jonathan Sterne, *MP3: The Meaning Of A Format*, 2012, p. 178.
23 Ibid.
24 Stephen Witt, *How Music Got Free: The Inventor, The Mogul, And The Thief*, 2016, p. 3.
25 Ibid., p. 18.
26 Ibid., p. 5.
27 Stephen Witt, *How Music Got Free: The Inventor, The Mogul, And The Thief*, 2016, p. 16.
28 Jonathan Sterne, *MP3: The Meaning Of A Format*, 2012, p. 145.
29 Stephen Witt, *How Music Got Free: The Inventor, The Mogul, And The Thief*, 2016, p. 20.
30 Ibid.
31 Jonathan Sterne, *MP3: The Meaning Of A Format*, 2012, p. 145.
32 Stephen Witt, *How Music Got Free: The Inventor, The Mogul, And The Thief*, 2016, p. 20.
33 Ibid., p. 22.
34 Jonathan Sterne, *MP3: The Meaning Of A Format*, 2012, pp. 199–200.
35 Ibid., p. 54.
36 Fred Goodman, *Fortune's Fool: Edgar Bronfman Jr., Warner Music, And An Industry In Crisis*, 2010, p. 126.
37 Stephen Witt, *How Music Got Free: The Inventor, The Mogul, And The Thief*, 2016, p. 55.
38 Ibid.
39 https://www.independent.co.uk/news/business/sony-may-buy-firm-that-poses-threat-to-music-industry-1449288.html
40 Stephen Witt, *How Music Got Free: The Inventor, The Mogul, And The Thief*, 2016, p. 56.
41 Jonathan Sterne, *MP3: The Meaning Of A Format*, 2012, p. 201.

42 Stephen Witt, *How Music Got Free: The Inventor, The Mogul, And The Thief*, 2016, p. 61.

43 https://www.npr.org/sections/therecord/2011/03/23/134622940/the-mp3-a-history-of-innovation-and-betrayal

44 Stephen Witt, *How Music Got Free: The Inventor, The Mogul, And The Thief*, 2016, p. 61.

45 Jonathan Sterne, *MP3: The Meaning Of A Format*, 2012, pp. 202–3.

46 Ibid., p. 198.

47 Stephen Witt, *How Music Got Free: The Inventor, The Mogul, And The Thief*, 2016, p. 61.

48 Ibid., p. 62.

49 Ibid., pp. 62–3.

50 Steve Knopper, *Appetite For Self-Destruction: The Spectacular Crash Of The Record Industry In The Digital Age*, 2009, p. 119.

51 https://www.npr.org/sections/therecord/2011/03/23/134622940/the-mp3-a-history-of-innovation-and-betrayal

52 https://www.techtimes.com/articles/207213/20170513/the-mp3-is-dead-heres-a-brief-history-of-mp3.htm

53 Stephen Witt, *How Music Got Free: The Inventor, The Mogul, And The Thief*, 2016, pp. 87–88.

54 Jonathan Sterne, *MP3: The Meaning Of A Format*, 2012, p. 134.

55 https://www.npr.org/sections/therecord/2011/03/23/134622940/the-mp3-a-history-of-innovation-and-betrayal

56 Jonathan Sterne, *MP3: The Meaning Of A Format*, 2012, p. 202.

57 Barry Kernfeld, *Pop Music Piracy: Disobedient Music Distribution Since 1929*, 2011, p. 204.

58 Jonathan Sterne, *MP3: The Meaning Of A Format*, 2012, p. 204.

59 Stephen Witt, *How Music Got Free: The Inventor, The Mogul, And The Thief*, 2016, p. 89.

60 Fred Goodman, *Fortune's Fool: Edgar Bronfman Jr., Warner Music, And An Industry In Crisis*, 2010, p. 127.

61 https://www.npr.org/sections/therecord/2011/03/23/134622940/the-mp3-a-history-of-innovation-and-betrayal

62 https://thequietus.com/articles/28561-mp3-vinyl-napster-music-industry

63 Ibid.

64 Stephen Witt, *How Music Got Free: The Inventor, The Mogul, And The Thief*, 2016, pp. 90–91.

65 Steve Knopper, *Appetite For Self-Destruction: The Spectacular Crash Of The Record Industry In The Digital Age*, 2009, p. 118.

66 Stephen Witt, *How Music Got Free: The Inventor, The Mogul, And The Thief*, 2016, p. 94.
67 Jonathan Sterne, *MP3: The Meaning Of A Format*, 2012, p. 27.
68 Ibid., p. 26.
69 Stephen Witt, *How Music Got Free: The Inventor, The Mogul, And The Thief*, 2016, p. 127.
70 Ibid., p. 128.
71 Jonathan Sterne, *MP3: The Meaning Of A Format*, 2012, p. 26.
72 Ibid., p. 208.
73 John Alderman, *Sonic Boom: Napster, P2P And The Future Of Music*, 2002, p. 13.
74 Steve Knopper, *Appetite For Self-Destruction: The Spectacular Crash Of The Record Industry In The Digital Age*, 2009, p. 119.
75 John Alderman, *Sonic Boom: Napster, P2P And The Future Of Music*, 2002, p. 14.
76 'Online revolution looms with the disc-free player', *Music Week*, 8 August 1998, p. 1.
77 'IFPI warns over danger from second MP3 player', *Music Week*, 26 September 1998, p. 3.
78 'Industry Is Hesitant With MP3', *Billboard*, 26 December 1998, pp. 5, 84.
79 'New Coalition Aims To 'Authenticate' Legit Online Music', *Billboard*, 6 February 1999, pp. 1, 74.
80 'Lads unite in bid to 'legitimise' MP3', *Music Week*, 6 February 1999, p. 7.
81 'Online Distrib On Fast Track As SDMI Moves Forward', *Billboard*, 13 March 1999, pp. 5, 106.
82 https://www.wired.com/1999/10/attack-on-mp3-piracy-escalates/
83 Ibid.
84 'Execs Predict Personalized Music Streams', *Billboard*, 13 November 1999, p. 60.
85 Ibid.
86 https://twitter.com/museumsound/status/1231865042469040128
87 Jonathan Sterne, *MP3: The Meaning Of A Format*, 2012, p. 26.
88 https://www.theregister.com/2008/03/10/ft_first_mp3_player/
89 'Online revolution looms with the disc-free player', *Music Week*, 8 August 1998, p. 1.
90 'The rapid spread in the use of MP3 files causes deep concern to record industry', *Music & Copyright*, 7 October 1998, pp. 3–4.
91 'IFPI warns over danger from second MP3 player', *Music Week*, 26 September 1998, p. 3.

92 David Arditi, *iTake-Over: The Recording Industry In The Streaming Era*, 2015, p. 38.
93 'RIAA wins TRO against MP3 player', *Music & Copyright*, 21 October 1998, p. 2.
94 https://variety.com/1998/music/news/riaa-sues-to-stop-rio-sales-1117481324/
95 'MP3 player comes to UK as US legal fight begins', *Music Week*, 24 October 1998, p. 6.
96 'MP3 players wins reprieve in California court', *Music & Copyright*, 4 November 1998, pp. 4–5.
97 'RIAA calls for online music discussion', *Music Week*, 7 November 1998, p. 5.
98 'BPI voices piracy concerns as Rio hits 25,000 UK sales', *Music Week*, 29 May 1999, p. 5.
99 Ibid.
100 Ibid.
101 'The New Punk Rock!', *Q*, May 1999, p. 148.
102 https://variety.com/1999/digital/news/it-s-a-rio-win-for-diamond-1117503116/
103 'Court Rules Against RIAA In MP3 Case', *Billboard*, 26 June 1999, pp. 3, 100.
104 https://archive.nytimes.com/www.nytimes.com/library/tech/99/07/cyber/cyberlaw/09law.html
105 Ibid.
106 David Arditi, *iTake-Over: The Recording Industry In The Streaming Era*, 2015, p. 38.
107 http://birrell.org/andrew/pjbwww/
108 Steve Levy, *The Perfect Thing: How the iPod Shuffles Commerce, Culture, and Coolness*, 2006, p. 13.
109 Ibid., p. 27.
110 Walter Isaacson, *Steve Jobs*, 2011, p. 354.
111 'Digital-Download Systems Spar For Dominance', *Billboard*, 24 April 1999, pp. 3, 88.

CHAPTER 7

1 https://www.mactech.com/1997/05/30/md1-filez-now-more-powerful/
2 Fred Goodman, *Fortune's Fool: Edgar Bronfman Jr., Warner Music, And An Industry In Crisis*, 2010, p. 127.
3 https://www.sequoiacap.com/people/doug-leone/
4 https://www.cnet.com/tech/services-and-software/mp3-com-gets-11-million-investment/

5 https://www.cnet.com/tech/services-and-software/mp3-com-gets-11-million-investment/
6 'Online Distrib On Fast Track As SDMI Move Forward', *Billboard*, 13 March 1999, pp. 5, 106.
7 'MP3 Files For IPO, Strikes Deal With No Limit Label', *Billboard*, 29 May 1999, p. 3.
8 'ASCAP, MP3.com Link Up', *Billboard*, 26 June 1999, p. 97.
9 John Alderman, *Sonic Boom: Napster, P2P And The Future Of Music*, 2002, p. 79.
10 *Mark Mulligan, Awakening: The Music Industry In The Digital Age*, 2015, p. 10.
11 *Billboard*, 28 August 1999, p. 10.
12 'Newsline . . .', *Billboard*, 23 October 1999, p. 103.
13 '2 Companies Offer Web Space For Fans' Downloads', *Billboard*, 23 October 1999, p. 3.
14 Brad Stone, *The Everything Store: Jeff Bezos And The Age Of Amazon*, 2013.
15 'Newsline . . .', *Billboard*, 30 October 1999, p. 71.
16 Fredric Dannen, *Hit Men: Power Brokers And Fast Money Inside The Music Business*, 1990.
17 'Newsline . . .', *Billboard*, 30 October 1999, p. 46.
18 'The rapid spread in the use of MP3 files causes deep concern to record industry', *Music & Copyright*, 7 October 1998, pp. 3–4.
19 Jeremy Silver, *Digital Medieval: The First Twenty Years Of Music On The Web . . . And The Next Twenty*, 2013, pp. 47–48.
20 https://www.theregister.com/1999/01/25/mp3_companies_to_launch_antipiracy/
21 Ibid.
22 https://www.wired.com/1999/01/liquefying-mp3/
23 https://www.cnet.com/tech/services-and-software/seal-of-approval-proposed-for-music/
24 http://edition.cnn.com/TECH/computing/9901/27/mp3.idg/index.html
25 https://www.mtv.com/news/fn08rq/new-coalition-aims-to-authenticate-digital-sound-files
26 Ibid.
27 Ibid.
28 https://www.mtv.com/news/4n46ve/companies-form-mp3-association
29 https://www.wired.com/1998/10/mp3-bands-together/
30 https://www.independent.co.uk/news/business/sony-may-buy-firm-that-poses-threat-to-music-industry-1449288.html
31 Ibid.
32 Ibid.

33 https://www.chicagotribune.com/news/ct-xpm-1995-01-31-9501310224-story.html
34 Ibid.
35 Ibid.
36 https://www.campaignlive.co.uk/article/interactive-cerberus-digital-jukebox/30034
37 https://www.soundonsound.com/techniques/musicians-diy-internet
38 'The Record Company Is Dead: Long Live The Internet', *NME*, 9 January 1999, pp. 6–7.
39 'The NME Face-Off: Chuck D', *NME*, 24 July 1999, pp. 22–23.
40 'Plug.In: Chuck D', *Billboard*, 17 July 1999, pp. 82, 90.
41 https://www.latimes.com/archives/la-xpm-1994-11-17-fi-63787-story.html
42 'Plug.In: Chuck D', *Billboard*, 17 July 1999, pp. 82, 90.
43 'RealNetworks, Thomson Products Open Mainstream Door To MP3', *Billboard*, 15 May 1999, pp. 5, 87.
44 https://www.mtv.com/news/vv91ef/free-tom-petty-track-pulled-from-mp3-site-but-still-available-online
45 https://www.mtv.com/news/zhizxh/petty-returns-to-mp3com
46 'Labels, Artists Clash Over MP3', *Billboard*, 1 May 1999, pp. 1, 74.
47 https://www.mtv.com/news/zhizxh/petty-returns-to-mp3com
48 'Web Raises New Contract Issues', *Billboard*, 19 June 1999, pp. 1, 75.
49 'Labels, Artists Clash Over MP3', *Billboard*, 1 May 1999, pp. 1, 74.
50 Ibid.
51 Ibid.
52 https://www.tampabay.com/archive/1999/05/03/singers-work-to-embrace-internet/?outputType=amp
53 https://www.wired.com/1999/04/mp3-com-signs-tori-and-alanis/
54 'Newsline . . .', *Billboard*, 18 September 1999, p. 100.
55 https://www.mtv.com/news/8l6nsr/tlc-announce-tour-post-new-song-at-mp3com
56 'Morissette Push Involves Multiple Media', Billboard, 30 October 1999, pp. 6, 74.
57 https://www.latimes.com/archives/la-xpm-2000-may-16-fi-30514-story.html
58 http://news.bbc.co.uk/1/hi/entertainment/126071.stm
59 https://www.theguardian.com/music/2020/aug/10/youve-been-smoking-too-much-the-chaos-of-tony-wilsons-digital-music-revolution
60 'Internet initiative for Superior Quality', *Music Week*, 27 March 1999, p. 8.
61 'MCPS sets 10p royalty rate for downloaded music', *Music Week*, 2 October 1999, p. 1.

62 Ibid.

63 'Has MCPS got its sums right?', *Music Week*, 2 October 1999, p. 4.

64 Ibid.

65 'AIM challenges MCPS 10p net rate', *Music Week*, 16 October 1999, p. 1.

66 Ibid.

67 'Supporting the MCPS 10p rate', *Music Week*, 23 October 1999, p. 10.

68 Ibid.

69 Ibid.

CHAPTER 8

1 https://labusinessjournal.com/news/atomic/

2 https://www.latimes.com/archives/la-xpm-1999-feb-12-fi-7341-story.html

3 'Labels, Artists Clash Over MP3', *Billboard*, 1 May 1999, pp. 1, 74.

4 'Plug.In: Chuck D', *Billboard*, 17 July 1999, pp. 82, 90.

5 'Did Atomic Pop's Public Enemy Web Exclusive Affect Retail?', *Billboard*, 7 August 1999, pp. 58, 60.

6 Ibid.

7 Ibid.

8 'Newsline . . .', *Billboard*, 16 October 1999, p. 70.

9 'Artists Take It To The Net', *Billboard*, 13 November 1999, pp. 63, 80.

10 'Creators Discuss Net Impact', *Billboard*, 11 December 1999, pp. 81, 86.

11 Ibid.

12 https://www.forbes.com/forbes/2000/0124/6502130a.html?sh=96161422a4cb

13 https://hitsdailydouble.com/news&id=274504&title=ATOMIC-POP-SHUTS-DOWN

14 https://www.zdnet.com/article/goodnoise-changes-tune-to-emusic-5000102445/

15 'Indies Jump Into Web Distribution', *Billboard*, 19 June 1999, pp. 8, 85.

16 'MP3 Supporters Look To Future', *Billboard*, 26 June 1999, pp. 1, 97.

17 https://www.zdnet.com/article/goodnoise-changes-tune-to-emusic-5000102445/

18 'Indies Jump Into Web Distribution', *Billboard*, 19 June 1999, pp. 8, 85.

19 Ibid.

20 Ibid.

21 Ibid.

22 'MP3 Supporters Look To Future', *Billboard*, 26 June 1999, pp. 1, 97.

23 Ibid.

24 'eMusic Buys Blues/R&B Masters', *Billboard*, 10 July 1999, pp. 6, 84.

25 'Newsline . . .', *Billboard*, 24 July 1999, p. 60.

26 'Newsline . . .', *Billboard*, 21 August 1999, p. 50.
27 https://money.cnn.com/1999/08/16/technology/aol/
28 https://money.cnn.com/1999/06/01/technology/aol/
29 'They Might Be Giants Make Versions Big Strides Without A Label', *Billboard*, 11 September 1999, pp. 73, 79.
30 'They Might Be Giants Top Downloaded Band in '99', *CMJ New Music Report*, 31 January 2000, p. 5.
31 https://www.mtv.com/news/33nj2r/bush-to-preview-single-online
32 'Newsline . . .', *Billboard*, 6 November 1999, p. 70.
33 https://www.ecommercetimes.com/story/emusic-com-adds-tunes-in-130m-deal-1857.html
34 https://www.cnet.com/tech/tech-industry/emusic-com-to-buy-cductive-com/
35 https://www.mtv.com/news/jqzlqv/emusic-buys-tunescom-rollingstonecom
36 'Newsline . . .', *Billboard*, 18 December 1999, p. 104.
37 'MP3 heralds the birth of a new sector for IT industry', *Financial Times*, 3 November 1999.
38 'Coming to the Crunch', *The Guardian*, 20 January 2000, p. 6.

CHAPTER 9

1 https://www.govinfo.gov/content/pkg/PLAW-105publ147/pdf/PLAW-105publ147.pdf
2 https://www.congress.gov/bill/105th-congress/house-bill/2265
3 'RIAA Targets Pirate Music Sites', *Billboard*, 13 February 1999, p. 72.
4 'Lycos Cooperating With RIAA Over New MP3 Database', *Billboard*, 13 February 1999, p. 111.
5 Ibid.
6 Ibid.
7 'IFPI Asks For Action Against Search Engine', *Billboard*, 3 April 1999, pp. 1, 93.
8 Ibid.
9 Ibid.
10 Ibid.
11 Ibid.
12 Fast Search & Transfer ASA was eventually acquired by Microsoft in 2008 and rebranded as Microsoft Development Center Norway – https://news.microsoft.com/2008/01/08/microsoft-announces-offer-to-acquire-fast-search-transfer/
13 'Newsline . . .', *Billboard*, 10 July 1999, p. 53.

14 https://grayzone.com/archives/grayzone-digests-1996-2011/grayzone-quarterly-digest-october-december-1999/recording-industry-aims-global-crackdown-on-internet-pirates/
15 https://www.wired.com/1999/11/university-snoops-for-mp3s/
16 Ibid.
17 Ibid.
18 https://www.mtv.com/news/gtbzxu/best-of-99-the-artist-sues-websites-fanzine
19 https://www.theregister.com/1999/09/16/student_not_guilty_of_copyright/
20 'IFPI Sweden Learns From Piracy Case', *Billboard*, 25 September 1999, p. 4.
21 https://www.theregister.com/1999/09/13/student_sued_for_sites_links/
22 'IFPI Sweden Learns From Piracy Case', *Billboard*, 25 September 1999, p. 4.
23 Ibid.
24 Ibid.
25 https://www.nytimes.com/2003/09/09/business/the-price-of-music-the-overview-261-lawsuits-filed-on-music-sharing.html
26 'Online Music: Is The Public Willing To Buy It?', *Billboard*, 11 December 1999, pp. 87, 97.
27 Ibid.
28 'CDs Most Tempting Prize For Shoplifters, Says Study', *Billboard*, 11 December 1999, p. 81.
29 https://thequietus.com/articles/28561-mp3-vinyl-napster-music-industry
30 Stephen Witt, *How Music Got Free: The Inventor, The Mogul & The Thief*, 2016, pp. 72-73.
31 https://torrentfreak.com/the-dawn-of-online-music-piracy-150620/
32 https://reverb.com/uk/news/how-the-mp3-accidentally-destroyed-the-music-industry
33 https://torrentfreak.com/the-dawn-of-online-music-piracy-150620/
34 Ibid.
35 Ibid.
36 https://content.time.com/time/subscriber/article/0,33009,998068,00.html

CHAPTER 10

1 https://www.jstor.org/stable/23012297
2 https://www.academia.edu/21671649/Angels_on_Pinheads_and_Needles_Points
3 https://www.travsonic.com/red-book-cd-format/
4 https://www.nytimes.com/2001/01/05/business/company-news-philips-says-royalty-revenue-to-drop-as-patents-expire.html

5 Phil Hardy, *Download! How The Internet Transformed The Record Business*, 2012, p. 95.
6 Ibid., p. 96.
7 Jeremy Silver, *Digital Medieval: The First Twenty Years Of Music On The Web . . . And The Next Twenty*, 2013, p. 54.
8 https://www.nytimes.com/2000/05/11/business/5-music-companies-settle-federal-case-on-cd-price-fixing.html
9 https://www.wired.com/1999/01/liquefying-mp3/
10 Ibid.
11 Jeremy Silver, *Digital Medieval: The First Twenty Years Of Music On The Web . . . And The Next Twenty*, 2013, p. 54.
12 'Worldwide industry initiative targets secure delivery on net', *Music Week*, 26 December 1998, p. 3.
13 'Majors prepare for digital delivery with SDMI', *Music & Copyright*, 13 January 1999, p. 4.
14 'Rise of new technologies dominates Cannes agenda', *Music Week*, 6 February 1999, p. 7.
15 'Online Distrib On Fast Track As SDMI Moves Forward', *Billboard*, 13 March 1999, pp. 5, 106.
16 Ibid.
17 Ibid.
18 Trevor Merriden, *Irresistible Forces: The Business Legacy Of Napster & The Growth Of The Underground Internet*, 2001, p. 161.
19 Ibid.
20 'Labels Cool To New Microsoft Technology', *Billboard*, 17 April 1999, pp. 1, 87.
21 Ibid.
22 'Anti-Copy Plan Would 'Filter' Downloads', *Billboard*, 29 May 1999, pp. 1, 97.
23 https://www.zdnet.com/article/sdmi-releases-secure-music-spec/
24 Ibid.
25 Ibid.
26 'SDMI plans gradually to phase out illegal online music files', *Music & Copyright*, 2 June 1999, p. 2.
27 'SDMI's First Step An Important One', *Billboard*, 10 July 1999, pp. 1, 90.
28 Ibid.
29 Ibid.
30 Ibid.
31 'Will Digital Players Carry Off Profits?', *Billboard*, 9 October 1999, pp. 1, 99.

32 Ibid.
33 'Support IFPI, Berman Tells U.K. Labels Group', *Billboard*, 9 October 1999, pp. 69, 88.
34 'SDMI Efforts Moving Ahead', *Billboard*, 11 December 1999, pp. 1, 108.
35 Ibid.
36 https://www.sony.com/en/SonyInfo/News/Press_Archive/199909/99-072A/
37 http://edition.cnn.com/TECH/computing/9909/28/walkman.tunes.idg/index.html
38 Paul Goldstein, *Copyright's Highway: From Gutenberg To The Celestial Jukebox*, 2003, p. 176.
39 Ibid., p. 177.
40 Ibid., p. 178.
41 Steve Knopper, *Appetite For Self-Destruction: The Spectacular Crash Of The Record Industry In The Digital Age*, 2009, p. 155.
42 https://www.theregister.com/2001/08/16/felten_spills_the_sdmi_beans/
43 Steve Knopper, *Appetite For Self-Destruction: The Spectacular Crash Of The Record Industry In The Digital Age*, 2009, pp. 150–51.
44 Ibid., p. 154.
45 https://www.theregister.com/2001/01/25/sdmi_boss_bails_out/
46 Steve Knopper, *Appetite For Self-Destruction: The Spectacular Crash Of The Record Industry In The Digital Age*, 2009, p. 156.
47 Mark Mulligan, *Awakening: The Music Industry In The Digital Age*, 2015, p. 22.
48 Ibid., p. 24.

CHAPTER 11

1 Brad Stone, *The Everything Store: Jeff Bezos And The Age Of Amazon*, 2013.
2 https://www.forbes.com/sites/forbeswealthteam/article/the-top-ten-richest-people-in-the-world/?sh=15fa448154dc
3 Clayton Christensen, *The Innovator's Dilemma: When New Technologies Cause Great Firms To Fail*, 1997, p. xv.
4 Ibid., p. xx.
5 Ibid., p. 121.
6 https://www.venturecapitaljournal.com/musicmaker-com-inc/
7 'Musicmaker.com Joins MP3 Fray', *Billboard*, 27 February 1999, pp. 12, 85.
8 Ibid.
9 https://www.washingtonpost.com/archive/business/1999/03/08/jumping-on-the-bandwagon-with-musicmakercom/6e4898c8-5119-42d5-b1b8-3567bef40645/

10 Ibid.
11 Ibid.
12 https://www.latimes.com/archives/la-xpm-1999-jun-11-fi-45310-story.html
13 'EMI Gets 50% Of Custom-CD Co.', *Billboard*, 19 June 1999, p. 8.
14 https://www.stereophile.com/news/10467/index.html
15 https://variety.com/1999/digital/news/emi-musicmaker-com-ink-5-yr-licensing-deal-1117502981/
16 https://www.latimes.com/archives/la-xpm-1999-jun-11-fi-45310-story.html
17 https://www.wired.com/1999/07/musicmaker-ipo-hits-a-high-note/
18 Ibid.
19 https://www.washingtonpost.com/archive/business/1999/05/03/musicmakercom-marches-to-its-own-tune-by-delaying-ipo/f103daf9-8c11-44a4-af04-22a06da9e278/
20 https://www.wsj.com/articles/SB931365923886588410
21 Ibid.
22 Ibid., p. 67.
23 Ibid., p. 69.
24 Ibid., p. 70.
25 https://www.theguardian.com/business/1999/nov/24/16
26 'New Media Boosts EMI's Bottom Line', *Billboard*, 4 December 1999, pp. 5, 143.
27 Ibid.
28 'EMI In Liquid Audio Pact', *Billboard*, 3 July 1999, p. 103.
29 https://money.cnn.com/1999/07/09/technology/liquid/
30 https://www.wsj.com/articles/SB931524332574467915
31 https://money.cnn.com/magazines/fortune/fortune_archive/1985/09/30/66485/index.htm
32 'Newsline . . .', *Billboard*, 4 September 1999, p. 86.
33 'Musicmaker.com Lands Big Acts In Deal', *Billboard*, 11 September, pp. 82, 85.
34 'Web Deal On Album', *Billboard*, 25 September, p. 6.
35 'Newsline . . .', *Billboard*, 25 September 1999, p. 80.
36 'Newsline . . .', *Billboard*, 2 October 1999, p. 115.
37 In August 2022, Bernardi, founder and former chief executive of email security company GigaMedia Access Corporation, pled guilty to one count of conspiracy to commit securities fraud. 'Robert Bernardi, founder and former CEO of Gigatrust, a purported market-leading provider of cloud-based content security solutions, used the prolific reputation of his company to secure upwards of $50 million in loans and investments,' said US Attorney Damian Williams. 'But as he admitted today, Bernardi's

representations to lenders and investors were just a house of cards built on a series of lies.' He was given a five-year prison sentence in January 2023. – https://www.justice.gov/usao-sdny/pr/former-ceo-email-security-company-pleads-guilty-50-million-scheme-defraud-investors-and / https://www.justice.gov/usao-sdny/pr/former-ceo-email-security-company-sentenced-five-years-prison

38 https://hitsdailydouble.com/news&id=273655&title=MUSICMAKER.COM+SPLITS+STOCK

39 https://www.washingtonpost.com/archive/business/2001/01/04/troubled-musicmaker-closes-its-web-site/58050e12-2b16-4674-b23e-253dceaad36d/

40 Ibid.

41 Ibid.

42 https://www.washingtontimes.com/news/2001/jan/9/20010109-020607-2071r/

43 https://money.cnn.com/2000/02/28/electronic/q_mp3/

44 'MP3 Files For IPO, Strikes Deal With No Limit Label', *Billboard*, 29 May 1999, p. 3.

45 Ibid.

46 https://money.cnn.com/1999/07/12/technology/mpthree/

47 https://www.latimes.com/archives/la-xpm-1999-jul-21-fi-58027-story.html

48 https://money.cnn.com/1999/07/21/markets/ipos/

49 https://www.hypebot.com/hypebot/2013/01/how-mp3coms-ipo-changed-sec-regulations.html

50 https://www.bloomberg.com/news/articles/2017-12-11/apple-buys-early-iphone-app-hit-shazam-to-boost-apple-music

51 https://www.apple.com/uk/newsroom/2018/09/apple-acquires-shazam-offering-more-ways-to-discover-and-enjoy-music/

52 https://www.theguardian.com/technology/2017/dec/11/apple-buys-shazam-music-app

CHAPTER 12

1 https://www.theguardian.com/music/2012/mar/25/spillers-cardiff-worlds-oldest-record-store

2 https://timesofmalta.com/articles/view/anthony-damato-owner-of-worlds-oldest-record-store-dies-aged-75.842763

3 https://adp.library.ucsb.edu/index.php/resources/detail/97

4 https://www.loc.gov/collections/edison-company-motion-pictures-and-sound-recordings/articles-and-essays/history-of-edison-sound-recordings/history-of-the-cylinder-phonograph/

5 https://www.theguardian.com/business/2023/apr/28/hmv-return-oxford-street-flagship-store-four-year-absence
6 https://www.fnacdarty.com/en/group/our-history/
7 https://towerrecords.com/cart/update
8 Richard Branson, *Losing My Virginity: The Autobiography*, 1998, p. 74.
9 Ibid., p. 72.
10 https://www.virgin.com/virgin-companies/virgin-megastore
11 Brian McLaughlin, *His Master's Voice: The Man Who Changed The Face Of Music Retail*, 2023.
12 https://www.billboard.com/music/music-news/hmv-coo-mclaughlin-to-retire-1437105/
13 https://www.nextplc.co.uk/about-next/our-history
14 https://www.musicweek.com/news/read/mcallister-remembered-as-man-who-took-hmv-global/025599
15 https://hmv.com/blog/music/100-years-of-hmv-our-story-so-far
16 https://www.thetimes.co.uk/article/hmv-quits-united-states-on-note-of-disappointment-nfrxf8thkj0
17 https://variety.com/2007/digital/features/how-dvds-became-a-success-1117963617/
18 https://www.bbc.co.uk/news/newsbeat-34919975
19 https://www.officialcharts.com/chart-news/elton-johns-candle-in-the-wind-1997-20-years-on-the-tribute-to-princess-diana-that-is-the-uks-biggest-selling-single-of-all-time__19805/
20 https://www.gartner.com/en/digital-markets/insights/growth-loops-vs-aarrr-funnel
21 'Virgin opts to shut Marble Arch outlet', *Music Week*, 23 January 1999, p. 5.
22 Ibid.
23 'New Virgin outlet to raise London stakes', *Music Week*, 5 June 1999, p. 1.
24 Ibid.
25 Ibid.
26 'HMV unveils £20m plan for millennium expansion', *Music Week*, 19 June 1999, p. 1.
27 'Newsline . . .', *Billboard*, 21 August 1999, p. 51.
28 'Newsline . . .', *Billboard*, 4 December 1999, p. 10.
29 'Get set for new Millennium blast off', *Music Week*, 11 September 1999, p. 1.
30 https://www.healthline.com/health/relationships/codependent-relationship#definition
31 https://www.theguardian.com/music/2016/may/06/album-music-records-archive

32 https://www.officialcharts.com/chart-news/the-first-ever-official-singles-chart-revisited-__2544/
33 Phil Hardy, *Download! How The Internet Transformed The Record Business*, 2012, p. 117.
34 Ibid.
35 David Arditi, *iTake-Over: The Recording Industry In The Streaming Era*, 2015, p. 13.
36 Steve Knopper, *Appetite For Self-Destruction: The Spectacular Crash Of The Record Industry In The Digital Age*, 2009, p. 81.
37 Ibid., p. 105.
38 https://european-union.europa.eu/institutions-law-budget/euro/history-and-purpose_en
39 https://eprints.mdx.ac.uk/29827/6/Richard%20Osborne-At_the_Sign_of_the_Swingin_Symbol.pdf
40 'Big-selling long-stayers increase chart stability on eve of millennium', *Music Week*, 16 January 1999, p. 6.
41 'Fewer singles enter chart as labels sharpen focus', *Music Week*, 27 February 1999, p. 3.
42 Ibid.
43 'Sony puts cap on low-priced singles', *Music Week*, 6 March 1999, p. 1.
44 Ibid.
45 https://www.officialcharts.com/chart-news/official-top-40-best-selling-singles-of-1999__33647/
46 'Sony puts cap on low-priced singles', *Music Week*, 6 March 1999, p. 1.
47 'Labels opt for higher price on new singles', *Music Week*, 10 April 1999, p. 5.
48 Ibid.
49 Ibid.
50 https://www.officialcharts.com/chart-news/official-top-40-best-selling-singles-of-1999__33647/

CHAPTER 13

1 Phil Hardy, *Download! How The Internet Transformed The Record Business*, 2012, p. 52.
2 Steve Knopper, *Appetite For Self-Destruction: The Spectacular Crash Of The Record Industry In The Digital Age*, 2009, p. 109.
3 Ibid., p. 110.
4 Phil Hardy, *Download! How The Internet Transformed The Record Business*, 2012, p. 121.

5 Ibid., p. 122.
6 Jason Olim (with Matthew Olim and Peter Kent), *The CDnow Story: Rags To Riches On The Internet*, p. 148.
7 Phil Hardy, *Download! How The Internet Transformed The Record Business*, 2012, p. 122.
8 Ibid., p. 123.
9 https://www.ftc.gov/news-events/news/press-releases/2000/05/record-companies-settle-ftc-charges-restraining-competition-cd-music-market
10 'Universal offers CD taster in £4m Crosse & Blackwell bid', *Music Week*, 4 September 1999, p. 5.
11 'EMI: putting the right price on history while embracing brave new future', *Music Week*, 2 October 1999, pp. 10–11.
12 Ibid.
13 'Asda extends low-price policy to online sales', *Music Week*, 23 October 1999, p. 1.
14 'Asda unveils plans to sell CDs direct online', *Music Week*, 30 October 1999, p. 4.
15 ' . . .as Boots slashes prices on top CDs', *Music Week*, 20 November 1999, p. 1.
16 Ibid.
17 Ibid.
18 'Asda plans US prices for CDs', *Music Week*, 27 November 1999, p. 1.
19 Ibid.
20 Ibid.
21 'How Supermarkets Stitched Up The Charts', *Q*, September 1999, pp. 34–35.
22 Ibid.
23 Ibid.
24 Ibid.
25 'Chain Provokes Used-CD Issue', *Billboard*, 23 January 1999, p. 52.
26 'Sale Of Used CDs Causes Stir In Canada', *Billboard*, 6 February 1999, pp. 8, 53.
27 'As Used-CD Biz Grows, Chains Get In On Act', *Billboard*, 10 July 1999, pp. 1, 92.
28 Ibid.
29 Jason Olim (with Matthew Olim and Peter Kent), *The CDnow Story: Rags To Riches On The Internet*, pp. 5–6.
30 Ibid., p. 213.
31 Ibid., p. 11.
32 Ibid., p. 16.

33 Ibid., pp. 39–41.

34 https://web.archive.org/web/20160305015154/http://www.thefreelibrary.com/NOW+OPEN!+MUSIC+BOULEVARD+AT+WWW.MUSICBLVD.COM+THE+INTERNET'S+LARGEST...-a017182281

35 https://www.fastcompany.com/3054025/youll-never-guess-what-the-first-thing-ever-sold-on-the-internet-was

36 https://www.theguardian.com/media/2001/apr/02/newmedia

37 Jason Olim (with Matthew Olim and Peter Kent), *The CDnow Story: Rags To Riches On The Internet*, p. 184.

38 Jason Olim (with Matthew Olim and Peter Kent), *The CDnow Story: Rags To Riches On The Internet*, p. 24.

39 Ibid,. pp. 79–80.

40 Ibid.

41 Ibid., p. 32.

42 Ibid., pp. 102–3.

43 Ibid., p. 137.

44 https://variety.com/1997/digital/news/cdnow-set-on-10-mil-track-1116678640/

45 https://www.cnet.com/tech/tech-industry/cdnow-goes-public-with-a-bang/

46 Jason Olim (with Matthew Olim and Peter Kent), *The CDnow Story: Rags To Riches On The Internet*, p. 24.

47 https://money.cnn.com/1998/10/23/deals/cdnow/

48 https://money.cnn.com/1999/03/18/technology/cdnow/

49 https://www.wired.com/1999/03/cdnow-now-is-the-time/

50 https://www.wsj.com/articles/SB921534997434346637

51 https://www.wired.com/1999/03/cdnow-now-is-the-time/

52 https://money.cnn.com/1999/03/18/technology/cdnow/

53 https://www.wired.com/1999/03/cdnow-now-is-the-time/

54 Jason Olim (with Matthew Olim and Peter Kent), *The CDnow Story: Rags To Riches On The Internet*, p. 130.

55 Ibid., p. 197.

56 Ibid., p. 194.

57 https://www.forbes.com/consent/ketch/?toURL=https://www.forbes.com/1999/06/29/feat.html

58 Ibid.

59 https://www.nytimes.com/2000/03/14/business/cdnow-deal-with-sony-and-time-warner-is-called-off.html

60 https://www.computerworld.com/article/2596168/struggling-cdnow-finally-finds-a-buyer.html

61 Brad Stone, *The Everything Store: Jeff Bezos And The Age Of Amazon*, 2013, p. 110.
62 'Top Web Shopping Sites In December Sold Music', *Billboard*, 6 February 1999, p. 55.
63 Ibid.
64 'Amazon.com Plans To Sell Digital Downloads', *Billboard*, 3 April 1999, p. 73.
65 'Amazon, RealNetworks Top Music Web Sites In March', *Billboard*, 1 May 1999, pp. 49, 54.
66 Brad Stone, *The Everything Store: Jeff Bezos And The Age Of Amazon*, 2013, p. 110.
67 'EMI, Amazon.com Link Sites On Web', *Billboard*, 8 May 1999, p. 56.
68 'RealNetworks, Thomson Products Open Mainstream Door To MP3', *Billboard*, 15 May 1999, pp. 5, 87.
69 'Newsline . . .', *Billboard*, 29 May 1999, p. 100.
70 'Internet's Impact On Retail Examined At ICSC Convention', *Billboard*, 12 June 1999, pp. 47, 51.
71 https://www.wsj.com/articles/SB932586424407318555
72 https://press.aboutamazon.com/1999/8/amazon-com-warner-music-group-realnetworks-and-liquid-audio-to-offer-exclusive-series-of-free-downloads-from-10-top-name-artists
73 'Amazon Offers Atlantic, Elektra Downloads', *Billboard*, 4 September 1999, p. 8.
74 'Majors' Fear Of Net Set Aside For Universal/Amazon Deal', *Billboard*, 4 September 1999, p. 88.
75 https://www.cnet.com/tech/tech-industry/amazon-sues-barnesandnoble-com-over-patent/
76 https://www.wsj.com/articles/SB1015466420659042800
77 https://press.aboutamazon.com/1999/10/amazon-com-announces-financial-results-for-third-quarter-1999
78 https://press.aboutamazon.com/2000/2/amazon-com-announces-profitability-in-u-s-based-book-sales-financial-results-for-fourth-quarter-1999
79 'Online giants target UK market', *Music Week*, 13 March 1999, p. 1.
80 'MW online retail review underlines service range', *Music Week*, 12 June 1999, p. 4.
81 'Music industry embraces online opportunities', *Music Week*, 27 November 1999 (Online Retailing supplement) pp. 3–11.
82 https://www.wsj.com/articles/SB931463953306260693
83 https://variety.com/2000/digital/news/boxman-feeling-boxed-in-1117787601/

84 https://www.theguardian.com/media/2000/oct/11/newmedia.internet
85 https://www.zdnet.com/article/e-tailer-boxman-seeks-liquidation-3002081886/
86 https://www.wsj.com/articles/SB972324096245929253
87 https://hmv.com/blog/music/100-years-of-hmv-our-story-so-far
88 http://news.bbc.co.uk/1/hi/business/616485.stm
89 https://www.theguardian.com/business/2002/apr/08/3
90 Jeremy Silver, *Digital Medieval: The First Twenty Years Of Music On The Web . . . And The Next Twenty*, 2013, p. 49.
91 'IBM Preps Madison Project', *Billboard*, 26 December 1998, pp. 1, 84.
92 https://www.theregister.com/1999/02/08/big_blue_big_five/
93 https://www.forbes.com/1999/02/09/mu2.html?sh=66f30c6324f6
94 Jeremy Silver, *Digital Medieval: The First Twenty Years Of Music On The Web . . . And The Next Twenty*, 2013, pp. 50–51.
95 Ibid., p. 51.
96 http://edition.cnn.com/TECH/computing/9904/14/musicwar.idg/
97 https://variety.com/1999/digital/news/getmusic-taps-nibley-1117755223/amp/
98 'Get Music Ramps Up', *Billboard*, 11 September 1999, p. 16.
99 'Universal, BMG Set Downloading Test', *Billboard*, 18 *December* 1999, pp. 8, 104.
100 Ibid.

CHAPTER 14

1 https://www.npr.org/2021/08/06/1025554426/a-look-back-at-the-very-first-website-ever-launched-30-years-later
2 'Sony stirs internet contract row', Music Week, 1 May 1999, p. 1.
3 Ibid.
4 Ibid.
5 'Website ownership is the new battleground', *Music Week*, 8 May 1999, p. 9.
6 Ibid.
7 Ibid.
8 Ibid.
9 'Web Raises New Contract Issues', *Billboard*, 19 June 1999, pp. 1, 75.
10 'Artists' Web Site Names An Ownership Issue', *Billboard*, 19 June 1999, p. 75.
11 Ibid.
12 Ibid.
13 https://www.independent.co.uk/arts-entertainment/arts-thunderbugs-are-go-1113085.html

14 https://www.officialcharts.com/artist/8256/thunderbugs/
15 https://www.winston.com/en/legal-glossary/cybersquatting.html#!/en/legal-glossary/:~:text=The%20term%20cybersquatting%20refers%20to,company%20names,%20or%20personal%20names.
16 https://nypost.com/1999/10/15/whats-in-a-name-a-lawsuit-celebrities-are-moving-in-on-websites-bearing-their-names/
17 Ibid.
18 'Yoakam Files Suit Against Web Site Operators', *Billboard*, 20 November 1999, p. 18.
19 'Farm Club' Sprouts On Web', *Billboard*, 20 November 1999, pp. 5, 18.
20 Rod McQueen, *The Icarus Factor: The Rise And Fall Of Edgar Bronfman Jr.*, 2004, p. 217.
21 'Farm Club' Sprouts On Web', *Billboard*, 20 November 1999, pp. 5, 18.
22 https://nypost.com/1999/11/14/jimmys-got-rhythm/
23 https://www.billboard.com/music/features/jimmy-iovine-doug-morris-ali-landry-remember-tv-show-farmclub-eminem-u2-6700596/
24 Fred Goodman, *Fortune's Fool: Edgar Bronfman Jr., Warner Music, And An Industry In Crisis*, 2010, p. 144.
25 https://www.claylacy.com/insights/business-jets-with-the-highest-roi-from-charter/
26 https://www.officialcharts.com/artist/614/marillion/
27 https://www.theguardian.com/music/2006/feb/03/pressandpublishing.popandrock
28 'Web-only tracks provide fan data', *Music Week*, 13 March 1999, p. 5.
29 'Marillion enhanced CD test pays off as online sales soar', *Music Week*, 10 July 1999, p. 5.
30 https://www.officialcharts.com/artist/7976/mero/
31 'Parlophone targets fans with e-mail for Blur single', *Music Week*, 3 July 1999, p. 5.
32 Ibid.
33 https://www.theguardian.com/media/2007/oct/02/digitalmedia.musicnews
34 'CD-on-demand vending machine offers personalised compilations', *Music & Copyright*, 21 May 1997, pp. 1, 4.
35 http://edition.cnn.com/TECH/computing/9906/14/sonykiosk.idg/index.html
36 'CD-on-demand vending machine offers personalised compilations', *Music & Copyright*, 21 May 1997, pp. 1, 4.
37 https://www.cnet.com/tech/services-and-software/cdnow-acquires-custom-cd-firm/
38 http://news.bbc.co.uk/1/hi/entertainment/126071.stm
39 'Sites + sounds' column, *Billboard*, 3 April 1999, p. 73.

40 'Newsline . . .', *Billboard*, 11 September 1999, p. 99.
41 'Newsline . . .', *Billboard*, 20 November 1999, p. 127.
42 'Sony licensing deal brings digital kiosks to High Street', *Music Week*, 19 June 1999, p. 5.
43 'Sony Takes Digital System To Stores', *Billboard*, 19 June 1999, pp. 1, 85.
44 'HMV trials burn-your-own CDs', *Music Week*, 31 July 1999, p. 1.
45 'Stores Test Digital Kiosks', *Billboard*, 28 August 1999, pp. 1, 108.
46 'Past failures ignored as new digital kiosk companies enter the market', *Music & Copyright*, 14 July 1999, pp. 3–4.
47 Ibid.
48 'Musicmaker unveils DIY compilation kiosks', *Music Week*, 30 October 1999, p. 3.
49 https://www.wired.com/2004/10/tail/
50 'HMV in Squeeze digital distribution trial', *Music Week*, 6 February 1999, p. 4.
51 'HMV's free internet service focuses online pricing issue', *Music Week*, 3 April 1999, p. 3.
52 'Music industry embraces online opportunities', *Music Week*, 27 November 1999 (Online Retailing supplement) pp. 3–11.
53 'Tower targets new markets with online retail campaign', *Music Week*, 6 November 1999, p. 3.
54 Ibid.
55 Ibid.
56 'Newsfile', *Music Week*, 20 November 1999, p. 5.
57 'Our Price giveaway to promote website', *Music Week*, 11 December 1999, p. 5.
58 https://www.bbc.co.uk/mediacentre/proginfo/2017/37/well-he-would-wouldnt-he
59 'Music Retailers Prep For A New Millennium, *Billboard*, 12 June 1999, pp. 1, 81.
60 Ibid.
61 'Sony Tries To Put Brakes On Int'l Net Sales Of Jamiroquai', *Billboard*, 29 May 1999, pp. 3, 101.
62 Ibid.
63 Ibid.
64 'Why Garth/Gaines Set, Single Aren't For Sale As Downloads', *Billboard*, 28 August 1999, p. 60.
65 Ibid.
66 As part of the Chris Gaines character on the sleeve of the album, Brooks

wore eyeliner, a soul patch chin beard and a dark wig styled messily that made him look like a lower-league grunge act.

67 https://www.cbc.ca/news/business/garth-brooks-to-launch-digital-download-service-ghosttunes-1.2830131
68 https://www.billboard.com/music/music-news/garth-brooks-ghost-tunes-folding-into-amazon-music-7655458/
69 https://uk.finance.yahoo.com/news/garth-brooks-says-wants-revive-192000979.html
70 https://www.forbes.com/sites/hughmcintyre/2016/10/25/garth-brooks-is-now-the-first-artist-with-7-diamond-certified-albums/
71 'Newsline . . .', *Billboard*, 27 November 1999, p. 89.
72 Ibid.
73 'Newsline . . .', *Billboard*, 2 October 1999, p. 82.
74 'EMI in retail website first', *Music Week*, 25 September 1999, p. 1.
75 Ibid.
76 'Dutch Retailer Threatens Boycott Over CD Cloning', *Billboard*, 20 February 1999, p. 39.
77 Ibid.
78 'Bard fires net broadside', *Music Week*, 2 October 1999, p. 1.
79 Ibid.
80 Ibid.
81 'Branson: back retail or we'll drop music', *Music Week*, 11 December 1999, p. 1.
82 Ibid.
83 Ibid.
84 'Branson: bluff or business?', *Music Week*, 11 December 1999, p. 4.

CHAPTER 15

1 https://www.rollingstone.com/music/music-news/david-bowie-to-release-entire-new-album-online-255118/
2 Ibid.
3 Ibid.
4 https://www.mtv.com/news/x8cpve/best-of-99-chili-peppers-def-leppard-to-preview-full-albums-online
5 'BPI highlights piracy risks of streamed audio on web', *Music Week*, 2 May 1998, p. 3.
6 https://www.mtv.com/news/x8cpve/best-of-99-chili-peppers-def-leppard-to-preview-full-albums-online
7 Ibid.
8 https://www.bbc.co.uk/news/av/entertainment-arts-35286749

9 Ibid.

10 'Net gets first taste of Bowie LP', *Music Week*, 14 August 1999, p. 5.

11 'Bowie album to debut on net', *Music Week*, 11 September 1999, p. 3.

12 'Virgin Pulls Out All Stops For Bowie Set', *Billboard*, 11 September 1999, pp. 19, 100.

13 Ibid.

14 Ibid.

15 Ibid.

16 Ibid.

17 *Billboard*, 25 September 1999, p. 5.

18 https://ultimateclassicrock.com/david-bowie-cyber-song/

19 https://www.davidbowie.com/1999/1999/06/17/david-bowie-to-include-whats-really-happening-the-track-written-in-the-cyber-song-bowienet-contest-on-forthcoming-album-titled-hours-due-out-october-5-on-virgin-records

20 'BARD Warns Labels Of Net Moves', *Billboard*, 9 October 1999, pp. 69, 88.

21 'Bard fires net broadside', *Music Week*, 2 October 1999, p. 1.

22 [The original piece was written in Dutch and I used Google Translate to convert quotes to English] https://www.quotenet.nl/entertainment/a171966/die-keer-dat-hans-breukhoven-alle-david-bowie-cd-s-uit-free-record-shop-haalde-171966/

23 'Retailers Seek Level Playing Field With Net Sellers', *Billboard*, 13 November 1999, pp. 1, 104.

24 Ibid.

25 Ibid.

26 'Bowie Predicts End Of Stores & Labels; Numbers Say Otherwise', *Billboard*, 13 November 1999, pp. 56, 58.

27 Ibid.

28 Ibid.

29 Ibid.

30 Ibid.

31 Ibid.

32 https://www.washingtonpost.com/archive/business/1992/03/07/thorn-emi-to-buy-virgin-music-group/2c1307b1-256a-44f6-a11c-c1d740512f2a/

33 Bowie Bonds were 'asset-backed securities' created in 1997 whereby Bowie let investors buy a share of his future royalties for 10 years. – https://www.bbc.co.uk/news/business-35280945

34 http://edition.cnn.com/TECH/computing/9902/12/globalnet.idg/index.html

35 https://archive.nytimes.com/www.nytimes.com/library/tech/99/11/biztech/articles/10net.html
36 http://allcharts.org/music/years/usa-albums-1999.htm
37 https://blog.roughtrade.com/gb/ranked-david-bowies-greatest-albums/
38 https://ultimateclassicrock.com/david-bowie-albums-ranked/
39 https://faroutmagazine.co.uk/david-bowie-albums-ranked-worst-to-best/

CHAPTER 16

1 Clayton Christensen, *The Innovator's Dilemma: When New Technologies Cause Great Firms To Fail*, 1997.
2 https://www.riaa.com/u-s-sales-database/
3 https://www.latimes.com/archives/la-xpm-1987-11-19-fi-22750-story.html
4 https://www.theguardian.com/music/musicblog/2012/sep/24/sony-minidisc-20-years
5 Ibid.
6 Ibid.
7 *Music Week*, 17 April 1999, p. 5.
8 'Now! debuts on MiniDisc', Music Week, 31 July 1999, p. 3.
9 'Now Warner set to join the MiniDisc fan club', *Music Week*, 18 September 1999, p. 3.
10 'Corrs lead Warner MiniDisc re-entry', *Music Week*, 30 October 1999, p. 5.
11 'MiniDisc Revival Brews Abroad', *Billboard*, 24 July 1999, pp. 1, 84.
12 'Japan: MiniDisc Tops Home Recording', *Billboard*, 24 July 1999, pp. 84–85.
13 'Music to play key role as DVD goes global', *Music Week*, 5 June 1999, p. 5.
14 'The DVD explosion' supplement, *Music Week*, 4 September 1999.
15 The company renamed itself One Little Independent Records in 2020 after criticism that its name and logo were offensive. 'I want to apologise unreservedly to anyone that has been offended by the name and the logo,' said label founder, Derek Birkett. 'I recognise now that both contribute to racism and should have been addressed a long, long time ago.' https://pitchfork.com/news/one-little-indian-changes-name-to-one-little-independent-records/
16 Ibid.
17 'Incentive Programs Arise As Video Market; Eagles Soar As Music DVD Sales Take Off', *Billboard*, 3 July 1999, p. 73.
18 https://www.cnbc.com/2019/11/08/the-death-of-the-dvd-why-sales-dropped-more-than-86percent-in-13-years.html
19 https://www.minitool.com/lib/sacd.html
20 'Sony releases first Super Audio CDs', *Music Week*, 11 September 1999, p. 4.

21 'Sony Presses On With SACD', *Billboard*, 11 September 1999, pp. 1, 108.
22 Ibid.
23 *Music Week*, 5 June 1999, p. 7.
24 Ibid.
25 https://www.discogs.com/release/7324423-Boyzone-Official-Interview-and-CD-ROM
26 https://www.discogs.com/release/1741455-Steps-Official-Interview-CD-And-CD-ROM
27 'Shape CD Sculpts Future Of Marketing', *Billboard*, 16 January 1999, pp. 63, 67.
28 Ibid.
29 Ibid.
30 Warner Music acquired Rykodisc in March 2006 for an estimated $67.5 million. – https://www.billboard.com/music/music-news/wmg-to-acquire-rykodisc-1356121/
31 Rhino was founded in 1978. Warner Music (via Atlantic Records) bought 50 per cent of the company in 1992 and acquired the remaining 50 per cent in 1998. – https://variety.com/1998/music/news/warner-bags-rhino-1117470997/
32 'Labels focus On Album Upgrades', *Billboard*, 10 April 1999, pp. 51–52.
33 Ibid.
34 Ibid.
35 https://www.riaa.com/u-s-sales-database/
36 Ibid.
37 'Cassette Campaign Relaunched', *Billboard*, 3 July 1999, p. 63.
38 *Billboard*, 24 July 1999, p. 61.
39 *Billboard*, 07 August 1999, p. 57.
40 *Billboard*, 14 August 1999, p. 82.
41 *Billboard*, 21 August 1999, p. 51.
42 *Billboard*, 28 August 1999, p. 58.
43 *Billboard*, 4 September 1999, p. 87.
44 https://www.riaa.com/u-s-sales-database/

CHAPTER 17

1 Joseph Menn, *All The Rave: the Rise And Fall Of Shawn Fanning's Napster*, 2003.
2 Adam Fisher, *Valley Of Genius: The Uncensored History Of Silicon Valley (As Told By The Hackers, Founders, And Freaks Who Made It Boom)*, 2018.
3 Joseph Menn, *All The Rave: The Rise And Fall Of Shawn Fanning's Napster*, 2003, p. 13.

4 Ibid., pp. 14–17.
5 Adam Fisher, *Valley Of Genius: The Uncensored History Of Silicon Valley (As Told By The Hackers, Founders, And Freaks Who Made It Boom)*, 2018, p. 285.
6 https://www.theguardian.com/theobserver/2000/may/21/features.review27
7 Trevor Merriden, *Irresistible Forces: The Business Legacy Of Napster & The Growth Of The Underground Internet*, 2001, p. 2.
8 https://www.zdnet.com/article/q-a-napster-creator-shawn-fanning-5000096066/
9 Joseph Menn, *All The Rave: The Rise And Fall Of Shawn Fanning's Napster*, 2003, p. 37.
10 Adam Fisher, *Valley Of Genius: The Uncensored History Of Silicon Valley (As Told By The Hackers, Founders, And Freaks Who Made It Boom)*, 2018, p. 287.
11 Steve Knopper, *Appetite For Self-Destruction: The Spectacular Crash Of The Record Industry In The Digital Age*, 2009, p. 123.
12 Trevor Merriden, *Irresistible Forces: The Business Legacy Of Napster & The Growth Of The Underground Internet*, 2001, pp. 4–5.
13 https://content.time.com/time/subscriber/article/0,33009,998068-4,00.html
14 Laura Robinson and David Halle, 'Digitization, the Internet, and the Arts: eBay, Napster, SAG, and e-Books', in *Qualitative Sociology*, Vol. 25, No. 3, Fall 2002, p. 378.
15 Joseph Menn, *All The Rave: The Rise And Fall Of Shawn Fanning's Napster*, 2003, pp. 53–54.
16 https://content.time.com/time/subscriber/article/0,33009,998068,00.html
17 https://torrentfreak.com/the-dawn-of-online-music-piracy-150620/
18 https://content.time.com/time/subscriber/article/0,33009,998068,00.html
19 Ibid.
20 Joseph Menn, *All The Rave: The Rise And Fall Of Shawn Fanning's Napster*, 2003, p. 57.
21 Ibid., p. 61.
22 https://content.time.com/time/subscriber/article/0,33009,998068,00.html
23 The term 'nappy' in reference to hair is now considered highly problematic depending on the use context. https://www.npr.org/sections/codeswitch/2019/08/09/412886884/the-racial-roots-behind-the-term-nappy
24 https://www.theguardian.com/theobserver/2000/may/21/features.review27
25 Trevor Merriden, *Irresistible Forces: The Business Legacy Of Napster & The Growth Of The Underground Internet*, 2001, p. 6.
26 Adam Fisher, *Valley Of Genius: The Uncensored History Of Silicon Valley (As Told By The Hackers, Founders, And Freaks Who Made It Boom)*, 2018, p. 288.

27 Steve Knopper, *Appetite For Self-Destruction: The Spectacular Crash Of The Record Industry In The Digital Age*, 2009, p. 124.
28 Joseph Menn, *All The Rave: The Rise And Fall Of Shawn Fanning's Napster*, 2003, p. 77.
29 Steve Knopper, *Appetite For Self-Destruction: The Spectacular Crash Of The Record Industry In The Digital Age*, 2009, p. 126.
30 Joseph Menn, *All The Rave: The Rise And Fall Of Shawn Fanning's Napster*, 2003, pp. 78, 83.
31 Ibid., p. 84.
32 Ibid.
33 Trevor Merriden, *Irresistible Forces: The Business Legacy Of Napster & The Growth Of The Underground Internet*, 2001, p. 10.
34 Steve Knopper, *Appetite For Self-Destruction: The Spectacular Crash Of The Record Industry In The Digital Age*, 2009, p. 129.
35 Joseph Menn, *All The Rave: The Rise And Fall Of Shawn Fanning's Napster*, 2003, p. 101.
36 Phil Hardy, *Download! How The Internet Transformed The Record Business*, 2012, p. 67.
37 Trevor Merriden, *Irresistible Forces: The Business Legacy Of Napster & The Growth Of The Underground Internet*, 2001, p. 16.
38 Ibid., p. 10.
39 Joseph Menn, *All The Rave: The Rise And Fall Of Shawn Fanning's Napster*, 2003, p. 107.
40 https://www.zdnet.com/article/q-a-napster-creator-shawn-fanning-5000096066/
41 Michael Wolff, *Burn Rate: How I Survived The Gold Rush Years On The Internet*, 1998, p. 22.
42 John Cassidy, *dot.con: The Greatest Story Ever Sold*, 2002, p. 144.
43 Adam Fisher, *Valley Of Genius: The Uncensored History Of Silicon Valley (As Told By The Hackers, Founders, And Freaks Who Made It Boom)*, 2018, p. 290.
44 https://www.latimes.com/archives/la-xpm-2003-apr-06-tm-napster14-story.html
45 https://fortune.com/2013/09/05/ashes-to-ashes-peer-to-peer-an-oral-history-of-napster/
46 Chris Blackwell, *The Islander: My Life In Music And Beyond*, 2022, p. 375.
47 Quoted in John Cassidy, *dot.con: The Greatest Story Ever Sold*, 2002, p. 254.
48 Trevor Merriden, *Irresistible Forces: The Business Legacy Of Napster & The Growth Of The Underground Internet*, 2001, p. 41.
49 https://fortune.com/2013/09/05/ashes-to-ashes-peer-to-peer-an-oral-history-of-napster/

50 https://www.salon.com/2000/05/01/rosen_2/
51 Phil Hardy, *Download! How The Internet Transformed The Record Business*, 2012, p. 67.
52 Adam Fisher, *Valley Of Genius: The Uncensored History Of Silicon Valley (As Told By The Hackers, Founders, And Freaks Who Made It Boom)*, 2018, p. 292.
53 Joseph Menn, *All The Rave: The Rise And Fall Of Shawn Fanning's Napster*, 2003, pp. 78, 124.
54 'RIAA Sues MP3 Search Site', *Billboard*, 18 December 1999, p. 8.
55 https://www.wired.com/1999/11/riaa-suing-upstart-startup/
56 Ibid., p. 125.
57 Mark Mulligan, *Awakening: The Music Industry In The Digital Age*, 2015, p. 13.
58 Jeremy Silver, *Digital Medieval: The First Twenty Years Of Music On The Web . . . And The Next Twenty*, 2013, p. 57.
59 Adam Fisher, *Valley Of Genius: The Uncensored History Of Silicon Valley (As Told By The Hackers, Founders, And Freaks Who Made It Boom)*, 2018, p. 292.
60 Ibid., p. 294.
61 https://www.sfgate.com/news/article/Assessing-Napster-10-years-later-3229454.php
62 Adam Fisher, *Valley Of Genius: The Uncensored History Of Silicon Valley (As Told By The Hackers, Founders, And Freaks Who Made It Boom)*, 2018, p. 302.

CHAPTER 18

1 https://www.rollingstone.com/music/music-news/clive-davis-ousted-payola-coverup-charged-37191/
2 Clive Davis (with Anthony DeCurtis), *The Soundtrack Of My Life*, 2012, p. 168.
3 Ibid., p. 170.
4 John Alderman, *Sonic Boom: Napster, P2P And The Future Of Music*, 2002, p. 164.
5 Clive Davis (with Anthony DeCurtis), *The Soundtrack Of My Life*, 2012, p. 441.
6 https://www.latimes.com/archives/la-xpm-1998-jul-29-fi-8088-story.html
7 https://variety.com/1998/music/news/zelnick-goes-global-at-bmg-1117478925/
8 Clive Davis (with James Willwerth), *Clive: Inside The Record Business*, 1974.
9 Clive Davis (with Anthony DeCurtis), *The Soundtrack Of My Life*, 2012, p. 435.
10 Clive Davis (with Anthony DeCurtis), *The Soundtrack Of My Life*, 2012, p. 435.

11 Reid eventually became chairman of Epic Records, part of Sony, but left in 2017 amid allegations of sexual harassment. – https://www.latimes.com/entertainment/music/la-et-ms-la-reid-sexual-harassment-allegations-20170516-story.html
12 Clive Davis (with Anthony DeCurtis), *The Soundtrack Of My Life*, 2012, pp. 435–36.
13 https://www.vanityfair.com/culture/2000/02/clive-david-bmg-entertainment-ceo-strauss-zelnick
14 Clive Davis (with Anthony DeCurtis), *The Soundtrack Of My Life*, 2012, p. 443.
15 https://www.vanityfair.com/culture/2000/02/clive-david-bmg-entertainment-ceo-strauss-zelnick
16 https://ew.com/article/1999/12/03/clive-davis-and-arista-records-overhaul/
17 Ibid., pp. 448–49.
18 https://www.theguardian.com/technology/2001/feb/12/copyright.news1
19 https://variety.com/2001/digital/news/napster-s-new-aim-1117801940/
20 John Alderman, *Sonic Boom: Napster, P2P And The Future Of Music*, 2002, p. 171.
21 https://money.cnn.com/2002/06/03/news/companies/napster_bankrupt/
22 https://www.billboard.com/music/music-news/roxio-to-acquire-napster-assets-73438/
23 https://www.latimes.com/archives/la-xpm-2000-nov-01-mn-45186-story.html
24 https://www.billboard.com/music/music-news/bertelsmann-pays-umg-60m-in-napster-settlement-1350776/
25 https://www.reuters.com/article/industry-bertelsmann-emi-napster-dc-idUKN2639765320070326
26 https://www.reuters.com/article/industry-warnermusic-bertelsmann-dc-idUSWNAS7367720070424
27 https://techcrunch.com/2008/09/15/best-buy-to-acquire-napster/
28 https://www.latimes.com/business/la-xpm-2011-oct-04-la-fi-ct-rhapsody-napster-20111004-story.html
29 https://www.theguardian.com/music/2020/aug/25/napster-sold-british-startup-melodyvr-surprise-deal
30 https://musically.com/2022/05/11/napster-gets-bought-again-this-time-with-a-web3-pivot-in-the-works/
31 https://www.wired.com/2000/01/riaa-sues-mp3-com/
32 John Alderman, *Sonic Boom: Napster, P2P And The Future Of Music*, 2002, p. 119.
33 https://www.latimes.com/archives/la-xpm-2000-apr-29-fi-24608-story.html

34 John Alderman, *Sonic Boom: Napster, P2P And The Future Of Music*, 2002, p. 143.
35 https://www.theguardian.com/technology/2000/jul/29/copyright
36 https://www.wsj.com/articles/SB966908032311770283
37 https://money.cnn.com/2000/11/14/bizbuzz/mp3/
38 https://www.billboard.com/music/music-news/vivendi-universal-acquires-mp3com-79680/
39 https://www.hollywoodreporter.com/business/business-news/hollywood-flashback-time-warner-aol-entered-a-doomed-182-billion-alliance-20-years-1267322/
40 https://www.theguardian.com/technology/2009/may/28/time-warner-aol-seperate
41 https://money.cnn.com/2000/06/20/worldbiz/vivendi_deal/
42 https://www.theguardian.com/media/2011/jan/21/edgar-bronfman-jr-vivendi
43 https://money.cnn.com/2001/05/01/europe/emi/index.htm
44 https://www.theguardian.com/business/2006/jun/28/money1
45 https://www.theguardian.com/media/2003/nov/24/citynews.business
46 https://edition.cnn.com/2003/BUSINESS/11/06/sony.bmg.reut/
47 https://www.sony.com/en/SonyInfo/IR/news/2004/qfhh7c000000hq9j-att/bmg_venture.pdf
48 Eamonn Forde, *The Final Days Of EMI: Selling The Pig*, 2019.
49 https://www.sonymusic.com/sonymusic/sony-completes-acquisition-of-bertelsmanns-50-stake-in-sony-bmg/
50 https://investors.wmg.com/news-releases/news-release-details/access-industries-acquire-warner-music-group-33-billion-all-cash
51 https://variety.com/2021/music/news/universal-music-shares-ipo-1235070391/
52 https://musicandcopyright.wordpress.com/2023/04/25/recorded-music-market-share-gains-for-sme-and-the-indies-publishing-share-growth-for-umpg-and-wcm/
53 https://money.cnn.com/2000/07/20/deals/bmg_cdnow/index.htm
54 https://www.theguardian.com/business/2006/oct/09/retail.usnews
55 https://www.marketingweek.com/virgin-megastores-to-be-rebranded-as-zavvi-after-sale/
56 https://www.theguardian.com/business/2009/feb/18/zavvi-job-losses
57 https://ew.com/article/2009/03/02/virgin-megastor/
58 https://www.goldmansachs.com/our-firm/history/moments/2000-dot-com-bubble.html
59 https://www.latimes.com/archives/la-xpm-2001-jan-25-fi-16735-story.html

60 https://www.riaa.com/wp-content/uploads/2023/03/2022-Year-End-Music-Industry-Revenue-Report.pdf
61 https://www.ifpi.org/wp-content/uploads/2020/03/Global_Music_Report_2023_State_of_the_Industry.pdf
62 https://www.apple.com/newsroom/2001/01/09Apple-Introduces-iTunes-Worlds-Best-and-Easiest-To-Use-Jukebox-Software/
63
64 https://www.apple.com/uk/newsroom/2015/06/08Introducing-Apple-Music-All-The-Ways-You-Love-Music-All-in-One-Place-/
65 https://www.bbc.co.uk/news/newsbeat-43240886
66 https://www.theguardian.com/technology/2011/jul/14/spotify-launch-us-record-labels
67 https://musically.com/2023/04/25/spotify-ended-q1-2023-with-515m-listeners-and-210m-subscribers/
68 https://www.theguardian.com/technology/2018/apr/03/spotify-stock-market-debut-all-you-need-to-know
69 https://www.musicbusinessworldwide.com/sony-has-cashed-in-50-of-its-spotify-shares-generating-around-750m/
70 https://variety.com/2018/biz/news/merlin-sells-all-of-its-spotify-shares-for-an-estimated-125-million-plus-1202810275/
71 https://variety.com/2018/biz/news/warner-music-group-sells-entire-stake-in-spotify-1202897605/
72 https://www.nytimes.com/2006/10/09/business/09cnd-deal.html
73 https://www.theverge.com/2022/11/9/23449067/youtube-music-premium-subscriber-growth-2022
74 https://www.ifpi.org/ifpi-global-music-report-global-recorded-music-revenues-grew-9-in-2022/

Index